VISUAL QUICKSTART GUIDE

InDesign CS2

FOR MACINTOSH AND WINDOWS

Sandee Cohen

Peachpit Press

Visual QuickStart Guide
InDesign CS2 for Macintosh and Windows
Copyright © 2006 by Sandee Cohen

Peachpit Press

1249 Eighth Street
Berkeley, CA 94710
800 283 9444 • 510 524 2178
fax 510 524 2221

Find us on the Web at http://www.peachpit.com.
To report errors, please send a note to errata@peachpit.com.

Peachpit Press is a division of Pearson Education.

Notice of Rights

Some halftone images courtesy of Hemera Photo-Objects 50,000 Volumes I and II
Some halftone images © copyright Photospin.com
Some line art © copyright www.arttoday.com

Notice of Liability

The information in this book is distributed on an "as is" basis, without warranty. Although every precaution has been taken in the preparation of this book, neither the author nor Peachpit Press shall have any liability to any person or entity with respect to any loss or damage caused or alleged to be caused directly or indirectly by the instructions contained in this book or by the computer software and hardware products described herein.

Trademarks

InDesign is a registered trademark of Adobe Systems, Inc.
Visual QuickStart Guide is a registered trademark of Peachpit Press, a division of Pearson Education.

Many of the designations used by manufacturers and sellers to distinguish their products are claimed as trademarks. Where those designations appear in this book, and Peachpit Press was aware of a trademark claim, the designations appear as requested by the owner of the trademark. All other product names and services identified throughout this book are used in editorial fashion only and for the benefit of such companies. No such use, or the use of any trade name, is intended to convey endorsement or other affiliation with the book.

Editor: Cary Norsworthy
Production Editor: Becky Winter
Compositor & Interior Design: Sandee Cohen
Cover Design: Peachpit Press
Cover Production: George Mattingly
Copy Editor: Sally Zahner
Proofreader: Leona Benten
Indexer: Joy Dean Lee

ISBN 0-321-32201-0

0 9 8 7 6 5 4 3 2 1

Printed and bound in the United States of America

DEDICATED TO

My Students
You ask all the right questions, so I have to
figure out the right answers.

THANKS TO

Nancy Ruenzel, publisher of Peachpit Press.

Cary Norsworthy, my editor at Peachpit Press. Cary really understands how to handle an overworked author.

Sally Zahner, copyeditor, whose patience and attention to detail was much appreciated!

Becky Winter, for her eagle production eye.

Leona Benten and **Evan Pricco** who blazed through the final pass of proof reading.

The staff of Peachpit Press, all of whom make me proud to be a Peachpit author.

Joy Dean Lee, indexer extraordinaire, who is so precise that she finds errors that all the editors missed.

Dave Awl who did a great job in dissecting all the new features and marking up the previous edition of the book.

David Van Ness who did an incredible job of taking the new screen shots.

Barry Anderson and **David Blatner** of the InDesign Conference and the Creative Suite Conference. Speaking at those events helps me write better.

Molly Ruff of the InDesign beta program who patiently answered questions and fielded complaints.

Peter Truskier of Premedia Systems (www.premediasystems.com) who created the script that automated my screen shot spotlights.

Dave Saunders who created my script to find all overset text boxes. Dave is a terrific scripter who can write custom scripts to order. Reach him at www.pdsassoc.com.

Hemera™ Technologies which gave me the use of their extensive Photo-Objects 50,000 collection of photographs. The DVDs and search engine made looking for artwork a real pleasure.

The InDesign team in Seattle, who continue to make InDesign my favorite program to use and to write about.

The **InDesign Talk List** of **Blueworld Listsearch. com**. You all have given me great insight as to what subjects I need to cover. You have also given me great tips in working with InDesign.

The **InDesign User to User forum**. We may not always agree, but we've created a great community of questions, comments, advice, complaints, and silly threads.

Netta Rabin and **Traci Levine** of Grosset & Dunlap. These two students were the shining stars in their class and came up with insights that I didn't even get. I take my hat off to them.

And a very special thanks to **David Lerner** of **Tekserve,** who once again helped me keep my computers running in the middle of the book crunch. Tekserve (www. tekserve.com) is the best place to buy, fix, or enhance Macintosh computers.

Colophon

This book was created using InDesign CS. The computers used were a G4 500 Mhz Powerbook, and a Gateway 200 XL. Screen shots were taken using Snapz Pro X (Macintosh) and Snaggit (Windows). Fonts used were Minion Pro and Futura Std from Adobe, Circle Negative from Myfonts.com, and a specialty "TIP" font I created using FontLab from FontLab Inc.

TABLE OF CONTENTS

	Introduction	**xiii**
Chapter 1	**Getting Started**	**1**
	Choosing Palettes	2
	Working with Palettes	10
	Using Workspaces	14
	Using the Toolbox	15
	Using Contextual Menus	16
Chapter 2	**Document Setup**	**17**
	Starting Documents	18
	Choosing Layout Options	20
	Changing Layout Options	23
	Using the Document Presets	24
	Using Document Rulers	26
	Working with Guides	28
	Working with Document Grids	32
	Changing the Magnification	33
	View and Pasteboard Controls	35
	Using the Zoom and Hand Tools	37
	Using the Navigator Palette	39
	Controlling Windows	41
	File Maintenance	42
	Working with Bridge	45
Chapter 3	**Basic Text**	**49**
	Creating Text Frames	50
	Typing Text	53
	Selecting Text	54
	Moving and Deleting Text	56
	Using the Character Palette	58
	Setting the Typeface and Point Size	59
	Styling Text	60
	Setting Line and Character Spacing	62
	Applying Text Distortions	64
	Setting the Language	65
	Applying Paragraph Formatting	66
	Setting Alignment and Indents	67
	Inserting a Manual Indent	69
	Setting Paragraph Effects	70
	Working with Hidden Characters	71
	Using the Glyphs palette	72

Working with Text Flow 75
Setting Text Frame General Controls 76
Using the Control Palette for Text 79
Using Special Text Characters. 80

Chapter 4   **Working with Objects** . . . . **.81**
Types of Frames 82
Creating Basic Shapes 83
Selecting Objects 85
Moving Objects. 86
Replicating Objects 88
Resizing Objects 90
Using the Transform Tools 91
Using the Transform Palette 96
Using the Transform Commands 100
Using the Arrange Commands 102
Aligning Objects 103
Grouping and Pasting Into Objects 106
Using the Control Palette for Objects 110
Using the Measure Tool 111
Using the Info Palette with Objects 113
Locking Objects 114
Selecting Frames 115

Chapter 5   **Working in Color** **117**
The Basics of Color 118
Using the Color Palette 120
Defining and Storing Swatches 124
Using Swatch Libraries. 132
Creating Mixed Inks. 134
Creating Tints 138
Using the Color Picker. 140
Creating Gradient Swatches 141
Using the Eyedropper 144
Overprinting Colors. 145

Chapter 6   **Styling Objects** **147**
Applying Fills 148
Applying Stroke Effects 152
Creating Custom Stroke Styles 159
Adding Arrows and Corner Effects 166
Applying Transparency 167
Adding Drop Shadows and Feathers 171
Using the Pathfinder Commands 173
Using the Eyedropper 176
Setting Object Defaults 178

Chapter 7	**Pen and Beziers**	**179**
	Pen Points	180
	Drawing Lines	181
	Drawing Curves	182
	Changing Curves and Corner Points	183
	Modifying Paths	184
	Modifying Points	186
	Using the Pencil Tool	188
	Using the Smooth Tool	190
	Using the Erase Tool	191
	Adding or Deleting Points on Paths	192
Chapter 8	**Imported Graphics**	**193**
	Placing Artwork	194
	Using Bridge to Place Artwork	196
	Specialty Frames	197
	Setting the Image Import Options	200
	Working with Images Inside Frames	204
	Using the Position Tool	206
	Fitting Graphics in Frames	207
	Nesting Graphic Elements	210
	Styling Placed Images	213
	Linking Graphics	214
	Embedding Graphics	218
	Setting Layer Visibility	219
	Using Clipping Paths	220
	Importing Transparent Images	224
	Viewing Images	226
	Applying Effects to Images	230
Chapter 9	**Text Effects**	**231**
	Wrapping Text	232
	Text on a Path	237
	Working with Paragraph Rules	240
	Inline and Anchored Objects	244
Chapter 10	**Pages And Books**	**251**
	Changing the Pages Palette	252
	Adding Blank Pages	253
	Navigating and Moving Pages	255
	Creating and Separating Spreads	259
	Importing Text	261
	Flowing Text	264
	Creating Text Breaks	268
	Working with Master Pages	269
	Adjusting Layouts	274

Table of Contents

		Working with Page Numbers	275
		Making Books	277
		Creating a Table of Contents	282
		Creating an Index	287
Chapter 11	**Layers**		**289**
		Creating and Deleting Layers	290
		Setting the Layer Options	292
		Working with Layers	295
Chapter 12	**Libraries and Snippets**		**297**
		Storing Items in a Library	298
		Applying Library Items to a Page	300
		Setting the Library Display	301
		Searching and Sorting Libraries	302
		Creating and Using Snippets	304
Chapter 13	**Tabs and Tables**		**305**
		Inserting Tab Characters	306
		Setting Tab Stops	307
		Creating Tab Leaders	310
		Creating and Using Tables	311
		Navigating Through Tables	316
		Selecting Tables	317
		Working with Rows and Columns	319
		Adjusting Tables within a Text Frame	325
		Working with Headers and Footers	326
		Adding Images to Tables	328
		Customizing Cells	329
		Setting Borders, Strokes, and Fills	332
		Alternating Strokes and Fills	335
		Adding Diagonal Lines in Cells	338
		Using the Table or Control Palettes	339
Chapter 14	**Automating Your Work**		**341**
		Changing Case	342
		Checking Spelling	342
		Finding and Changing Text	346
		Find Dialog Box Settings	350
		Finding and Changing Text (continued)	352
		Using the Story Editor	353
		Bullets and Numbering	354
		Footnotes	356
		Creating Tagged Text	359
		Using Find Font	361
		Keeping Lines Together	362

Table of Contents

	Using the Eyedropper on Text	363
	Using Scripts	365
Chapter 15	**Text and Object Styles**	**367**
	Defining Text Styles	368
	Text Style Categories	370
	Defining Text Styles (continued)	373
	Loading and Importing Styles	378
	Applying Styles and Style Overrides	382
	Clearing Style Overrides	383
	Redefining and Deleting Styles	385
	Automatic Drop Cap Styling	387
	Using Nested Styles	389
	Defining Object Styles	393
	Object Style Categories	394
	Defining Object Styles (continued)	396
	Working with Object Styles	397
	Using the Quick Apply Feature	398
Chapter 16	**Typography Controls**	**399**
	Optical Margin Alignment	400
	Using Adobe Paragraph Composer	401
	Applying Justification Controls	402
	Controlling Hyphenation	406
	Baseline Grid	408
	Balancing Ragged Lines	411
	Using OpenType	411
	Open Type Categories	413
Chapter 17	**Color Management**	**415**
	Choosing Color Settings	416
	Saving and Loading Color Settings	420
	Working with Profiles	422
Chapter 18	**Interactive PDF Elements**	**423**
	Types of Interactive Elements	424
	Defining Hyperlinks	425
	Working with Hyperlinks	434
	Working with Bookmarks	435
	Adding Sounds	438
	Adding Movies	440
	Movie Display Options	443
	Creating Buttons	445
	General Button Properties	447
	Setting the Button States	448
	Applying Behaviors	453
	Button Behaviors	454

Table of Contents

Applying Behaviors (continued). 456
Deleting or Deactivating Behaviors 457
Exporting Interactive PDFs. 458

Chapter 19   **Output**. **459**
Printing a Document 460
Print Dialog Box Categories 461
Setting the General Print Options 463
Choosing the Setup Controls 464
Tiling Pages 465
Setting Marks and Bleed 467
Setting the Output Controls 469
Working with Separations Preview 471
Separations Preview Plate Settings. 472
Working with Separations Preview (continued) 473
Color Separations and Ink Manager 474
Setting the Graphics Options 476
Setting the Advanced Options 477
Flattener Presets and Preview. 478
Working with Print Presets. 482
Creating a Print Summary 484
Creating PostScript Files 485
Creating a Preflight Report 486
Packaging a Document 489

Chapter 20   **Exporting** **491**
Setting the Export File Options 492
Creating PDF Files 493
PDF Export Options 493
General PDF Options 495
Compression PDF Options 498
Output PDF Options 501
Advanced PDF Options 503
Security PDF Options 504
Working with PDF Presets 506
Creating EPS Files 508
InDesign Interchange Format. 511
JPEG Options 511
Exporting SVG Files. 513
Exporting Text 516
Packaging for GoLive 517

Chapter 21   **Customizing InDesign** **519**
Modifying Keyboard Shortcuts 520
Setting the Preferences Categories. 523
The Preference Categories 523

General Preferences Controls. 527
Type Preferences 529
Advanced Type Preferences 531
Composition Preferences 532
Units & Increments Preferences. 534
Grids Preferences 535
Guides & Pasteboard Preferences 536
Dictionary Preferences. 537
Spelling Preferences 540
Autocorrect Preferences 541
Story Editor Display Preferences 542
Display Performance Preferences 543
Appearance of Black Preferences 545
File Handling Preferences 546
Trashing Preferences 547
Configuring Plug-Ins 548

Index **549**

Table of Contents

INTRODUCTION

Welcome to the *InDesign CS2 Visual QuickStart Guide*, my fourth version of the book. It's hard to believe how quickly InDesign has become a major force in desktop publishing and page layout. I feel very lucky to have been working with and teaching InDesign since its very first version. In fact, this is the only third-party book that has had editions for all four versions of InDesign.

Rarely has an application caused as much excitement as InDesign. The first version, released in April 2000, was hailed for its innovative typographic features. Version 1.5, which came out in December of 2000, added more tools and text controls. With version 2, InDesign created great excitement by adding transparency effects. With InDesign CS, Adobe added new automation features such as nested styles and PDF interactive features.

Now, with InDesign CS2, Adobe has added the long-requested object styles as well as pathfinder commands, and sophisticated inline and anchored objects. InDesign is now even better integrated with other Creative Suite 2 applications and can change the visibility of Photoshop and Acrobat layers within the InDesign document.

Using This Book

If you have used any of the other Visual QuickStart Guides, you will find this book to be similar. Each chapter is divided into different sections that deal with a specific topic — usually a tool or command. For instance, the chapter on text has sections on creating text frames, typing text, selecting text, and so on.

Each of the sections contains numbered exercises that show you how to perform a specific technique. As you work through the steps, you gain an understanding of the technique or feature. The illustrations help you judge if you are following the steps correctly.

I've also sprinkled sidebars, printed in gray boxes, throughout the chapters. Some of these sidebars give you a bit of history or background for a specific feature. Other times, I've written out humorous stories about desktop publishing. These sidebars are the same as the little stories and anecdotes I tell my students in the classes I teach.

Instructions

You will find it easier to use this book once you understand the terms I am using. This is especially important since some other computer books use terms differently. Therefore, here are the terms I use in the book and explanations of what they mean.

Click refers to pressing down and releasing the mouse button on the Macintosh, or the left mouse button on Windows. You must release the mouse button or it is not a click.

Press means to hold down the mouse button, or a keyboard key.

Press and drag means to hold the mouse button down and then move the mouse. I also use the shorthand term *drag*. Just remember that you have to press and hold as you drag the mouse.

Menu Commands

InDesign has menu commands that you follow to open dialog boxes, change artwork, and initiate certain actions. These menu commands are listed in bold type. The typical direction to choose a menu command might be written as **Object > Arrange > Bring to Front**. This means that you should first choose the Object menu, then choose the Arrange submenu, and then choose the Bring to Front command.

Keyboard Shortcuts

Most of the menu commands for InDesign have keyboard shortcuts that help you work faster. For instance, instead of choosing New from the File menu, it is faster and easier to use the keyboard shortcut (Cmd-N on the Macintosh and Ctrl-N on Windows). Often these shortcuts use multiple keystroke combinations.

The modifier keys used in keyboard shortcuts are sometimes listed in different orders by different software companies or authors. The order that you press those modifier keys is not important. However, it is very important that you always add the last key (the letter or number key) after you press the other keys.

Learning Keyboard Shortcuts

While keyboard shortcuts help you work faster, you really do not have to start using them right away. In fact, you will most likely learn more about InDesign by using the menus. As you look for one command, you may see another feature that you would like to explore.

Once you feel comfortable working with InDesign, you can start adding keyboard shortcuts to your repertoire. My suggestion is to look at which menu commands you use most often. Then each day choose to use one of those shortcuts. For instance, if you import a lot of art from other programs, you might decide to learn the shortcut for the Place command (Cmd-D on the Mac; Ctrl-D on Windows). For the rest of that day use the shortcut every time you import text or art. Even if you have to look at the menu to refresh your memory, use the keyboard shortcut to actually open the Place dialog box. By the end of the day you will have memorized the Place shortcut. The next day you can learn a new one.

Cross-Platform Issues

One of the great strengths of InDesign is that it is almost identical on both the Macintosh and Windows platforms. In fact, at first glance it is hard to tell which platform you are working on. However, because there are some differences between the platforms, there are some things you should keep in mind.

Modifier Keys

Modifier keys are always listed with the Macintosh key first and then the Windows key second. So the instruction "Hold the Cmd/Ctrl key" means hold the Cmd key on the Macintosh platform or the Ctrl key on the Windows platform. When the key is the same on both computers, such as the Shift key, only one key is listed.

Generally the Cmd key on the Macintosh (sometimes called the Apple key) corresponds to the Ctrl key on Windows. The Opt key on the Macintosh corresponds to the Alt key on Windows. The Control key on the Macintosh does not have an equivalent on Windows. Notice that the Control key for the Macintosh is always spelled out while the Ctrl key for Windows is not.

Platform-Specific Features

A few times in the book, I have written separate exercises or instructions for the Macintosh and Windows platforms. These exercises are indicated by (Mac) and (Win).

Most of the time this is because the procedures are so different that they need to be written separately. Some features exist only on one platform. Those features are then labeled as to their platform.

Whether you're learning InDesign in a class or on your own, I hope this book helps you master the program. Just don't forget to have fun!

Sandee Cohen

(Sandee@vectorbabe.com)
September, 2005

GETTING STARTED 1

One of the reasons why InDesign has become so popular is that it uses many of the same tools, palettes, and onscreen elements that are found in Adobe Photoshop and Adobe Illustrator. So you may be tempted to skip this chapter which covers those onscreen elements.

However, despite the fact that InDesign comes from Adobe, it has features that you won't find in those other Adobe applications.

So, although you may think you know everything in this chapter, take a quick look at these pages. You may discover some things you didn't realize were in InDesign.

Of course, if this is your first introduction to an Adobe product, you'll want to read this chapter very carefully, as you will learn techniques you can use for either Illustrator or Photoshop.

Choosing Palettes

Most of the commands and features that control InDesign are found in the onscreen palettes. Each of the palettes covers special features. The palettes are similar to those found in other Adobe applications. Although they first appear the way Adobe arranges them, we'll look at them in alphabetical order.

Align palette

The Align palette ❶ (**Window > Object & Layout > Align**) aligns and distributes objects on a page *(see Chapter 4, "Working with Objects")*.

Attributes palette

The Attributes palette ❷ (**Window > Attributes**) allows you to set fills and strokes to overprint *(see Chapter 5, "Working in Color")*. It also lets you create non-printing objects *(see Chapter 19, "Output")*.

Bookmarks palette

The Bookmarks palette ❸ (**Window > Interactive > Bookmarks**) allows you to define pages as bookmarks. These bookmarks are then used as navigation aids in PDF documents *(see Chapter 18, "Interactive PDF Elements")*.

Character palette

The Character palette ❹ (**Window > Type & Tables > Character** or **Type > Character**) controls character-level attributes such as the typeface and point size *(see Chapter 3, "Basic Text")*.

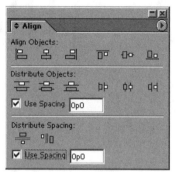

❶ *Use the **Align palette** to align the edges and centers of objects or to distribute the space between objects.*

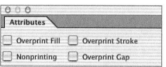

❷ *The **Attributes palette** lets you set the overprinting controls for fills and strokes or set objects to not print.*

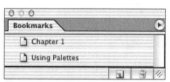

❸ *The **Bookmarks palette** lets you create navigation bookmarks that are used in Adobe PDF documents.*

❹ *Use the **Character palette** to format the appearance of text characters.*

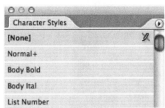

❺ *Use the* **Character Styles palette** *to automate the formatting of text characters.*

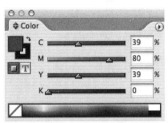

❻ *The* **Color palette** *is used to mix colors to apply to text and objects.*

❼ *The* **Control palette** *changes its options depending on the selected object.*

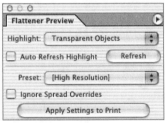

❽ *The* **Flattener Preview palette** *is used to see how the transparency effects will affect objects and images.*

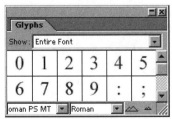

❾ *The* **Glyphs palette** *lets you insert characters from a font.*

Character Styles palette

The Character Styles palette **❺** (**Window > Type & Tables > Character Styles** or **Type > Character Styles**) lets you define and work with character styles (*see Chapter 14, "Automating Your Work"*).

Color palette

The Color palette **❻** (**Window > Color**) allows you to mix or apply colors (*see Chapter 5, "Working in Color"*).

Control palette

The Control palette **❼** (**Window > Control**) changes its layout depending on the object selected on the page. If you are working with text, the Control palette shows a combination of the Paragraph and Character palettes. If you are working with objects, the palette shows a combination of the Transform and Stroke palettes. The Control palette is covered in Chapters 3, 4, and 13.

Flattener Preview palette

The Flattener Preview palette **❽** (**Window > Output > Flattener**) lets you display the page as it would look after flattening has been applied during the printing process (*see Chapter 19, "Output"*).

Glyphs palette

The Glyphs palette **❾** (**Window > Type & Tables > Glyphs** or **Type > Glyphs**) lets you insert or replace characters from a font (*see Chapter 3, "Basic Text"*). The Glyphs palette also helps you work with OpenType features (*see Chapter 16, "Typography Controls"*).

Choosing Palettes

Gradient palette

The Gradient palette ⑩ (**Window** > **Gradient**) lets you define and control the appearance of gradients or color blends *(see Chapter 5, "Working in Color")*.

Hyperlinks palette

The Hyperlinks palette ⑪ (**Window** > **Interactive** > **Hyperlinks**) is used to create links that let you easily navigate around PDF and HTML documents *(see Chapter 18, "Interactive PDF Elements")*.

Index palette

The Index palette ⑫ (**Window** > **Type & Tables** > **Index**) lets you create cross-referenced index entries for a document or book *(see Chapter 10, "Pages and Books")*.

Info palette

The Info palette ⑬ (**Window** > **Info**) gives you feedback on the type of object selected, and the action taken on that object *(see Chapter 4, "Working with Objects")*.

Even More Palettes?

Your copy of InDesign may display even more palettes. These may be part of third-party plug-ins that give you features not found in the basic InDesign program.

Third-party palettes are not available in the ordinary installation. You need to install the plug-ins for those features. *(See Chapter 21, "Customizing InDesign," for information on installing plug-ins.)*

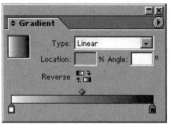

⑩ *The* **Gradient palette** *lets you create color blends.*

⑪ *Use the* **Hyperlinks palette** *to create and store links to other pages in a PDF document or on the Web.*

⑫ *The* **Index palette** *lets you create and manage index entries for a document or book.*

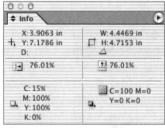

⑬ *The* **Info palette** *shows the attributes of objects. These attributes change depending on the object chosen.*

Choosing Palettes

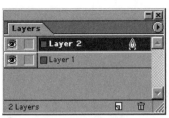

⓮ *Use the* **Layers palette** *to add layers and change their display.*

⓯ *Create a* **Library palette** *to store commonly used items and add them to documents.*

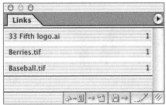

⓰ *The* **Links palette** *displays a list of all the imported graphics and text files.*

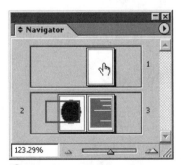

⓱ *Use the* **Navigator palette** *to see a preview of your document and move around the pages.*

Layers palette

The Layers palette **⓮** (**Window > Layers**) controls the stacking order and visibility of different layers *(see Chapter 11, "Layers")*.

Library palette

The Library palette **⓯** (**File > New > Library**) lets you store and re-use elements *(see Chapter 12, "Libraries and Snippets")*.

Links palette

The Links palette **⓰** (**Window > Links**) controls the status of placed images *(see Chapter 8, "Imported Graphics")*.

Navigator palette

The Navigator palette **⓱** (**Window > Object & Layout > Navigator**) lets you see the layout of pages *(see Chapter 2, "Document Setup")*.

Screen Real Estate

Your workspace may feel cramped with so many palettes on your screen. One way I solved the problem was to invest in a small, second monitor.

That way I can set up InDesign so that the palettes are displayed on the second monitor while the Toolbox and the document window are displayed on my main monitor.

This gives me much more room to work on my documents.

Choosing Palettes

Object Styles palette

The Object Styles palette ⓲ (**Window >
Object Styles**) lets you quickly apply formatting to text and graphic frames (*see Chapter 14, "Automating Your Work"*).

Pages palette

The Pages palette ⓳ (**Window > Pages**) lets
you add and control pages and master pages,
as well as move from one page to another (*see
Chapter 10, "Pages and Books"*).

Paragraph palette

The Paragraph palette ⓴ (**Window > Type &
Tables > Paragraph**) controls paragraph-level
attributes such as the alignment and margin
indents (*see Chapter 3, "Basic Text"*).

Paragraph Styles palette

The Paragraph Styles palette ㉑ (**Window >
Type & Tables > Paragraph Styles**) lets you
define and apply paragraph styles (*see Chapter 14, "Automating Your Work"*).

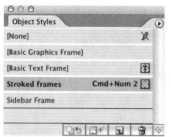

⓲ *The* **Object Styles palette** *lets you
create and apply object styles for frames.*

⓳ *The* **Pages palette** *lets you add and
delete pages, apply master pages, and
move through the document.*

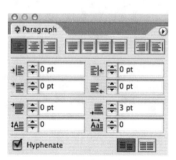

⓴ *The* **Paragraph palette** *contains all the
formatting controls for text paragraphs.*

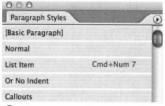

㉑ *The* **Paragraph Styles palette**
*makes it easy to apply complex
formatting to paragraphs.*

Choosing Palettes

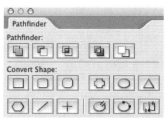

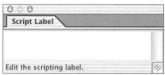

㉒ *The* **Pathfinder palette** *allows you to easily change the shape of objects.*

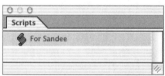

㉓ *The* **Script Label palette** *allows you to edit the labels applied to objects in a script.*

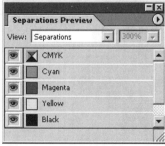

㉔ *The* **Scripts palette** *allows you to run scripts directly within InDesign.*

㉕ *The* **Separations Preview palette** *lets you see the color plates that are in a document.*

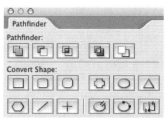

㉖ *Use the* **Story palette** *to apply the optical margin alignment for hanging punctuation.*

Pathfinder palette

The Pathfinder palette **㉒** (**Window > Object & Layout > Pathfinder**) allows you to apply the Pathfinder and Convert Shape commands that change the shapes of objects *(see Chapter 4, "Working with Objects")*.

Script Label palette

The Script Label palette **㉓** (**Window > Automation > Script Label**) lets you edit labels that are applied to objects as part of scripts.

Scripts palette

The Scripts palette **㉔** (**Window > Automation > Scripts**) displays the scripts that have been placed inside the Scripts folder. These scripts can be run directly from within InDesign *(see Chapter 14, "Automating Your Work")*.

Separations Preview palette

The Separations Preview palette **㉕** (**Window > Output > Separations**) lets you change the display for the color plates in the document. This lets you see the individual color separations *(see Chapter 19, "Output")*.

Story palette

The Story palette **㉖** (**Window > Type & Tables > Story**) lets you change the automatic margin alignment to an optical margin alignment that adjusts the position of punctuation and serifs *(see Chapter 14, "Automating Your Work")*.

Choosing Palettes

Stroke palette

The Stroke palette  (**Window > Stroke**) controls attributes such as stroke width, dashes, and end arrows and symbols (*see Chapter 6, "Styling Objects"*).

Swatches palette

The Swatches palette ❷❽ (**Window > Swatches**) stores the colors and gradients used in a document (*see Chapter 5, "Working in Color"*).

Table palette

The Table palette ❷❾ (**Window > Type & Tables > Table**) contains the formatting and controls for creating tables within text frames (*see Chapter 13, "Tabs and Tables"*).

Tabs palette

The Tabs palette ❸⓪ (**Window > Type & Tables > Tabs** or **Type > Tabs**) controls the position of the tab stops for text (*see Chapter 13, "Tabs and Tables"*).

❷❼ The **Stroke palette** *controls the appearance of rules and lines around objects.*

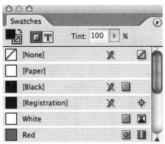

❷❽ The **Swatches palette** *stores colors and gradients.*

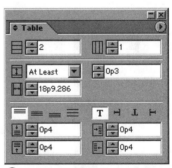

❷❾ Use the **Table palette** *to format tables and table cells.*

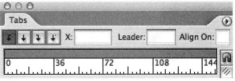

❸⓪ The **Tabs palette** *lets you position and format tabs within text.*

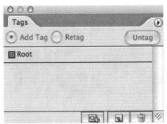

❸❶ *Use the* **Tags palette** *to control XML tags in a document.*

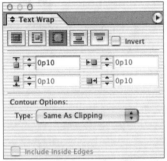

❸❷ *Use the* **Text Wrap palette** *to control how text wraps around objects and images.*

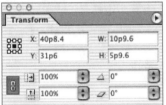

❸❸ *The* **Transform palette** *lets you control the position and size of objects.*

❸❹ *Use the* **Transparency palette** *to change the opacity and appearance of objects.*

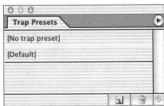

❸❺ *The* **Trap Presets palette** *lets you store trapping settings to apply to various objects.*

Tags palette

The Tags palette **❸❶** (**Window > Tags**) lets you apply and control XML (extensible markup language) tags in a document. Working with tags is beyond the scope of this book. For more information on using XML tags, see *Real World InDesign CS2,* by Olav Martin Kvern and David Blatner, published by Peachpit Press in association with Adobe Press.

Text Wrap palette

The Text Wrap palette **❸❷** (**Window > Text Wrap**) controls how text wraps around objects and placed images *(see Chapter 9, "Text Effects").*

Transform palette

The Transform palette **❸❸** (**Window > Object & Layout > Transform**) lets you see the size and position of objects. You can also use the Transform palette to apply transformations such as scaling and rotation *(see Chapter 4, "Working with Objects").*

Transparency palette

The Transparency palette **❸❹** (**Window > Transparency**) contains the controls for opacity and blend modes *(see Chapter 6, "Styling Objects").*

Trap Presets palette

The Trap Presets palette **❸❺** (**Window > Output > Trap Presets**) is used to store different settings for how colors are trapped between one object and another. Setting traps is not covered in this book. Talk to the print shop that will ouput your file before you attempt to set traps in InDesign.

Choosing Palettes

Working with Palettes

If you don't see a palette onscreen, you can open it by choosing the command in the Window menu.

To open a palette:

◆ Choose the name of the palette from the Window menu.

TIP Palettes that control type, such as Character and Paragraph, are also listed in the Type menu.

To close a palette:

◆ Click the close box in the title bar **36**.

If you can't afford a second monitor, you can quickly hide your palettes and Toolbox.

To hide palettes:

1. Make sure an insertion point is not within a text frame to avoid inserting a tab character into your text.

2. Press Shift+Tab key. This hides all the palettes.

   or

   Press the Tab key. This hides all the palettes including the Toolbox.

TIP Press the commands again or choose the palette command from the Window menu to reveal the palettes.

In addition to the palette buttons and fields, each palette contains a menu.

To display the palette menus:

1. Click the palette menu button to open the palette menu **37**.

2. Choose a command from the menu.

Mac close box

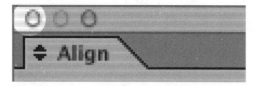

36 *Click the* **close box** *to close a palette.*

Palette menu button

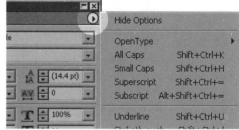

37 *Click the* **palette menu button** *to display the menu for a palette.*

First click
Second click
Third click

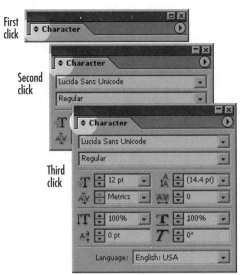

⑱ *Each click on the palette options arrow changes the display of a palette.*

Mac zoom button

Windows collapse box

⑲ *Click the* **collapse box** *to shorten the display of a palette.*

Some palettes display only some of their features when first opened. These palettes contain up/down arrows next to the name of the palette. You can access the optional features by clicking the up/down arrows in the palette tab.

To reveal the palette options:

1. Click the up/down arrow in the palette tab to expand the palette to reveal the options for the palette **⑱**.

2. Continue to click the arrow to toggle through each of the palette display states.

TIP The palette menu also contains a Show Options command that toggles between the palette display states.

You can also shrink a palette so that it only displays the palette tab.

To shrink a palette display:

◆ Click the collapse box (Win) or zoom button (Mac) **⑲** to collapse the palette.

To expand a palette display:

◆ If the palette is collapsed, click the collapse box to expand the palette.

Working with Palettes

Some of the palettes allow you to display smaller palette rows, which helps you save screen space.

To display small palette rows:

◆ Choose Small Palette Rows from the palette menu to display the smaller text and symbols 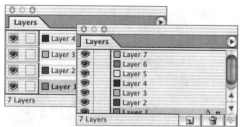 for that palette.

⑩ Small palette rows *(lower window) display more information in the same size palette.*

Another way to save screen space is to move one palette so that it is located within the boundaries of another. This is called *nesting*.

To nest palettes:

1. Position the cursor over the palette tab.

2. Drag the tab so that the outline is inside another palette. A black rectangle around the inside perimeter of the palette indicates that the two palettes will be nested 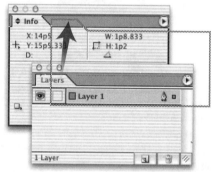.

3. Release the mouse button. The palette appears next to the other item 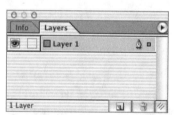.

⑪ *Drag the palette tab into another palette area to* **nest palettes**.

To unnest palettes:

1. Drag the palette tab so that the outline is completely outside the other palette.

2. Release the mouse button. The palette appears as a separate onscreen item.

⑫ *The results of nesting one palette into another.*

Another way to arrange palettes is to create side tabs that adhere to the sides of your screen.

To create a side tab:

1. Drag the palette tab to the left or right side of the screen. A vertical outline of the tab appears at the edge of the screen 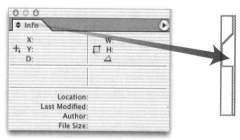.

2. Release the mouse. This adheres the palette to the side of the screen.

⑬ *Drag the palette tab to the left or right side of the screen to create a* **side tab**.

Collapsed side tabs

Expanded
side tabs

⊕ *Click the side tab on its name to* **expand or collapse the palette** *to the side of the monitor.*

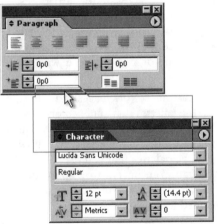

⊕ *Drag the palette tab to the bottom edge of another palette to* **dock the palettes** *together.*

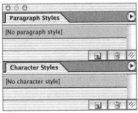

⊕ *Docked palettes are displayed together.*

To collapse and expand side tabs:

◆ If the side tab is in its collapsed state, click on the side tab palette name to expand it from the side of the screen **⊕**.

If the side tab is in its expanded state, click on the side tab palette name to collapse it to the side of the screen **⊕**.

TIP Side tabs can also be nested with other palettes.

TIP As you move palettes around the screen, you'll notice that the palettes snap to the edges of the monitor screen. I don't find any big benefit to this except it keeps things neat and tidy.

You can also dock palettes so they open, close, and move together. The palettes take up less space than if they were separated, yet unlike nested palettes, both can be seen at once.

TIP As you drag to nest and dock palettes, make sure you drag by positioning your cursor on the palette's name. If you drag from the top bar, you will move the palette, but you won't be able to dock or nest it.

To dock a palette:

1. Drag one palette tab to the bottom edge of another palette **⊕**. A dark line appears at the bottom of the palette area.

2. Release the mouse. This docks the palette underneath the top palette **⊕**.

To undock palettes:

1. Drag one palette tab so that the outline is completely outside the other palette.

2. Release the mouse button. The palette appears as a separate palette.

Working with Palettes

Using Workspaces

I don't know any two InDesign users who agree as to how to arrange their palettes. Although my palettes may start out neatly arranged, within a short time I've got them scattered all over my screen — especially if I am demonstrating in front of a class.

Fortunately, you can arrange and save your palette arrangements into workspaces that you can call up at any time.

TIP InDesign ships with a workspace labeled Default. This is the workspace that the palettes revert to if you delete the InDesign preferences.

To save a custom workspace:

1. Arrange your palettes as you want them to appear on the screen.

2. Choose **Window > Workspace > Save Workspace**. The Save Workspace dialog box appears ➍.

3. Enter a name for the workspace.

4. Click the Save button. The name of the workspace appears in the Workspace menu.

To apply a workspace:

◆ Choose the custom workspace from the Workspace menu.

To delete a workspace:

1. Choose **Window > Workspace > Delete**. The Delete Workspace dialog box appears ➎.

2. Use the pop-up menu to choose the workspace you want to delete.

3. Click the Delete button to delete the workspace.

TIP You cannot delete the Default workspace.

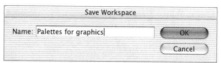

➍ The **Save Workspace dialog box** *lets you name the custom workspace configuration.*

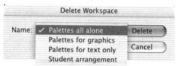

➎ The **Delete Workspace dialog box** *lets you choose the workspace you want to delete.*

Suggestions for Using Workspaces

Workspaces save all the attributes, appearances, and positions of the palettes. This means that you can have a workspace that closes all the palettes except one or two that you want to use.

You can have workspaces that show just the palettes that apply colors, gradients, and other object attributes. You can have other workspaces that show only the palettes that you use for text. You can even have a workspace that puts all the palettes on the left for left-handed users.

You can apply workspaces at any time as you are working — even with a document open. It's very soothing to see all your palettes rearrange into orderly groups.

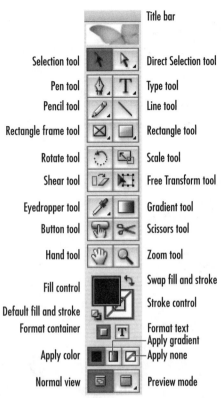

Title bar

Selection tool

Pen tool

Pencil tool

Rectangle frame tool

Rotate tool

Shear tool

Eyedropper tool

Button tool

Hand tool

Direct Selection tool

Type tool

Line tool

Rectangle tool

Scale tool

Free Transform tool

Gradient tool

Scissors tool

Zoom tool

Fill control

Default fill and stroke

Format container

Apply color

Normal view

Swap fill and stroke

Stroke control

Format text
Apply gradient

Apply none

Preview mode

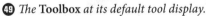

49 *The* **Toolbox** *at its default tool display.*

Using the Toolbox

The Toolbox contains the tools for working in InDesign, as well as controls for applying the colors of fills and strokes **49**. Some of the tools have fly-out panels that let you access the other tools in the category **50**. *(See the exercise on the next page for how to access the fly-out panels.)*

To choose a tool:

◆ Click the tool in the Toolbox.

or

Tap the individual keyboard shortcuts for each of the tools.

TIP You can change the arrangement of the Toolbox using the preferences *(see page 528)*.

or

Double-click the title bar on the Toolbox to change the arrangement.

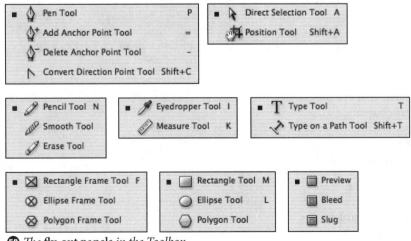

- Pen Tool   P
- Add Anchor Point Tool   =
- Delete Anchor Point Tool   –
- Convert Direction Point Tool Shift+C

- Direct Selection Tool   A
- Position Tool   Shift+A

- Pencil Tool   N
- Smooth Tool
- Erase Tool

- Eyedropper Tool   I
- Measure Tool   K

- Type Tool   T
- Type on a Path Tool Shift+T

- Rectangle Frame Tool   F
- Ellipse Frame Tool
- Polygon Frame Tool

- Rectangle Tool   M
- Ellipse Tool   L
- Polygon Tool

- Preview
- Bleed
- Slug

50 *The* **fly-out panels** *in the Toolbox.*

Tools that have a small triangle in their box have other tools hidden in a fly-out panel.

To open the related tools:

1. Press the fly-out triangle on the tool slot. The fly-out panel appears ❺❶.

2. Choose one of the tools listed in the fly-out panel.

To see the tool keyboard shortcuts:

◆ Move the cursor over the tool and pause. A tool tip appears with the name of the tool and the keyboard shortcut ❺❷.

TIP If you don't see the tool tip after pausing for a moment, make sure the Tool Tips control is turned on in the application preferences (*see Chapter 21, "Customizing InDesign"*).

TIP You can change or add keyboard shortcuts for tools using the keyboard shortcut controls (*see Chapter 21, "Customizing InDesign"*).

Using Contextual Menus

Contextual menus are menus that change depending on the type of object selected or where the mouse is positioned ❺❸. The benefit of contextual menus is that you don't have to move all the way up to the menu bar to invoke a command. Also the menu changes to provide you commands that are appropriate for the type of object chosen.

To display contextual menus:

◆ (Mac) Hold the Control key and click the mouse button.

or

(Win) Click the right mouse button.

TIP The contextual menu cursor appears as you hold the Control key.

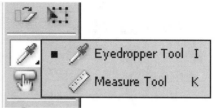

❺❶ *The* **fly-out panel** *displays the additional tools for that slot in the Toolbox.*

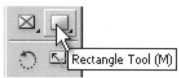

❺❷ *Pause over a tool to see the* **tool tip** *with the tool name and keyboard shortcut.*

Contextual cursor

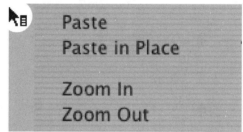

❺❸ *The* **contextual menu** *changes depending on what type of object is selected.*

DOCUMENT SETUP 2

Billions of years ago, when dinosaurs ruled the earth — or 19 years ago, before the start of desktop publishing — people prepared documents for printing using pieces of stiff board. They marked up the boards with special blue pencils to indicate the edges of the pages. They drew marks that specified where the margins and columns should be and how the pages should be trimmed. This board, called a *mechanical,* was used as the layout for the document.

Unlike the board mechanicals of the past, InDesign documents are electronic layouts. Just as with the board mechanicals, you need to set the page sizes, margins, and column widths. However, since you are not using a pencil but a computer, you have additional controls for how the document is laid out.

Of course, changing an electronic layout takes far less time than it did with the board mechanicals that old dinosaurs like me used to use.

Starting Documents

When you create a new document, you have the opportunity to set many options in the New Document dialog box.

To set the basic options for a new document:

1. Choose **File > New > Document**. This opens the New Document dialog box ❶.

2. Type the number of pages in your document in the Number of Pages field.

3. Check Facing Pages to set your document with left-hand and right-hand pages. *(See page 20 for more information on facing pages.)*

4. Check Master Text Frame to make it easy to flow text onto pages. *(See page 269 for more information on master text frames.)*

5. Use the Page Size pop-up list to set the size of your page. *(See page 20 for more information on the page size.)*

6. Set the Orientation to portrait or landscape. *(See page 21 for more information on the page orientation.)*

7. Enter the size of the margins in the Margins fields. *(See page 21 for more information on setting the margins.)*

8. Set the number of columns and the gutter width in the Columns Number and Gutter fields. *(See page 22 for more information on columns and gutters.)*

9. Click OK. The document appears in the window ❷.

TIP See the section "Working with Document Presets" on page 24 for information about the Document Presets and Save Preset buttons.

TIP The pages are surrounded by an area called the pasteboard. Like a drawing table, you can set items there for later use. Items on the pasteboard do not print.

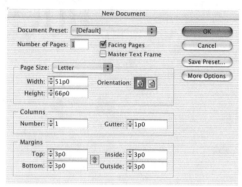

❶ *The* **New Document dialog box** *set for the basic layout options.*

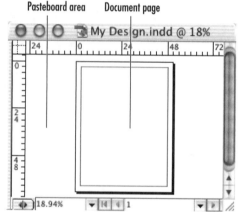

❷ *Each document page is surrounded by the* **pasteboard area** *where you can temporarily store objects for use later.*

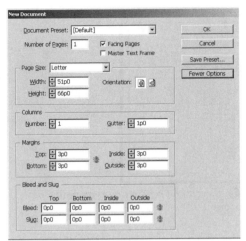

❸ The **New Document dialog box** *set for the advanced layout options.*

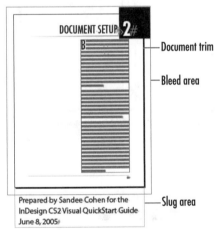

❹ *A document with* **bleed and slug areas.**

You can also set the advanced options for a document. The first is the area around the page, called a *bleed*. When you set a bleed, you define an area outside the trim of the page where objects will still print. The second area is called a *slug*. This is an area outside the page that may or may not print. Slugs are often used by advertising agencies to list insertion dates and the name of the product, manufacturer, and ad agency.

TIP The following exercise lets you set the options as part of the New Document dialog box. See page 23 for how to change the options for an existing document.

To set the advanced options for a new document:

1. Click the More Options button in the New Document dialog box. The advanced options for Bleed and Slug dimensions appear at the bottom of the dialog box **❸**.

2. Set the amounts for the size of the bleed area around the document **❹**. *(See the sidebar on page 468 for a description of why you need to set a bleed area.)*

3. Set the amounts for the size of the slug area around the document. The slug area is displayed outside the document trim **❹**.

TIP Click the Make Same Size icon *(see page 21)* for the Bleed or Slug to automatically set all the dimensions to the same size.

Starting Documents

Choosing Layout Options

The term *facing pages* refers to documents such as this book where pages on one side of its spine face the pages on the other side. (This is also called a *spread*.) Single pages, such as advertisements, are set with facing pages turned off.

To set facing pages:

◆ With the Document Setup dialog box open, click Facing Pages. This changes the document from single page to facing pages ❺ and ❻.

TIP When a document is set for facing pages, the names in the dialog box for the Left and Right margins change to Inside and Outside margins ❻.

The page size is the size of the individual pages of the document.

To set the size of the page:

◆ Choose one of the following 11 choices from the Page Size menu ❼:

- **Letter**, 8½ by 11 inches.
- **Legal**, 8½ by 14 inches.
- **Tabloid**, 11 by 17 inches.
- **Letter–Half**, 8½ by 5½ inches.
- **Legal–Half**, 8½ by 7 inches.
- **A4**, 21 by 29.7 centimeters.
- **A3**, 29.7 by 42 centimeters.
- **A5**, 14.8 by 21 centimeters.
- **B5**, 17.6 by 25 centimeters.
- **Compact Disc**, 4.7222 by 4.75 inches.
- **Custom**, which allows you to enter your own specific values.

TIP The A4, A3, A5, and B5 sizes are used primarily outside of the United States.

TIP If you change the values in the Width or the Height field, the Page Size automatically switches to the Custom setting.

Choosing Layout Options

Left margin   Right margin

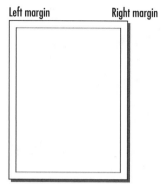

❺ *The left and right margins on* **nonfacing pages**.

Outside margin   Inside margins   Outside margin

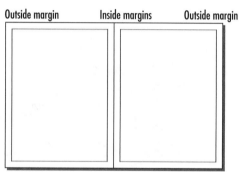

❻ *The outside and inside margins on* **facing pages**.

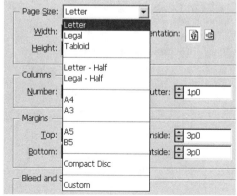

❼ *The* **Page Size menu** *offers standard U.S. and international paper sizes, as well as customization controls.*

Portrait   Landscape

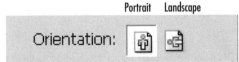

8 *The* **Orientation choices** *let you set the position of the page.*

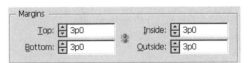

9 *The margin settings for a document with facing pages.*

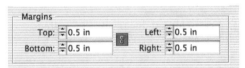

10 *The margin settings for a document with nonfacing pages.*

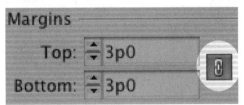

11 *Click the* **Make Same Size icon** *to automatically enter the same amount for all four margins.*

The term *orientation* refers to how the page is positioned, either up and down or sideways.

To set the orientation:

◆ Click the Portrait orientation to create a document where the width is always less than the height **8**.

or

Click the Landscape orientation to create a document where the width is always greater than the height **8**.

To set the margins:

1. Click the field arrows or enter an amount for the Top and Bottom fields.

2. If the document is set for facing pages, click the field arrows or enter an amount for the Inside and Outside fields **9**.

or

If the document is not set for facing pages, click the field arrows or enter an amount for the Left and Right margins **10**.

TIP For a facing page document, you can set the outside margin to be twice the size of the inside margin. That way the two inside margins combine around the gutter to be the same size as the outside margin.

TIP When you finish typing in one of the fields, press the Tab key to jump to the next field.

TIP Click the Make Same Size icon in the Margins area to control how the margins are created **11**. When the icon displays a link, all the margins will be the same size. When the icon displays a broken link, you can enter different sizes for each margin.

Choosing Layout Options

You can also set visible guides for columns and the *gutters* (or spaces) between the columns.

To set the columns and gutters:

1. Click the field arrows or enter an amount for the number of columns .

2. Click the field arrows or enter an amount for the gutter .

TIP The columns and gutters act as guidelines on your page 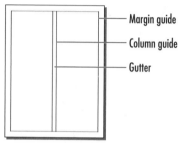. You can still place text or graphics across or outside the columns or gutters.

Wouldn't it be nice if the New Document dialog box remembered your favorite setup so you wouldn't have to change the settings each time you start a new document? It can, and that's called setting the *defaults*.

To set the document defaults:

1. Close all InDesign documents, leaving just the application open.

2. Choose **File > Document Setup**. The Document Setup dialog box appears.

3. Make whatever changes you want to the options in the Document Setup dialog box.

4. Click OK. The settings you have chosen become the default for any new documents.

TIP You can also specify a Document Preset *(see page 24)* to use as the document default.

⑫ *The* **column settings** *let you set the number of columns and the amount of space for the gutter between the columns.*

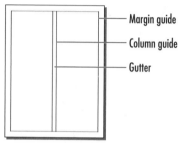

⑬ *A* **two-column document** *with margin, column, and gutter guidelines.*

Setting Other Defaults

As you work in InDesign, you will discover other areas where you would like to set defaults. Perhaps you'd like certain colors to appear (or not appear) in each new document. Or you would like certain text options to appear automatically.

Just as you can set the Document Setup options with no document open, you can also set other defaults.

With no document open, go to the menu and choose those options you would like to set as a default. Whatever is available for you to choose can then be set as a default.

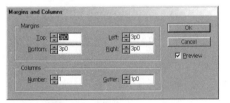

⓮ *The* **Document Setup** *dialog box for an existing document.*

⓯ *The* **Margins and Columns** *dialog box for an existing document.*

Changing Layout Options

You may discover that you need to change some of the settings of an existing document. When you start a new document, all the settings appear in one dialog box. However, after you begin working on the document you must use two separate controls to make changes to the document.

To change the document setup:

1. Choose **File > Document Setup** to open the Document Setup dialog box ⓮.

2. Make whatever changes you want to the following settings:
   - **Number of Pages**
   - **Facing Pages**
   - **Page Size**
   - **Orientation**
   - **Bleed** and **Slug**

3. Click OK to apply the changes to the document.

To change the margins and columns:

1. Choose **Layout > Margins and Columns** to open the Margins and Columns dialog box ⓯.

2. Make whatever changes you want to the following settings:
   - **Margins**
   - **Number of columns**
   - **Gutter** (the width of the space between the columns)

3. Click OK to apply the changes to the document.

   TIP Changing the margins and columns while on a page or spread changes the settings only for that page or spread. To change the settings for all the pages, you need to work with the Master Page. *(See Chapter 10, "Pages and Books," for more information on master pages.)*

Changing Layout Options

Using the Document Presets

You may want to save all the settings for certain types of documents so they can easily be applied when you start new documents. For instance, my Visual QuickStart books require different settings than the handouts I use when teaching. Document presets make it easy to apply the different settings when I create new documents.

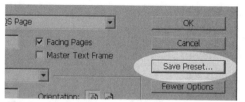

16 *Click the* **Save Preset button** *in the New Document dialog box to save the current settings as a preset.*

To save the document settings as document preset:

1. Choose **File > New > Document** and set the options in the New Document dialog box.

2. Click the Save Preset button **16**. This opens the Save Preset dialog box **17**.

3. Enter a name for the preset in the Save Preset As field and click OK. This adds the preset to the Document Preset menu in the New Document dialog box.

17 *Enter a name for a document preset in the* **Save Preset As** *field.*

To apply a document preset:

◆ Choose the document preset from the Document Preset menu in the New Document dialog box **18**.

 or

 Choose **File > Document Presets** and then choose one of the presets listed in the menu. This opens the New Document dialog box with that preset chosen.

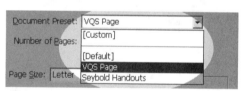

18 *You can apply presets using the* **Document Preset menu** *in the New Document dialog box.*

To edit a document preset:

1. Choose **File > Document Presets > Define**. This opens the Document Presets dialog box.

2. Choose the document preset in the Document Presets dialog box, and click the Edit button **19**. This opens the Edit Document Preset dialog box **20**.

3. Make whatever changes you want. Click OK to save the changes in the preset.

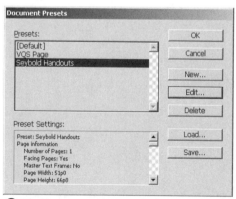

19 *The* **Document Presets dialog box** *lets you edit, delete, and create new document presets.*

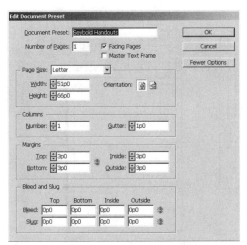

20 *Use the* **Edit Document Preset dialog box** *to make changes to existing document presets.*

You can also use the Document Presets dialog box to create document presets without going through the New Document dialog box.

To create a new document preset:

1. Choose **File > Document Presets > Define**. This opens the Document Presets dialog box.

2. Click the New button to open the New Document Presets dialog box.

TIP This dialog box is similar to the Edit Document Preset dialog box.

3. Use the dialog box to name and set the options for the new preset.

4. Click OK to save the preset.

To delete a document preset:

◆ Choose the document preset, and click the Delete button.

TIP You can't delete the [Default] preset.

You can also export document presets into a file that can be shared with others.

To export document presets:

1. Click the Save button in the Document Presets dialog box.

2. Name and save the document preset file.

You can also import document presets from others.

To import document presets:

1. Click the Load button in the the Document Presets dialog box.

2. Naviagate to find the document preset file.

3. Click the Open button. The document presets are imported into InDesign.

Using the Document Presets

Using Document Rulers

Designers need to measure things on pages. Rather than hold a ruler up to your monitor, you can use InDesign's electronic rulers.

To show and hide the document rulers:

◆ To see the rulers along the top and left edges of the document window, choose **View > Show Rulers ㉑**.

or

To hide the rulers, choose **View > Hide Rulers**.

You can change the rulers to display different units of measurement. This is helpful if you receive instructions written in measurements with which you are not familiar.

To change the unit of measurement:

1. Choose **Edit > Preferences > Units & Increments** (Win) or **InDesign > Preferences > Units & Increments** (Mac). This opens the Units & Increments dialog box.

2. For the Horizontal and Vertical settings, choose one of the measurements from the pop-up lists ㉒.

TIP You can have different units for the horizontal and the vertical rulers. For instance, the vertical ruler can match the document's leading so that each unit equals each line of copy. The horizontal unit can be in inches or picas.

3. If you choose Custom, enter the number of points for each unit on the ruler.

TIP You can also change the units with the ruler contextual menus ㉓. *(See page 16 for more information on how to access contextual menus.)*

TIP The Units & Increments preferences also let you set your own value for the number of points per inch. *(See page 534 for more information on setting this preference.)*

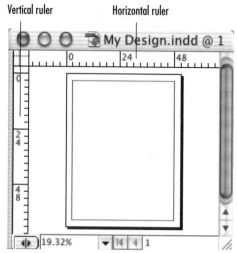

Vertical ruler · Horizontal ruler

㉑ *The* **horizontal and vertical rulers**.

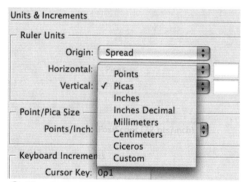

㉒ *The choices for the* **ruler's units of measurement**.

㉓ *The contextual menu when you click over a ruler.*

Using Document Rulers

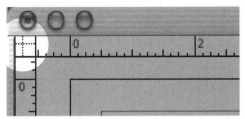

24 *The* **zero point indicator** *of the rulers.*

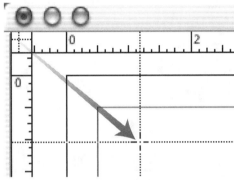

25 *You set the ruler's* **zero point** *by dragging the zero point indicator to a new position on the page.*

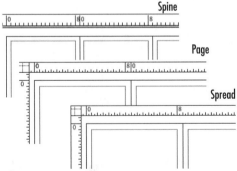

26 *You can control if the the rulers reset for each spine or each page. They can also be set to stay across a spread.*

The rulers start numbering at the top-left corner of the page. You may want to move this point, called a *zero point*, to a different position. This might help you judge how much space you have from one spot of the page to another.

To reposition the zero point:

1. Position the cursor over the zero point crosshairs at the upper-left corner of the rulers **24**.

2. Drag the zero point to the new position on the page **25**.

3. Release the mouse button to position the zero point.

TIP Double-click the zero point crosshairs in the corner of the rulers to reset the zero point to the upper-left corner.

If you are working on a project such as an advertising spread, it may be easier to position objects if the rulers continue across the *spine* of the pages. *(The spine is where the pages of a book, magazine, or other multipage document are bound together.)* InDesign lets you customize the origin of the rulers.

To set the origin of the rulers:

1. Choose **Edit > Preferences > Units & Increments** (Win) or **InDesign > Preferences > Units & Increments** (Mac).

2. Set the Ruler Units Origin menu to Page, Spread, or Spine **26**.

   or

   Choose a setting from the ruler contextual menu **23**.

TIP There is no difference between the page or spine settings unless there are more than two pages to the spread.

Using Document Rulers

Working with Guides

Guides are nonprinting lines that help you position objects. InDesign has many different types of guides that you can work with 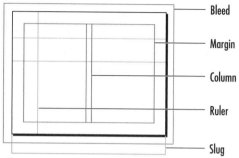.

- **Ruler guides** can be positioned anywhere on the page or pasteboard.
- **Margin guides** show the settings of the margins for the document.
- **Column guides** show the column settings for a page or master page (see Chapter 10, "Pages and Books").
- **Bleed guides** show the bleed area for the document.
- **Slug guides** show the slug area for the document.

InDesign gives you options for how to work with guides.

To change the guide preferences:

1. Choose **Edit > Preferences > Guides & Pasteboard** (Win) or **InDesign > Preferences > Guides & Pasteboard** (Mac) to open the Guides & Pasteboard Preferences 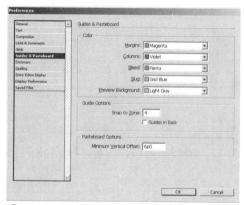.

2. Use each of the menus to set the colors of the guides.

3. Check Guides in Back to position the guides behind text and graphics on the page 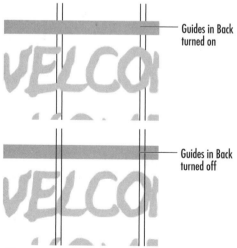.

4. Enter an amount in the Snap to Zone field. This is the distance, in pixels, for how close an object must be before it will snap or jump to align with a guide.

To show and hide guides:

- To see the margin, column, and ruler guides, choose **View > Grids & Guides > Show Guides**.

    or

    To hide the guides, choose **View > Grids & Guides > Hide Guides**.

27 *Examples of the various* **types of guides** *on a page.*

Labels: Bleed, Margin, Column, Ruler, Slug

28 *The dialog box for the* **guides preferences**.

Labels: Guides in Back turned on, Guides in Back turned off

29 *The* **Guides in Back command** *changes how guides are displayed as they pass through text and artwork.*

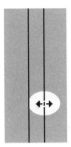

③⓪ *The* **two-headed arrow** *indicates that a column guide can be moved.*

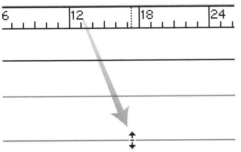

③① *You can drag ruler guides out from the horizontal ruler or vertical ruler.*

Objects can be set to automatically snap to guides as you move them. This makes it easier to align objects to guides.

To make objects snap to guides:
◆ Choose **View > Grids & Guides > Snap to Guides.**

TIP Choose the command again to turn off the feature.

There may be times when you want to move a column guide manually. This results in a custom guide setting.

To unlock and move column guides:
1. If **View > Grids & Guides > Lock Column Guides** is checked, choose the command to unlock the column guides.
2. Position the cursor over the guide you want to move.
3. Press the mouse button. The cursor turns into a two-headed arrow that indicates that the column has been selected **③⓪**.
4. Drag the column guide to the new position.

TIP You cannot change the width of the gutter space between the columns by moving a column guide. But you can change it in the Margins and Columns dialog box *(see page 23)*.

Ruler guides are more flexible than margin or column guides and can be positioned anywhere on the page to help with object placement.

To create ruler guides:
1. Position the cursor over the horizontal or vertical ruler. *(See page 26 for how to display the rulers.)*
2. Press the mouse button. The cursor turns into a two-headed arrow.
3. Drag to pull the guide out onto the page **③①**.

Working with Guides

Rather than pulling guides out one at a time, you can also create a series of ruler guides in rows and columns.

To create rows and columns using guides:

1. Choose **Layout > Create Guides.** This opens the Create Guides dialog box 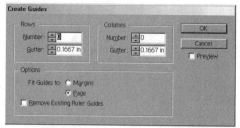.

2. Enter the number of rows (horizontal guides) in the Rows Number field.

3. Enter the amount for the space between the rows in the Rows Gutter field.

4. Enter the number of columns (vertical guides) in the Columns Number field.

5. Enter the amount for the space between the columns in the Columns Gutter field.

6. Choose between Fit Guides to Margins or Fit Guides to Page ③③.

7. Check Remove Existing Ruler Guides to delete all the ruler guides that were previously on the page. This includes ruler guides that were manually added to the page.

8. Click OK to apply the guides.

TIP Check Preview to see the guides on the page change as you enter the values within the dialog box.

TIP If you set the Number fields to zero for both the Rows and Columns, you can use the Remove Existing Ruler Guides setting as a quick way to delete all the ruler guides on the page.

To reposition ruler guides:

1. Position the cursor over the guide you want to move.

2. Press the mouse button. The cursor turns into a two-headed arrow and the guide changes to a darker color. This indicates that the guide has been selected.

3. Drag the ruler guide to a new position.

③② The Create Guides dialog box *lets you automatically add many guides on a page.*

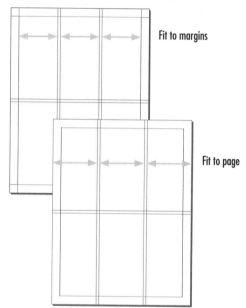

Fit to margins

Fit to page

③③ Fit Guides to Margin *spaces the guides equally inside the page margins.* **Fit Guides to Page** *spaces the guides equally inside the page trim.*

Working with Guides

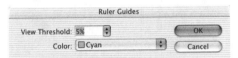
34 *Use either of the* **Selection tools** *to select a ruler guide.*

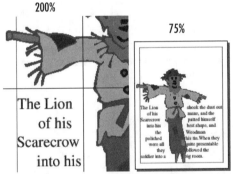
35 *Use the* **Ruler Guides dialog box** *to change the color of the ruler guides. You can also set the threshold to determine at what magnification the guides are visible.*

200%

75%

The Lion
of his
Scarecrow
into his

36 *A* **view threshold** *of 200% means the guides are visible only when the magnification is 200% or higher.*

You can also manually move or delete ruler guides.

To move existing ruler guides:

◆ Use either of the Selection tools to drag the ruler guide to a new position **34**.

To delete ruler guides:

1. Click the ruler guide with one of the Selection tools. The ruler guide turns a darker color, indicating it is selected.

2. Press the Delete/Backspace key. This deletes the ruler guide.

You may want to lock your ruler guides so they don't move inadvertently.

To lock guides:

◆ Choose **View > Grids & Guides > Lock Guides.**

TIP Choose the command again to unlock the guides.

You can change the color of ruler guides. You can also set the magnification at which the guides are not visible.

To change the appearance of ruler guides:

1. Choose **Layout > Ruler Guides** to open the dialog box **35**.

2. Use the Color pop-up list to pick the color for the ruler guides.

3. Set a percentage for the View Threshold. This sets the amount of magnification below which the ruler guides are not displayed **36**.

TIP Increase the View Threshold if you have many guides on the page. This hides the guides at low magnifications and shows them at higher ones. *(See page 33 for setting the view magnifications.)*

Working with Guides

Working with Document Grids

Ruler guides aren't the only way to align objects. The document grid can also be used as a structure for designing pages. The baseline grid is used to keep lines of text even. *(See page 409 for how to align text to the baseline grid.)*

To display the grids:

◆ Choose **View** > **Grids & Guides** > **Show Document Grid 37** or **View** > **Grids & Guides** > **Show Baseline Grid.**

To hide the grids:

◆ Choose **View** > **Grids & Guides** > **Hide Document Grid** or **View** > **Grids & Guides** > **Hide Baseline Grid.**

To change the grid apperance:

1. Choose **Edit** > **Preferences** > **Grids** (Win) or **InDesign** > **Preferences** > **Grids** (Mac) to open the Grids Preferences dialog box **38**.

2. Use the Color pop-up list to change the grid color.

3. Enter an amount in the Horizontal and Vertical Gridline Every fields to set the distance between the main gridlines.

4. Enter an amount in the Subdivisions field to create lighter gridlines between the main gridlines.

5. Enter an amount in the Start field to set where the baseline grid should start.

6. Use the Relative To list to position the start of the grid relative to the top of the page or the top margin.

7. Enter a percentage in the View Threshold field. This sets the lowest magnification at which the grid is visible.

8. Check Grids in Back to position the gridlines behind objects on the page, as shown on page 28 in figure **29**.

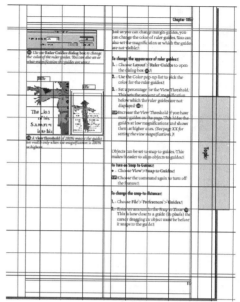

37 *Choose* **Show Document Grid** *to see the horizontal and vertical gridlines.*

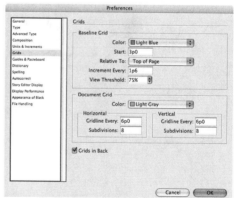

38 *The* **Grids Preferences dialog box** *lets you control the display and arrangement of the document grid.*

Working with Document Grids

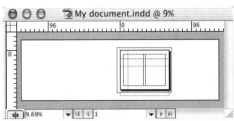

39 *The* **Entire Pasteboard command** *shows the page as well as the pasteboard.*

InDesign's "Smart" View Commands

If you have not used other page layout programs, you may not realize how smart some of InDesign's View commands are. These are the commands Fit Page in Window, Fit Spread in Window, and Entire Pasteboard.

In most other programs, if you choose the Fit Page in Window command, the magnification changes to show the entire page. If you then change the size of the window, the magnification is no longer the correct size to show the entire page.

InDesign, however, is much smarter. When you choose those three View commands, InDesign continues to display the entire page, spread, or pasteboard even if you resize the window. The magnification dynamically changes as you change the size of the window.

The command will stay active until you choose a new view or manually change the magnification. That's pretty smart!

To turn on Snap to Grid:

◆ Choose **View > Grids & Guides > Snap to Document Grid.** If Snap to Document Grid is checked, the feature is already turned on.

Changing the Magnification

Magnification refers to the size of the document as it appears on your screen. InDesign gives you many ways to change the magnification setting. Some of the quickest and easiest ways to change the magnification settings are to use View commands.

To zoom with the View commands:

1. To increase the magnification, choose **View > Zoom In.**

2. To decrease the magnification, choose **View > Zoom Out.**

3. To see all of the current page, choose **View > Fit Page In Window.** This changes the magnification setting to whatever amount is necessary to see the entire page.

TIP A small monitor forces you to use small magnifications to see the entire page. A larger monitor allows you to set its resolution so that it shows the entire page at magnifications that are easier to read.

4. To see all of the current spread, choose **View > Fit Spread in Window.** *(See page 20 for more information on working with spreads.)*

5. To see the document at 100% magnification, choose **View > Actual Size.**

6. To see the entire pasteboard area, choose **View > Entire Pasteboard 39.**

InDesign lets you view the page with a wide range of magnification settings. You can select a specific magnification amount from the magnification list.

To use the magnification list:

1. Click the control at the bottom-left corner of the document window to display the magnification list 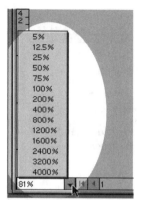.

2. Choose one of the magnifications in the list.

40 *The* **magnification list** *at the bottom of the document window.*

You can also view specific magnifications not in the list.

To enter a specific magnification amount:

1. Double-click or drag across the magnification shown in the bottom-left corner of the document window.

2. Type a number between 5 and 4000.

TIP It is not necessary to type the % sign.

3. Press Return or Enter to apply the setting.

Magnification Shortcuts

Because the View commands are used so often, the keyboard shortcuts are listed here. You can also find these shortcuts listed on the View menu.

Mac Commands

Zoom In	Cmd-=
Zoom Out	Cmd-hyphen
Fit Page in Window	Cmd-0
Fit Spread in Window	Cmd-Opt-0
Actual Size	Cmd-1

Windows Commands

Zoom In	Ctrl-=
Zoom Out	Ctrl-hyphen
Fit Page in Window	Ctrl-0
Fit Spread in Window	Ctrl-Alt-0
Actual Size	Ctrl-1

Changing the Magnification

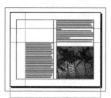

41 *Click the* **Normal View Mode icon** *to see all the elements of the document.*

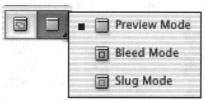

42 *The* **Normal View Mode** *shows all the elements of the document.*

43 *Choose one of the view modes to see specific areas in a Preview Mode.*

44 *The* **Preview Mode** *shows only the printing elements and hides the pasteboard.*

45 *The* **Bleed Mode** *shows only the printing elements and the bleed area.*

46 *The* **Slug Mode** *shows only the printing elements and the slug area.*

View and Pasteboard Controls

As you work, you may want to view your document in different ways. The four View modes provide different ways of looking at your document.

To choose the four View modes:

- Click the Normal View Mode icon at the bottom of the Toolbox **41**.

  - **Normal View Mode** is the default view and shows you all the guides in the document as well as the pasteboard, bleed, and slug areas **42**.

    or

  Choose one of the view modes from the fly-out panel at the bottom of the Toolbox **43**.

  - **Preview Mode** shows only the area inside the page boundaries. All guides are automatically hidden **44**.
  - **Bleed Mode** adds the area inside the bleed to the Preview Mode **45**.
  - **Slug Mode** adds the area inside the slug to the Preview Mode **46**.

View and Pasteboard Controls

When you switch to the Preview Mode the pasteboard is replaced by a colored background. The default color is gray; but you can change that to any color you like.

To change the Preview Background color:

1. Choose **Edit** > **Preferences** > **Guides & Pasteboard** (Win) or **InDesign** > **Preferences** > **Guides & Pasteboard** (Mac) to open the Guides & Pasteboard Preferences.

2. Use the Preview Background list to set the color for the background **47**. This changes the color shown in the Preview Mode **48**.

TIP Restrain yourself from changing the color to something extremely intense. A vivid color around a document can change how colors on the page appear.

The area above and below the document is controlled by the Minimum Vertical Offset. You can make that area larger.

To change the Minimum Vertical Offset:

1. Choose **Edit** > **Preferences** > **Guides & Pasteboard** (Win) or **InDesign** > **Preferences** > **Guides & Pasteboard** (Mac) to open the Guides & Pasteboard Preferences.

2. Enter an amount in the Minimum Vertical Offset field **49**. This increases the pasteboard above and below the page **50**.

TIP Some people who come to InDesign from other programs want to increase the vertical offset of the pasteboard to avoid problems when rotating objects so that they stick off the pasteboard. Their old program wouldn't let them rotate objects in that manner. Fortunately, InDesign lets you rotate objects outside the pasteboard.

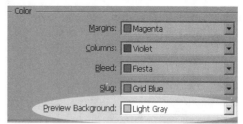

47 *Use the* **Preview Background list** *to change the color of the pasteboard area shown in the Preview Mode.*

48 *A* **black background in the pasteboard area** *presents your work with a more dramatic appearance.*

49 *Use the* **Minimum Vertical Offset field** *to increase the size of the pasteboard above and below the document.*

50 *The effects of increasing the size of the Minimum Vertical Offset.*

51 *Use the* **Zoom tool** *to change the magnification of the page.*

52 **Drag the Zoom tool** *diagonally to magnify a specific area. The marquee indicates the area to be selected.*

53 *The selected area fills the window after you release the mouse button.*

Using the Zoom and Hand Tools

The Zoom tool lets you jump to a specific magnification and position on the page. The Hand tool moves the view to a new position.

To use the Zoom tool:

1. Click the Zoom tool in the Toolbox **51**. The cursor turns into a magnifying glass.

2. Click the Zoom tool on the area you want to zoom in on. Click as many times as is necessary to change the magnification.

TIP Press Cmd/Ctrl and Spacebar to access the Zoom tool without leaving the tool that is currently selected.

TIP Each click of the Zoom tool changes the magnification to the next setting in the magnification list.

TIP Press the Opt/Alt key while in the Zoom tool to decrease magnification. The icon changes from a plus sign (+) to a minus sign (–).

TIP Double-click the Zoom tool in the Toolbox to set the view to the actual size (100%).

A *marquee zoom* allows you to zoom quickly to a certain magnification and position.

To create a marquee zoom:

◆ Drag the Zoom tool diagonally across the area you want to see. Release the mouse button to zoom in **52** and **53**.

Using the Zoom and Hand Tools

You can also use the Hand tool (sometimes called the *Grabber* tool) to move around within the area of the document. This is more flexible than using the scrollbars, which only go up and down or left and right.

To use the Hand tool:

1. Click the Hand tool in the Toolbox ⑤⑷.
2. Drag the Hand tool to move around the page.

TIP Double-click the Hand tool in the Toolbox to fit the entire page in the window.

If you want to become a true InDesign power user, you need to use keyboard shortcuts. One of the primary shortcuts you should learn is how to temporarily access the Hand tool without leaving the current tool. This lets you scroll around a document very quickly.

To temporarily access the Hand tool:

◆ Press the Opt/Alt plus Spacebar keys. This gives you the Hand tool in all situations.

TIP You can also access the Hand tool by pressing just the Opt/Alt key if you are working in a text frame.

⑤⑷ *Use the* **Hand tool** *to move the page around the window.*

Playing the Keyboard "Bass Notes"

I confess! I haven't chosen the Zoom or Hand tools in years. Rather than move the mouse all the way over to the toolbox, I use the keyboard short-cuts.

On the Mac, I keep my fingers lightly resting on the Cmd, Opt, and Spacebar keys. By changing which keys are pressed, I alternate between the Zoom In, Zoom Out, and Hand tools.

On Windows, I do the same thing with the Ctrl, Alt, and Spacebar keys.

So, as my right hand moves the mouse around and taps other keys on the keyboard, my left hand is always playing the three bass notes of the keyboard.

Magnification field | Zoom out | Zoom slider

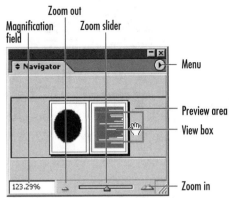

Menu

Preview area

View box

Zoom in

55 *The elements of the **Navigator palette**.*

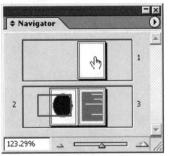

56 *When View All Spreads is chosen, the Navigator displays all the spreads in the document.*

Using the Navigator Palette

The Navigator palette combines the functions of both the Zoom and Hand tools. As you change the views in the Navigator, you change the views in your document.

TIP Enlarge the size of the Navigator palette to see more details in your document.

To use the Navigator zoom buttons:

1. If the Navigator palette is not already open, choose **Window > Object & Layout > Navigator**. This opens the Navigator palette **55**.

2. Click the Zoom In button to increase the magnification.

3. Click the Zoom Out button to decrease the magnification.

To set a specific magnification:

1. Highlight the value in the Magnification field and enter the specific magnification.

2. Press Return or Enter.

To use the Zoom slider:

◆ Drag the Zoom slider to the right to increase the magnification.

   or

   Drag the slider to the left to decrease the magnification.

The Navigator palette can display a single spread or all the spreads in the document.

To change the view spread options:

◆ Choose View All Spreads from the Navigator palette menu. This displays all the spreads in the document **56**.

TIP When you choose View All Spreads, the menu choice changes to View Active Spread. This displays only the currently selected spread. *(See Chapter 10, "Pages and Books," for more information on working with spreads.)*

Using the Navigator Palette

The Preview area within the Navigator palette can also be used to move around the document.

To move using the Navigator Preview area:

1. Position the cursor inside the Preview area of the Navigator palette. The cursor changes into a hand **57**.

2. Drag the Hand cursor around the Preview area. The Preview Box moves to change the area displayed within the document window.

TIP Notice how the Hand cursor turns into an animated fist as it grabs the page to move around the document. *Cute!*

The View Box is the rectangle that shows the size of the area displayed in the document window. You can change the color of that rectangle so that it is more easily seen against the color of your document pages.

To change the color of the View Box:

1. Choose Palette Options from the Navigator menu. This opens the Palette Options dialog box **58**.

2. Use the Color list to pick a new color.

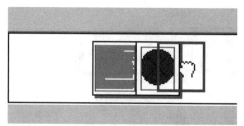

57 *The* **Hand cursor** *inside the Preview area of the Navigator palette.*

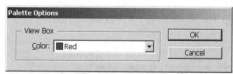

58 *The* **Palette Options** *let you change the color of the View Box inside the Navigator palette.*

Too Many Navigation Choices

Between the document scrollbars, the Hand tool, the Navigator palette, and the page controls *(covered in Chapter 10, "Pages and Books")*, you may feel a little overwhelmed by all your choices for moving around a document. Here are some guidelines for when to use what:

- Use the Hand tool for short distances.
- Use the Navigator palette if you need some visible clues as to where you are moving.
- Use the page controls such as the Pages palette if you need to jump across many pages in a document.

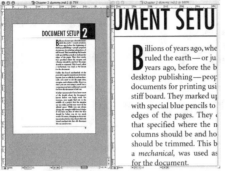

⑤ *Two views of the same document set as tiled windows.*

Controlling Windows

The window commands let you view one document in two windows and control the display of multiple windows.

To see a document in two windows:

1. Choose **Window > Arrange > New Window.** This creates a second window containing the document.

2. Choose **Window > Arrange > Tile.** This changes the size of the two windows and positions them side by side on your screen **⑤**.

   or

   Choose **Window > Arrange > Cascade.** This stacks all the open windows so that their title bars are visible.

In the Macintosh OS X operating system, the windows for InDesign documents may be obscured by other application windows. Fortunately there is a command that lets you move all the InDesign windows to be seen at the front of the screen.

To control the order of documents (Mac):

◆ Choose **Window > Arrange > Bring All To Front.** This moves all the InDesign documents to the front of the stacking order of all other applications.

File Maintenance

After you work on a document for even a little while, you must save your work to a hard drive or disk. This is vital so that you don't lose important information should your computer crash in a power blackout or you do something stupid.

To save and name a file (Win):

1. Choose **File** > **Save** or **File** > **Save As.** This opens the Save As dialog box **60**.

2. Use the Save In field to choose a destination disk and folder for the file.

3. Use the File Name field to name the file.

4. Use the Save As Type field to choose between an InDesign document and an InDesign template.

5. Click Save to save the file and close the dialog box.

To save and name a file (Mac):

1. Choose **File** > **Save** or **File** > **Save As.** This opens the Save As dialog box **61**.

2. Use the Macintosh navigational elements to choose a destination disk and folder for the file.

3. Use the Name field to name the file.

4. Use the Format pop-up list to choose between an InDesign document and an InDesign template.

TIP The template format saves the file so that each time it is opened, it opens as an untitled document. This protects the document from inadvertent changes.

5. Click Save to save the file and close the dialog box.

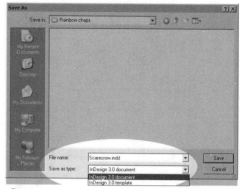

60 *The* **Save As** *dialog box (Win).*

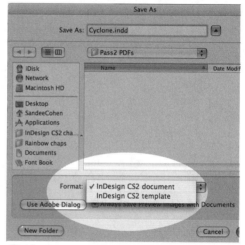

61 *The* **Save As** *dialog box (Mac).*

OS or Adobe Dialog Box?

There's an option in the Save and Open dialog boxes to use the Adobe dialog box or the OS (operating system) dialog box. The Adobe dialog box is another way of displaying the information in your computer. You should also choose the Adobe dialog box if you are using Version Cue.

However, for this book I will use the OS dialog boxes.

The Three Different Save Commands

The first time you look under the File menu you may be a little confused by the three different commands for saving documents. What are the differences between Save, Save As, and Save a Copy?

The first time you save an untitled document, there is no difference between choosing **File > Save** and **File > Save As**. Both commands bring up the Save As dialog box.

Once you have named a file, the Save command adds new work to the file without changing the file's name. The Save As command will always open the dialog box where you can change the file's name or location.

I use the Save command almost all the time. That way I only have to remember one keystroke combination: Cmd/Ctrl-S. The only time I use the Save As command is if I want to change the name of a document or save it somewhere else.

The **File > Save A Copy** command is different. When you save a copy, you can save the file under a new name. However, unlike the Save As command, you continue to work on the file you were working on.

I use the Save a Copy command when I am about to do something strange or bizarre to my work. The Save a Copy command lets me create a version of the file that I know I can fall back on.

As you work, you may want to spin off a copy of your document under another name. The Save a Copy command makes this easy to do.

To create a copy of a document:

1. Choose **File > Save a Copy**. This opens the Save As dialog box.

2. Use the same steps as described in the two previous exercises to save the file.

3. Click Save. The copy of the document is saved while you can continue to work on your current file.

There may be times when you want to revert to the previously saved version of a document without saving any changes.

To go back to the saved version of a document:

◆ Choose **File > Revert**. The file closes and then reopens to where it was when last saved.

To undo the steps you have done:

◆ Choose **Edit > Undo [Action]**.

TIP Repeat this command as often as necessary.

To redo the steps you have done:

◆ Choose **Edit > Redo [Action]**.

To close a document:

◆ Choose **File > Close**.

   or

   Click the Close box in the document window.

File Maintenance

It happens — someday, somehow your computer will crash, a blackout will hit your city, or you will be forced to restart the computer without saving your work. Fortunately, InDesign has an automatic recovery option that can save your work.

To recover a file:

1. Restart the computer after the crash or data loss.

2. Start InDesign. Any files that were open when the crash occurred will be automatically opened.

3. Choose **File > Save As** to save the file with a new name and destination.

TIP The restored data is a temporary version of the file and must be saved in order to ensure the integrity of the data.

InDesign gives you options for opening and closing files.

To open a file within InDesign:

1. Choose **File > Open**.

2. Use the navigation controls to select the file you want to open.

TIP You can also open a document by double-clicking its icon.

To open recently saved documents:

◆ Choose **File > Open Recent** and then choose one of the files listed in the submenu.

TIP InDesign lists the ten last-opened documents in the submenu.

File Maintenance

Opening QuarkXPress or PageMaker Files

InDesign can convert documents and templates from QuarkXPress 3.3 (or later) and Adobe PageMaker 6.5 (or later). Simply choose **File > Open** and choose the file. InDesign converts the file into a new InDesign document.

How good is the conversion? It's great for templates that consist of the layout without any text. All the master pages *(see page 269)* are converted along with the style sheets *(see page 378)* and colors *(see Chapter 5, "Working in Color")*. This lets you use your old templates to produce new work in InDesign. Graphics that were pasted via the clipboard into QuarkXPress or PageMaker — and not placed using the Place or Get Picture commands — are not converted.

The conversion may change documents with lots of text. For instance, InDesign arranges type with a very sophisticated composition engine *(see page 401)*. This means that text could move to new lines when it appears in the InDesign document.

If you need to make just one or two small changes to an old document, you're better off opening the file in QuarkXPress or PageMaker and making the changes to the original files.

However, if you need to completely redo a document, export the text from the file, and then use InDesign to convert the template into an InDesign file. You can then use that template for all new documents.

Installing Adobe Bridge

Don't panic if you can't remember installing Adobe Bridge. Bridge is installed automatically when you install InDesign or any of the other CS2 applications.

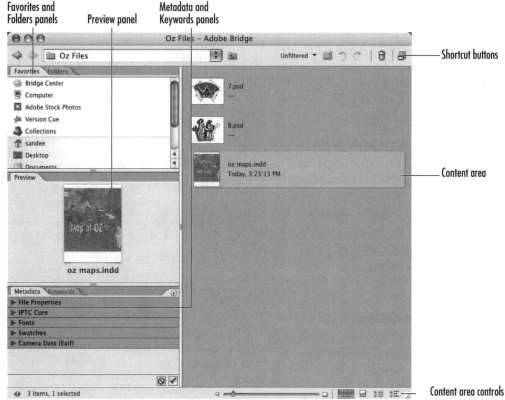

62 *Click the* **Bridge icon** *in InDesign's Control palette to launch or switch to Bridge.*

Working with Bridge

Adobe Bridge is a command center for all the products in the Adobe Creative Suite 2. You can launch Bridge through InDesign or as a separate application.

To launch and use Bridge:

◆ Click the Bridge icon **62** in the Control palette.

or

Use the Start menu (Windows) or Dock (Mac) to launch Bridge (or use any of the other operating system methods for launching an application).

TIP If a Bridge window **63** does not appear, choose **File > New Window** from the Bridge application menu.

Favorites and Folders panels   Preview panel   Metadata and Keywords panels

Shortcut buttons

Content area

Content area controls

63 *The* **Bridge window** *displays the files of your Creative Suite 2 products.*

Bridge has three different display options 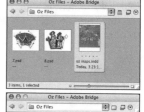. Each one changes the amount of information visible in Bridge.

To change Bridge display options:

◆ If Bridge is in the Compact Mode, click the Full Mode icon **65** to display all the panels of the Bridge window.

or

If Bridge is in the Full Mode, click the Compact Mode icon **65** to display only the content area.

or

If Bridge is in the Compact Mode, click the Ultra-Compact Mode icon **65** to display only the window title bar and navigation controls.

Bridge acts as a special Adobe version of the Macintosh Finder or the Windows Explorer. You can use Bridge to navigate through your computer directories or you can view files through a display of your favorite folders and servers.

To choose the Bridge navigation options:

◆ Click the Folders tab **66** to view the standard computer drives and network devices.

or

Click the Favorites tab **66** to view those drives and directories that you have added to the Favorites area.

To open InDesign files via Bridge:

◆ Double-click the file in the Preview panel or in the content area. The file opens as it would if you were using the operating system windows.

Working with Bridge

Full Mode

Compact Mode

Ultra-Compact Mode

64 *The* **Full Mode, Compact Mode,** *and* **Ultra-Compact Mode** *displays for the Bridge window.*

Ultra-Compact Mode icon   Full Mode or Compact Mode icon

65 *The* **mode icons** *for the Bridge displays.*

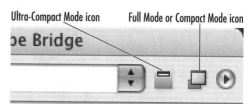

66 *The* **Favorites and Folders tabs** *allow you to change the navigation controls for Bridge.*

67 *Change the size of the* **Preview panel** *to change the size of the preview of a selected item.*

68 *Use the* **Preview Slider** *to change the size of the items in the main window.*

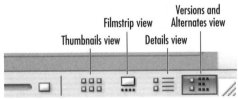

Versions and
Alternates view
Filmstrip view
Thumbnails view | Details view

69 *The* **view icons** *for the Bridge main window displays.*

One of the reasons I now use Bridge to open files instead of my operating system is that Bridge provides previews of all the Adobe Creative Suite 2 files — even if those files don't ordinarily display previews. I also have more control over the appearance of those previews.

To change the preview display in Bridge:

1. Select an item in the main window area. The item appears in the Preview panel.

2. Change the size of the Preview panel to increase or decrease the preview of the selected item **67**.

You can also change the preview and arrangement of items in the main window.

To change the main window displays:

◆   Use the Preview Slider to increase or decrease the size of items in the main window **68**.

You can also change how items in the main window are arranged.

To change the arrangement of main window items:

◆   Click one of the arrangement icons **69**:

   • **Thumbnails view** arranges the files in a grid.
   • **Filmstrip view** displays the files as a horizontal scrolling list with a large preview of the selected item.
   • **Details view** displays a list of the thumbnails along with information about the selected file.
   • **Versions and Alternates view** displays a list of the files, together with their Version Cue information.

Working with Bridge

Other Uses for Bridge

Adobe Bridge is expansive (pun intended). Covering all the features is beyond the scope of this book; and in fact many Bridge features don't pertain to InDesign. However, I will cover additional relevant features in other chapters as we get to those subjects.

You can use Bridge to view, search, sort, manage, and process image files, as well as to create folders, move and delete files, rotate images, and run batch commands.

Bridge also contains the link to the Adobe Stock Photos controls. You can use this service to search leading stock photo libraries for images. You can download low-resolution, complimentary versions of the images and try them out in your projects before purchasing them.

Adobe Creative Suite 2 offers additional Bridge features not available in the version of Bridge installed in the individual products. One such feature is the Bridge Center. This acts as a special Adobe Web browser where you can view newsreaders, see your most recent activity, read tips and tricks for using Adobe products, save groups of files, and more.

Creative Suite 2 users can also use Bridge to specify color management settings and access scripts that help automate workflow.

BASIC TEXT 3

When I started in advertising around twenty-five years ago, setting type was an involved process. First, the copywriter typed out the text on pieces of paper. The art director or typographer then marked up the page of copy with a red pencil to indicate the typeface, point size, leading, and so on. Then, the copy was sent to a typesetting house where a typesetter retyped the text into a special typesetting machine. The text was printed onto special photographic paper and sent back the next morning. The copywriter then had to proof the text to make sure that there were no errors.

That's why I am amazed every time I use a program such as InDesign to set text. I don't type the copy onto a piece of paper; I type right onto my actual layout. I don't have to send the copy out overnight; it's right there on my computer screen. And I know that the only mistakes are the ones I make myself!

Creating Text Frames

InDesign holds text in objects called *frames*. Before you can start typing text, you need to create a text frame. The easiest way to do this is with the Type tool.

❶ *Choose the* **Type tool** *in the Toolbox to work with text.*

TIP You can resize or reshape text frames like you can other objects. *(See Chapter 4, "Working with Objects," for more details on creating and working with objects.)*

❷ *The cursor set to create a text frame.*

To create a text frame with the Type tool:

1. Click the Type tool in the Toolbox ❶.
2. Move the cursor to the page. The cursor changes to the Type tool cursor ❷.
3. Drag diagonally to create the frame ❸.

TIP The frame starts from the horizontal line that intersects the text frame cursor.

4. Release the mouse button. The text frame appears with an insertion point that indicates you can type in the frame.

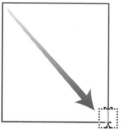

❸ *Drag diagonally* with the Type tool to **create a text frame.**

The Type tool will always create rectangular frames. However, you can use the frame tools to create other geometric shapes such as ellipses and polygons to hold text.

TIP The frame tools also let you use numerical settings to specify the exact dimensions of a frame *(see page 52).*

❹ *The* **Ellipse tool** *in the Toolbox.*

To draw an elliptical frame:

1. Click the Ellipse tool in the Toolbox ❹.
2. Drag diagonally to create the ellipse ❺.
3. Release the mouse button when the ellipse is the correct size.
4. Click the Type tool inside the frame to convert it to a text frame.

❺ *Drag diagonally to* **create an ellipse.**

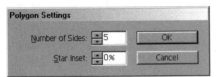

⑥ *The* **Polygon tool** *in the Toolbox.*

⑦ *Use the* **Polygon Settings dialog box** *to change the shape and the number of sides of a polygon.*

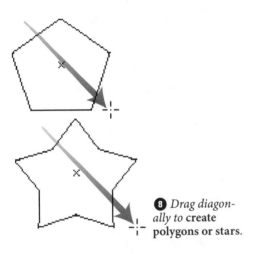

⑧ *Drag diagonally to* **create polygons or stars**.

Unassigned Frames

The Ellipse, Polygon, and Rectangle tools create frames that are unassigned. This means they hold neither text nor graphics. But don't let the unassigned designation mislead you. It doesn't really matter if a frame is unassigned or not.

You can convert unassigned frames to hold text *(see page 52)*, or you can convert unassigned frames to hold graphics *(see page 195)*.

The Polygon tool also lets you draw stars as well as ordinary polygons.

To draw a polygon frame:

1. Double-click the Polygon tool in the Toolbox **⑥**. This opens the Polygon Settings dialog box **⑦**.
2. Enter a number in the field for the number of sides.
3. Leave the Star Inset amount as 0%. If you increase the star inset, you create a star. (See the next exercise.)
4. Drag across the page to create the polygon **⑧**.

TIP Press the up or down arrow keys as you drag to increase or decrease the number of sides of the polygon.

5. Release the mouse button when the polygon is the correct size.
6. Click the Type tool inside the frame to convert it to a text frame.

To create a star frame:

1. Double-click the Polygon tool in the Toolbox to open the Polygon Settings dialog box **⑦**.
2. Enter a number in the Number of Sides field for the number of outer points.
3. Enter a value for the Star Inset amount. The greater the amount, the sharper the points will be.
4. Drag to create the star **⑧**.

TIP Press the up or down arrow keys as you drag to increase or decrease the number of points of the star.

TIP Press the left or right arrow keys as you drag to increase or decrease the star inset.

5. Release the mouse button when the star is the correct size.
6. Click the Type tool inside the frame to convert it to a text frame.

Creating Text Frames

You can also create rectangular frames using the Rectangle tool.

To draw a rectangular frame:

1. Click the Rectangle tool in the Toolbox .

2. Drag diagonally to create the rectangle ⑩.

3. Release the mouse button when the rectangle is the correct size.

4. Click the Type tool inside the frame to convert it to a text frame.

The Ellipse and Rectangle frame tools let you numerically specify the frame size.

To set the size of a frame numerically:

1. Choose the Ellipse or Rectangle tool from the Toolbox.

2. Position the cursor where you want to create the frame.

3. Click. A dialog box appears ⑪.

4. Set the Width and Height of the frame.

5. Click OK. The frame appears with its upper-left point where you first clicked.

TIP Hold the Opt/Alt key as you click to position the centerpoint of the frame at that point.

Frames created with the Ellipse, Polygon, and Rectangle tools must be converted to use as text frames.

To convert unassigned frames:

1. Select the frame you want to convert.

2. Choose the Type tool and click inside the frame.

   or

   Choose **Object > Content > Text.** An insertion point appears indicating that you can begin typing.

⑨ *The* **Rectangle tool** *in the Toolbox.*

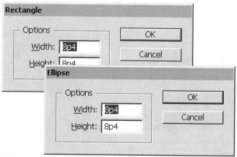

⑩ *Drag diagonally to* **create a rectangle**.

⑪ *The* **Ellipse and Rectangle dialog boxes** *let you specify the width and height of a frame.*

Tips for Drawing Frames

There are several keyboard shortcuts you can press as you draw frames:

- Hold the **Shift key** to constrain the frame to a square, circle, or uniform polygon.
- Hold the **Opt/Alt key** to draw the frame from the center outward.
- Hold the **Spacebar** to reposition the frame as you draw.

Creating Text Frames

⑫ *The* **overflow symbol** *indicates that there is more text than will fit in the frame.*

⑬ *The* **blinking insertion point** *indicates where text will be added.*

Typing Text

The two most important parts of working with text are typing the text and then selecting it to make changes.

To type text:

1. Click with the Type tool in a frame.
2. Begin typing.
3. Press Return to begin a new paragraph.

   or

   Press Shift-Return to begin a new line without starting a new paragraph.

TIP InDesign automatically wraps text within the text frame.

TIP If the text frame is too small to display all the text, an overflow symbol appears **⑫**. You can reshape the frame *(see page 90)* or flow the text into a new frame *(see page 75)* to eliminate the overflow.

To add text into a passage you have already typed, you move the *insertion point* to where you want to place the new material. The point blinks to help you find it **⑬**.

To move the insertion point:

1. Position the Type tool cursor where you want the insertion point.
2. Click to set the insertion point.

To move the point using the keyboard:

1. Use the arrow keys to move the insertion point left or right one character at a time or up and down one line at a time.
2. Use the Cmd/Ctrl key with the arrow keys to move the insertion point one word or one paragraph at a time.

Typing Text

Selecting Text

The simplest way to select text is to use the mouse.

To select text using the mouse:

◆ Press and drag across the text. The highlight indicates which text is being selected.

TIP You don't have to drag from left to right to select multiple lines. Simply drag down.

Like other programs, InDesign has special techniques to select words, lines, and paragraphs with the mouse.

To select a single word:

◆ Double-click within a word to select it **⑭**.

TIP Although only the word is selected, if you hit the Delete key, the word and the space after it will be deleted.

To select a single line:

◆ Triple-click within the line **⑮**.

TIP Turn on **Triple Click to Select a Line** in the Text preferences (see page 529).

To select a paragraph:

◆ If **Triple Click to Select a Line** is turned off, triple-click within the paragraph **⑯**.

or

If **Triple Click to Select a Line** is turned on, quadruple-click in the paragraph.

To select all the text in a frame or story:

◆ If **Triple Click to Select a Line** is turned off, quadruple-click within any paragraph.

or

If **Triple Click to Select a Line** is turned on, quintuple-click in any paragraph.

Dorothy began to sob for she felt lonely among all these **strange** people. The kind-hearted Munchkins immediately took out their handkerchiefs and began to weep also.

⑭ *Double-click to* **select a single word,** *which is then highlighted.*

Dorothy began to sob for she felt lonely among all these strange people. The **kind-hearted Munchkins** immediately took out their handkerchiefs and began to weep also.

⑮ *A triple-click* **selects a single line** *in a paragraph.*

Dorothy began to sob for she felt lonely among all these strange people. The kind-hearted Munchkins immediately took out their handkerchiefs and began to weep also.

⑯ *An example of how a triple-click or quadruple-click can* **select a paragraph.**

Keyboard, Mouse, or Menu?

One of the hot topics in working with software is the keyboard-versus-mouse debate. If you are a fast typist, you will work faster using keyboard shortcuts. There are times when you may consider using a mouse.

If my hands are already on the keyboard, I try to keep them there to select text or apply a formatting change.

But if my hands are on the mouse, I try to use it. So if I've just finished moving a text frame to a new position, I can easily highlight the text with the mouse.

Menu commands are another matter entirely. I try whenever possible to learn the keyboard shortcuts for menu commands.

That way I don't have to move the mouse all the way up to the top of the page to choose a command such as Cut, Copy, or Paste *(see page 88)*.

Quick Guide to the Shortcuts

Here are some easy ways to understand the selection shortcuts:

- The up, down, left, and right arrow keys all jump around the text.
- Add the Cmd/Ctrl keys to make the bigger jumps. Instead of a character, you jump a word. Instead of a line, you jump a paragraph. (Remember: you have more power when you take *Command* or *Control!*)
- Adding the Shift key lets you select the text. The *S* in *Shift* stands for *Select*.

If you spend a lot of time typing and modifying text, you should learn the following techniques for selecting text.

To select text using keyboard shortcuts:

1. Use the following keyboard commands to select text using the keyboard:

Keystroke	Selects
Shift key and tap the left or right arrow key	Single character.
Shift key and tap the up or down arrow key	One line of text. Repeat to select additional lines.
Cmd/Ctrl+Shift keys and tap the left or right arrow key	One word and the space following it.
Cmd/Ctrl+Shift keys and tap the up or down arrow key	Paragraph.
Shift key and tap the Home or End key	All the text to the beginning or end of a line.
Cmd/Ctrl+Shift keys and tap the Home or End key	All the text to the beginning or end of a text frame or story.
Cmd/Ctrl+A	All the text within an entire text frame or story.

2. Repeat any of the above commands to select additional text.

TIP You can switch commands to first select a line and then the following word.

TIP Once text is selected, you can use the above commands in reverse to deselect the text.

TIP You can quickly switch to editing inside a text frame by double-clicking with either selection tool. The tool will switch to the Type tool and place an insertion point where you double-clicked.

Selecting Text

Moving and Deleting Text

You can copy or move text from one place and then paste it into another. Text that is copied or cut is stored on the computer *clipboard. (See the sidebar on this page for an explanation of how the clipboard works.)*

To copy and paste text:

1. Select the text or text frame ⓱.

2. Choose **Edit > Copy** or **Cut**.

> **TIP** If you choose Cut, the highlighted text disappears and the remaining text reflows.

3. Position the insertion point where you want to put the copied or cut text ⓲.

4. Choose **Edit > Paste**. The text is inserted into the new position ⓳.

   or

   Choose **Edit > Paste Without Formatting** to paste the text so that its formatting (point size, typeface, style, etc.) matches the text it is being pasted into.

> **TIP** The Paste Without Formatting command is very helpful if you want the text from one place to be pasted into a paragraph that has different formatting.

> **TIP** You can select text before pasting to replace the selected text with the copied text.

⓱ *Select text in order* **to copy or cut** *it from one position to another.*

⓲ *Click to put the insertion point where you want* **to insert the copied or cut text.**

⓳ *The* **Paste command** *inserts the copied or cut text at the insertion point.*

What Is the Computer Clipboard?

The Copy command places the copied objects into an area of the computer memory called the *clipboard.* The contents of the clipboard stay within the memory until a new copy or cut command is executed or until the computer is turned off.

The clipboard can hold only one set of information at a time. So if you copy one sentence, you will lose it from the clipboard if you copy or cut something else later on.

⑳ *Press on highlighted text to display the* **Drag-and-Drop Text cursor**.

㉑ *Drag to display the* **destination insertion point** *for drag-and-drop text.*

㉒ *Release the mouse button to* **drop the text** *into its new position.*

You can also use the mouse to drag text from one place to another. Drag-and-drop text can be set to be active in the Story Editor and/or the Layout View. *(See page 530 to set the preference to control drag-and-drop text.)*

To drag text from one place to another:

1. Select the text so that it is highlighted within the frame.

2. Position the cursor inside the highlighted text. The cursor changes to a curved arrow with the letter T next to it **⑳**.

3. Press with the mouse and drag to the new position. An insertion point appears at the new location **㉑**.

4. Release the mouse to move the text to the new position **㉒**.

TIP Hold the Opt/Alt key as you drag the text to create a copy of the original text in the new location.

The Duplicate command copies and pastes in one step. It also leaves the contents of the clipboard untouched.

To duplicate text:

1. Select the text or text frame.

2. Choose **Edit > Duplicate**. The copied text is duplicated as follows:

   • A text frame is created slightly offset from the original object.

   • Text inside a frame is pasted immediately following the original text.

TIP The Duplicate command does not replace the contents of the clipboard.

Moving and Deleting Text

Using the Character Palette

Character formatting refers to attributes that can be applied to a single character or *glyph* in a paragraph without applying that formatting to the entire paragraph. The Character palette controls character attributes.

TIP As you work with text frames, the Control palette changes to display many of the text controls found in the Character palette. This makes it possible to style text using just the Control palette. See "Using the Control Palette for Text" at the end of this chapter for how to use the Control palette to style text.

To work with the Character palette:

1. If the Character palette is not visible, choose **Window > Type & Tables > Character** or **Type > Character**. This opens the Character palette 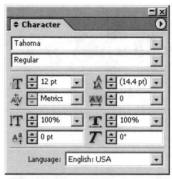.

   or

   Click the Character palette tab to move it to the front of a set of nested palettes.

2. Click the palette tab to reveal all the palette options.

   or

   Choose Show Options from the Character palette menu **24**.

TIP The Character palette menu also contains additional controls for formatting text.

23 The **Character palette** *lets you change the character attributes.*

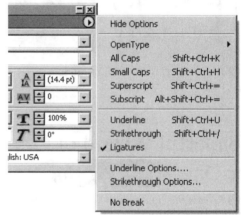

24 The **Character palette menu** *contains additional controls for formatting text.*

Setting the Text Defaults

When you first open InDesign, text frames are set with the fonts that the Adobe folks thought you'd like to work with. You don't have to live with those settings.

Deselect all objects and change the text settings to whatever you like. Those settings will become the defaults for that document. You can also set the defaults for all new documents by changing the settings with no document open.

25 *The* **font menu** *in the Character palette lets you choose the typeface for text. The style menu next to each font name displays the style choices.*

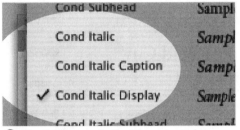

26 *The* **style menu** *in the Character palette lets you choose the proper style choices for a typeface.*

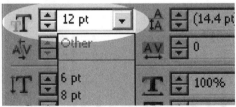

27 *The* **point size menu** *in the Character palette lets you choose common point sizes or enter a specific size in the field.*

Setting the Typeface and Point Size

The design of type is called the *typeface*. The typeface you are reading now is called Minion. The typeface of the subhead below is called Futura Condensed Bold.

To choose a font (typeface):

1. Choose **Type > Font** and then choose the typeface from the font menu. The font menu can be set to preview the typefaces *(see page 529).*

    or

    In the Character palette, choose a typeface from the font menu **25**.

2. If necessary, choose the styling for the font from the style menu next to the name of the font.

    or

    Use the style list in the Character palette to choose the styling **26**.

TIP The style list changes depending on the typeface and the fonts you have installed. If you do not have the bold version of a font, it will not be listed.

TIP You can use the keyboard commands to apply styling such as regular, bold, italic, and bold italic.

The size of type is measured using a system called *points*. There are 72 points per inch. The point size of this text is 10.25.

TIP Use the preferences to change this value to the more traditional setting 72.27 points per inch *(see page 534).*

To change the point size:

◆ Choose **Type > Size** and then choose a point size from the list **27**.

    or

    Use the point size field controls to enter a custom point size.

Styling Text

InDesign also lets you apply electronic styling such as All Caps, Small Caps, Subscript, and Superscript. *(See page 65 for a discussion about electronic styling.)*

To apply electronic styles:

♦ Choose one of the styles listed in the Character palette menu **28**. The text changes to the style chosen **29**.

  - **All Caps** converts lowercase letters to all capital letters.
  - **Small Caps** converts lowercase letters to reduced capitals.
  - **Superscript** reduces and raises the text above the baseline.
  - **Subscript** reduces and lowers the text below the baseline.
  - **Underline** draws a line under the text. *(See the next page for how to customize the appearance of the underline.)*
  - **Strikethrough** draws a line through the text. *(See the next page for how to customize the appearance of the strikethrough line.)*
  - **Ligatures** automatically substitutes the combined letterforms for characters such as fi and fl **30**.

TIP The All Caps style has no effect on text typed with the Caps Lock or Shift key held down.

TIP The sizes of the Small Caps, Subscript, and Superscript are controlled in the text preferences *(see page 531)*.

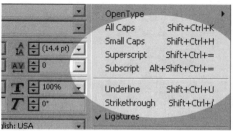

28 *The* **electronic style options** *in the Character palette menu.*

Dorothy and TOTO — All caps

L. FRANK BAUM — Small caps

Emerald City® — Superscript

H_2O — Subscript

Tin Woodman — Underline

~~Cowardly~~ Lion — Strikethrough

29 *Examples of the electronic styles applied to text.*

30 *Applying the* **Ligatures command** *to the top text replaces specific pairs of letters with combination letter forms such as those on the bottom.*

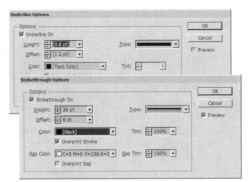

㉛ *The* **Underline Options** *and* **Strikethrough Options dialog boxes** *let you customize the appearance of the Underline and Strikethrough effects.*

Underlines as Highlights!

One of the most exciting uses for the custom underlines and strikethrough effects is to use them as highlights for individual lines or words of text. This is something designers have wanted to do for years.

All you have to do is set the weight of the line to slightly thicker than the text point size. And use the offset to position the line around the text. You can then apply these custom underlines as highlights for text. You can also combine the underline and strikethrough lines above and below the text **㉜**.

The Wonderful
Wizard of OZ

㉜ *An example of how custom underlines and strikethrough settings can be used for highlights and other special effects.*

As mentioned on the previous page, you can change the appearance of the Underline and Strikethrough effects.

To customize Underline and Strikethrough Options:

1. Select the text.

2. Choose Underline Options or Strikethrough Options from the Character palette menu. The Underline Options or Strikethrough Options dialog box appears **㉛**.

3. Click Underline On or Strikethrough On to turn on the effect.

   TIP The effect will already be on if it was applied in the Character palette menu.

4. Use the Weight controls to set the thickness of the line.

5. Use the Offset controls to move the line as follows:
   - **Positive underline numbers** move the line *below* the baseline.
   - **Positive strikethrough numbers** move the line *above* the baseline.

6. Choose one of the rules from the Type list *(see page 157 for working with rules).*

7. Choose a color and tint from the Color and Tint lists.

8. If your line type has a gap, such as in a dashed line, use the Gap Color and Gap Tint lists to color the gap.

9. If desired, check the Overprint Stroke and Overprint Gap options. *(See page 145 for more information on overprinting colors.)*

Styling Text

Setting Line and Character Spacing

Leading is the space between lines of type within a paragraph 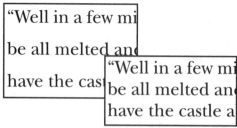. (It is pronounced *led-ding*, which refers to the metal formerly used to set type.) Leading is specified as an absolute point size or as auto leading. The leading of this paragraph is 10.75 points.

To set the leading:

1. Select the paragraph of text.

2. Use the leading controls in the Character palette to enter an amount of leading .

   or

   Set the leading to Auto to have the leading automatically change to an amount based on the point size.

   TIP The amount of the auto leading is set in the Paragraph palette's Justification menu *(see page 405).*

Kerning is the space between two letters. It is applied so letters fit snugly together .

To set kerning:

1. Select the text you want to kern, or place an insertion point between the letters.

2. To use the kerning pairs in the typeface, choose Metrics from the kerning list .

   or

   Choose Optical to adjust the kerning using a visual representation of the text.

   TIP Use optical kerning when there are no built-in font metrics, for instance, when you combine two different typefaces.

3. To apply a specific kerning amount, use the kerning controls or pop-up menu to apply a numerical amount.

   TIP Positive numbers increase the space. Negative numbers decrease the space. Zero indicates no kerning is applied.

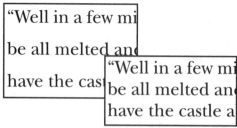

The 24-point leading (top) has more line space than the 16-point leading (bottom).

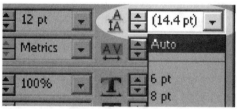

*The **leading controls** in the Character palette let you change the amount of space between lines.*

A comparison of the different kerning settings: 0 (top), Metrics (middle), Optical (bottom).

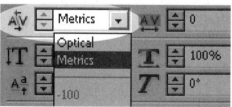

*The **kerning controls** in the Character palette change the space between characters.*

The Emerald City
The Emerald City

③ *Tracking of 100 increases the space along all the letters.*

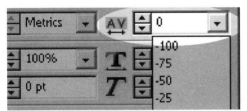

③ *The* **tracking controls** *in the Character palette change the space across a sequence of letters.*

Wonderful Wizard

④ *A negative baseline shift lowers the capital letters from the rest of the characters.*

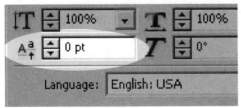

④ *The* **baseline shift controls** *in the Character palette move text above or below the line.*

Tracking is similar to kerning; however, unlike kerning, which applies to letter pairs, tracking is applied to a range of letters **③**. Tracking is very useful, because as you increase the space between the letters, you don't lose the relative spacing that is applied by kerning.

To set tracking:

1. Select the text you want to track.
2. Use the tracking field controls in the Character palette to set the amount of tracking **③**.

TIP Positive numbers increase the space between letters. Negative numbers decrease the space. Zero indicates no tracking is applied.

Baseline shift moves text up or down from the *baseline*, or the imaginary line that the letters sit on. Baseline shift is often applied to shift bullets or parentheses so they sit better next to text. It can also be used for special effects in display or headline text **④**.

To set the baseline shift:

1. Select the text that you want to reposition.
2. Use the baseline shift controls in the Character palette to move the text away from the baseline **④**.

TIP Positive numbers move the text up. Negative numbers move the text down.

Applying Text Distortions

InDesign also lets you apply horizontal or vertical scaling to text. This distorts the text to increase its height or width ➍. This changes the type from the original design of the characters. Typographic purists (such as this author) disdain distorting text.

To apply horizontal scaling:

1. Select the text that you want to distort.
2. Use the horizontal scale field controls in the Character palette to change the width of the text ➋.

To apply vertical scaling:

1. Select the text that you want to distort.
2. Use the vertical scale field controls in the Character palette ➌.

Skewing allows you to slant or tilt text ➍. This is also called *false italic* because it resembles the slant of italic text.

To skew text:

1. Select the text that you want to skew.
2. Enter an angle in the skew field in the Character palette to specify how much the text should be slanted ➎.
- **TIP** Positive numbers to 180 degrees tilt the text to the left. Negative numbers to 180 degrees tilt the text to the right.

DOROTHY   Vertical scale
DOROTHY   Normal
DOROTHY   Horizontal scale

➍ *The effects of applying either vertical scaling or horizontal scaling to text.*

➋ *Use the* **horizontal scale controls** *in the Character palette to distort the width of text.*

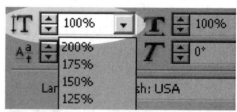

➌ *The* **vertical scale controls** *in the Character palette let you distort text height.*

CYCLONE!

➍ *You can apply negative and positive skew to text to create a special effect.*

➎ *The* **skew controls** *in the Character palette let you create fake oblique and slanted text.*

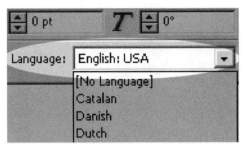

46 *The **Language menu** lets you set the language used for spelling checks as well as for typographer quotes.*

Setting the Language

You can also set the language. This ensures that foreign words as well as your native language are spell-checked and hyphenated using the proper dictionary. (Sorry, but changing the language doesn't translate the text.)

TIP If you have [No Language] selected, InDesign can't substitute typographer's quotes ("curly" quotes) for the ordinary typewriter quotes ("dumb" quotes).

To set the language:

1. Select the text that you want to set the language for.
2. Choose the language from the pop-up menu in the Character palette **46**.

Electronic Styling: Myths and Realities

As you set type using programs such as InDesign, people may tell you *never* to style fonts electronically. So if you use the Roman version of a font (such as Minion), you should never press the keyboard shortcut for italic. You should only choose the actual typeface (Minion Italic) from the font menu.

This rule emerged because some typefaces do not have an italic or bold version. The styling shows on the screen, but it doesn't print. Techno or Zapf Dingbats are examples of fonts that shouldn't be styled electronically. When people see their printed samples, they're disappointed that there is no bold or italic appearance.

Fortunately, InDesign prevents you from making errors like that. If you apply the shortcut for italic, InDesign applies the actual italic version. If there is no version, InDesign does not change the font. So there is no harm styling electronically using InDesign.

I've also heard people advise to avoid all caps, subscript, small caps, and other electronic styles on type. In most cases, there is nothing wrong with applying those styles, and InDesign allows you to apply those electronic styles to text.

In some cases you'll have better results with a small-caps version of a font than with the electronic style for small caps. However, a special small-caps font offers a subtle effect that few people will recognize. *(For an excellent discussion on how to use electronic small caps, see* The Non-Designer's Type Book, *by Robin Williams, published by Peachpit Press.)*

I personally hate the electronic styling for Vertical and Horizontal Scale. They distort the type horribly. The Skew command is even worse! However, I do accept that there might be times (grotesque Halloween cards?) where those distortions are acceptable.

Setting the Language

Applying Paragraph Formatting

Paragraph formatting refers to the attributes that are applied to the paragraph as a whole. For instance, you cannot have half of the paragraph centered and the other half on the left size of the page. The alignment must be applied to the whole paragraph. InDesign paragraph formatting is applied using the Paragraph palette.

TIP As you work with text frames, the Control palette changes to display many of the text controls found in the Character palette. This makes it possible to style text using just the Control palette. See "Using the Control Palette for Text" at the end of this chapter for information on using it to style text.

To work with the Paragraph palette:

1. If the Paragraph palette is not visible, choose **Window > Type & Tables > Paragraph** or **Type > Paragraph**. This opens the Paragraph palette **47**.

   or

   Click the Paragraph palette tab to move it to the front of a set of tabbed palettes.

2. To display all the paragraph formatting controls, choose Show Options from the Paragraph palette pop-up menu.

TIP The Paragraph palette menu also contains additional controls for formatting text **48**. *(See Chapter 16, "Typography Controls," for more on working with the Paragraph palette menu.)*

TIP The following techniques are useful when applying paragraph attributes:

- To apply attributes to a single paragraph, click to place an insertion point within the paragraph.
- To apply attributes to more than one paragraph, select a portion of the first and last paragraphs and the paragraphs in between.

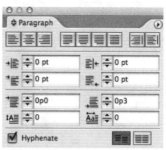

47 *The* **Paragraph palette** *controls attributes that are applied to the whole paragraph.*

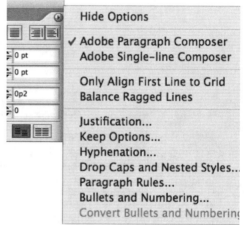

48 *The* **Paragraph palette menu** *contains additional controls for paragraph attributes.*

49 *The* **Alignment buttons** *on the Paragraph palette control how the type is aligned to the frame edges.*

Setting Alignment and Indents

In addition to the common paragraph alignment controls found in page layout or word processing programs, InDesign offers some special controls for setting alignment.

To set paragraph alignment:

1. Select the paragraphs.

2. Click one of the seven Alignment buttons **49** to set the alignment as follows:

Alignment	Icon	Example	Description
Flush Left		I have been wicked in my day but I never thought a little girl like you would be able to melt me.	Sets the text to align at the left margin.
Centered		I have been wicked in my day but I never thought a little girl like you would be able to melt me.	Sets the text to align at the center of the paragraph.
Flush Right		I have been wicked in my day but I never thought a little girl like you would be able to melt me.	Sets the text to align at the right margin.
Justified Last Left		I have been wicked in my day but I never thought a little girl like you would be able to melt me.	Sets the text to align at both the left and right margins, but aligns the last line flush left.
Justified Last Centered		I have been wicked in my day but I never thought a little girl like you would be able to melt me.	Sets the text to align at both the left and right margins, but centers the last line.
Justified Last Right		I have been wicked in my day but I never thought a little girl like you would be able to melt me.	Sets the text to align at both the left and right margins, but aligns the last line flush right.
Justified All		I have been wicked in my day but I never thought a little girl like you would be able to melt me.	Sets the text to align at both the left and right margins.
Align Towards Spine		I have been wicked in my day but I never thought a little girl like you would be able to melt me.	Sets the text to align along the spine of the document. This flips the alignment on recto and verso pages.
Align Away From Spine		I have been wicked in my day but I never thought a little girl like you would be able to melt me.	Sets the text to align toward the outside edge of the pages. This flips the alignment on recto and verso pages.

TIP Look closely and you'll see that the lines in the alignment buttons resemble how the alignment changes the position of the text.

Setting Alignment and Indents

You might want to indent a paragraph so that it stands out from the rest of the text. Or you might want to indent the first line of each paragraph to make text easier to read. These looks are created by the margin indents.

To set the margin indents:

1. Select the paragraphs.

2. Use the margin indent controls ⑤ to move the text as follows ⑤:

   - **Left Indent** moves the left side of the paragraph away from the left side of the text frame.
   - **First Line Left Indent** moves the first line of the paragraph away from the rest of the paragraph.
   - **Right Indent** moves the right side of the paragraph away from the right side of the text frame.
   - **Last Line Left Indent** moves the last line of the paragraph away from the right side of the text frame.

Another look you can create is to hang elements on the first line outside the rest of the paragraph ⑤.

To create a hanging bullet or numbered list:

1. Select the paragraphs.

2. Set the Left indent to the amount that the body of the paragraph should be indented.

3. Set the First Line indent to a negative amount. This hangs the first line outside the main body of the paragraph.

4. Insert a tab character *(see page 306)* to separate the bullet or number from the rest of the first line.

TIP The order of these steps is important because the First Line indent cannot have a negative amount until the Left indent has been created.

TIP A negative number for the Last Line Left Indent combined with a positive Right Indent lets you hang items on the last line outside the rest of the paragraph ⑤.

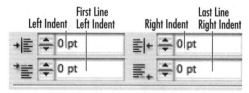

⑤ The **margin indents** *control the space around a paragraph and the first and last lines.*

Left indent

First line indent   Right indent

> Well in a few minutes I shall be all melted and you shall have the castle all to yourself. I have been wicked in my day but I never thought a little girl like you would be able to melt me and end my life.

⑤ *The effect of applying margin indents to text inside a text frame.*

First line indent (-1p6)

Left indent (1p6)

- Take balloon out of storage and inflate.

- Wind clock and set the correct time.

⑤ *The margin indent settings for a* **hanging bullet**. *Notice that the First Line indent has a negative value.*

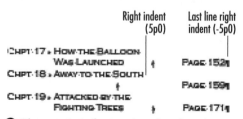

⑤ *The margin indent settings for a* **hanging last line item**. *Notice that a right-indent tab has been inserted before the page number.*

54 *The* **Indent to Here character** *is indicated by the small dagger symbol. It automatically creates a hanging indent for the drop cap.*

Pros and Cons of Indent to Here Character

When should you use the Indent to Here character? When should you use the paragraph margin indents?

The Indent to Here character is an excellent solution for setting off a drop cap. Because it is not set by a measurement, it doesn't need to be adjusted if you change the drop cap letter from a wide letter such as *M* to a thin one such as *I* or *J*.

However, the Indent to Here character is not a good solution for long documents with outdented characters. Margin indents applied to style sheets *(see page 370)* are more useful for those situations. For instance, all the numbered lists, bulleted lists, and tip characters in this book have been formatted using margin indents — not the Indent to Here character.

Inserting a Manual Indent

The Indent to Here character allows you to set an indent command that is tied to the position of the character.

TIP The Indent to Here character makes it easy to set a hanging indent for a drop cap or bulleted list.

To use the Indent to Here character:

1. Click inside a text frame where you would like the indent to occur.

TIP The insertion point is placed not in the lines that you want to indent, but inside the line that serves as the model. This is usually the first line of text.

2. Type Cmd/Ctrl-\ (backslash).

   or

   Choose **Type > Insert Special Character > Indent to Here**. This inserts a character that creates an indent at that point **54**.

TIP The Indent to Here character is indicated by a dagger symbol when the Show Hidden Characters command is chosen *(see page 71)*.

To remove the Indent to Here character:

1. Place the insertion point to the right of the Indent to Here character.

2. Press the Delete/Backspace key.

Setting Paragraph Effects

The paragraph effects are available when Show Options is chosen in the Paragraph palette menu. One of the paragraph effects is to add space above and below a paragraph ⑤⑤. For instance, the space between this paragraph and the one following is controlled by adding space below.

To add space between paragraphs:

1. Select the paragraphs that you want to add space above or below.

2. Use the Space Before field controls to add space before the paragraphs ⑤⑥.

3. Use the Space After field controls to add space after the paragraphs ⑤⑥.

TIP Never insert paragraph returns to add space between paragraphs. That can cause problems later if text reflows!

Drop caps increase the size of the first character or characters and positions them so that they drop down into the rest of the paragraph ⑤⑦. The opening page for each chapter of this book contains a paragraph that has a drop cap applied.

To create drop caps:

1. Select the paragraph you want to set with a drop cap.

2. Use the Drop Cap Number of Lines field to set the number of lines that the letter should occupy ⑤⑧.

3. Use the Drop Cap Number of Characters field to set how many characters of the text should have the drop cap applied ⑤⑧.

TIP If you want the drop cap to have a different typeface, you can select and change the letter manually. You can also use the automatic drop cap character style controls *(see page 387)*.

"At the East, not far from here," said one, "there is a great desert, and none could live to cross it." _____ Paragraph space

"It is the same at the South," said another, "for I have been there and seen it. The South is the country of the Quadlings."

"I am told," said the third man, "that it is the same at the West and that country, where the Winkies live, is ruled by the Wicked Witch of the West, who would make you her slave if you passed her way."

⑤⑤ *An example of adding space between paragraphs.*

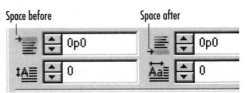
Space before — Space after

⑤⑥ *Use the **Paragraph Space controls** to add space before or after a paragraph.*

Dorothy lived in the midst of the great Kansas prairies, with Uncle Henry, who was a farmer, and Aunt Em, who was the farmer's wife.

⑤⑦ *An example of a **drop cap** set for one character and three lines.*

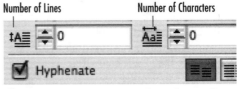
Number of Lines — Number of Characters

⑤⑧ *Use the **Drop Cap controls** to change the appearance of a paragraph drop cap.*

Setting Paragraph Effects

The Munchkins immediately took out their handkerchiefs and began to weep.

The Munchkins immediately took out their handkerchiefs and began to weep.

⑤⑨ *The effects of the* **Hyphenate command** *turned off (top) and turned on (bottom).*

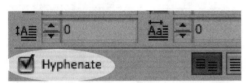

⑥⓪ *Use the* **Hyphenate checkbox** *to hyphenate words at the ends of lines.*

Tab   Space

» I · have ¦ been· wicked · but · I · never· thought · a · little · girl· like · you · would · end, ——— New line
my·life.¶——————— End of paragraph
#————————————— End of story

⑥① *An assortment of the* **hidden characters** *displayed within text.*

You can also control if the text within a paragraph should be hyphenated **⑤⑨**.

To turn on hyphenation:

1. Select the paragraphs you want to set the hyphenation for.

2. To turn on hyphenation, click the Hyphenate checkbox in the Paragraph palette **⑥⓪**. Depending on what words are hyphenated, the text may reflow. *(See Chapter 15, "Typography Controls," for information on controlling the number of hyphens in a paragraph.)*

Working with Hidden Characters

Every time you tap the Spacebar, Tab key, Return key, or Enter key, you create an nonprinting character in the text. These hidden characters, (sometimes called *invisibles*) can be turned on to let you see where the spaces, tab characters, and paragraph returns fall in the text.

To show or hide hidden characters:

◆ Choose **Type** > **Show Hidden Characters**. This displays the characters in the same color as the highlight for the layer **⑥①**.

or

◆ Choose **Type** > **Hide Hidden Characters** to hide the hidden characters.

TIP Hidden characters are also hidden when you turn on Overprint Preview *(see page 145).*

To change the colors of the hidden characters:

◆ Change the Layer color in the Layers palette *(see page 292).*

Paragraph Effects; Hidden Characters

Using the Glyphs Palette

Quick — what's the keystroke for a trademark symbol? The Euro symbol or Japanese Yen symbol? If you can't remember the keystrokes for all the characters you use, then you need to open the Glyphs palette. The Glyphs palette lets you easily see all the characters in a typeface. You can also use the palette to display the alternate letterforms in OpenType fonts *(see page 411)*.

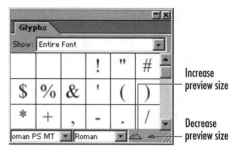

Increase preview size
Decrease preview size

62 *Use the* **Glyphs palette** *to insert characters from different fonts.*

To insert characters:

1. Place the insertion point where you would like the character to be inserted.

2. Choose **Type > Glyphs**. This opens the Glyphs palette **62**.

3. Choose the typeface and style of the character you want to insert.

4. Scroll through the Preview area to find the character you want to insert.

TIP Use the Preview Size controls to increase or decrease the size of the preview.

5. Double-click the character you want to insert.

6. Repeat step 5 to insert any additional characters.

TIP The Glyphs palette allows you to insert characters that are not usually available for certain operating systems. For instance, Macintosh users can insert fractions and Windows users can insert ligatures.

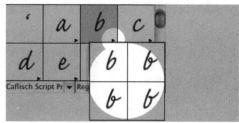

63 *Press the* **triangle under the glyph** *to display the alternatives for the glyph.*

To access alternative characters:

1. Place your insertion point where you want to insert the alternative characters.

2. Press the small triangle next to the glyph in the Glyphs palette **63**. This opens the alternative letterforms for that character.

3. Choose the alternative character. This inserts the character into the text.

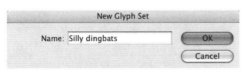

64 *The* **New Glyph Set dialog box** *lets you name the new glyph set.*

So What's a Glyph?

If you're like me, you're probably wondering about the word *glyph*. Why use that word? Why not call it the Character palette?

The answer has to do with being precise. You know what a letter is: a, b, c, X, Y, or Z. You wouldn't call things like 1, @, ? or $ letters, though. They're characters.

Well, glyphs are the proper name for everything including letters, characters, and alternative letterforms for things like ligatures and swashes.

So rather than call it the Insert Letters/Characters/Alternative Letterforms palette, Adobe calls it the Glyphs palette.

I could have sworn that the word glyph was some special Adobe typographic term; but then one of my students reminded me of Egyptian hieroglyphics and Hawaiian petroglyphs.

So glyph really isn't as strange a word as I originally thought.

As you hunt through the Glyphs palette, you may find there are too many glyphs to look through. Fortunately you can use the palette to create custom glyph sets. These sets can contain collections of your favorite glyphs.

To create a glyph set:

1. Choose New Glyph Set from the Glyphs palette menu.
2. Name the set in the New Glyph Set dialog box **64**.
3. Click OK.

TIP You can have many different glyph sets. Organize them however you want.

Once you have created a glyph set, you can add your favorite characters from any font into the glyph set.

To add characters to a glyph set:

1. Use the Glyphs palette to select the character you want to add to an existing glyph set.
2. Choose Add to Glyph Set > [Set Name] from the Glyphs palette menu. The character appears in the glyph set.

TIP The Add to Glyph Set command also appears in the contextual menu that appears when you right-mouse-click or Ctrl-click (Mac) over the Glyphs palette.

Using the Glyphs Palette

To insert characters in a glyph set:

1. Choose the glyph set from the Glyph Set menu in the Glyphs palette.

2. Double-click to insert the glyph.

Once you have created a glyph set, you can edit the items in the set.

To edit the characters in a glyph set:

1. Choose **Edit Glyph Set** > [Set Name] from the Glyphs palette menu. The Edit Glyph Set dialog box appears ⑥⑤.

2. Select the glyph item that you want to edit.

3. Choose Remember Font with Glyph to set the glyph to a specific font. This means the glyph does not change to match the font in the text it's inserted into.

   or

   Deselect Remember Font with Glyph to use the unicode value of the current font. This option lets you match a character such as the Euro symbol to the text it is inserted into.

4. If you have selected Remember Font with Glyph, you can change the typeface and style in the Edit Glyph dialog box.

5. Click the Delete from Set button to delete a glyph from a set.

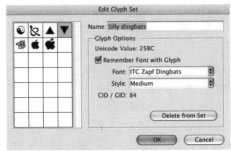

⑥⑤ *The* **Edit Glyph Set** *dialog box lets you delete or modify the glyphs in a custom glyph set.*

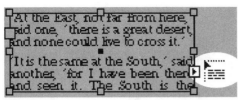

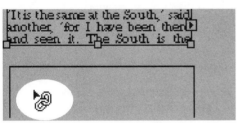

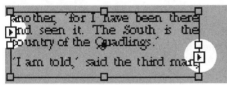

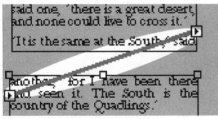

66 *The* **load text cursor** *indicates that you can continue the overflow text in another frame.*

67 *The* **link text cursor** *indicates you can click to fill the next frame with text.*

68 *The* **link indicators** *show that the text flows into and out of the text frame.*

69 *The* **text threads** *show the links between frames.*

Working with Text Flow

As mentioned earlier *(see page 53),* if text overflows its text frame, you can link the text into another frame.

To link text between frames:

1. Click the overflow symbol. The cursor changes to the load text cursor **66**.

2. Move the cursor over to the frame you want to flow the text into. The cursor changes to the link text cursor **67**.

TIP Unlike with QuarkXPress, the second text frame does not have to be empty.

3. Click in the text frame. The link indicators show that the text in the frame flows to or from another frame **68**.

TIP You can use the same steps to link empty text frames. This makes it easy to flow text into the layout later.

To change the link between frames:

1. Click the link indicator in the frame where you want to break the link. The cursor turns into a link text cursor.

2. Click in a new text frame to flow the text into a new frame.

   or

   Click inside the text frame to keep all the text within that frame. (The overflow symbol appears.)

InDesign also displays *text threads,* which show you the links between text frames.

To show the links between frames:

1. Select the text frame that you want to see the links for.

2. Choose **View > Show Text Threads.** This displays lines that show which frames are linked together **69**.

Working with Text Flow

Setting Text Frame General Controls

Once you create a text frame, you can still control the flow of text within the frame. This is similar to creating a mini-layout within the text frame.

To create text frame columns:

1. Select the text frame.

2. Choose **Object > Text Frame Options**. This opens the Text Frame Options dialog box ⑦⓪.

3. Click the General tab.

4. Make whatever changes you want to the settings.

TIP As you modify the text frame options, click the Preview checkbox to see the effects of your changes.

You can create columns within a text frame.

To create text frame columns:

◆ Set the following options in the Columns areas ⑦①:

- **Number** sets the number of columns.
- **Width** sets the column width.
- **Gutter** controls the space between the columns.

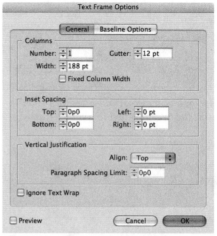

⑦⓪ *The* **Text Frame Options dialog box** *controls the flow of text within a frame.*

⑦① *The* **Columns settings** *for the Text Frame Options dialog box.*

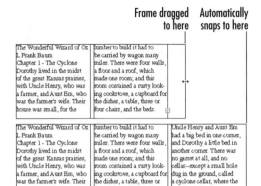

Frame dragged   Automatically
to here   snaps to here

⓲ *Applying* **Fixed Column Width** *ensures that the columns in a text frame are always the same size.*

⓳ *The* **Inset Spacing settings** *for the Text Frame Options dialog box.*

"At the East, not far from here," said one, "there is a great desert, and none could live to cross it."
"It is the same at the South," said another, "for I have been there and seen it. The South is the country of the Quadlings."
"I am told," said the third man, "that it is the same at

⓴ *A text frame with inset spacing has space between the text frame and the text.*

InDesign also has a powerful feature that helps you maintain a fixed column width when working with a text frame. This is very helpful for magazine and newspaper layouts where all text is in the same column width.

To use Fixed Column Width:

1. Click Fixed Column Width in the Text Frame Options dialog box.

2. Drag to resize the frame width. The width automatically jumps to whatever size can accommodate an additional column **⓲**.

You can also add space between the text and the frame. This is called the *inset spacing.*

To control the frame inset:

1. Select the text frame and open the Text Frame Options dialog box.

2. Enter the values in the Inset Spacing controls to control the amount of space between the top, bottom, left, and right edges of the frame **⓳**.

3. Click OK to apply the changes to the column **⓴**.

TIP If you have applied a stroke to a frame, you will most likely want to create an inset spacing so that the text does not touch the stroke.

Setting Text Frame General Controls

The vertical justification of a text frame controls where the text is positioned from the top to the bottom of the frame.

To set the vertical justification:

1. Select the text frame and open the Text Frame Options dialog box *(see page 76)*.

2. Choose one of the four options in the Vertical Justification Align pop-up list 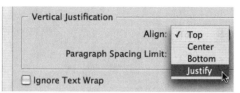:

   - **Top** positions the text so that the first line sits at the top of the frame 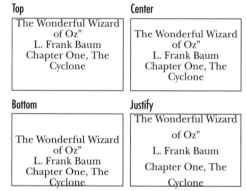.
   - **Center** positions the text so it is centered between the top and bottom of the frame 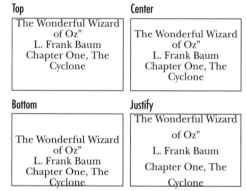.
   - **Bottom** positions the text so that the last line sits at the bottom of the frame 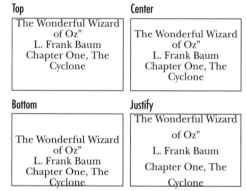.
   - **Justify** positions the text so that it fills the entire frame from top to bottom 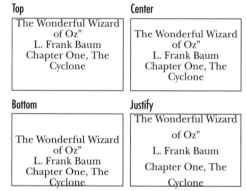.

   TIP The vertical justification options are only available for rectangular text frames. If the frame is another shape or has corner effects applied, the vertical justification options are dimmed out.

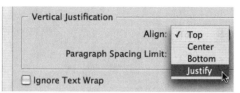

⑦⑤ *The* **Vertical Justification Align menu** *lets you choose where text is positioned vertically.*

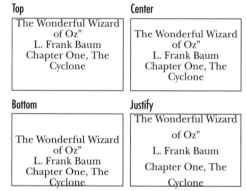

⑦⑥ *The four* **vertical alignment settings** *change the position of text within a frame.*

When you set the vertical alignment to Justify, you can set how the space between paragraphs is applied.

To set the paragraph spacing limit:

1. Set the Vertical Justification Alignment to Justify.

2. Set an amount in the Paragraph Spacing Limit field ⑦⑦. The higher the number, the more space between paragraphs and the less likely the leading between the lines will be affected by justifying the text vertically.

   TIP Set an amount equal to the height of the text frame to add space only between the paragraphs, not between the lines ⑦⑧.

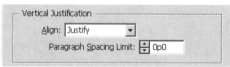

⑦⑦ *The* **Paragraph Spacing Limit** *for justified vertical alignment controls how much space will exist between paragraphs before the leading is increased.*

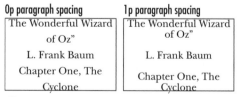

⑦⑧ *A paragraph spacing limit of 0p causes the leading to increase. A limit of 1p only adds space between the paragraphs, not the leading.*

Setting Text Frame General Controls

Character icon

79 *Click the* **Character icon** *to display the character attributes in the Control palette.*

Paragraph icon   Columns   Horizontal cursor position

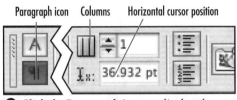

80 *Click the* **Paragraph icon** *to display the paragraph attributes in the Control palette.*

Using the Control Palette for Text

As mentioned previously, the Control palette changes its settings depending on the type of object selected. For example, when a text object is selected, the Control palette displays a combination of the Character and Paragraph palette controls.

To use the Control palette for character settings:

1. Use the Type tool to create an insertion point within a text frame. The Control palette displays the text options.

2. Click the Character icon to display the character attribute settings **79**.

TIP Cmd-Opt-7 (Mac) or Ctrl-Alt-7 (Win) switches the focus between the Character and Paragraph settings in the Control palette.

To use the Control palette for paragraph settings:

1. Use the Type tool to create an insertion point within a text frame. The Control palette displays the text options.

2. Click the Paragraph icon to display the paragraph attribute settings **80**.

TIP The paragraph settings also let you control the number of columns in a text frame *(see page 76 for more information on setting columns in a text frame).*

TIP Look at the paragraph settings to see the horizontal position of the cursor in the text frame.

Using the Control Palette for Text

Using Special Text Characters

Text does not consist of just alphabetical characters. There are special characters and spaces that are used as part of professional typography. InDesign lets you insert those characters into your documents.

TIP See the next page for a list of the special characters and white space characters and their default keyboard shortcuts.

To insert special characters:

1. Place the insertion point where you want to insert the special character.

2. Choose **Type > Insert Special Character**.

   or

   Control-click (Mac) or right-mouse click (Win) and choose Insert Special Character from the contextual menu.

3. Choose a character listing from the submenu.

You can insert white space characters, which are fixed spaces such as *em* and *en* spaces. You can also insert a nonbreaking space that forces two words to stay together.

To insert special space characters:

1. Place the insertion point where you want to insert the special character.

   TIP You can highlight a regular space to replace it with a white space character.

2. Choose **Type > Insert White Space**.

   or

   Control-click (Mac) or right-mouse click (Win) and choose Insert White Space from the contextual menu.

3. Choose a white space character listing from the submenu.

How Wide are the Spaces?

While some of the white space character widths are obvious, others need some definition.

- An *em space* is the size of the letter M at that point size. In traditional typesetting, an em space was often used as the indent for a paragraph.

- An *en space* is one-half of an em space. An en space is often used as a fixed-width space between bullets and the next character of text.

- A *thin space* is one-eighth of an em space. I use a thin space on either side of an em dash or the greater than (>) sign in menu commands such as **File > New**.

- A *hair space* is one-twenty-fourth of an em space. A hair space is used when extremely small spaces are needed.

- A *figure space* is the width of a number in the same typeface. This is used to help align numbers in financial tables.

- A *punctuation space* is the width of a period or comma.

- A *flush space* is a variable space that is used with the Justify All paragraph alignment setting. When flush space is inserted, the space between the characters will automatically expand so that the line of text fills the entire column width. A flush space character ensures that the justification of the text comes from the word spacing and not letterspacing.

WORKING WITH OBJECTS 4

Back in the old days of board mechanicals, advertising agencies and design studios had a production area called the bullpen. It was the people in the bullpen — called bullpen artists — who actually created the mechanical. Most of them were kids just out of design school; the bullpen was usually their first step up the ladder in advertising or design.

The kids in the bullpen were quite amazing. Although not professional illustrators, they could create all sorts of artwork for the layout.

The same is true with InDesign. While InDesign is not a full-fledged drawing program such as Adobe Illustrator, you can use InDesign's tools to create a wide variety of effects by distorting, moving, resizing, duplicating, and aligning objects. It's your electronic bullpen.

Types of Frames

Frames are the containers in which you place graphics or text. Frames can also be used as graphic shapes. There are three types of frames you can create: unassigned, graphic, and text.

TIP There is a difference in how frames are displayed depending on if you have selected them with the Selection tool or the Direct Selection tool. See the table at the end of this chapter for a chart that shows the differences in how frames look when they are selected.

Unassigned frames

Unassigned frames are created with the Rectangle, Ellipse, and Polygon tools *(see pages 51 – 52)* ❶. These frames are useful for adding color to your layout or a stroke around an area without inserting a graphic or text.

Graphic frames

Graphic frames are created with the Rectangle Frame, Ellipse Frame, and Polygon Frame tools *(see the following section)*. When you create a graphic frame, diagonal lines inside the frame indicate that you can insert a graphic inside the frame ❶.

TIP Although most people insert images inside graphic frames, there is nothing to prevent you from flowing text inside a graphic frame.

Text frames

Text frames are created using the Text tool or by converting frames *(see page 52)*. When you create a text frame, two link boxes appear on the sides of the frame in addition to the bounding box handles. Text frames also display a blinking insertion point when they are selected ❶.

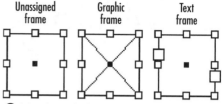

Unassigned frame   Graphic frame   Text frame

❶ *The three different types of frames: unassigned, graphic, and text.*

Diagonal Lines in Graphic Frames?

The diagonal lines inside a graphic frame come from a convention that was used in traditional pasteboard mechanicals.

When pasteboard artists drew the lines on mechanicals, they would often block off an area with diagonal lines to indicate that a picture or graphic was to go in that area.

Electronic page-layout programs such as QuarkXPress and Adobe InDesign use the same convention. The diagonal lines indicate where scanned images or graphics need to be inserted.

However, there is absolutely no rule that says you can only place images in graphic frames. You can place text in graphic frames or images in unassigned frames. The choice is yours.

---

② *The* **Rectangle Frame tool** *in the Toolbox creates rectangular graphic frames.*

③ *The* **Ellipse Frame tool** *in the Toolbox creates elliptical graphic frames.*

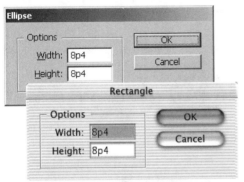

④ *The* **Ellipse and Rectangle dialog boxes** *let you create frames with precise width and height measurements.*

Creating Basic Shapes

You use the rectangle, ellipse, and polygon frame tools to create graphic frames into which you place images. You can also combine and intersect frames into other shapes using the Pathfinder palette *(see page 173)*.

TIP If another tool is visible, press the corner triangle to reveal the toolset.

To create a rectangular graphic frame:

1. Click the Rectangle Frame tool in the Toolbox **②**.
2. Drag across the page to create the rectangle.

TIP Hold the Opt/Alt key to draw the object from the center.

3. Release the mouse button when the rectangle is the correct size.

TIP Hold the Shift key to constrain the rectangle into a square.

To create an elliptical graphic frame:

1. Click the Ellipse Frame tool in the Toolbox **③**.
2. Drag across the page to create the ellipse.

TIP Hold the Opt/Alt key to draw the object from the center.

3. Release the mouse button when the ellipse is the correct size.

TIP Hold the Shift key to constrain the ellipse into a circle.

You can also create rectangles and ellipses by specifying their size numerically.

To create objects numerically:

1. Click with either the rectangle or ellipse tools. A dialog box appears **④**.
2. Enter the width and height amounts.
3. Click OK. The object appears where the mouse was clicked.

To create a polygon graphic frame:

1. Double-click the Polygon Frame tool in the Toolbox **⑤**. This opens the Polygon Settings dialog box **⑥**.

2. Enter a number in the field for the Number of Sides in the polygon.

3. To create a star, change the amount in the Star Inset field from 0% to a higher number.

TIP A star inset of 0% creates a basic polygon. As you increase the percentage, the points of the star become more pronounced.

4. Drag across the page to create the polygon or star.

TIP Hold the Opt/Alt key to draw the object from the center.

TIP Hold the Shift key to constrain the width and height of the object to the same amount.

5. Release the mouse button when the polygon or star is the correct size.

⑤ *Use the* **Polygon Frame tool** *to create polygon and star graphic frames.*

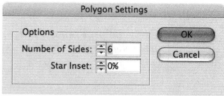

⑥ *The* **Polygon Settings dialog box** *creates either polygons or stars.*

⑦ *The* **Line tool** *in the Toolbox creates straight lines.*

InDesign is definitely the program for anyone who says they can't even draw a straight line. The Line tool makes it easy.

To create straight lines:

1. Click the Line tool in the Toolbox **⑦**.

2. Position the cursor where you want the line to start.

TIP Hold the Opt/Alt key to draw the line from its centerpoint.

3. Drag to create a line.

4. Release the mouse where you want the line to end.

TIP Hold the Shift key to constrain the lines to 45-degree angles.

Converting Shapes

So what if you've created a circle and later on realize you need a rectangle? What do you do?

Simple, you can use the Pathfinder Convert Shape commands *(see page 173)* to change an object from one shape to another.

Creating Basic Shapes

Selection tool — Direct Selection tool

❽ *The Selection tool in the Toolbox selects entire objects. The Direct Selection tool selects a point on an object or images inside objects.*

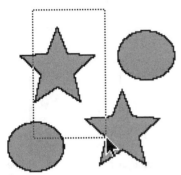

❾ *Drag to create a marquee to select objects.*

What Are The Differences Between the Selection Tools?

Perhaps the most confusing part of InDesign is the difference between the Selection tool (black arrow) and the Direct Selection tool (white arrow) **❽**.

If you are familiar with QuarkXPress, you can think of the Selection tool as Quark's *Object* tool. It will always select the object as a whole. Use this tool when you want to manipulate the entire object.

Think of the Direct Selection tool as Quark's *Content* tool. It selects the points that make up a frame or the image that is pasted inside a frame. Use this tool when you want to select inside a frame. For more information on working with the Direct Selection tool, see page 108.

Selecting Objects

Once you've created objects, you can use different techniques to select them.

To select by clicking:

1. Choose the Selection tool (black arrow) in the Toolbox **❽**.
2. Click the object you want to select.
3. Hold the Shift key to select any additional objects.

TIP Hold the Shift key and click on a selected object to deselect that object.

TIP To select objects behind others, hold the Command/Ctrl key as you click the mouse button.

You can also select objects by dragging an area, or *selection marquee,* around the object.

To select by dragging a marquee:

1. Choose the Selection tool.
2. Drag along a diagonal angle to create a marquee around the objects you want to select **❾**.

TIP You do not need to marquee the entire object to select it. Objects are selected if any portion is within the marquee.

TIP Hold the Shift key and drag around another area to add to a selection.

You can also use a menu command to select all the objects on a page.

To select all the objects on a page:

♦ Choose **Edit > Select All**.

TIP This command works only if you do not have an insertion point blinking inside a text frame *(see page 50)*.

Selecting Objects

Moving Objects

The simplest way to position an object on a page is to drag it to a new position, but you can also move objects by using menu and keyboard commands, or by typing specific numerical locations into a dialog box, as you'll learn later in this chapter.

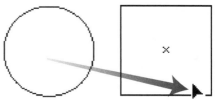

⑩ *Quickly drag to see the bounding box of the object being moved.*

To move an object by dragging:

1. Choose the Selection tool in the Toolbox.

2. Click the object you want to move. A bounding box with eight handles appears around the object. This indicates the object is selected.

3. Position the Selection tool on the edges of the bounding box (but not on the handles of the bounding box).

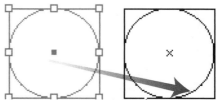

⑪ *Pause before you drag to see a preview of the object being moved.*

TIP If an object has a fill color, gradient, or image inside it, you can drag with the Selection tool directly inside the object. Otherwise, you must drag by the stroke or bounding box.

4. Drag to move the object. If you drag quickly, you will see only a bounding box preview of the object being moved **⑩**.

   or

   Press and pause for a moment before you drag the object. The pause lets you see a preview of the actual object as you move it **⑪**.

Moving Objects

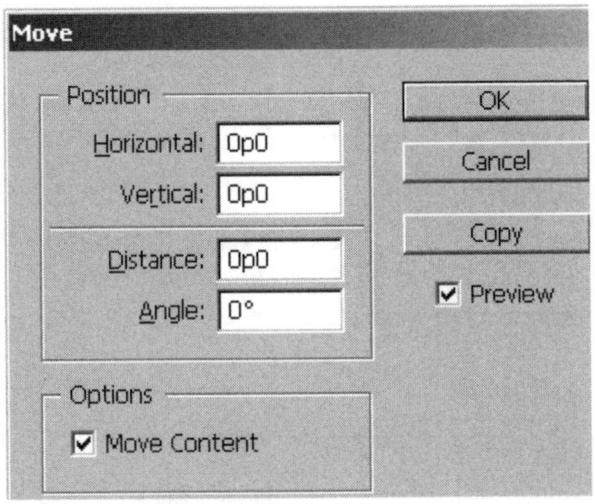

⓬ *The* **Move dialog box** *gives you numerical controls for moving objects.*

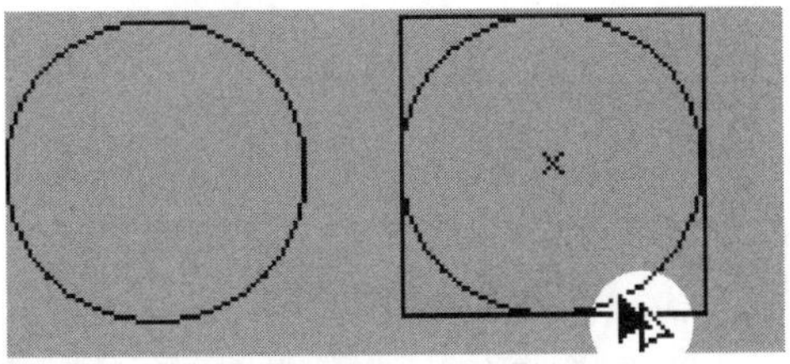

⓭ *The* **double-headed arrow** *indicates that a copy is being created of the moved object.*

You can also move an object more precisely. One way to do this is with the Move command in the Transform menu.

To use the Move command:

1. Select the object or objects.
2. Choose **Object > Transform > Move.** This opens the Move dialog box ⓬.

TIP This command is also available in a contextual menu *(see page 26).*

TIP Click the Preview checkbox to see the results of your actions as you enter numbers in the dialog box.

3. Use the Horizontal and Vertical fields to move the object along those axes.
4. Use the Distance field to move the object an absolute distance.
5. Use the Angle field to set the angle along which the object moves.
6. Check Move Content to also move any placed graphics.
7. Click OK to move the original object.

   or

   Click Copy to create a duplicate of the object in the new position.

To copy an object as you drag:

1. Hold the Opt/Alt key before you start the move.
2. Move the object as described on the opposite page. A double-headed arrow indicates that a copy is being created ⓭.
3. Release the mouse button. The copy will appear in the new position.

Moving Objects

Replicating Objects

There are several commands you can use to create duplicates of objects. Use the Copy command when you want to put the object on the clipboard *(see page 56)* so you can paste it somewhere else.

To copy objects:

1. Select an object to copy.
2. Choose **Edit > Copy**.

Use the Cut command to remove the object from the page so it can be pasted elsewhere.

To cut objects:

1. Select an object to cut.
2. Choose **Edit > Cut**.

Use the Paste command to see the contents of the clipboard.

To paste objects:

- Choose **Edit > Paste**. The contents of the clipboard appear in the center of the window area ⓮.

   or

   Choose **Edit > Paste in Place**. The contents of the clipboard appear in the same location as when they were originally selected.

The Duplicate command makes a copy without changing the contents of the clipboard.

To duplicate objects:

1. Choose the object to duplicate.
2. Choose **Edit > Duplicate**. The selected object appears on the page slightly offset from the original ⓯.

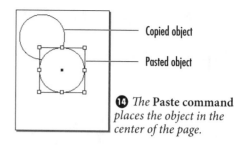

Copied object

Pasted object

⓮ *The* **Paste command** *places the object in the center of the page.*

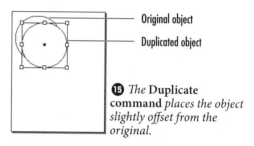

Original object

Duplicated object

⓯ *The* **Duplicate command** *places the object slightly offset from the original.*

Using Paste in Place

I always wondered just how useful the Paste in Place command is. After all, if you already have a copy of an object in one place, why would you need a second copy right over it?

That's not the point of Paste in Place. The power of the command is that you can paste an object in the same place on different pages. You can even paste in the same place in different documents.

PageMaker users will recognize this as the Powerpaste command. Quark-XPress users will wonder how they ever got along without it.

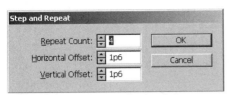

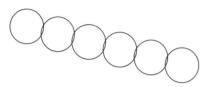

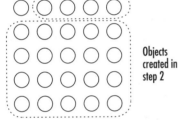

16 *Use the* **Step and Repeat dialog box** *to make multiple copies of an object positioned at specific horizontal and vertical intervals.*

17 *The Step and Repeat command created five copies of the first circle.*

Objects created in step 1

Objects created in step 2

18 *An example of how to use the Step and Repeat command to create a grid of objects.*

You can also duplicate many objects at once.

To duplicate multiple objects:

1. Choose an object.

2. Choose **Edit > Step and Repeat.** The Step and Repeat dialog box appears **16**.

3. In the Repeat Count field, enter the number of duplicates that you want to create in the top row.

4. In the Horizontal Offset field, enter a distance for the horizontal space between duplicates.

5. In the Vertical Offset field, enter a distance for the vertical space between duplicates.

TIP If you want space between the objects, make the offset at least the width or height of the object plus the amount of space between the objects.

6. Click OK. The selected object is duplicated in the desired positions **17**.

TIP The Horizontal and Vertical Offsets are remembered when you choose Edit > Duplicate. The offset is also remembered when you duplicate an object using Opt/Alt+drag.

You might want to duplicate objects so they form a horizontal and vertical grid **18**.

To create a grid of objects:

1. Set the Step and Repeat dialog box as follows:
   • In the Repeat Count field, enter the number of duplicates for the top row.
   • Enter the distance for the Horizontal Offset.
   • Leave the Vertical Offset as zero.

2. Select all the objects in the row, and set the Step and Repeat dialog box as follows:
   • In the Repeat Count field, enter the number for the additional rows.
   • Leave the Horizontal Offset as zero.
   • Enter a distance for the Vertical Offset.

Replicating Objects

Resizing Objects

Very often things need to be made bigger or smaller. InDesign gives you several different ways to scale objects. You can also use the bounding box handles to change the dimensions of the object visually. This is the easiest way to quickly resize an object.

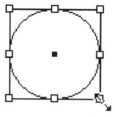

⑲ *Use the bounding box handles to resize an object.*

To resize using the bounding box handles:

1. Choose the Selection tool.
2. Choose which handle to drag based on the following options **⑲**:
   - Drag the corner handles to change both the width and height.
   - Drag the top or bottom handles to change the height only.
   - Drag the left or right handles to change the width only.
3. Drag the handle. If you drag quickly, you will see only the bounding box of the object **⑳**.

   or

   Press and hold for a moment and then drag the handle. This shows a preview of the object as you resize the bounding box **㉑**.

TIP Hold down the Shift key as you drag a corner to keep the original proportions of the width and height.

TIP Hold the Cmd/Ctrl key as you drag to resize any images placed inside the object (*see page 194*).

4. Release the mouse button when the object is the correct size.

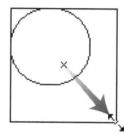

⑳ *If you drag quickly, you **only see a box** as you resize an object.*

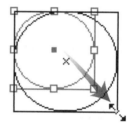

㉑ *If you press and pause a moment, you **see an actual preview** as you resize an object.*

Resizing or Scaling?

While you and I might feel the words are the same, InDesign treats them differently. When you *resize* an object, you change its width or height. The amount of scaling stays the same in the Control palette or the Transform palette. You have to resize the object again to get it back to its original size.

When you *scale* an object, the width and height change, and the amount of scaling applied to the object is shown in the Scale fields in the Control palette or Transform palette. You can convert the object back to its original size by setting the scaling to 100%.

22 Objects selected with the Selection tool *have both the object and its content transformed by the transform tools.*

23 Objects selected with the Group Selection tool *have only the object transformed by the transform tools.*

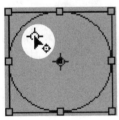

24 *The indicator that the transformation point can be moved to a new position.*

Using the Transform Tools

The transform tools resize and distort objects. You can transform the object itself or the object as well as any content. How you select objects changes the effect of the transform tools.

To control the effect of the transform tools:

◆ Select the object using the Selection tool. This type of selection causes the transform tools to affect both the object and any text or images inside it **22**.

or

Hold the Opt/Alt key as you click the frame with the Direct Selection tool. This causes the transformation to affect only the object, not any text or images inside the object **23**.

TIP The plus (+) sign next to the Direct Selection tool indicates that the tool is the Group Selection tool.

All the transformations take place in relation to a transformation point. Each object has a default transformation point, but you can change it if necessary.

To control the transformation point:

1. Select the object to be transformed.

2. Choose one of the transform tools. A transformation point appears inside the object.

3. Move the cursor near the transformation point. A small icon appears next to the cursor that indicates you can move the transformation point **24**.

4. Drag the transformation point to a new position.

or

Click to position the transformation point in a new position.

The Scale tool lets you increase or decrease the size of objects.

To scale objects visually using the Scale tool:

1. Select the object or objects.
2. Choose the Scale tool in the Toolbox .
3. If necessary, change the position of the transformation point *(see previous page).*
4. Move the cursor away from the transformation point, and drag to scale the object .

TIP Hold down the Shift key to constrain the tool to horizontal, vertical, or proportional scaling.

TIP To see a preview of the image as you scale, press and hold the mouse button for a moment before you start to drag.

TIP Hold down the Opt/Alt key to copy the object as you scale it.

If you prefer, you can enter the resize objects numerically using the Scale command.

To scale objects using the Scale command:

1. Select the object or objects.
2. Choose **Object > Transform > Scale.** This opens the Scale dialog box 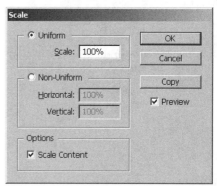.
3. Use the Uniform Scale field to scale the object proportionally.

   or

   Use the Non-Uniform Horizontal and Vertical fields to scale the object non-proportionally.
4. Check Scale Content to also scale any graphics that are placed inside it *(see Chapter 8, "Imported Graphics")* .
5. Click OK to scale the object.

   or

   Click Copy to create a scaled copy of the object.

25 *The* **Scale tool** *in the Toolbox is used to change the size of objects.*

26 *The* **arrowhead** *appears while scaling an object.*

27 *The* **Scale dialog box** *lets you scale objects using numerical values.*

28 *When* **Scale Content is turned on**, *the placed image scales along with the frame.*

(Sidebar, left margin:) Using the Transform Tools

㉙ *The* **Rotate tool** *in the Toolbox is used to change the orientation of objects.*

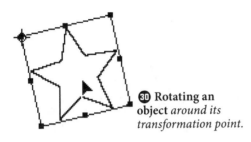

㉚ *Rotating an* **object** *around its transformation point.*

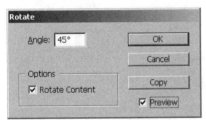

㉛ *The* **Rotate dialog box** *lets you rotate objects using numerical values.*

Rotate content on   Rotate content off

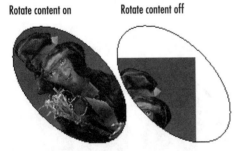

㉜ *When* **Rotate Content is turned on**, *the placed image rotates along with the frame.*

To scale objects numerically using the Scale tool:

1. Select the object or objects.

2. Choose the Scale tool in the Toolbox.

3. Hold the Opt/Alt key and click to designate the position of the transformation point. This opens the Scale dialog box **㉗**.

4. Set the dialog box controls as described in the previous exercise.

The Rotation tool changes the orientation, or angle, of the object on the page.

To rotate objects visually using the Rotate tool:

1. Select the object or objects.

2. Click the Rotation tool in the Toolbox **㉙**.

3. If necessary, change the default transformation point *(see page 91)*.

4. Move the cursor away from the transformation point, and drag to rotate the object **㉚**.

TIP Hold down the Shift key to constrain the rotation to 45-degree increments.

TIP Hold down the Opt/Alt key *after* you start the rotation to copy as you rotate.

To rotate objects using the rotate command:

1. Select the object or objects.

2. Choose **Object > Transform > Rotate**. This opens the Rotate dialog box **㉛**.

3. Use the Angle field to set how much the object should rotate.

4. Check Rotate Content to also rotate any graphics placed inside the object **㉜**.

5. Click OK to rotate the object.

   or

   Click Copy to create a copy as you rotate the object.

To rotate objects numerically using the Rotate tool:

1. Select the object or objects.

2. Choose the Rotate tool in the Toolbox.

3. Hold the Opt/Alt key and click to set the position of the transformation point. This opens the Rotate dialog box ❸❶.

4. Set the dialog box controls as described in the previous exercise.

The Shear tool distorts the shape of objects.

To shear objects visually using the Shear tool:

1. Select the object or objects.

2. Click the Shear tool in the Toolbox ❸❸.

3. If necessary, change the transformation point by dragging it to a new position *(see page 91)*. The cursor indicates the transformation point can be moved.

4. Move the cursor away from the transformation point, and drag to shear the object ❸❹.

To shear objects using the Shear command:

1. Select the object or objects.

2. Choose **Object > Transform > Shear.** This opens the Shear dialog box ❸❺.

3. Use the Shear Angle field to set the amount of distortion.

4. Check one of the Axis options:
   • **Horizontal** shears along the horizontal axis.
   • **Vertical** shears along the vertical axis.
   • **Angle** shears along a specific angle.

5. Check Shear Content to also distort any graphics placed inside the object ❸❻.

6. Click OK to shear the object.

   or

   Click Copy to create a sheared copy of the object.

❸❸ *Use the **Shear tool** in the Toolbox to distort objects.*

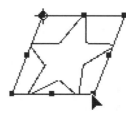

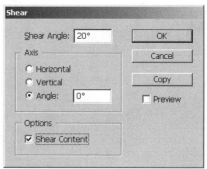

❸❹ *Shearing an object around the transformation point.*

❸❺ *The **Shear dialog box** lets you distort objects using numerical values.*

Shear content on   Shear content off

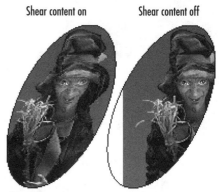

❸❻ *The difference between shearing an object with Shear content on and off.*

Using the Transform Tools

37 *Choose the* **Free Transform tool** *in the Toolbox to both scale and rotate objects.*

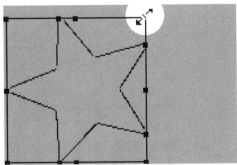

38 *The* **double-headed arrow** *indicates that the Free Transform tool is in the scale mode.*

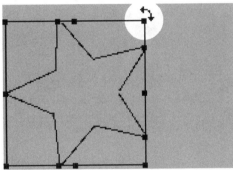

39 *The* **curved double-headed arrow** *indicates that the Free Transform tool is in the rotation mode.*

To shear objects numerically using the Shear tool:

1. Select the object or objects.
2. Choose the Shear tool in the Toolbox.
3. Hold the Opt/Alt key and click to set the position of the transformation point. This opens the Shear dialog box **35**.
4. Set the dialog box controls as described in the previous exercise.

Rather than switching between the Scale and Rotate tools, you can use the Free Transform tool to both scale and rotate.

To scale using the Free Transform tool:

1. Select the object or objects.
2. Click the Free Transform tool in the Toolbox **37**. A bounding box appears around the object.
3. Place the cursor on one of the handles of the bounding box. The cursor changes to a double-headed arrow **38**.
4. Drag to increase or decrease the size of the object.

To rotate using the Free Transform tool:

1. Select the object or objects.
2. Click the Free Transform tool in the Toolbox **37**. A bounding box appears around the object.
3. Place the cursor outside one of the handles of the bounding box. The cursor changes to a curved double-headed arrow **39**.
4. Drag to rotate the object clockwise or counter-clockwise.

Using the Transform Tools

Using the Transform Palette

The Transform palette allows you to move, scale, rotate, and shear objects precisely, using numerical values.

TIP When you have objects selected, the Control palette displays many of the controls that are found in the Transform palette. *(See the section "Using the Control Palette for Objects" on page 110.)*

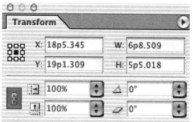

40 *The* **Transform palette** *is a command center for positioning and transforming objects.*

To open the Transform palette:

◆ Choose **Window > Object & Layout > Transform** to open the palette **40**.

or

If the Transform palette is behind other palettes, click the Transform palette tab.

As you work with the Transform palette, it is important to know the reference point on the object. This is the same as the transformation point used with the transform tools.

To set the Transform palette reference point:

1. Select the object or objects that you want to transform.

2. Click the reference point control on the Transform palette to choose the point around which the object moves **41**.

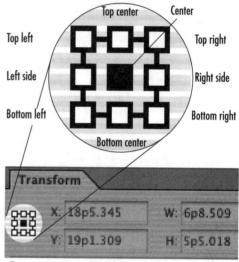

41 *The* **Reference point** *controls where in the object the transformation occurs.*

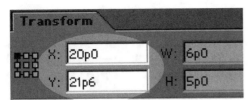

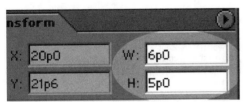

You can use the Transform palette to move objects numerically.

To move an object with the Transform palette:

1. Select the object or objects that you want to move.

2. To move the object horizontally, enter an amount in the X field .

TIP As you increase the numbers, the object moves to the right.

3. To move the object vertically, enter an amount in the Y field .

TIP As you increase the numbers, the object moves down.

4. Press Enter or Return to apply the changes.

You can use the Transform palette to resize an object numerically. This does not change the scaling amount applied to the object.

To resize with the Transform palette:

1. Select the object or objects.

2. If necessary, change the reference point as explained on the preceding page.

3. To change the width of the object, enter an amount in the W field .

4. To change the height of the object, enter an amount in the H field .

5. Press Enter or Return to resize the object.

You can resize proportionally even if you know the size for only one side of the object.

To resize proportionally:

1. Select the object or objects.

2. Enter the new size in the W field or H field .

3. Do not change the amount in the other field.

4. Hold Cmd/Ctrl as you press Enter or Return. The amount in both the W and H fields changes proportionally.

The X and Y fields in the Transform palette control the position of an object.

The W and H fields in the Transform palette control the width and height of objects.

Using the Transform Palette

You can also scale objects using the Transform palette.

To scale with the Transform palette:

1. Select the object or objects.

TIP Use the Selection tool to scale the object and its contents. Use the Direct Selection tool to scale only the object.

2. If necessary, change the reference point as explained on the preceding page.

3. To change the horizontal size, enter a percentage in the Scale X field .

4. To change the height of the object, enter a percentage in the Scale Y field .

TIP The Scale X and Y fields also have pop-up lists from which to choose the amount of scaling.

5. Press Enter or Return to apply the changes 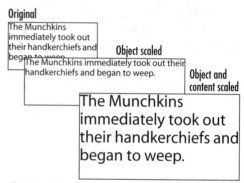.

TIP You can also scale text within a text frame by dragging on the edge of the frame while holding the Cmd/Ctrl key. Hold Cmd/Ctrl-Shift and drag by a corner point to scale proportionally. This also applies to text frames in groups.

To scale proportionally with the Transform palette:

1. Select an object or objects.

2. If the Link icon is in the open state, click to close it .

3. Enter an amount in either the **Scale X** or **Scale Y** fields. You do not have to enter an amount in both fields. The closed Link icon forces both fields to display the same amount.

4. Press Enter or Return to apply the changes.

TIP Hold the Cmd/Ctrl key as you press the Enter or Return key to scale proportionally even if the Link icon is in the open state.

Scale width Scale height

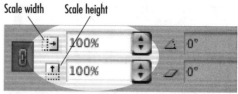

44 *The* **Scale width and height fields in the Transform palette** *let you apply percentage amounts to scale objects.*

Original

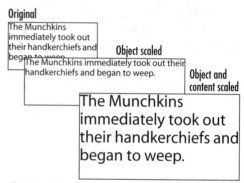

The Munchkins immediately took out their handkerchiefs and began to weep.

Object scaled

The Munchkins immediately took out their handkerchiefs and began to weep.

Object and content scaled

The Munchkins immediately took out their handkerchiefs and began to weep.

45 *The difference between scaling an object or scaling an object and its content.*

Closed state   Open state

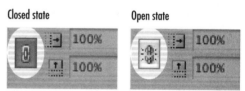

46 *The* **Link icon** *in the closed state forces both the Scale X and the Scale Y fields to the same amount. In the open state, you can enter different amounts for the Scale X and Scale Y fields.*

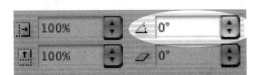

47 *The* **Rotation Angle** *field in the Transform palette lets you change the angle of objects.*

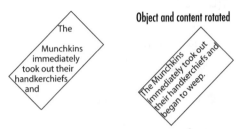

Object and content rotated

48 *The difference between rotating an object or rotating an object and its content.*

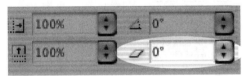

49 *The* **Shear** *field in the Transform palette lets you distort the shape of objects.*

Object sheared

The Cyclone

Object and content sheared

The Cyclone

50 *The difference between shearing an object or shearing an object and its content.*

You can also rotate objects using the Transform palette.

To rotate with the Transform palette:

1. Select the object or objects.

TIP Use the Selection tool to rotate the object and its contents. Use the Direct Selection tool to rotate only the object. *(See page 85 for more information on selecting objects.)*

2. If necessary, change the transformation point, as explained on page 91.

3. Enter the amount of rotation in the Rotation field **47**.

TIP The Rotation Angle field also has a pop-up list from which to choose the amount of rotation.

4. Press Enter or Return to apply the changes **48**.

You can also shear objects using the Transform palette.

To shear with the Transform palette:

1. Select the object or objects.

TIP Use the Selection tool to shear the object and its contents. Use the Direct Selection tool to shear only the object.

2. If necessary, change the transformation point, as explained on page 91.

3. Enter the amount of distortion in the Shear field **49**.

TIP The Shear field also has a pop-up list from which to choose the amount of shearing.

4. Press Enter or Return to apply the changes **50**.

Using the Transform Palette

Using the Transform Commands

In addition to the transform tools and transform fields, there are a whole bunch of transform commands you can use on objects. These commands make it easy to perform commonly used transformations, such as rotating and flipping objects.

To rotate with the Transform commands:

1. Select an object or objects.

2. Click to open the Transform palette menu.

   or

   Click to open the Control palette menu.

3. Choose one of the rotation settings as follows ⑤:

   - **Rotate 180°.**
   - **Rotate 90° CW** (clockwise).
   - **Rotate 90° CCW** (counter-clockwise).

To flip objects using the Transform commands:

1. Select an object or objects.

2. Click to open the Transformation palette menu.

   or

   Click to open the Control palette menu.

3. Choose one of the flip settings as follows ⑤:

   - **Flip Horizontal.**
   - **Flip Vertical.**
   - **Flip Both.**

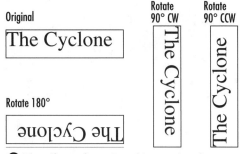

⑤ The effects of **rotating objects** using the Transform submenu.

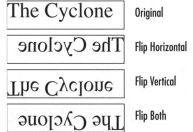

⑤ The effects of **flipping objects** using the Transform submenu.

Circle moved to new position

Transform Again command applied to triangle

53 *The* **Transform Again** *command allows you to duplicate transformation commands applied to objects.*

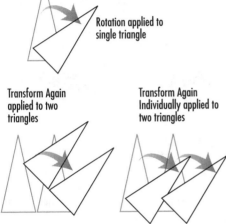

Rotation applied to single triangle

Transform Again applied to two triangles

Transform Again Individually applied to two triangles

54 *The differences between the* **Transform Again** *command and the* **Transform Again Individually** *when applied to multiple objects.*

When you perform a transformation on an object, that transformation is stored in InDesign's memory. You can then perform the same transformation again on another object — even in another document! This is similar to Illustrator's Transform Again command.

To repeat transformations:

1. Use any of the transform commands on a selection.

2. Select a different object or objects.

3. Choose one of the following from the **Object > Transform Again** submenu.

   - **Transform Again** applies the last single transform command to the selection as a whole **53**.
   - **Transform Again Individually** applies the last single transform command to each object in the selection **54**.
   - **Transform Sequence Again** applies the last set of transformation commands to the selection as a whole.
   - **Transform Sequence Again Individually** applies the last set of transformation commands to each object in the selection.

TIP InDesign remembers all the transformation commands until you select a different object or perform a different task.

TIP InDesign can even remember an Opt/Alt-drag transformation that duplicated an object.

Using the Transform Commands

Using the Arrange Commands

Objects in InDesign are layered on top of one another in the same order they were created. (This is sometimes called the *stacking order.*) The first object created is behind the second, the second behind the third, and so on. Though you may not see the layering when objects are side by side, it is apparent when they overlap **55**.

TIP The layering of objects is not the same as the layers of a document. *(See Chapter 11, "Layers," for more information on working with layers.)*

The Arrange commands allow you to move objects through the stacking order.

To move up or down one level in a stack:

1. Select the object you want to move.
2. Choose **Object > Arrange > Bring Forward** to move the object in front of the next object in the stacking order **56**.

   or

   Choose **Object > Arrange > Send Backward** to move the object behind the next object in the stacking order **57**.

To move up or down the entire stack:

1. Select an object you want to move.
2. Choose **Object > Arrange > Bring to Front** to move the object in front of all the others in its layer **58**.

   or

   Choose **Object > Arrange > Send to Back** to move the object behind all the others in its layer **59**.

55 *When two objects overlap, it is obvious which object is in front of the other.*

Star in back — Bring Forward applied

56 *The effects of the* **Bring Forward command.**

Star in front — Send Backward applied

57 *The effects of the* **Send Backward command.**

Star in back — Bring to Front applied

58 *The effects of the* **Bring to Front command.**

Star in front — Send to Back applied

59 *The effects of the* **Send to Back command.**

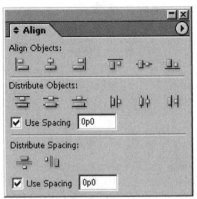

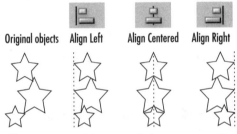

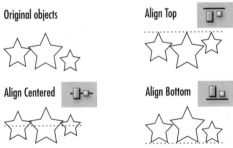

60 *Use the* **Align palette** *to arrange objects in an orderly fashion.*

61 *The effects of the* **vertical align commands.**

Original objects

Align Top

Align Centered

Align Bottom

62 *The effects of the* **horizontal align commands.**

Aligning Objects

The Align palette provides commands that align objects or distribute them evenly along a horizontal or vertical axis.

To work with the Align palette:

1. Choose **Window** > **Object & Layout** > **Align**. This opens the Align palette **60**.

   or

   If the Align palette is behind other palettes, click the Align palette tab.

2. Choose Show Options from the Align palette menu to see all the commands in the palette.

To align objects:

1. Select two or more objects.

2. Click an alignment icon as follows:

   • Click a vertical alignment icon to move the objects into left, centered, or right alignment **61**.

   • Click a horizontal alignment icon to move the objects into top, centered, or bottom alignment **62**.

TIP The align commands move objects based on the best representation of the controls. For instance, the Align Left command uses the left-most object; Align Top uses the top-most object, and so on.

TIP You can use the Lock command to force one object to be the reference object for others *(see the sidebar on page 114).*

You can also move objects so the spaces between certain points of the objects are equal. This is called *distributing* objects.

To distribute objects:

1. Select three or more objects.
2. Click a distribute icon as follows:
   - Click a vertical distribute icon to move the objects so that their tops, centers, or bottoms are equally distributed ⓺.
   - Click a horizontal distribute icon to move the objects so that their left edges, centers, or right edges are equally distributed ⓺.

You can also distribute objects based on their size. This ensures that the space between the objects is equal.

To distribute the space between objects:

1. Select three or more objects.
2. Click a distribute space icon as follows:
   - Click the vertical space icon to move objects so the vertical spaces between them are equal ⓺.
   - Click the horizontal space icon to move objects so the horizontal spaces between them are equal ⓺.

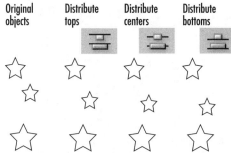

⓺ *The effects of the* **vertical distribute commands**. *Notice that the middle object changes position to create an even distribution.*

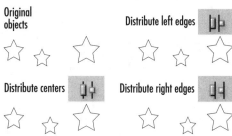

⓺ *The effects of the* **horizontal distribute commands**. *Notice that the middle object changes position to create an even distribution.*

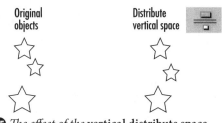

⓺ *The effect of the* **vertical distribute space command**.

⓺ *The effect of the* **horizontal distribute space commands**.

(Aligning Objects — side tab)

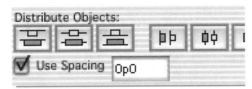

67 *The* **Use Spacing** *option for Distribute Objects lets you set a specific distance between the tops, centers, bottoms, or sides of objects.*

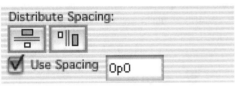

68 *The* **Use Spacing** *option for Distribute Spacing lets you set a specific distance between objects.*

Setting the Anchor Object for Alignment

The Align palette doesn't let you designate which object should be used as the reference object for the alignment commands. So what if you want to designate a specific object to be used as the alignment reference object?

Select the object you want to use and apply the Lock command *(see page 114)*. Then select all the objects and apply the alignment.

The locked object remains stationary and forces the other objects to align to it. Then if you need to, unlock the object to move it and the others.

The Align palette also has controls to space objects numerically. You can apply a numerical distance between the tops, centers, bottoms, or sides of objects.

To use spacing to distribute objects:

1. Select two or more objects.
2. Check Use Spacing in the Distribute Objects section of the Align palette **67**.
3. Enter the numerical distance in the Use Spacing field.
4. Click one of the Distribute Objects icons. Now the objects are separated by a specific space inserted between the tops, centers, bottoms, or sides of the objects.

TIP If a positive number moves the objects in the wrong direction, use a negative number.

You can also set a specific numerical distance between the objects themselves. This is very useful when you want the same amount of space between objects, but the objects themselves have different sizes.

To set the spacing between objects:

1. Select two or more objects.
2. Check Use Spacing in the Distribute Spacing section of the Align palette **68**.
3. Enter the numerical distance in the Use Spacing field.
4. Click one of the Distribute Spacing icons. Now a specific amount of space is added between the objects horizontally or vertically.

TIP If a positive number moves the objects in the wrong direction, use a negative number.

Aligning Objects

Grouping and Pasting Into Objects

You can group objects so you can easily select and modify them as a unit.

To group objects:

1. Select the objects you want to group.

2. Choose **Object > Group.** A dotted-line bounding box encloses all the objects **69**.

TIP The Selection tool selects all the objects in a group as a single unit.

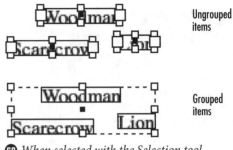

Ungrouped items

Grouped items

69 *When selected with the Selection tool, grouped items display a bounding box around the entire group.*

You can also create groups within groups. This is called *nesting*.

To nest groups:

1. Select the grouped objects.

2. Hold the Shift key and select another object or group.

3. Choose **Object > Group.**

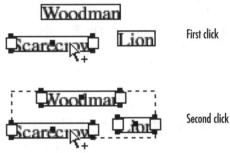

First click

Second click

70 **Selecting nested groups** *with the Opt/Alt key and Direct Selection tool.*

Once you have grouped objects, you can select individual objects within the group.

To select objects within groups:

1. Choose the Direct Selection tool.

2. Click to select one object in the group.

3. Hold the Opt/Alt key and click the same object again **70**. This selects the entire group.

TIP The plus (+) sign next to the Direct Selection tool cursor indicates the Group Selection tool.

4. If the group is nested within other groups, click again on the same object to select the next level of the nest.

Grouping and Pasting Into Objects

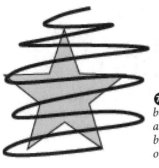

71 *An object to be pasted into another should be positioned over the other.*

72 *The* **Paste Into** command *displays the content only within the borders of the container.*

You can also use menu commands to select items within a group.

To use commands to select objects within groups:

1. Use the Selection tool to select the entire group.

2. Choose **Object > Select > Content**. This selects the top-most object in the group.

3. Choose **Object > Select > Previous Object in Group**. This selects the object that is directly below the selected object.

   or

4. Choose **Object > Select > Next Object in Group**. This selects the object that is directly above the selected object.

TIP These commands are also available in the Control palette when groups are selected.

To ungroup objects:

1. Select the group.

2. Choose **Object > Ungroup**.

3. If you have nested groups, continue to ungroup the objects as necessary.

You can also take one object and paste it into the frame of another object. This is similar to the concept of *masks* in illustration programs. InDesign refers to the object that is pasted as the *content*. It refers to the frame that holds the object as the *container*.

To paste an object into another:

1. Select the first object and position it over the second object **71**.

2. Choose **Edit > Cut** to place the first object on the computer clipboard.

3. Select the second object and choose **Edit > Paste Into**. The content appears within the borders of the container **72**.

TIP To paste multiple objects into another, group the multiple objects together.

Grouping and Pasting Into Objects

There are some special techniques for selecting just the container or the content of pasted-in objects.

TIP You can also use these techniques with placed images inside a frame. *(See Chapter 8, "Imported Graphics," for working with placed images.)*

To select just the container object:

♦ Hold the Opt/Alt key and click with the Direct Selection tool to select the container **73**.

or

Select the entire object with the Selection tool and then choose **Object > Select > Container**.

To select just the content object:

♦ Hold the Opt/Alt key and click with the Direct Selection tool to select the content **74**.

or

Select the entire object with the Selection tool and then choose **Object > Select > Content**.

Once you have pasted one object into another, you use special techniques to move the content inside the container.

To move only the content object:

1. Select the content object.

2. Use either the Direct Selection or the Selection tool to drag the content by its center point **75**. The content moves within the container.

To move only the container:

1. Select the container object.

2. Use either the Direct Selection or the Selection tool to drag the container by its center point **76**. The container moves without disturbing the content.

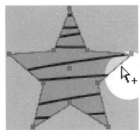

73 *Hold the Opt/Alt key and click with the Direct Selection tool to* **select just the container that holds the pasted-in object**.

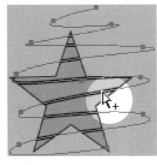

74 *Click with the Opt/Alt key and Direct Selection tool to* **select the content inside a container**.

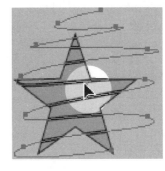

75 *Move the content inside a container by* **dragging the center point of the content object**.

76 *Move the container without disturbing the content by* **dragging the center point of the container**.

Why Use Groups?

The concept of groups comes from illustration programs. In those programs you might have an illustration that contains hundreds, if not thousands, of individual objects. It would be cumbersome to have to select those objects individually to move or modify the artwork. That's why groups were created — to make it easier to quickly select all the individual elements in artwork.

Page-layout programs rarely deal with that many objects on a page. So why is it important to group objects?

I use groups for the illustrations and captions that appear in this book. By grouping the objects together, I know the artwork won't inadvertently get separated from the captions that describe it.

I also need to group them when I apply the Distribute Spacing command. This way the illustration and caption are treated as one object to be separated from the other illustrations on the page.

Of course, you can also move the pasted-in content along with the container.

To move the pasted-in content and the container:

1. Click with the Selection tool to select both the container and the pasted-in content.

2. Drag the objects to a new position.

Finally, you may want to remove the content within a container or swap one pasted-in content for another.

To remove a pasted-in content:

1. Use the Direct Selection tool to select the pasted-in content.

2. Choose **Edit > Cut**.

TIP The pasted-in content can be placed back on the page by choosing **Edit > Paste**.

To swap one pasted-in content for another:

1. Position the new object over the frame.

2. Choose **Edit > Cut**.

3. Select just the frame that holds the pasted-in content.

4. Choose **Edit > Paste Into**. The object on the clipboard replaces the content within the frame.

Grouping and Pasting Into Objects

Using the Control Palette for Objects

The Control palette is context sensitive. This means it displays different commands depending on the number of objects or if the objects are grouped or pasted-in.

To use the Control palette with a single object:

◆ Select a single object. The Control palette displays the basic Transform palette and stroke options ⑦. *(See Chapter 6, "Styling Objects," for more information on working with strokes.)*

To use the Control palette with multiple objects:

◆ Select multiple objects. The Control palette displays icons for the basic Align palette options in addition to the Transform palette options ⑱.

To use the Control palette with grouped or pasted-in objects:

◆ Select a grouped or a pasted-in object. The Control palette displays the icons for the Select commands in addition to the Transform palette options ⑲.

TIP These Select commands can also be used with placed images *(see Chapter 8, "Imported Graphics")*.

TIP The Control palette also displays the Fitting commands *(covered on page 207)*.

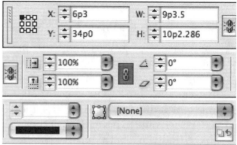

⑦ *The Control palette displays the* **basic Transform** *(top and middle) and* **Stroke** *palette options (bottom) when a single object is selected.*

⑱ *The Control palette adds the* **basic Align** *palette options when multiple objects are selected.*

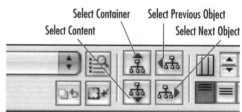

⑲ *The Control palette adds the* **Select Object** *options when groups or containers or content objects are selected.*

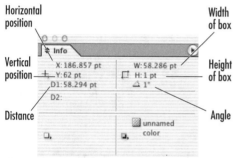

⑧⓪ *The* **Measure tool** *in the Toolbox.*

⑧① *Drag the Measure tool to measure the distance between two points.*

Horizontal position

Vertical position

Distance

Width of box

Height of box

Angle

⑧② *The* **measurements displayed in the Info palette** *for the measuring line drawn with the Measure tool.*

Using the Measure Tool

There are many places where you can find the numerical sizes of items. You can use the rulers; you can place guides; you can look at the Control palette; and so on. But what if you want to measure the distance of one point in an object to a different point in another one? That's where the Measure tool is so helpful.

To measure distances using the Measure tool:

1. Choose **Window > Info** to open the Info palette.

TIP All amounts measured by the Measure tool are displayed in the Info palette.

2. Click the Measure tool in the Toolbox ⑧⓪.

TIP The Measure tool is behind the Eyedropper tool in the Toolbox.

3. Place the Measure tool on the start point and drag to the end point. A measuring line appears on the page ⑧①. The Info palette displays the following attributes of the measurement ⑧②:

- **Horizontal position** displays the X coordinate of the first point in the line or whichever point is then moved.
- **Vertical position** displays the Y coordinate of the first point in the line or whichever point is then moved.
- **Distance** shows the length of the line.
- **Width** shows the width of the bounding box that would enclose the line.
- **Height** shows the height of the bounding box that would enclose the line.
- **Angle** shows the angle on which the line was drawn.

Using the Measure Tool

Once you have drawn a measuring line, you can move it to other areas of the page.

To move a measuring line:

1. With the Measure tool still selected, position the cursor over the measuring line.

2. Drag the line to a new position 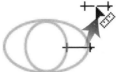.

TIP Do not position the cursor over the start or end points of the measuring line.

You can also change the start or end points of the measuring line.

To reposition the points of the measuring line:

1. With the Measure tool still selected, position the cursor over either point in the measuring line.

2. Drag the point to a new position.

You can also extend a second line out from the origin of the measuring line to create an electronic protractor to measure angles.

To measure angles:

1. Drag the first line with the Measure tool.

2. Hold the Opt/Alt key and move the Measure tool back to the origin of the first line. An angle cursor appears **84**.

3. Drag to create a second line extending out from the origin point **85**. The Info palette displays the distance of the second line, as well as the angle between the measuring lines **86**.

TIP No bounding box is displayed when two measuring lines are created.

83 Drag the line segment *of the measuring line to move it to a new position.*

84 *The angle cursor indicates that you are about to create a second measuring line.*

85 Two measuring lines *let you measure angles with the Measure tool.*

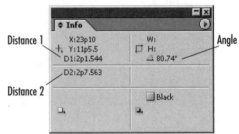

86 *The Info palette display for* two measuring lines.

Using the Measure Tool

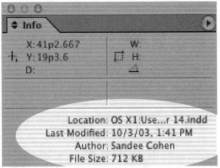

87 *With no objects selected, the Info palette displays* **document information.**

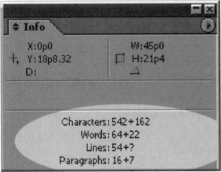

88 *With text selected, the Info palette displays* **text information.**

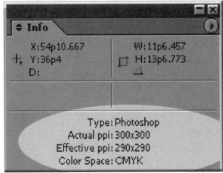

89 *With a placed image selected, the Info palette displays* **placed image information.**

Using the Info Palette with Objects

The Info palette also gives you important information about the document, text, and placed images.

To see the document information:

◆ Deselect any objects on the page. The Info palette displays the following information **87**:

- **Location** of the file on the computer.
- **Last Modification** date and time.
- **Author** as entered in the File Info (**File > File Info**) dialog box.
- **File size**.

To see the text information:

◆ Place your insertion point inside a text frame.

or

Highlight the text in the frame. The Info palette displays the following information **88**:

- **Character** in the frame or selection.
- **Words** in the frame or selection.
- **Lines** in the frame or selection.
- **Paragraphs** in the frame or selection.

TIP If there is any overflow text in the frame, the amounts are displayed as a number with a plus sign.

To see the placed object information:

◆ Select a frame that contains a placed image, or the placed image itself. The Info palette displays the following information **89**:

- **Type** of placed image.
- **Actual ppi** (**points per inch**) resolution of the image.
- **Effective ppi** resolution of the image if you have scaled the image in InDesign.
- **Color Space** of the image.
- **ICC Profile** (if applicable) may also be shown.

Locking Objects

You can also lock objects so they cannot be moved or modified. This prevents people from inadvertently destroying your layout.

TIP Locking objects is not the same as locking the layers of a document. *(See Chapter 11, "Layers," for more information on working with layers.)*

To lock the position of an object:

1. Select the objects you want to lock.
2. Choose **Object > Lock Position.** A small padlock appears if you try to move or modify the object **90**.

TIP Locked objects can be selected, copied, and pasted, and their colors and contents can be modified.

To unlock objects:

1. Select the objects you want to unlock.
2. Choose **Object > Unlock Position.**

90 *The* **Padlock cursor** *indicates that the Lock Position command has been applied.*

How Safe Are Locked Objects?

I sincerely hope that you lock your front door more securely than the Lock Position command locks objects, although what's bad for your home can be good for your layouts.

The Lock Position command only locks the position of the object. The object can still be selected using either the selection tools or the Select All command.

If there is text within the selected object, the text can be selected and otherwise modified.

If there is a placed image within the selected object, the image can be replaced by choosing a new object with the Place command *(see page 194).*

If you need more security for your objects — for instance, to avoid inadvertently changing the color of an object — then you should lock the object's layer *(see page 292).*

Locking Objects

Selecting Frames

Use this chart as a guide to let you know what type of object you have selected and which parts of the object can be selected using the Selection tool or the Direct Selection tool.

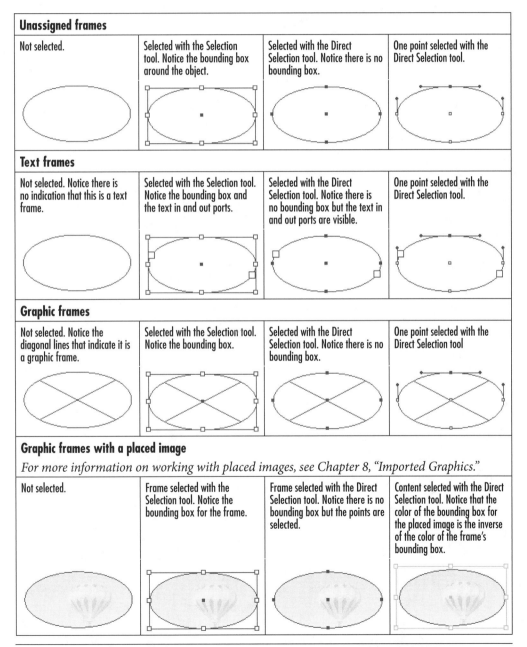

Unassigned frames			
Not selected.	Selected with the Selection tool. Notice the bounding box around the object.	Selected with the Direct Selection tool. Notice there is no bounding box.	One point selected with the Direct Selection tool.

Text frames			
Not selected. Notice there is no indication that this is a text frame.	Selected with the Selection tool. Notice the bounding box and the text in and out ports.	Selected with the Direct Selection tool. Notice there is no bounding box but the text in and out ports are visible.	One point selected with the Direct Selection tool.

Graphic frames			
Not selected. Notice the diagonal lines that indicate it is a graphic frame.	Selected with the Selection tool. Notice the bounding box.	Selected with the Direct Selection tool. Notice there is no bounding box.	One point selected with the Direct Selection tool

Graphic frames with a placed image

For more information on working with placed images, see Chapter 8, "Imported Graphics."

Not selected.	Frame selected with the Selection tool. Notice the bounding box for the frame.	Frame selected with the Direct Selection tool. Notice there is no bounding box but the points are selected.	Content selected with the Direct Selection tool. Notice that the color of the bounding box for the placed image is the inverse of the color of the frame's bounding box.

WORKING IN COLOR 5

When I first started in advertising, only the senior creative teams could work in color. The junior teams were assigned only black-and-white ads. Later on they might be able to work on a two-color job, but the four-color work was handled by senior art directors.

Fortunately, you're not limited by such constraints. InDesign gives you, right from the first day you use it, all the color controls you could ever wish for. However, with that power comes some responsibility.

When you define colors and use them on your pages, you are wearing two hats. Your first hat is that of a designer who looks at the aesthetics of the page and then applies colors. This is where you have fun with your creativity.

Your second hat is that of production manager. Wearing that hat you need to understand some of the priniciples of color and printing color documents. You also need to make sure your colors are defined so they print correctly.

The Basics of Color

Here's a quick primer to help you understand what happens when you define and apply colors in your InDesign layout, as well as other programs. For more information on working with color in computer graphics applications, I recommend *The Non-Designer's Scan and Print Book,* by Sandee Cohen and Robin Williams, published by Peachpit Press. I also recommend *Pocket Pal Graphic Arts Production Handbook*, now in its nineteenth edition, published by International Paper. You can order Pocket Pal at www.ippocketpal.com.

Type of color	How it is used	How it is created	Comments
CMYK	CMYK stands for the cyan, magenta, yellow, and black inks that are combined to create other colors. Also called process color, this is the primary type of color used in color printing. Most magazines and brochures are printed using the four process color inks.	Use the Color palette set to CMYK or the New Color Swatch dialog box set to CMYK or the Color Picker in the CMYK mode.	Color images are saved in the CMYK mode before they are imported into InDesign.
RGB	RGB stands for the red, green, and blue lights that are used in computer monitors to display colors. Because RGB colors are based on lightwaves, not inks, there will always be a slight difference between colors defined as RGB and those defined as CMYK. RGB colors can be used to define colors for documents that will be displayed onscreen. But you should not use them for print work.	Use the Color palette set to RGB or the New Color Swatch dialog box set to RGB or the Color Picker in the RGB mode.	Most scanners save images as RGB files. You must use a program such as Adobe Photoshop to convert those images to CMYK.

Type of color	How it is used	How it is created	Comments
LAB	The LAB is another light-based color model that uses luminance (L) combined with green to red (A) plus yellow to blue (B). As with RGB, you should not define print colors using this system.	Use the Color palette set to LAB or the New Color Swatch dialog box set to LAB or the Color Picker in the LAB mode.	
Spot colors	Spot colors are specialty colors that are printed without using the four process color inks. For instance, a metallic gold in a brochure is printed using metallic gold ink, not a combination of CMYK colors. Spot colors can be mixed to display colors that could not be created using simple CMYK colors.	Use the New Color Swatch dialog box set to Spot.	Spot colors can be defined by the user or you can use the commercial spot color libraries produced by companies such as Pantone and Dicolor and Toyo. Other names for spot colors are specialty, second color, fifth or sixth color, or flat colors.
Tints	Tints are colors that have been screened so that only a percentage of their color appears on the page.	Tints can be created from named colors using the New Tint dialog box.	
Mixed inks	Mixed inks are combinations of at least one spot color and another spot or process color.	Mixed inks can be created using the Swatches palette menu. One spot color must also have been previously defined.	Mixed Ink Groups are combinations of different percentages for Mixed ink colors.

The Basics of Color

Using the Color Palette

There are three different models for defining colors: CMYK, RGB, and LAB. Each model is used for different purposes. You choose the color mode and mix colors in the Color palette. *(See Chapter 6, "Styling Objects," for how to apply colors to objects and text.)*

To choose the options in the Color palette:

1. If the Color palette is not visible, choose **Window > Color** to open the palette ❶.

    or

    If the Color palette is behind other palettes, click the Color palette tab.

2. If the color sliders are not visible, click the palette tab or choose Show Options from the Color palette menu ❷.

    TIP Hold the Shift key as you drag one slider to have the others move along with it.

The CMYK color model is used primarily for print work. CMYK colors are mixed using percentages of the four inks used in process printing: cyan, magenta, yellow, and black.

To define CMYK colors:

1. Choose CMYK from the Color palette menu. This opens the palette in the CMYK mode ❸.

2. Choose one of the following methods to define the amount of cyan, magenta, yellow, or black ink in the color:

    *   Type a value from 0 to 100% in each of the four color fields.
    *   Drag the sliders for each of the four color fields.
    *   Click a color in the CMYK spectrum area.

    TIP Click the solid white or black rectangles to the right end of the spectrum to quickly get 100 percent black or white.

❶ *The* **Color palette** *with the options turned off shows only the spectrum or ramp for choosing colors.*

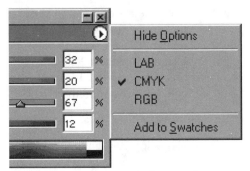

❷ *The* **Color palette menu** *lets you choose among the three color models.*

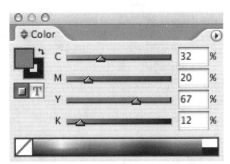

❸ *The* **Color palette with the CMYK (cyan, magenta, yellow, and black) color controls**.

The Black Color Palette

If your Color palette displays a single slider for Black, it is because the Black color in the Swatches palette is your default color. Simply change it to CMYK to get the full set of CMYK color sliders.

Understanding CMYK Color

Each of the colors in CMYK corresponds to one of the inks used in typical four-color printing. Cyan is a shade of blue. Magenta is a shade of red. Yellow is…well, yellow. And black is black—I want my baby back.

If you are creating print documents, you will want to define your colors using CMYK colors. Not only is the CMYK system overwhelmingly used for print work, it is the system you are most familiar with, whether you're aware of it or not. Yellow and cyan make green; magenta and yellow make orange, and so on.

In theory, you shouldn't need more than three colors for printing. If you mix cyan, magenta, and yellow together, you should get a solid black color. In reality, however, those inks are not pure enough to create solid black; instead they create a dark brown.

That's why process printing uses four colors. In addition to cyan, magenta, and yellow, a fourth *key color*—black, indicated by the letter K—is added to create the really black areas. That's where the term CMYK comes from.

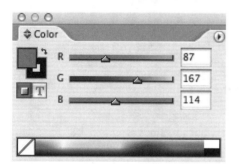

❹ *The Color palette set for mixing* **RGB (red, green, blue) color controls** *for onscreen display such as Web sites.*

Mixing Colors in RGB

Maybe some Web designers and video engineers can think in RGB, but I confess, I can't. With the RGB sliders, red plus green creates yellow; green plus blue creates a shade of cyan, and all three colors together create white. To create black, you set all three colors to zero. It's the exact opposite of CMYK where the four colors combine to create black.

The RGB color model is used primarily for onscreen work such as presentations and Web sites. The RGB colors — red, green, and blue — are mixed using representations of the three colors of light. This is what you see on television screens and computer monitors. RGB colors have a wider range of colors than CMYK colors.

To mix RGB colors:

1. Choose RGB from the Color palette menu. This opens the palette in the RGB mode **❹**.

2. Choose one of the following methods to define the amount of red, green, or blue in the color:
   - Type the value from 0 to 255 in each of the three color fields.
   - Drag the sliders for each of the three color fields.
   - Click a color in the RGB spectrum area.

The LAB color model defines colors according to a *luminance* (lightness) component, and two color components, *a* and *b*. The *a* component defines the green to red values. The *b* component defines the blue to yellow values. LAB colors are designed to be device-independent so that the color does not change from one source to another.

TIP The proper name for LAB is L*A*B and is pronounced by spelling out the name (*el-ay-bee*), not by saying the word "lab."

To mix LAB colors:

1. Choose LAB from the Color palette menu. This opens the palette in the LAB mode ❺.

2. Choose one of the following methods to define the three components of the color:

   - Type the value from 0 to 100 in the L field or type the value from -128 to 127 in the *a* or *b* field.
   - Drag the sliders for each of the fields.
   - Click a color in the LAB spectrum area.

The out-of-gamut symbol appears if you choose an RGB or LAB color that cannot be printed using process inks ❻.

To convert out-of-gamut colors:

- Click the small square next to the out-of-gamut symbol. This converts the color to the closest process-color equivalent.

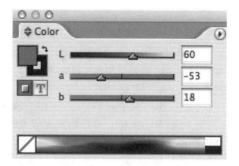

❺ *The* **LAB Color palette** *mixes colors that look consistent no matter whether you print them or display them onscreen.*

Out-of-gamut symbol
Color conversion square

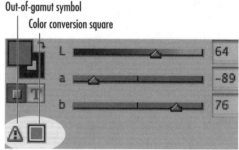

❻ *The* **out-of-gamut symbol** *for RGB or LAB colors indicates that the color shown on screen will not print as seen using process color inks.*

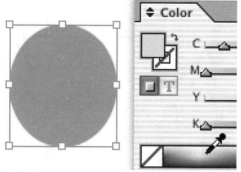

⑦ *With an object selected,* **click the color ramp** *in the Color palette to apply a color to an object.*

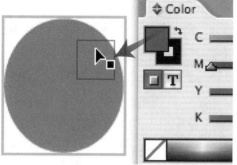

⑧ **Drag a color from the Color palette** *to apply a color to an object.*

You can use the Color palette to apply colors to selected objects.

TIP This technique, while convenient to use, creates unnamed colors or colors that are not listed in the Swatches palette. *(See the sidebar on page 131 for why creating unnamed colors can be a problem.)*

To apply colors to a fill or stroke:

◆ With an object or text selected, use the Color palette to define a fill color. This applies the unnamed color to the fill of the object or text. *(See page 148 for how to set the fill color of an object.)*

or

With an object or text selected, use the Color palette to define a stroke color. This applies the unnamed color to the stroke of the object or text. *(See page 152 for how to set the stroke color of an object.)*

TIP You can choose colors by clicking the ramp section of the Color palette **⑦**.

TIP You can also drag a color directly from the Color palette onto objects **⑧**. This also creates unnamed colors.

TIP A square dot appears next to the cursor when you drag a swatch color onto objects. This indicates you are dragging a fill color onto the object.

You can add colors from the Color palette to the Swatches palette so you can easily reuse them. *(See the next section for more techniques to store colors.)*

To transfer colors from the Color palette:

1. Define the color in the Color palette.

2. Choose Add to Swatches from the Color palette menu. The color appears as a new color swatch in the Swatches panel.

Using the Color Palette

Defining and Storing Swatches

Although it is very quick to create a color using the Color palette, you will find it more efficient to create color *swatches*. A swatch is a color that has been defined and is stored in the Swatches palette.

TIP Unnamed colors are not available for all places where you use colors. For instance, only named color swatches can be used as part of text styles.

To work with the Swatches palette:

1. If the Swatches palette is not visible, choose **Window > Swatches** to open the palette ❾.

   or

   If the Swatches palette is behind other palettes, click the Swatches palette tab.

2. To see the different types of swatches, click the icons at the bottom of the palette as follows:

   • **Show All Swatches** displays both the color and the gradient swatches.
   • **Show Color Swatches** displays only the color swatches.
   • **Show Gradient Swatches** displays only the gradient swatches *(see page 141)*.

3. To change the display of the swatches in the palette, choose the following from the Swatches palette menu ❿:

   • **Name** displays a list of the swatch names in a large typeface.
   • **Small Name** uses a more compact typeface to display the swatch names.
   • **Small Swatch** displays only the square of the swatch color or gradient.
   • **Large Swatch** displays a larger square of the swatch color or gradient.

   TIP Each icon for the types of swatches has its own display setting. So the color swatches can be displayed in the Small Name view while the gradients are shown in the Large Swatch display.

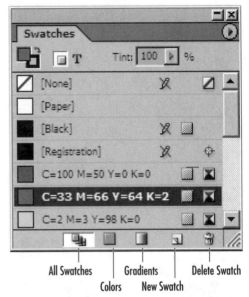

All Swatches • Colors • Gradients • New Swatch • Delete Swatch

❾ *The* **Swatches palette** *shows all the saved colors.*

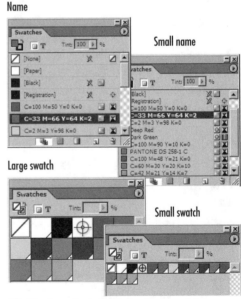

Name • Small name • Large swatch • Small swatch

❿ *The four choices for the display of the Swatches palette.*

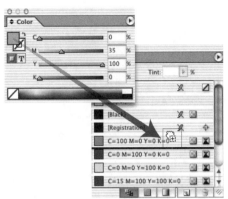

⑪ *You can* **drag colors from the Color palette** *into the Swatches palette.*

The Color "Paper"

The swatch labeled [Paper] in the Swatches palette allows you to change the background color of the pages in your document. This can be helpful if your document will be printed on colored paper, specialty paper, or even newsprint that is not completely white. You can modify the paper color to help judge how your images will look when printed.

The Registration Color

"Registration" is a color that is set to print on all plates of a document. For instance, if your document will be printed using process colors, you might want to create a note or mark that should be seen on all four plates. Rather than make the note in a combination of cyan, magenta, yellow, and black, you can apply the color Registration to the text for the note. This prints the note as a combination of all four inks.

Although you can apply colors to objects and text directly from the Color palette, this is not considered a good production workflow. Instead, use the Swatches palette to add the color currently defined in the Color palette.

TIP If you apply colors from the Color palette, they are called unnamed colors. Unnamed colors can cause production problems later on and should be avoided. *(See "Avoiding Unnamed Colors" on page 131.)*

To add a color to the Swatches palette:

1. Use the Color palette to define a color *(see page 120)*.

2. Click the New Swatch icon at the bottom of the palette. The new color, named with the color values, is automatically added to the Swatches palette.

TIP You can also add colors to the Swatches palette using the Color Picker *(see page 140)*.

InDesign also lets you drag colors from the Color palette into the Swatches palette.

To drag colors into the Swatches palette:

1. Create the color in the Color palette.

2. Drag the color from the Color palette fill or stroke box to the bottom of or between two colors in the Swatches palette.

3. Release the mouse when a black line appears in the Swatches palette ⑪. The new color is added and automatically takes its name from the color values.

TIP The cursor displays a plus sign as you drag the color into the Color palette. On the Mac the cursor is the image of a fist. On Windows the cursor is an arrow.

You can define and add new colors to your document using only the Swatches palette.

To define a new color swatch:

1. Choose New Color Swatch from the Swatches palette menu. This opens the New Color Swatch dialog box .

   or

   Opt/Alt-click the New Swatch icon at the bottom of the Swatches palette.

2. To name the color swatch yourself, deselect the checkbox for Name with Color Value and then type a name in the Swatch Name field.

   or

   Leave the setting checked to name the color swatch using the values that define the color. This option is not available for spot colors.

3. Choose Process or Spot from the Color Type pop-up list . *(See the sidebar "Process or Spot?" on the next page for an explanation of the difference between process and spot color.)*

4. Choose LAB, CMYK, or RGB from the Color Mode menu 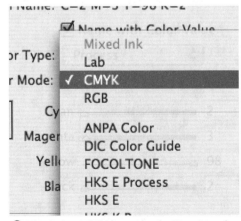. *(See "The Basics of Color" on page 118 for a description of the three color modes.)*

   or

   Choose one of the Swatch Libraries at the bottom of the Color Mode menu 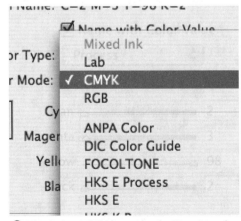. *(See "Using Swatch Libraries" on page 132 for how to use these types of colors.)*

5. If you have chosen LAB, CMYK, or RGB, use the sliders to change the values from the ones originally defined.

6. Click OK. This adds the swatch and closes the dialog box.

   or

   Click Add to add the swatch without closing the dialog box. This allows you to define additional colors.

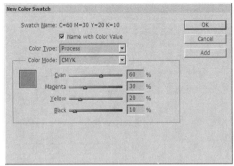

 Use the **New Color Swatch dialog box** *to define colors to be added to the Swatches palette.*

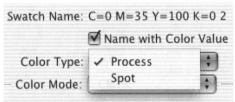 *Use the* **Color Type menu** *to choose either process or spot colors.*

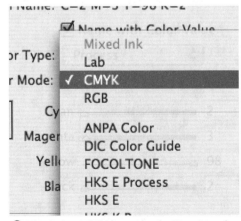 *The* **Color Mode menu** *in the New Swatch dialog box.*

Defining and Storing Swatches

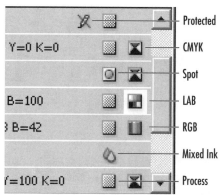

Protected

CMYK

Spot

LAB

RGB

Mixed Ink

Process

⑮ *The* **icons in the Swatches palette** *identify the different types of colors and color modes.*

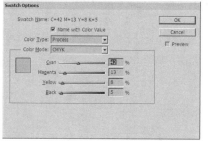

⑯ *Once you define a swatch, you modify it in the* **Swatch Options dialog box**.

The colors that appear in the Swatches palette are displayed with icons that give you information about the type of color, the color mode, and other attributes **⑮**. Of course, once you have defined a color swatch, you can modify its color definition. This changes the appearance of all text and objects that use that color, even if they are not selected.

TIP The color Black is protected and cannot be modified. If you need a variation of Black, create a new color swatch.

To modify a color swatch:

1. Select the swatch and choose Swatch Options from the Swatches palette menu. This opens the Swatch Options dialog box **⑯**. These are the same controls as in the New Color Swatch dialog box.

   or

   Double-click the swatch in the palette.

2. Make changes to the color.

TIP Click the Preview checkbox to see how the changes affect the colors applied to objects in the document.

3. Click OK to apply the changes.

TIP The Swatch Options dialog box does not have an Add button. This is because you use this dialog box only to modify existing colors — not to add new ones.

Defining and Storing Swatches

Process or Spot?

Process colors are those printed using small dots of the four process inks: cyan, magenta, yellow, and black. Spot colors are printed using special inks. For example, if you look at the process-color green printed in a magazine, that color is actually a combination of cyan and yellow printed together in a series of dots. However, a spot-color green is printed by using actual green ink.

One benefit of spot colors is that you can exactly match a special color or use specialty colors such as fluorescents or metallics that could never be created using process inks. You can also use a spot color together with black as a two-color job. This is cheaper than printing four-color process colors. The benefit of process colors is that you use just four inks to create thousands of different color combinations.

Once you create color swatches, you can apply them via the Fill and Stroke controls in the Toolbox or Color palette.

To apply a swatch color:

1. Create the object or text that you want to color.

2. Select either the Fill or Stroke icons in the Color palette or Toolbox. *(See Chapter 6, "Styling Objects," for more information on the Fill or Stroke icons.)*

3. In the Swatches palette, click the color you want. This applies the swatch to the object.

To delete swatches:

1. Select the color you want to delete.

TIP To select a series of adjacent swatches, select the first swatch and then hold the Shift key and select the last swatch in the series. This highlights the first and last swatch and all the swatches in between.

TIP Hold the Command/Ctrl key to select nonadjacent swatches.

2. Click the Delete Swatch icon **17** or choose Delete Swatch from the Swatches menu.

3. If the swatch is used within the document, the Delete Swatch dialog box appears, asking how you want to replace the deleted swatch **18**:

   • To swap the color with one from the Swatches palette, choose Defined Swatch and then pick a swatch from the pop-up list.

   • To leave the color as an unnamed color applied to the object, choose Unnamed Swatch. *(See page 131 for more information on unnamed colors.)*

TIP The default swatches None, Paper, Black, and Registration cannot be deleted.

17 *Click the* **Delete Swatch icon** *to delete the selected swatches.*

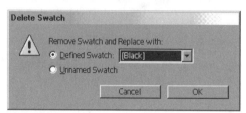

18 *The* **Delete Swatch dialog box** *controls what happens to colors when they are deleted from a document.*

Defining and Storing Swatches

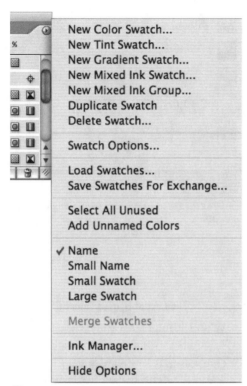

New Color Swatch...
New Tint Swatch...
New Gradient Swatch...
New Mixed Ink Swatch...
New Mixed Ink Group...
Duplicate Swatch
Delete Swatch...

Swatch Options...

Load Swatches...
Save Swatches For Exchange...

Select All Unused
Add Unnamed Colors

✓ Name
Small Name
Small Swatch
Large Swatch

Merge Swatches

Ink Manager...

Hide Options

⓳ *The* **Swatches palette menu** *contains the commands for working with color swatches.*

If you have many colors in your document that you are not using, you may want to delete them to avoid confusion when the file is sent to a print shop.

To delete all unused swatches:

1. Choose Select All Unused in the Swatches palette menu **⓳**.
2. Click the Delete Swatch icon or use the Delete Swatch command in the Swatches palette menu.

You can also select several swatches and merge them into one color.

TIP The Merge Swatches command makes it easy to globally replace all instances of one defined color with another.

To merge swatches:

1. Click to select the first color. This is the final color that you want the other colors to change to.
2. Hold the Cmd/Ctrl key and click to select another swatch. This is the color that you want to delete.

   or

   Hold the Shift key and click to select a range of swatches. These are the swatches you want to delete.

3. Choose Merge Swatches from the Swatches palette menu **⓳**. This deletes all the swatches except the swatch that was first selected. That swatch is applied to all text and objects that used the deleted swatches.

The position that swatches occupy in the palette comes from the order in which they were created. You can easily change the order of the swatches.

To move swatches to new positions:

1. Select a swatch in the palette.
2. Drag the swatch to a new position. A black line indicates where the swatch will be located ⑳.
3. Release the mouse button.

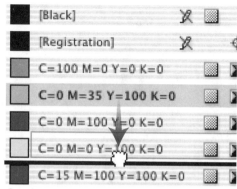

⑳ *Drag a swatch to move it from one position to another.*

You may find it easier to duplicate a swatch and modify it than to start from scratch.

To duplicate a swatch:

◆ Select the swatch and choose Duplicate Swatch from the Swatches palette menu.

   or

   Select the swatch and click the New Swatch icon.

   or

   Drag the swatch onto the New Swatch icon.

You can save a selection of swatches for use in other InDesign documents, or in Adobe Illustrator or Adobe Photoshop documents.

To save selected swatches:

1. Select the swatches in the Swatches palette that you want to save.
2. Choose Save Swatches For Exchange from the Swatches palette menu.
3. Use the operating system dialog box to save the swatches as an Adobe Swatch Exchange (.ase) file.

The Cost of Unused Colors

Why is it important to delete unused colors?

One reason is if you are going to send your documents to a service bureau or print shop for final output. It can be confusing to the people who are going to open your file if they see many colors in a document that's supposed to be printed in black and white.

At the very least, they're going to wonder if they've received the right instructions. At the worst, they'll delay printing the file until they talk to someone to make sure.

Also, it may seem like a little thing, but every color adds to the size of the file. Even in these days of huge hard drives, it's always better to keep your files as lean as possible.

Defining and Storing Swatches

> **Avoiding Unnamed Colors**
>
> Why do I warn you against creating unnamed colors? Why may your service bureau warn you not to create unnamed colors?
>
> Your job will most certainly print, even with unnamed colors. The problem comes when someone checks to make sure all your colors are defined correctly.
>
> Because the unnamed colors don't appear in the Swatches palette, there is no way for someone to easily find or make a universal change to the colors in your document. So the checker will have to search, page by page, to see if there are any unnamed colors.
>
> So although there is nothing actually wrong with unnamed colors, it is better to always use the Swatches palette to apply colors. That way you'll have more control over the colors in your document.

You can import the swatches from one InDesign document into another. You can also import the swatches from an Adobe Swatch Exchange file.

To import swatches from other documents:

1. Choose Load Swatches from the Swatches palette menu. The operating system dialog box appears.
2. Navigate to find the document or Adobe Swatch Exchange file you want to import swatches from.
3. Click Open. The swatches are imported into the current document.

Unnamed colors are colors that are applied to objects directly from the Color palette or the Color Picker instead of through the Swatches palette. It is a good idea not to have unnamed colors floating around your document. Fortunately, you can easily convert unnamed colors into named colors.

To name unnamed colors:

- Choose Add Unnamed Colors from the Swatches palette menu. All unnamed colors are added to the palette and named with their percentage values.

You can create colors that are available as the default colors for all new documents.

To create default colors:

1. Close all documents but leave InDesign running.
2. Use any of the methods in this section, "Defining and Storing Swatches" to define and store a color in the Swatches palette. The color will appear in the Swatches palette of all new InDesign documents.

Using Swatch Libraries

Rather than defining your own color mixtures, you can use the swatch libraries from professional color systems from companies such as Pantone or Trumatch. These color libraries usually have printed samples that you can refer to in order to see how the color will appear when printed.

To add colors from swatch libraries:

1. Open the New Swatch dialog box *(see page 126)* or the Swatch Options dialog box *(see page 127)*.

2. Choose one of the swatch libraries listed in the Color Mode list ❿. This displays the colors in the library ❷.

3. Scroll through the library to select the color you want to add to your document.

   or

   Instead of scrolling through a long list, type the name or number associated with the color in the Swatch Library field.

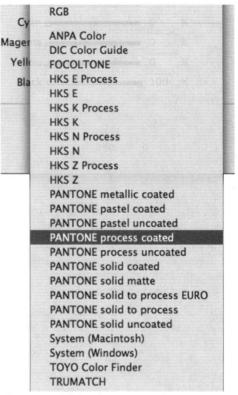

❿ *The* **swatch libraries** *in the Color Mode list.*

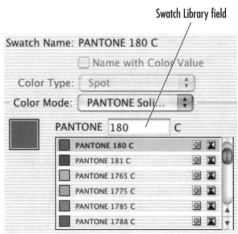

❷ *An example of the window that displays a swatch library, such as the Pantone Solid Coated colors.*

The Swatch Libraries

InDesign ships with a collection of third-party swatch libraries that contain the color definitions used by professional color systems. Here is a description of each of the types of libraries.

ANPA Color is commonly used for newspaper production. The colors can be found in the ANPA Color Newspaper Color Ink Book.

DIC Color Guide contains spot colors used mainly in Japan. These colors can be matched using the color guides from from Dainippon Ink and Chemicals, Inc.

Focoltone holds the process colors that can be matched using materials that are available from Focoltone International, Ltd. These colors are very popular in both France and the United Kingdom.

HKS is a system of process and spot colors used in Europe.

Pantone is the major color-matching system company used in North America. All Pantone colors can be matched to materials available from Pantone, Inc.

System (Macintosh) includes the colors of the Macintosh operating system.

System (Windows) includes the colors of the Windows operating system.

Toyo consists of spot colors used primarily in Japan. Color matching materials are available from the Toyo Ink Manufacturing Co., Ltd.

Trumatch provides a library of process colors. These colors have been specially designed for digital prepress as well as desktop color printers and copier machines. Color matching materials are available from Trumatch, Inc.

Web consists of the 216 colors that are shared by both the Macintosh and Windows system colors. These are sometimes called the Web-safe colors.

You can use the swatch libraries to open color palettes from other InDesign documents and Adobe Illustrator documents.

To import swatches from other documents:

1. Choose Other Library from the Color Mode list **㉑**.

2. Navigate to select the InDesign or Illustrator document. The colors appear in the window.

Using Swatch Libraries

Creating Mixed Inks

Mixed inks is the term InDesign uses for a color that combines a spot color with other spot colors or process colors. (QuarkXPress calls this type of color a *multi-ink*.) Mixed inks give you more flexibility in creating colors, especially for two-color jobs.

To create a single Mixed Ink swatch:

1. Choose New Mixed Ink Swatch from the Swatches palette menu. This opens the New Mixed Ink Swatch dialog box 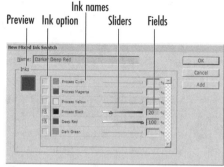.

   TIP The command to create mixed inks is not available unless you have first defined a spot color in the Swatches palette.

2. Enter a name for the mixed ink swatch.

3. Click the ink controls to select the colors in the mixed ink swatch. You must choose two inks, and one of them must be a spot color ink 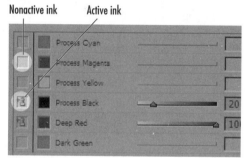.

4. Use the sliders or fields to set the amount of each ink in the swatch.

5. Click the OK button to create the mixed ink swatch.

   or

   Click the Add button to create the mixed ink swatch and then use the dialog box to define a new mixed ink swatch.

Ink names
Preview   Ink option   Sliders   Fields

㉓ *The* **New Mixed Ink Swatch dialog box** *allows you to combine a spot color with other colors.*

Nonactive ink   Active ink

㉔ *Use the* **ink controls** *to define the colors in the mixed ink swatch.*

Using Mixed Ink Swatches

Mixed ink swatches have a variety of uses. Perhaps the most common use is to define a mixed ink as a single spot color plus a percentage of process black. This allows you to create a slightly darker version of a spot color. I find this extremely helpful when working on two-color jobs where I need to darken my spot color.

You can also use mixed ink swatches to combine two spot colors. For instance, you can combine a spot yellow with a spot blue to create a green mixed ink swatch. However, be careful when you try to mix spot colors. The color in the preview box is only a very rough representation of the actual color on press.

Finally, you can use mixed inks to combine varnishes with process colors. This is a sophisticated technique and you should consult with your print shop.

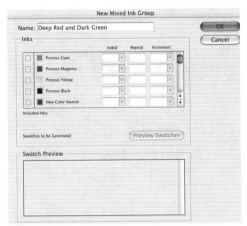

25 *The* **New Mixed Ink Group dialog box** *allows you to automatically create a series of mixed inks.*

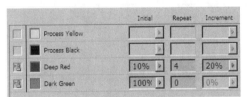

26 *Use the* **Inks controls** *to set the mixed ink colors, the initial amounts, the repetitions, and the increments by which they change.*

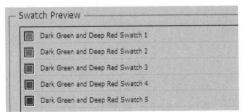

27 *The* **Swatch Preview area** *displays the mixed ink swatches created by the Mixed Ink Group controls.*

28 *A* **Mixed Ink Group** *creates a group listing, as well as individual mixed ink swatches.*

You might want to create a collection of mixed inks that combine colors in an increasing series of mixtures. InDesign calls this a Mixed Ink Group and makes it easy to automatically create the mixtures of colors.

TIP A Mixed Ink Group makes it easy to create a variety of mixed inks that can be quickly applied as you work.

To create a Mixed Ink Group:

1. Choose New Mixed Ink Group from the Swatches palette menu. The New Mixed Ink Group dialog box appears **25**.

2. Enter a name for the group in the Name field.

3. Click the Inks controls to select the colors in the mixed ink swatch. You must choose at least two inks and one of them must be a spot color ink.

4. Use the Initial field to define the amount of color that the first instance of an ink has **26**.

5. Use the Repeat field to set how many new mixed inks will be created with the color.

TIP Set the Repeat to zero to keep that color constant throughout the mixed ink group.

6. Use the Increment field to set the color increases for each new mixed ink.

7. Click the Preview Swatches button to see the result of the settings in the Swatches **27**.

8. Click OK to create the Mixed Ink Group. The group appears in the Swatches palette **28**.

Creating Mixed Inks

Once you have created a mixed ink group, you can make changes to the entire group or the individual swatches in the group.

To modify all the swatches in a mixed ink group:

1. Select the mixed ink group in the Swatches palette and choose Swatch Options from the Swatches palette menu.

   or

   Double click the name of the mixed ink group in the Swatches palette. The Mixed Ink Group Options dialog box appears **29**.

2. Use the Name field to change the name of the group.

3. Use the ink controls to delete inks from the mixed ink group.

   TIP While you can delete inks from the group, you cannot add inks. So a two-ink group can't be changed to a three-ink group.

4. Use the Inks list to swap one ink for another **30**. The list shows both the process and spot colors in the document.

5. If desired, check Convert Mixed Ink Swatches to Process. This changes all the colors in the mixed ink swatches to their process color equivalents.

   TIP The option to convert the colors to process is permanent and cannot be changed except as part of InDesign's undo chain.

6. Click OK. The changes are applied to the inks used in the mixed ink swatches that you originally created.

   TIP Watch out! Once you have deleted inks from the mixed ink group, you can't go back and add them to the mixed ink group. You'll have to regenerate the entire mixed ink group.

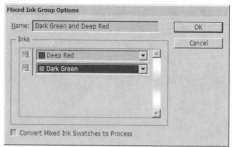

29 *Use the* **Mixed Ink Group Options dialog box** *to make changes to the inks used in a mixed ink group.*

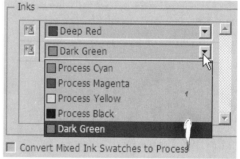

30 *Use the* **Inks list** *to change the colors used in a mixed ink group.*

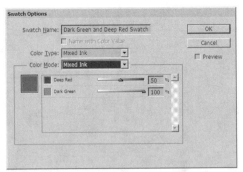

*Use the **Swatch Options dialog box** to make changes to individual swatches.*

*Use the **Color Type list** to change the mixed ink swatch to either a process or a spot color.*

*Use the **Color Mode list** to choose the color mode or to select one of the swatch libraries.*

Once you have created a mixed ink swatch, you can modify any of its attributes such as the name, color type, or ink percentages.

To modify a mixed ink swatch:

1. Select the mixed ink swatch in the Swatches palette and choose Swatch Options from the Swatches palette menu.

    or

    Double-click the name of the mixed ink swatch in the Swatches palette. The Swatch Options dialog box appears ③.

2. Use the Color Type list to change the type of swatch from Mixed Ink to either Process or Spot ②.

3. Use the Name field to change the name of the swatch.

4. If you have changed the color type to Process, you can select the option for Name with Color Value.

5. Use the Color Mode list to change the color to LAB, CMYK, or RGB ③.

    or

    Choose one of the Swatch Libraries.

    TIP Changes to the Color Mode and Color Type remove the swatch from the mixed ink group. These colors cannot be converted back into mixed inks.

6. Use the sliders to change the amount of inks in the mixed ink swatch.

    TIP If you change only the sliders for the mixed ink swatch, the color retains its connection to the inks defined in the Mixed Ink Group Options.

7. Click OK to apply the changes.

Creating Mixed Inks

Creating Tints

Tints are screened, or lighter, versions of colors. Spot color tints create screens of the base color. Process color tints reduce the amounts of the process inks that define the color.

To create a tint swatch:

1. Select the *base color,* that is, the swatch color that you want to tint.

2. Use the Tint field in the Swatches palette to create a screen of the swatch color ③④.

3. Click the New Swatch icon to store the tint percentage as a swatch in the Swatches panel.

TIP The tint swatch appears in the Swatches palette with the same name as the base color but with the tint percentage listed ③⑤.

TIP The tint field percentage continues to tint other swatches in the palette until you reset the field to 100%.

As you select a color swatch as a base color, the Color palette displays a slider and a ramp of the color.

To tint a swatch using the Color palette:

1. Select the swatch color that you want to tint.

2. In the Color palette, use the slider or click in the ramp to create a percentage of the base color ③⑥.

3. Click the New Swatch icon to create a tint swatch of the percentage you defined.

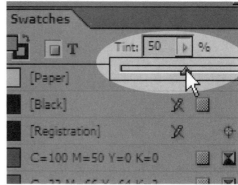

③④ *Use the* **Tint field** *to create a screened version of a swatch color.*

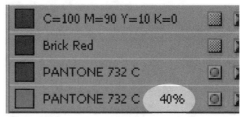

③⑤ *A* **tint swatch** *is listed with the same name as the base color and the tint percentage.*

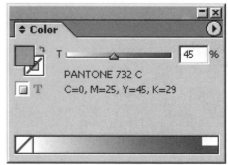

③⑥ *The Color palette displays* **a slider and tint ramp** *when a base color is chosen.*

Creating Tints

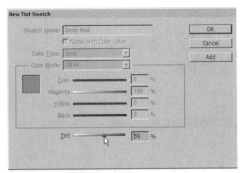

❸❼ *The* **New Tint Swatch dialog box** *lets you set the percentage of a tint.*

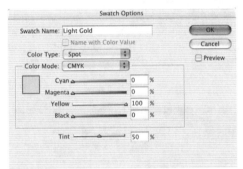

❸❽ *The* **Swatch Options** *for a tint swatch let you change the tint percentage or modify the base color of the tint.*

You can also create a tint swatch using the Swatches palette menu.

To store a tint swatch of a color:

1. In the Swatches palette, select the *base color,* that is, the color you want to tint.

2. Choose New Tint Swatch from the Swatches palette menu. The New Tint Swatch dialog box appears **❸❼**.

3. Adjust the tint slider to a percentage.

4. Click OK. The tint swatch appears in the Swatches palette with the same name as the base color but with the tint percentage listed.

   or

   Click Add to add the tint to the Swatches palette and then create additional tints.

Once you store a tint swatch, you can modify the tint percentage. This updates all the objects that use that tint swatch.

To modify tint swatches:

1. Double click the name of the tint swatch in the Swatches palette. This opens the Swatch Options dialog box for tints **❸❽**.

   TIP This dialog box is slightly different from the ordinary Swatch Options dialog box, which does not have a tint slider.

2. To change the tint value, adjust the Tint slider at the bottom of the dialog box.

   TIP You can also modify the sliders for the base color when you open the Swatch Options dialog box to modify a tint.

3. Click OK to apply the changes.

   TIP Anytime you modify the swatch used as a base color, all tints of that color update automatically.

Creating Tints

Using the Color Picker

If you have used Photoshop, you are probably familiar with Photoshop's Color Picker which is accessed through the foreground or background color icons in the Toolbox. InDesign also has a Color Picker, which is opened through the Toolbox.

To define a color using the Color Picker:

1. Double-click either the Fill icon or the Stroke icon in the Toolbox ㉟. This opens the Color Picker.

2. Use the RGB, LAB, or CMYK fields (㊵ – ㊷)to define the color.

3. Click OK to apply the color to the current fill or stroke.

TIP When you click the RGB or LAB controls, the Color Picker displays one of those color controls. When you click the CMYK controls, however, the Color Picker does not display the CMYK color controls.

To define a color swatch using the Color Picker:

1. Double-click either the Fill icon or the Stroke icon in the Toolbox to open the Color Picker.

2. Use the RGB, LAB, or CMYK fields to define the color.

3. Click the Add [RGB, LAB, or CMYK] Swatch button to add the color to the Swatches palette.

4. Click OK to close the Color Picker.

㉟ The **Fill and Stroke icons** *in the Toolbox or Color palette let you open the Color Picker.*

RGB controls

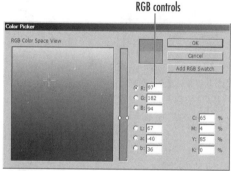

㊵ The **Color Picker in the RGB mode** *lets you define and store RGB colors.*

LAB controls

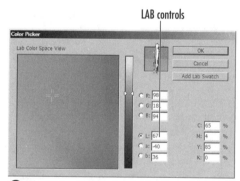

㊶ The **Color Picker in the LAB mode** *lets you define and store LAB colors.*

CMYK controls

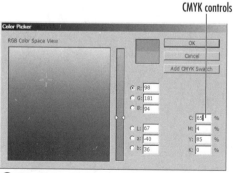

㊷ The **Color Picker in the CMYK mode** *lets you define and store CMYK colors.*

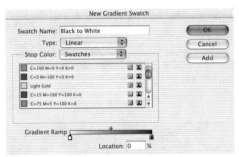

43 *Use the* **New Gradient Swatch dialog box** *to define a gradient of blended colors.*

Linear gradient　　　　**Radial gradient**

44 *A* **linear gradient** *changes colors along a line. A* **radial gradient** *changes colors in a circular pattern.*

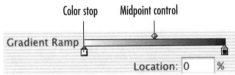

45 *Use the* **color stops and midpoint controls** *along the gradient ramp to modify the gradient.*

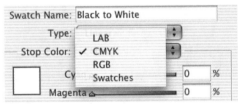

46 *Use the* **Stop Color menu** *to choose the format for the colors used for the color stops.*

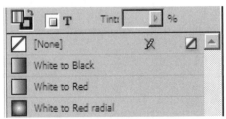

47 *Gradients are* **stored in the Swatches palette.**

Creating Gradient Swatches

Gradients are blends that change from one color into another. InDesign creates gradients as swatches that can then be applied to objects. *(See Chapter 6, "Styling Objects," for information on applying gradients.)*

To define a gradient:

1. Choose New Gradient Swatch from the Swatches palette menu. The New Gradient Swatch dialog box appears **43**.

2. Enter a name for the gradient in the Swatch Name field.

3. Choose Linear or Radial in the Type field **44**.

4. Click a color stop on the gradient ramp to define a color in the gradient **45**.

   TIP You **must select a color stop** in order to see the Stop Color list.

5. Choose the type of color for the selected stop from the Stop Color list **46**:
   - **Swatches** shows you the list of colors in the Swatches palette.
   - **LAB, CMYK,** or **RGB** displays the sliders that let you define the color using the LAB, CMYK, or RGB values.

6. Click the other gradient stop to define a color for it.

7. Adjust the midpoint control to change the position where the two colors blend equally.

8. Click OK to add the gradient to the Swatches palette **47**.

   or

   Click the Add button to add the current gradient to the Swatches palette and continue defining additional gradients.

   TIP If you don't see the gradient listed in the Swatches palette, click either the Show All Swatches or Show Gradient Swatches icon at the bottom of the Swatches palette.

All gradients must have at least two colors. However, you can easily add more colors to a gradient by using the color stops.

To add gradient color stops:

1. Open the New Gradient Swatch or the Gradient Options dialog box.

2. Click the area below the gradient ramp. This adds a color stop to the ramp area **48**.

3. Make whatever changes you want to the color stop.

4. If necessary, move the color stop to a new position.

5. Click OK to apply the changes to the gradient swatch.

To delete a gradient color stop:

◆ Drag the color stop away from the ramp area and release the mouse **49**. The gradient reblends according to the colors that remain.

TIP You can't have fewer than two color stops in a gradient.

To modify a gradient swatch:

1. Select the gradient swatch and choose Swatch Options from the Swatches palette menu. This opens the Gradient Options dialog box.

   or

   Double-click the gradient in the palette.

TIP Use the Preview checkbox to see how the changes affect the gradients in the document.

2. Adjust the midpoint, color stops, or gradient type.

3. Click OK to apply the changes.

48 *Click under the gradient ramp to add a color stop to the gradient.*

49 *Drag a color stop off the gradient ramp to delete that color from the gradient.*

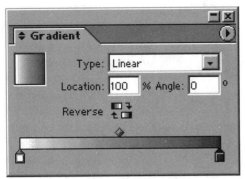

50 *Use the* **Gradient palette** *to create unnamed gradients.*

Process and Spot Colors in Gradients

A gradient that's defined using process colors is separated onto CMYK plates.

A gradient that contains two tints of the same spot color will be separated onto the single spot color plate. If you want the gradient to fade to white, create a gradient between the spot color and a 0% tint of the spot color.

You can create a gradient between two spot colors. However, to avoid moiré patterns in the gradient, you must assign different screen angles to those spot colors in the Inks dialog box.

For instance, if you had a gradient of spot red to spot yellow, you would want to make sure each color had a screen angle that was 45 degrees different from the other. Ask your print shop for details on setting the screen angles for spot colors.

A gradient that contains both spot and process colors will be separated onto both the spot and process color plates.

Just as you can create unnamed colors, you can also create unnamed gradients. These are gradients that are created only within the Gradient palette and are not stored in the Swatches palette.

TIP Like unnamed colors, I don't recommend working with unnamed gradients.

To work with the Gradient palette:

1. If the Gradient palette is not visible, choose **Window > Gradient** to open the palette **50**.

   or

   If the Gradient palette is behind other palettes, click the Gradient palette tab.

2. Choose Show Options from the Gradient palette menu to see all the controls in the palette.

TIP If the color stops are not visible, click the area under the ramp to display the color stops in the Gradient palette.

To create unnamed gradients:

1. Use the Type pop-up list to choose between Linear and Radial.

2. Select a color stop and adjust the sliders in the Color palette to define the color at that position.

   or

   Hold the Opt/Alt key and click the name of a swatch in the Swatches palette.

3. Select another color stop and use the sliders in the Color palette to define the color at that position.

4. Set the angle of the gradient in the Angle field.

TIP Click the Reverse icon to reverse the positions of the color stops.

Creating Gradient Swatches

Once you have a defined a gradient in the Gradient palette, you can store it as a swatch.

To store an unnamed gradient:

1. Create the gradient in the Gradient palette.

2. Click the New Swatch icon in the Swatches palette.

   or

   Drag the preview of the gradient from the Gradient palette into the Swatches palette.

3. Double-click the name of the gradient in the Swatches palette to rename it.

Using the Eyedropper

The Eyedropper tool lets you sample colors from graphics that are placed in your document. *(See Chapter 8, "Imported Graphics," for more information on placing graphics.)*

To sample and store colors from placed graphics:

1. Click the Eyedropper tool in the Toolbox ❺❶.

2. Move the Eyedropper cursor over the color of a placed graphic ❺❷.

3. Click to sample the color.

TIP If you have already used the Eyedropper to sample a color, hold the Opt/Alt key to sample a new color.

4. Click the New Swatch icon in the Swatches palette. The sampled color is stored as a color swatch.

TIP The Eyedropper samples the color in the same color mode as the placed graphic. So RGB images yield RGB colors, and CMYK images yield CMYK colors.

TIP The Eyedropper can also sample and apply fills, strokes, and transparency attributes of objects and text formatting. *(See Chapter 6, "Styling Objects," and Chapter 14, "Automating Your Work.")*

❺❶ *The* **Eyedropper tool** *lets you sample colors from placed images.*

❺❷ *Click with the* **Eyedropper tool** *over an area of an image that you want to sample.*

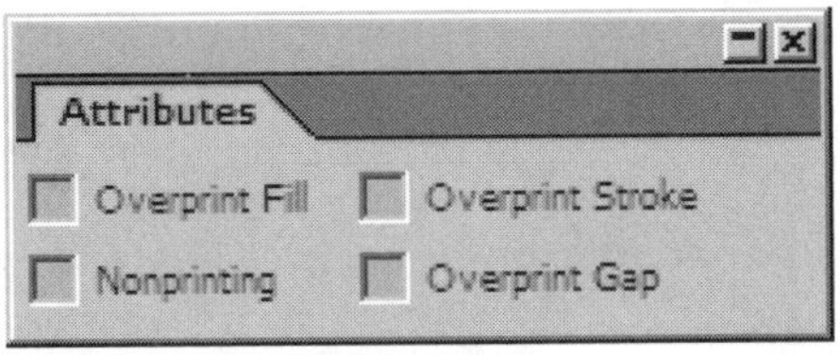

(53) *Use the* **Attributes palette** *to set an object to overprint.*

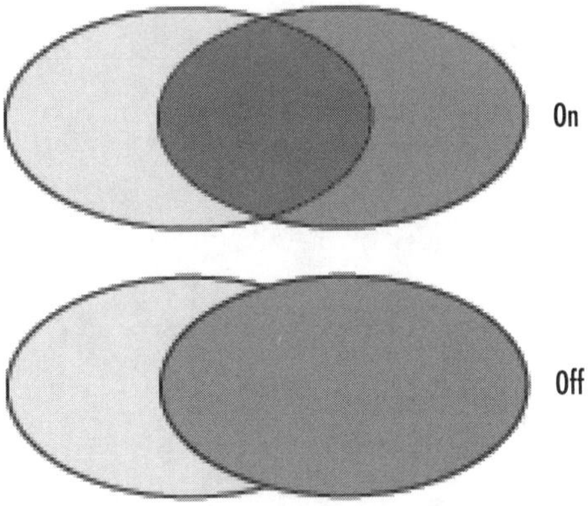

(54) *Turn on the* **Overprint Preview command** *to see the effects of overprinting onscreen.*

> **Rules of Overprinting**
>
> You may come across a situation where the overprint preview doesn't seem to work. Most likely there's nothing wrong with the preview—it's how the color values were defined.
>
> The rules of overprinting state that a color only overprints if it *doesn't share a common plate* with the color below. So, 100% cyan will overprint with 100% yellow to form green; however as soon as you add any percentage of yellow to the cyan, then the top color no longer overprints the bottom.

Overprinting Colors

Overprinting is a technique that allows you to set the color of one object to mix with any colors underneath. For instance, without overprinting, a yellow object placed over a blue background knocks out the blue and prints as yellow. But with overprinting turned on, the yellow object mixes with the blue background to create green.

To set a fill or stroke to overprint:

1. Select the object.
2. If the Attributes palette is not visible, choose **Window > Attributes** to open the palette (53).

   or

   If the Attributes palette is behind other palettes, click the Attributes palette tab.
3. Check Overprint Fill to set the object's fill color to overprint.
4. Check Overprint Stroke to set the object's stroke color to overprint.
5. Check Overprint Gap to set the color of the gap applied to stroke effects to overprint *(see page 157 for how to apply a gap color to strokes)*.

TIP Check Nonprinting in the Attributes palette to set an object not to print. This is helpful if you want to add comments for production use that aren't meant to be seen in the finished piece.

In the past, the only way to see the effects of setting an object to overprint was to wait until the object was separated and printed by a commercial printer. InDesign lets you see a simulation of overprinting onscreen.

To turn on the overprint preview:

- Choose **View > Overprint Preview.** InDesign shows the effects of those colors set to overprint (54).

STYLING OBJECTS 6

Here's where you get a chance to express your creativity. Styling refers to applying fills, strokes, gradients, and effects to frames, lines, and text. If you're bored with plain black text on a white background, InDesign lets you change the text and background colors to almost anything you can imagine.

Most other graphics programs let you style objects and text with fills, strokes, and gradients. InDesign certainly does that also.

However, InDesign has broken new ground in offering sophisticated effects such as transparency, drop shadows, and glows. These are the effects that art directors and designers could only dream about creating with other page-layout programs.

With InDesign, they can make those dreams a reality.

Applying Fills

Fills are the effects applied to objects, which can be the interior of frames or text within a frame. So you can apply one color fill to the text inside a frame and another color fill to the frame itself. A fill can be a solid color or a gradient. *(See Chapter 5, "Working in Color," for more information on defining colors and gradients.)*

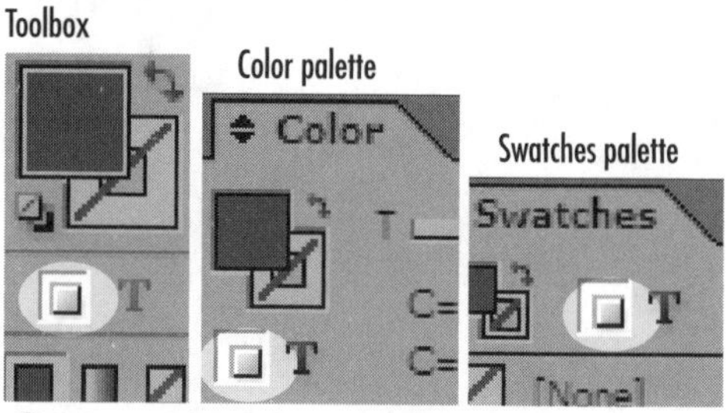

❶ *The* **Container icons** *(circled) indicate an effect will be applied to an object, not text.*

To apply a fill to an object:

1. Select an object.
2. Make sure the Container icon is chosen in the Toolbox or the Swatches or Color palette ❶. This indicates that the object will be modified.
3. Click the Fill icon in the Toolbox or in the Swatches or Color palette ❷.
4. Choose a color or gradient in the Color, Gradient, or Swatches palettes.

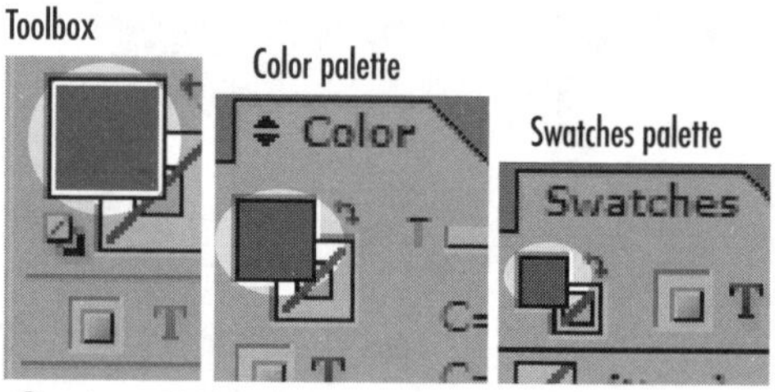

❷ *The* **Fill icons** *(circled) indicate an effect will be applied inside an object.*

You don't have to select an object to apply a fill. You can just drag a swatch onto any object to apply a color or a gradient.

To drag fill effects onto objects:

1. Drag a gradient or color swatch from the Toolbox or the Color, Gradient, or Swatches palette onto the object ❸.
2. Release the mouse button when the swatch is inside the object. A square dot appears to indicate you are inside the object.

TIP If you release the mouse button when the swatch is on the edge of the object, you will apply the effect to the object's stroke *(see page 152)*.

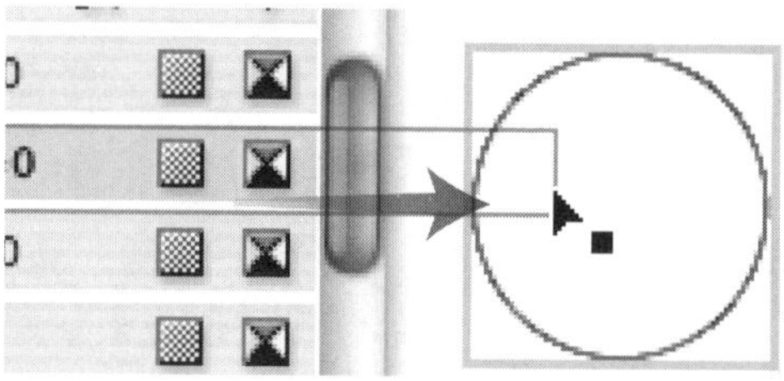

❸ *You can drag a swatch inside an object to apply a fill.*

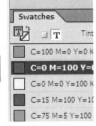

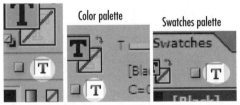

❹ *Choose a swatch to apply the color or gradient to selected text.*

Toolbox

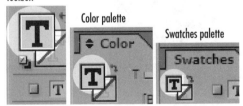

❺ *The Text icons (circled) set an effect to be applied to all the text within a frame.*

Toolbox

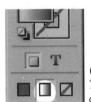

❻ *The T inside the Fill icon (circled) indicates that text is going to be styled.*

❼ *The Gradient icon in the Toolbox indicates that a color or gradient will be applied.*

❽ *The gradient in the Fill box indicates that the gradient will be applied as a fill.*

You can also apply fill colors to selected text in a text frame.

To apply a fill to selected text:

1. Use the Text tool to highlight the text.
2. Click the Fill icon in the Toolbox or the Swatches or Color palette.
3. Choose a swatch in the Color, Gradient, or Swatches palette **❹**.

TIP When text is highlighted, the color of the text is inverted. Deselect to see the actual text color.

You can also apply a fill to all the text in a frame with just the frame selected.

To apply a fill to all the text in a frame:

1. Select the text frame that contains the text to which you want to apply the fill.
2. Click the Fill icon in the Toolbox or the Swatches or Color palette.
3. Click the Text icon in the Toolbox or the Swatches or Color palette **❺**.

TIP The *T* inside the Fill icon indicates the text will be affected, not the frame **❻**.

4. Choose a swatch in the Color, Gradient, or Swatches palette.

You can also apply a gradient to text or objects.

To apply a gradient fill:

1. Click the Fill icon in the Toolbox or the Swatches or Color palette with the container or text icons selected.
2. Click the Gradient icon in the Toolbox **❼**.

   or

   Click a gradient in the Swatches or Gradient palette. The gradient is displayed in the Fill box **❽**.

Applying Fills

Once you have applied a gradient to an object or text, you can modify how it is applied using the Gradient tool.

To adjust a gradient fill:

1. Select the object that contains the gradient you want to modify.

2. Choose the Gradient tool in the toolbox ❾.

3. Drag the Gradient tool along the angle that the linear gradient should follow ❿.

   or

   Drag the Gradient tool to define the start and end points of a radial gradient ⓫.

TIP The start of the drag positions the first color. The end of the drag positions the final color.

TIP You can create a 3D sphere effect by positioning the start of a radial gradient slightly off-center in an ellipse. If the center color is lighter than the outside color, the sphere appears to bulge toward the viewer. If the center color is darker than the outside color, the sphere appears to bulge away from the viewer.

❾ *The* **Gradient tool** *in the Toolbox lets you modify the appearance of gradients.*

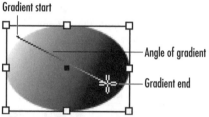

Gradient start

Angle of gradient

Gradient end

❿ *Drag the Gradient tool to set the start and end points and the angle of a linear gradient.*

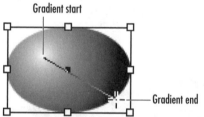

Gradient start

Gradient end

⓫ *Drag with the Gradient tool to set the start and end points of a radial gradient.*

Applying Fills

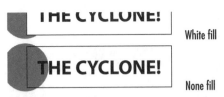

White fill

None fill

⑫ *The difference between a text frame with a white fill and a none fill.*

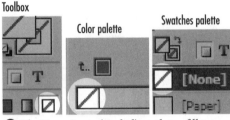

Toolbox

Color palette

Swatches palette

⑬ *The **None** icons(circled) apply no fill to an object.*

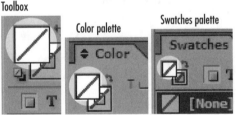

Toolbox

Color palette

Swatches palette

⑭ *The **None** symbol in the Fill icon(circled) indicates there is no fill applied to the object.*

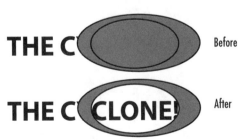

Before

After

⑮ *An example of how **a compound path** creates a hole in an object.*

You can also apply a fill of None to an object. This makes the background of the object transparent **⑫**.

To apply a fill of None:

1. Select the object.
2. Click the None icon in the Toolbox or the Swatches or Color palette **⑬**.

TIP If the object is not in front of others, you may not see a difference between a white and none fill. Check the icon to be sure **⑭**.

Another way to style objects is to create a compound path. A compound path allows one path to punch a hole in another. This makes the inside path transparent while the outside path is solid **⑮**.

TIP Compound paths are also used as part of the Pathfinder commands that allow you to combine and intersect objects *(see page 173)*.

To create a compound path:

1. Select two paths that overlap.
2. Choose **Object > Compound Paths > Make.**

TIP If the second object is not completely contained inside the first, the hole appears only where the objects overlap.

TIP Compound paths must contain the same fill and stroke effects.

You can release a compound path back to separate objects to restore the inside path to a solid color.

To release a compound path:

1. Select the compound path.
2. Choose **Object > Compound Paths > Release.**

Applying Fills

Applying Stroke Effects

Strokes are the effects applied to the edge of objects and text, or along lines.

TIP In QuarkXPress, stroke effects are called frames or line effects.

To apply a stroke to an object:

1. Select the object.

2. Make sure the Container icon is chosen in the Toolbox or the Swatches or Color palette ❶. This indicates that the object will be modified.

3. Click the Stroke icon in the Toolbox or the Swatches or Color palette ⓰.

4. Choose a swatch in the Color, Gradient, or Swatches palette.

You can also apply a stroke color by dragging a swatch onto the edge of any object on the page.

To drag stroke effects onto objects:

1. Drag a gradient or color swatch from the Toolbox or the Color, Gradient, or Swatches palette onto the edge of the object.

2. Release the mouse button when you see a small line appear next to the mouse cursor ⓱. This applies the color or gradient to the stroke.

TIP If you release the mouse button when the swatch is inside the object, you apply the effect to the object's fill *(see page 148)*.

InDesign makes it easy to swap the fill and stroke colors applied to an object.

To swap the fill and stroke settings:

◆ Click the double-headed arrow in the Toolbox ⓲. This switches the colors of the fill and stroke applied to the object.

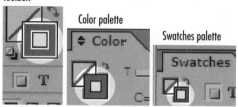

Toolbox

Color palette

Swatches palette

⓰ The **Stroke icons** *(circled) set an effect to be applied to the outside of an object or text.*

⓱ **Drag a swatch onto the edge** *to apply a stroke effect to an object.*

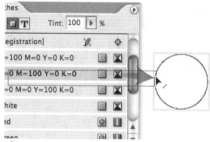

⓲ *Click the* **Swap Fill and Stroke icon** *in the Toolbox to switch the settings.*

Applying Stroke Effects

Dorothy
Dorothy

⑲ *A stroke effect applied to text.*

Toolbox

Color palette

Swatches palette

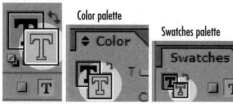

⑳ *The* **outlined T in the Stroke icon** *(circled) indicates that a stroke has been applied to text.*

㉑ *The effect of a linear gradient applied as a stroke with three different types of fills.*

Permission to Stroke Text

If you have worked with other desktop publishing programs, you may have found that strokes applied to text deform the shape of the characters. This happens because the stroke is applied on both the outside and the inside of the text. As a result, most teachers like me warned our students never to add a stroke to text — not in headlines and never in body copy.

InDesign, however, places strokes only on the outside of text. This means that it does not distort the characters. So you have complete permission to stroke headline text in InDesign. (Body text is too small to stroke.)

You can also add a color or gradient stroke to the outside edges of text with a color or gradient **⑲**.

To apply a stroke to selected text:

1. Use the Text tool to highlight the text.
2. Click the Stroke icon in the Toolbox or Color palette **⑳**.
3. Choose a swatch in the Color, Gradient, or Swatches palette.

To apply a stroke to all the text in a frame:

1. Select the text frame that contains the text to which you want to apply the stroke.
2. Click the Text button in the Toolbox or Color palette.
3. Click the Stroke icon in the Toolbox or Color palette.
4. Choose a swatch in the Color, Gradient, or Swatches palette.

You can also apply a gradient as a stroke to text or objects.

To apply a gradient stroke:

1. Click the Stroke icon in the Toolbox or the Swatches or Color palette.
2. Click the Gradient icon in the Toolbox or the Swatches or Gradient palette.
3. Use the Gradient tool to modify the angle or length of the gradient applied to a stroke *(see page 150)*.

TIP A linear gradient applied as a stroke creates a beveled effect. This may be combined with a solid or gradient fill for a three-dimensional effect **㉑**.

Color is only one aspect of a stroke effect. The Stroke palette controls the rest of the stroke attributes.

To work with the Stroke palette:

◆ If the Stroke palette is not visible, choose **Window > Stroke** to view it ㉒.

or

If the Stroke palette is behind other palettes, click the Stroke palette tab.

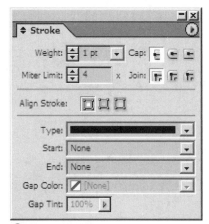

㉒ *The* **Stroke palette** *with all its options displayed.*

One of the most important attributes of a stroke is its thickness. This is controlled by changing the stroke weight ㉓.

To set the stroke weight (thickness):

1. Select the object.
2. Use the Weight field controls to set the thickness of the stroke ㉔.

TIP The stroke can be positioned on the outside, in the center, or inside the path using the Align Stroke controls *(see page 156)*.

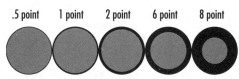

㉓ *Different* **stroke weights**.

If you scale a stroked object with the Scale Strokes setting turned on in the Transform palette, the size of the stroke changes, but the stroke weight displayed stays the same. This can create objects that have half-inch-thick strokes that read 1 point. You can eliminate this confusion by resetting the stroke weight so that it shows the actual thickness after scaling.

㉔ *The* **Weight controls** *let you change the stroke thickness.*

To reset the stroke weight:

1. Select the object.
2. Choose Reset Scaling to 100% from the Transform palette menu.

(vertical text in left margin:) **Applying Stroke Effects**

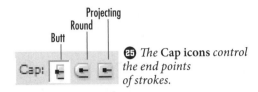

25 *The* **Cap icons** *control the end points of strokes.*

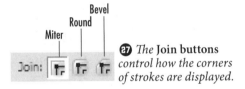

26 *The three Cap settings applied to strokes.*

27 *The* **Join buttons** *control how the corners of strokes are displayed.*

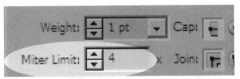

28 *The three Join settings applied to strokes.*

29 *The* **Miter Limit field** *controls how long a miter point may extend.*

A stroke's style is also controlled by the end caps and joins, which form points and corners.

To set the caps and joins:

1. Select an object that has a stroke applied to it.

2. In the Stroke palette, use the Cap icons **25** to change the way the ends of open paths are treated **26**:
   - **Butt** ends the stroke in a square. This is the default setting for a plain stroke.
   - **Round** ends the stroke in a semi-circle.
   - **Projecting** ends the stroke in a square that extends out from the end point.

   TIP The Cap settings have no effect on closed paths such as rectangles, ellipses, and polygons.

3. Use the Join buttons **27** to change the way two segments of a path meet at corners **28**:
   - **Miter** joins the segments at an angle.
   - **Round** joins the segments with a curve.
   - **Bevel** joins the segments with a line between the segments.

   TIP The join commands affect only corner points. *(See Chapter 7, "Pen and Beziers," for information on the types of points.)*

Sometimes a mitered join becomes too long and pointed. Fortunately, you can stop the point from becoming too long by setting the miter limit.

To set the miter limit:

1. Select an object with a mitered join.

2. In the Stroke palette, increase the amount in the Miter Limit field to control the size of the angle between the segments **29**.

   TIP If the size of the angle exceeds the miter limit, a bevel is substituted **28**. It does not mean a shorter point is substituted.

Applying Stroke Effects

In traditional drawing programs, a stroke is distributed evenly on the outside and inside of its path. InDesign lets you choose the alignment of the stroke on the path ⓪.

TIP This is different than the position of a stroke applied to text *(see page 153)*.

To set the alignment of a stroke:

1. Apply a stroke to an object.

2. Choose one of the three alignment options for the stroke as follows ㉛:

   • **Center** aligns the stroke so that half the stroke weight is inside the path and half is outside the path.

   • **Inside** aligns the stroke so that the entire thickness of the stroke weight is inside the path.

   • **Outside** aligns the stroke so that the entire thickness of the stroke weight is outside the path.

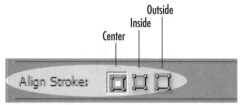

⓪ *Set the **Align Stroke controls** to set the position of the stroke along the path.*

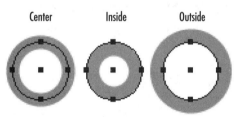

㉛ *Examples of how the Align Stroke controls change the position of the stroke on the path.*

Uses for the Stroke Alignment

Most people will find they don't ever need to change the alignment options for a stroke. They use the traditional Center alignment all the time. However, for many others, the ability to specify where the stroke aligns on the path is a real benefit.

Say you have a placed image inside a frame *(see Chapter 8 "Imported Graphics," for more information on working with imported graphics)*. After you import the graphic, you may want to add a stroke to its frame, but you don't want the stroke to cover any part of the placed image.

If you applied a stroke with the traditional Center alignment, you would then have to enlarge the size of the frame by half the size of the stroke. By setting the stroke alignment to Outside, you ensure that the stroke does not cover any part of the image.

Or say you want to apply a stroke to an object without increasing its size. With the Center alignment, every time you change the stroke weight, the size of the object would increase or decrease. By setting the stroke alignment to Inside, the stroke only appears inside the object and doesn't add to the size of the object.

Applying Stroke Effects

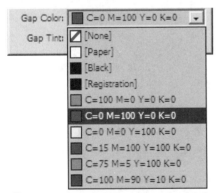

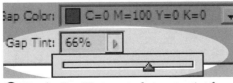

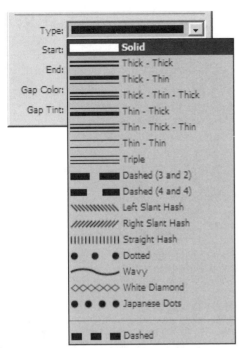
32 *The 18 default strokes in the* **Stroke Type** **menu** *in the Stroke palette.*

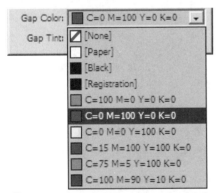
33 *Use the* **Gap Color menu** *in the Stroke palette to set the color of the clear areas of a stroke.*

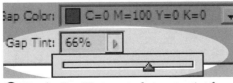
34 *Use the* **Gap Tint controls** *to set a tint for the gap color.*

The default setting for strokes is a solid line. However, you can choose one of the specialty strokes such as stripes, dashes, hashes, dots, or diamonds. You can even pick a stroke that curves up and down along the path.

To apply stroke styles to strokes:

1. Apply a stroke to an object.
2. Choose one of the styles from the Stroke Type menu **32**.

As described on page 152, the color of the stroke comes from choosing the Stroke icon and then picking a color. This method only colors the solid portion of a stroke. For strokes such as stripes and dashes, you can also color the gap, or the clear area between the solid colors of the stroke.

TIP This is the same technique used to set the gap color for the underline and strikethrough effects *(see page 61)*.

To set a stroke gap color:

1. Choose one of the specialty strokes that have both solid and clear areas.
2. Use the Gap Color menu to choose the color for the clear areas of the stroke **33**.

TIP This list contains the same colors and gradients as the Swatches palette.

3. If necessary, use the Gap Tint controls to set a screen for the gap color **34**.

Applying Stroke Effects

The stroke list contains a dashed stroke that you can customize to set the size of the dashes and the gaps between them.

To create custom dashed strokes:

1. Apply a stroke to an object.

2. Choose Dashed from the Stroke Type pop-up menu. The dashed settings appear at the bottom of the Stroke palette ③⑤.

TIP The dashed settings only appear when you select the stroke style named Dashed and not the ones labeled Dashed (3 and 2) or Dashed (4 and 4).

3. Enter an amount in the first dash field for the length of all of the dashes in the line.

4. Enter an amount in the first gap field for the size of the space between all of the dashes.

5. To create a series of dashes and gaps with irregular lengths, enter other values in the rest of the dash and gap fields.

TIP Apply round caps to add round ends to the dashes.

6. If necessary, use the Corners list ③⑥ to adjust the dashes and gaps ③⑦:

   • **None** leaves the dashes and gaps as they are. This can cause unequal dashes at the corners.

   • **Adjust dashes** changes the stroke so that the corner dashes are equal.

   • **Adjust gaps** changes the stroke so that the gap lengths are equal.

   • **Adjust dashes and gaps** changes the stroke to make the best fit so that both the corner dashes and gaps are equal.

TIP Although you can't customize them, you can also choose one of the preset dashes from the Stroke Type menu:

   • **Dash (3 and 2)** creates a dash that is 3 times the stroke weight with a gap that is 2 times the stroke weight ③⑧.

   • **Dash (4 and 4)** creates dashes and gaps that are 4 times the stroke weight ③⑧.

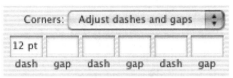

③⑤ *The* **Dashed settings** *at the bottom of the Stroke palette. These only appear when the Dashed stroke type is chosen.*

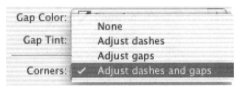

③⑥ *Use the* **Corners menu** *to adjust how dashes and gaps are distributed on a stroke.*

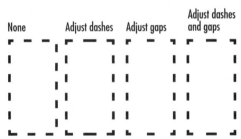

③⑦ *Examples of how the Corners settings affect the appearance of a dashed stroke.*

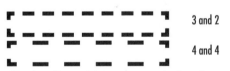

③⑧ *The effects of the two preset dash styles on 3-point strokes.*

Applying Stroke Effects

39 *Choose* **Stroke Styles** *from the Stroke palette to open the Stroke Styles dialog box.*

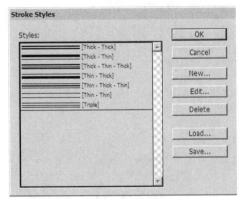

40 *The* **Stroke Styles dialog box** *lets you create, edit, and manage custom stroke styles.*

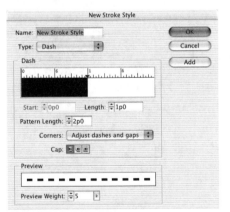

41 *The* **New Stroke Style dialog box** *is where you define the pattern for a custom stroke.*

42 *Use the* **Type menu** *to choose the type of custom stroke style.*

Creating Custom Stroke Styles

The Strokes palette menu contains a Stroke Styles feature that allows you to create custom stripes, dashes, and dots that you can add to your Strokes palette for reuse.

To create custom styles for strokes:

1. Choose Stroke Styles from the Stroke palette menu **39**. The Stroke Styles dialog box appears **40**.

TIP This dialog box contains the seven default stripe styles. You can't edit these default stripes, but you can use them as the basis for new stripe styles.

2. Click the New button to open the New Stroke Style dialog box **41**.

   or

   Choose one of the default stripes and then click the New button. This opens the New Stroke Style dialog box with the stripe style already set as the starting pattern.

3. Use the Name field to enter a name for the custom stroke style.

4. Choose the type of stroke style from the Type menu as follows **42**:

   - **Stripe** allows you to create multiple lines that run parallel to each other along the stroked path.
   - **Dotted** creates a series of dots repeated along the path.
   - **Dash** creates a single line that is broken into a series of individual elements.

5. The dialog box changes its controls according to the stroke style chosen in the Type menu. The following exercises show how to set the controls for each type of stroke.

6. When you have finished setting the stroke style, click OK to create the style.

   or

   Click the Add button to create the style and then define additional styles.

To create a custom stripe stroke style:

1. Choose Stripe from the Type menu of the New Stroke Style dialog box. The stripe controls appear **43**.

2. Click inside the Stripe area to add a stripe to the stroke.

TIP New stripes appear in the Stripe area with no width and need to be adjusted in order to appear as part of the finished stroke.

3. Drag the Start control triangle on the percentage ruler or enter an amount in the Start field to set the initial position for the stripe on the stroke **44**.

TIP A setting of 0% positions the stripe to start at the very top of the stroke width.

4. Drag the Width control triangle on the percentage ruler or enter an amount in the Width field to set the width of the stripe **44**.

TIP The width of the stripe is a percentage of the final stroke weight of the stroke. For example, a stripe width of 50% applied to a 4-point stroke creates a 2-point stripe.

5. Drag the stripe itself up or down in the Stripe area to position it without changing its width.

6. If you need to delete a stripe, drag it up or down so that it is off the Stripe area.

7. Use the Preview control to increase or decrease the size of the preview for the stroke style **45**.

TIP A larger preview helps you see small elements added to the custom stroke style. However, it does not change the appearance of the stroke used in the document.

TIP See the special exercise on pages 164 and 165 for how to use striped strokes for a special knockout rule.

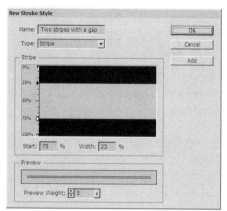

43 *The* **New Stroke Style dialog box** *set for the* **Stripe controls**.

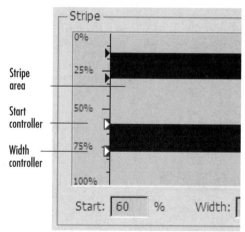

Stripe area

Start controller

Width controller

44 *The* **stripe controls** *in the New Stroke Style dialog box.*

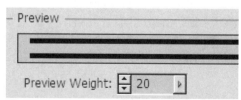

45 *Use the* **Preview display and Preview Weight** *to see what the stripe style will look like.*

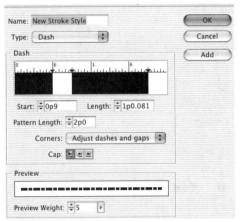

46 *The* **New Stroke Style dialog box** *set for the* Dash *controls.*

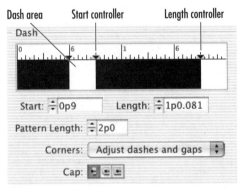

47 *The* **Dash controls** *in the New Stroke Style dialog box.*

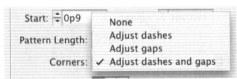

48 *Use the* **Corners list** *to choose how dashes are distributed along a stroke.*

49 *Use the* **Preview display and Preview Weight** *to see what the dash style will look like.*

To create a custom dashed stroke style:

1. Choose Dash from the Type menu of the New Stroke Style dialog box. The dash controls appear **46**.

2. Click inside the Dash area to add a dash to the stroke **47**.

TIP New dashes appear in the Dash area with no length and need to be adjusted in order to appear as part of the finished stroke.

3. Drag the Start control triangle on the percentage ruler or enter an amount in the Start field to set the initial position for the dash **47**.

TIP Unlike the Stripe controls, the length of a dash is set as an absolute amount, not a percentage of the stroke width.

4. Drag the dash itself to move it without changing its width.

5. Use the Pattern Length field to increase the length of the space that the dashes repeat within **47**.

6. If you need to delete a dash, drag it up or down so that it is off the Dash area.

7. Use the Corners list to choose how the dashes should be arranged around corners **48**. *(See page 158 for a complete description of the Corners choices and their appearances.)*

8. Choose a Cap style to set how the dashes appear on the stroke. *(See page 155 for a complete description of the Cap style choices.)*

9. Use the Preview control to increase or decrease the size of the preview for the stroke style **49**.

Creating Custom Stroke Styles

To create a custom dotted stroke style:

1. Choose Dotted from the Type menu of the New Stroke Style dialog box. The dotted controls appear ⑩.

2. Click inside the Dotted area to add a dot to the stroke ⑪.

3. Drag the Center control triangle on the ruler or enter an amount in the Center field to set the initial position for the dot ⑪.

4. Use the Pattern Length field to increase the length of the space that the dots repeat within ⑪.

5. If you need to delete a dot, drag it up or down so that it is off the Dotted area.

6. Use the Corners list to choose how the dots should be arranged around corners ⑫.

TIP Unlike the choices for dashes, the Corners list for dots only allows you to adjust gaps, as the dots themselves cannot change their length. *(See page 158 for a complete description of the Corners choices and their appearances.)*

7. Use the Preview control to increase or decrease the size of the preview for the stroke style ⑬.

To edit a stroke style:

1. Select the custom stroke style in the Stroke Styles dialog box and choose Edit. The Edit Stroke Style dialog box appears.

TIP The Edit Stroke Style dialog box is the same as the New Stroke Style dialog box, except that there is a Preview button to help you see what your changes do to the stroke ⑭. Also, the Edit Stroke Style dialog box does not have an Add button.

2. Click OK to apply the changes.

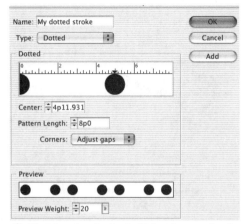

⑩ *The* **New Stroke Style dialog box** *set for the* **Dotted controls**.

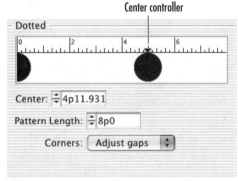

⑪ *The* **Dotted controls** *in the New Stroke Style dialog box.*

⑫ *Use the* **Corners menu** *to control how dotted styles are applied to corners.*

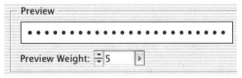

⑬ *Use the* **Preview display and Preview Weight** *to see how a dotted style will look.*

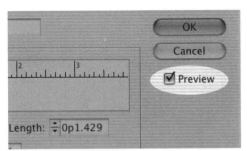

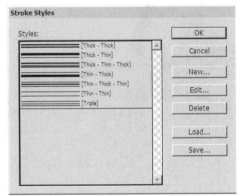

❺❹ *Click the* **Preview checkbox** *to see how the stroke edits appear when applied to objects.*

❺❺ *The* **Stroke Styles dialog box** *lets you create, edit, and manage custom stroke styles.*

Once you have defined a stroke style, it appears in the Type menu of the Stroke palette for that document. You may want to transfer strokes from one document to another. You do so using the Stroke Styles dialog box **❺❺**.

To save strokes for use in another document:

1. Choose Stroke Styles from the Stroke palette menu.

2. Select the custom strokes that you want to transfer to another document.

TIP Hold the Shift key to select a range of strokes.

TIP Hold the Cmd/Ctrl key and click to select noncontiguous strokes.

3. Click the Save button. A dialog box appears where you can save the strokes as an .inst file, which contains the custom stroke definitions.

To transfer strokes from another document:

1. Choose Stroke Styles from the Stroke palette menu.

2. Click Load from the Stroke Styles dialog box.

3. Navigate to find the .inst file that contains the custom stroke definitions.

4. Click the Open button to add the strokes to the document.

TIP You can copy and paste objects that contain a custom stroke from one document to another. This adds the custom stroke to the Stroke palette.

To delete a stroke from document:

1. Choose Stroke Styles from the Stroke palette menu.

2. Select the stroke or strokes you want to delete.

3. Click the Delete button.

TIP You can't delete the seven default strokes.

Creating Custom Stroke Styles

My Favorite Use for Custom Strokes

You have no idea how excited I am to see custom strokes in InDesign. This was one of the features I have wanted in the program since it first was released. Fortunately, they were introduced in InDesign CS. Here is a little lesson that explains my favorite way to use custom strokes and shows why this seemingly small feature is so important.

Look at the illustration in figure ⑤⑥. Notice how the callout lines indicating the eye and button get lost as they move over the dark areas of the image. That's a real problem for people who do lots of book illustrations.

In the old days of pasteboard mechanicals we used to have special striped rules that were black with a white line on either side. What I need today is a way to create that look electronically.

One of the ways I fixed this before InDesign CS was to create two rules. I started with a half-point black rule. I then copied the black rule, pasted the copy behind it, and set the copy to 1-point with a white stroke. This gave me a half-point rule with a quarter-point white stroke on either side.

The white stroke became the knockout that helped keep the black from getting lost. Unfortunately, the technique was cumbersome and very awkward to work with if I had to move objects. Eventually it became so difficult to work with the multiple rules that I gave up altogether.

Now look at the illustration in figure ⑤⑦. See how much easier it is to follow the

continues on next page

⑤⑥ *Notice how the black callout rules get lost as they pass over the dark areas of the image.*

⑤⑦ *Notice how a white line on either side of the black rule makes it easier to follow the rule as it passes over the dark areas of the image.*

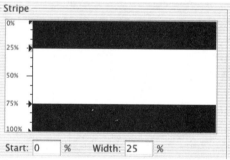

⑤⑧ *Two stripes that take up 25% of the stroke width leave a 50% gap.*

Creating Custom Stroke Styles

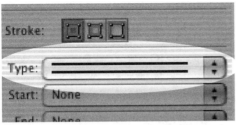

59 *The custom stripe appears in the Type menu in the Stroke palette.*

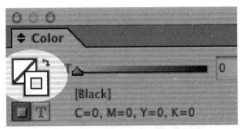

60 *A white stroke color was applied to the white stripes of the custom stroke.*

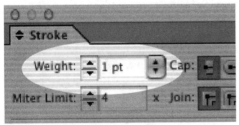

61 *A 1-point stroke weight becomes a half-point gap color for the custom stroke.*

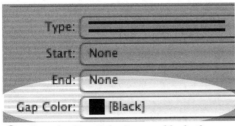

62 *When the Gap Color is set to black, the custom stripe shows a black line with two white stripes.*

callout across the image. That's because there's a special custom stroke applied to the rules.

Here's how I created it. I made a custom stroke style which consists of two 25% stripes on either side of a 50% gap as seen in figure **58**. I saved this custom stroke.

I drew the callout rules in the layout and applied the custom stroke from the Type menu in the Stroke palette **59**.

I set the stroke color as white **60**. Since the two stripes are set for 25% of the stroke width, I set the stroke weight to 1 point **61**. That made each side of the white knockout a quarter of a point.

I then needed to set the gap color in the Stroke palette to black **62**. Since the gap had been set for 50% of the stroke width, that made the black gap a half-point width.

The benefits of this custom stroke are great. I only need to draw one object to apply two colors. And I can use this custom stroke for straight line rules as well as curves, rectangles, or any object that has to pass over multiple colors.

In case you're wondering, I could have also defined the stroke as a single 50% stripe with two 25% gaps on top and bottom. In that case I would have used a black stroke with a white gap.

Look carefully at the callout lines in this book. They have been set using a 1-point rule set with a single 50% black stripe with two 25% paper gaps around it. This rule was saved as my "Knockout Rule."

Creating Custom Stroke Styles

Adding Arrows and Corner Effects

You can add arrowheads and other shapes to the open-ended objects that have strokes applied to them 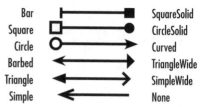.

To add arrowheads and end shapes:

1. Select an object with open ends.

2. Add a graphic to the beginning of the object by choosing a shape from the Start menu in the Stroke palette 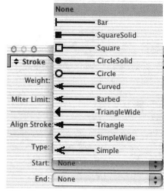.

3. Add a graphic to the end of the object by choosing a shape from the End menu.

InDesign can modify the shape of objects by adding special corner effects. You can apply these effects to any object that has corner points — even open-ended objects.

TIP You can change a star's points to curves by applying a rounded corner effect. Or you can convert an L-shaped line into a soft curve.

To apply corner effects:

1. Select an object with corner points.

2. Choose **Object > Corner Effects**. The Corner Effects dialog box appears .

3. Choose one of the effects from the Effect menu.

4. Set the size of the effect.

TIP Check Preview so you can see how the settings look.

5. Click OK to apply the settings 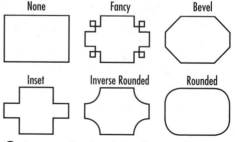.

TIP You can change corner effects later by selecting the object and reopening the dialog box. However, the individual points within the effect cannot be manipulated.

⑥ *The 12 different types of* **arrowhead styles** *for paths.*

⑥ *Choose an arrowhead style from the* **Start** *or* **End menu** *in the Stroke palette.*

⑥ *The* **Corner Effects dialog box** *lets you apply different corners to objects.*

⑥ *An example of applying the special corner effects to rectangles.*

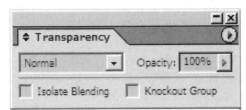

67 *The* **Transparency palette** *controls the object's opacity and its interaction with other objects.*

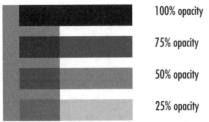

100% opacity

75% opacity

50% opacity

25% opacity

68 *An example of how different opacity settings change the display of an object filled with black.*

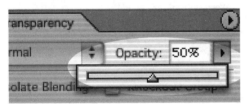

69 *The* **Opacity slider** *in the Transparency palette lowers the visibility of objects.*

70 *An example of how a white frame set to 50% opacity creates a ghost area in the image.*

Applying Transparency

When designers have requested transparency in a page-layout program, all they've thought about was seeing through objects. InDesign offers much more in its Transparency controls. The command center of all the transparency controls in InDesign is located in the Transparency palette.

To open the Transparency palette:

◆ Choose **Window** > **Transparency** to open the palette **67**.

or

If the Transparency palette is behind other palettes, click the Transparency palette tab.

Ever since desktop publishing began, designers have requested some way to see through one object to the others behind it. One way to do this is to reduce the opacity, or increase the translucence, in an object **68**.

To reduce an object's opacity:

1. Select the object that you want to see through.

2. Use the Opacity slider in the Transparency palette to reduce the visibility of the object **69**.

TIP Once you have activated the Opacity field or slider, you can use the up and down arrow keys on the keyboard to increase or decrease the amount of opacity.

TIP Place a white frame at a reduced opacity over an image to "ghost" that area in the image **70**. You can then add a text frame over the ghosted area. *(See the sidebar on page 172 as to why you need to add a separate text frame over the ghosted area.)*

Applying Transparency

If you've used Adobe Photoshop, you should be familiar with the Blend Mode menu. This feature allows the colors and shades in one object to interact with the objects beneath.

To add a blend mode to objects:

1. Select the object that you want to have interact with the objects beneath it.

2. Choose a blend mode from the list in the Transparency palette ⓴. *(See the opposite page for a description and display of the blend modes.)*

As you apply a blend mode or an opacity setting, you may need to control how the transparency is applied. One such control is called a *knockout group*. Objects in a knockout group display their blend modes or opacity settings on other objects, but not with each other ⓲.

To create a knockout group:

1. Apply a blend mode or opacity setting to an object.

2. Repeat for any additional objects.

   TIP Each object can have its own blend mode or opacity setting, or they all can have the same settings.

3. Use the Selection tool to select the objects that have the blend mode or opacity settings applied. These are the objects you *don't* want to have interact with each other.

4. Choose **Object > Group**.

5. With the group selected, click the Knockout Group checkbox in the Transparency palette ⓳.

   TIP If the Knockout Group checkbox is not visible, click the palette tab or choose Show Transparency Options from the Transparency palette menu.

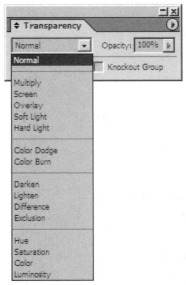

⓴ *The **Blend Mode menu** lets you change the interaction between objects.*

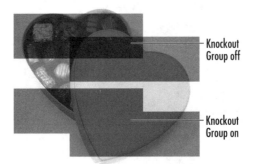

⓲ *With the **Knockout Group** turned on, blended objects do not interact with each other.*

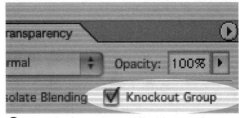

⓳ *The **Knockout Group checkbox** in the Transparency palette changes the interaction of grouped objects among each other.*

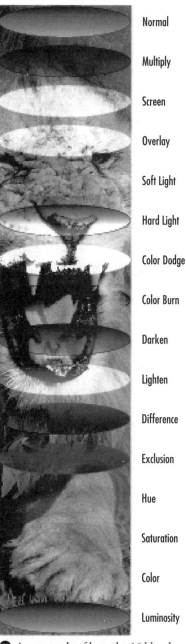

Normal

Multiply

Screen

Overlay

Soft Light

Hard Light

Color Dodge

Color Burn

Darken

Lighten

Difference

Exclusion

Hue

Saturation

Color

Luminosity

⑦ *An example of how the 16 blend modes interact when placed over an image.*

Applying Transparency

Understanding the Blend Modes

The best way to understand the blend modes is to experiment and explore by applying them to objects. Here's a quick rundown of how they work **⑦**.

- **Multiply** multiplies the bottom color with the top color.

- **Screen** is the inverse of Multiply.

- **Overlay** preserves the highlights and shadows of the base color while mixing in the top color.

- **Soft Light** is similar to shining a diffused spotlight on the artwork.

- **Hard Light** is similar to shining a harsh spotlight on the artwork.

- **Color Dodge** lightens the bottom color to reflect the top color.

- **Color Burn** darkens the bottom color to reflect the top color.

- **Darken** displays either the bottom or top color — whichever is darker.

- **Lighten** selects the bottom or top color — whichever is lighter.

- **Difference** subtracts one color from another depending on which has the greater brightness.

- **Exclusion** is similar to Difference but is lower in contrast.

- **Hue** replaces the hue of the bottom object with the hue of the top one.

- **Saturation** replaces the saturation of the bottom object with the top.

- **Color** colorizes the bottom object with the top color.

- **Luminosity** changes the bottom object's luminence with the top.

Difference, Exclusion, Hue, Saturation, Color, and Luminosity modes do not blend spot colors, only process colors.

The other control for transparency is the Isolate Blending command. This creates the opposite effect of a Knockout group. With this command, the objects in the group display their blend modes with each other, but not with objects outside the group ⑦⑤.

TIP The Isolate Blending command only affects the blend mode settings, not any opacity settings.

To isolate the blending in objects:

1. Apply a blend mode to an object.

2. Repeat for any additional objects.

TIP Each object can have its own blend mode, or all objects can have the same settings.

3. Use the Selection tool to select the objects that have the blend mode. These are the objects that you *don't* want to interact with the other objects.

4. Choose **Object > Group**.

5. Keep the group selected, click the Isolate Blending checkbox in the Transparency palette ⑦⑥. The objects in the group interact with each other, but not with other objects on the page.

Isolate
Blending
off

Isolate
Blending
on

⑦⑤ *With the* **Isolate Blending command** *turned on, blended objects only interact with each other, not the objects below.*

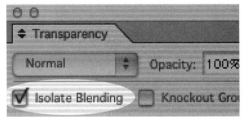

⑦⑥ *The* **Isolate Blending checkbox** *in the Transparency palette limits grouped objects to interact only with each other.*

Applying Transparency

DOROTHY

77 *An example of a drop shadow applied to text.*

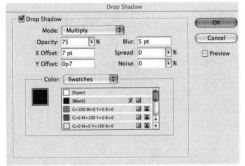

78 *An example of a drop shadow applied to text and positioned over a placed image.*

79 *An example of a drop shadow applied to a placed image.*

Adding Drop Shadows and Feathers

One of the most desired features in graphics programs is an automatic drop shadow that is cast behind objects, text, or images **77** – **79**. While it's been very easy to add drop shadows in Adobe Photoshop or Adobe Illustrator, it has not been easy to do so in page-layout programs — that is until InDesign.

To add a drop shadow to an object:

1. Select the object, text frame, or placed image to which you want to add a drop shadow.

2. Choose **Object > Drop Shadow**. This opens the Drop Shadow dialog box **80**.

3. Click the Drop Shadow checkbox. This activates the drop shadow controls.

4. Set the controls as follows:

   • Use the Mode list to choose the blend mode for the shadow. These are the same as the blend mode settings in the Transparency palette *(see pages 168 and 169)*.

   • Set the Opacity amount for how transparent the shadow should be.

   • Set the *X* Offset and *Y* Offset to create the distance between the shadow and the object.

   • Set the Blur amount for how soft the edges of the drop shadow should be.

   • Set the Spread amount to increase the size of the shadow.

   • Noise adds artifacts to the shadow, giving it a rougher or grainier texture. This is especially helpful to avoid banding when the shadow is printed.

   • Use the Color list to set a color for the shadow.

   TIP You can use the Swatches list to choose named colors or switch to CMYK, RGB, or LAB colors.

5. Click OK to apply the shadow.

80 *The* **Drop Shadow dialog box** *controls how shadows are applied to objects, text, and images.*

Adding Drop Shadows and Feathers

To remove a drop shadow from an object:

1. Select the object that has the drop shadow applied.

2. Choose **Object > Drop Shadow**. This opens the Drop Shadow dialog box.

3. Uncheck the Drop Shadow checkbox. This turns off the drop shadow effect.

⬤ *The* **Feather dialog box** *controls the softness of edges that are applied to objects, text, and images.*

InDesign lets you apply feather commands to objects. This softens the edges of the images.

To add a feathered edge to an object:

1. Select the object, text frame, or placed image you want to have a feathered edge.

2. Choose **Object > Feather**. This opens the Feather dialog box **⬤**.

3. Click the Feather checkbox. This displays the rest of the feather controls.

4. Use the Feather Width controls to set how thick the feather should appear.

5. Choose one of the settings in the Corners list as follows **⬤**:

   - **Sharp** feathers by closely following the contours of the object.
   - **Round** feathers by rounding off any sharp corners in the image.
   - **Diffuse** makes the edges of the object fade from opaque to transparent. This is the same as the Feather command applied to objects in Adobe Illustrator.

6. Use the Noise field to add grain to the feathering. This helps avoid banding when printing.

7. Click OK to apply the feather.

To remove a feather from an object:

1. Select the object that has the feather.

2. Choose **Object > Feather**. This opens the Feather dialog box.

3. Uncheck the Feather checkbox. This turns off the feather effect.

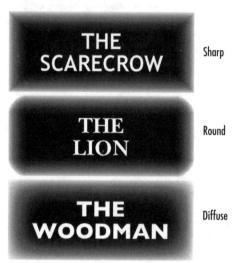

Sharp

Round

Diffuse

⬤ *The* **three different corner settings** *for applying a feather effect.*

Applying Transparency and Effects

You can apply any of the transparency effects — opacity, blend modes, feather, and drop shadow — to any object, including frames, images, and text frames. However, you should remember that the transparency effect will be applied to the object as a whole.

This means that if you apply an opacity setting to a frame that contains a fill color and text, the opacity will be applied to both the fill and the text.

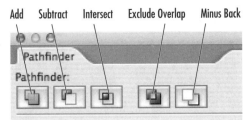

Add Subtract Intersect Exclude Overlap Minus Back

83 *Click the* **Pathfinder icons** *in the Pathfinder palette.*

Command	Objects before	Objects after
Add		
Subtract		
Intersect		
Exclude Overlap		
Minus Back		

84 *Examples of how the Pathfinder commands change selected objects.*

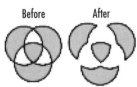

Before   After

85 *An example of how the* **Exclude Overlap command creates separate objects** *when the Compound Path is released.*

Using the Pathfinder Commands

Sometimes the easiest way to create shapes is to have one frame interact with others. For instance, rather than struggle to create a crescent moon, you can let one circle punch a hole in another. That's what the Pathfinder commands in the Pathfinder palette do.

To use the Pathfinder commands:

1. Select the objects that you want to have interact with each other. You must select at least two objects.

2. Click one of the Pathfinder icons at the top of the Pathfinder palette **83**.

   or

   Choose one of the following from the **Object > Pathfinder** menu:

   - **Add** combines the outer edges of the objects in a single shape **84**.
   - **Subtract** uses the frontmost objects as cookie cutters that change the shape of the backmost object **84**.
   - **Intersect** creates a new shape based on the area intersected by the objects **84**.
   - **Exclude Overlap** creates a hole where the objects overlap **84**.
   - **Minus Back** uses the backmost objects as cookie cutters that change the shape of the frontmost object **84**.

Depending on the command and the position of the objects, you may create a compound path. For instance, the Exclude Overlap command always creates compound paths. If you want to separate the objects, you need to release the compound path:

To separate the results of the Pathfinder commands:

1. Select the objects created by the Pathfinder command.

2. Choose **Object > Compound Paths > Release**.

3. Deselect the objects and then move each one to new positions **85**.

You can use the Convert Shape commands to change objects from one shape to another.

To change the shape of objects:

1. Select the object that you want to convert.

2. Click one of the Convert Shape icons in the Pathfinder palette 86 and 87.

   or

   Choose one of the following from the **Object > Convert Shape** menu:

   - **Rectangle** converts to a rectangle.
   - **Rounded Rectangle** converts to a rectangle with rounded corners.
   - **Beveled Rectangle** converts to a rectangle with flat, angled corners.
   - **Inverse Rounded Rectangle** converts to a rectangle with inverted rounded corners.
   - **Ellipse** converts the object to an ellipse.
   - **Triangle** converts to a triangle.
   - **Polygon** converts to a polygon using the current settings for the Polygon tool.
   - **Line** converts the object to a line. The length is the diagonal of the bounding box of the object.
   - **Orthogonal Line** converts the object to a line. The length is the width or height of the bounding box, whichever is greater.

   TIP The size of the corner effects comes from the current corner radius setting in the Corner Effects.

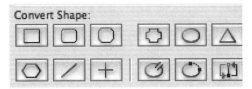

86 *The* **Convert Shape icons** *in the Pathfinder palette allow you to change the shape of objects.*

Icon	Function
▢	Rectangle
▢	Rounded Rectangle
▢	Beveled Rectangle
▢	Inverse Rounded Rectangle
◯	Ellipse
△	Triangle
⬡	Polygon
╱	Line
＋	Orthogonal Line
◔	Open Path
◯	Close Path
⟲	Reverse Path

87 *The Convert Shape icons and their functions.*

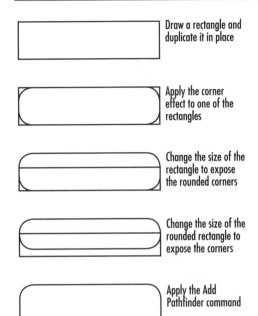

Draw a rectangle and duplicate it in place

Apply the corner effect to one of the rectangles

Change the size of the rectangle to expose the rounded corners

Change the size of the rounded rectangle to expose the corners

Apply the Add Pathfinder command

88 *The steps used to create* **a rectangle with two rounded corners.**

Three of the icons in the Convert Shape area are actually path modification commands.

To modify paths:

1. Select the object that you want to modify.
2. Click one of the Convert Shape icons in the Pathfinder palette **86** and **87**.

   or

   Choose one of the following from the **Object > Paths** menu:

   - **Open Path** opens a closed path at a point.
   - **Close Path** creates a segment between the end points of a path.
   - **Reverse Path** changes the direction of a path.

TIP Apply the Close Path command to expand the electronic corner effects into actual points on the path. This is similar to applying Illustrator's Object > Expand command.

Creating Special Shapes

The Pathfinder and Convert Shape commands can be used to create special shapes. Here are a few ideas for working with those commands.

You can use the Pathfinder commands to merge two different shapes into one. For instance, many people want to create a rectangle with only two rounded corners. That shape is easily created by applying the Pathfinder > Add command to merge an ordinary rectangle with a rounded-corner rectangle. **88**.

Using the Pathfinder Commands

Using the Eyedropper

Imagine you've finished styling an object with exactly the right combination of fill, stroke, and transparency attributes. And now you'd like to apply those same settings to a different object. That's where the Eyedropper tool comes to the rescue. First you have to set which attributes the Eyedropper tool will sample.

To set the eyedropper options:

1. Double-click the Eyedropper tool in the Toolbox **89**. This opens the Eyedropper Options dialog box **90**.

2. Click the triangles to open each of the attribute categories.

TIP The object settings categories are Fill, Stroke, and Transparency. *(See page 363 for information on working with the text categories, character and paragraph.)*

3. Use the checkboxes to choose which attributes you want the Eyedropper tool to sample.

4. Click OK to set the options.

Once you set the eyedropper options, you can sample and apply object attributes.

To sample and apply object attributes:

1. Choose the Eyedropper tool.

2. Click the white eyedropper cursor inside the object that you want to sample **91**. The cursor changes from white to black.

TIP If an object has a stroke, but no fill, click the object's outline to sample its stroke.

3. Click the black eyedropper cursor inside the object that you want to change **92**. This applies the first object's attributes to the second.

4. Click the eyedropper inside any other objects that you want to change.

89 *The* **Eyedropper tool** *in the Toolbox lets you sample object attributes.*

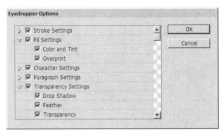

90 *Use the* **Eyedropper Options dialog box** *to set which attributes the Eyedropper will sample and apply.*

91 *The* **white eyedropper** *lets you sample the object attributes.*

92 *The* **black eyedropper** *applies object attributes from one object to another.*

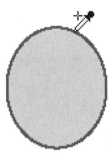

93 *The* **white precision eyedropper** *allows you to sample a specific color.*

94 *The* **black precision eyedropper** *lets you apply a specific color to either the fill or a stroke.*

As you work with the Eyedropper tool, you may change your mind and want to unload one set of attributes to sample new ones.

To sample new attributes:

1. Hold the Opt/Alt key. The eyedropper cursor changes to white.

2. Click the cursor inside a new object that you want to sample.

3. Release the Opt/Alt key to apply the new attributes to objects.

You may not want to sample all the attributes in an object — just the fill or stroke. That's when you can use the Eyedropper tool in its precision mode. The precision mode allows you to sample and apply just the color to either a fill or a stroke.

To use the precision eyedropper:

1. Choose the Eyedropper tool. Hold the Shift key. A plus sign appears next to the white eyedropper cursor **93**. This indicates that the Eyedropper tool is in the precision mode.

2. Click the precision white eyedropper cursor on the fill or stroke color you wish to sample. The cursor turns into the precision black eyedropper **94**.

3. Click the precision eyedropper on either a fill or a stroke of the object that you want to change. Only the fill or stroke is changed.

Using the Eyedropper

Setting Object Defaults

You can make any of the object settings the default for any new objects you create. You can set the object defaults for the current document or globally for all new documents.

95 *Click the* **Default Fill and Stroke icon** *in the Toolbox to set the fill to none and stroke to black.*

To set current document defaults:

1. With a document open, deselect any objects.
2. Make whatever changes you want in the Stroke palette or other palettes. This sets the defaults for the open document.
3. Set whatever amounts you want for the Drop Shadow, Feather, or Corner Effects dialog boxes.

To set global defaults:

◆ With no document open, make whatever changes you want in the Stroke or other palettes. This sets the global defaults for all new documents.

InDesign also has its own default fill and stroke setting of a black stroke and no fill. These are separate from the defaults you set yourself. This can be easily applied to objects.

To apply the InDesign fill and stroke defaults:

◆ Click the Default Fill and Stroke icon in the Toolbox **95**.

PEN AND BEZIERS 7

I remember the first time I tried to use the Pen tool in a computer graphics program. I clicked the tool and dragged across the screen in the way I thought would create a simple curve. Instead, I got a wild series of lines that shot out in different directions. When I tried to change the shape of the curves, things got even worse. I was so startled I immediately closed up the program and didn't use the Pen tool for a long, long time.

However, I really wanted to use the Pen tool, as I knew it was the best way to create curved shapes. So I forced myself to try the tool again. It took a lot of trial and error but eventually I was able to understand the Pen and Bezier controls. Later on, working with tools such as the Pencil and Eraser made it even easier to work with Bezier curves.

Once I got it, I realized the principles are simple. Even better, if you have used the Pen tool in Adobe Illustrator or Adobe Photoshop, you will find InDesign's Pen tool almost the same.

I just wish someone had written out easy to understand, step-by-step instructions. So think of this chapter as the instructions for the Pen tool that I wish I had had back then.

Multimedia Pen Lessons

This chapter contains everything you should need to master the Pen tool in InDesign. However, if you would like to learn the Pen tool using movies and audio narration, may I suggest you visit www.zenofthepen.org. It has an online tutorial you can purchase that can help you learn the Pen tool in InDesign, as well as in other programs such as Adobe Illustrator.

Pen Points

One of the most important tools in any graphics program is the Pen tool. Fortunately InDesign has a Pen tool that lets you create much more sophisticated shapes in your layout than can be created with the basic shape tools. *(See Chapter 4, "Working with Objects," for more information on working with the basic shapes.)*

TIP If you are familiar with the Pen tool in Adobe Illustrator or Macromedia FreeHand, you will find it very easy to master the Pen in InDesign.

If you've never used a Pen tool in any graphics program, you will understand more if you first become familiar with the elements of paths.

Elements of Paths

Paths are defined by points and line segments. When you draw with the Pen tool you create the following:

- **Anchor points** define a path at points where the path changes **1**. These can be plain corner points, smooth curve points, and corner curve points as explained on the following pages.

- **Segments** are the paths that connect anchor points **1**.

- **Control handles** extend out from anchor points; their length and direction control the shape of the segment's curves **1**.

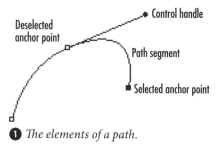

1 The elements of a path.

Deselected anchor point · Control handle · Path segment · Selected anchor point

---

The Father of Bezier Curves

Some people call the curves created by the Pen tool *Bezier curves*. This is in honor of Pierre Bézier (*Bay-zee-ay*), the French mathematician.

Monsieur Bézier created the system of mathematics that is used to define the relationship of the control handles to the shape of the curve.

Adobe Systems, Inc., adopted this mathematical system when it created the PostScript language which is used as the basis of graphics programs. InDesign, along with many other programs, uses Bezier curves as the mathematics behind each curve.

Drawing in a Page Layout Program?

I limit using InDesign's Pen tool to simple things. If I need some sort of curved or wavy line, I use InDesign's Pen tool. For instance, all the curved arrows in this book were created with the Pen tool. However, if I want a perfect spiral, I use Illustrator's Spiral tool. *(See Chapter 8, "Imported Graphics," for how to bring Illustrator paths into InDesign.)*

If I need to jazz up some text, I stay within InDesign. But if I need a complete map of New York State with highways, rivers, and scenic attractions, I work in Illustrator.

Pen Points

2 *Click the* **Pen tool** *in the Toolbox to create lines.*

 3 *The* **start icon** *for the Pen tool.*

 4 *Click with the Pen tool to* **create a corner point,** *shown as a small square.*

5 **Straight lines** *extend between the plain corner points.*

 6 *The small circle next to the Pen cursor indicates that you will* **close the path.**

Drawing Lines

Different types of anchor points create different line shapes. Straight lines are formed by creating *plain corner points.*

To create straight lines:

1. Click the Pen tool in the Toolbox **2**.

2. Position the cursor where the path should start. A small *X* appears next to the Pen, which indicates that you are starting the path **3**.

3. Click. A plain corner point appears as a colored square. The Pen cursor is displayed without any symbol next to it **4**.

4. Position the cursor for the next point and click. This creates another plain corner point with a straight line that connects the first point to the second.

TIP Hold the Shift key to constrain the straight lines to 45-degree angles.

5. Continue clicking until you have created all the straight-line sides of the object **5**.

TIP If you have not closed the path *(see the next exercise)*, hold the Cmd/Ctrl key and click with the Selection tool. This deselects the path and allows you to start a new one.

To close a path with a straight line:

1. Move the Pen over the first point. A small circle appears next to the Pen **6**. This indicates that you can close the path.

2. Click. This closes the path with a plain corner point and allows you to start a new path.

Drawing Curves

Smooth curve points create curves like the track a roller coaster follows. There are no abrupt changes from one curve to another.

To create smooth curves:

1. Drag the Pen tool where you want to start the curve. Handles extend out from the point.

TIP The length and angle of the handle control the curve's height and direction.

2. Release the mouse button.

TIP You do not see a curve until you create the next point of the path.

3. Move the cursor to where you want the next part of the curve. Drag to create the curved segment between the two smooth curve points ❼.

4. Continue to create curved segments by repeating steps 2 and 3 ❽.

To close a path with a smooth curve:

1. Move the Pen over the first point. A small circle appears, indicating that you can close the path.

2. Drag backwards to close the path ❾.

A *corner curve point* creates curves with an abrupt change in direction. The path of a bouncing ball illustrates a corner curve.

To create a corner curve:

1. With the Pen tool active, drag to create an anchor point with control handles.

2. Without releasing the mouse button, hold the Opt/Alt key and then drag to pivot the second handle ❿.

3. Release the mouse button when the second handle is the correct length and direction.

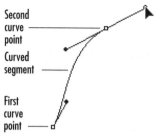

❼ *Drag with the Pen tool to create* **smooth curves.**

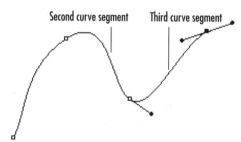

❽ *A path with a series of curved segments.*

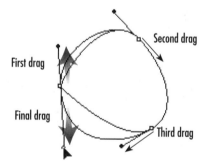

❾ **Dragging backwards closes a path** *with a smooth curve.*

❿ **Hold the Opt/ Alt key** *to pivot the handles, which creates a corner curve.*

⓫ *Move the cursor back over a point and* **click to retract a handle** *along a curve.*

⓬ *Drag with the Pen tool over an existing anchor point to* **extend a handle out** *from the point.*

General Pen Rules

As you work with the Pen tool, there are some rules you should follow:

- Use the fewest number of points to define a path. Too many points add to the size of the file and make it difficult to edit the path later.

- Try to limit the length of the control handles to one-third the length of the curve. This is sometimes called the *One-Third Rule*. The One-Third Rule makes it easier to edit and control the shape of curves.

Changing Curves and Corner Points

If you retract the handle that extends out from a curve point, the next segment becomes a straight line.

To retract a handle:

1. Drag to create a smooth curve point.

2. Move the Pen cursor back over the anchor point. A small angle symbol appears next to the cursor.

3. Click. The handle retracts back into the anchor point. The point is now a corner point with only one handle ⓫.

4. Continue the path with either a straight line or a curved line.

TIP Click to make the next path segment straight. Drag to make the next path segment curved.

If you create a corner point with no control handles, you can extend a single handle out from that anchor point.

To extend a handle from a point:

1. Click to create a corner point with no handles.

2. Move the Pen cursor back over the anchor point you just created. A small angle symbol appears next to the cursor.

3. Drag to pull a single handle out from the anchor point ⓬.

4. Continue the path with a curved line.

Changing Curves and Corner Points

Modifying Paths

Once you create a path, you can still change its shape and the position of the points. You can also split a path into two separate segments or join two segments together. When you move points, you use the Direct Selection tool.

To move individual points:

1. Click the Direct Selection tool in the Toolbox ⓭.

2. Position the tool over the point you want to move.

3. Drag the point to the new position.

To select and move multiple points:

1. Click the Direct Selection tool in the Toolbox.

2. Drag to create a rectangular marquee around the points you want to select ⓮. The selected points appear solid. The unselected points appear hollow.

   or

   Hold the Shift key as you click to select the points.

   TIP You can select points in one path or multiple paths.

3. Drag the point to the new position.

The Direct Selection tool also lets you change the length and direction of the control handles.

To move control handles:

1. Click the Direct Selection tool in the Toolbox.

2. Click a point on the path. This displays the control handles for that point.

3. Position the Direct Selection tool over the end point of the handle.

4. Drag the handle to the new position ⓯.

⓭ *The* **Direct Selection tool** *in the Toolbox; use it to move points.*

⓮ **Drag a marquee to select multiple points.** *The center point does not turn black.*

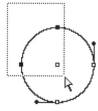

⓯ *The Direct Selection tool* **changes the length and position** *of a control handle.*

⓰ *The* **Scissors tool** *in the Toolbox allows you to snip paths in two.*

⓱ *The Scissors tool* **splits a path into two points,** *one on top of the other.*

⓲ *The* **Close Path command** *joins the two endpoints of a path.*

⓳ *The results of applying the* **Reverse Path command** *to a path with an arrowhead.*

You may want to separate one path into two parts — for instance, to separate two halves of a circle. The Scissors tool makes it easy to split or break a path into segments.

To split paths:

1. Select the path.
2. Click the Scissors tool in the Toolbox **⓰**.
3. Position the cursor where you want to split the path.
4. Click to split the path at that point.

TIP The Scissors tool splits the path by creating two points, one on top of the other. Use the Direct Selection tool to move one point away from the other **⓱**.

TIP Paths that contain text cannot be split into two distinct segments.

To open paths using a command:

1. Select the path.
2. Choose **Object > Path > Open Path**. This opens the path by creating two points, one on top of the other. Use the Direct Selection tool to move one point away from the other.

To close paths using a command:

1. Select the path.
2. Choose **Object > Path > Close Path**. This closes the path by creating a line segment between the start and end points of the path **⓲**.

The direction of a path comes from the order in which you draw the path. You can change the path direction.

To change the path direction:

1. Use the Direct Selection tool to select the path.
2. Choose **Object > Path > Reverse Path**. This switches the start and end points of the path **⓳**.

Modifying Paths

Modifying Points

So what happens if you create the wrong point with the Pen tool? Are you stuck? Does it mean you have to redraw the entire path? Thankfully, no—there are many ways to change the paths made with the Pen tool, as well as paths made with other tools. *(See Chapter 4, "Working with Objects," for more information on working with the basic shapes.)*

A simple way to change a path is to add a point. This helps you turn one shape into another.

To add points to a path:

1. Select the path.
2. Choose the Add Anchor Point tool in the Toolbox **20**.
3. Click the path where you want to add the point.

TIP The Pen tool automatically changes to the Add Anchor Point tool when positioned over a selected path segment **21**.

You can delete points from a path without causing a break in the path.

To delete points from a path:

1. Select the path.
2. Choose the Delete Anchor Point tool in the Toolbox **22**.
3. Click to delete the point of the path.

TIP The Pen tool changes to the Delete Anchor Point tool when positioned over a point on a selected path **23**.

20 *The* **Add Anchor Point tool** *in the Toolbox.*

21 *The* **Add Anchor Point tool** *over a path segment.*

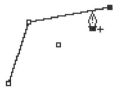

22 *The* **Delete Anchor Point tool** *in the Toolbox.*

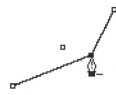

23 *The* **Delete Anchor Point tool** *over a point.*

Modifying Points

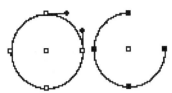

24 *When you select and* **delete a segment**, *you keep the points on either side of the segment.*

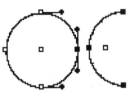

25 *When you select and* **delete a point**, *you delete both segments that were attached to the point.*

26 *The* **Convert Direction Point tool** *in the Toolbox.*

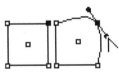

27 *Drag with the Convert Direction Point tool to* **change a corner point into a smooth curve point**.

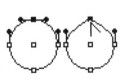

28 *Click with the Convert Direction Point tool to* **change a smooth curve point into a corner point**.

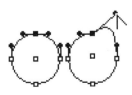

29 *Drag a handle with the Convert Direction Point tool to change a* **smooth curve point into a corner curve point**.

You may also want to create an open path by deleting a segment or the point between two segments.

To delete a segment in a path:

1. Use the Direct Selection tool to select the segment that you want to delete.

2. Press the Delete key or choose **Edit > Clear**. This deletes the segment and opens the path **24**.

TIP If you select a point with the Direct Selection tool, the two segments on either side of the point can be deleted **25**.

You can also change the control handles around an anchor point. This changes the shape of the segments controlled by that anchor point.

To modify an anchor point:

1. Select the path.

2. Choose the Convert Direction Point tool in the Toolbox **26**.

3. Use the tool as follows to change the anchor points:

   - Press and drag a corner point to create a smooth curve point with two handles **27**.
   - Click a smooth curve point to create a corner point with no handles **28**.
   - Drag one of the handles of a smooth curve point to create a corner curve point **29**.

Modifying Points

Using the Pencil Tool

Unlike the Pen tool, which uses mathematical principles to draw paths, InDesign's Pencil tool works more like a traditional Pencil. However, the Pen tool is a little more precise than the Pencil.

TIP If you are familiar with the Pencil tool in Adobe Illustrator, you will find you already know how to work with InDesign's Pencil tool.

To draw with the Pencil tool:

1. Click the Pencil tool in the Toolbox **30**. A small cross next to the Pencil cursor indicates that you are about to start the path **31**.
2. Press and drag with the Pencil **32**.
3. To close the path, hold the Opt/Alt key **33**. A small circle next to the cursor indicates that the path will be closed.
4. Release the mouse to create the path.

The Pencil tool can also be used to edit existing paths and reshape paths.

To edit paths with the Pencil tool:

1. Select the path that you want to reshape.

TIP The Pencil tool can edit paths created by tools such as the Pen or the frame tools.

2. Move the Pencil tool near the selected path. The cross next to the cursor disappears. This indicates that you are about to edit the path.
3. Drag along the path. When you release the mouse button, the path is reshaped **34**.

TIP If you don't get the results you expect, drag the Pencil tool in the opposite direction.

30 *The* **Pencil tool** *in the Toolbox.*

31 *The cross next to the Pencil cursor indicates that you are about to* **start a new path.**

32 *Press and drag to create a path with the Pencil tool.*

33 *The circle next to the Pencil cursor indicates that the Opt/Alt key will* **close the path.**

34 *Drag the Pencil tool next to a selected path to* **reshape the path.**

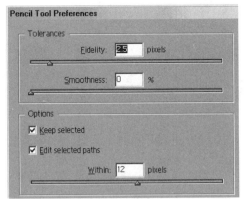

35 *The* **Pencil Tool Preferences dialog box** *allows you to control the appearance of the path.*

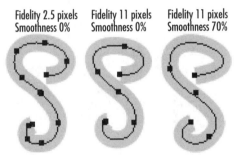

Fidelity 2.5 pixels   Fidelity 11 pixels   Fidelity 11 pixels
Smoothness 0%   Smoothness 0%   Smoothness 70%

36 *The Pencil tool Fidelity and Smoothness settings change the appearance of the path.*

You can change how the Pencil tool responds to the movements of the mouse as you drag. The preferences also control how the Pencil tool edits paths.

To set the preferences for the Pencil tool:

1. Double-click the Pencil tool in the Toolbox. This opens the Pencil Tool Preferences dialog box **35**.

2. Set the amount of Fidelity using the slider or field. The lower the amount of Fidelity, the more the path will follow the motions of the mouse **36**.

3. Set the amount of Smoothness using the slider or field. The higher the setting for Smoothness, the more the path will follow curved shapes **36**.

4. Check Keep Selected to keep the path selected after you have drawn it. This makes it easier to reshape the path.

5. Check Edit Selected Paths to turn on the reshape option.

6. If the Edit Selected Paths option is turned on, use the slider or field to set how close the Pencil tool must come, in pixels, to the path you want to reshape.

Using the Pencil Tool

Using the Smooth Tool

Once you have created a path, you may want to delete extra points so that the path is smoother.

TIP If you are familiar with Illustrator's Smooth tool, you will find it easy to use the Smooth tool in InDesign.

To smooth paths with the Smooth tool:

1. Select the path that you want to smooth.
2. Click the Smooth tool in the Toolbox .
3. Press and drag the Smooth tool along the path.
4. Release the mouse. The path is redrawn with fewer points ⬤.

You can change how the Smooth tool responds to the movements of the mouse as you drag.

To set the preferences for the Smooth tool:

1. Double-click the Smooth tool in the Toolbox to open the Smooth Tool Preferences dialog box ⬤.
2. Use the slider or field to set the Fidelity amount. The lower the amount, the more the new path will follow the original path.
3. Use the slider or field to set the Smoothness amount. The higher the setting, the more curved the path.
4. Check Keep Selected to keep the path selected after you have smoothed it. This makes it easier to increase the smoothness of the path.

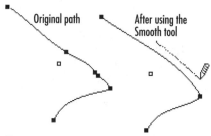

⬤ *The* **Smooth tool** *in the Toolbox.*

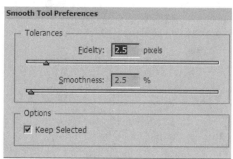

⬤ *Drag the Smooth tool along a path to* **remove points and eliminate small bumps** *and curves.*

⬤ *The* **Smooth Tool Preferences** *allow you to control how much the Smooth tool affects the appearance of paths.*

40 *The* **Erase tool** *in the Toolbox.*

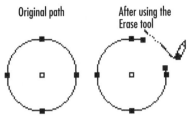

Original path   After using the
                  Erase tool

41 *The Erase tool deletes points as you drag it along a path.*

**Deleting or Removing Points:
Which tools or commands do what?**

You may find yourself confused by all the different tools and commands for deleting or removing points and segments.

When does the action cause a break in a path? When does an action remove points without opening the path?

See the table on the next page for a review of how points are removed from paths, and the result.

Using the Erase Tool

You may want to delete parts of paths. Rather than selecting and deleting individual points, you can use the Erase tool to drag to delete parts of a path.

TIP If you are familiar with the Erase tool in Adobe Illustrator, you will find it easy to use the Erase tool in InDesign.

To delete paths with the Erase tool:

1. Select the path that you want to delete parts of.

2. Choose the Erase tool in the Toolbox **40**.

3. Press and drag the Erase tool along the path.

4. Release the mouse to display the new path **41**.

TIP The Erase tool will always open a closed path.

TIP If you drag the Erase tool over the middle of an open path, you create two separate open paths. Both open paths will be selected.

Adding or Deleting Points on Paths

The following table compares the different tools and commands as to their effect when adding or deleting points on a path.

Tool or Command	Action	Result
Add Anchor Point tool	Click a segment on the path	Always adds a point to the path.
Delete Anchor Point tool	Click an existing point on the path	Deletes the point. Path reshapes without any break.
Erase tool	Drag along a path	Creates a break in the path
Scissors tool	Click a point or a segment	Creates two end points at that position. Points can then be separated to create a break in the path.
Open Path command	Applied to a path	Creates two end points at the origin of the path. Points are indicated by selection. Points can then be separated to create a break in the path.
Close Path command	Applied to a path	Creates a segment that joins two end points of a path.
Delete command	Applied to points or segments selected with the Direct Selection tool	If applied to a selection in the middle of a path, the command breaks the path into two segments. If applied to a selection at the end of a path, the command shortens the path.

Adding or Deleting Points on Paths

IMPORTED GRAPHICS 8

One reason desktop publishing became so popular is how easy it made combining graphics such as photographs and illustrations with type for layouts.

In the years before personal computers, specialized workers, toiling under the exotic name *strippers*, manually trimmed away the blank areas around graphics so that text could be placed around the image. (The name stripper is derived from combining strips of film together.)

Even more complicated was placing text over an illustration. The image and text had to be combined by photography and then stripped into the layout.

Certainly you expect InDesign to import images in the formats that are used by other page-layout programs. But since this is *Adobe* InDesign, you also get some special benefits when working with other Adobe products.

Here's where you learn how to add imported artwork to your page layouts. It only takes a few clicks of a mouse to combine type and artwork together. It's enough to make old-time strippers hang up their tassels!

Placing Artwork

Most artwork that's used in InDesign comes from other sources such as scanners or digital cameras. Artwork can also be created using programs such as Adobe Photoshop, Adobe Illustrator, Macromedia FreeHand, or Adobe Acrobat. The easiest way to place artwork is to automatically create the frame that contains it when you import the artwork.

To place artwork without drawing a frame:

1. Choose **File > Place**. This opens the Place dialog box .

2. Navigate to find the file you want to import. *(See "File Formats" on the next page for a list of the file types you can place in InDesign.)*

3. Check Show Import Options to open the Import Options dialog box before you place the file. *(See page 200 for more information on working with Import Options.)*

4. Click Open to load the graphic into an image cursor .

   TIP Hold the Shift key as you click Open to open the Import Options dialog box, even if the option is not checked.

5. Click the cursor to place the graphic in a rectangular frame the same size as the artwork.

   or

   Drag the image cursor to define the size of the rectangular frame.

   or

   Position the cursor over an existing frame to place the image inside the frame ❸.

   TIP Only the frame is sized when you drag the image cursor. The artwork stays at its actual size. *(See page 205 for how to change the size of an image inside a frame.)*

❶ *Use the **Place dialog box** to open a file you wish to place. Check Show Import Options to make refinements to the imported file.*

❷ *The **loaded image cursor** appears when you prepare to place artwork.*

❸ *The **curved loaded image cursor** appears when you position the loaded cursor over an existing frame.*

File Formats

A wide variety of graphic formats can be added to InDesign documents. These formats are recommended for professional printing:

- **Adobe Illustrator** (AI)
- **Adobe Photoshop** (PSD)
- **Encapsulated PostScript** (EPS)
- **Desktop Color Separation** (DCS)
- **Joint Photographic Experts Group** (JPEG)
- **Portable Document Format** (PDF)
- **Portable Network Graphics** (PNG)
- **PostScript** (PS)
- **Scitex Continuous Tone** (SCT)
- **Tagged Image File Format** (TIFF)

Although the following formats can be inserted into InDesign documents, they are not recommended for use in commercially printed documents. These formats are acceptable for low-resolution, onscreen PDF review, or non-PostScript printers:

- **Enhanced Metafiles** (EMF)
- **Macintosh Picture** (PICT)
- **Graphics Interchange Format** (GIF)
- **PC Paintbrush** (PCX)
- **Windows Bitmap** (BMP)
- **Windows Metafile** (WMF)

Placing JPEGs from Digital Cameras

In earlier versions of InDesign, JPEG photos from a digital camera might appear at a huge size. InDesign now computes a more reasonable size so that you no longer need to lower the size of the image.

You can also place artwork into an existing frame. This is handy if you have set up empty frames as placeholders for graphics.

To place artwork into an existing frame:

1. Use one of the tools to create a rectangular, elliptical, or polygonal frame.

TIP You can use either the frame tools that create graphic frames or the tools that create unassigned frames *(see page 82)*.

2. Use either the Selection or Direct Selection tool to select the frame.

3. Choose **File > Place** and navigate to find the image you wish to place in the frame.

4. Click Open in the Place dialog box. The file automatically is inserted within the frame.

TIP You can also use the Pen tool to create frame shapes *(see Chapter 7, "Pen and Beziers")*.

To replace the artwork in an existing frame:

1. Use either Selection tool to select the frame that contains the artwork you want to replace.

2. Choose **File > Place** and navigate to find the image you wish to place.

3. Click Replace Selected Item in the Place dialog box ❶.

4. Click Open in the Place dialog box. The new image automatically replaces the contents of the frame.

To move or copy artwork between frames:

1. Use the Direct Selection tool to select the artwork you want to replace.

2. Choose **Edit > Cut** or **Edit > Copy**. This places the artwork on the clipboard.

3. Select the frame that you want to move the artwork into.

4. Choose **Edit > Paste Into**. The contents of the clipboard are pasted into the frame.

Placing Artwork

Using Bridge to Place Artwork

Adobe Bridge not only lets you organize and view artwork, it also lets you drag graphics directly onto InDesign pages.

To place artwork from Bridge:

1. Position the Bridge and InDesign windows so that both are visible.

2. Drag the file from Bridge onto an empty area of the InDesign page. This places the file into a new graphic frame, the same size as the image ❹. The straight lines in the cursor indicate that a new frame will be created ❺.

   or

   Drag the file from Bridge onto a pre-existing frame on the InDesign page. This places the file into the frame ❻. The curved lines in the cursor indicate that the image will be placed into the frame ❼.

3. Release the mouse button to place the image.

TIP When Bridge is in the Compact Mode, you can choose Compact Window Always on Top to keep the Bridge window visible over the InDesign document window.

Using Bridge to Place Artwork

❹ **Drag an image from Adobe Bridge** *to place it onto an InDesign page.*

❺ **The straight lines in the cursor** *indicate that the image dragged from Bridge will appear in a new frame.*

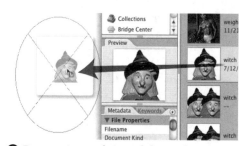

❻ **Drag an image from Adobe Bridge** *to place it onto an InDesign page.*

❼ **The curved lines in the cursor** *indicate that the image dragged from Bridge will appear in an existing frame.*

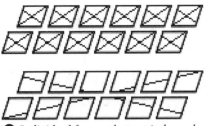

❽ *Individual frames that act independently display diagonal lines within each object (top). A* **compound shape** *displays the diagonal lines across the entire set of frames (bottom).*

❾ *A placed image is seen across all the items in a compound shape.*

Specialty Frames

Frames don't have to be single items drawn from scratch. You can join frames into one compound shape or you can convert text into frames that can hold images. You can also bring paths from other programs into InDesign to act as frames.

You can make multiple frames act as a single item by converting them to a compound shape. Frames combined into a compound shape display a single image across all the items in the compound.

To create a compound shape:

1. Select the frames you want to combine into a compound shape.

TIP If the frames overlap, InDesign displays a transparent area *(see page 151)*.

2. Choose **Object > Compound Paths > Make**. If the frame is a graphic frame, the diagonal lines cross through all the frames in the compound **❽**.

To add an image to a compound shape:

1. Use either Selection tool to select the compound shape.

2. Use any of the techniques described on the previous pages to place the image in the selected frame. The image tiles across the spaces between the elements of the compound shape **❾**.

To split a compound shape:

1. Select the compound shape.

2. Choose **Object > Compound Paths > Release**. The image is shown only through the first frame; the rest of the compound frames are available to hold other images.

Specialty Frames

You can also create unique frame shapes by converting text to frames so graphics assume the shapes of letters.

TIP If you can't draw for beans, you can convert the characters in dingbat or symbol fonts into graphic shapes such as hearts, arrows, snowflakes, and so on.

To convert text to frames:

1. Use the Selection tool to select the frame that contains the text.

   or

   Highlight the selected text within the frame.

2. Choose **Type** > **Create Outlines.** Each character of text is converted to paths that can be modified .

TIP You can also place images into the converted text paths as you can with compound shapes .

TIP The converted paths are created as compound paths. If you want to place different images or colors in each of the frames, release the compound shape first *(see the previous page).*

TIP If you select only a portion of the text within the frame, the highlighted text is converted to inline graphics within the frame. *(See page 244 for more information on working with inline graphics.)*

Frame

Paths

⑩ *The* **Create Outlines command** *converts text into paths that can then be modified.*

⑪ *Text converted to paths can also hold imported graphics.*

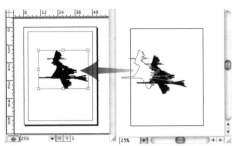

⑫ *Artwork can be* **dragged from a vector program** *and converted into InDesign frames.*

⑬ *Graphics converted to frames can hold images or text.*

Dragging from Illustrator

If you want to import paths from Adobe Illustrator, you need to make sure that Illustrator's preferences are set correctly.

Choose File Handling And Clipboard in Illustrator's Preferences dialog box. Under the Clipboard section, check the AICB (no transparency setting) option. Then click the Preserve Paths button.

If this is not done, the Illustrator paths will not be converted to frames.

If you work with a vector-drawing program such as Adobe Illustrator or Macromedia FreeHand, you can also convert the paths in those programs to InDesign frames.

TIP In addition to Illustrator and FreeHand, this technique can be used with any other program that copies paths using the AICB (Adobe Illustrator Clipboard). Check your vector-drawing program manual for more information.

To import paths as frames:

1. Position the windows of the vector-drawing program and InDesign so they are both visible onscreen.

2. Select the paths in the vector-drawing program with the appropriate tool in that application.

3. Drag the paths from the vector-drawing program onto the window of the InDesign document.

4. When a black line appears around the perimeter of the InDesign window, release the mouse button. The paths are converted to InDesign unassigned frames **⑫**.

TIP If you don't have the screen space to see both windows at once, you can also use the clipboard to copy the paths from the vector program and paste them in InDesign.

TIP Once the vector path has been converted to an InDesign frame, it can be used to hold an image or text **⑬**.

Setting the Image Import Options

When you import a graphic, you can use the Image Import Options dialog box to control how that image is placed.

TIP The following chart shows which types of import options are applied to pixel images.

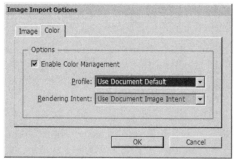

⑭ *The* Image Import Options dialog box for TIFF and JPEG images.

Import Options for Placed Images	
TIFF	Image Import Options with controls for Image and Color
JPEG	Image Import Options with controls for Image and Color
PSD	Image Import Options with controls for Image, Color, and Layers
EPS	EPS Import Options
Illustrator	PDF Import Options
PDF	PDF Import Options

To set the options for TIFF and JPEG images:

1. In the Place dialog box, check Import Options.

2. Choose a TIFF or JPEG image and click Open. This opens the Image Import Options dialog box for TIFF or JPEG images **⑭**.

3. Select the Image tab. If the image has a clipping path, you can choose Apply Photoshop Clipping path *(see page 220)*.

4. Select the Color tab. If the image has a color profile, you can turn on its color management settings *(see page 422)*.

5. Click OK to place the image.

Best File Format from Adobe Illustrator?

If you work in Adobe Illustrator, you will notice that there are several file formats you can choose from when you save your work: native Illustrator, EPS, or Adobe PDF. Which one works best with InDesign?

All three file formats can be placed into InDesign documents. However, native Illustrator files have the best preview.

You may have old Illustrator documents that were saved as EPS files. There's no need to resave them. You can place them into InDesign too.

However, you may see a white background behind artwork that has been saved on a Macintosh as an EPS. If that is a problem, use the Rasterize the PostScript option during import to eliminate the white background.

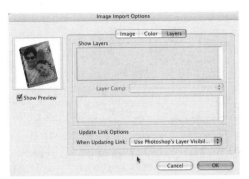

⑮ *The* **Image Import Options for Photoshop** files.

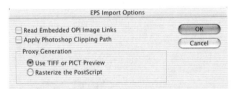

⑯ *The* **EPS Import Options dialog box** *lets you control imported EPS files.*

Working with Photoshop Layer Comps

A layer comp is a snapshot of a state of the Layers palette. Layer comps record the visibility, position and appearance of the layers in a Photoshop file.

You create layer comps in Photoshop. The names of the layer comps are then available within InDesign.

Using layer comps makes it possible to have several variations of the same file within InDesign.

To set the options for PSD images:

1. In the Place dialog box, check Show Import Options.

2. Choose a Photoshop image and click Open. This opens the Image Import Options dialog box for Photoshop files **⑮**.

3. Choose Show Preview to see a preview of the file.

4. Select Image Settings. If the image has a clipping path, you can choose Apply Photoshop Clipping path *(see page 220)*.

5. Select Color Settings. If the image has a color profile, you can turn on its color management settings *(see page 422)*.

6. Select Layers. If the images has layers or layer comps, you can choose which layers are visible in the InDesign layout *(see page 219)*.

7. Click OK to place the image.

To set the import options for EPS images:

1. In the Place dialog box, check Show Import Options.

2. Choose an EPS file. This opens the EPS Import Options dialog box **⑯**.

3. Don't check Read Embedded OPI Image Links unless your service bureau has instructed you to have InDesign perform the image swapping.

4. If the image has a clipping path, you can choose Apply Photoshop Clipping Path *(see page 220)*.

5. Set the options in the Proxy Generation to control the preview of the image:

   • **TIFF or PICT Preview** uses the preview that was created with the file.

   • **Rasterize the PostScript** displays the actual PostScript data as a preview. This lets you see custom PostScript code such as is found in FreeHand.

6. Click OK to place the image.

Setting the Image Import Options

InDesign also lets you place PDF files as graphics.

To set the options for PDF files:

1. In the Place dialog box, check Show Import Options.
2. Choose a PDF file. This opens the Place PDF dialog box .
3. Choose Show Preview to see a preview of each page of the PDF.
4. Use the page selectors to select the page you want to place . If you select multiple pages, use the following exercise to place the multiple pages.
5. Click the General tab to see those options.
6. Use the "Crop to" list to determine how the PDF should be cropped within the frame 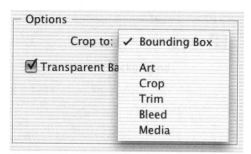. Choose the crop options:

   - **Bounding Box** crops to the active page elements, which includes printer marks.
   - **Art** crops to the area defined as placeable art.
   - **Crop** crops to only the printable area, not to the printer marks.
   - **Trim** crops to the area that is the final trim size.
   - **Bleed** crops to the area that is the total size of the image if a bleed area has been specified.
   - **Media** crops to the page size of the original document.

7. Choose Transparent Background to show only the elements of the page, without the opaque background .

   TIP If you choose Transparent Background, you can make it opaque by adding a fill color to the frame that contains the PDF.

8. Click the Layers tab to set the layers for the PDF (see page 219).
9. Click OK to place the image.

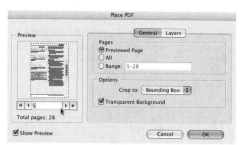

⑰ The **Place PDF dialog box** lets you preview and control the options for PDF files.

⑱ The **page selectors** let you preview the pages of a multipage PDF.

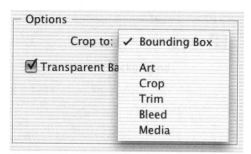

⑲ The **"Crop to" menu** in the Place PDF dialog box controls the size of the placed artwork.

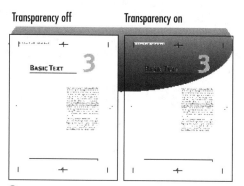

⑳ The effect of the **Transparent Background** on a placed PDF image.

Setting the Image Import Options

The **plus sign (+) in the PDF cursor** *indicates that you can place multiple pages from the PDF.*

PDF documents can contain more than one page. If you want, you can place those multiple pages all at once, without having to go back to the Place PDF dialog box.

To place multiple pages from a PDF:

1. In the Place PDF dialog box, choose one of the following:
   - **Previewed Page** selects whatever page is selected in the Preview area.
   - **All** selects all the pages in the document.
   - **Range** allows you to specify individual pages or a range of pages. Use commas to separate individual pages; use a hyphen to specify a range of pages.
2. Click OK to load the cursor.

TIP The cursor for a PDF displays a plus (+) sign when it is loaded with multiple pages .

3. Click as many times as necessary to load all the pages. When the plus sign disappears from the cursor, you have reached the last page to be placed.

Working with Images Inside Frames

After you place an image, you may want to move or modify it. Which tool you use and where you click affects what will be selected.

To select and move both the frame and the image:

1. Use the Selection tool and click the frame holding the image. A bounding box appears that indicates that the frame and its content are selected 🥈.

2. Press and drag the selection to move both the frame and the image.

TIP If you move quickly, you will see only a bounding box of the moved items 🥉. If you press and pause for a moment, you will see a preview of the items being moved 🥈.

To select the image within the frame:

1. Use the Direct Selection tool and click inside the frame where the image is visible. A bounding box for the image appears 🥈.

TIP If the image is larger than the frame, this bounding box will appear outside the boundaries of the frame.

2. Press and drag the image to move it without disturbing the frame.

TIP As you press, the areas of the image that are outside the frame are displayed lighter than the area within the frame 🥈.

To select and move just the frame:

1. Use the Direct Selection tool and click the edge of the frame. The points on the frame appear 🥈.

2. Hold the Opt/Alt key and click the frame again to select all the points.

3. Release the Opt/Alt key and drag the frame to move it to reveal a new part of the image.

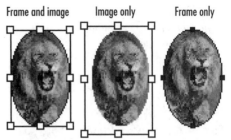

Frame and image   Image only   Frame only

🥈 *The display of the bounding boxes and points indicates what items are selected.*

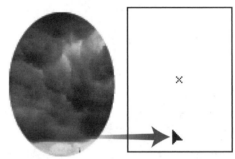

🥉 *If you move an object quickly, you see only a bounding box as the item is being moved.*

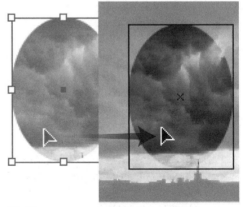

🥈 *If you press and pause before you move, you see a preview of the image being moved.*

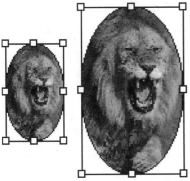

25 *The* **Transform Content command** *allows you to modify a frame and a placed image at the same time.*

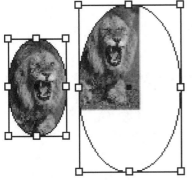

26 *With* **Transform Content turned off**, *the frame is modified but the image remains its original size.*

27 *With just the image selected, the transform tools and commands modify the image, but not the frame.*

When you apply transformations to frames that contain placed images, you have a choice as to which objects — the frame, the image, or both — are transformed. Here are some helpful guides.

TIP If you pause before you drag with any of the transform tools, you will see a preview of the image as you transform it.

To transform both the frame and the placed image:

1. Use the Selection tool to select both the frame and the placed image.

2. Make sure that Transform Content is chosen in the Transform or Control palette menus.

3. Use any of the Transform palette fields or transform tools **25**.

To modify the frame only:

1. Turn off Transform Content in the Transform or Control palette menu.

2. Use any of the Transform palette fields or transform tools to modify only the selected frame **26**.

To modify the placed graphic only:

1. Use the Direct Selection tool to select the artwork within the frame.

2. Use any of the Transform palette fields or transform tools to modify only the selected image **27**.

Using the Position Tool

The Position tool works like a combination of the Selection and Direct Selection tools. Originally created for PageMaker users who missed that feature when they switched to InDesign, the Position tool may be the solution for confused editors *(see sidebar on the opposite page)* who don't know which tool to use for what purpose.

To use the Position tool:

1. Click the Position tool in the Toolbox ㉘.
2. Use the Position tool with a graphic frame as follows:
   - Move the cursor over the edge of a frame to select the frame. A square next to the cursor indicates that the frame will be selected ㉙.
   - Move the cursor over one of the bounding boxes of the frame. The double-headed arrow indicates that both the frame and the graphic can be resized ㉚.
   - Move the cursor over the center point of the frame. The curved arrow indicates that you can move the frame and its contents ㉛.
   - Move the cursor over the placed graphic within the frame. The Hand cursor indicates that the graphic may be repositioned inside the frame ㉜.
   - Click the Hand cursor inside the frame. The bounding box for the placed graphic indicates that the graphic may be resized.
   - Move the cursor over the bounding box for the graphic. The double-headed arrow indicates that the graphic can be resized ㉝.

TIP The Position tool does not allow you to reshape frames.

㉘ *The* **Position tool** *in the Toolbox works as a combination of the Selection and Direct Selection tools.*

㉙ *Place the* **Position tool over the edge of a frame** *to select the frame.*

㉚ *Place the* **Position tool over the bounding box** *to resize a frame and graphic*

㉛ *Place the* **Position tool over the center point** *to move a frame.*

㉜ *Place the* **Position tool over the image** *to move the graphic inside a frame.*

㉝ *Place the* **Position tool over the bounding box for a graphic** *to resize the graphic.*

Before　　　　　After

③④ *The effect of the* **Fit Content to Frame** command.

Before　　　　　After

③⑤ *The effect of the* **Fit Content Proportionally** command.

"Why Does the Frame Say 100% Even Though I Resized the Image?"

Here's something that confuses my students. They import an image into a frame, and then choose Fit Content Proportionally to shrink the image.

When they look at the Control palette the frame size is listed at 100%. That seems impossible; how can the image which has just been shrunk down still be listed as 100%? The answer is that the *frame* may be listed as 100%, but if you select the *image* with the Direct Selection tool, you'll see the percentage that the image was scaled.

"OK," my student says, "but how come sometimes the frame *does* show something less than 100% for the size of the frame as well as the image?"

That happens under a very specific set of circumstances: You have applied a stroke to the frame and you have chosen Scale Strokes from the Control palette menu. When that happens, and the frame is resized, the percentage for the frame size appears in the Control palette.

Fitting Graphics in Frames

Placed images don't always fit perfectly into preexisting frames. InDesign gives you several commands that let you quickly position and resize artwork in frames.

To resize the graphic to the frame size:

1. Use either selection tool to select the frame or the graphic inside the frame.

2. Choose **Object > Fitting > Fit Content to Frame.** This changes the size of the graphic to fit completely within the area of the frame **③④**.

TIP This command does not preserve the proportions of the artwork; the artwork may become distorted.

To proportionally resize to the frame size:

1. Use either selection tool to select the frame or the graphic inside the frame.

2. Choose **Object > Fitting > Fit Content Proportionally.** This changes the size of the graphic to fit completely, and without distortion, within the frame **③⑤**.

TIP Use the Fit Frame to Content command *(see the next page)* to resize the frame to the size of the graphic.

Fitting Graphics in Frames

The Fit Content Proportionally command usually leaves some empty space between the graphic and the frame. What if you want to resize the image so that it fills the entire frame? That's where the Fill Frame Proportionally command comes to the rescue.

To resize the graphic to fill the frame:

1. Use either selection tool to select the frame or the graphic inside the frame.

2. Choose **Object > Fitting > Fill Frame Proportionally.** This changes the size of the graphic to fit completely, and without distortion, within the frame ⑯.

To resize the frame to the graphic size:

1. Use either selection tool to select the frame or the graphic inside the frame.

2. Choose **Object > Fitting > Fit Frame to Content.** This changes the size of the frame so that the artwork fits completely within the area of the frame ⑰.

TIP The Fit Frame to Content command is also available for text frames.

To center the graphic within the frame:

1. Use either selection tool to select the frame or the graphic inside the frame.

2. Choose **Object > Fitting > Center Content.** This centers the graphic within the frame without changing the size of either the graphic or the frame ⑱.

TIP The Fitting commands are also available on the Control palette ⑲.

Before   Fit Content Proportionally   Fill Frame Proportionally

⑯ *The Fit Content Proportionally command may leave a gap between the frame and the image. The Fill Frame Proportionally command always fills the frame.*

Before   After

⑰ *The effect of the* **Fit Frame to Content** *command.*

Before   After

⑱ *The effect of the* **Center Content command.**

Fit Content Proportionally
Fit Content to Frame   Fill Frame Proportionally
Fit Frame to Content   Center Content

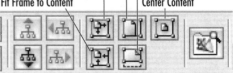

⑲ *Use the* **Fit icons in the Control palette** *to modify placed images and frames.*

Fitting Graphics in Frames

Content offset on   Absolute offset

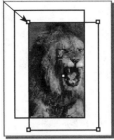

⓿ **Content offset** *positions the graphic relative to the frame.* **Absolute offset** *positions the graphic relative to the page.*

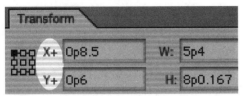

㊶ *The* **plus signs (+) next to the X and Y coordinates** *indicate that the position of the object is relative to the frame.*

In addition to the commands that position graphics, you can also position images numerically within frames using the X and Y coordinates in the Transform palette.

To numerically position graphics within frames:

1. Check Show Content Offset in the Transform palette menu.

2. Use the Direct Selection tool to select the graphic inside the frame.

3. Enter the X and Y coordinates in the Transform palette. The image moves to a new position relative to the frame **⓿**. This is called the *content offset.*

TIP Small plus signs (+) next to the X and Y coordinates in the Transform palette indicate that Show Content Offset is turned on **㊶**.

To numerically position graphics on the page:

1. Uncheck Show Content Offset from the Transform palette menu.

2. Use the Direct Selection tool to select the graphic inside the frame.

3. Set the X and Y coordinates in the Transform palette. The image moves to a new position relative to the page rulers. This is called the *absolute offset.*

Of course you can use any of the transformation commands to scale, rotate, and shear objects within the frame. This allows you to scale images numerically within a frame.

To transform images within a frame:

1. Use the Direct Selection tool to select the graphic inside the frame.

2. Use any of the transform tools or the Transform palette described on pages 91 – 100.

Fitting Graphics in Frames

Nesting Graphic Elements

Once you have an image in a frame, you can then paste it into another frame. This technique is called *nesting elements* and it allows you much more flexibility in assembling various images than other programs. *(This is similar to the paste-into techniques covered on pages 107 and 108.)*

TIP For instance, you can use nested elements to put a placed image inside a circular frame and then put that circular frame inside a rectangular frame. The top rectangular frame crops the circular frame while the circular frame crops the placed image.

To create a nested frame:

1. Use the Selection tool to select the element to be nested inside the frame **42**.

TIP A nested element can be a graphic or text frame.

2. Cut or copy the element to the clipboard.

3. Select the frame that is to hold the nested element.

4. Choose **Edit > Paste Into**. This pastes the element inside the frame **43**.

TIP The Selection tool moves all the elements in the nest.

TIP Frames can hold multiple levels of nested frames. So you can have a frame within a frame within a frame, and so on.

TIP Use the Fit Content commands to automatically position the nested frame inside the parent frame *(see page 207)*.

42 *Before nesting, the circular frame with the placed image is a separate object.*

43 *After nesting, the circular frame is the content inside the rectangular frame.*

44 *The first click with the* **Direct Selection tool** *selects the placed image inside a nest.*

45 *The next click with the* **Group Selection tool** *selects both the frame and the placed image.*

46 *Use the* **Selection tool to drag the center point** *of the selected frame to move the selected items of the nested elements.*

Once you have created nested elements, you can use the Direct Selection tool to select and move the items within the nest.

TIP In the example given on the previous page, you might want to move the placed image and the circular frame without moving the rectangular frame that holds those elements.

To select and move nested elements:

1. Use the Direct Selection tool to select the nested element.

TIP If the item contains a placed image, the image is selected and the hand cursor displayed **44**.

2. Hold the Opt/Alt + Shift keys. This changes the Direct Selection tool to the Group Selection tool *(see page 106)*.

TIP The plus (+) sign next to the white arrow indicates the Group Selection tool.

3. Click with the Group Selection tool to select both the placed image and the frame **45**.

4. If you have many levels of nested elements, click with the Group Selection tool as many times as necessary to select up through the nest levels.

5. Switch to the Selection tool when you have selected all the nested elements you want to move.

6. Drag the center point of the selected nested elements. This allows you to move the selected nested elements together **46**.

TIP If you drag the bounding box handles instead of the center point, you change the size of the nested element.

You can also select nested elements using the Select commands. These commands make it very easy to select pasted-in elements and graphics.

To use the Select commands for nested elements:

1. Use the regular Selection tool to select the object. This selects the main container that holds the nested elements .

2. Choose **Object > Select > Content**. This selects the item that was pasted into the main container. In the case of a nested element, this is the frame that holds the placed graphic.

TIP Use the Selection tool to move this object by dragging its center point.

3. You can choose **Object > Select > Content** again to select the placed graphic.

TIP If you have selected objects within the nested elements, you can choose **Object > Select > Container** to select upward through the nested elements.

TIP The Select commands are also available as icons on the Control palette .

47 *The first click with the **Selection tool** selects the frame that holds the nested image.*

Select container   Select content

48 *You can also use the **Select command icons** in the Control palette.*

49 *When a frame is selected, choosing a fill color changes the background color of the frame.*

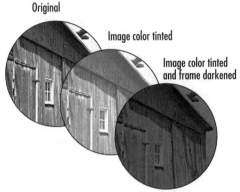

Original

Image color tinted

Image color tinted and frame darkened

50 *You can change the appearance of a grayscale image by changing the image color or the fill color of the frame.*

Colorizing Grayscale Images

Your service bureau may instruct you not to colorize grayscale images. Or you may get a warning from a pre-flight program that checks your document before printing.

In theory there is nothing wrong with colorizing grayscale images, but individual production workflows may not be able to handle the images.

If you get a warning about colorizing grayscale images, check with your print shop or service bureau to see whether or not it can handle them.

Styling Placed Images

Once you have placed a graphic within a frame, you can employ many techniques to style the frame or the image. For instance, you can change the color of the frame or the color of the image.

To color the frame fill or stroke:

1. Use the Selection tool to select the frame.
2. Click the Fill icon in the Toolbox or Color or Swatches palette.

   or

   Click the Stroke icon in the Toolbox or Color or Swatches palette.
3. Choose a color in the Swatches palette. If the Fill icon is chosen, you'll see the fill color wherever the image doesn't fill the frame **49**.

If you import a grayscale image, you can add color to it, so you change the black values in the image.

To color a grayscale image:

1. Use the Direct Selection tool to select the grayscale image.
2. Choose the Fill icon in the Color palette or Toolbox.

   TIP The default fill color for grayscale images is black.
3. Change the tint value to lighten the image.

   or

   Choose a color in the Color or Swatches palette. The grayscale values change to a tint of the color chosen **50**.
4. Use the steps in the previous exercise to change the fill color of the frame. This colorizes the white areas of the image.

Styling Placed Images

Linking Graphics

When you place an image, you don't actually place the image into the document. You place a screen preview of the image that links to the original graphic. In order to print the file, InDesign needs to follow that *link* to the original graphic.

TIP It is possible to link text files as well as graphics, but those are primarily used together with InCopy.

To examine the links in a document:

1. Choose **Window > Links**. This opens the Links palette ⑤. The Links palette shows all the linked images in the document with their page numbers. Special icons indicate the status of the image ⑤.

   - **Missing Link** indicates that InDesign can't find the original graphic.
   - **Modified Link** indicates that the graphic has changed and has a different modification date from when it was originally placed.

2. Use the Links palette menu to sort the list of graphics as follows:

   - **Sort By Name** arranges the graphics in alphabetical order.
   - **Sort By Status** arranges the missing or modified graphics together.
   - **Sort By Page** arranges the graphics according to the page they are on.

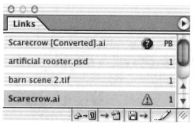

⑤ *The* **Links palette** *displays the placed images in the document.*

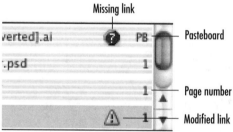

⑤ *The* **icons and page numbers** *next to a listing in the Links palette tell you the status of a placed image.*

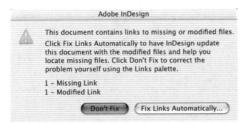

53 *The* **Missing or Modified Links notice** *appears when you open a file that has a missing link to a text or graphics file.*

Pixels or Vectors?

There are two main types of graphics in desktop publishing. Pixel-based images (sometimes called *bitmapped,* or *raster* images) display images as an arrangement of small rectangles. Scanners and digital cameras all capture images in pixels. Adobe Photoshop lets you paint or modify pixels.

Vector images display artwork according to paths filled with colors. They are the same as the vector shapes in InDesign. Programs such as Adobe Illustrator and Macromedia FreeHand create vector images.

Pixel-based images are usually used for photographs or images with blends. Vector images are usually used for more precise images such as maps or technical drawings.

One of the big benefits of working with vector images is that they can be scaled up or down without losing any details. Pixel-based images can lose detail if they are scaled up too high.

The Missing or Modified Links notice appears when you open a file whose link is missing or has been changed **53**.

To relink graphics when you open a document:

1. Click the Fix Links Automatically button in the Missing or Modified Links notice. All modified graphics are automatically updated.

2. If there are missing links, the operating system navigation dialog box opens. Use it to find each missing graphic.

TIP It is not necessary to find missing links as you work on a document. For instance, if you only need to work on text, you don't need to find missing graphics. However, you must fix all links before you send out a document to be printed.

If you open a document without choosing the Fix Links Automatically button, you can use the Links palette to find missing graphics and relink them to the screen preview.

TIP Using the Links palette lets you carefully check each graphic to make sure it is the one you want to modify.

To relink a missing graphic:

1. Select the missing link in the Links palette.

TIP You can also select multiple links. Shift-click to select a range of links. Cmd/Ctrl-click to select noncontiguous links.

2. Click the Relink button. This opens the navigation dialog box, which you can use to find the missing file.

   or

   Choose Relink from the Links palette menu.

3. Navigate to find the missing file.

4. Click OK to relink the graphic.

If a graphic has been modified, you can use the controls at the bottom of the Links palette to update the link.

To update modified links:

1. Select the modified link in the Links palette.
2. Click the Update Link button .

   or

   Choose Update Link from the Links palette menu.

TIP You can select more than one graphic to update multiple links. Shift-click to select a range of links. Cmd/Ctrl-click to select noncontiguous links.

The Links palette also lets you move quickly to a specific graphic.

To jump to a linked graphic in the document:

1. Select the link in the Links palette.
2. Click the Go to Link button ⑤④.

   or

   Choose Go to Link from the Links palette menu.

The Links palette can also be used to open and edit a graphic.

To edit a linked graphic:

1. Select the graphic you want to place.
2. Choose Edit Original from the Links palette menu.

   or

   Click the Edit Original icon in the Links palette ⑤④. The graphic opens in the program that created it.

TIP You can also edit the graphic in its original program by holding the Opt/Alt key and double-clicking the graphic on the page.

Go to Link   Edit Original
Relink | Update Link |

⑤④ *The* **icon commands in the Links palette** *allow you to access frequently used commands.*

Links for Text Files

InDesign also has a preference *(see page 530)* that automatically creates a link for placed text files. With the preference turned on, if you modify the original text file that was placed in the InDesign document, you see a notice when you open the file that links are missing or modified.

It might seem like a good idea to use the Update Link command to update the text within the InDesign document. However, if you do, you will lose any formatting or changes you have applied within InDesign.

In most cases it is not necessary to keep the link for text files. You are probably better off embedding the text file within the document *(see page 218)*.

However, if you are working with InCopy or some other sort of workgroup software, you may not be able to embed text files within the document. In that case, check with your workgroup supervisor for the proper procedures.

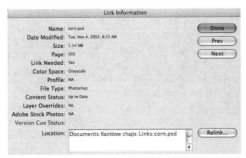

55 *The* **Link Information dialog box** *gives you information about a placed graphic.*

You may want to find a placed image in the Macintosh Finder, Windows Explorer, or Bridge window.

To find the linked file:

1. Select the graphic in the Links palette.
2. Choose one of the following:
   - **Reveal in Finder** (Mac) or **Reveal in Explorer** (Win) to select the file in the operating system directory.
   - **Reveal in Bridge** to select the file in the Bridge window.

The Link Information dialog box gives you information about an imported graphic.

To see the link information:

1. Select the graphic in the Links palette.
2. Choose Link Information from the Links palette menu. This opens the Link Information dialog box **55**.
3. If necessary, use the Relink button to find missing graphics.
4. Use the Next or Previous buttons to move to other graphics in the Links palette.
5. Click the Done button when finished.

Linking Graphics

Embedding Graphics

Usually, only the preview of a graphic is contained within an InDesign file. You can, however, embed a graphic within the InDesign file. This means that all the information necessary to print the file is contained within the InDesign document.

TIP Embedded graphics will increase the size of the InDesign file.

To embed placed images or text:

1. Select the placed image.

or

Select the frame that contains the imported text.

2. Choose Embed File from the Links palette menu. If you have selected a graphic, the Embed icon appears next to the file name in the Links palette **56**.

or

If you have selected text, the file name disappears from the Links palette.

TIP Embedded text files do not add to the size of the InDesign file.

TIP Once you embed a graphic, InDesign no longer needs to find the original file on your hard disk.

To unembed images:

1. Select the embedded image.

2. Choose Unembed File from the Links palette menu. The Unembed alert box appears **57**.

3. Click Yes to link the embedded graphic back to the original file that was placed into InDesign.

or

Click No. A dialog box appears asking you to choose the destination for a new file.

56 The **Embed icon** in the Links palette indicates that all the information necessary to print the graphic is stored in the InDesign file.

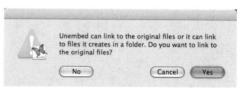

57 The **Unembed alert box** lets you choose to link back to the original file or create a new file.

When to Embed Graphics

You may be tempted to embed many, if not all, of your graphics within the InDesign document. After all, it makes it much easier to send a file to the service bureau if you don't have to remember to send the graphic files along with it. *(For more information on preparing files for printing, see Chapter 19, "Output.")*

Embedding graphics increases the size of the InDesign file. Just a few large graphics can make the InDesign file balloon in size. This means the file will take a long time to open or save.

You shouldn't have problems, though, if you embed small graphics, such as logos. Just remember that each time you embed a small graphic, it adds to the file size. Page after page of small graphics adds up.

My own feeling is to avoid embedding graphics. That way I don't have to worry about the file size. But I do have to remember to send the necessary files along to the printer.

Embedding Graphics

Show/Hide Layer Icons

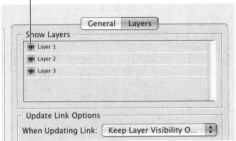

58 *The* **Layer controls** *of the Place PDF dialog box.*

Layer Comp description

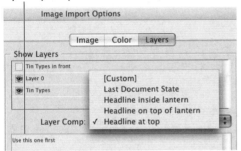

59 *The* **Layer Comp list** *of the Image Import Options for a Photoshop file.*

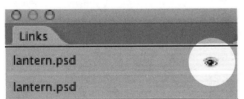

60 *The* **Eyeball icon** *in the Links palette indicates that the visibility of the layers is different from the saved state in Photoshop*

Setting Layer Visibility

When you import Photoshop and PDF files, you have the opportunity to set the visibility of the layers in those files. This makes it possible to import one file, but then use it with various combinations of the layers turned on or off.

To set the layer options as you import files:

1. Choose Show Import Options when you place a layered Photoshop or PDF file.

2. Click the Layers option in the Show Import Options dialog box **58**.

3. Click the visibility icon for each layer to show or hide that layer.

4. If you have chosen a Photoshop file with layer comps, use the Layer Comps list to choose the layer comp that you want to apply to the image **59**.

TIP Notice that the description for the layer comp appears in the field under the Layer Comp list.

5. Select one of the following from the When Updating Link list:

   - **Use Photoshop's/PDF's Layer Visibility** resets any overrides you have made in InDesign to the settings in the original Photoshop or PDF file.

   - **Keep Layer Visibility Overrides** maintains any layer settings you have made in InDesign.

TIP A symbol appears in the Links palette if you have set the layers differently from the saved state of the file **60**.

Once you have imported a layered file. you can change the visibility of the layers.

To edit the layer options of a placed file:

1. Select the place image.

2. Choose **Object > Object Layer Options**.

3. Make whatever changes you want.

Setting Layer Visibility

Using Clipping Paths

Raster images saved as TIFF or EPS files are always rectangular. If you want to see only part of the image you import, you can create a *clipping path* that surrounds the part of the image that you want to see. The rest of the image becomes transparent. One way to create a clipping path is to use Adobe Photoshop to create paths for the file.

To import a file with a clipping path:

1. In Photoshop, use the Path tools to create a path around the image ⬤.

   TIP Although you will not see the clipping effect in Photoshop itself, the areas of the image inside the path will be visible in InDesign. The areas outside the path will be invisible.

2. Use Photoshop's Paths palette menu to designate the path as a clipping path.

3. Save the file as a TIFF, EPS, or Photoshop file.

   TIP You can have many paths saved as part of a Photoshop file, but only one path can be designated as a clipping path.

4. In InDesign, choose **File** > **Place** and choose the file you have created.

5. In InDesign's Import Options, check Apply Photoshop Clipping Path ⬤. The image is automatically clipped so that only the areas inside the path are visible in the layout ⬤.

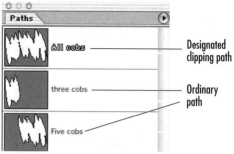

Designated clipping path

Ordinary path

⬤ **Photoshop's Paths palette** *shows the paths saved with the file. Clipping paths are shown in outlined type.*

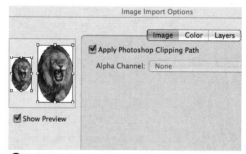

⬤ *InDesign's* **Image Import Options dialog box** *lets you choose to apply a clipping path to a file.*

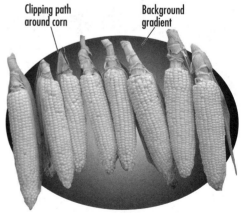

Clipping path around corn

Background gradient

⬤ *An example of how a* **clipping path** *allows an image to have a transparent background to show other objects behind it.*

Using Clipping Paths

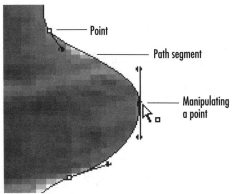

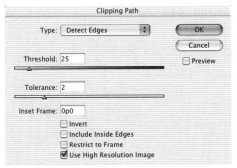

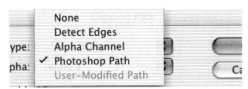

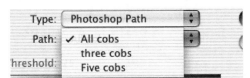

64 *Use the Direct Selection tool to manipulate the shape of a clipping path around an image.*

65 *The* **Clipping Path dialog box** *lets you create or modify a clipping path for a graphic.*

66 *Use the* **Clipping Path Type list** *to choose which type of clipping path to apply.*

67 *Use the* **Path list** *to choose a specific path attached to a graphic.*

Once you have a clipping path applied to a graphic, you can change the shape of the path to hide or show more of the image.

To modify the shape of a clipping path:

1. Use the Direct Selection tool to select the placed image. If the image has a clipping path, the path appears as a series of points and path segments **64**.

2. Use any of the path techniques to change the shape of the clipping path. *(See Chapter 7, "Pen and Beziers" for information on working with paths.)*

You can also turn a clipping path into a frame. This lets you apply a stroke to the path.

To convert a clipping path into a frame:

1. Use either selection tool to select the image with the clipping path.

2. Right-click (Win) or Control-click (Mac) to open the contextual menu.

3. Choose Convert Clipping Path to Frame. The clipping path is converted.

You don't have to designate a clipping path in Photoshop. InDesign lets you select any path, saved with the image file, as a clipping path.

To choose a path as an InDesign clipping path:

1. Select the placed image that includes a path.

2. Choose **Object > Clipping Path.** The Clipping Path dialog box appears **65**.

3. Use the Type menu in the Clipping Path dialog box to select the Photoshop Path option **66**. *(See the next page for using the Detect Edges and Alpha Channel options.)*

4. Use the Path menu to select which path should be used as a clipping path **67**.

5. Click the Preview button to see the effects of choosing a path.

6. Click OK to apply the path.

Using Clipping Paths

What happens, though, if an image doesn't contain a clipping path? Fortunately, InDesign can create a clipping path from the edges — or the differences between the dark and light colors — of the image.

To create a clipping path from an image:

1. In the Clipping Path dialog box, choose Detect Edges from the Type menu 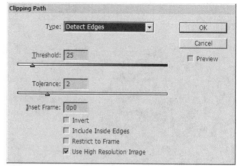.

2. Adjust the Threshold slider to define the color that is used as the area outside the clipping path; 0 is pure white.

3. Adjust the Tolerance slider to allow a slight variation in the Threshold color. A high number for the tolerance often smooths out small bumps in the path.

The Clipping Path dialog box gives you controls for creating a clipping path based on the appearance of the image.

You can also use an alpha channel, saved with the file, as a clipping path.

TIP Alpha channels are grayscale images that are saved along with the color or black channels of an image.

To choose an alpha channel as a clipping path:

1. Use the Type menu in the Clipping Path dialog box to select Alpha Channel.

2. Use the Alpha menu to select which channel should be used as a clipping path.

3. Because alpha channels can contain shades of gray, adjust the Threshold slider to define the color that is used as the area outside the clipping path; 0 is pure white.

4. Adjust the Tolerance slider to allow a slight variation in the Threshold color. A high number for the tolerance often smooths out small bumps in the path.

Using Clipping Paths

69 *The* **Include Inside Edges** *in a clipping path creates transparent areas within the image such as the area inside the basket handles.*

The End of the Clipping Path?

Clipping paths are not suitable for many types of images. A clipping path acts like a knife that cuts out the background of an image. This is good if you need a really sharp edge on an image. However, soft, curly hair may need variations in transparency that a clipping path can't provide.

Fortunately, InDesign lets you use the transparency in Photoshop files to make parts of an image transparent *(see the next page)*.

All clipping paths can be further modified by using the controls at the bottom of the Clipping Path dialog box.

To modify the effects of a clipping path:

1. Type a positive value in the Inset Frame field to shrink the entire path into the image.

   or

   Type a negative value to expand the path outside the image.

2. If necessary, check Invert to switch which areas the path makes visible and which areas it leaves invisible.

3. Check Include Inside Edges to add areas to the clipping path that are enclosed by the foreground image **69**.

4. Check Use High Resolution Image to create the path from the high-resolution version of the file rather than the preview. This is a slower but more accurate way of calculating the path.

5. Check Restrict to Frame to prevent the clipping path frame from displaying any part of the image that is outside the frame that holds the image.

To delete the clipping path around an image:

1. Select the placed image.

2. Choose **Object > Clipping Path.** The Clipping Path dialog box appears.

3. Choose None from the Type pop-up list.

Using Clipping Paths

Importing Transparent Images

InDesign offers you a special advantage when you place native Photoshop (PSD) or Illustrator (AI) files. If there is any transparency in the placed image, InDesign displays the image with the same transparency as in the original file.

To use the transparency in a Photoshop file:

1. In Photoshop, use any of the tools to silhouette or fade the edges of the image. The Photoshop transparency grid indicates which parts of the image are transparent.

2. Save the file as a Photoshop (PSD) file.

3. Choose **File > Place** to import the file into the InDesign document.

TIP The Image Import Options dialog box automatically sets the Alpha Channel import option to Transparency. You do not have to set the transparency option for native Photoshop files.

4. Click to place the file. The areas that were transparent in Photoshop will be transparent in InDesign **70**.

TIP You can combine the use of a Photoshop path together with transparency to create a silhouette with a see-through transparency.

To use the transparency in an Illustrator file:

1. In Illustrator, use any of the commands to apply transparency to the artwork.

2. Save the file as an Illustrator (AI) file.

3. Make sure that the PDF Compatibility option is checked in the Save dialog box.

4. Import the file into the InDesign document. The areas that were transparent in Illustrator will be transparent in InDesign.

70 A transparent Photoshop file lets you see through the glass to the text behind the image.

Importing Transparent Images

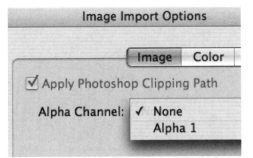

⓲ *Use the* **Alpha Channel menu** *in the Image Import Options to apply the channel to an image.*

In addition to importing Photoshop files with transparent layers, InDesign can also apply an alpha channel saved with flattened files. This allows you to display transparency in file formats that do not support layers or a transparency grid.

To apply an alpha channel to an image:

1. Add an alpha channel to the image in Photoshop. The alpha channel should be created as follows:
   - Black designates those areas that are not transparent.
   - White designates those areas that are completely transparent.
   - Shades of gray are used for those areas that are partially transparent.

2. Save the file as a TIFF, GIF, JPEG, or BMP file.

3. Choose **File** > **Place** to import the file into the InDesign document.

4. Use the Show Import Options checkbox to open the Image Import Options dialog box.

5. Choose the name of the alpha channel from the Alpha Channel menu and click OK to place the file ⓲.

6. If necessary, click to place the file on the page. The alpha channel is applied to the image to create opaque, transparent, and semi-transparent areas.

Importing Transparent Images

Viewing Images

When you have a large document with a lot of images in it, you might find that the redraw time is delayed as you move around. However, you can set preferences for how your images are displayed by lowering some of the image detail for increased speed as you move through pages. These display settings can be applied to the entire document or to individually selected objects.

TIP The display settings for images don't affect how the document will print.

To set the default appearance of previews:

1. Choose **Edit > Preferences > Display Performance** (Windows).

    or

    Choose **InDesign > Preferences > Display Performance** (Mac OS X). This opens the Display Performance Preferences dialog box **72**.

2. Choose one of the three options from the Default View Settings menu **73**.

    *   **Fast** is used when you want fast screen redraw and the best performance.
    *   **Typical** is used when you want a better representation of the images.
    *   **High Quality** is used when you want to see as much detail as possible onscreen. This option may cause InDesign to work slower than it will with the other choices.

    TIP Each of the menu choices corresponds to one choice in the Adjust View Settings list.

3. Check Preserve Object-level Display Settings to use the display settings that have been applied to individual images *(see the next page)* **74**.

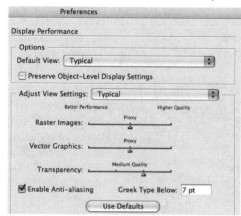

72 *The* **Display Performance Preferences** dialog box *controls how images and transparency effects are displayed.*

73 *The* **Default View Settings list** *lets you choose which display performance setup is applied to images.*

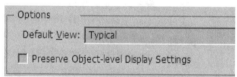

74 *Check* **Preserve Object-level Display Settings** *to let each object's settings override the overall document display setting.*

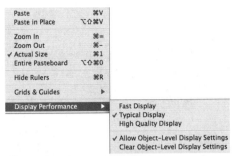

75 *The* **Display Performance contextual menu** *settings let you quickly switch from one display performance setup to another.*

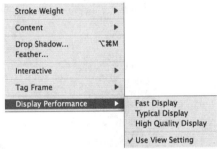

76 *The* **Display Performance contextual menu** *for an object lets you change the display performance for that object.*

As you work, you can switch between the menu commands without having to open the Display Performance Preferences dialog box.

To switch the default view setting:

1. With no object selected, Right-click (Win) or Control-click (Mac). This opens a contextual menu **75**.

2. Choose one of the view settings from the Display Performance submenu.

3. Choose Allow Object-level Display Settings to override any individual image previews *(see the next exercise).* This does not delete those individual settings, it only overrides them.

4. Choose Clear Object-level Display Settings to delete any individual image previews.

TIP You can also use the View menu to choose the view settings or to override any individual image previews.

You can also set each individual image to its own display setting. This lets you set one large image to faster screen redraw while showing more detail in other objects.

To set individual image previews:

1. Select the image.

2. Right-click (Win) or Control-click (Mac). This opens the contextual menu for the display of that object **76**.

3. Choose one of the options from the Display Performance submenu of the contextual menu.

TIP The Use View Setting command sets the object back to the current View Setting in the Display Performance Preferences.

TIP You can also use the **Object > Display Performance** submenu to choose the view settings for a selected object.

Viewing Images

The labels Fast, Typical, and High Quality are merely guides. You can customize the specific displays for raster images, vector art, and transparency effects in the Adjust View Settings area of the Display Performance Preferences.

To set the raster and vector displays:

1. Choose Edit > Preferences > Display Performance (Win).

   or

   Choose InDesign > Preferences > Display Performance (Mac).

2. Choose one of the radio button settings in the Adjust View Settings menu **77**.

3. Drag the slider for the Raster Images or Vector Graphics as follows **78**:

   • **Gray Out** (far left) displays a gray background instead of the image **79**. This is the fastest performance.

   • **Proxy** (middle) displays a 72-ppi screen preview of the image **80**. This setting provides the best performance that still shows what the image looks like.

   • **High Resolution** (far right) displays the maximum resolution for the image **80**.

4. Repeat the process for each of the other menu settings.

TIP Raster Images and Vector Graphics settings don't have to be set for the same resolution. This allows you to have a faster redraw for large raster files, and more details in the lines of vector graphics.

77 *The* **Adjust View Settings menu** *gives you three display settings to apply to a document or individual images.*

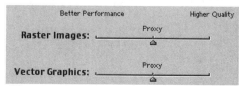

78 *The* **Raster Images and Vector Graphics sliders** *let you control how those formats are displayed.*

79 *An example of the* **Gray Out view setting.**

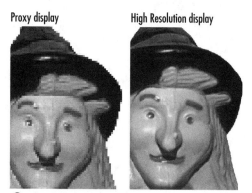

80 *The difference between the Proxy setting and the High Resolution setting.*

Viewing Images

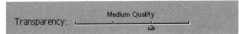

81 *The* **Transparency slider** *lets you control the display of drop shadows, feathers, and transparency effects. The setting labels appear as you move the slider.*

You can also adjust the display for the transparency effects as well as the drop shadows and feather effects.

To set the transparency effects displays:

1. Choose one of the listings in the Adjust View Settings menu.
2. Drag the Transparency slider to each notch setting as follows **81**: (The labels appear as you drag the slider.)
    *   **Off** (far left) displays no transparency effects. This is the fastest performance.
    *   **Low Quality** (second from left) displays basic opacity and blend modes. Drop shadows and feathers are displayed in low resolution only. Some blend modes may change in the final output.
    *   **Medium Quality** (second from right) displays drop shadows and feathers in low resolution.
    *   **High Quality** (far right) displays high resolution drop shadows and feathers. Blend modes appear in their correct CMYK color display.
3. Repeat the process for each of the other Adjust View menu items.

Viewing Images

Applying Effects to Images

It makes a difference if you apply a drop shadow to the frame or to the image inside the frame.

To apply effects to imported images:

◆ Select the object with the Selection tool to apply the effect to the frame that contains the image ❽❷.

or

Select the image with the Direct Selection tool to apply the effect to the image within the frame ❽❷.

TIP If you apply a drop shadow to an image, you may need to enlarge the size of the frame in order to see the shadow.

Image Selected   Frame Selected

❽❷ *The difference between applying a drop shadow to an image versus a frame.*

TEXT EFFECTS 9

Go back and look at the newspaper and magazine advertisements created in the 1800s. (Yes, that was *before* I worked in advertising.) In those ads, the text marches along in a straight line without swerving toward or moving around the images.

In those days, it was extremely difficult to wrap text around an image. Each line of text had to be cut and pasted around the edges of an image.

The paste-up artists never dreamed of setting text along a path so that it follows the shape of a rollercoaster — that would have been far too much work!

Adding short horizontal rules to divide one paragraph from another was another tedious task. In fact, if you look closely at some old advertisements, you can see that the rule isn't perfectly centered in the column.

Fortunately, electronic page-layout programs such as InDesign make it easy to do all these special text effects with incredible precision.

Wrapping Text

One of my favorite effects to apply to text is to arrange it to flow around images and other objects. This is called *text wrap*. (If you are familiar with some other programs, you might call this *text runaround*; but InDesign doesn't give you the runaround.) InDesign gives you many different options for wrapping text around either objects you create in InDesign or imported graphics.

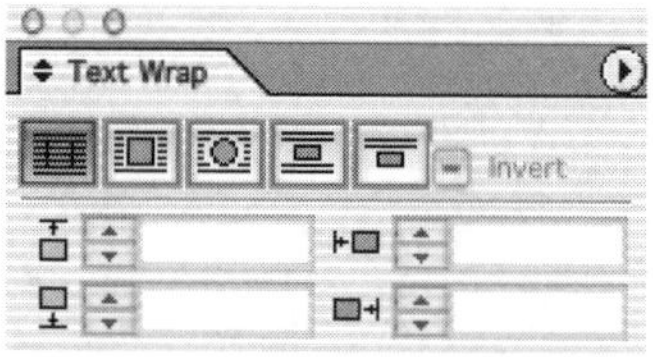
Text Wrap
Invert

❶ *The* **Text Wrap palette** *controls the settings for how text flows around an object.*

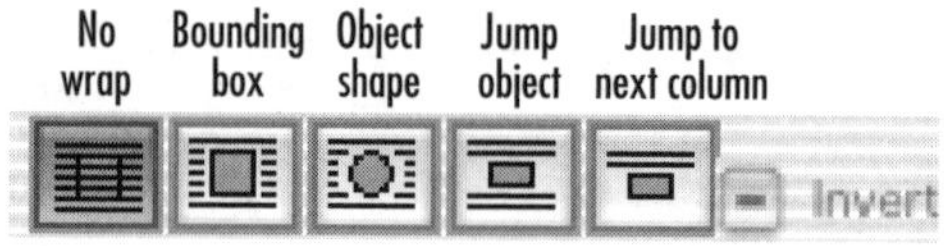
No wrap
Bounding box
Object shape
Jump object
Jump to next column
Invert

❷ *The five different* **text wrap buttons** *let you choose how the text wraps around objects.*

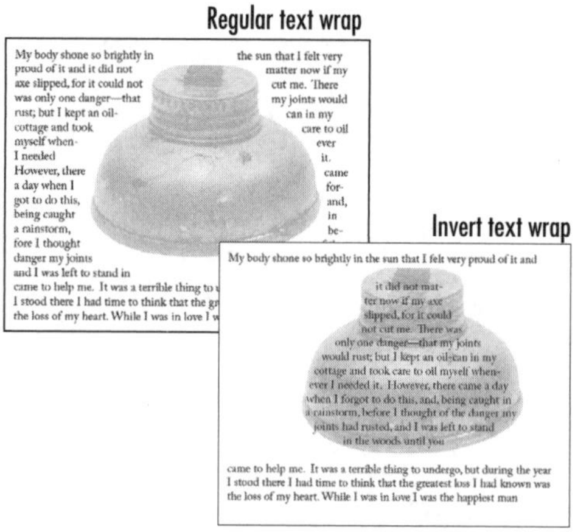
Regular text wrap
Invert text wrap

❸ *When the* **Invert command** *is turned on, the text wrap causes the text to flow inside, not outside, an object.*

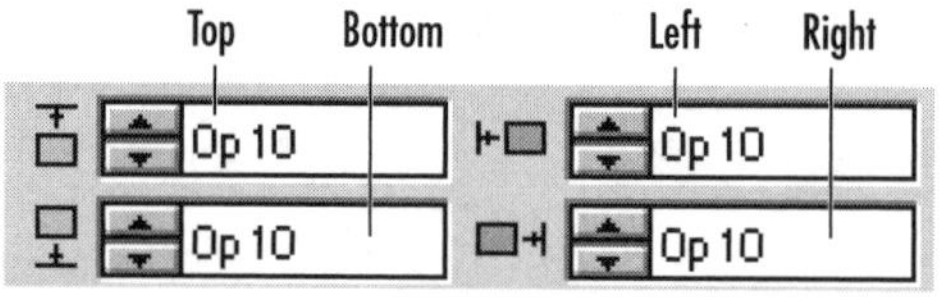
Top
Bottom
Left
Right
0p10
0p10
0p10
0p10

❹ *The text wrap* **Offset controls** *allow you to set the distance between the text and a graphic.*

To apply a text wrap:

1. Select the object that you want the text to wrap around. This can be an imported graphic, a text frame, or an unassigned frame.
2. Choose **Window > Type & Tables > Text Wrap.** This opens the Text Wrap palette ❶.
3. Choose one of the following options for how the text should flow around the object ❷. *(See the chart opposite for a visual representation of each text wrap.)*
   - **No wrap** lets the text flow across the object.
   - **Bounding Box** flows the text around the bounding box for the object.
   - **Object Shape** flows the text around the shape of the frame or the shape of the placed graphic. *(See the exercise on page 234 for more information on setting the Object Shape text wrap.)*
   - **Jump Object** flows the text to the next available space under the object.
   - **Jump to Next Column** flows the text to the next column or text frame.
4. Check Invert to force the text to flow inside the object ❸.
5. Enter an amount in the offset fields to control the distance between the text and the object ❹.

TIP The number of available offset fields depends on the type of text wrap you choose.

Wrap Chosen	Offset available	Results
No Wrap	No offset options available.	There were only four witches in all the Land of Oz, and two of them, those who live in the North and the South, are witches. I know this is true, for I am one of them myself, and cannot be mistaken.
Bounding Box	Top, bottom, left, and right offset options available.	There were only four witches in all the Land of Oz, and two of them, those who live in the North and the South, are good witches. I know this is true, for I am one of them myself, and cannot be mistaken.
Object Shape	Top offset option is the only one available. The amount is used as the space around the entire graphic.	There were only four witches in all the Land of Oz, and two of them, those who live in the North and the South, are good witches. I know this is true, for I am one of them myself, and cannot be mistaken.
Jump Object	Top, bottom, left, and right offset options available. However only the top and bottom offsets affect the text.	There were only four witches in all the Land of Oz, and two of them, those who live in the
Jump to Next Column	Top, bottom, left, and right offset options available. However only the top offset affects the text.	There were only four witches

TIP Unless you change the preference setting *(see page 533)*, lines that wrap below the text wrap object skip to the next available leading increment below the object.

Wrapping Text

When you choose Object Shape for the text wrap, InDesign lets you set the contour options for that shape. This gives you more control over the shape of the text wrap.

To set the text wrap contour options:

1. Use the Direct Selection tool to select the image.

2. Click the Object Shape text wrap button in the Text Wrap palette.

3. Choose Show Options from the Text Wrap palette menu to display the Contour Options at the bottom of the Text Wrap palette.

4. Use the Contour Options Type menu to choose the type of element that should be used to create the text wrap 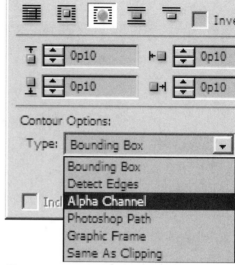:

   - **Bounding Box** uses the rectangle that contains the image.
   - **Detect Edges** uses the differences between the pixels of the image and its background.
   - **Alpha Channel** lets you choose an embedded alpha channel.
   - **Photoshop Path** lets you choose an embedded path.
   - **Graphic Frame** uses the shape of the frame that contains the image.
   - **Same As Clipping** uses whatever shape has been designated as the clipping path for the image *(see page 220)*.

5. If you choose Alpha Channel or Photoshop Path, use the second pop-up menu to choose a specific channel or path.

6. Check Include Inside Edges to make the text wrap inside any holes in the image, path, or alpha channel .

5 *The* **Contour Options Type menu** *lets you choose what type of element controls the shape of the text wrap.*

Finally she picked up her basket. "Come along, Toto," she said. "We will go to the Emerald City

6 *Use the* **Include Inside Edges option** *to have text wrap within the edges of the image, such as within the handles of the basket.*

Wrapping Text

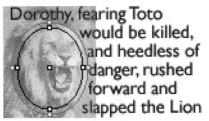

 An example of how an invisible object can be used to create a text wrap.

A text wrap doesn't have to be around visible objects. You can use an object with no fill or stroke as the shape to wrap text around . This creates a special effect for text around an image.

To wrap text around an invisible object:

1. Draw an object with no fill or stroke.

2. Set the Text Wrap to Object Shape.

 *Use the Direct Selection tool to* change the shape of a text wrap path.

Once you set a text wrap, you can still manipulate it so that the text reads more legibly or fits more attractively into the contour of the object. This is called a *custom text wrap*.

To create a custom text wrap:

1. Use either selection tool to select the object that has the text wrap applied to it.

   TIP Apply the Object Shape text set for Graphics Frame *(see page 232)* to create a simple text wrap without a lot of points.

2. Use the Direct Selection tool to move the points on the text wrap path .

   TIP You can preview how the text reflows around the text wrap. Press and hold for a moment before you move the point of the text wrap. You can then see the text reflow as you move the point.

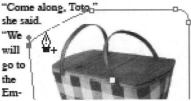

 The plus sign next to the Pen tool *indicates that you can add a point to the text wrap path.*

3. Click the Pen tool between points on the text wrap path to add a new point to the path .

4. Click the Pen tool on a point on the text wrap path to delete the point from the path .

   TIP Hold the Cmd/Ctrl key to access the Direct Selection tool while using the Pen tool.

 *Position the Pen tool over a point and click to* delete points from a text wrap path.

You may find that you don't want some text to be affected by a text wrap. For instance, you might want to have the body text in one frame run around an image but have the text label in another frame appear over the image ⑪. That's when you need to direct the text frame to ignore a nearby text wrap.

To ignore the text wrap:

1. Select the text frame that contains the text that you don't want affected by the text wrap command.

2. Choose **Object > Text Frame Options**. This opens the Text Frame Options dialog box ⑫.

3. Check Ignore Text Wrap. The text in that frame is unaffected by any objects that have a text wrap applied.

TIP Text wrap is applied even if the object that has the wrap is on a hidden layer. Use the Layer Options dialog box to change this so that hidden layers do not exert a text wrap *(see Chapter 11, "Layers," for more information on working with layers)*.

TIP Ordinarily, InDesign's text wrap is applied to text both above and below the object that has the text wrap turned on. Use the text wrap setting in Composition preferences *(see page 533)* to have the text wrap applied only to text below the object. This is closer to how QuarkXPress applies text wrap.

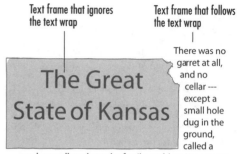

Text frame that ignores the text wrap

Text frame that follows the text wrap

There was no garret at all, and no cellar --- except a small hole dug in the ground, called a cyclone cellar, where the family could go in case one

⑪ *An example of how* **Ignore Text Wrap** *keeps the map title from being affected by the text wrap applied to the outline of the state.*

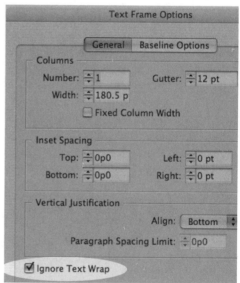

⑫ *The* **Ignore Text Wrap checkbox** *in the Text Frame Options dialog box prevents text from being affected by any text wrap settings.*

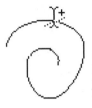

⓭ *The* **Path Type tool** *in the Toolbox is used to add text to a path.*

⓮ *The plus sign next to the Path Type cursor indicates you can click to add text to a path.*

⓯ *Drag the indicator line to move the text along a path.*

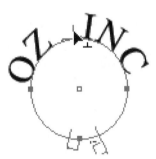

⓰ *The* **center point indicator** *allows you to move text or flip it from one side of the path to another.*

Text on a Path

When you create an object such as a text frame, the outside shape of the frame is considered the object's path. Not only can InDesign fit text inside a text frame, it also lets you position text so that it runs along the outside of the frame.

To run text on the outside of a path:

1. Choose the Path Type tool in the Toolbox **⓭**.
2. Move the tool so that it is near the path. A small plus sign appears next to the tool cursor **⓮**.
3. Click with the Path Type tool. A blinking insertion point appears on the path.
4. Type the text. Use any of the text controls to select or modify the text.

TIP Use the Direct Selection tool to select the path and change its fill or stroke to None to make the path invisible. *(See Chapter 7, "Pen and Beziers," for more information on modifying paths.)*

Once you apply text to a path, you can drag to position the text.

To position text on a path:

♦ Drag the indicator at the start or end of the text on a path to change the start or end point of the text **⓯**.

or

Drag the small indicator within the text to change the center point of the text. **⓰**

TIP You can also drag the center point indicator to the other side of the path.

TIP You can use the Paragraph palette *(see page 67)* to change the alignment of the text between the start and end indicators.

Text on a Path

To apply effects to text on a path:

1. Choose **Type > Type on a Path > Options**. This opens the Path Type Options dialog box ⑰.

2. Use the Effect menu ⑱ to control how the text is positioned in relationship to the path ⑲.

   - **Rainbow** positions the text in an arc along any curves in the path.
   - **Skew** distorts the text vertically as it is positioned along curves in the path.
   - **3D Ribbon** distorts the text horizontally as it is positioned along curves in the path.
   - **Stair Step** aligns the individual baselines of each letter so that the text stays vertical as it is positioned along curves in the path.
   - **Gravity** uses the distortion of the path to distort the text as it is positioned along curves in the path.

3. Click the Flip checkbox to position the text on the other side of the path.

4. If the spacing of the text is uneven, use the spacing control to tighten the character spacing around sharp turns and acute angles on the path.

TIP Higher values remove more space from between the characters.

⑰ *The* **Path Type Options dialog box** *allows you to control how text is applied to a path.*

⑱ *The* **Effect menu** *controls the appearance of the text on the path.*

⑲ *The* **five effect settings** *applied to text on a path.*

Text on a Path

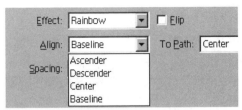

@ *The **Align menu** controls how the text is positioned in relationship to the path.*

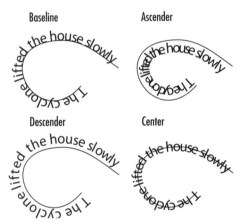

@ *The **Align choices** applied to text on a path.*

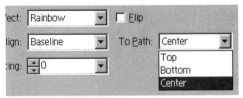

@ *The **To Path menu** positions the vertical alignment of the text on the path.*

@ *The effect of the To Path settings on the position of text on a stroked path.*

You can also control where the letters are positioned vertically on the path.

To set the vertical alignment of text on a path:

1. Use the Align menu @ to control how the text is positioned in relationship to the path @.

   - **Ascender** positions the text so that the tops of the tallest letters touch the path.
   - **Descender** positions the text so that the bottoms of the lowest letters touch the path.
   - **Center** positions the text so that the middle of the text touches the path.
   - **Baseline** positions the text so that the baseline of the text touches the path.

2. Use the To Path menu to position the vertical alignment in one of the following positions @:

   - **Top** positions the text relative to the top of the path's stroke weight @.
   - **Center** positions the text in the middle of the path's stroke weight @.
   - **Bottom** positions the text relative to the bottom of the stroke weight @.

TIP If you do not see any changes between the To Path settings, try increasing the thickness of the stroke weight.

TIP You can also use the Baseline Shift controls *(see page 63)* to move the text up or down relative to the path.

Working with Paragraph Rules

The correct way to create a line above or below a paragraph is with paragraph rules. These are lines that travel with the paragraph and that can be applied as part of style sheets *(see page 368).*

To apply paragraph rules:

1. Select the paragraph to which you want to apply the rule and choose Paragraph Rules from the Paragraph palette menu 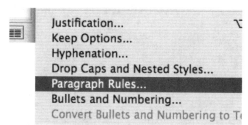. This opens the Paragraph Rules dialog box .

2. Choose Rule Above or Rule Below to specify whether the rule appears before or after the selected paragraph .

3. Check Rule On to activate the rule.

TIP If you want rules both above and below the paragraph, repeat steps 2 and 3.

Why Use Paragraph Rules?

If you want a line (technically called a *rule*) to appear above or below a paragraph, you might draw a line using the Pen or the Line tool. Unfortunately, if the text reflows, that line does not travel with the text. You could also paste the line into the text as an inline graphic *(see page 244)*, but you would not have much control over that line.

The proper way to create lines above or below paragraphs is to use the Paragraph Rules commands. Because the rules are applied as part of the paragraph settings, they automatically move if the paragraph moves. In addition, they can be precisely positioned in relationship to the paragraph.

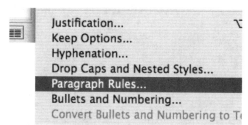

② Use the **Paragraph palette menu** *to open the Paragraph Rules.*

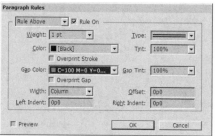

② *The* **Paragraph Rules dialog box** *controls the settings for paragraph lines.*

② *Choose* **Rule Above or Rule Below** *to position the line above or below a paragraph.*

27 *Use the* **Weight control** *to define the thickness of the paragraph rule.*

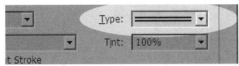

28 *Use the* **Type list** *to choose the stroke style for the paragraph rule.*

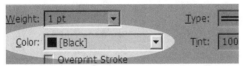

29 *Use the* **Color list** *to choose the main color for the paragraph rule.*

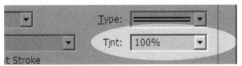

30 *Use the* **Tint control** *to set the screen for the color of the paragraph rule.*

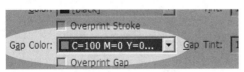

31 *Use the* **Gap Color list** *to set the secondary color of the paragraph rule.*

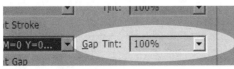

32 *Use the* **Gap Tint control** *to set the screen for the gap color of the paragraph rule.*

Once you have turned on the rule, you can style its appearance. This is somewhat similar to styling the stroke for an object.

To style the appearance of a rule:

1. Set an amount for the weight (or thickness) of the rule **27**.

2. Use the Type list to choose a stroke style for the rule **28**.

TIP In addition to the default stroke styles, this list also displays the custom stroke styles you define for the document *(see page 159)*.

3. Use the Color list to apply a color or gradient swatch to the rule **29**.

TIP The available swatches are those previously defined in the Swatches palette.

TIP Use the Text Color setting to have the color of the rule change automatically if the text color changes.

4. If desired, check Overprint Stroke to set the ink to overprint *(see page 145 for setting overprints)*.

5. If you have chosen a color for the rule, use the Tint controls to create a shade of the color **30**.

6. If you have chosen a rule style that has a gap, use the Gap Color list to apply a color or gradient swatch to the gap **31**. This is similar to setting the Gap Color for strokes, strikethroughs, and underlines.

7. If you have chosen a gap color for the rule, use the Gap Tint controls to create a shade of the gap color **32**.

8. If desired, check Overprint Gap Color to set the gap ink to overprint.

Working with Paragraph Rules

The length of a rule (called its width) can be set to cover the width of the column or the width of the text. The rule can also be set to be indented from the column or text margins.

To control the width of a rule:

1. Choose from the Width list in the Paragraph Rules dialog box as follows ③:

   - **Column** creates a rule that is the same width as the column that holds the text ③.
   - **Text** creates a rule that is the same width of the closest line of text ③.

   TIP If you set a rule below a paragraph that ends in a short line, the rule will be the same length as the last line.

2. Set the Left Indent to the amount that the rule should be indented from the left side of the column or text ③.

3. Set the Right Indent to the amount that the rule should be indented from the right side of the column or text ③.

   TIP Use positive numbers to move the rule in from the margin ③. Use negative numbers to move the rule outside the margin. The rule can extend outside the text frame.

By default the paragraph rule is positioned on the baseline of the text. You can control the position above or below the baseline ③. This is called the *offset* of the rule.

To control the offset of a rule:

- In the Paragraph Rules dialog box, enter a value in the Offset field.

  - For a Rule Above, positive numbers raise the rule above the baseline.
  - For a Rule Below, positive numbers lower the rule below the baseline.

  TIP Negative numbers move rules in the opposite direction.

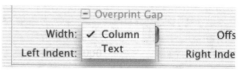

③ *The* **Width list** *lets you choose the length of paragraph rules.*

> "From the Land of Oz," said Dorothy gravely. "And here is Toto, too. And oh, Aunt Em! I'm so glad to be at home again!"   Column

> "From the Land of Oz," said Dorothy gravely. "And here is Toto, too. And oh, Aunt Em! I'm so glad to be at home again!"   Text

③ **Column width** *fits the rule to the width of the column.* **Text width** *fits the rule to the neighboring text.*

③ *The* **Left Indent and Right Indent** fields *let you modify the length of a rule.*

> "From the Land of Oz," said Dorothy gravely. "And here is Toto, too. And oh, Aunt Em! I'm so glad to be at home again!"   No indent

> "From the Land of Oz," said Dorothy gravely. "And here is Toto, too. And oh, Aunt Em! I'm so glad to be at home again!"   Left and right indents

③ *How changing the* **Left and Right Indent** *settings changes the look of rules.*

> "From the Land of Oz," said Dorothy gravely. "And here is Toto, too. And oh, Aunt Em! I'm so glad to be at home again!   No offset

> "From the Land of Oz," said Dorothy gravely. "And here is Toto, too. And oh, Aunt Em! I'm so glad to be at home again!   0p8 offset

③ *Change the* **Offset amount** *to move a rule up or down relative to the text.*

Working with Paragraph Rules

The Guardian of the Gate

It was some time before the Cowardly Lion awakened, for he had lain among the poppies a long while.

35 *A paragraph rule can create the effect of reversed text.*

39 *A dialog box showing the sample settings for a paragraph rule that create the effect of reversed text.*

True Story

When I first started learning page layout software, I used the art director's computer at the advertising agency where I worked. I stayed after hours to explore the programs and create my own documents.

When I saw the command "Rules" in the menu, I figured that was where they kept the laws governing the program. Since I didn't want to mess up the art director's machine, I never chose the command.

It was several years later (and several horrible jobs without any paragraph rules) that I discovered what the "Rules" were.

You can create many special effects with paragraph rules. One of the most common is to superimpose text inside paragraph rules to create the effect of reversed text. Most reversed text is white type inside a black background. However, any light color can be used inside any dark background **35**.

TIP Don't forget that you can also use the underline or strikethough styles to create reversed text *(see page 61)*.

To reverse text using rules:

1. Apply a light color to a line of type.

2. Open the Paragraph Rules dialog box.

3. Create a Rule Below.

4. Set the weight of the rule to a point size large enough to enclose the text. For instance, if the text is 12 points, the rule should be at least 12 points.

TIP If you have more than one line of text, you need to calculate the size of the leading times the number of lines.

5. Set a negative number for the offset value.

TIP The offset amount should be slightly less than the weight of the rule. For instance a rule of 14 points might take an offset of -11 points.

6. Check Preview so you can see the effect of the weight and offset settings you choose.

7. Adjust the weight and offset, if necessary.

8. Click OK to apply the rule **39**.

Working with Paragraph Rules

Inline and Anchored Objects

Another type of nested element is called an *inline object*. An inline object is a frame that is pasted as a character into the actual text.

TIP An inline object can also be used to add images to a table *(see Chapter 13, "Tabs and Tables")*.

To create an inline object:

1. Select the element that you want positioned.

2. Cut or copy the element to the clipboard.

3. Click to place an insertion point where you want the inline object to be positioned.

4. Choose **Edit > Paste**. The element is pasted into the text and flows along with any changes to the text **40**.

TIP Use the Direct Selection tool to move the graphic within its inline frame.

TIP Use the Selection tool to select and move inline objects up or down inside the text.

TIP Use any of the Text Wrap commands to force text around the inline object *(see page 232)*.

You can also place an image directly into the text as an inline object.

To import an image directly as an inline object:

1. Place your insertion point where you would like the graphic to appear.

2. Choose **File > Place** and select the image you want to import. The image appears inside an inline frame.

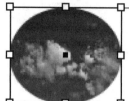

who walked in the forest
This was m
years ago,
before Oz
out of the c
to rule over this land.
"There lived here then,

40 *An* **inline object** *flows along with the text.*

Uses for Inline Objects

The biggest problem with inline objects is that most people forget they are available.

Have you ever wanted to use a little picture instead of a plain bullet? Inline graphics make it easy to add the picture so it flows along with the text.

You can also use an inline object to keep a picture of an author along with her biography.

Inline objects don't have to be graphic elements. You can insert an inline text frame to create two columns of text within a single column story.

Finally, you can paste a horizontal line as an inline graphic to make the fill-in-the-blank lines in a coupon.

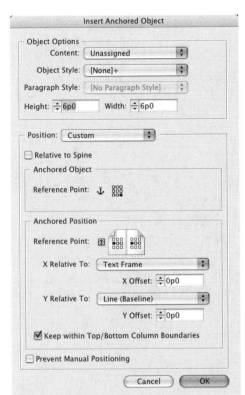

❹ *The* **Insert Anchored Object dialog box** *lets you control the options for an anchored object.*

❷ *The* **Content list** *lets you choose the type of anchored object.*

In addition to inline objects, InDesign also allows you to insert anchored objects into text flow. Anchored objects require a little more preparation but are much more powerful than inline objects.

To create an anchored object:

1. Place the insertion point in the text where you want to anchor the object.

TIP This does not have to be the exact position where you want the anchored object to appear.

2. Choose **Object > Anchored Object > Insert**. The Anchored Object dialog box appears **❹**.

3. Set each of the options for the Anchored Object as described in the following exercises.

4. Click OK to insert the anchored object into the story. An anchored object hidden character symbol appears in the text.

To set the Object Options for an anchored object:

1. Use the Content list to choose the type of object to be anchored. These are the same as the **Object > Content** options.

2. Use the Object Style list to choose a graphic style for the object **❷**. *(See Chapter 15, "Text and Object Styles," for more information on graphic styles.)*

3. If you select Text as the content, use the Paragraph Style list to choose the style for the text. *(See Chapter 15, "Text and Object Styles," for more information on text styles.)*

4. Use the Height and Width controls to set the size of the anchored object.

TIP Anchored objects are always defined as rectangles. You can use any of the drawing tools or the Convert Shape commands to change the rectangle to other shapes.

I divide anchored objects into two different types based on their position on the page.

To set the Position for the anchored object:

◆ Use the Position list to choose the type of positioning for the anchored object 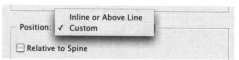:

- **Inline or Above Line** positions the anchored object within the text frame. *(This is similar to the simple inline graphic described on page 244.)*
- **Custom** allows you to position the anchored object outside the text frame.

Once you have chosen the positioning for the anchored object, you can set the options for the location of the anchored object 🄬.

To set the options for inline objects:

1. Click the Inline radio button to specify that option for the object. This removes all the options except the Y Offset.

2. Use the Y Offset controls to move the object above or below the baseline of the text.

TIP Positive numbers move the object above the baseline. Negative numbers move the object below the baseline.

🄬 The **Position list** *lets you choose the location for anchored objects.*

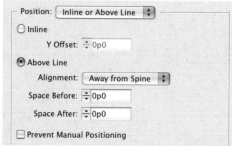

🄬 The Position options for **Inline or Above Line anchored objects**.

Anchored object indicator in the text

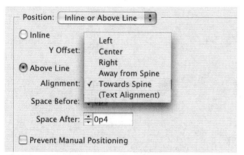

⑤ *An* **Above Line anchored object** *inside a text frame.*

⑥ *The* **Alignment list** *for Above Line anchored objects.*

To set the options for Above Line objects:

1. Click the Above Line radio button to position the object above the line that contains the anchor insertion point **⑤**.

2. Use the Alignment list to position the object in the text frame as follows **⑥**:
   - Right aligns the object on the right.
   - Left aligns the object on the left.
   - Center aligns the object in the center.
   - Text Alignment uses whatever alignment was set for the paragraph that contains the anchored object.

   If you have a facing-page document, you have two additional options. These options flip the anchored object if it is a left- or right-hand page.

   - Away From Spine positions the object so that it is furthest away from the spine.
   - Towards Spine positions the object so that it is closest to the spine.

3. Use the Space Before or Space After control to add space above or below the object.

4. Check the Prevent Manual Positioning option to stop the object from being moved with any of the selection tools.

Inline and Anchored Objects

The other type of anchored object is the custom object. This option offers the most choices for positioning the anchored object.

TIP Honestly, I find the Custom Anchored Objects dialog box baffling **47**. The only way I can apply the settings is to first insert the anchored object and then close the dialog box. Next, with the anchored object still selected, I choose **Object > Anchored Object > Options**. This opens the Options dialog box that has a Preview that lets me see what the settings are doing.

To set the options for custom objects:

1. Use the Anchored Object Reference Point proxy box to choose which point on the anchored object should be used as the orientation of the anchored object.

2. If the document has facing pages, you can choose Relative to Spine to allow the settings to flip depending if they are left- or right-hand pages.

3. Click the Anchored Position Reference Point to choose the position on the page where the object should align.

4. Use the X Relative To list to set the point from which the horizontal axis should start **48**.

5. Use the Y Relative To list to set the point from which the vertical axis should start **49**.

6. Use the X Offset and Y Offset controls to move the anchored object from the X and Y reference points.

7. Select Keep With Top/Bottom Column Boundaries to insure that the anchored object does not move above or below the frame that contains the text.

8. Select Prevent Manual Positioning to prevent the object from being moved.

TIP Custom anchored objects are indicated on the page by a little anchor *(cute)* **50**.

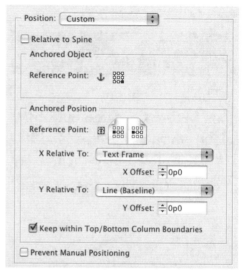

47 The **Custom Anchored Objects dialog box.**

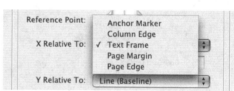

48 The **X Relative list** *for custom anchored objects.*

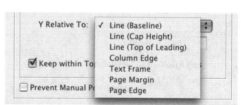

49 The **Y Relative list** *for custom anchored objects.*

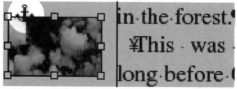

50 The **indicator for custom anchored objects.**

(side tab) Inline and Anchored Objects

Tips for Using for Anchored Objects

Although the settings for custom anchored objects may take a while to master, you should not give up learning to use them. There are quite a few ways to use custom anchored objects.

It is important to remember that custom anchored objects can be positioned well outside the frame of text that contains the anchor position. This lets you use the custom anchored object for marginalia notes or images. Many textbooks, for example, require notes for teacher editions. Custom anchored objects make it easy to insert those notes.

Anchored objects have to start off as rectangles, but once you insert the object, you can apply any of the Convert Shape commands to change their shape. My favorite is to use the Orthogonal Line command to change the anchored object into a stroked line that I can extend down the side of the text frame. This makes it easy to highlight important paragraphs.

Also, you may feel limited that you can insert only one anchored object in the text flow. For example, the illustrations in this book consist of both a graphic frame and a text frame. Fortunately, both of those elements can be made into an anchored object by grouping them and then pasting them into the anchored object.

As I said on the previous page, it's a lot easier to set the options for a custom anchored object if you edit the settings for an existing anchored object.

To edit the settings for an anchored object:

1. Use the Selection tool to select the anchored object.

2. Choose **Object > Anchored Object > Options**. This opens the Anchored Object Options dialog box, which gives you a Preview option in addition to all the settings to control the anchored object.

So what if you want to convert the anchored object into a regular object but position it in the same spot as when it was anchored? I thought I could cut and paste the object to get it out of the text flow. Nope; instead you need to release the anchored object.

To release an anchored object:

1. Use the Selection tool to select the anchored object.

2. Choose **Object > Anchored Object > Release**. This converts the anchored object into an ordinary object.

Inline and Anchored Objects

PAGES AND BOOKS 10

Most people who lay out documents work on projects that have more than one page — booklets, brochures, newsletters, menus, proposals, magazines, books, and so on. Even a lowly business card has two pages if you design a front and back.

When you work with multipage documents, you need to add pages, flow text, apply page numbers, and force text to move to certain pages.

If you are working on very complex documents, you need to make sure all the pages have the same structure.

If you are working on a book, you will want to join individual chapters together. You may also want to automate the process of creating a table of contents or an index.

Here's where you'll learn how to automate and organize working with multipage layouts. In addition, you'll learn how to use InDesign's Book features to synchronize multiple documents in a large project. You'll also discover special features for creating a table of contents from text.

Changing the Pages Palette

You may want to change the display of the Pages palette.

To open the Pages palette:

◆ If the Pages palette is not visible, choose **Window > Pages** to open the palette ❶.

To control the display of the Pages palette:

1. Choose Palette options from the Pages palette menu. This opens the Pages Options dialog box ❷.

2. Use the Pages Icon Size menu to change the size of the document pages icons as they appear in the Pages palette. The four choices are Small, Medium, Large, and Extra Large.

   TIP Small allows you to fit the most number of pages in the smallest palette area.

3. Use the Masters Icon Size menu to change the size of the master page icons. These choices are the same as the Pages Icon Size menu.

4. Uncheck Show Vertically to display the pages horizontally in the palette ❸.

   TIP Turning the Show Vertically option off makes it easier to fit more pages in a smaller palette area.

5. Choose Pages on Top to position the document pages at the top of the palette ❹.

6. Choose Masters on Top to position the master pages at the top of the palette.

7. Use the Resize list to control what happens when you resize the palette:

   • **Proportional** maintains the same relative area as you change the size of the palette.
   • **Pages Fixed** adds new space only to the masters area.
   • **Masters Fixed** adds new space only to the pages area.

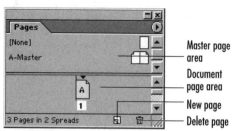

Master page area
Document page area
New page
Delete page

❶ The **Pages palette** *is the command center for multipage documents.*

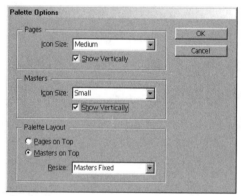

❷ The **Palette Options dialog box** *lets you control the appearance of the Pages palette.*

Horizontal arrangement   Vertical arrangement

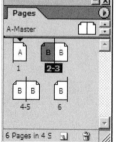 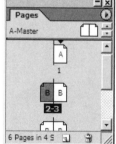

❸ *The Pages palette when* **Show Vertically** *is turned off (left) and turned on (right). More pages are visible in the horizontal orientation.*

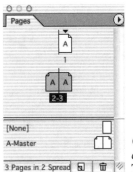

4 *An example of choosing* **Pages on Top.**

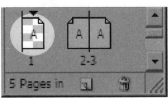

5 *The* **checkerboard grid over a page** *indicates that an effect such as a transparency or a drop shadow has been applied to that page.*

6 *Drag a master page from the master page area of the Pages palette to the document area to add pages to a document.*

Adding Blank Pages

Although you probably specified a certain number of pages before you started your document, you might need to add more pages after you've started working on it. You can add pages as you work or you can add a particular number of pages at a precise location.

TIP A checkerboard grid over the page display in the Pages palette indicates that an effect that requires flattening *(see page 478)* such as a transparency, drop shadow, feather, or Photoshop transparency has been applied on that page **5**.

If you need to add just a few pages, you can add them one by one, manually.

To manually add pages:

1. Click the New Page icon in the Pages palette to add a single page.

   or

   Drag a master page or a nonmaster page from the master page area to the document area of the palette **6**. *(See page 269 for how to work with master pages.)*

2. Repeat as many times as necessary until you have added all the pages you need.

Glossary of Page Terms

As you work with pages and the Pages palette, it helps if you understand the following:

- **Document pages:** The main pages of your document. These are the pages that contain your project. Items that are on the document pages are *document page items.*
- **Master pages:** The pages that contain elements that are repeated on all the document pages. Items that are on the master pages are called *master page items.*
- **Local Overrides:** Normally you cannot select or modify master page items. However, if you apply a local override to the master page items on a specific document page, they can be modified on the document page.

Adding Blank Pages

If you need to add many pages, rather than dragging pages over and over in the Pages palette, you can add them using the Insert command. This also lets you specify where to add the pages.

To add pages using the Insert command:

1. Choose Insert Pages from the Pages palette menu. The Insert Pages dialog box appears .

2. Type the number of pages you want to insert in the Pages field.

3. Choose where to add the pages within the document from the Insert menu as follows 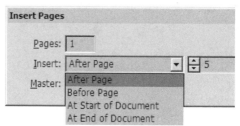:

   - **After Page** lets you insert new pages after a specific page.
   - **Before Page** lets you insert new pages before a specific page.
   - **At Start of Document** inserts new pages at the beginning of the document.
   - **At End of Document** inserts new pages at the end of the document.

4. Use the Master menu to choose the master page that the new pages should be based on.

   or

   Choose None from the Master menu to have an empty page that does not act as a master applied to the new pages.

5. Click OK. The new pages appear in the Pages palette.

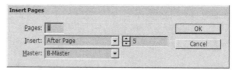

7 The **Insert Pages dialog box** lets you add many pages at once to a document.

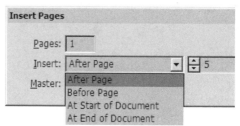

8 The **Insert menu** *gives you specific choices as to where to insert pages.*

Adding Blank Pages

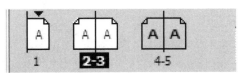

⑨ *The colored highlight on the* **targeted pages** *(pages 4-5) shows they are not the active pages (pages 2-3).*

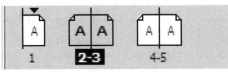

⑩ *The highlight on both the page number and the page for the* **active pages** *(pages 2-3) shows they are both targeted and active.*

Navigating and Moving Pages

As you work with pages in the Pages palette, you should understand the difference between targeting a page and working on a page. The active page is the page you are currently working on. The targeted page is the page chosen in the Pages palette.

To target a page:

◆ Click the page in the Pages palette. A highlight appears on the page **⑨**.

TIP When a page is targeted, it means you can apply a command in the Pages palette even without working on the page.

To work on a page:

◆ Double-click the page number or name of the master page spread in the Pages palette. A highlight appears on the number or name of the page **⑩**.

TIP When you work on the page, that page or spread is centered within the document window.

InDesign has several different ways to move from page to page. If you are accustomed to using QuarkXPress, you may want to navigate using the Pages palette. This method is also handy, as you can position the Pages palette anywhere you want on the screen.

To move to a specific page using the Pages palette:

◆ Double-click the page in the Pages palette that you want to move to. The page is centered within the document window.

or

Double-click the name of the spread to fit both pages in the document window.

TIP You can also scroll or use the Hand tool to move through the document.

Navigating and Moving Pages

You can also use the navigation controls if you don't mind moving down to the bottom of the document window.

To navigate using the window page menu:

◆ Click a page number in the window page menu to navigate through the document **⑪**.

or

Enter a number in the Page field to move to a specific page.

To use the navigation controls:

◆ Click each of the navigation arrows to move through the document **⑫**.

You can also navigate using the commands in the Layout menu in the menu bar at the top of the application.

TIP The major benefit to using the Layout menu commands is that they can be applied using keyboard shortcuts. This makes it easy to move through the document when your hands are on the keyboard.

To navigate using the Layout menu:

◆ Choose one of the following:

* **Layout > First Page** moves to the first page of the document.
* **Layout > Previous Page** moves to the previous page.
* **Layout > Next Page** moves to the next page.
* **Layout > Last Page** moves to the last page of the document.
* **Layout > Next Spread** moves to display the next spread of pages.
* **Layout > Previous Spread** moves to display the previous spread of pages.
* **Layout > Go Back** moves to the page that was previously active.
* **Layout > Go Forward** moves to the page that was active before the Go Back command was applied.

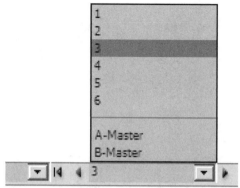

⑪ *The* **pop-up page list** *at the bottom of the document lets you navigate through the document.*

First page Previous page   Next page Last page

⑫ *Use the* **navigation controls** *at the bottom of the document window to move through the document.*

Navigating and Moving Pages

Normally, only 100 pages are seen in the page list. Documents with more than 100 pages will not display some pages. If you hold the Opt/Alt key as you open the Page list, you will see all the pages no matter how long the document is.

If you don't hold the Opt/Alt key, the list will always show the current page, the first and last pages, and five pages before and after the current page.

Once those pages are shown, the list displays all the pages in the document proportionally on either side of the current page. That means if the current page is closer to the end of the document, there will be more pages shown before the current page.

You can also use the Pages palette to duplicate and delete pages from the document.

To duplicate pages:

1. Select the page or spreads you want to duplicate.
2. Drag the pages onto the New Page icon.

   or

   Choose Duplicate Spread from the Pages palette menu.

To delete pages:

1. Use the Pages palette to select the pages.

   TIP Hold the Shift key to select contiguous pages. Hold the Cmd/Ctrl key to select noncontiguous pages.

2. Choose Delete Pages from the Pages palette menu.

   or

   Click the Delete Page icon at the bottom of the Pages palette ❶.

   TIP The command may change to Delete Spreads if you have a spread or spreads selected.

3. When the confirmation dialog box appears, click OK to confirm your choice.

   TIP Hold the Opt/Alt key to bypass the confirmation dialog box.

Navigating and Moving Pages

You can use the Pages palette to change how pages are arranged in the document.

To rearrange pages in a document:

♦ Drag a page next to or between the pages of a spread as follows ⓭:

- With Allow Pages to Shuffle turned on, the new page forces other pages to a new spread ⓮.
- With Allow Pages to Shuffle turned off, the new page is added to the existing spread without moving the other pages ⓯.

TIP The arrow cursor indicates which side of a spine the new page is inserted on ⓭.

One of the limitations of the Pages palette is that it doesn't scroll as you rearrange pages. This makes it difficult to drag pages from one position to another. That's when you should use the Move Pages command.

To move pages in a document:

1. Choose Move Pages from the Pages palette menu. This opens the Move Pages dialog box ⓰.

2. Use the Move Pages field to list the pages you want to move.

TIP Use hyphens to designate contiguous pages. Use commas to separate noncontiguous pages.

3. Use the Destination list to choose one of the following:

- After Page
- Before Page
- At Start of Document
- At End of Document

4. If you have chosen After Page or Before Page, enter the page number in the field.

5. Click OK to move the pages.

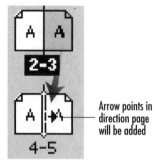

Arrow points in direction page will be added

⓭ *Pages can be moved by dragging their icons in the Pages palette.*

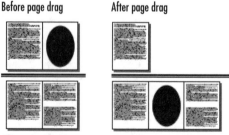

Before page drag   After page drag

⓮ When **Allow Pages to Shuffle is turned on,** *a page moved between two other pages forces one of the pages to the next spread.*

Before page drag   After page drag

⓯ When **Allow Pages to Shuffle is turned off,** *a page moved between other pages is added between the two pages in the spread.*

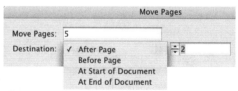

Move Pages

Move Pages: 5
Destination: ✓ After Page   2
              Before Page
              At Start of Document
              At End of Document

⓰ *The* Move Pages *dialog box.*

(sidebar) **Navigating and Moving Pages**

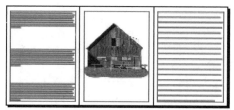

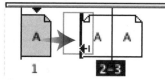

⑰ *An example of how three pages can be put together to form an* **island spread**.

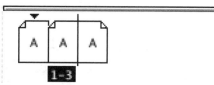

⑱ *The* **thick vertical line** *indicates that the new page will be added as an island spread.*

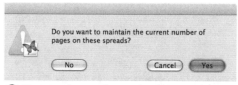

⑲ *An example of an* **island spread** *in the Pages palette.*

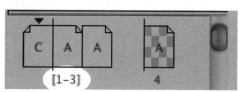

⑳ *You can dismantle an island spread by changing the number of pages in the spread.*

㉑ *The* **brackets around the page numbers** *indicate that the Keep Spread Together option has been applied to the pages.*

Creating and Separating Spreads

Most documents are either single-page or facing-page documents. However, you can create spreads with more than one or two pages. These are *island spreads,* like the fold-outs found in special issues of magazines **⑰**.

To create an island spread:

1. Deselect Allow Pages to Shuffle in the Pages palette menu.

TIP This command is turned off so that the pages that are already in the spread do not move to new positions.

2. Drag a page from the pages area, or a master page, next to the spread. *(See page 268 for working with master pages.)*

3. Release the mouse when the vertical line appears next to the spread **⑱**. This adds the page to the island spread **⑲**.

To dismantle an island spread:

1. Drag each page outside the spread.

   or

   Choose Allow Pages to Shuffle from the Pages palette menu. A dialog box asks if you want to maintain the current number of pages in the spread **⑳**.

2. Click the No button. This dismantles the island spread into the default number of pages per spread in the document.

You can also control whether or not the pages in a spread are kept together or allowed to separate.

To keep the pages in a spread together:

1. Select the spread you want to protect.

2. Choose Keep Spread Together from the Pages palette menu. Brackets appear around the page numbers **㉑**. This prevents the spread from separating if you add pages.

Creating and Separating Spreads

The reverse of keeping spreads together is to separate them from the spine. This method is often used if you need to bleed artwork into the inside margin of a page. If the pages are not separated, artwork that bleeds from a left-hand page would appear on the right-hand page. When the pages don't touch at the spine, the bleed from one page doesn't appear on the other.

TIP This technique is also helpful if you want to rearrange pages as part of manually imposing them into printer spreads.

To separate spread pages:

1. Deselect Allow Pages to Shuffle in the Pages palette menu.

2. Drag a left-hand page to the left of the spread.

   or

   Drag a right-hand page to the right of the spread.

3. Release the mouse button when you see the vertical line outside the spread ㉒. The page will be separated from the other page in the spread ㉓.

To join pages together into a spread:

1. Deselect Allow Pages to Shuffle in the Pages palette menu.

2. Drag a page next to the spine of another page.

3. Release the mouse button as follows:
   • When you see an arrow at the spine point to the right, release the mouse button to create a right-hand page ㉔.
   • When you see an arrow at the spine point to the left, release the mouse button to create a left-hand page ㉕.

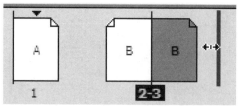

㉒ **Drag a page outside a spread** *to separate a page from the spine of the other page in the spread.*

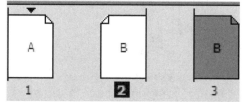

㉓ *The results of* **separating a page** *from the spine of the other page in the spread.*

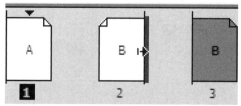

㉔ *You can* **rejoin a page as a right-hand page** *by dragging so that you see an arrow pointing to the right of the spine.*

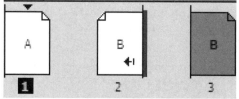

㉕ *You can* **rejoin a page as a left-hand page** *by dragging so that you see an arrow pointing to the left of the spine.*

Creating and Separating Spreads

☑ Show Import Options
☑ Replace Selected Item

26 The **Import options** *in the Place dialog box.*

 27 The **loaded text cursor** *indicates that you can place the imported text.*

Importing Text Files

InDesign lets you import text files saved from Microsoft Word 98 or higher *(see the next page)*. You simply save the file and import it into InDesign.

If you have an earlier version of Word, you should save the text as a RTF (Rich Text Format) document. RTF files retain most of their original formatting and can be imported by InDesign.

InDesign can also import ASCII text. *ASCII* stands for American Standard Code for Information Interchange. This is a standard character-coding scheme used by most computers to display letters, digits, and special characters. It is the most primitive computer text format. For example, when text is saved in the ASCII format, any italic or bold formatting is lost.

Although ASCII text is stripped down, it is useful for importing text from databases or Internet sites. However, you do have to reformat text imported in the ASCII format.

Importing Text

If you have a short amount of text, you can easily type it directly in InDesign's text frames. However, if you are working with long amounts of text, most likely you will want to import the text from a word processing program. You will also want to place the text so that it flows from page to page.

To import text:

1. Choose **File > Place**. The options for placing text are at the bottom of the Place dialog box **26**.

2. Navigate to find the file you want to import.

3. Click Show Import Options to open the specific import options for that type of text file. *(See the next two exercises for specifics on importing Microsoft Word and Microsoft Excel files.)*

4. Click Replace Selected Item to replace the contents of a selected text frame with the new text.

5. Click Open to load the text into a text cursor **27**. *(See pages 264 – 267 for working with the text cursors.)*

TIP If you hold the Shift key as you click Choose, you open the Import Options dialog box even if the option is not checked.

TIP If the text file uses fonts not installed on your computer, an alert box informs you that the fonts are missing. *(See page 361 for more information on replacing missing fonts.)*

Importing Text

The options for importing text change depending on which type of text file you choose to import.

To set the import options for Microsoft Word files:

1. Choose Import Options to open the Microsoft Word Import Options dialog box 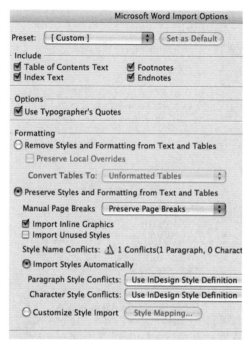.

2. Choose which of the following to include:
   - Table of Contents Text
   - Index Text
   - Footnotes
   - Endnotes.

3. Choose whether quotes should be converted into typographer quotes.

TIP You may want to turn this option off if the text uses plain quote marks to indicate feet (') or inches (").

4. Select Remove Styles and Formatting from Text and Tables to remove the formatting that was applied in Word.

5. If you choose to remove styles and formatting, you can select Preserve Local Overrides to keep attributes such as italic and bold.

6. Use the Convert Table To list to choose one of the following 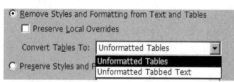:
   - **Unformatted Tables** creates a table with InDesign's default settings.
   - **Unformatted Tabbed Text** converts tables into tab-delimited text.

7. Use the Manual Page Breaks list to control how Word page break commands are handled 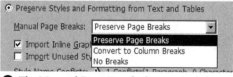.

8. Select Import Inline Graphics to include images inserted into the Word text.

9. The rest of the Word import options deal with text styles. *(See Chapter 15, "Text and Object Styles," for more information on these settings.)*

TIP The import options for RTF files contain the same options as the Microsoft Word Import Choices.

29 *The* **Microsoft Word Import Options** **dialog box** *is used to import Word files.*

29 *The* **Convert Tables To list** *controls how Word tables are converted.*

30 *The* **Manual Page Breaks list** *controls how Word page breaks are converted.*

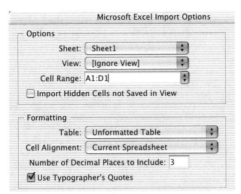

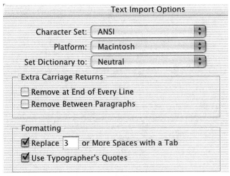

⚃ *The* **Microsoft Excel Import Options dialog box** *is used to import Excel tables.*

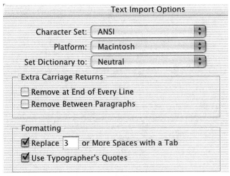

⚄ *The* **Text Import Options dialog box** *is used to import raw ASCII text files.*

You can also set the options for how Microsoft Excel files are imported.

To set the options for Microsoft Excel files:

1. Choose Import Options to open the Microsoft Excel Import Options **⚃**.

2. Choose which parts of the spreadsheet, view, and cells you want to import.

3. Choose what formatting should be imported along with the cells.

TIP Excel files are imported as InDesign tables *(see Chapter 13, "Tabs and Tables").*

Plain text files, such as ASCII files, can also be imported *(see the sidebar, "Importing Text Files," on page 261).*

To set the options for ASCII files:

1. Choose Import Options to open the Text Import Options dialog box **⚄**.

2. Choose the character set, platform, and dictionary to ensure that special characters are imported correctly.

3. Choose how to handle extra carriage (paragraph) returns at the end of lines and paragraphs.

4. Choose how to delete extra spaces inserted into the text.

TIP Most of the extra carriage returns and spaces are created when text is imported from Web pages.

Importing Text

Flowing Text

Once you have imported the text into the loaded text cursor *(see page 261)*, you can choose how the text flows into the document. This allows you to flow text and create pages at the same time.

To import text into a new frame:

◆ Drag the loaded text cursor to create a text frame that contains the text . The straight lines indicate the text will be placed into a new frame.

or

Click the loaded text cursor on the page. InDesign creates a text frame the width of the margins of the page.

TIP To unload the text cursor, choose any tool in the toolbox.

You can place text automatically into text frames that are master page items. This makes it easy to flow text from page to page.

To create master text frames:

◆ Choose Master Text Frame when you first create the document 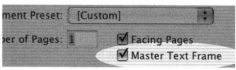. This creates a text frame that fits within the margins of the master page.

To import text into an existing or master frame:

1. Move the loaded text cursor inside the frame.

TIP The text frame does not have to be selected.

TIP The curved lines around the cursor indicates that the text will flow into that frame .

2. Click the loaded text cursor inside the frame. The text flows into the frame.

㉝ *The* **straight lines around the loaded text cursor** *indicates that the text will be placed into a new text frame.*

㉞ *Apply the* **Master Text Frame** *option when you create a new document.*

㉟ *The* **curved lines around the loaded text cursor** *indicates that the text will be placed into an existing frame.*

What Can You Do With a Loaded Cursor?

Once you load a cursor with text, it may seem like all you can do is click to place the text. However, there are some things you can do without losing the text loaded into the cursor. You can:

• Use any of the menu or Pages palette commands to add pages to the document.

• Use the keyboard shortcuts to zoom in or out.

• Use the scroll bars to move through the page or the document.

• Move the onscreen elements, such as the palettes, to new positions.

And remember, never point a loaded cursor at anyone!

Move the loaded cursor inside an existing or master frame to flow text onto a page.

If there is more text than can fit on the page, an overflow (plus sign) symbol appears at the bottom of the frame.

Click the overflow symbol to manually load the overflow text into the cursor.

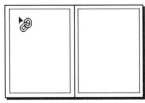

Click the link cursor to flow the text to the next page.

The text flows onto the next page.

If you want, you can import many pages of text so they're linked from one page to another. There are several techniques for flowing the text. The manual method lets you choose exactly where the text should appear. For instance, you can use this method to place text onto noncontiguous pages.

TIP While it is possible to flow text from page to page without a master text frame, it is easier if you have chosen to use a master text frame.

To manually flow text:

1. Import the text so that you have a loaded cursor.

2. Move the cursor inside the area where the master text frame is located.

TIP The cursor displays curved lines when it is within the area of the master text frame **36**.

3. Click inside the area where the master text frame is located. The text fills the frame. If there is more text, an overflow symbol appears at the bottom of the frame **37**.

4. Click the overflow symbol to load the overflow text into the cursor **38**.

5. Move to another page. The cursor changes to a link symbol **39**. Click to flow the text onto that page **40**.

6. If there is additional overflow text, repeat steps 3, 4, and 5 until all the text has been manually flowed onto the pages.

Flowing Text

Flowing text manually is tedious and cumbersome. Rather than manually load the overflow text onto the cursor, you can use the semi-autoflow command to easily load the cursor with the overflow text.

To semi-autoflow text:

1. Import the text so that you have a loaded cursor.

2. Hold the Opt/Alt key to display the semi-autoflow cursor **41**.

TIP The cursor displays curved lines if you place it inside an existing frame **42**.

3. Click inside an existing frame or drag to create a text frame. The semi-autoflow cursor automatically loads any overflow text into a new cursor, which can be placed into a new frame **43**.

4. Hold the Opt/Alt key and click or drag to create another text box linked to the first.

5. Repeat step 4 as many times as necessary to place all the text in the story **44**.

  41 *The* **semi-autoflow cursors** *let you flow text page by page.*

42 *The* **semi-autoflow cursor** *indicates that the text will automatically load any overflow into the text cursor.*

43 *After clicking with the semi-autoflow cursor the text is automatically loaded into a new cursor.*

44 *Each click with the semi-autoflow cursor loads the text onto new pages.*

Flowing Text

Use the **autoflow cursors** *to create all the pages necessary to hold the imported text.*

The **autoflow cursor** *indicates that new pages will be created as the text is imported.*

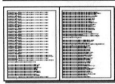

After clicking with the autoflow cursor new pages are created to hold the text.

Use the **fixed-page autoflow cursors** *to flow text only onto the existing pages.*

The **fixed-page autoflow cursor** *indicates the text will flow only onto existing pages in the document.*

The semi-autoflow command may not be practical for flowing more than a few pages of text. If you have many pages of text, you can automatically flow the text and create new pages at the same time using the autoflow feature.

To autoflow pages with text:

1. Import the text so that you have a loaded cursor.

2. Hold the Shift key. This cursor changes to the autoflow text cursor ⑤.

3. Move the cursor over the area inside the margins of the page. The curved autoflow cursor appears ⑥.

4. Click the mouse button. This flows the text onto that page and creates as many additional pages as are necessary to hold all the text ⑦.

TIP Do not select the master text frame before you flow the text or you will lose the ability to autoflow the text.

What if you want to automatically flow text onto the existing pages of a document without adding any new pages? That's what the fixed-page autoflow cursor does. This allows you to import text onto a fixed number of pages and then format the text so that it fits within that number of pages.

To flow text onto a fixed number of pages:

1. Import the text so that you have a loaded cursor.

2. Hold the Shift+Opt/Alt keys. The cursor changes to the fixed-page autoflow cursor ⑧.

3. Click anywhere inside the margins of the page ⑨. This flows the text automatically onto as many pages as are in the document. If there is more text, an overflow symbol appears on the last page.

Flowing Text

You can import dummy text into a frame instead of importing real text.

To add placeholder text:

1. Click inside a frame.

2. Choose **Type** > **Fill with Placeholder Text**. The dummy text fills the frame 🔟.

TIP You can use text for the placeholder by saving a file named placeholder.txt in the InDesign application folder.

Creating Text Breaks

InDesign has special characters that force the text to break to a new position.

To insert break characters:

1. Place the insertion point where you want to jump to the next location.

2. Choose **Type** > **Insert Break Character**.

   or

   Control-click (Mac) or right-click (Win) to choose Insert Break Character from the contextual menu.

3. Choose one of the following from the Insert Break Character menu:

> Lore dionsectet, velit num nit prat verosto eu facin ullan ex ex ero enis at. Duisismod lesequamet eum delisim nisl exeriureet acing ercilla alissed tat.
>
> Lor ad te mincillan hendre feugiat praestio ea amet ip estrud dit in hendignis enim delenim ver sit velisi bla feugue delesequipit ulluptat alis nostrud doluptat. Ut prat luptat alit

🔟 *A sample of the* **placeholder text** *that is used to fill text frames.*

Insert Break Character Shortcuts

Use the following shortcuts to insert break characters:

- **Enter** inserts a column break.
- **Shift-Enter** inserts a frame break.
- **Cmd-Enter** (Mac) or **Ctrl-Enter** (Win) inserts a page break.

Break character	Description	Symbol in text
Column break	Jumps text to the next column. If there is no column in the frame, the column break forces the text to the next page.	⌄
Frame break	Jumps text to the next frame.	⌄⌄
Page break	Jumps text to the next page.	●⌄
Odd page break	Jumps text to the next odd page.	▪⌄
Even page break	Jumps text to the next even page.	▪▪⌄

TIP To see a representation of the break characters, choose **Type** > **Show Hidden Characters**.

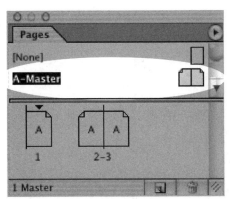

Double-click a master page in the Pages palette to view that **master page in the document window.**

Working with Master Pages

Every new document includes a master page. When you add objects to the master page, they appear on all the document pages based on that master page.

To add objects to a master page:

1. In the Pages palette, double-click the name of the master page 🔵. This opens the master page in the document window.

2. Add text boxes, graphics, or any other elements you want on the master page.

TIP If the document has been set for facing pages, there are two sides to the master page, left-hand and right-hand. The left-hand master page governs the left-hand document pages. Similarly, the right-hand master page governs the right-hand document pages.

3. Double-click the name of the document page to make it the active page. Any items placed on the master page now appear on the document page.

TIP Reopen the master page to make any changes to the master-page elements. Those changes appear on the document pages.

> ### Uses for Master Pages
>
> Master pages allow you to automate page layout changes. For instance, if you have a hundred-page book, you wouldn't want to have to draw a text frame on every page and type the name of the chapter or book title.
>
> Master pages allow you to place an object or frame on the master page and have it appear on all the document pages.
>
> If you place an object on the master page, it will always be positioned in exactly the same spot on every page that has that master applied.
>
> You can also use master pages to store design alternatives such as different column layouts or margin settings.
>
> Think of master pages as the style sheets for pages.

Working with Master Pages

You can have many master pages in a document. This allows you to have different layouts for different parts of your document.

To create new master pages:

1. Choose New Master from the Pages palette menu. This opens the New Master dialog box .
2. Choose a letter for the prefix for the master page.

TIP The prefix is the letter that appears inside the pages that have that master page applied to them.

3. Enter a name for the master page.
4. Use the pop-up menu to set which master page, if any, the new master page should be based on.

TIP Basing one master page on another allows you to make changes on one master page that are applied to the other.

5. Enter the number of pages for the master. This allows you to create spreads that serve as master pages.

TIP To create a new master page without opening the New Master dialog box, hold the Cmd/Ctrl key and click the New Page icon at the bottom of the Pages palette.

As you work, you might want to convert a document page into a master page. InDesign makes it easy to turn a document page into a master page.

To convert a document page to a master page:

1. Select the page or pages.
2. Drag the page or pages from the document area to the master page area 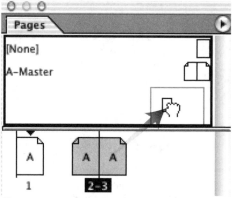.

   or

   Choose Save as Master from the Pages palette menu.

The New Master dialog box allows you to set the attributes for the master page.

Drag a document page into the master page area to convert the document page to a master.

Strategies for Basing Master Pages on Each Other

I have three master page spreads for this book. One master — the main master — holds only the guides and page numbers for the book. The master for ordinary pages is based on that main master. The master for the chapter opener is also based on that main master.

That way, if I need to move the page numbers I only need to change the page number on the main master. The other masters update automatically.

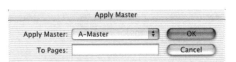

54 *The* **Apply Master dialog box** *allows you to change the master that governs pages.*

55 *The* **rectangle around the single page** *indicates that the master will be applied to that page only.*

56 *The* **rectangle around the spread** *indicates that the master will be applied to the spread.*

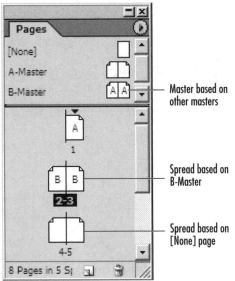

Master based on other masters

Spread based on B-Master

Spread based on [None] page

57 *The* **letters inside the page icons** *indicate what masters are applied to pages or other masters.*

New pages are based on the master page applied to the last existing page of the document. You can easily change the master page that governs pages.

To apply a new master to a page:

1. Select the page or pages.
2. Choose Apply Master to Pages from the Pages palette. This opens the Apply Master dialog box **54**.
3. Use the Apply Master menu to apply a master to the pages.
4. Use the To Pages field to change the selected pages.

TIP Selecting None creates pages that have no master page applied.

To apply masters with the Pages palette:

◆ Drag the master page onto the document pages as follows:
   • To apply to a single page, drag the master page icon onto the page. A rectangle appears around the page **55**.
   • To apply to a spread, drag the master page icon onto the spread. A rectangle appears around the spread **56**.

You can also base one master page on another using the Pages palette.

To base masters on existing masters:

1. Create a new master or spread.
2. Drag one master page onto another.
   • To base the spread on the master, drag the master onto the spread.
   • To base one page on the master, drag the master onto a single page.
3. Release the mouse button. The prefix of the master appears inside the second master page **57**. The prefix indicates that the master page governs the other master page.

Working with Master Pages

Ordinarily you modify the elements of a master page only on the master page itself. The elements on the document pages are protected from being selected or modified. However, you can release that protection and modify the master elements by creating local overrides.

To modify master elements on document pages:

1. Hold Cmd/Ctrl-Shift and click the element you want to modify. This releases the protection and selects the element.

2. Make any local override changes to the element.

TIP An object can still have some links to the master page even if local overrides have been applied (*see "Overriding Master Page Elements" on this page*).

You might want to modify all the master elements on a page. Rather than release each item one by one, InDesign lets you do it with a single command.

To release all master elements on a page:

♦ Choose Override All Master Page Items from the Pages palette menu. This releases the objects so they can be modified on the document page.

Once you have created a local override on a master page element, it may still have links to the original master page item. If you want, you can completely sever all ties between the master page item and the item on the document page.

To separate an item from the master item:

1. Select the object that has been released from the master page.

2. Choose Detach Selection From Master in the Pages palette menu. Any changes you make on the master page will no longer be applied to that object.

Overriding Master Page Elements

If you modify a master page element on a document page, the local override loses its link to the master page element. However, the element may have partial links to the master page element.

Let's say you add a stroke to an object on the document page. From that point on, the stroke of the element is removed from the control of the element on the master page.

But other attributes of the element maintain their link to the master page item. For instance, the position of the element maintains a link to the master page item. So if you move the element on the master page, the item on the document page also moves.

Similarly, the fill color of the elements on the document pages changes if you change the master page element. Only the formatting for the stroke is separated from the master page element.

How Many Master Pages?

While it may seem like a lot of work to set up master pages, the more masters you have the easier it is to lay out complicated documents.

A weekly magazine can easily have 50 or more master pages — some for special editorial spreads and others for different types of advertising spaces.

Some publishers insist that every page must be based on a master and do not allow any modifications of the master page elements. Others let the designers override the master pages.

You decide which way best suits your work habits and the project.

Stacking Order of Master Page Items

The items on the master page are always behind any new items you may put on a page. But when you release the master page items from the master page, they always spring to the front of the document page.

If you want, you can use the Object > Arrange menu to change the stacking order of the items. However, if you release many items on many pages, it may seem cumbersome to move them backwards.

Instead, create two layers in your document (*see Chapter 11, "Layers"*). Put all the master page elements on the bottom layer, and your regular document objects on the top layer. That way when you release the master page items, they will not move in front of your regular page items.

Of course you can also separate all the objects on a page from their links to the master page items.

To separate all the master items on a page:

1. Use the command, Override All Master Page Items, to first release all the master page items from the master page.

2. Choose Detach All Objects From Master in the Pages palette menu. This severs any remaining link between the item and the master page.

TIP Only those items that were released from the master page can then be detatched from the master page. If an item is unreleased from the master page, it cannot be detatched.

You can also hide master page items on document pages so they do not print.

To change the display of master page items:

◆ Choose Hide Master Items from the Pages palette menu.

or

Choose Show Master Items from the Pages palette menu.

InDesign also lets you quickly clear all local overrides and reapply the master page items to the document page.

To remove local overrides and reapply the master:

◆ Choose Remove All Local Overrides in the Pages palette menu. All local override elements will be deleted and the master page items will be reapplied.

Adjusting Layouts

You certainly are not expected to set layouts perfectly the first time, or every time. Fortunately, InDesign has a powerful layout adjustment feature that moves and resizes objects as you change the page size or margins.

Once layout adjustment is turned on, any changes to the layout will alter the position of the elements on both the master pages and the document pages.

To set the layout adjustment options:

1. Choose **Layout > Layout Adjustment.** This opens the Layout Adjustment dialog box 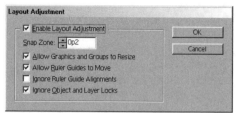.

2. Check Enable Layout Adjustment so that elements change position when page size, orientation, margins, or columns are changed ⑤.

3. Set a value for the Snap Zone to specify how close an object must be before it will align and move to a margin or column guide, or page edge.

4. Check Allow Graphics and Groups to Resize so that elements change size as well as move during the adjustment.

5. Check Allow Ruler Guides to Move to have ruler guides move as part of the layout adjustment.

6. Check Ignore Ruler Guide Alignments to keep objects from moving along with ruler guides.

7. Check Ignore Object and Layer Locks to move objects that are locked or on locked layers.

8. Click OK to set the options. The document will change according to the new settings when the document setup or margins are changed.

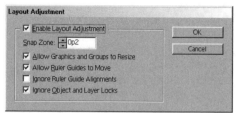

⑤ *The* **Layout Adjustment dialog box** *controls which elements change if you change document attributes such as the page size or margins.*

⑤ *When* **Enable Layout Adjustment** *is turned on, the items on the page adjust their size and position when the margins and page size are changed.*

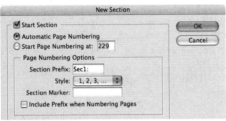

60 *The* auto page number character *appears as a letter on master pages but as a number on document pages.*

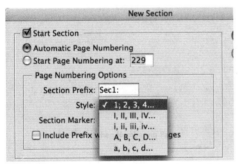

61 *The* **New Section** *dialog box lets you change the formatting and numbering of pages.*

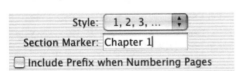

62 *The* **Style menu** *allows you to choose different formats for page numbering of a section.*

| Style: | 1, 2, 3, ... |
| Section Marker: | Chapter 1 |

☐ Include Prefix when Numbering Pages

63 *The entry in the* **Section Marker** field *allows you to create custom labels for pages.*

Working with Page Numbers

The most common element that is added to a master page is the page-number character.

To add automatic page numbering:

1. Draw a text frame on the master page where you want the page number to appear.

2. Choose **Type > Insert Special Character > Auto Page Number**. This inserts a special character in the text frame **60**.

TIP The auto page number character is the prefix for the master page *(see page 269)*.

3. If the master page is a facing-page master, repeat steps 1 and 2 for the other side.

You may want to change the format of page numbers or the number they start from. You do that by creating a new *section*.

To create a document section:

1. Move to the page where you want the section to start.

2. Choose **Layout > Numbering & Section Options**. The New Section dialog box appears **61**.

3. Check Start Section to open the options.

4. Type the label (up to five characters) for the section in the Section Prefix field.

5. Choose Include Prefix when Numbering Pages to add the section prefix to the page number.

6. Use the Style pop-up list to set the format for the numbering **62**.

7. Choose the Page Numbering options:
   - **Automatic Page Numbering** continues the count from the previous pages.
   - **Start Page Numbering At** lets you enter a specific number to start the section from.

8. Enter a label for the Section Marker **63**. *(See the steps on the next page for how to work with the section marker.)*

Working with Page Numbers

Once you have created an entry for the section marker *(see previous page)*, you need to insert a section marker character to see the entry on document pages.

To add a section marker character:

1. Place the insertion point in a text frame where you want the section marker to appear.

TIP The text frame can be on a master page or a document page.

2. Choose **Type** > **Insert Special Character** and then choose Section Marker from the menu.

TIP If the text frame is on the master page, the word "Section" appears on the master page. If the text frame is on the document page, the label for the section marker appears ⓺.

You can also insert special characters that create jump lines that show the page where the text flow continues to or from.

To create a continued to/from page number:

1. Place the insertion point in a text frame that touches the frame that holds the story.

2. Choose **Type** > **Insert Special Character** and then choose one of the following:

   • **Next Page Number** inserts the number of the page that the text jumps to or continues on ⓺.

   • **Previous Page Number** inserts the number of the page that the text continued from ⓺.

TIP The continued to/from character needs a separate text frame so that if the text reflows, the continued to/from character doesn't move along with the text.

TIP The continued to/from characters only insert the page number. You have to type "Continued on" or "Continued from" yourself.

⓺ *The* **section marker** *appears as the word "Section" on master pages but as the label on document pages.*

⓺ *The* **Next Page Number** *character shows the page number that the story is continued on. The overlapping area is where the page number frame touches the story frame.*

⓺ *The* **Previous Page Number** *character shows the page number that the story comes from. The overlapping area is where the page number frame touches the story frame.*

Absolute or Section Numbering?

What if you create a document that has its first section start on page i and then starts a new section that starts on page 1? This could create some confusion if you try to print page "one." Which "one" would you print?

Fortunately, InDesign has a preference setting that allows you to change the section numbering to absolute numbering *(see page 527)*. This makes it easier to avoid confusion if a document has multiple sections that start with the same number.

Working with Page Numbers

The Wizard of Oz

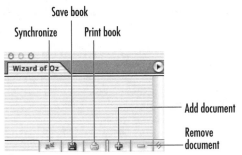

⑥⑦ *A saved book document has its own document icon.*

⑥⑧ *An empty* **Book palette** *displays the name of the book on its palette tab.*

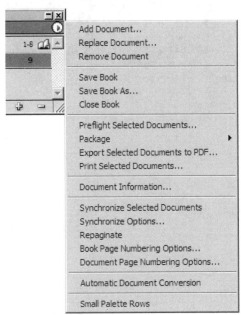

⑥⑨ *The* **Book palette menu** *contains commands for working with books and book documents.*

Making Books

Most people who create long documents break them up so that each chapter is contained in its own document. They need a way to coordinate the page numbers, colors, and styles. An InDesign *book* is an electronic file that keeps track of all those documents.

To create an electronic book file:

1. Choose **File > New > Book**.

2. Use the dialog box to name the book document and save it in a location **⑥⑦**. The Book palette appears **⑥⑧**.

TIP The tab for the Book palette contains the name of the book.

Once you have created the book file, you can then add documents that make up the book.

TIP You don't have to create the book file first. For instance, I created these chapters before I added them to a book document.

To add documents to a book:

1. Click the Add Document button at the bottom of the Book palette.

   or

   Choose Add Document from the Book palette menu **⑥⑨**.

2. Use the dialog box to find the document you want to add to the book. The name of the chapter appears in the Book palette.

3. Repeat steps 1 and 2 to add other documents to the book.

To remove documents from a book:

1. Select the documents you want to remove.

2. Click the Remove Document button at the bottom of the Book palette.

   or

   Choose Remove Document from the Book palette menu.

Making Books

You can use the Book palette and Book palette menu to open, rearrange, and control the documents that make up the book.

To open documents in a book:

◆ Double-click the name of a document in the Book palette. The open book symbol next to the name indicates that the document is open 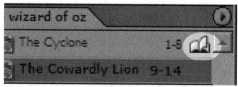.

⑦⓪ *The* **open book icon** *indicates that a document of the book is open.*

The order that documents are listed in the Book palette determines the page numbers of the book.

To change the order of the documents in a book:

◆ Drag the name of a document in the Book palette to a new position in the palette 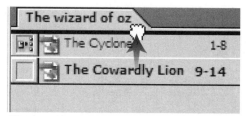.

⑦① **Drag a listing in the Book** *palette to change the order that the document appears in the book.*

One of the benefits of creating a book document is that you can have one file control the style sheets *(see page 368)* and colors *(see Chapter 5, "Working in Color")* for the other documents in the book. If you make changes to the style source file, all the other files synchronize to that file.

To set the style source for a book document:

◆ Click the Style Source box next to the name of the file that you want to control the rest of the documents in the book 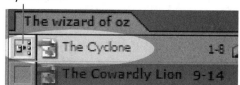.

Style source icon

⑦② *The* **style source file** *is used to synchronize the style sheets and colors for other documents in a book.*

To synchronize files to the style source:

◆ Click the Synchronize button in the Book palette.

or

Choose Synchronize Book in the Book palette menu.

TIP The menu command says Synchronize Selected Files if only some of the files in the book are selected.

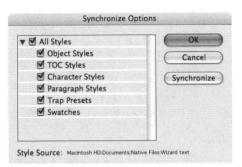

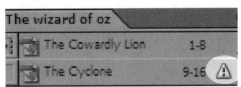

Style Source: Macintosh HD:Documents:Native Files:Wizard text

73 *Use the* **Synchronize Options dialog box** *to set which attributes of the style source file will be applied to the files in the book.*

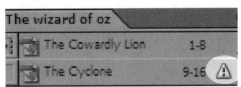

74 *The* **Alert icon in the Book palette** *indicates that the file has been modified.*

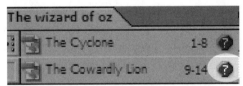

75 *The* **Missing icon in the Book palette** *indicates that the file has been moved after it was imported into the book.*

To set the synchronizing options:

1. Choose Synchronize Options from the Book palette menu. The Synchronize Options dialog box opens **73**.

2. Choose the options that you want to apply from the style source document.

If the book is closed when you modify the files in the book, you need to update them when you do reopen the book document.

TIP This step is not necessary if you modify book files while the book document is open.

To update files in a book:

1. Choose **File > Open** and then navigate to the book document you want to work on.

2. Use the Book palette to open, then modify any files in the book document. An Alert icon appears next to the modified files **74**.

   or

   Use the Open command in the File menu to open, then modify any files in the book document.

3. If necessary, synchronize the files to the style source document *(see previous exercise)*.

You can also replace missing files in a book or swap one file for another.

TIP A Missing icon indicates that the file has been moved after being added to the book **75**. The Replace command lets you relink the missing file to the Book palette.

To replace a file in a book:

1. Select the file in the Book palette that you want to replace.

2. Choose Replace Document from the Book palette menu.

3. Navigate to find the file you want to replace or relink.

4. If necessary, synchronize the files.

Making Books

Files in a book automatically run in consecutive numbers. As you add or delete pages in one document, the page numbers in the rest of the book adjust. You can control how the page numbers are adjusted.

To set how page numbers are adjusted:

1. Choose Book Page Numbering Options from the Book palette menu to open the dialog box ⓰.

2. Choose the Page Order options as follows:

   - **Continue from previous document** starts new pages sequentially from the end of the previous listing.
   - **Continue on next odd page** always starts new pages on an odd number.
   - **Continue on next even page** always starts new pages on an even number.

3. If using the odd or even options results in a skipped page, check Insert Blank Page.

4. Deselect Automatic Pagination to stop InDesign from automatically numbering the files in a book.

To set the numbers for each document in a book:

1. Choose Document Page Numbering Options from the Book palette menu to open the dialog box ⓱.

2. Choose Automatic Page Numbering to number pages as they appear in the Book palette.

   or

   Choose Start Page Numbering At to set a specific page number to start that document on.

3. Set the rest of the options as described on page 275.

To force the pagination in a book:

◆ Choose Repaginate from the Book palette menu.

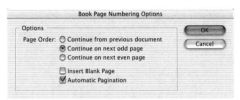

⓰ *Use the* **Book Page Numbering Options** **dialog box** *to set how pages shall be numbered in a book.*

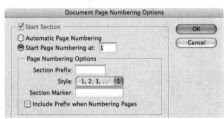

⓱ *Use the* **Document Page Numbering** **Options dialog box** *to set how an individual document is numbered in a book.*

Making Books

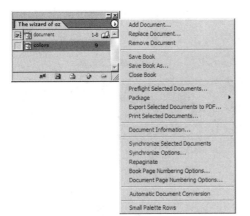

78 *If you select individual files in the Book palette list, the Book palette commands are applied only to the selected files.*

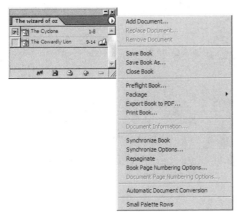

79 *With no document files selected, the Book palette commands are applied to all the book files.*

The Book palette also lets you apply printing and output commands to all the files in a book.

To print a book:

◆ Choose Print Book from the Book palette menu. *(See Chapter 19, "Output," for more information on printing files.)*

or

Click the Print icon in the Book palette.

To preflight a book:

◆ Choose Preflight Book from the Book palette menu. *(See page 486 for more information on the preflight command.)*

To package a book:

◆ Choose Package from the Book palette menu. *(See page 489 for more information on the package command.)*

To export the book files as a PDF:

◆ Choose Export Book to PDF from the Book palette menu. *(See page 493 for more information on the exporting as a PDF.)*

The Book palette menu commands change depending on which files are selected in the Book palette **78**.

To control what parts of a book are changed:

◆ Select the files in the book as follows:
  - Hold the Shift key and click to select contiguous files.
  - Hold the Cmd/Ctrl key and click to select noncontiguous files.
  - Click the area below the files to deselect the file. This applies commands to all the files in the book **79**.

Making Books

Creating a Table of Contents

InDesign creates a table of contents (TOC) by looking at the styles applied to paragraphs and then listing the text and page numbers for those paragraphs. The TOC for this book lists the chapters and the section heads ⑧⓪.

To prepare a document for a table of contents:

1. Add the page or pages that will hold the TOC.

TIP Most tables of contents are part of the frontmatter of a book and are numbered separately without affecting the regular page numbering.

TIP If the document is part of a book, make sure the book's pagination is current.

2. Apply paragraph styles to the paragraphs that you want to appear in the TOC. *(See page 368 for more information on paragraph styles.)*

To define the styles for TOC entries:

1. Choose **Layout > Table of Contents** to open the Table of Contents dialog box ⑧①.

2. Set the Title and Listing controls as described in the exercises that start on the next page.

3. Click Save Style. This opens the Save Style dialog box ⑧②.

4. Name the style and click Save.

To generate the TOC:

1. Choose **Layout > Table of Contents** to open the Table of Contents dialog box.

2. Set each of the controls as described in the following exercises.

3. Click OK. This closes the dialog box and creates a loaded text cursor that contains the TOC.

4. Click or drag the loaded cursor to apply the TOC text where you want it to appear in the document.

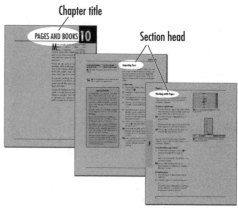

Chapter title

Section head

⑧⓪ *The paragraph styles applied to chapter titles and section heads in this book can be used to create a table of contents.*

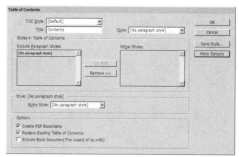

⑧① *The* **Table of Contents dialog box** *lets you select and format listings for a table of contents.*

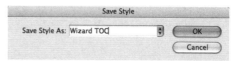

⑧② *The* **Save Style dialog box** *lets you save the settings from the Table of Contents dialog box.*

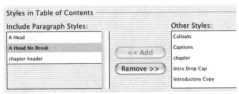

83 *Use the* **Title field in the Table of Contents** *dialog box to enter the text you want to appear before the listings.*

84 *Move styles from the Other Styles list to the* **Include Paragraph Styles list** *to choose which paragraphs are added to the table of contents.*

Benefits of an Automatic TOC

If all this seems like too much work just to create a short table of contents, you may be tempted to create one by hand—manually entering the items in the TOC.

For instance, I could easily create the TOC for this book by hand.

But there is a big benefit in creating an automatic TOC. When you export PDF files with an automatically created TOC, they will have hyperlinks from the TOC to the document pages. *(See Chapter 18, "Interactive PDF Elements," for more information on adding hyperlinks and other interactive elements to InDesign files.)*

This means someone reading the PDF document can just click on the page number listed in the TOC to go to that specific page. Without the electronic TOC, you'd have to manually add all those links in Acrobat.

The title is the label that is applied before each entry in the table of contents. You can set the type for the title as well as the paragraph style that formats the title.

To enter the title of the table of contents:

1. Type the text for the title in the Title field **83**.

2. Use the Style menu to the right of the Title field to choose which paragraph style is applied to format the title.

You choose the entries for a table of contents by selecting the paragraph style sheets that were applied to those sections of your documents.

To choose the listings for the table of contents:

1. Select a paragraph style listed in the Other Styles area of the Table of Contents dialog box **84**.

2. Click the Add button. This moves the style to the Include Paragraph Styles list.

3. Repeat steps 1 and 2 for any additional styles.

Most likely you will want to format the entries in a table of contents with a different style than the one used within the document.

To format the entries in the table of contents:

1. Select the entry listing in the Include Paragraph Styles area.

2. Choose a paragraph style sheet from the Entry Style menu under the Style: [Name] in the Table of Contents dialog box ⑧⑤.

3. Repeat steps 1 and 2 for any additional styles.

The Table of Contents dialog box has additional controls for more advanced options such as formatting the page numbers for each entry.

To open the additional table of contents controls:

◆ Click the More Options button in the Table of Contents dialog box ⑧⑥. This opens the advanced options at the bottom of the dialog box ⑧⑦.

TIP If the button says Fewer Options, then the dialog box already shows the advanced options.

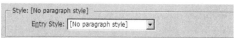

⑧⑤ *Use the* **Entry Style menu** *to choose a style sheet that you have created to format the listing as it should appear in the table of contents.*

⑧⑥ *Click the* **More Options button** *to expand the controls in the Table of Contents dialog box.*

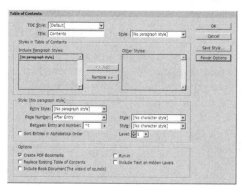

⑧⑦ *The* **Table of Contents dialog box** *with all the options available.*

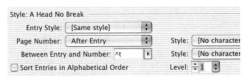

88 *The* **Style options area** *gives you controls to format how the entries are formatted and arranged in the TOC.*

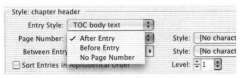

89 *The* **Page Number menu** *controls where the page number will appear in the TOC listings.*

Other Uses for a Table of Contents

You're not limited to using the Table of Contents commands just for listings of chapters and section heads.

If you have a sales catalog you can use the commands to create a list of all the items, which can be used as a price list. I could generate a separate file for this book that lists all the titles for sidebars such as this one. In a book of illustrations, you can use it to create a list of names of all the artists for each illustration.

The only thing you need to remember is to assign a style sheet to each item that you want to appear in the table of contents.

With the advanced options open, you have additional controls for the style for each entry in the TOC **88**. This gives you greater control over where the page numbers appear and how they are formatted.

To set the advanced Style options for each entry:

1. Choose one of the styles in the Include Paragraph Styles list *(on page 368)*. The style name appears in the Style options area.

2. If you have not already applied a listing from the Entry Style menu, do so as explained on the previous page.

3. Use the Page Number menu to choose a position for the entry's page number **89**:
   - **After Entry** positions the number after the entry.
   - **Before Entry** positions the number before the entry.
   - **No Page Number** lists the entry without any page number.

4. If desired, choose a character style for the page number from the Style list to the right of the Page Number menu.

   TIP The character style lets you apply formatting to the page number for each entry. *(See page 375 for working with character styles.)*

You can also control how the entry name and the page number are separated from each other.

To control the separator character:

1. Select one of the character options from the Between Entry and Number menu **88**. The character symbol appears in the field.

2. If you want, type additional text before or after the character symbol. This lets you add a label before the page number.

3. If desired, apply a style from the Style menu for the Between Entry and Number character **88**.

A table of contents doesn't have to be organized in the order that the items appear.

To alphabetize the table of contents:

◆ Check Sort Entries in Alphabetical order from the advanced options area ⓫.

To indent the entries in a table of contents:

◆ Use the Level controls to indent each table of contents entry ⓫.

TIP Each entry in the Include Paragraph Styles list is automatically indented. This is for display purposes in that dialog box and does not affect the final TOC.

There are additional options you can set for a table of contents ⓽.

To set the table of contents options:

◆ Select each of the table of contents options at the bottom of the Table of Contents dialog box as follows:

 • **Create PDF Bookmarks** adds bookmarks to the PDF that is created from the TOC. This is in addition to any hyperlinks within the TOC.
 • **Replace Existing Table of Contents** lets you update or change the table of contents that has already been placed in the document.

TIP This option is only available if a table of contents has already been generated.

 • **Include Book Documents** lets you create a table of contents for all the documents in a book.
 • **Run-in** creates a single paragraph table of contents with each entry divided by a semicolon (;) and a space.
 • **Include Text on Hidden Layers** uses text that is on layers that are not visible. *(See the sidebar on this page to see how option this could be used.)*

Options
- ☑ Create PDF Bookmarks
- ☐ Replace Existing Table of Contents
- ☐ Include Book Documen(The wizard of oz.indb)
- ☐ Run-in
- ☐ Include Text on Hidden Layers

⓽ *The* **TOC Options area** *lets you control more of the table of contents.*

A TOC of Nonexisting Items

The following tip comes from *Real World InDesign CS2,* by Olav Martin Kvern and David Blatner (Peachpit Press, copyright 2006). I strongly recommend this book for anyone who wants a deeper understanding of InDesign.

The items in a TOC don't have to be from items that are visible on each page. For instance, let's say you want a list of all photographers in your book and where their pictures appear. Simply put the names of the photographers next to their photos, but set the names to not print *(see page 460)* or on a layer set to not print *(see page 293)*.

Then, run the TOC for the items. You get a list of the photographers' names, even though those names don't actually appear on the printed pages.

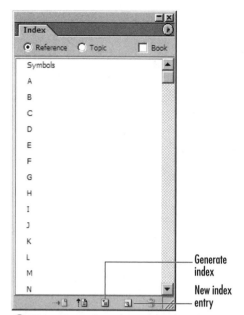

⑨ *The* **Index palette** *lets you define those items that should be part of the index.*

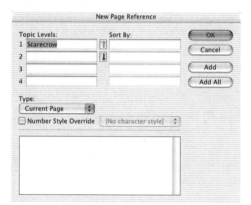

⑨ *Use the* **New Page Reference dialog box** *to add specific index entries to the Index palette.*

From the far north they hear
Uncle Henry and Dorothy co
waves before the coming sto

⑨ *An* **index reference marker** *is visible in the text when Show Hidden Characters is chosen.*

Creating an Index

There are different ways to create an index in InDesign. The simplest way is to add index references to the words or phrases you want to appear in the index.

TIP The following exercises are just the start of working with indexes. For more information, see *Real World Adobe InDesign CS2,* published by Peachpit Press.

To apply an index reference to text:

1. Highlight the text entry that you want to be indexed. For instance, if you want to find all instances of "Aunt Em" in the Wizard of Oz, you would highlight a single instance of "Aunt Em" in one place.

2. Choose **Window > Type & Tables > Index** to open the Index palette **⑨**.

TIP The palette does not show the alphabet until you have already entered one reference.

3. Click the Reference button at the top of the palette.

4. Click New Index Entry or choose New Page Reference in the Index palette menu. The New Page Reference dialog box appears **⑨**.

5. Click the Add button to add just that instance of the text to the Index palette.

   or

   Click the Add All button to add all the instances of the text to the Index palette.

6. Click Done to return to the document. An index reference marker appears before the referenced text **⑨**.

7. Repeat these steps for each entry that you want added to the Index palette.

TIP The Index palette shows referenced text along with the page numbers that the text appears on.

Once you have all the index references in the document, you can then generate the index text file.

To generate an index file:

1. Click the Generate Index button.

   or

   Choose Generate Index from the Index palette menu. The Generate Index dialog box appears .

2. In the Title field, enter the text that you want for the title of the index .

3. Use the Title Style menu to choose a paragraph style for the formatting of the index title.

4. If you have already created an index, check the Replace Existing Index to replace the original index.

5. If the document is part of a book, check Include Book Documents to add those documents to the index.

6. Check Include Entries on Hidden Layers to include the text on hidden layers in the index.

7. Click OK. This closes the dialog box and creates a loaded text cursor that contains the index.

8. Click or drag to apply the index text where you want it to appear in the document.

94 *The* **Generate Index dialog box** *lets you create the index text file.*

95 *The* **index options** *in the Generate Index dialog box.*

The Art of an Index

An index is much more than just a list of entries in a document. There is an art to creating a good index. You need to understand the meaning of the index entries and anticipate the terms readers will want to search for.

Quite frankly, most designers are not prepared to create a truly elegant and useful index. In fact, I hire a professional indexer who reads my books and creates an index for me. The result is not electronic, but I wouldn't do it any other way. Thanks, Joy!

LAYERS 11

When I was in advertising, we used to lay clear acetate sheets over our mechanical board as a way to create variations for our layouts. One acetate layer might have copy and prices for a test market newspaper ad. Another piece of acetate might have prices for a special Sunday-circular ad. Yet another might have copy without prices for the national magazine ads. The artwork and other graphics stayed on the bottom layer and were visible through the acetate layers.

When the mechanical was sent to be printed, the print shop workers flipped the different acetate sheets on or off the board to create the different types of ads. Because a new mechanical didn't have to be created for each variation, it saved a lot of time and effort.

InDesign gives you the same sort of flexibility with electronic layers. You may have just two layers — one for text, the other for graphics. Or you may have a document with hundreds of different layers.

For instance, if you have English and French versions of a document, you can put the text for each language on its own layer. You can then display just one version at a time.

Creating and Deleting Layers

Every InDesign document opens with a default layer in the Layers palette. You don't have to do anything special to work with this default layer. It is instantly active, and everything you do is automatically on that layer.

To open the Layers palette:

◆ If the Layers palette is not visible, choose **Window>Layers** to open it **❶**.

As you work, you may want additional layers in your document.

To create new layers:

1. Choose New Layer from the Layers palette menu **❷**. This opens the New Layer dialog box.

or

Click the New Layer icon. This creates a new layer without opening the New Layer dialog box.

2. Set the layer options as described in the next section.

3. Click OK to create the layer.

TIP You can open the layer options at any time by double clicking the name of the layer in the Layers palette or by choosing Layer Options from the Layers palette menu.

It may be easier to create different versions of a document by duplicating a layer, as well as the objects on that layer.

To duplicate a layer:

◆ Drag the layer onto the New Layer icon **❸**. This creates a copy of the layer, as well as all objects on that layer.

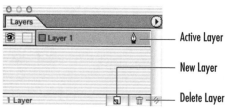

❶ *The* **Layers palette** *for all new documents contains one layer.*

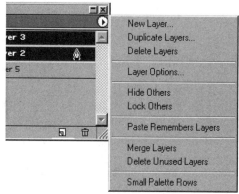

❷ *The* **Layers palette menu** *contains the commands for working with layers.*

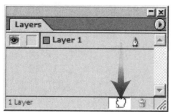

❸ *You can duplicate a layer by dragging it onto the* **New Layer icon**.

Creating and Deleting Layers

Before paste

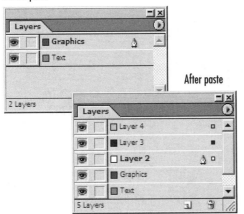

After paste

④ *The* **Paste Remembers Layers command** *adds new layers when objects are pasted from one document to another.*

Adobe InDesign

⚠ The layer "Layer 2" contains one or more objects. Delete the layer anyway?

OK   Cancel

⑤ *An alert dialog box makes sure you don't inadvertently delete artwork when you delete a layer.*

You can also import the layers automatically when you paste items from one document to another. This behavior is controlled by the Paste Remembers Layers command.

To create new layers while pasting:

1. Choose Paste Remembers Layers from the Layers palette menu. If there is a check mark next to the command, then it is already turned on.

TIP When turned on, this command is applied to all open documents.

2. Drag and drop or copy and paste the items from one document into a second document. New layers are created in the second document as follows **④**:

   - The layers from the first document are added as new layers if they do not have the same name as the layers in the second document.
   - The layers from the first document are merged with the layers if they have the same name as layers in the second document.

TIP If Paste Remembers Layers is turned off, the items are pasted onto the single active layer in the second document.

As you work, you may want to delete a layer. This deletes all objects on the layer.

To delete a layer:

1. Select the layer you want to delete.

TIP Shift-click to select multiple layers.

2. Click the Delete Layer icon. If there are items on the layer an alert box appears **⑤**.

TIP Opt/Alt-click the Delete Layer icon to bypass the alert box.

If you have layers with no objects on them, you can quickly delete those layers.

To delete all unused layers:

   ◆ Choose Delete Unused layers from the Layers palette menu.

Creating and Deleting Layers

Setting the Layer Options

The Layer Options dialog box contains some housekeeping options that make it easier to organize and work with layers . *(See the previous section for how to open the Layer Options dialog box.)*

⑥ *The* **Layer Options dialog box** *is the command center for all the attributes of a layer.*

To name a layer:

◆ Use the Name field to name the layer.

TIP If you have many layers, you should use descriptive names instead of the default names Layer 1, Layer 2, etc.

Each layer has a color associated with it. This is the color used to highlight object frames and paths.

To set the highlight color for a layer:

◆ Choose a color from one of the 37 colors in the Color list **⑦**.

TIP Each new layer is automatically assigned the next color in the Color list. This means you can have 37 layers without ever repeating a color.

TIP Select Custom to choose your own color for a layer.

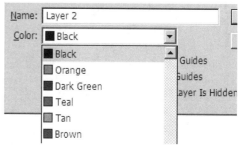

⑦ *The* **Color list** *contains all the choices for highlighting objects.*

Layers help you organize your documents. For instance, if you lock a layer you lock all the objects, so they cannot be selected, moved, modified, or deleted.

To lock a layer:

1. Choose Lock Layer from the Layer Options dialog box.

   or

   Click the Toggle Lock space in the Layers palette **⑧**. A pencil with a slash indicates that the layer is locked. A blank space indicates the layer is unlocked.

TIP Use the Lock Others command from the Layers palette menu or Opt/Alt-click the Toggle Lock space in one layer to lock all the other layers in the document **⑨**.

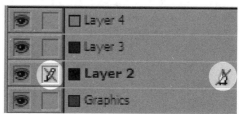

⑧ *Click the* **Toggle Lock space** *to lock the layer. The spotlighted icons indicate that the layer is locked.*

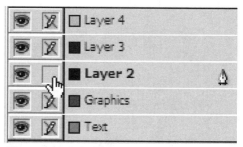

⑨ *Opt/Alt-click the* **Toggle Lock space** *to lock all the other layers in the document.*

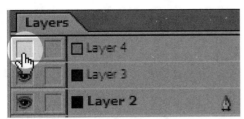

⑩ *Click the* **Toggle Visibility space** *to hide or show the layer.*

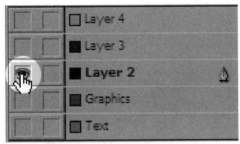

⑪ *Opt/Alt-click the Toggle Visibility space to hide all the other layers in the document.*

You can also use layers to hide and show the information on the layer. This can make it easy to focus on certain information. Hidden layers do not print.

To hide a layer:

◆ Deselect Show Layer from the Layer Options dialog box.

   or

   Click the Toggle Visibility space in the Layers palette so that the space is blank **⑩**. When the space is blank, the layer is invisible.

TIP You cannot work on invisible layers.

TIP Use the Hide Others command from the Layers palette menu or Opt/Alt-click the Toggle Visibility space in one layer to hide all the other layers in the document **⑪**.

To show a layer:

◆ Select Show Layer from the Layer Options dialog box.

   or

   Click the Toggle Visibility space in the Layers palette. When the eyeball is visible, the layer is visible.

So What About the Photoshop Layers?

If you've read anything about the features in InDesign CS2, you've probably seen that InDesign allows you to manipulate the layers in placed Photoshop files. What does that mean and why haven't I covered the feature in this chapter?

The reason is that the Photoshop layers are not controlled using the Layers palette. The Photoshop layers are controlled using the Image Import Options.

The layers in Photoshop are not the same as the layers in InDesign. *(To find out how you can manipulate the layers in Photoshop, see page 219.)*

Setting the Layer Options

Although hidden layers don't print, you can control some of their on-screen attributes in the Layer Options dialog box such as whether the guides are visible or not, and how the text wraps on a hidden layer.

To control the guides on a layer:

1. Choose Show Guides in the Layer Options dialog box to display the guides for that layer.

2. Choose Lock Guides to protect the guides on the layer from being changed.

The Layer Options dialog box contains the Suppress Text Wrap When Layer Is Hidden setting which controls what happens if you turn off the visibility for a layer that has a text wrap applied to images 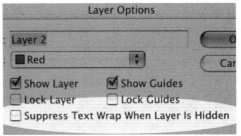.

To control the text wrap for hidden layers:

1. Apply a text wrap to an image that is on one layer.

2. Create text that is on another layer 🔞.

3. Set the Layer Options dialog box as follows:

   • Turn off Suppress Text Wrap When Layer Is Hidden to maintain the text wrap when the layer is visible 🔞.

   • Turn on Suppress Text Wrap When Layer Is Hidden to discard the text wrap when the layer is not visible 🔞.

⑫ *The* **Suppress Text Wrap When Layer Is Hidden** option *controls what happens to the text wrap for hidden layers.*

> When Dorothy stood in the doorway and looked around, she could see nothing but the great gray prairie on every side. Not a tree nor a house broke the broad sweep of flat country that reached to the edge of the sky in all directions. The sun had baked the plowed land into a gray mass, with little cracks running through it. Even the grass was not green, for the sun

⑬ *An image with a text wrap is placed on one layer affecting the text on another layer.*

> When Dorothy stood in the doorway and looked around, she could see nothing but the great gray prairie on every side. Not a tree nor a house broke the broad sweep of flat country that reached to the edge of the sky in all directions. The sun had baked the plowed land into a gray mass, with little cracks running through it. Even the grass was not green, for the sun

⑭ *When the layer is hidden, the wrap continues to affect text when the* **Suppress Text Wrap option is turned off.**

> When Dorothy stood in the doorway and looked around, she could see nothing but the great gray prairie on every side. Not a tree nor a house broke the broad sweep of flat country that reached to the edge of the sky in all directions. The sun had baked the plowed land into a gray mass, with little cracks running through it. Even the grass was not green, for the sun had burned the tops

⑮ *When the layer is hidden, the wrap does not affect text when the* **Suppress Text Wrap option is turned on.**

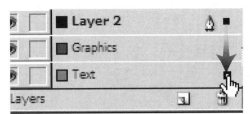

⑯ Drag the proxy square *to move an object from one layer to another.*

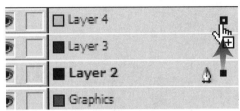

⑰ *Hold the Opt/Alt key as you drag the proxy square to copy an object from one layer to another.*

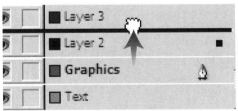

⑱ *Drag a layer up or down in the Layers palette to change the order of the layers.*

Working with Layers

Once you've created additional layers in your document, you can move objects onto the new layers.

To apply objects to layers:

◆ Click the layer in the Layers palette so that it's highlighted, and then create the object.

Rather than cutting or copying the object, selecting the new layer, and pasting it, you can use the Layers palette to move the object between layers.

To move objects from one layer to another:

1. Select the object. A square object proxy appears next to the name of the layer in the Layers palette.

2. Drag the object proxy from one layer to another **⑯**. This moves the object to a new layer.

TIP Hold the Opt/Alt key as you drag the proxy to create a copy of the object on the new layer **⑰**. The original object stays on its layer.

To reorder layers:

◆ Drag one layer above or below another to change the order in which objects appear in the document **⑱**.

You may want to combine the contents of one layer with another. This is called *merging* layers.

To merge layers:

1. Select the layers you want to merge.

2. Choose Merge Layers from the Layers palette menu. All the objects on the layers are combined onto one layer.

Working with Layers

LIBRARIES AND SNIPPETS 12

Back when I worked in advertising, I noticed that the art directors would stick little bits and pieces of type and logos on their mechanical board, drafting table, lamp, and wall. This made it easy to grab an often-used logo or piece of art.

Similarly, when you work with electronic page layouts, you use certain elements over and over. For instance, if you're working on a magazine, you might want to have a series of different-sized frames to hold frequently used ads.

Rather than copying and pasting the frames from one part of the document to another, you can use InDesign's libraries or snippets to hold the elements you use repeatedly.

Then, when you need to use an item from the library or the saved snippet file, you can simply drag it onto the page.

Storing Items in a Library

A library allows you to store elements, such as text frames, images, or empty frames. When elements are in a library, they can be dragged easily into open documents. Libraries are especially useful when you need to use the same element in many different places.

TIP Libraries appear as palettes that float above the open InDesign documents. Libraries are available to use with any InDesign document.

To create a library:

1. Choose **File > New > Library.** This opens the New Library dialog box.

2. Use this dialog box to name the library file and select its location.

TIP The name of the library file appears in the tab of the Library palette.

3. Click Save. The library appears as a floating palette ❶.

To add items to a library:

1. With a library open, select the item you want to insert in it.

2. Click the Add Item button at the bottom of the Library palette.

   or

   Drag the item into the library ❷. The item appears in the Library palette.

   or

   Choose Add Item from the Library palette menu ❸.

TIP Multiple objects are always entered as a single library item. If you want individual objects, you need to select and add them to the library one by one.

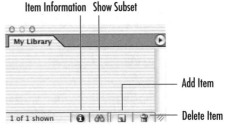

Item Information   Show Subset
Add Item
Delete Item

❶ *A new* **Library palette** *does not contain any items.*

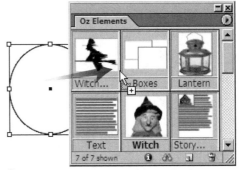

❷ *You can add items to a library by dragging them from the page into the Library palette.*

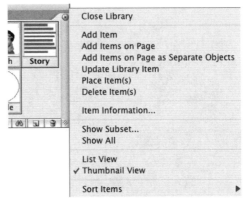

❸ *The* **Library palette menu** *contains the commands for working with a library.*

Strategies for Using Libraries

Libraries can be used in many different ways. I use a library to store items that I use often in a document.

For instance, I have one library labeled IDCS2VQS for this Visual QuickStart book. One of the elements is a graphic frame with a text frame underneath. I drag that out for the illustrations and captions.

Other elements are the empty circles, lines, and curved arrows I use to point to elements in the figures.

Another element is a gray text frame with a stroke around it. I drag it out when I write sidebars such as this.

You can also add all the items on a page to a library.

To add a page to a library:

1. With a library open, move to the page you want to add to the library.

2. Choose Add Items on Page from the Library palette submenu.

TIP The Add Items on Page command automatically labels the entry as a single page in the library Item Information dialog box *(see page 301)*.

Instead of the Add Items on Page command *(described above),* you may want to add all the items on a page as individual library entries. Instead of dragging them one by one into the Library palette, you can add the items as separate elements.

To add all the items on a page separately:

1. With a library open, move to the page that contains all the items that you want to add to the library.

2. Choose Add Items on Page as Separate Objects from the Library palette menu.

To delete items from a library:

1. Select the item in the library.

2. Click the Delete Item icon.

   or

   Choose Delete Item(s) from the Library palette menu.

3. A dialog box appears asking for confirmation that you want to delete the items. Click Yes.

TIP Hold the Opt/Alt key to bypass the dialog box when you delete a library item.

Applying Library Items to a Page

Libraries can be opened and the elements in the libraries dragged onto any InDesign documents.

To add library items to a document:

1. Select the item in the library.

TIP Shift-click to select multiple contiguous entries in the Library palette.

TIP Cmd/Ctrl-click to select multiple non-contiguous entries in the Library palette.

2. Drag the items from the library onto the page **④**.

   or

   Choose Place Item(s) from the Library palette menu.

TIP The Place Item(s) command adds the library item in the same position it was in when first defined.

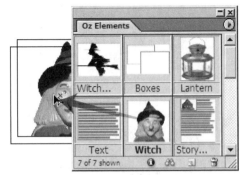

④ *Items can be dragged from a library onto a document.*

You may want to modify an item in a library with a new object, text, or image. The Update Library Item command makes this easy to do.

To update an item in a library:

1. Select the item on the page that you want to use as the replacement in the library.

2. Select the item in the library that needs to be updated.

3. Choose Update Library Item from the Library palette menu. The library thumbnail updates to display the new item.

Libraries in the Bridge

Libraries appear in the Adobe Bridge *(see page 45)* as icons, not previewed documents.

Library icons can be opened through the Bridge as you would any InDesign file.

Although you can add descriptions to the items in a library *(see the facing page)*, the library items in the Adobe Bridge cannot have keywords or other XMP metadata applied to them.

Applying Library Items to a Page

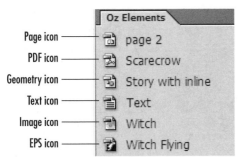

Page icon — page 2
PDF icon — Scarecrow
Geometry icon — Story with inline
Text icon — Text
Image icon — Witch
EPS icon — Witch Flying

⑤ *The* **List View** *shows the name of the item and an icon that shows the type of item.*

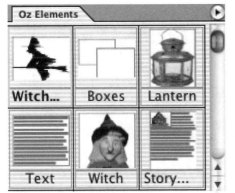

⑥ *The* **Thumbnail View** *shows the name of the item and a preview of the item.*

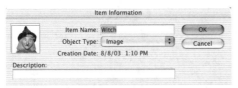

⑦ *The* **Item Information** *dialog box lets you change the information assigned to each item.*

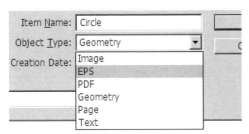

⑧ *Use the* **Object Type** *list to apply a label for the library element.*

Setting the Library Display

If you have many items in a library, you may want to change how the items are displayed.

To change the library display:

◆ Choose List View in the Library palette menu to see the item name and an icon that indicates the type of item **⑤**.

or

Choose Thumbnail View to see the name and a small preview of the item **⑥**.

You can also add information such as file type and keywords that makes it easy to search for library entries.

To modify the library item information:

1. Select the item.

2. Click the Library Item Information icon.

   or

   Choose Item Information from the Library palette menu. This opens the Item Information dialog box **⑦**.

3. Enter the name in the Item Name field.

4. Use the Object Type list to choose the following categories **⑧**:

   - **Image** contains raster images, such as Photoshop or TIFF files.
   - **EPS** contains EPS files.
   - **PDF** contains PDF files.
   - **Geometry** includes frames and rules that do not contain images or text.
   - **Page** is an entire page.
   - **Text** contains text frames.

   TIP InDesign assigns a category when items are entered into a library. You can change that listing to any category you want.

5. Enter a description for the item.

   TIP The description can be keywords or other information that helps identify the item.

Searching and Sorting Libraries

If you have many items in a library, you may find it difficult to find specific library entries. InDesign has a powerful search feature that makes it easy to locate specific items in a library.

To search within a library:

1. Click the Show Library Subset icon.

   or

   Choose Show Subset from the Library palette menu. This opens the Subset dialog box **9**.

2. Choose Search Entire Library to search all entries in the library **10**.

   or

   Choose Search Currently Shown Items to search through only those items currently displayed in the library.

3. Use the Parameters menu and fields to set the search criteria **11**.

4. Click More Choices to add up to five choices to the parameters list.

5. Choose Match All to choose only those items that match all the search parameters **12**.

   or

   Choose Match Any One to find items that meet at least one of the search parameters.

6. Click OK to display the items that meet the search criteria.

TIP Use the Back or Forward button to move through the search settings in the Subset dialog box.

9 *The* **Subset dialog box** *lets you find specific library items.*

10 *The* **search criteria** *in the Subset dialog box let you specify where to search in the library.*

11 *The* **Parameters menu** *lets you choose which part of the Item Information is searched.*

12 *The* **match criteria** *in the Subset dialog box control how the search items are matched.*

Libraries or Snippets?

As you read about libraries and snippets *(discussed on the following pages)* you may wonder which one you should use. I agree that the two features are very similar. But I have noticed a few significant differences.

Unlike library items, snippets can be dragged from the Bridge onto an InDesign document and always appear on the page in exactly the same spot where they originated. Library items cannot be dragged onto the page in the same position. They must be added using the Place command.

Also, snippets have smaller file sizes than Libraries. Snippets should be used when you need to save just a few items from a page.

Finally, snippets have a more fun name. I like reading the word *snippets*. I like writting the word *snippets*. I like saying the word *snippets*! Snippets make me happy.

Once you have sorted a library, you may need to show all the items at some other time.

To display all the library entries:

◆ Choose Show All from the Library palette submenu.

You can also control the order in which the library items are displayed. This makes it easier to find items in large libraries.

To sort library entries:

◆ Choose one of the Sort Items options from the Library palette menu:

- **By Name** arranges the items in alphabetical order.
- **By Oldest** arranges the items in the order they were added with the oldest items first.
- **By Newest** arranges the items in the order they were added, with the newest items first.
- **By Type** arranges the items in groups according to their categories *(see page 301)*.

Searching and Sorting Libraries

Creating and Using Snippets

Snippets are exactly what they sound like — little bits of a page that you snip off to use somewhere else. There are two ways to create snippets.

Creating snippets using the Export command:

1. Select the items on the page that you want to turn into a snippet.
2. Choose File > Export.
3. In the Export dialog box choose InDesign Snippet from the Format list 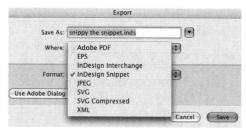.

TIP The InDesign Snippet option is not available if you are within a text frame. You cannot drag portions of text as a snippet, only the entire frame.

4. Name and save the file. The snippet icon appears in the directory.

Creating snippets by dragging:

1. Select and drag the items that you want to turn into a snippet onto the desktop. The Snippet icon appears with a bizarre temporary name.
2. Change the name to something more understandable.

Once you have created snippets, you can drag them onto a page.

Dragging snippets onto a page:

1. Select the snippet on the desktop or in the file directory.
2. Drag the Snippet icon onto the InDesign document page. The snippet items appear on the page in the same position they were in when first created.

TIP Snippets also can be be dragged from the Adobe Bridge onto a page.

⑬ *The* **Export dialog box** *lets you save items as InDesign snippets.*

TABS AND TABLES 13

Before tabs and tables, there was chaos. Well, perhaps not chaos, but it was difficult to line columns of text in an orderly fashion.

The word "tab" comes from the tabulator key on a typewriter. (Does anyone still use a typewriter?) The tabulator key moved the carriage return a certain number of spaces.

The tabulator key was named because it allowed typists to create tabular data. Tabular data is information arranged in systematic rows and columns — otherwise known as a table.

However, mathematical information isn't the only thing arranged in tables. Resumes, menus, train schedules, calendars, and even classified ads are all arranged in some form of table.

Anytime you need to keep text or graphics aligned in either columns or rows, consider using the tabs and tables features in InDesign.

Not only can you align text using tabs, but you can create tab leaders that make it easy to read across the lines of text. You can also create tables with repeating headers and footers and add custom strokes and fills to the tables.

Inserting Tab Characters

There are two parts to working with tabs. The first part is to insert the *tab characters* that force the text to jump to a certain position.

To insert tab characters into text:

1. Position the insertion point where you want the tab character to be located.

2. Press the Tab key on the keyboard. This creates a tab character in the text ❶.

TIP Choose Type > **Show Hidden Characters** to see the display of the tab character within the text.

TIP InDesign recognizes tab characters in imported text.

InDesign also has a special type of tab character called a right tab. This tab character automatically sets the text to the rightmost position in the frame ❷.

To insert a right tab character:

1. Place the insertion point where you want the right tab character.

2. Press Shift-Tab.

   or

   Use the contextual menu to insert a right tab character from the Insert Special Character menu.

Frank⟨»⟩Writer

❶ *A* **tab character** *is displayed as part of the hidden characters in text.*

Chapter·one ⸽ 5¶
Chapter·two ⸽ 45¶
Chapter·three ⸽ 62#

❷ *The* **right tab character** *automatically moves the text to the right side of the text frame.*

Inserting Tabs in Text

It's actually very simple to insert a tab character into text. Just tap the Tab key. However, there are some guides for working with tabs.

Insert only one tab character for each column. Even if the text doesn't line up correctly, don't add another tab character. Use the Tab palette and tab stops to line up the columns.

If you're over a certain age, you may have been taught to put a tab at the beginning of a paragraph to indent the first line. Don't do it! As mentioned in Chapter 3, "Basic Text," you can use the first line indent to format paragraphs.

Inserting Tab Characters

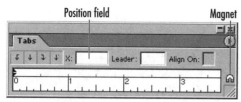

❸ *The* **Tabs palette** *contains the controls for inserting tab stops and aligning the tabs.*

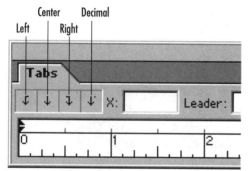

❹ *Choose one of the four* **tab alignment icons** *to control how the text is aligned.*

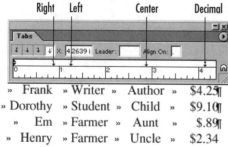

» Frank	» Writer	» Author	» $4.25¶
» Dorothy	» Student	» Child	» $9.10¶
» Em	» Farmer	» Aunt	» $.89¶
» Henry	» Farmer	» Uncle	» $2.34

❺ *Examples of how the four tab alignments control the text.*

Setting Tab Stops

The next — and most important — part to working with tabs is to set the *tab stops* or the formatting controls that set where the text should stop after it is forced to jump to a new position. This alignment is controlled using the Tabs palette.

To open the Tabs palette:

◆ Choose **Type > Tabs.** The Tabs palette appears above the text frame **❸**.

TIP The Tabs palette can be kept onscreen like any other palette.

TIP If the Tabs palette is not positioned above the text, click the Magnet icon in the palette to automatically move the palette to the correct position.

To set tab stops:

1. Select the text.

2. Choose the type of tab alignment from the four tab icons in the ruler **❹**. The four alignments work as follows **❺**:

   • **Left** aligns the left side of the text at the tab stop.

   • **Center** centers the text on either side of the tab stop.

   • **Right** aligns the right side of the text at the tab stop.

   • **Decimal** aligns the text at the decimal point or period of the text.

3. Click the ruler area where you want the tab stop to be positioned.

   or

   Type a number in the Position field. A small tab arrow corresponding to the tab type appears that indicates the position of the tab stop.

TIP The default tab stops are invisible left-aligned tabs positioned every half inch. Adding tab stops to the ruler overrides all tab stops to the left of the new tab.

Setting Tab Stops

To change tab settings:

1. Select the text.

2. Open the Tabs palette.

3. To change the alignment of a tab stop, select the tab arrow and then click a new alignment icon.

   or

   Hold the Opt/Alt key and click the tab arrow in the ruler.

4. To change the position of a tab stop, drag the tab arrow to a new position.

TIP As you move a tab stop along the ruler, a line extends through the text, even if the Tabs palette is not aligned to the text frame ❻. This helps you judge the position of the tab stop.

Many times you will want to have tab stops repeated at the same interval. InDesign makes it easy to set repeating tabs.

To set a repeating tab:

1. Position the first tab stop on the ruler.

2. With the tab stop still selected, choose Repeat Tab from the Tabs palette menu ❼. This adds new tab stops at the same interval along the ruler ❽.

TIP The tab stops created by the Repeat Tab command are not linked and move independently.

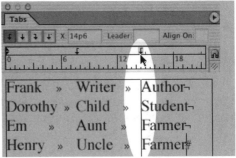

❻ *As you move a tab stop,* **a line extends through the text** *to help you position the tab stop correctly.*

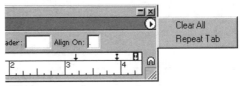

❼ *The* **Tabs palette menu** *gives you two important commands for working with tabs.*

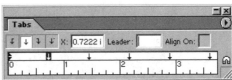

❽ *The* **Repeat Tab command** *allows you to easily add tab stops at the same interval along the ruler.*

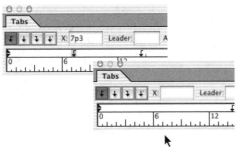

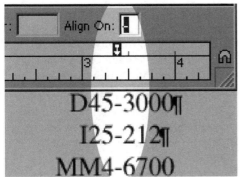

⑨ *To remove a tab stop, drag it off the Tabs palette ruler.*

⑩ *You can enter a custom alignment character for the* **Align On** *field. Here the text aligns to the hyphen.*

Once you have added tab stops to the Tabs palette ruler, you can remove them easily.

To remove tab stops:

1. Select the tab stop on the Tabs palette ruler.

2. Drag the tab stop off the ruler. This deletes the tab stop **⑨**.

TIP If there are no tab stops to the left of the one you removed, this restores the invisible, default tab stops at the nearest half-inch position.

If you have many tab stops on the Tabs palette ruler, it may be easier to delete all the tab stops with a single command.

To clear all the tabs off the ruler:

◆ Choose Clear All from the Tabs palette ruler **⑦**. This restores the invisible, default tab stops at every half-inch mark.

The Decimal tab aligns numerical data to a decimal point. However, you may need to align text to a different character. For instance, some European currency uses a comma instead of a decimal. InDesign lets you set a custom alignment character.

To set a custom alignment character:

1. Choose the Decimal Tab icon.

2. Add a tab stop to the ruler.

3. Replace the period in the Align On field with a different character. The text aligns around that character **⑩**.

Setting Tab Stops

Creating Tab Leaders

A *tab leader* allows you to automatically fill the space between the tabbed material with a repeating character. Tab leaders are often used in the tables of contents of books *(such as the one in this book).*

TIP Tab leaders are added when the reader needs to move horizontally across a wide column from one entry to another. The tab leader helps the reader's eye stay on the correct line of text.

To add tab leaders:

1. Select the tab stop arrow on the Tabs palette ruler.

2. Type up to eight characters in the Leader field of the Tabs palette.

TIP Add spaces between characters in the Leader field to give the leader a more pleasing look 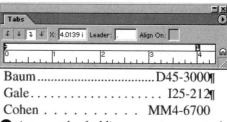.

TIP Press the Tab key on the keyboard to preview the characters in the Leader field.

TIP You can select the characters in a tab leader as you would ordinary text and change the point size, kerning, or other attributes.

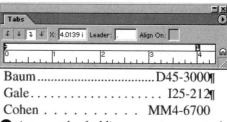

Baum .... D45-3000¶
Gale .... I25-212¶
Cohen MM4-6700

⓫ *An example of adding spaces to separate the tab leader.*

Choosing Between Tabs and Tables

For as long as I can remember, designers have wanted an easy way to create tables in page-layout documents. Now that InDesign lets you create tables, is there any reason to still use tabs?

Absolutely! I use tabs in this book to separate numbers from the text in the exercises. I also use tabs with leaders for the listings in the table of contents.

I use tables whenever I need side-by-side paragraphs such as in a resume. I also use tables whenever I need to separate the information with horizontal and vertical lines.

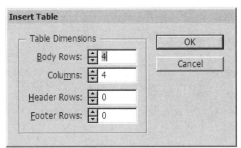

⓬ *Use the* **Insert Table dialog box** *to create an empty table in a text frame.*

Table Styles

InDesign's table features are very powerful. There are all sorts of controls for how the table is formatted. Unfortunately, InDesign CS2 doesn't have any sort of styles to let you quickly apply intricate formatting to tables and cells.

If you work with a lot of tables, you should seriously consider investing in a plug-in to help automate table formatting. One of the plug-ins I have found useful is TableStyles and CellStyles from Teacup Software (www.teacupsoftware.com).

Not only does this plug-in let me quickly apply very intricate table formatting, it also lets me update all the tables in a document at once.

Creating and Using Tables

Tabs limit you to lining up only a single line of text. Tables let you line up text so it can extend down into several lines. Tables also let you add borders to the cell that contains the text or add fills of color behind the text.

To create a new table in a text frame:

1. Place an insertion point inside a text frame.

2. Choose **Table > Insert Table**. The Insert Table dialog box appears **⓬**.

3. Use the Body Rows control to set the number of rows in the table.

4. Use the Columns control to set the number of columns.

5. Use the Header Rows control to set the number of rows across the top of the table.

6. Use the Footer Rows control to set the number of rows across the bottom of the table.

TIP Headers and footers are special cells that are repeated when the table is divided between frames or pages. *(See page 326 for more information on working with headers and footers in tables.)*

7. Click OK. InDesign creates a table that fills the text frame as follows:

   • The width of the table is set to fill the width of the text frame.

   • The table columns are distributed evenly across the table.

   • The height of the table is set at the size of the default text size plus 8 points to accomodate the cell inset *(see page 330)*.

   • If the default height of the table is greater than the size of the text frame, an overflow symbol appears indicating that the table can flow to another frame *(see page 53)*.

Creating and Using Tables

Many times you will import text that you'd like to be converted into a table. Fortunately, this is rather easy to do.

To convert text into a table:

1. Select the text.

2. Choose **Table > Convert Text to Table**. The Convert Text to Table dialog box appears ⓭.

3. Use the Column Separator menu to choose which character should be used as the marker for each column in the table.

   or

   Type the character that you would like as the marker in the Column Separator field.

   TIP If you have imported tabbed delimited text, this is most likely a tab character although paragraph returns and spaces are sometimes used.

4. Use the Row Separator menu to choose which character should be used as the marker for each row in the table.

   or

   Type the character that you would like as the marker in the Row Separator field.

   TIP For most text, this is the paragraph symbol.

5. If you have chosen anything except a paragraph symbol for the Row Separator, use the Number of Columns field to choose how many columns there should be in the table.

6. Click OK to create the table ⓮.

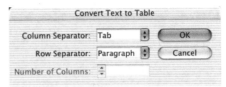

⓭ *The* **Convert Text to Table** *dialog box lets you choose how text is converted to a table.*

April#	May#	June#
12#	67#	54#
6#	7#	2#

April » May » June¶
12 » 67 » 54¶
6 » 7 » 2#

⓮ *The* **Convert Text to Table command** *transforms tabs and paragraphs into rows and columns.*

Creating and Using Tables

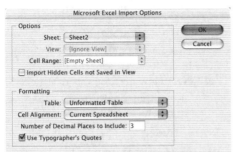

⑮ *The* **Microsoft Excel Import Options** *dialog box lets you choose which worksheet and cells are imported from an Excel document.*

⑯ *The* **Microsoft Word Import Options** *dialog box lets you choose how Word tables are imported into the InDesign document.*

Most people use Microsoft Word and Excel to create text and spreadsheets. InDesign lets you import the tables created by both Word and Excel.

To import a table from Word or Excel:

1. Place an insertion point inside a frame.

    or

    Deselect any text frame. This creates a loaded text cursor.

2. Choose **File > Place** and navigate to the Word or Excel file.

3. If necessary, use the Microsoft Excel Import Options **⑮** or the Microsoft Word Import Options **⑯** to control how the file will be imported, as described on the next two pages. Click OK.

4. The imported document is inserted into the selected text frame.

    or

    Click or drag the loaded text cursor.

When you import from Excel, InDesign automatically chooses all the cells in the worksheet that contain data. However, you can customize which cell data is imported.

To choose the cells that should be imported:

1. Use the Sheet menu to choose which worksheet should be imported.

2. If you have specified a custom view in Excel, use the View menu to choose that view.

3. Use the Cell Range field to specify a set of cells.

4. If desired, check the Import Hidden Cells not Saved in View box.

Creating and Using Tables

To set the formatting for Excel cells:

1. Use the Table menu to change the formatting options as follows:

   - **Formatted Table** imports the cells with whatever formatting was applied in Excel.
   - **Unformatted Table** imports the cells with no formatting except a stroke around each InDesign cell.
   - **Unformatted Tabbed Text** converts the cells into text divided by tab characters.

2. Choose the options in the Cell Alignment menu as follows:

   - **Current Spreadsheet** imports the text aligned with whatever alignment was set in the spreadsheet.
   - **Left** imports the text aligned to the left side of each cell.
   - **Center** imports the text aligned to the center of each cell.
   - **Right** imports the text aligned to the right side of each cell.

3. Use Number of Decimal Places to Include to set how many decimal places to include in the imported cells.

4. If desired, check Use Typographer's Quotes to convert straight "quotes" (like these) into open and closed "quotes" (like these).

Importing from Spreadsheets

Most likely, if you need to import data from Excel spreadsheets, the files have been created by accountants or others who know little about graphic design or page layout.

Try to talk to them before they send you the file for layout. Explain that they should not format their document using the controls in Microsoft Excel. Most of the time you will just have to strip out that formatting in order to make the file work in your layout.

You may also want to ask them for a test file so you can see how the information will be imported.

Creating and Using Tables

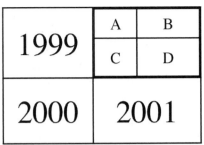

1999	A	B
	C	D
2000	2001	

⑰ *An example of how a table can be inserted inside a cell of another table.*

Summer Schedule#	Closed#	
June#	July#	July 4#
Aug.#	Sept#	Sept. 1#

Summer Schedule » Closed¶
June » July » July 4¶
Aug. » Sept » Sept. 1#

⑱ *The* **Convert Table to Text command** *transforms table rows and columns into tabs and paragraph returns.*

You can also control how table information in Word documents is imported. *(See page 262 for information on setting the inline graphic options for Word files.)*

To set the formatting for Word tables:

1. Select Remove Text and Table Formatting in the Microsoft Word Import Options dialog box to change the original formatting applied in Word.

TIP Use this option to remove some of the hideous formatting that may have been applied to Word tables.

2. If you have set the option to remove the formatting, choose one of the following from the Convert Tables To menu:

   - **Unformatted Tables** imports the Word table with no formatting except a stroke around each cell.
   - **Unformatted Tabbed Text** converts the cells into text divided by tab characters.

To place a table in a table cell:

1. Click with the Text tool to place an insertion point inside a table cell.

2. Use the Insert Table command or a Place command to create a table within that cell **⑰**.

To convert a table to text:

1. Place an insertion point in any cell inside the table.

2. Choose Table > Convert Table to Text.

3. Use the Convert Table to Text dialog box to choose what elements should be used to designate the column and row separators **⑱**:

   - You can convert columns and rows to tabs, commas, or paragraph returns.
   - You can type your own character in the field to customize the conversion.

Navigating Through Tables

As you work with tables, you will want to add content to the cells, move from cell to cell, and select cells, rows, and columns.

⑲ *Press the Tab key to* **jump forward from one cell to another** *in a table.*

To insert text into table cells:

1. Place an insertion point inside a table cell.
2. Type the text for the cell.

   or

   Choose **File > Place** to insert imported text in the cell.

TIP Press Opt/Alt-Tab to insert a tab character inside a cell.

⑳ *Press Shift-Tab to* **jump backward from one cell to another** *in a table.*

To move from one cell to another:

◆ Press the Tab key to jump forward from one cell to another **⑲**.

   or

   Press Shift-Tab to move backward from one cell to another **⑳**.

Since you navigate through a table using the Tab character, you need some special techniques to insert actual tab characters into a table.

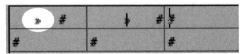

㉑ *Press Opt/Alt-Tab to* **insert a tab character** *into a table.*

To insert a tab character into a table:

◆ Press Opt/Alt-Tab to insert a tab character inside a cell **㉑**.

   or

   Choose **Type > Insert Special Character > Tab Character**.

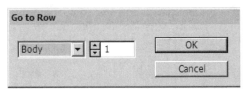

㉒ *The* **Go to Row dialog box** *lets you quickly jump from one row to another.*

To jump to a specific row:

1. Choose **Table > Go to Row**. The Go to Row dialog box appears **㉒**.
2. Use the menu to move to the body, header, or footer of the table.
3. Enter the number for the row you want to move to.

Text only selected

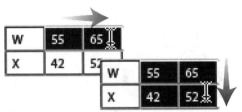

Cell selected

23 *When the text in a cell is selected, only the text is highlighted. When the entire cell is selected, the entire cell area is highlighted.*

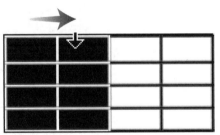

24 *Drag across and then down to select a specific group of cells in a table.*

25 *The* **down arrow cursor** *indicates you can click to select an entire column in a table.*

Selecting Tables

By clicking and dragging your cursor, you can select cells, columns, row, or the entire table.

TIP When the entire cell, rows, columns, or combination of cells are selected, you can copy and paste cells from one part of a table to another *(see page 322).*

To select text in a table cell:

1. Place an insertion point inside a table cell.
2. Drag across the cell until all the text in the cell is highlighted.

   or

   Choose **Edit > Select All** to select all the text within that cell.

TIP There is a difference in the appearance between just the text selected and the entire cell selected **23**.

To select text in multiple table cells:

1. Use the Text tool to drag across to select the cells in specific columns **24**.
2. If you want, continue to drag down to select the cells in additional rows.

To select a table column:

1. Place the Text tool cursor at the top of the table. A down arrow cursor appears.
2. Click the down arrow. The entire column is selected **25**.
3. Drag across with the down arrow cursor to select any additional columns.

   or

   Move the down arrow to another column and Shift-click to select multiple columns.

Selecting Tables

To select a table row:

1. Place the Text tool cursor at the left side of the table. A left arrow cursor appears.

2. Click the left arrow. The entire row is selected 26.

3. Drag down with the left arrow cursor to select any additional rows.

   or

   Move the down arrow to another row and Shift-click to select multiple rows.

To select the entire table:

1. Place the Text tool cursor at the top corner of the table. A slanted arrow cursor appears.

2. Click the slanted arrow. The entire table is selected 27.

To use the table selection commands:

1. Place the insertion point in a cell in the table.

2. Choose one of the following commands:
   - **Table > Select > Cell** selects the cell.
   - **Table > Select > Row** selects the row that contains the cell.
   - **Table > Select > Column** selects the column that contains the cell.
   - **Table > Select > Table** selects the entire table.

   TIP The table selection commands are very helpful for applying borders and fills to table cells *(see page 332)*.

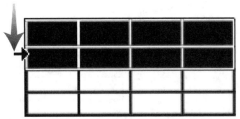

26 *The* **left arrow cursor** *indicates you can click to select an entire row in a table.*

27 *Positioning the cursor at the upper-left corner and clicking will select the entire table.*

Selecting Tables

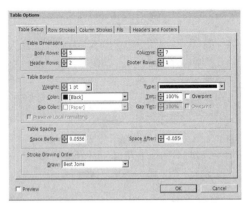

28 *The* **Table Setup dialog box** *contains the basic options for a table's appearance.*

29 *The* **Table Dimensions area** *lets you set the number of rows, columns, header rows, and footer rows.*

Working with Rows and Columns

Once you've created a table, you may want to change the number of rows and columns in the table.

TIP In addition to the Table menu and dialog boxes, many adjustments to tables can be made using the Table palette or Control palette. *(See the section "Using the Table or Control Palettes" at the end of this chapter for more information on modifying tables with those onscreen elements.)*

To change the number of rows and columns:

1. Select the entire table or any part of the table.

2. Choose **Table > Table Options > Table Setup** to open the Table Setup dialog box **28**.

3. Set the Body Rows controls in the Table Dimensions area to increase or decrease the number of rows in the main section of the table **29**.

4. Set the Header Rows controls to increase or decrease the number of rows in the header section of the table **29**. *(See page 326 for more information on working with headers and footers.)*

5. Set the Columns controls to increase or decrease the number of columns in the table **29**.

6. Set the Footer Rows controls to increase or decrease the number of rows in the footer section of the table **29**.

TIP Use the Preview control at the bottom of the Table Setup dialog box to see the results of changing the controls.

TIP The commands in the Table Dimensions section always add rows and columns at the end of the table sections. The next exercise explains how to insert rows and columns into a specific location in the table.

Working with Rows and Columns

You can also insert columns and rows into a specific location in a table.

To insert columns into a table:

1. Place an insertion point where you want to insert the columns.

2. Choose **Table** > **Insert** > **Column**. The Insert Columns(s) dialog box appears 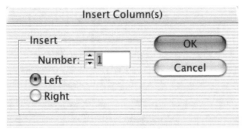.

   or

   Choose **Insert** > **Column** from the Table palette menu.

3. Use the Number field to set the number of rows.

4. Choose either Left or Right to specify where the new rows should be inserted ㉛.

To insert rows into a table:

1. Place an insertion point where you want to insert the rows.

2. Choose **Table** > **Insert** > **Row**. The Insert Row(s) dialog box appears ㉜.

   or

   Choose **Insert** > **Row** from the Table palette menu.

3. Use the Number field to set the number of rows.

4. Choose either Above or Below to specify where the new rows should be inserted.

   TIP The Insert Row(s) dialog box inserts rows into the header, footer, or main section of a table.

To insert rows as you type:

1. Place the insertion point in the final cell of the last row of the table main body, header, or footer.

2. Press the Tab key. A new row is automatically inserted.

㉚ *Use the* **Insert Column(s) dialog box** *to add columns at a specific location within a table.*

Original table

	A	B	C	D
Y	84	94	34	55
Z	22	33	44	55
	AA	BB	CC	DD

Selected cell

After column is inserted   New column

	A	B		C	D
Y	84	94		34	55
Z	22	33		44	55
	AA	BB		CC	DD

㉛ *An example of how a column is added to the left of the selected cell.*

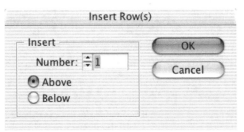

㉜ *Use the* **Insert Row(s) dialog box** *to add rows at a specific location within a table.*

33 *Hold the Opt/Alt key as you drag across to* **add columns** *to a table.*

34 *Hold the Opt/Alt key as you drag down to* **add rows** *to a table.*

Selected cells   After deleting content

35 *An example of how you can* **delete the content of selected cells.**

To add columns as you drag the table edge:
1. Drag the last column of the table.
2. Press the Opt/Alt key as you drag. This expands the size of the table by adding columns **33**.

To add rows as you drag the table edge:
1. Drag the last row of the table.
2. Press the Opt/Alt key as you drag. This expands the size of the table by adding rows **34**.

To delete table columns:
1. Select the columns you want to delete.
2. Choose **Table > Delete > Column**.

To delete table rows:
1. Select the rows you want to delete.
2. Choose **Table > Delete > Row**.

To delete the entire table:
1. Select the table.
2. Choose **Table > Delete > Table**.

You may want to delete the content inside a cell without deleting the cell itself.

To delete the content in table cells:
1. Select the cells, columns, or rows.
2. Press the Delete/Backspace key or choose **Edit > Clear**.

TIP The content is deleted but the cells themselves remain in place **35**.

Working with Rows and Columns

You can't move cells from one place to another, but you can copy and paste cells and their content to new locations.

To copy and paste the content in table cells:

1. Select the cells, columns, or rows that you want to move to a new position.

2. Choose **Edit > Copy** or **Edit > Cut**. This puts the selected cells on the clipboard.

3. Select the new cells, columns, or rows.

TIP You should select at least the same number of cells, columns, or rows, that were selected in step 1.

4. Choose Edit > Paste. The content on the clipboard is pasted into the selected cells **36**.

TIP If you selected more cells than were selected in step 1, the excess cells are not changed.

Select and copy cells

Select and copy empty cells

Paste cells to new position

36 *The three-step process to* **copy and move cells** *from one position to another.*

When you create a table, all the columns and rows are evenly spaced. However, you can modify the size of the rows and columns.

TIP A red dot inside a table cell indicates there is an overflow of text **37**. You can change the size of the cell to display the overflow text.

July	August	Sep-
34	45	785
453	499	644

37 *A red dot inside a table cell indicates that there is an overflow of text inside the cell.*

To change a single row height visually:

1. With the Text tool selected, place the cursor along the border of the row you want to adjust. The cursor changes to an up/down arrow **38**.

2. Drag to adjust the height of the row.

April	May	June
12	67	54
6	7	2

38 *The Up/ Down arrow indicates you can adjust the row height.*

To change all the rows visually:

1. Place the cursor along the bottom border of the table. The cursor changes to an up/down arrow.

2. Hold the Shift key as you drag to adjust the height of all the rows in the table.

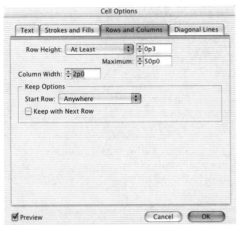

39 *The* **Rows and Columns category** *of the Cell Options dialog box.*

40 *The* **Left/ Right arrow** *indicates you can adjust the column width.*

41 *The* **Column Width control** *of the Cell Options dialog box.*

To set the row height numerically:

1. Select the rows you want to adjust.
2. Choose **Table** > **Cell Options** > **Rows and Columns** to open the Cell Options dialog box to the Rows and Columns options **39**.
3. Set the Row Height menu as follows:
   - **At Least** sets a row height that can increase to hold text or an image.
   - **Exactly** sets a row height that does not get larger.
4. Enter an amount in the Row Height field.
5. Use the Maximum field to prevent the row from becoming too tall.

To change the column width visually:

1. With the Text tool selected, place the cursor along the border of the column you want to adjust. The cursor changes to a left/right arrow **40**.
2. Drag to adjust the width of the column.

To set the column width numerically:

1. Select the columns you want to adjust.
2. Enter an amount in the Column Width field **41**.

You can adjust columns or rows so their spacing is evenly distributed.

To automatically distribute columns:

1. Set the rightmost column to the position it should be after the adjustment.

2. Select the columns you want to adjust.

3. Choose **Table** > **Distribute Columns Evenly**. The column widths adjust ㊷.

To automatically distribute rows:

1. Set the bottommost column to the position it should be after the adjustment.

2. Select the rows you want to adjust.

3. Choose **Table** > **Distribute Rows Evenly**. The row heights adjust so they are the same size ㊸.

If you want, you can control when and how the rows of a table break across text frames. This is called the *keep options* for rows.

To set the keep options for rows:

1. Select the rows you want to control.

2. Choose **Table** > **Cell Options** > **Rows and Columns**.

3. Choose from the Start Row menu as follows ㊹:

   • **Anywhere** lets the row start anywhere in a text frame.

   • **In Next Text Column** forces the row to the next column in the frame or the next text frame.

   • **In Next Frame** forces the row to the next text frame.

   • **On Next Page** forces the row to the next page.

   • **On Next Odd Page** forces the row to the next odd-numbered page.

   • **On Next Even Page** forces the row to the next even-numbered page.

4. Check Keep with Next Row to make sure one row doesn't separate from another ㊺.

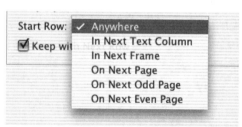

㊷ *The results of using the* **Distribute Columns Evenly** *command.*

㊸ *The results of using the* **Distribute Rows Evenly** *command.*

㊹ *The* **Start Row menu** *lets you choose where that row starts.*

㊺ *Check* **Keep with Next Row** *to force one row to always stay with the next one.*

Working with Rows and Columns

Here are the dates for the Spring classes.¶

April#	May#
12#	67#

No space around table

Here are the dates for the Summer classes.¶

June#	July#
12#	22#

Space added around table

46 *Add some space around a table to keep it from colliding with text.*

47 *The* **Table Spacing controls** *let you set the amount of space before and after a table.*

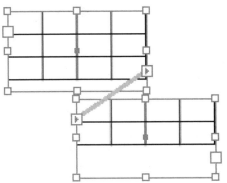

48 *The text threads show how tables can flow from one frame to another.*

Adjusting Tables within a Text Frame

Tables are always contained within text frames. You can control how much space there is between the table and the text that precedes or follows it **46**.

To set the spacing around a table:

1. With the table selected, choose **Table > Table Options > Table Setup**. The Table Options dialog box appears.

2. Use the Table Spacing control for Space Before to set the amount of space between text and the top of the table **47**.

3. Use the Table Spacing control for Space After to set the amount of space between the bottom of the table and the text that follows it.

TIP A table is inserted into a text frame as an inline object in its own paragraph. This means that any space before or after the paragraph that holds the table is added to the space set by the Table Spacing controls.

If a table extends longer than a text frame, you get a text frame overflow. You can easily flow the rest of the table from frame to frame across pages.

To flow tables between frames:

1. Use the Selection tool to load the overflow cursor.

2. Click the overflow cursor inside the new frame to flow the rest of the table into the frame **48**.

Working with Headers and Footers

Tables with lots of data often flow from one location to another. For easy navigation, you can repeat the first and last rows of the table each time it appears in a new place. When the first row of a table repeats, it is called a *header*. When the last row repeats, it is called a *footer*. You can create headers and footers when you first define a table *(see page 311)* or add or modify them in an existing table.

To add a header or footer to a table:

1. With the table selected, choose **Table > Table Options > Headers and Footers**. The Table Options dialog box opens to the Headers and Footers tab 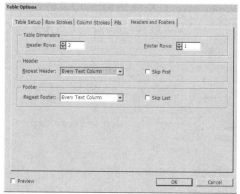.

2. Use the Header Rows controls to set the number of repeating rows added to the top of the table .

3. Use the Footer Rows controls to set the number of repeating rows added to the bottom of the table.

TIP To turn off a header or footer, set the Header Rows or Footer Rows to zero.

TIP You can also set the number of header and footer rows in the Table Setup.

To set the repeat options for headers and footers:

1. Use the Repeat Header or Repeat Footer menu as follows 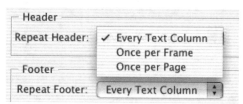:

    -   **Every Text Column** repeats the header or footer whenever the table appears.
    -   **Once per Frame** repeats the header or footer only once in the same frame. This is useful when a table flows from one column to another.
    -   **Once per Page** repeats the header or footer only once in the same page. This is useful when a table flows into multiple frames on the same page.

2. Check Skip First (header) or Skip Last (footer) to display the header or footer only after the first instance of the table.

49 *The* **Headers and Footers area** *in Table Options lets you control the appearance of headers and footers in the table.*

50 *Use the* **Table Dimensions for Headers and Footers** *to control the number of header and footer rows.*

51 *Use the* **Repeat Header menu** *to set how frequently the header appears.*

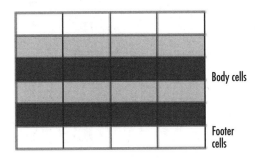

Body cells

Footer cells

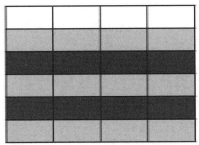

52 *An example of what happens when a row is* **converted from body cells to header cells.** *Notice that the footer takes on the alternating fill.*

As you work, you may want to convert body table cells into a header or footer.

To convert cells into a table header:

1. Select the rows that you want to convert. These rows must be the first rows of the table.

2. Choose **Table > Convert Rows > To Header**. The rows are converted from the body of the table to the table header **52**.

TIP If there already is a header for the table, the cells are added to the bottom of the existing cells.

To convert cells into a table footer:

1. Select the rows that you want to convert. These rows must be the last rows of the table.

2. Choose **Table > Convert Rows > To Footer**. The rows are converted from the body of the table to the table footer.

TIP If there already is a footer for the table, the cells are added to the top of the existing cells.

Finally, you may want to convert the rows in a header or footer into the body of the table.

To convert header or footer cells into body cells:

1. Select the rows that you want to convert.

TIP The rows must be the bottom rows of the header or the top rows of the footer.

2. Choose **Table > Convert Rows > To Body**.

Working with Headers and Footers

Adding Images to Tables

Although table cells are created to hold text, you can easily add images as inline graphics to each cell. *(See page 244 for more information on working with inline graphics.)*

To insert a graphic into a table cell:

1. Place an insertion point inside a table cell.

2. Choose **File > Place** to insert an image into the cell .

   or

   Paste a graphic copied to the clipboard into the cell.

TIP Graphics in cells are pasted as inline graphics.

If the graphic is larger than the size of the cell, some of the graphic may stick out beyond the cell. You use the Clipping setting to control whether placed graphics are seen outside a cell.

To control the display of a graphic inside a cell:

1. Place your insertion point inside the cell that contains the placed graphic.

2. Choose **Table > Cell Options > Text**. This opens the Cell Options dialog box .

3. Select Clip Contents to Cell to limit the display of the graphic to inside the cell 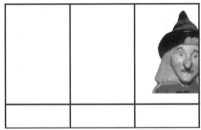.

   or

   Deselect Clip Contents to Cell to allow the graphic to be displayed outside the cell .

TIP In addition to allowing a graphic to appear outside the cell boundaries, you can also drag a table so that the table itself extends outside the text frame.

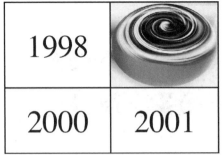
53 *An example of how a placed image can be inserted into a table cell.*

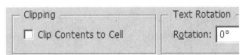
54 *The **Clip Contents to Cell** option for inline graphics in a cell.*

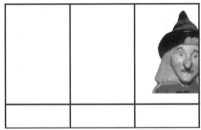
55 *With the **clip options turned on**, an inline graphic is confined to the boundaries of the cell.*

56 *With the **clip options turned off**, an inline graphic extends outside the boundaries of the cell.*

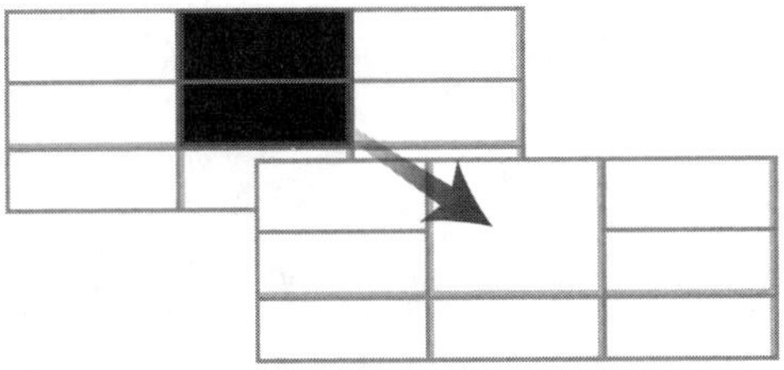

(57) *The results of using the* **Merge Cells** command.

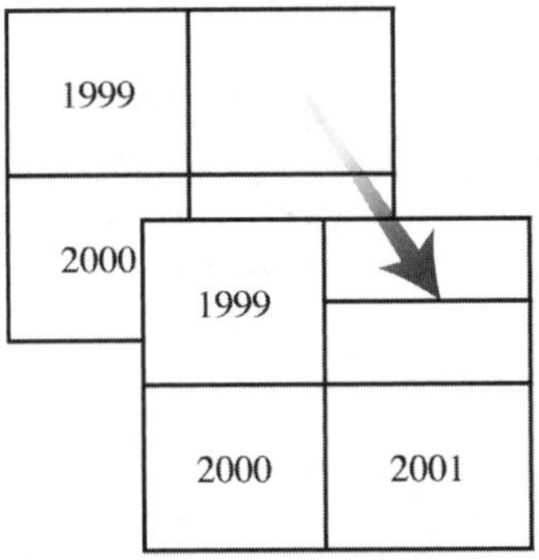

(58) *The results of using the* **Split Cell Horizontally** command.

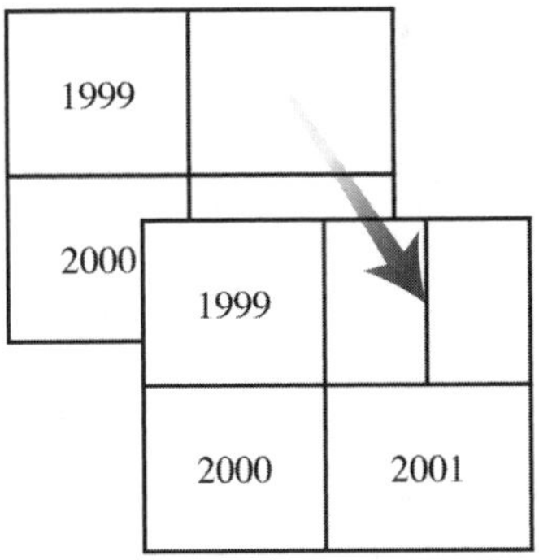

(59) *The results of using the* **Split Cell Vertically** command.

Customizing Cells

In addition to setting the controls for the entire table, you can also make settings for individual cells. You can customize the arrangement of rows and columns by merging or splitting cells. You may want to merge cells to fit more text within a cell. You can also change the space of text within a cell.

To merge cells:

1. Select the cells you want to merge.
2. Choose **Table > Merge Cells**. The dividers between the cells are deleted (57).

TIP If the merged cells contain text, the text will be divided into paragraphs.

To unmerge cells:

1. Select the cells you want to unmerge.
2. Choose **Table > Unmerge Cells**.

To split cells:

1. Select the cell you want to split.
2. Choose **Table > Split Cell Horizontally** or **Table > Split Cell Vertically** (58) or (59).

You can also control how text is positioned horizontally and vertically with each cell.

TIP These settings also control how inline graphics are positioned within frames.

To set the cell options for text:

1. Select the cells you want to adjust.

2. Choose **Table > Cell Options > Text**. This opens the Cell Options for text controls 🗿.

3. Use the four Cell Insets fields to adjust the amount of space between the text and the top, bottom, left, and right sides of the cells 🗿.

4. Choose one of the four settings from the Text Rotation menu to rotate the text in 90° increments.

You can also set the vertical alignment for where the text is positioned in the cell.

To set the text vertical alignment:

1. Select the cells you want to adjust.

2. Choose **Table > Cell Options > Text**. This opens the Cell Options dialog box for text controls.

3. Use the Vertical Justification Align menu to choose one of the four alignment options as follows:

   - **Top** positions the text at the top edge of the cell.
   - **Center** positions the text in the middle of the cell.
   - **Bottom** positions the text at the bottom edge of the cell.
   - **Justify** distributes the lines of the text evenly so that it extends from the top to the bottom of the cell.

TIP The Justify setting overrides any leading applied to the text.

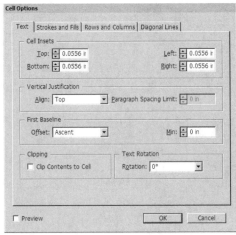

🗿 *The* **Text area of the Cell Options** *controls how text is positioned within each cell.*

🗿 *The* **Cell Insets controls** *let you specify how far away text sits from the edge of the cell.*

Customizing Cells

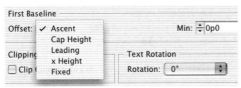

62 *When the Justify option is chosen in the Vertical Justification Align menu, the* **Paragraph Spacing Limit control** *is available.*

63 *The* **First Baseline controls** *let you set the position of the first baseline of text within a cell.*

If you choose Justify for the vertical alignment, you can then control the space between the lines or paragraphs.

To set the vertical justification spacing:

1. Select the cells you want to adjust.

2. Choose **Table > Cell Options > Text**. This opens the text controls for the cells.

3. Choose Justify from the Vertical Justification list.

4. Set an amount for the Paragraph Spacing Limit **62**.

TIP Increase the value for the paragraph spacing to avoid increasing the space between the lines within the paragraph.

Just as you can control where the first baseline of text appears in a text frame, you can also control the position of the text baseline within a cell.

To control the first baseline in a cell:

1. Select the cells you want to control.

2. Choose **Table > Cell Options > Text**. This opens the text controls for the cells.

3. In the First Baseline area, use the Offset menu to choose a setting **63**.

4. In the Min field, set the minimum amount of space for the first baseline.

Customizing Cells

Setting Borders, Strokes, and Fills

One of the benefits of using tables instead of tabs is how easy it is to add lines and colors to the table. (The line around a table is called the *border*. Lines around cells are called *strokes*. Colors inside the cells are called *fills* 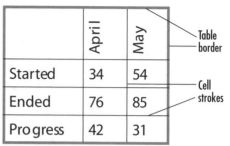.)

To add a border around the table:

1. Select at least one cell in the table.
2. Choose **Table > Table Options > Table Setup**. The Table Options dialog box opens with the Table Setup options selected .
3. In the Table Border category, use the Weight field to set the thickness of the border/line .
4. Use the Color menu to set the color of the border/line.
5. Use the Tint field to apply a screen to the color.
6. If desired, check overprint for the color *(see page 145)*.
7. Use the Type menu to set a stripe pattern for the border.

If you have applied a stroke to a cell that touches the table border, the Preserve Local Formatting checkbox controls how the table border changes the local settings to cells.

To preserve the formatting applied to cells:

1. Apple a stroke to the cells *(see the next page for how to apply strokes to cells)*.
2. In the Table Options dialog box, select Preserve Local Formatting to maintain the appearance of the cell edges that touch the table border 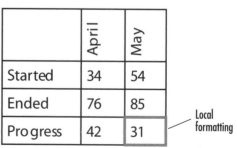.

   or

   Deselect Preserve Local Formatting to allow the table border to override the stroke applied to the cell.

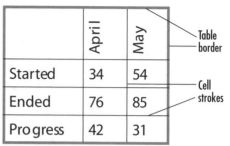

⑭ *The* **table border** *goes around the outside of a table.*

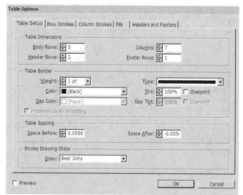

⑮ *The* **Table Setup dialog box** *lets you apply a border around the entire table.*

⑯ *You can format the line around a table with the* **Table Border** *controls.*

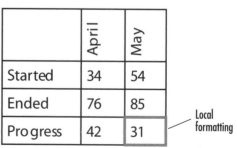

⑰ *The* **Preserve Local Formatting option** *maintains the appearance of cells that touch the table border.*

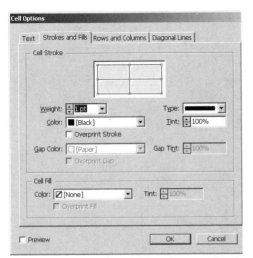

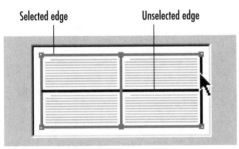

Tables are automatically created with strokes around the cells. You can remove those cell strokes, apply new ones, or customize them as you see fit.

To customize the strokes around individual cells:

1. Select the cells you want to modify.

2. Choose **Table > Cell Options > Strokes and Fills**. The Cell Options dialog box appears with the Strokes and Fills options selected 🔟.

3. Click the proxy lines in the cell preview to select which edges of the selected cells should be formatted 🔟. The top, bottom, left, and right edges of the preview area correspond to the position of the edges in the selected cells.

🔲 *Important!* Select and deselect the proxy lines in the cell preview *before* you change any of the settings in the dialog box. This avoids applying partial settings to the cells.

🔲 The cell preview area changes depending on the combination of cells, rows, or columns you have selected 🔟.

4. Set the controls under Cell Stroke to format the appearance of the selected edges.

5. Click OK to apply the settings.

🔟 *The* **Strokes and Fills controls** *under Cell Options let you format cells in a table.*

🔟 *Click the* **proxy lines for the cell stroke** *to control which edges of the cell are stroked. The colored lines indicate the edge is selected.*

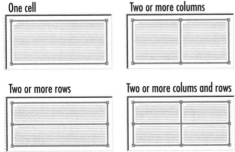

🔟 *The* **cell preview area** *changes depending on how many cells, rows, or columns are selected.*

Setting Borders, Strokes, and Fills

If all your strokes are the same solid color, you don't have to worry about how the table is drawn, But as soon as you mix strokes or use nonsolid strokes, you need to set preferences for how the strokes appear when they cross each other.

To set the stacking order for the border and strokes:

1. Select at least one cell in the table.

2. Choose **Table > Table Options > Table Setup**. The Table Options dialog box appears.

3. Choose one of the following from the Draw menu 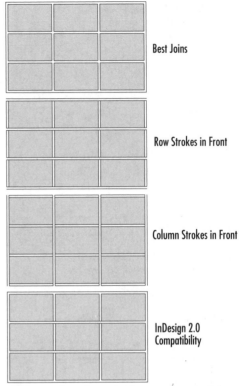:

   - **Best Joins** lets InDesign create the best possible appearance for how the strokes intersect.
   - **Row Strokes in Front** moves the strokes for the rows in front of the strokes for the columns.
   - **Column Strokes in Front** moves the strokes for the columns in front of the strokes for the rows.
   - **InDesign 2.0 Compatibility** uses a combination of the Best Joins for the table border and the rows in front of the strokes for the interior cells.

Best Joins

Row Strokes in Front

Column Strokes in Front

InDesign 2.0 Compatibility

71 *Examples of how the* **Draw menu settings** *are applied to tables.*

You can also fill the inside of a cell with a color or gradient.

To customize the fill inside individual cells:

1. Select the cells you want to modify.

2. Choose **Table > Cell Options > Strokes and Fills**. The Cell Options dialog box opens set to Strokes and Fills.

3. Set the controls under Cell Fill to format the color inside the selected cells **72**.

TIP If you have already defined a gradient swatch, you can fill the selected cells with a gradient.

72 *The* **Cell Fill controls** *let you apply colors to individual cells in a table.*

Setting Borders, Strokes, and Fills

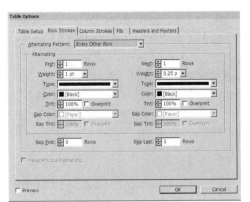

73 *The* **Table Options for Row Strokes** *allow you to apply alternating patterns for the strokes applied to rows.*

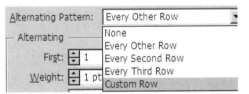

74 *The* **Alternating Pattern menu** *for setting table rows.*

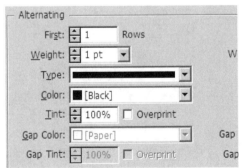

75 *The* **Alternating controls** *allow you to choose the appearance for the alternating row strokes.*

Alternating Strokes and Fills

Many people who work with tables find it helpful to set alternating strokes or fills for entire rows or columns in repeating patterns. This can help readers easily navigate down the column or across the row in lengthy tables.

TIP Even if you insert or delete rows or columns, the Alternating Pattern feature automatically reapplies the correct sequence of fills to your table.

To alternate repeating strokes for rows:

1. Select at least one cell in the table.

2. Choose **Table** > **Table Options** > **Alternating Row Strokes**. The Table Options dialog box opens set to the Row Strokes tab **73**.

3. Use the Alternating Pattern menu to choose how frequently the row strokes will alternate **74**.

4. Set the controls on the left side of the Alternating area to format the stroke appearance for the first set of rows **75**.

5. Set the controls on the right side of the Alternating area to format the appearance of the stroke for the next or second set of rows.

6. Use the Skip First and Skip Last fields to omit certain columns at the start and end of the table from the alternating count.

TIP If you have applied custom strokes to individual cells and want to override the local formatting, uncheck the Preserve Local Formatting checkbox.

Alternating Strokes and Fills

To alternate repeating strokes for columns:

1. Select at least one cell in the table.

2. Choose **Table > Table Options > Alternating Column Strokes**. The Table Options dialog box opens set to Column Strokes **76**.

3. Use the Alternating Pattern menu to choose how many column strokes will alternate **77**.

4. Set the controls on the left side of the Alternating area to format the appearance of the stroke for the first set of columns **78**.

5. Set the controls on the right side of the Alternating area to format the appearance for the second set of columns.

6. Use the Skip First and Skip Last fields to omit certain columns at the start and end of the table from the alternating count.

TIP If you have applied strokes to individual cells, the Preserve Local Formatting command controls whether the alternating strokes for columns override that local formatting.

76 *The* **Column Strokes controls** *under Table Options let you apply automatic alternating strokes to table columns.*

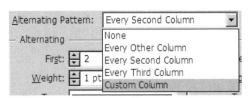

77 *The* **Alternating Pattern menu** *for table columns.*

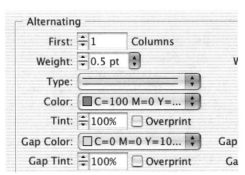

78 *The* **Alternating controls** *allow you to choose the appearance for the alternating column strokes.*

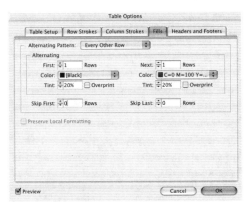

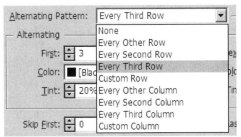

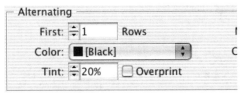

79 *The **Fills controls** under Table Options let you apply automatic alternating fills to table rows or columns.*

80 *The **Alternating Pattern menu** for setting table fills.*

81 *The **Alternating controls** allow you to choose the appearance for the alternating fills.*

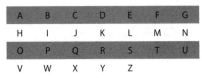

82 *An example of a table that uses the **alternating fills** for repeating rows.*

To alternate repeating fills:

1. Select at least one cell in the table.

2. Choose **Table > Table Options > Alternating Fills**. The Table Options dialog box appears set to Fills **79**.

   or

   Choose **Table Options > Alternating Fills** from the Table palette.

3. Use the Alternating Pattern menu to choose how many row or column fills will alternate **80**.

4. Set the controls on the left side of the Alternating area to format the appearance of the fill for the first set of columns or rows **81**.

5. Set the controls on the right side of the Alternating area to format the appearance of the second set of columns or rows.

6. Use the Skip First and Skip Last fields to omit certain rows or columns at the start and end of the table from the alternating count.

TIP If you have applied fills to individual cells, the Preserve Local Formatting command controls whether the alternating fills override that local formatting.

TIP My own personal favorite is to set repeating fills of light and dark rows **82**.

Alternating Strokes and Fills

Adding Diagonal Lines in Cells

Many people who design tables use diagonal lines to indicate empty data or corrected information. InDesign lets you apply diagonal lines inside cells.

To add diagonal lines in cells:

1. Select the cells you want to modify.

2. Choose **Table > Cell Options > Diagonal Lines**. The Cell Options dialog box opens with the Diagonal Lines options selected **83**.

3. Click one of the direction controls to set the direction of the diagonal lines **84** and their styles **85**.

4. Set the Line Stroke options to format the appearance of the line **86**.

5. Choose one of the following from the Draw menu:

   • **Content in Front** positions the diagonal line behind any text in the cell.

   • **Diagonal in Front** positions the diagonal line in front of any text in the cell.

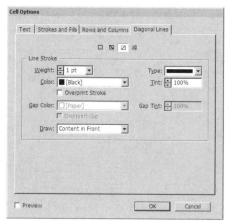

83 *The* **Diagonal Lines controls** *under Cell Options let you add diagonal lines to cells.*

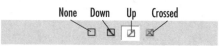

84 *The* **direction controls** *for the diagonal lines in cells.*

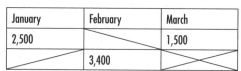

85 *Examples of how the diagonal lines can be used in cells.*

86 *The* **Line Stroke controls** *for diagonal lines let you style the appearance of the diagonal lines inside cells.*

Table palette menu

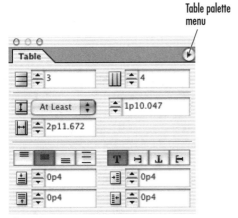

87 *The* **Table palette** *provides an onscreen palette to modify many of the table controls.*

88 *When a table is selected, the Control palette displays some of the* **table controls.**

Using the Table or Control Palettes

You can also work with the Table palette or the Control palette to modify the number of columns and rows, their width and height, and other settings in tables.

To work with the Table palette or Control palette:

1. Select the table or cells in the table.

2. Choose **Window > Type & Tables > Table.** This opens the Table palette **87**.

   or

   Choose **Window > Control.** This opens the Control palette **88**.

3. Use the controls, fields, and icons as shown in the following chart.

Table feature	Icon
Number of rows	▤ ⬍ 4
Number of columns	▥ ⬍ 3
Row height menu	⯐ Exactly ▼
Row height	⬍ 1p4.32
Column width control	⊟ ⬍ 6p5.75
Text vertical justification	≡ ≡ ≡ ≣
Text rotation	T ⊣ ⊥ ⊢
There are four controls that are found only in the Table palette:	
Top cell inset	⬍ 0p4
Bottom cell inset	⬍ 0p4
Left cell inset	⬍ 0p4
Right cell inset	⬍ 0p4

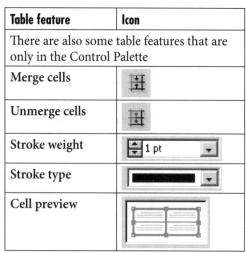

Table feature	Icon
There are also some table features that are only in the Control Palette	
Merge cells	
Unmerge cells	
Stroke weight	
Stroke type	
Cell preview	

TIP You can also use the commands in the Table palette menu or Control palette menu to modify the table.

AUTOMATING YOUR WORK 14

I have a general rule about working with a computer. Anytime I find myself doing the same thing more than ten times in a row, I stop. Most likely there is a command or tool that I can use to automate the process.

That's what this chapter is about — learning how to automate InDesign so the application does the dull, tedious chores for you. (Sadly, I can't apply this rule to other parts of my life, such as washing dishes, cleaning the litter box, or folding socks.)

There are many different automation features. You can use Find/Change, Spell Check, Footnotes, and Find Font to quickly change text formatting. Footnotes make it possible to Simply choose the command and let InDesign do its stuff.

As amazing as these features are, they are not the ultimate in automation. The next chapter shows how text and object styles are even more powerful automation tools.

Of course, you're not required to learn any of these automation features. You are perfectly welcome to modify text by hand, one word at a time — especially if you don't care about doing anything else in your life.

Changing Case

InDesign gives you a command to quickly change text case.

To change text case:

1. Select the text you want to change.
2. Choose **Type** > **Change Case** and then choose one of the following: lowercase, Title Case, Sentence case, or UPPERCASE from the submenu.

Checking Spelling

One of the most popular features of page layout programs is the spelling checker, which searches a document for misspelled words.

To use the spell check command:

1. To check the spelling in a specific text frame or linked frames, click to place an insertion point anywhere within the text.
2. Choose **Edit** > **Check Spelling.** The Check Spelling dialog box appears ➊.
3. In the Search list, choose where the spelling check should be performed:
   - **All Documents** checks all open documents.
   - **Document** checks the entire active document.
   - **Story** checks all the linked frames of the selected text.
   - **To End of Story** checks from the insertion point.
   - **Selection** checks only the selected text.
4. Check the Case Sensitive option to require a match for upper- and lowercase characters.
5. Click Start to begin the spelling check. InDesign searches through the text, then stops and displays each error it finds.
   - **TIP** InDesign displays words that aren't in its dictionary, duplicate words, and capitalization errors.

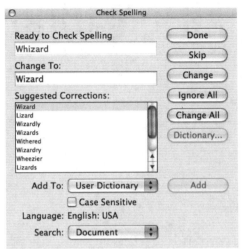

➊ *The* **Check Spelling dialog box** *is the command center for a spelling check.*

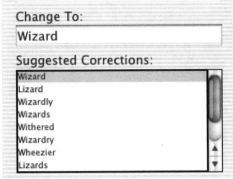

Change To:

Wizard

Suggested Corrections:

Wizard
Lizard
Wizardly
Wizards
Withered
Wizardry
Wheezier
Lizards

② *InDesign gives you a list of* **suggested corrections** *for the unknown words found during a spelling check.*

The Limitations of the Spelling Check

Every once in a while, I read an article about how the use of spelling checkers in computers is contributing to the death of proper writing and language. It's true; too many people run a spelling check and don't bother to actually read the document. Consider the following text:

Their is knot any thing wrung with using a spelling cheque on a sent tents in a doc you mint. Ewe just haft to clique the write butt ends.

Obviously the paragraph is utter nonsense. Yet InDesign's spelling checker (as well as the spelling checker in most other programs) wouldn't flag a single word as being incorrect.

A spelling checker only flags words it doesn't recognize; but since everything in the paragraph is an actual word, InDesign doesn't see any problems. So, please, don't skip a session with a proofreader just because you've run a spelling check.

The spelling checker may display a word that is correctly spelled. This could be a specialized term (like *InDesign*) or a proper name (like *Sandee*). If you have words like that, you will want to instruct the spelling checker to ignore those specialized words.

To ignore a specialized word:

◆ Click Skip to continue the spelling check without changing that instance of the text.

or

Click Ignore All to continue the spelling check without changing any instance of that text.

TIP Once you press the Start button, it then turns into the Skip button.

Of course, the spelling checker wouldn't be very helpful if it couldn't make changes to suspect words.

To correct the error displayed:

1. Type a correction in the Change To box.

or

Select a word from the Suggested Corrections list **②**.

2. Click Change to change only that instance of the word in the text.

or

Click Change All to change all instances of the word in the text.

Checking Spelling

The Ignore commands only work during a particular session of InDesign. If you use specialized words frequently, you should add them to the dictionary that InDesign uses during a spell check.

To add words to the spelling check dictionary:

◆ Click Add when the word is displayed during the spelling check.

To edit the dictionary:

1. Choose **Edit > Spelling > Edit Dictionary** to open the Dictionary dialog box ❸.

TIP You can also open the Dictionary by clicking the Dictionary button in the Check Spelling dialog box ❶.

2. Use the Target list to choose which dictionary you want to add the words to. *(See page 538 for how to create multiple dictionaries.)*

3. Choose the language from the Language list.

TIP If you have only one language in the Language list, you need to do a custom installation of InDesign to install the rest of the language dictionaries.

4. Choose Added Words, Removed Words, or Ignored Words from the Dictionary List.

5. Check the Case Sensitive option to ensure that the case of the word as entered in the dictionary is used during the spelling check.

6. Type the word you want to add in the Word field.

   or

   Click the word you want to remove.

7. Click the Add or Remove button.

TIP The words in the Dictionary also help you control hyphenation. *(See Chapter 16, "Typography Controls," more information on working with hyphenation.)*

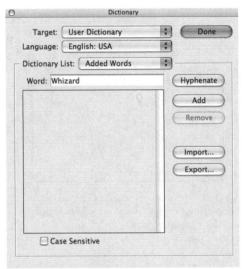

❸ *The* **Dictionary dialog box** *allows you to add or delete words in the dictionary used for a spelling check.*

Checking Spelling

dorothy and
the the Munchkins.

❹ *The* **wavy underlines** *indicate which words have been flagged by the dynamic spelling checker.*

dorothy and teh Munchkins As typed

Dorothy and the Munchkins After the autocorrection

❺ *An example of how the* **Autocorrect** *feature corrects the capital letter and the misspelled words.*

You may want to send your dictionary list to others. To do this, you can export the list.

To export entries in the spelling check dictionary:

1. Click the Export button.
2. Name the file and save it.

To import entries into a spelling check dictionary:

1. Click the Import button.
2. Find the file you wish to import.

InDesign also flags suspect words in the layout or Story Editor the same way it would in the spelling checker.

To use the dynamic spelling:

◆ Choose **Edit** > **Spelling** > **Dynamic Spelling**. The dynamic spell checker displays unknown words and other spelling errors with wavy underlines **❹**. *(See Chapter 21, "Customizing InDesign," for how to set the preferences for the spelling and dynamic spelling checkers.)*

You can also set InDesign to automatically correct spelling errors as you type. This is called the Autocorrect feature.

To automatically correct spelling errors as you type:

◆ Choose **Edit** > **Spelling** > **Autocorrect**. A check appears in front of the command to indicate that Autocorrect is turned on.

TIP The Autocorrection feature only corrects words that are in the Autocorrect preferences *(see page 541)* or wrongly capitalized words **❺**. It does not automatically correct unknown words or repeated words.

Checking Spelling

Finding and Changing Text

InDesign has a powerful Find/Change command that lets you find all instances of text or formatting and make changes to the found items. The simplest Find/Change command looks for certain characters of text, called *text strings,* and changes them. For instance, you can change *Sept.* into *September.*

To set the Find/Change text strings:

1. To find and change within a specific text frame or linked frames, click to place an insertion point within the text.

2. Choose **Edit > Find/Change.** The Find/Change dialog box appears 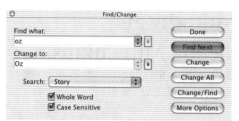.

3. In the Find What field, type or paste the text you want to search for.

4. In the Change To field, type or paste the text to be inserted.

5. In the Search pop-up list, choose where the search should be performed:
   - **All Documents** checks all open documents.
   - **Document** checks the entire active document.
   - **Story** checks all the linked frames of the selected text.
   - **To End of Story** checks from the insertion point.
   - **Selection** checks only the selected text.

6. Select Case Sensitive to limit the search to text with the same capitalization. For instance, a case-sensitive search for "InDesign" does not find "Indesign."

7. Select Whole Word to disregard the text if it is contained within another word. For instance, a whole-word search for "Design" omits the instance in "InDesign."

8. Click Start. InDesign looks through the text and selects each matching text string it finds.

⑥ *The* **Find/Change dialog box** *allows you to set the controls for searching for and replacing text.*

Finding and Changing Text

7 *Press the controls next to the Find What and Change To fields to open the* **metacharacters menus***.*

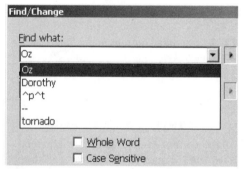

8 *InDesign keeps a record of the past 15 text strings in the Find What or Change To fields.*

As you run a Find/Change search, you can choose whether or not to apply changes.

To apply the Find/Change changes:

◆ Click Change to change the text without moving to the next instance.

or

Click Change/Find to change the text and move to the next instance.

or

Click Change All to change all the instances in the text.

You can tell InDesign to ignore or skip a Find/Change instance.

To ignore a Find/Change instance:

◆ Click Find Next to avoid changing that instance of the found text and skip to the next occurrence.

InDesign also lets you search for special characters such as spaces, hyphens, paragraph returns, tab characters, or inline graphic markers. These are called *metacharacters* for the Find/Change commands.

To Find/Change metacharacters:

1. Choose the character you want to look for in the Find What menu **7**.

2. Choose the character you want to substitute in the Change To menu.

3. Apply the Find/Change commands as described on the opposite page.

TIP InDesign also keeps a list of the past 15 text strings for both the Find What and the Change To fields. You can use that list to quickly reapply searches **8**.

Finding and Changing Text

The Find What menu has three special meta-characters called *wildcard* characters. The wildcard characters allow you to search for items that are defined as a range of characters.

To search for wildcard characters:

1. Choose one of the wildcard characters from the Find What menu:
   - **Any Character** finds any character including spaces, tabs, returns, or text.
   - **Any Digit** searches for any number from 0 to 9.
   - **Any Letter** searches for any alphabetical letter from A to Z.
2. Set the Change To options.
3. Run the search.

TIP You can only use wildcard characters in the Find What field, not in the Change To field.

The Find/Change dialog box has additional options that let you search for more than just text strings. You can use the Find/Change dialog box to search for formatting options.

To expand the Find/Change options:

- Click More Options in the Find/Change dialog box. This opens the format options that let you change formatting attributes such as typestyle, size, paragraph attributes, character colors, and so on ❾. *(See the next exercises for setting the format options.)*

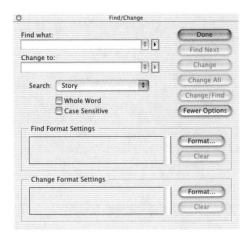

❾ *The* **expanded options** *in the Find/Change dialog box.*

Working with Wildcard Characters

You cannot insert wildcard characters in the Change To field. However, that should not discourage you from working with wildcard characters.

The numbers for the steps of this book are an example of how I can format using wildcard characters. In the Find What field I enter ^9.^t, which is the code for any digit (^9), followed by a period (.), and the code for a tab (^t).

I set the formatting for the number style in the Change To field. InDesign searches for any number followed by a period and a tab and applies the proper formatting as set in the Change To field.

In addition to text strings, you can also Find/Change formatting. This helps when making changes to text that has been imported from word-processing programs.

Finding and Changing Text

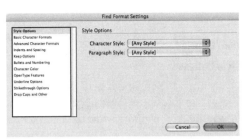

⓾ *The* **Find Format Settings dialog box** *lets you search for specific formatting options.*

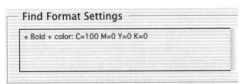

⓫ **Formatting criteria** *appear in the Find Format Settings area of the Find/Change dialog box.*

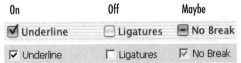

⓬ *The* **three states for checkboxes** *in the Find/Change dialog box. Notice the difference between the Maybe state for the Mac (top) and Windows (bottom).*

With the Find/Change dialog box expanded, you can set the formatting options for either the Find or Change field.

To search for formatting options:

1. Click the Format button in the Find Format Settings area of the Find/Change dialog box. This opens the Find Format Settings dialog box **⓾**.

2. Choose those formatting categories on the left side of the Find Format Settings dialog box **⓾**. *(See the chart on the following pages for an explanation of what each category controls.)*

3. Enter the criteria you want to search for in the fields for the chosen category.

TIP For instance, if you want to search for all 12-point text, you would choose the Basic Character category and then enter 12 for the point size.

4. Click OK. The search criteria are displayed in the Find Format Settings area **⓫**.

TIP Leave the Find What field blank to search for formatting without looking for specific text.

TIP There are three ways to set checkboxes in the Find/Change dialog box. Click three times to cycle through the choices **⓬**:

- **On** means the attribute will be searched or replaced. Use this to look for an attribute that has been applied to the text or to apply the attribute.
- **Off** means the attribute will not be searched or replaced. Use this to look for an attribute that has not been applied to the text or to remove the attribute.
- **Maybe** means the attribute may or may not be searched or replaced. Use this if you don't want to change the attribute from its current state.

Finding and Changing Text

Find Dialog Box Settings

Find Format Settings dialog box appearance	Find/Change Features
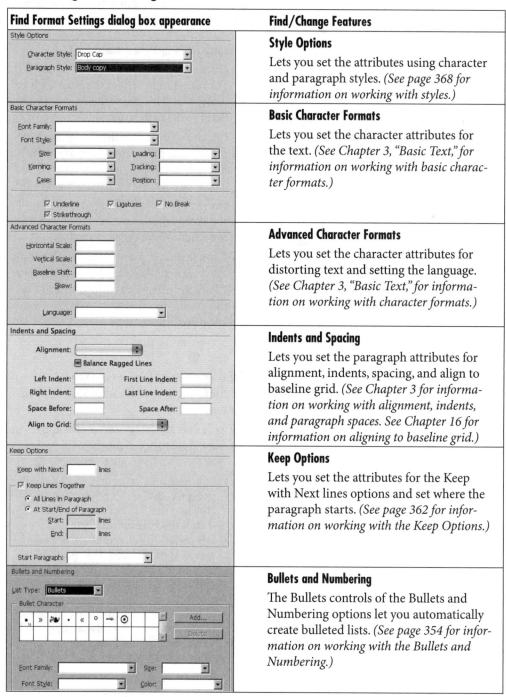	**Style Options** Lets you set the attributes using character and paragraph styles. *(See page 368 for information on working with styles.)*
	Basic Character Formats Lets you set the character attributes for the text. *(See Chapter 3, "Basic Text," for information on working with basic character formats.)*
	Advanced Character Formats Lets you set the character attributes for distorting text and setting the language. *(See Chapter 3, "Basic Text," for information on working with character formats.)*
	Indents and Spacing Lets you set the paragraph attributes for alignment, indents, spacing, and align to baseline grid. *(See Chapter 3 for information on working with alignment, indents, and paragraph spaces. See Chapter 16 for information on aligning to baseline grid.)*
	Keep Options Lets you set the attributes for the Keep with Next lines options and set where the paragraph starts. *(See page 362 for information on working with the Keep Options.)*
	Bullets and Numbering The Bullets controls of the Bullets and Numbering options let you automatically create bulleted lists. *(See page 354 for information on working with the Bullets and Numbering.)*

Find Dialog Box Settings

Find Format Settings dialog box appearance	Find/Change Features
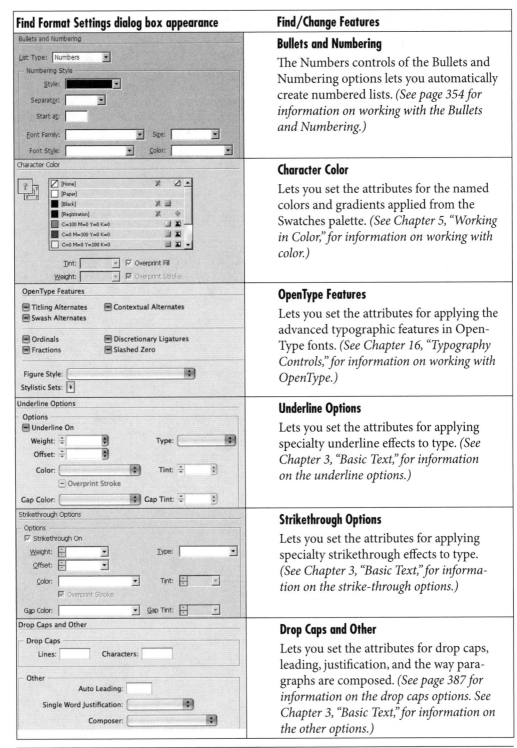	**Bullets and Numbering** The Numbers controls of the Bullets and Numbering options lets you automatically create numbered lists. *(See page 354 for information on working with the Bullets and Numbering.)*
	Character Color Lets you set the attributes for the named colors and gradients applied from the Swatches palette. *(See Chapter 5, "Working in Color," for information on working with color.)*
	OpenType Features Lets you set the attributes for applying the advanced typographic features in Open-Type fonts. *(See Chapter 16, "Typography Controls," for information on working with OpenType.)*
	Underline Options Lets you set the attributes for applying specialty underline effects to type. *(See Chapter 3, "Basic Text," for information on the underline options.)*
	Strikethrough Options Lets you set the attributes for applying specialty strikethrough effects to type. *(See Chapter 3, "Basic Text," for information on the strike-through options.)*
	Drop Caps and Other Lets you set the attributes for drop caps, leading, justification, and the way paragraphs are composed. *(See page 387 for information on the drop caps options. See Chapter 3, "Basic Text," for information on the other options.)*

Find Dialog Box Settings

Finding and Changing Text (continued)

With the Find/Change dialog box expanded, you can set the formatting options for either the Find or the Change field.

To set the replacement formatting options:

1. Click the Format button in the Change Format Settings area of the Find/Change dialog box. This opens the Change Format Settings dialog box.

TIP This dialog box is identical to the Find Format Settings dialog box.

2. Choose the formatting categories on the left side of the Change Format Settings dialog box.

3. Enter the criteria you want to replace in the fields for the chosen category.

TIP For instance, if you want to make all the found text italic, you would choose the Basic Character category and then enter "italic" in the style.

4. Click OK. The replaced criteria are displayed in the Find Style Settings area.

TIP An alert symbol next to the Find What or Change To fields indicates that formatting options are part of the Find/Change criteria .

TIP If you click the Fewer Options button, you reduce the size of the Find/Change box, although you can still search for the Formatting options that are hidden.

To delete the formatting options:

◆ Click the Clear button to delete all the formatting in the Find Format Settings or Change Format Settings area.

🔞 *The* **alert symbol next to the Find What and Change To fields** *indicates that formatting options have been chosen as part of Find/ Change.*

Finding and Changing Text

THE WONDERFUL WIZARD OF OZ

Chapter 1
The Cyclone

Dorothy lived in the midst of the great Kansas prairies, with *Uncle Henry*, who was a farmer, and *Aunt Em*, who was the farmer's wife. Their house was small, for the lumber to build it had to be carried by wagon many miles. There were four walls, a

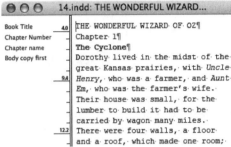

		14.indd: THE WONDERFUL WIZARD...
Book Title	4.0	[THE· WONDERFUL· WIZARD· OF· OZ¶
Chapter Number		Chapter· 1¶
Chapter name		**The· Cyclone¶**
Body copy first		Dorothy· lived· in· the· midst· of· the·
	9.4	great· Kansas· prairies,· with· *Uncle·*
		Henry,· who· was· a· farmer,· and· *Aunt·*
		Em,· who· was· the· farmer's· wife.··
		Their· house· was· small,·· for· the·
		lumber· to· build· it· had· to· be·
		carried· by· wagon· many· miles.··
	12.2	There· were· four· walls,· a· floor·
		and· a· roof,· which· made· one· room;

14 *Text is displayed in the* **Story Editor** *without most of its special formatting. This makes it easier to make changes to the text.*

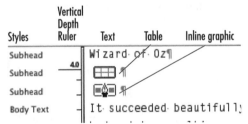

Styles	Vertical Depth Ruler	Text	Table	Inline graphic
Subhead	4.0	Wizard· of· Oz¶		
Subhead				
Subhead				
Body Text		It· succeeded· beautifully		

15 *The Story Editor displays the various elements within the story.*

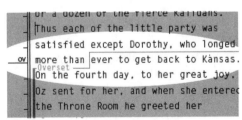

or· a· dozen· of· the· fierce· Kalidahs.
Thus· each· of· the· little· party· was
satisfied· except· Dorothy,· who· longed
ov more· than ever· to· get· back· to· Kansas.
Overset
On· the· fourth· day,· to· her· great· joy,
Oz· sent· for· her,· and· when· she· entered
the· Throne· Room· he· greeted· her

16 *The* **Overset Text indicator** *shows where the text extends outside the visible area of the text frame.*

Using the Story Editor

For people like me, one of the *good* things about electronic page layout is that I edit text as it appears on the page.

For others, one of the *bad* things about electronic page layout is that they edit text as it appears on the page. Those people like to edit text without seeing images, typefaces, sizes, and other design elements **14**. For those people, InDesign has a Story Editor.

To use the Story Editor:

1. Select the text frame that contains the text you want to edit, or place your insertion point inside the text.

2. Choose **Edit > Edit in Story Editor**. The Story Editor opens.

3. Use the right side of the Story Editor to make changes to the text. Any changes you make in the Story Editor appear on the document page.

4. Use the left side of the Story Editor to view the paragraph styles that may have been assigned to the text **15**. *(See page 368 for information on styles.)*

5. If your text is overset inside the text frame, the Overset Text indicator displays where the overset appears **16**.

TIP The text within tables cannot be displayed in the Story Editor.

TIP The Story Editor appears as a separate window from your document page. You don't have to close the Story Editor to move back to the document. Just click the document page to work on it; then click to move back to the Story Editor.

TIP You can change the display of the Story Editor by changing the preference settings *(see page 542).*

Bullets and Numbering

InDesign can also automatically add bullets and numbers in front of paragraphs. This makes it easier to create and format those paragraph lists.

To add bullets to a paragraph:

1. Choose Bullets and Numbering from the Paragraph palette menu. The Bullets and Numbering dialog box appears.

2. Choose Bullets from the List Type menu. This displays the bullets options 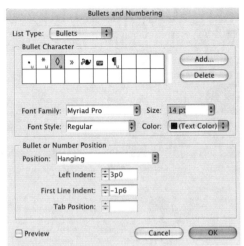.

3. Choose a bullet from the Bullet Character.

4. Use the Font Family, Font Style, Size, and Color controls to style the bullet.

TIP See the exercise on the following page for how to set the position of the bullet.

TIP The letter **u** under the character indicates that the bullet can be styled with any font. Bullets without a **u** are set to one font.

TIP You can also click the Bullets icon in the Control palette . This applies the last-used setting of the bullet options.

To add bullet characters:

1. Click the Add button in the Bullets and Numbering dialog box. The Add Bullets dialog box opens 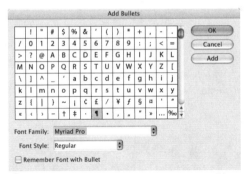.

2. Use the glyphs area to choose the character for the bullet.

3. If you want, choose the Font Family and Font Style for the bullet.

4. To set the bullet to a specific font, click Remember Font with Bullet.

5. Click Add or OK to add the character to the bullet list and choose new characters.

6. Click OK to quit the dialog box.

Bullets are just one type of character that can be added to paragraphs. You can also automatically create numbered lists with the Bullets and Numbering controls.

⑰ *The* **Bullets options** *of the* **Bullets and Numbering dialog box** *let you select and format bullets automatically.*

⑱ *The* **Bullets icon** *in the Control palette quickly applies bulleted lists.*

⑲ *The* **Add Bullets dialog box** *lets you add new bullet characters.*

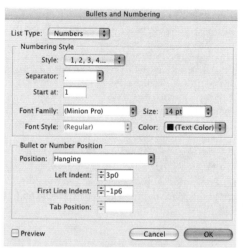

20 *The* **Numbers options** *of the* **Bullets and Numbering dialog box** *lets you select and format numbers automatically.*

21 *The* **Numbers icon** *in the Control palette quickly applies numbered lists.*

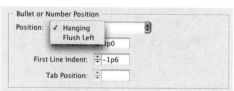

22 *The* **Position controls** *of the* **Bullets and Numbering dialog box**.

To create automatic numbered lists:

1. Choose Bullets and Numbering from the Paragraph palette menu. The Bullets and Numbering dialog box appears.

2. Choose Numbers from the List Type menu to display the numbers options **20**.

3. Use the Separator control to choose a character that follows the number. You can also type your own character.

4. Use the Start At field to designate what number the list should start with.

5. Use the Style list to choose Roman or Arabic numerals, or letters, for the list.

6. Use the Font Family, Font Style, Size, and Color controls to style the number.

TIP You can also click the Numbers icon in the Control palette **21**. This applies the last setting of the numbers options.

To set the position of bullets or numbers:

1. Use the Position list to choose one of the following **22**:
   - **Hanging** positions the character to the left of the text in the paragraph.
   - **Flush Left** positions the character within the left indent of the paragraph.

2. If you choose Hanging, use the First Line Indent control to set the indent for the left side of the text.

3. If you choose Hanging, use the Start At field to designate what number the list should start with.

4. If you choose Flush Left, use the Tab Position field to set the position of the first character after the bullet or number.

To convert bullets or numbers to text:

- Choose Convert Bullets and Numbering to Text from the Paragraph palette menu:

TIP Use this command if you are going to export the text or save the document to a previous version of InDesign.

Bullets and Numbering

Footnotes

Footnotes are the tiny reference markers inserted into text that correspond to comments usually inserted at the bottom of that column of text. InDesign makes it easy to insert, format, and update footnotes.

To insert a footnote into text:

1. Position the insertion point where you want the footnote reference to appear.

2. Choose **Type > Insert Footnote**. The reference appears in the text and the insertion point appears in the footnote position at the bottom of the text ㉓.

3. Type or paste the text for the footnote.

You can also format the style for the reference and the footnote.

To format the style of the footnote:

1. Choose **Type > Document Footnote Options**.

2. Click the Numbering and Formatting tab to display those options ㉔.

3. Use the Style list to choose Roman or Arabic numerals, symbols, letters, or asterisks for the reference ㉕.

4. Use the Start At field to set what number the footnotes should start with.

5. If desired, click the options for Restart Numbering Every and then choose Page, Spread, or Section.

6. If desired, turn on the option for "Show Prefix/Suffix in" and then choose Footnote Reference, Footnote Text, or Both Reference and Text.

7. Use the Prefix field to choose a special character or to type in your own prefix for the reference.

8. Use the Suffix field to choose a special character or to type in your own suffix for the reference.

Reference   Footnote

According to Littlefield, Baum wrote the book as a parable of the Populists, an allegory of their failed efforts to reform the nation in 1896.[1] Scholars soon began to find additional correspondences between Populism and The Wonderful Wizard of Oz. Richard Jensen, in a 1971 study of Midwestern politics and culture, devoted two pages to Baum's story.[2]

1 *Littlefield, "Parable on Populism," 50, 58.*
2 *Richard Jensen, The Winning of the Midwest: Social and Political Conflict, 1888-1896 (Chicago, 1971), 282-83.*

㉓ **Footnotes** *within text allow you to easily insert reference markers and the footnote text.*

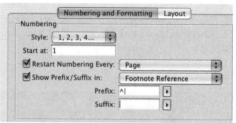

㉔ *The* **Numbering controls** *of the Footnote Options dialog box.*

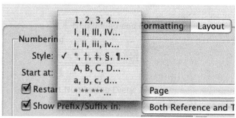

㉕ *The* **Style options** *for the footnote reference.*

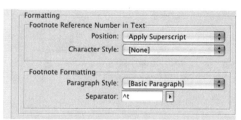

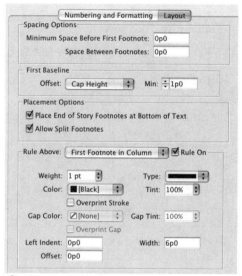

The Formatting controls *of the Footnote Options dialog box.*

The Layout controls *of the Footnote Options dialog box.*

You can also control the appearance of the reference and the footnote text.

To format the reference:

1. Click the Numbering and Formatting tab to open the Formatting controls ㉖.

2. Use the Position list to Apply Superscript, Apply Subscript, or Apply Normal position.

3. Use the Character Style list to apply a previously defined character style *(see page 382)*.

To format the footnote:

1. Click the Numbering and Formatting tab to open the Formatting controls ㉖.

2. Use Paragraph Style list to apply a previously defined paragraph style *(see page 382)*.

3. Use the Separator field to enter a tab or space between the footnote reference and the footnote text.

TIP You can enter your own character in this field, as well as have multiple characters in the field.

In addition to the Numbering and Formatting controls, you can also control the appearance and position of the layout of the footnote.

To control the spacing options for the footnote:

1. Click the Layout tab of the Footnote Options dialog box to open the Layout controls ㉗.

2. Use the Minimum Space Before First Footnote field to control how much space separates the bottom of the column and the first footnote.

3. Use the Space Between Footnotes field to control the distance between the last

Footnotes

paragraph of one footnote and the first paragraph of the next.

You can also control the position of the first baseline of the footnote.

To set the first baseline of the footnote:

1. Use the Offset list to choose the vertical alignment for the baseline.

2. Use the Min. field to increase or decrease this setting.

To set the placement options:

1. Check Place End of Story Footnotes at Bottom of Text to force a footnote that appears at the end of a story to the bottom of the text frame.

2. Check Allow Split Footnotes to permit long footnotes to flow from their original column to the next.

To set the controls for the footnote rule:

1. Choose if a separator rule is applied to one of the following:

   • **First Footnote in Column** applies the rule to the first footnote in the text column .

   • **Continued Footnotes** applies the rule to footnotes that are continued from previous columns or pages .

2. Check Rule On to apply the rule.

3. Use the rest of the controls to style the appearance of the rule *(see page 368 for information on styling paragraph rules)*.

28 *The* **Layout controls** *of the Footnote Options dialog box.*

Importing Footnotes from Microsoft Word

When you import Word documents *(see page 262)*, the Word Import Options dialog box lets you import footnotes and endnotes.

The footnotes in Word documents are converted into electronic footnotes in InDesign documents.

Endnotes, however, are imported as ordinary text. This means that although you may see the reference in the text and the footnote at the end of the story, there is no electronic link between the reference and the footnote. Unlike electronic footnotes, if you delete the reference, you won't delete the endnote at the end of the text.

Footnotes

```
<ASCII-MAC>
<dps:Normal=<Nextstyle:Normal><ct:>>
<ctable:=<Black:COLOR:CMYK:Process:0.0000
00,0.000000,0.000000,1.000000>>
<pstyle:Normal>The <ct:Bold>Scarecrow<ct:>
did not mind how long it took him to fill the
basket, for it enabled him to <ct:Italic>keep
away from the fire.<ct:> So he kept a good
distance away from the flames.
```

🕸 *The* **tagged text codes** *as they appear outside InDesign.*

The **Scarecrow** did not mind how long it took him to fill the basket, for it enabled him to *keep away from the fire.* So he kept a good distance away from the flames.

🕸 *The same text as it appears on the InDesign page.*

🕸 *The* **Export Options dialog box** *for setting the Tagged Text options.*

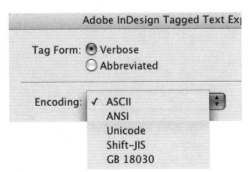

🕸 *The* **Encoding menu** *for how tagged text should be exported.*

Creating Tagged Text

If you import text from Microsoft Word, InDesign reads the paragraph and character styles applied in Word. But what happens if you want to import text from an application such as a database that doesn't have style sheets? Tags let you add the codes for styles 🕸 so that the correct formatting imports with the text 🕸.

You can learn the correct tags for different formatting by exporting tags from InDesign.

To export tags from InDesign:

1. Select the text you want to export.

2. Choose **File > Export.**

3. Choose Adobe InDesign Tagged Text from the Save as File Type (Win) or Format (Mac) menu.

4. Click Save. The Export Options dialog box appears 🕸.

5. Choose the type of tag:
   - **Verbose** shows the longer version of the tags.
   - **Abbreviated** shows the short version of the tags.

6. Choose the type of encoding 🕸:
   - **ASCII,** for most English language files.
   - **ANSI,** for most international characters.
   - **Unicode,** a standard for most languages.
   - **Shift-JIS,** for Japanese characters.
   - **GB 18030,** for Chinese characters.

Creating Tagged Text

You can import tagged text as ordinary text. However, there are some special import options for tagged text.

To import tagged text:

1. Choose **File** > **Place**.
2. Navigate to find the text-only file with the tagged text codes.
3. If you want to control how the text is placed, click Show Import Options.
4. Click Open. The Adobe InDesign Tagged Text Import Options dialog box appears ⓷.

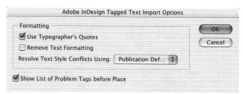

⓷ *The* **Adobe InDesign Tags Import Options dialog box** *controls how tagged text is imported.*

The tagged-text import options control how any conflicts and missing tags are treated ⓸.

To set tagged-text import options:

1. Check Use Typographer's Quotes to import text with the proper smart quotes.
2. Check Remove Text Formatting to import the text without any local formatting applied.
3. Use the Resolve Text Style Conflicts Using list to choose how to treat conflicts between the styles in the original document and those in the tagged text file:
   - **Publication Definition** uses the style as it is already defined in the document.
   - **Tagged File Definition** uses the style as defined in the tagged text. This adds a new style to the document with the word "copy" added to the style name.
4. Check Show List of Problem Tags before Place to display a list of incorrect or unrecognized tags.

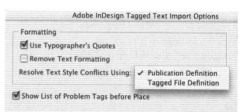

⓸ *The* **Resolve Text Style Conflicts Using menu** *lets you determine how two conflicting styles should be resolved.*

Creating Tagged Text

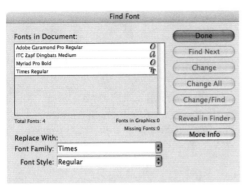

35 The **Find Font dialog box** *lets you make global changes to the fonts in a document.*

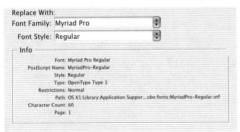

36 The **Find Font icons** *tell you the status and type of fonts used in the document.*

Copperplate Gothic	⚠	Missing font
Minion	*O*	OpenType font
Minion Bold	*a*	Type 1 font
Times Roman	T	TrueType font
Myriad-Bold		Font in graphic

37 The **Info area** *of the Find Font dialog box gives you more information about the font.*

Using Find Font

In addition to the Find/Change commands for text, InDesign lets you make global changes for font families. This helps if you open documents that contain missing fonts.

To make changes using Find Font:

1. Choose **Type > Find Font**. The Find Font dialog box appears **35**.

2. Select the font that you want to change in the list.

TIP The icons next to each font display the type of font and its status **36**.

3. Use the Replace With list to choose a replacement for the selected font.

4. Click Find First to find the first instance of the font. InDesign highlights the first place the font is used.

TIP When you find the first instance, the Find First button changes to Find Next.

5. Click one of the following options:
   - **Find Next** skips that instance.
   - **Change** replaces that instance.
   - **Change/Find** replaces that instance and finds the next instance.
   - **Change All** changes all the instances of the font.

6. Use the More Info button to find more information, such as if the fonts can be embedded in PDF documents **37**.

7. Use the Reveal in Finder (Mac) or Reveal in Explorer (Windows) to locate where the font is on the computer.

To replace missing fonts:

1. Open the document. If fonts are missing, an alert box appears.

2. Click Find Font to open the Find Font dialog box.

3. Choose the missing font and follow the steps in the previous exercise.

Keeping Lines Together

Another automation technique is to specify how many lines of text must remain together in a column or page. InDesign does this using the Keep Options controls.

To set the Keep Options for a paragraph:

1. Choose Keep Options from the Paragraph palette menu. This opens the Keep Options dialog box .

2. Enter a number in the Keep With Next Lines field to force the last line in a paragraph to stay in the same column or page with the specified number of lines.

TIP This option ensures that subheads or titles remain in the same column as the body copy that follows.

3. Click Keep Lines Together and set one of these options :

   - **All Lines in Paragraph** prevents the paragraph from ever breaking.
   - **At Start/End of Paragraph** lets you set the number of lines that must remain together for the start and the end of the paragraph.

4. Use the Start Paragraph menu to choose where the lines must jump to 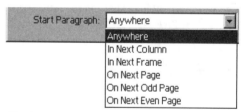.

   - **Anywhere** allows the text to jump anywhere.
   - **In Next Column** forces the text to the next column or page.
   - **In Next Frame** forces the text to the next frame or page.
   - **On Next Page** forces the text to the next page.
   - **On Next Odd Page** forces the text to the next odd-numbered page.
   - **On Next Even Page** forces the text to the next even-numbered page.

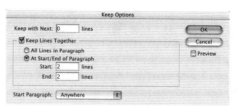

38 *The* **Keep Options dialog box** *controls how paragraphs break across columns or pages.*

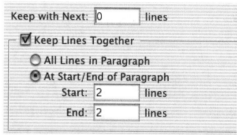

39 *The* **Keep Lines Together controls** *of the Keep Options dialog box.*

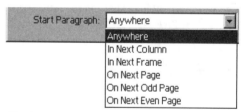

40 *The* **Start Paragraph list** *lets you choose where the next lines of the paragraph appear.*

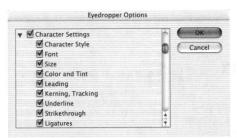

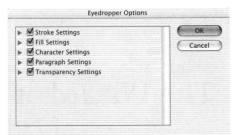

Using the Eyedropper on Text

The Eyedropper tool lets you quickly grab the formatting from one part of the text and apply it to another. *(See page 144 and page 176 for more information on how to use the eyedropper to sample colors, fills, and stroke attributes.)*

To set the eyedropper options for text:

1. Double-click the Eyedropper tool in the Toolbox ❹❶. This opens the Eyedropper Options dialog box.

2. Click the triangle control to open the Paragraph Settings from the list ❹❷.

3. Check which paragraph attributes you want the Eyedropper tool to sample.

4. Click the triangle control to open the Character Settings from the list ❹❸.

5. Check which character attributes you want the Eyedropper tool to sample.

❹❶ *The* **Eyedropper tool** *in the Toolbox lets you sample and apply text formatting.*

❹❷ *The* **Eyedropper Options dialog box** *contains the controls for text as well as object styling.*

❹❸ *Use the checkboxes to set the* **Paragraph Settings** *or the* **Character Settings**.

Using the Eyedropper on Text

Once you have set the eyedropper options, you can sample and apply paragraph or character attributes.

TIP Deselect the text frame as you use the Eyedropper tool to avoid styling the text frame itself.

To sample and apply paragraph attributes:

1. Choose the Eyedropper tool.

2. Click the white eyedropper inside the paragraph that you want to sample **44**. The eyedropper changes from white to black.

3. Click the black eyedropper inside the paragraph that you want to change **45**. This changes the paragraph attributes.

TIP The black eyedropper does not apply character attributes when clicked unless a paragraph style was already applied to the sampled text.

4. Click the eyedropper inside any additional paragraphs that you want to change.

To sample and apply character attributes:

1. Choose the Eyedropper tool.

2. Click the white eyedropper inside the text that you want to sample **46**. The eyedropper changes from white to black.

3. Drag the black eyedropper across the exact text you want to change. This highlights the text **47**.

4. Release the mouse to apply the changes.

To sample new text attributes:

1. Hold the Opt/Alt key as you click the Eyedropper tool. The Eyedropper cursor changes to white.

2. Click the eyedropper inside the new text that you want to sample.

44 *Click the white eyedropper to sample the right alignment of the paragraph attributes.*

45 *Click the black eyedropper to apply the right alignment of the paragraph attributes.*

46 *Click the white eyedropper to sample local character attributes.*

47 *Drag the black eyedropper to apply character attributes to text.*

Using the Eyedropper on Text

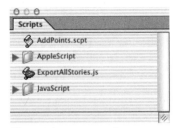

 *Use the **Scripts** palette to run scripts from within InDesign.*

My Favorite Script

My favorite script was written for me by Peter Truskier of Premedia Systems (www.premediasystems.com). This script automates the process of creating the special spotlight used on certain screen shots in this book. *(See page 353, figure ⑯ for an example of the effect.)*

With Peter's marvelous script, I can do in just a single click that which used to take me almost a minute for each illustration. Ordinarily, it costs big bucks to hire people to write scripts for you, but if you go to the Adobe Studio Exchange, (www.adobestudioexchange.com) you will find other similarly wonderful scripts that are free to download.

Using Scripts

Perhaps the most powerful way to automate working in InDesign is with AppleScripts on the Macintosh or VisualBasic scripts in Windows. You can also use JavaScripts, which work on both platforms. While you need to know code to *write* scripts, it's very easy to *run* scripts in InDesign. Writing code is much too difficiult for me. Running scripts is totally easy. (Honestly, if I can do it, anyone can!)

To run scripts in InDesign:

1. Place the script file or the folder containing the script file inside the following directory path:

   InDesign Application Folder: Presets: Scripts.

2. Choose **Windows > Automation > Scripts** to open the Scripts palette ⑱.

3. If you have placed a folder inside the Scripts directory, click the triangle controller to open the scripts in the folder.

4. Double-click the script that appears in the palette.

TIP Certain scripts require an object or text to be selected. Follow any onscreen prompts that occur.

Using Scripts

TEXT AND OBJECT STYLES 15

Last year I taught an InDesign class to a group of designers that included a young woman who was responsible for a yearly 100-page catalog of her company's products. When I got to the part of the class where I showed what text styles could do, she began to cry.

I'd never had a student break down and cry in a class, so I was very concerned. I didn't know what to do. "What's wrong?" I asked.

It took her a while to speak, but she eventually explained that it was "those styles." Turns out she had never been taught what styles did and she had been formatting the thousands of entries in the catalog by hand.

She now realized just how much time she could have saved by using text styles. Of course, this was before InDesign added object styles.

I dedicate this chapter to all of you who have been slaving away, working without text and object styles. May the techniques you learn here bring smiles, not tears, to your faces.

Defining Text Styles

InDesign has two types of text styles. *Paragraph styles* apply formatting for both character and paragraph attributes. *Character styles* apply formatting for only character attributes.

The Basic Paragraph style is the style that is always part of a document and is automatically applied to all new text 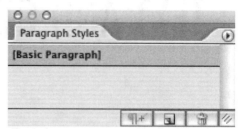. When you change the definition of the Basic Paragraph style, it automatically updates all text that has been styled with the Basic Paragraph style.

To set the Basic Paragraph attributes by example:

1. Click inside a text frame and use the Control palette, Character palette, or Paragraph palette to change the text attributes.

2. A plus sign (+) appears next to the Basic Paragraph listing in the Paragraph Styles palette 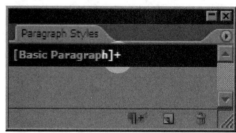. This indicates that local formatting has been applied to the Basic Paragraph.

3. Choose Redefine Style from the Paragraph Styles palette menu. This changes the definition of the Basic Paragraph to match the local formatting. The plus sign disappears.

To set the Basic Paragraph attributes by definition:

1. Double-click the Basic Paragraph listing in the Paragraph Styles palette. This opens the Paragraph Styles Options dialog box.

2. Make whatever changes to the style definition you like as explained on the following pages.

3. Click OK to make the changes.

TIP The Basic Paragraph style can be modified but not deleted.

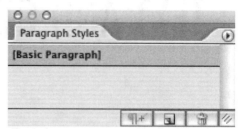

① *The* **Basic Paragraph** *is the default style that appears in all new documents.*

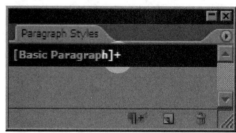

② *The* **plus sign (+) next to the style name** *indicates that local formatting has been applied to the text.*

New Style icon

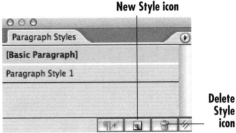

Delete Style icon

❸ *The* **Paragraph Styles palette** *lets you define and apply paragraph styles.*

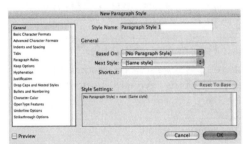

❹ *The* **New Paragraph Style dialog box** *set to the General options.*

General
Basic Character Formats
Advanced Character Formats
Indents and Spacing
Tabs
Paragraph Rules
Keep Options
Hyphenation
Justification
Drop Caps and Nested Styles
Bullets and Numbering
Character Color
OpenType Features
Underline Options
Strikethrough Options

❺ *Click each* category in the Paragraph Styles *dialog box to set the format of the style.*

You can use the Paragraph Styles palette to define new paragraph styles for a document.

To define a paragraph style manually:

1. Choose **Type** > **Paragraph Styles.** This opens the Paragraph Styles palette **❸**.

2. Choose New Paragraph Style from the Paragraph Styles palette menu.

   or

   Opt/Alt-click the New Style icon in the Paragraph Styles palette. This opens the New Paragraph Style dialog box set to the General options **❹**.

3. Use the Style Name field to name the style.

4. Set the Based On, Next Style, and Shortcuts options as described on pages 376 and 377.

5. Click each category on the left side of the dialog box and set the criteria for each one **❺**. *(See the chart on the following pages for more information on each category.)*

6. Click OK to define the style. The name of the style appears in the Paragraph Styles palette.

Defining Text Styles

Text Style Categories

Paragraph and Character Style Features

These are categories that you set for paragraph and character styles. All these categories apply for paragraph styles; they apply for character styles where indicated.

Dialog box options	Description
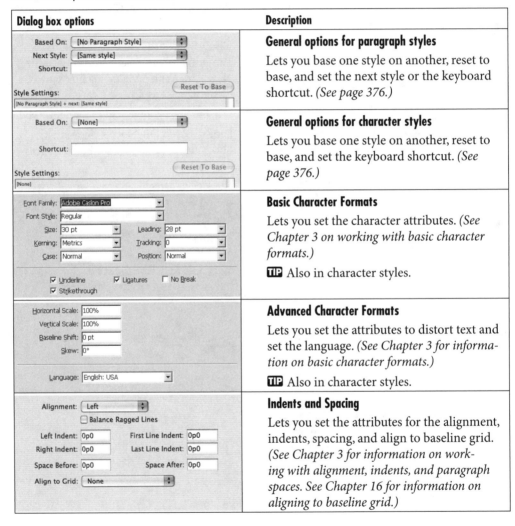	**General options for paragraph styles** Lets you base one style on another, reset to base, and set the next style or the keyboard shortcut. *(See page 376.)*
	General options for character styles Lets you base one style on another, reset to base, and set the keyboard shortcut. *(See page 376.)*
	Basic Character Formats Lets you set the character attributes. *(See Chapter 3 on working with basic character formats.)* **TIP** Also in character styles.
	Advanced Character Formats Lets you set the attributes to distort text and set the language. *(See Chapter 3 for information on basic character formats.)* **TIP** Also in character styles.
	Indents and Spacing Lets you set the attributes for the alignment, indents, spacing, and align to baseline grid. *(See Chapter 3 for information on working with alignment, indents, and paragraph spaces. See Chapter 16 for information on aligning to baseline grid.)*

Dialog box options	Description
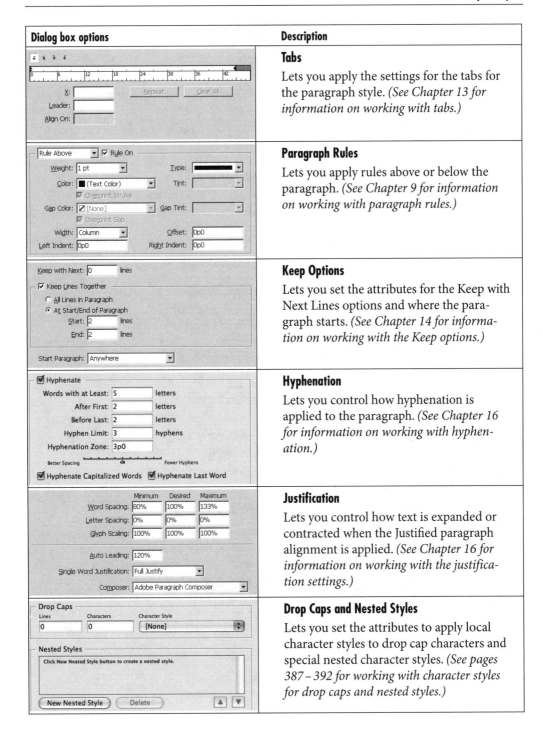	**Tabs** Lets you apply the settings for the tabs for the paragraph style. *(See Chapter 13 for information on working with tabs.)*
	Paragraph Rules Lets you apply rules above or below the paragraph. *(See Chapter 9 for information on working with paragraph rules.)*
	Keep Options Lets you set the attributes for the Keep with Next Lines options and where the paragraph starts. *(See Chapter 14 for information on working with the Keep options.)*
	Hyphenation Lets you control how hyphenation is applied to the paragraph. *(See Chapter 16 for information on working with hyphenation.)*
	Justification Lets you control how text is expanded or contracted when the Justified paragraph alignment is applied. *(See Chapter 16 for information on working with the justification settings.)*
	Drop Caps and Nested Styles Lets you set the attributes to apply local character styles to drop cap characters and special nested character styles. *(See pages 387–392 for working with character styles for drop caps and nested styles.)*

Text Style Categories

Text Style Categories

Dialog box options	Description
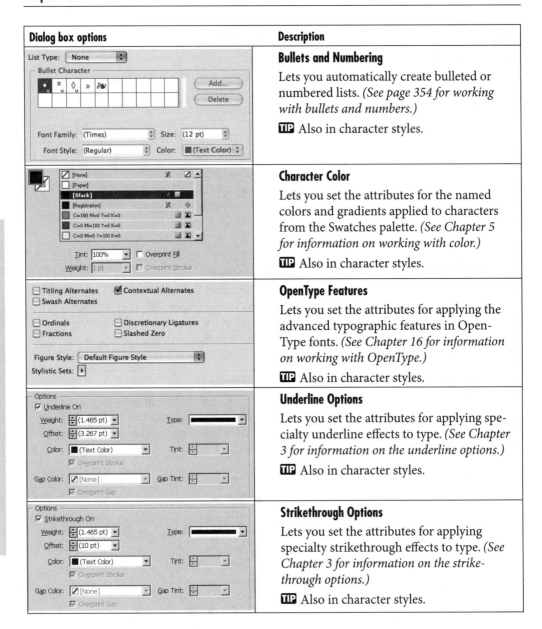	**Bullets and Numbering**
	Lets you automatically create bulleted or numbered lists. *(See page 354 for working with bullets and numbers.)*
	TIP Also in character styles.
	Character Color
	Lets you set the attributes for the named colors and gradients applied to characters from the Swatches palette. *(See Chapter 5 for information on working with color.)*
	TIP Also in character styles.
	OpenType Features
	Lets you set the attributes for applying the advanced typographic features in Open-Type fonts. *(See Chapter 16 for information on working with OpenType.)*
	TIP Also in character styles.
	Underline Options
	Lets you set the attributes for applying specialty underline effects to type. *(See Chapter 3 for information on the underline options.)*
	TIP Also in character styles.
	Strikethrough Options
	Lets you set the attributes for applying specialty strikethrough effects to type. *(See Chapter 3 for information on the strikethrough options.)*
	TIP Also in character styles.

Based On:
Next Style:
Shortcut:

[Same style]
[No Paragraph Style]
✓ Body Text
Body plain
[Basic Paragraph]

⑥ *The* **Next Style menu** *lets you choose the same style or an already defined style.*

Checking Spelling

Next style
applied

One of the most popular features of page layout programs is the Spelling Checker that checks a document for misspelled words.

To use the spell check command:

1. To check the spelling in a specific text frame or linked frames, click to place an insertion point within the text.

Same
style
applied

2. Choose Edit > Check Spelling. The Check Spelling dialog box appears **②**.

3. In the Search list, choose where the spelling check should be performed **③**:

❼ *The* **Next Style command** *automatically changes the paragraph style when a paragraph return is pressed (curved arrows). The* **Same Style command** *keeps the style when the paragraph return is pressed (straight arrows).*

Defining Text Styles (continued)

The easier way to define a style is to format the text and define the style by example.

To define a paragraph style by example:

1. Select a sample paragraph.

2. Use the Character and Paragraph palettes and any other commands to format the text.

3. Leave the insertion point in the formatted paragraph.

4. Choose **Type > Paragraph Styles**.

5. With the insertion point blinking in the formatted text, click the New Style icon. This adds a new style to the Paragraph Styles palette.

TIP Double-click to rename the style created by the New Style icon.

The Next Style command has two features. For typists who enter text directly into InDesign, it allows you to automatically switch to a new style as you type text. For instance, as I type this paragraph, I press the paragraph return after the period. This automatically switches to the next style, which is the exercise header.

To set the next paragraph style:

1. Select the General category in the New Paragraph Style dialog box.

2. Choose a style from the Next Style list in the New Paragraph Style dialog box **⑥**. The chosen style is applied to the next paragraph when you press the Return key **❼**.

   or

   Choose Same Style from the Next Style list **⑥**. This retains the original style until you manually change the style.

Defining Text Styles

The Next Style feature does even more magic when you use it to apply the next style to selected text. This allows you to format many paragraphs in one simple click.

To apply the Next Style to multiple paragraphs:

1. Highlight the text that you want to style.

   or

   Select the text frame that contains the text that you want to style.

2. Position your cursor over the name of the paragraph style that you want to apply to the first paragraph.

3. Right-click (Windows) or Control-click (Mac) the name of the style. A contextual menu appears ❽.

4. Choose Apply "name of style" then Next Style. This styles the text according to the Next Style controls ❾.

TIP The command to apply the Next Style is only available if a Next Style has been defined for the paragraph style. If the style has Same Style for the Next Style, then the contextual menu will not display the Next Style option.

❽ *The* **contextual menu over a style name** *allows you to apply a paragraph style and then the Next Style to the rest of the selected text.*

FRIDAY

The Princess Bride (1987) Directed by: Rob Reiner

SATURDAY

On the Waterfront (1954) Directed by: Elia Kazan

SUNDAY

The Wizard of Oz (1939) Directed by: Victor Fleming, Richard Thorpe

❾ *An example of how the* **Next Style** *command applies one style and then the next and the next and so on. Here the style for the day changes to the movie listing, then back to the day, and then to the listing, and so on.*

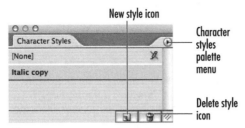

New style icon

Character styles palette menu

Delete style icon

⓾ *The* **Character Styles palette** *lets you define and apply character styles.*

⓫ *The* **New Character Style dialog box** *lets you specify settings for each of the categories for character styles.*

General
Basic Character Formats
Advanced Character Formats
Character Color
OpenType Features
Underline Options
Strikethrough Options

⓬ *Click each* **category** *in the Character Style dialog box to set the format of the style.*

Character styles allow you to set specific attributes that override the paragraph style character attributes. For instance, **this bold text** was set by applying a character style to the paragraph style.

To define a character style:

1. Choose **Type** > **Character Styles.** This opens the Character Styles palette **⓾**.
2. Choose New Character Style from the Character Styles palette menu. This opens the New Character Style dialog box **⓫**.
3. Name the style.
4. Set the Based On and Shortcut controls as described on pages 376 and 377.
5. Click each category to set the character attributes **⓬**.
6. Click OK to define the style. The name of the style appears in the Character Styles palette.

You can also format the text and then define a character style by example.

To define a character style by example:

1. Select a sample paragraph.
2. Use the Character palette and other commands to format the text.

   TIP It does not matter what paragraph attributes are applied to this text. Only the character attributes are set by example.
3. Leave the insertion point in the newly formatted text.
4. Choose **Type** > **Character Styles.**
5. Click the New Style icon. This adds a new style to the Character Styles palette.

Defining Text Styles

Basing one style on another makes it easy to coordinate multiple text styles.

To base one style on another:

1. Start with at least one paragraph or character style.

2. Open the New Character Style dialog box to define a new style.

3. From the Based On pop-up menu, choose the style you want to use as the foundation of the new style.

4. Make changes to define the second style's attributes.

TIP The changes to the second style are displayed in the Style Settings area **⑬**.

TIP Any changes you make later to the original style also affect the second style.

If you have based one style on another, you may want to remove any changes to the style so that it is like the first. This is called resetting to the base style.

To reset to the base style:

◆ Click the Reset To Base button.

Rather than create a new style from scratch, it may be easier to duplicate an existing style and then redefine it.

To duplicate a style:

1. Select the style.

2. Drag the style onto the New Style icon in the Paragraph Styles palette.

   or

   Choose Duplicate Style from the Paragraph Styles palette menu.

Style Settings:

Body Text + next: [Same style] + size: 14 pt + color: C=0 M=100 Y=0 K=0

⑬ *When you base a new style on an existing style, you can see how they differ in the Style Settings field of the New Character Style dialog box.*

Basing Styles

The style for the numbers of the exercises in this book is based on the style of the subheads. If I change the style for the subheads, the number style and the numbers change automatically.

Similarly, the style for the exercises is based on the style for the body copy. So if my publisher asks me to make the copy a little smaller, I only have to change the point size for one style.

Limit how many levels you use when you base one style on another. Theoretically, you can base one style on another, which is based on another, which is based on another, and so on. However, this can be confusing if you go down too many levels.

I always use one style as the main one and base others on it. I think of the main style as the hub of a wheel, and the others are the spokes around it.

Defining Text Styles

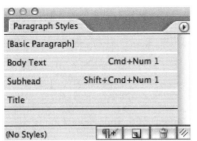

⑭ *The* **keyboard shortcut for a style** *is listed next to the name of the style.*

You can also set keyboard shortcuts for paragraph and character styles. This makes it easy to apply text styles as you type.

To set style keyboard shortcuts:

1. Open the New Paragraph Style or New Character Style dialog box.

   or

   Double-click the name of the style to open the Paragraph Style Options or Character Style Options dialog box.

2. Place an insertion point in the Shortcut field.

3. Press a keyboard modifier plus a number from the number pad. The keyboard modifiers can be a combination of one or more of the following keys:

   - Cmd (Mac) or Ctrl (Win) keys.
   - Shift key.
   - Opt (Mac) or Alt (Win) keys.

   TIP In Windows, the Num Lock key must be turned on to set keyboard shortcuts.

   TIP The keyboard shortcut appears next to the style name in the Paragraph Styles or Character Styles palette **⑭**.

Defining Text Styles

Loading and Importing Styles

You can transfer or load text styles from one document into another.

To transfer text styles into an InDesign document:

1. Choose one of the following from the Paragraph Styles or Character Styles palette menu:

   - **Load Character Styles** transfers the character styles.
   - **Load Paragraph Styles** transfers the paragraph styles.
   - **Load All Styles** transfers both character and paragraph styles.

2. Navigate to find the document with the text styles you want to import.

3. Click Open. The text styles are added to the current document.

TIP Text style names are case-sensitive. Therefore, a paragraph style name of *Body Text* will be added as a separate style to a document that already has a paragraph style named *body text* 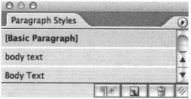.

⓯ **Style names are case sensitive,** *so two styles can have the same name but different character cases.*

How Many Styles?

I was taught to create a unique style for each type of element in my document. For instance, I might have a paragraph that I use in these sidebars that looks identical to the paragraph I use in the regular body text.

Some people might be tempted to define only one style and apply it to both paragraphs. That's not how I work. Instead, I have a unique paragraph style for each type of element.

There are two reasons for this. The first reason is that if I ever decide to change the appearance of one type of paragraph, I have that flexibility. The other reason comes from using styles as the tags that give my document structure.

With this type of structure applied to the text, I can export the text and reuse it in an XML workflow. While XML is way beyond the scope of this book, the concept of tagging each type of element with its own style is a good practice to learn.

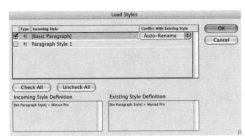

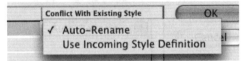

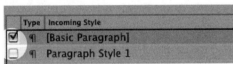

16 *The* **Load Styles dialog box** *allows you to choose how style conflicts should be resolved.*

17 **A checkmark next to the style name** *indicates the incoming style definition should be used.* **No checkmark** *indicates the existing style definition should be used.*

18 *Use the* **Conflict With Existing Style menu** *to resolve a style conflict.*

When you load styles from one document to another, there may be times when the styles coming into the document have the same name, but different definitions. This is called a style conflict. When this happens you need to resolve the conflict between the styles.

To resolve style conflicts:

1. Choose one of the Load Styles commands described above. If there are conflicts, the Load Styles dialog box displays the incoming styles that have the same name as the existing styles **16**.

2. Check the styles that you want to load into the document, and resolve the conflict **17**.

   or

   Uncheck the styles that you don't want to load into the document.

   TIP Use the Check All or the Uncheck All button to quickly make choices in a long list of styles.

3. For all the checked styles choose one of the following from the Conflict With Existing Style menu **18**:

   - **Auto-Rename** imports the style with a suffix to differentiate it from the existing style.
   - **Use Incoming Style Definition** changes the existing style to match the imported style definition.

Loading and Importing Styles

When you place text from word processing programs such as Microsoft Word into InDesign, the text styles from the imported text are added to the document.

To import styles in Microsoft Word text:

1. Choose **File > Place** and navigate to find the Word file you want to import.

2. Check Show Import Options and click Open. This opens the Microsoft Word Import Options dialog box 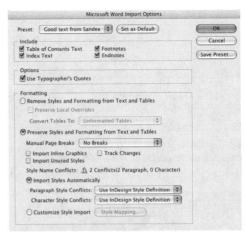.

3. Check Preserve Styles and Formatting from Text and Tables.

4. Check Import Styles Automatically.

   or

   Check Customize Style Import.

If you chose to import the styles automatically, you can choose how style conflicts are resolved.

To resolve style conflicts automatically:

1. To resolve paragraph style conflicts, choose one of the following from the Paragraph Style Conflicts menu ⑳.

   • Choose **Use InDesign Style Definition** to have the InDesign style override the incoming style.
   • Choose **Redefine InDesign Style** to have the incoming style override the InDesign style.
   • Choose **Auto Rename** to add the incoming style to the list of styles in the InDesign style palette.

2. To resolve character style conflicts choose from the Character Style Conflicts menu.

TIP A disk icon indicates that the style definition came from the imported text ㉑.

TIP The disk icon disappears if you modify the imported style.

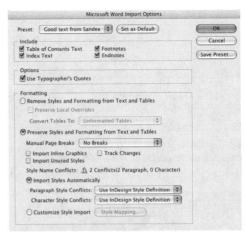

⑲ *The* **Microsoft Word Import Options** dialog box *allows you to control how styles are imported from Word files.*

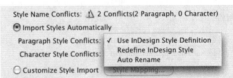

⑳ *Use the* **Paragraph Style Conflicts** *or* **Character Style Conflict menu** *to resolve a style conflict.*

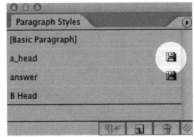

㉑ *The* **disk icon** *indicates that the style definition came from an imported text file.*

22 *Choose Customize Style Import to click the* **Style Mapping button**.

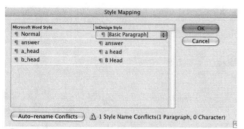

23 *The* **Style Mapping dialog box** *lets you choose how each Microsoft Word style should be applied.*

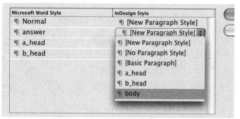

24 *The* **style choices list** *lets you map one style to another. Here the Word style* **answer** *has been mapped to the InDesign style* **body**.

What if you have a style name in Word that is totally different from the name of the style in the InDesign document? You need a way to tell InDesign which existing style to apply to the Word text. The custom style mapping controls let you change an incoming style to a specific existing style.

To map one style to another:

1. In the Microsoft Word Import Options dialog box, check Customize Style Import **22**. This makes the Style Mapping button available.

2. Click the Style Mapping button. This opens the Style Mapping dialog box **23**.

3. Under the InDesign Style column, choose one of the styles from the pop-up menu for each of the incoming Word styles **24**.

4. Click OK to close the Style Mapping dialog box.

TIP Only paragraph styles are shown in the pop-up menu for incoming Word paragraph styles. Similarly, only character styles are shown in the pop-up menu for incoming Word character styles.

5. Click OK to close the Style Mapping dialog box.

6. Click OK in the Microsoft Word Import Options dialog box to import the text.

Loading and Importing Styles

Applying Styles and Style Overrides

Defining text styles is just half of the process. You reap the benefits of your planning when you apply styles to text.

You can apply paragraph and character styles as you type new text, or you can add the styles to existing text **25**.

To apply paragraph styles:

1. Select the paragraphs.

TIP You do not need to select entire paragraphs. As long as a portion is selected, the paragraph style will be applied to the entire paragraph.

2. Click the name of the paragraph style.

   or

   Type the keyboard shortcut.

You can override the paragraph style by applying a character style or local formatting.

To apply local formatting:

1. Select the text.

2. Use the Control Palette or Character palette to format the text.

TIP A plus (+) sign next to the paragraph style name indicates that local formatting has been applied to the text **26**.

Rather than use local formatting, I prefer to use character styles on text. That way if I want to make changes later on, I can just redefine the character style.

To apply character styles:

1. Select the text.

TIP You must select all the text you want to format with a character style.

2. Click the name of the character style.

   or

   Type the keyboard shortcut.

Character styles

2. Navigate to find the document that —**Paragraph style** contains the styles you want to import.

3. Click **Open**. The styles are *automatically* added to the current document.

25 *An example of paragraph and character styles applied to text.*

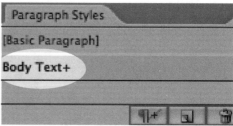

26 *The* **plus sign next to the paragraph style name** *indicates that local formatting has been applied to the text.*

Character Style Strategies

InDesign character styles only need to be defined with a single change from the paragraph attributes.

For instance, if you want to change text to italic, define a character attribute with just italic as the definition.

You can then apply the italic character attribute to many different paragraph styles, even if they are different typefaces or point sizes.

You can even define a character style with no attributes. That type of character style can be used to tag text so that it is easily found later.

This is very different from the character style sheets in QuarkXPress. In that program you need a different character style sheet to apply italics to each different typeface.

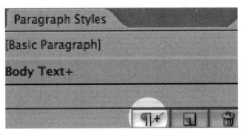

27 *The* **Clear Overrides button** *lets you remove local formatting applied to text.*

Clearing Style Overrides

When you apply local formatting or character styles, you have several different ways to clear those style overrides.

You can use the Clear Overrides button to clear the overrides in a text selection.

To clear the local formatting in a text selection:

1. Select the text you want to clear.
2. Click the Clear Overrides button in the Paragraph Styles palette **27**. This changes the local formatting in the selection to the underlying paragraph style.

You may find that you want to clear just the character attributes that were applied as local formatting, but you want to keep any paragraph attributes.

To clear only local character formatting in a text selection:

1. Select the text you want to clear.
2. Hold Cmd/Ctrl and click the Clear Overrides button. This changes the local character formatting in the selection to the underlying paragraph style.

A Summary for Clearing Overrides	
To do this:	**Do this:**
Clear all the local formatting in a selection	Click the Clear Overrides button
Clear the local character formatting in a selection	Hold Cmd/Ctrl and click the Clear Overrides button
Clear the local paragraph formatting in a selection	Hold Cmd/Ctrl-Shift and click the Clear Overrides button
Clear all the local formatting applied to a paragraph	Hold Opt/Alt and click the name of the paragraph style
Clear all the local formatting and the character styles applied to a paragraph	Hold Opt/Alt-Shift and click the name of the paragraph style

The opposite to the previous exercise allows you to clear just the paragraph attributes that were applied as local formatting, but keep any character attributes.

To clear only local paragraph formatting in a text selection:

1. Select the text you want to clear.
2. Hold Cmd/Ctrl-Shift and click the Clear Overrides button. This changes the local paragraph formatting in the selection to the underlying paragraph style.

You can also remove all local formatting without making a specific text selection.

To override local formatting:

1. Place your insertion point in the paragraph you want to override.
2. Hold the Opt/Alt key as you click the name of the paragraph style ㉘.

You may want to clear the characters styles and local formatting applied to the text.

To override character styles and local formatting:

1. Place your insertion point in the paragraph you want to override.
2. Hold the Opt/Alt and Shift keys as you click the name of the paragraph style. This deletes both the character styles and the local formatting applied to the text ㉙.

To break the link to a style:

1. Place your insertion point in the paragraph you want to override.
2. Choose Break Link to Style from the Paragraph Styles or Character Styles palette. This removes the style from the text, but does not change the formatting.

Original text with local formatting

Dorothy lived with **Uncle Henry**, and **Aunt Em**. Their house was small.

Opt/Alt-click removes local formatting

Dorothy lived with Uncle Henry, and Aunt Em. Their house was small.

㉘ Opt/Alt-click a paragraph style name *to remove any local formatting applied to text.*

Original text with character style applied

Their house was small. There were four *walls*, a *floor*, and a *roof*.

Opt/Alt-Shift-click removes character style

Their house was small. There were four walls, a floor, and a roof.

㉙ *Press* **Opt/Alt-Shift** and click a paragraph style name *to remove character styles and local formatting.*

Clearing Style Overrides

Redefining and Deleting Styles

One of the advantages of using paragraph or character styles is that when you redefine the style, it changes all the existing text that has that style applied to it.

To redefine a paragraph or character style:

1. Double-click the style name in the palette. This opens the Paragraph or Character Style Options dialog box, where you can change the attributes of the style.

2. Click OK. The style is redefined, and the text updates to reflect the new definition of the style.

To redefine a style by example:

1. Use the Control palette, Paragraph palette, or Character palette to make any changes to text that has the style applied to it.

2. Select the modified text.

3. Choose Redefine Style from the Styles palette. The style is redefined based on the modified example.

You may have styles that you do not need in your InDesign document. You can shorten the styles list by deleting unused styles.

To delete unused styles:

1. Select the styles you want to delete.

2. Drag the styles onto the Delete Style icon.

    or

    Choose Delete Styles from the Style palette menu.

TIP Use Select All Unused Styles to delete all the unused styles from a document.

Redefining and Deleting Styles

You can also delete styles that are being used in the document. In that case, you have a choice as to how to handle the text that has the style applied to it.

To delete paragraph styles that are in use:

1. Select the style you want to delete.
2. Delete the style as described in the previous exercise. An alert box appears ⑳.
3. Use the pop-up menu in the alert box to choose [No Paragraph Style], [Basic Paragraph], or one of the other paragraph styles.

To delete character styles that are in use:

1. Select the style you want to delete.
2. Delete the style as described in the previous exercise. An alert box appears ㉛.
3. Use the pop-up menu in the alert box to choose [None] or one of the other character styles.
4. Check Preserve Formatting to convert the character style into local formatting.

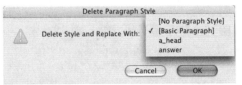

⑳ *The* **Delete Paragraph Style alert box** *lets you assign another paragraph style to replace a deleted style.*

㉛ *The* **Delete Character Style alert box** *lets you assign another character style to replace a deleted style.*

Redefining and Deleting Styles

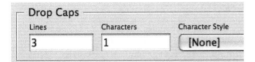

32 *The* **Drop Caps and Nested Styles dialog box** *allows you to automate the style applied to drop caps.*

33 *Set the* **Lines and Characters fields** *to the number of lines for the drop cap and the number of characters to be formatted.*

34 *Use the* **Character Style menu** *to assign a character style to format the drop cap character.*

Automatic Drop Cap Styling

If you look at the opening paragraph of each chapter of this book, you'll notice that the typeface for the drop cap is not the same as the rest of the text in the paragraph. In early editions of this book, I had to manually drag across every single drop cap character and change it to a character style. These days InDesign has a feature that makes it possible to automatically style the drop cap character.

TIP Use this technique if you want to apply an automatic drop cap without defining a paragraph style. Use the exercise on the next page if you want to apply the automatic drop cap as part of a paragraph style.

To apply automatic drop cap character styling:

1. Define a character style *(see page 375)* that contains the formatting for the drop cap character.

2. Place your insertion point anywhere inside the paragraph that you want to style with the drop cap.

TIP Nope, you don't have to put the insertion point at the front of the paragraph.

3. Choose Drop Caps and Nested Styles from the Paragraph palette menu. The Drop Caps and Nested Styles dialog box appears **32**.

4. Use the Lines field to set the number of lines that the drop cap character will descend into the text **33**.

5. Use the Characters field to set the number of characters that will be turned into a drop cap character **33**.

6. Use the Character Style menu to choose the predefined character style to assign to the drop cap character **34**.

7. Click OK. The drop cap with the character style is applied to the selected paragraph.

The previous exercise works great if you have only one drop cap paragraph you need to style. But if you're working with many paragraphs that need to be formatted, you're much better off making the automatic drop cap part of a paragraph style sheet. That way you can style all the text with a single, magical click.

To apply automatic drop cap in a paragraph style:

1. Define a character style *(see page 375)* that contains the formatting for the drop cap character.

2. Choose to define a new paragraph style *(see page 369)*.

3. Choose the Drop Caps and Nested Styles category from the Paragraph Styles dialog box 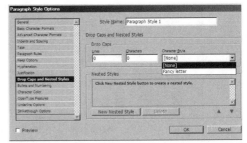. The Drop Caps controls appear .

4. Set the Lines field as described on the previous page.

5. Set the Characters field as described on the previous page.

6. Set the Character Style menu as described on the previous page.

7. Set whatever other formatting you want in the Paragraph Styles dialog box.

8. Click OK to define the paragraph style.

9. Use the Paragraph Styles palette to assign this paragraph style to text. This allows you to assign the automatic drop cap to make paragraphs.

35 *The* **Drop Caps and Nested Styles category** *for paragraph styles allows you to automate drop cap characters as you apply a paragraph style.*

36 *The controls for automatic* **Drop Caps within the Paragraph Style Options dialog box.**

Automatic Drop Cap Styling

Dorothy·Gale:·(620)·555-5432¬
3·Farmhouse·Lane,·Very·Small·Town,
KA,·12345¶
Scarecrow:·(620)·555-5432¬
Middle·of·Cornfield,·Very·Small·
Town,·KA,·12345¶
Woodman:·(620)·555-5432¬
Deep·in·Forest,·Very·Small·Town,·
KA,·12345¶

③ *An example of the kind of formatting that can be automated using nested styles. In this case there are predictable elements that can be used to apply the automatic formatting.*

Searching for Repeating Elements

It may seem difficult to find repeating elements, but they are much easier to find than you might think.

Consider the steps in my exercises. The numbers are always separated from the rest of the body copy by a tab character. So I can easily set the tab as the repeating element for a nested style.

If you are formatting any text that comes from databases, it is extremely easy to have the people who create the database add tab characters to divide the different parts of the text. Then you can use the repeating tab characters to format with the nested styles.

Using Nested Styles

Every once in a while I see a feature that is revolutionary in the field of desktop publishing. Nested styles are such a feature. Nested styles allow you to automate how character styles are applied to paragraphs.

Imagine you are formatting a phone directory. Each paragraph starts with a person's name followed by a colon. After that comes a phone number, and then a new line symbol forces the rest of the address to the end of the paragraph. These are repeating elements that you can reliably count on to use as markers for formatting using nested styles.

You want the person's name to be italic, the phone number to be bold, and the text after the new line symbol to be the regular paragraph style.

Before nested styles, you would have had to manually highlight each element in the paragraph and apply a character style. With nested styles all the formatting is applied in one fell swoop **③**!

TIP As you work with nested styles, remember that you need predictable elements that you can use as part of the automatic formatting. If you can't predict where the elements will be in the text, you probably can't use nested styles for that text.

To prepare to use nested styles:

◆ Define all the character styles that will be used to apply the formatting for nested styles.

TIP You can only use character styles as part of nested styles, not local formatting from the Character palette.

Once you have defined the character styles, you can apply them using the Nested Styles command.

To apply the Nested Styles command to text:

1. Place your insertion point inside the paragraph that you want to format.

2. Choose Drop Caps and Nested Styles from the Paragraph palette menu. The Drop Caps and Nested Styles dialog box appears ⓸.

3. Click the New Nested Style button. This adds a new listing under the Nested Styles area ⓹.

4. Use the Character Style menu to choose which character style will be applied to the repetitive element ⓺.

5. Use the Duration menu to choose the extent to which the character style is applied ⓻:

   • **Through** applies the style so it includes the repeating character.

   • **Up to** applies the style so it ends before the repeating character.

6. Use the Count field to set how many repeating characters should occur before the character style ends.

7. Use the Repeating Element menu to set which element controls the nested style ⓼. *(See the next exercise for how to set the repeating elements.)*

8. Click OK to apply the nested style.

   or

   Click the New Nested Style button to add more nested styles for other parts of the text.

⓸ *The Nested Styles area of the* **Drop Caps and Nested Styles dialog box** *allows you to apply multiple character styles to predictably occurring text elements.*

Style menu   Duration menu   Count field   Repeating Element

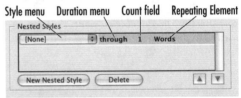

⓹ *The* **New Nested Style button** *creates a new listing in the Nested Styles area.*

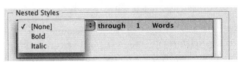

⓺ *Click the* **Character Style menu** *to choose the character style that should be applied as the formatting for the nested style.*

⓻ *Click the* **Duration menu** *to set the extent to which the formatting is applied.*

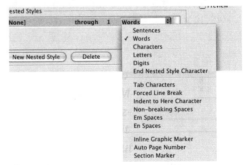

⓼ *Click the* **Repeating Element menu** *to choose the element that ends the nested style.*

Using Nested Styles

Small Town, KA, 123

43 *The* **End Nested Style Here character** *can be inserted to end the effects of a nested style.*

Using the End Nested Style Here Character

When might you need to insert the End Nested Style Here character? Imagine that you want to style the last set of information in an address such as a zip code or postal code.

You can't rely on a certain number of commas appearing before the zip code appears, nor can you rely on the code to only have numbers if you have a mixture of U.S. and European addresses.

That's when you want to insert the End Nested Style Here character in front of the code.

If necessary, you can ask the editorial department that generates the text to insert a special character before the code. For instance, the zip code 10003 might appear as CODE10003. You can then use the Find/Change command to change the word *CODE* into the End Nested Style Here character.

To set the repeating elements in a nested style:

◆ Click the Repeating Element menu and choose one of the listings from the menu.

or

Type a single character in the field.

TIP A character typed into the field can be text, punctuation, or numbers.

TIP If you type multiple characters in the field, InDesign will use any of those characters as the repeating element.

There may be times that you don't have any repeating element that you can rely on to appear in the text. In that case you can insert the End Nested Style Here Character to control the end of a nested style.

To manually insert the End Nested Style Here Character:

1. Place your insertion point where you want the End Nested Style Here Character to appear.

2. Choose **Type > Insert Special Character > End Nested Style Here**. This inserts the End Nested Style Here character into the text **43**.

TIP The End Nested Style Here character can be seen if you choose **Type > Show Hidden Characters**.

TIP You can also use the Special menu in the Change field to insert the End Nested Style Here character into text.

Using Nested Styles

If you have multiple nested styles in the Nested Styles area, you can move them up or down to change the order in which they are applied.

To change the order of multiple nested styles:

1. Select the nested style that you want to move.

2. Click the up or down arrow to move the nested style to a new position 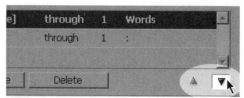.

44 *Use the* **up/down arrows** *to change the order of nested styles.*

The Drop Caps and Nested Styles command in the Paragraph palette is applied as local formatting. It is rather easy to create a paragraph style that contains the nested style. This makes it possible to apply nested styles by simply applying a paragraph style to the text.

To apply nested styles in a paragraph style:

1. Define the character styles *(see page 375)* for the nested style.

2. Choose to define a new paragraph style *(see page 369)*.

3. Choose the Drop Caps and Nested Styles category from the New Paragraph Style dialog box **45**.

4. Add and define the nested styles as described on page 389.

5. Add any additional nested styles as necessary.

6. Set whatever other formatting you want in the New Paragraph Style dialog box.

7. Click OK to define the paragraph style.

8. Use the Paragraph Styles palette to assign this paragraph style to text.

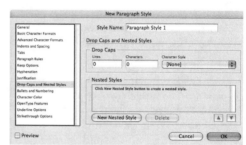

45 *The* **Drop Caps and Nested Styles area** *of the New Paragraph Style dialog box.*

Using Nested Styles

New Style icon

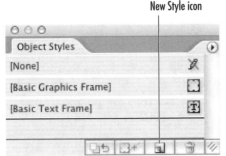

46 *The* **three built-in object style settings** *in the Object Styles palette.*

47 *The* **Object Style Options dialog box** *lets you modify the object style attributes.*

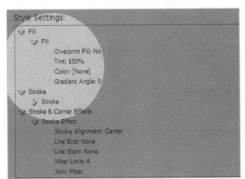

48 *Click the* **Style Settings controls** *to see the description of the settings for each category.*

Defining Object Styles

Just as character and paragraph styles make it easy to apply formatting to text, object styles make it easy to apply formatting to objects. InDesign comes with three built-in object style settings.

TIP If you understand the principles of text styles, it will be easy to work with object styles.

To apply the built-in object styles:

1. Select the object you want to style.

2. Choose Window > Object Styles to open the Object Styles palette **46**.

3. Click one of the following in the Object Styles palette:

   - **[Basic Graphics Frame]** applies the default object settings for graphic frames. *(See the chart on the following pages for which settings are included.)*
   - **[Basic Text Frame]** applies the default settings for text frames. *(See the chart on the following pages to see which settings are included.)*
   - **[None]** removes all formatting from the object.

To modify the default styles:

1. Double-click the Basic Graphics Frame or Basic Text Frame style. This opens the Object Style Options dialog box.

TIP The [None] style can't be modified.

2. Click each of the categories on the left side of the dialog box. This displays the settings for each category **47**. *(See the chart on the following pages for details of each category.)*

3. Make whatever changes you like to each of the category settings.

4. Use the Style Settings controls to see a description of the settings for each category **48**.

Defining Object Styles

Object Style Categories

These are the categories for object styles.

Dialog Box Options	Description
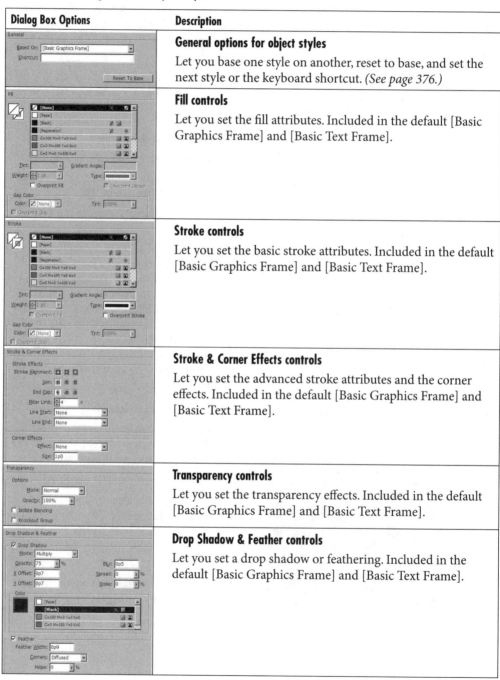	**General options for object styles** Let you base one style on another, reset to base, and set the next style or the keyboard shortcut. *(See page 376.)*
	Fill controls Let you set the fill attributes. Included in the default [Basic Graphics Frame] and [Basic Text Frame].
	Stroke controls Let you set the basic stroke attributes. Included in the default [Basic Graphics Frame] and [Basic Text Frame].
	Stroke & Corner Effects controls Let you set the advanced stroke attributes and the corner effects. Included in the default [Basic Graphics Frame] and [Basic Text Frame].
	Transparency controls Let you set the transparency effects. Included in the default [Basic Graphics Frame] and [Basic Text Frame].
	Drop Shadow & Feather controls Let you set a drop shadow or feathering. Included in the default [Basic Graphics Frame] and [Basic Text Frame].

Dialog Box Options	Description
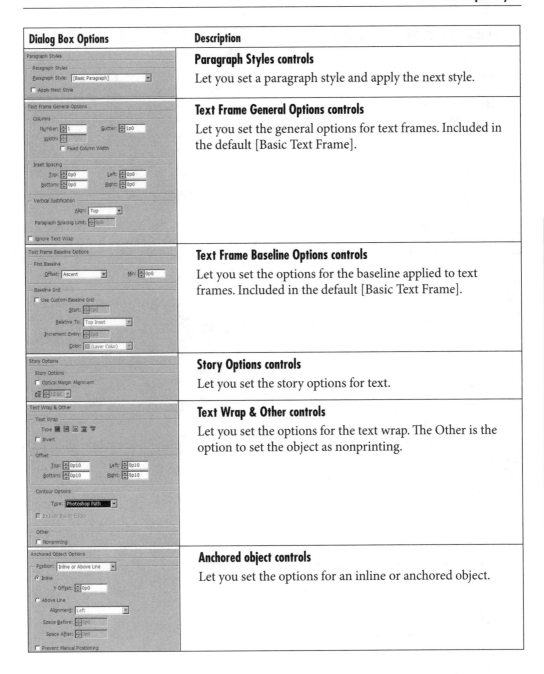	**Paragraph Styles controls** Let you set a paragraph style and apply the next style.
	Text Frame General Options controls Let you set the general options for text frames. Included in the default [Basic Text Frame].
	Text Frame Baseline Options controls Let you set the options for the baseline applied to text frames. Included in the default [Basic Text Frame].
	Story Options controls Let you set the story options for text.
	Text Wrap & Other controls Let you set the options for the text wrap. The Other is the option to set the object as nonprinting.
	Anchored object controls Let you set the options for an inline or anchored object.

Defining Object Styles (continued)

You will most likely want to create your own object styles.

To create a new object style:

1. Choose New Style from the Object Styles palette menu.

   or

   Hold the Opt/Alt key and click the New Style icon in the Object Styles palette. The New Object Styles dialog box appears ㊾.

2. Use the Name field to name the style.

3. Use the checkboxes to control which categories are part of the style ㊿. Unchecked categories are not part of the style ㊿.

4. Use the Based On field to base one style on another.

5. Click the Reset To Base button to remove all differences between one style based on another.

6. Click OK to create the style.

The easier way to define an object style is to format the object and define the style by example.

To define an object style by example:

1. Select a sample object.

2. Use the palettes and commands to format the object.

3. Choose New Style from the Object Styles palette menu.

   or

   Hold the Opt/Alt key and click the New Style icon in the Object Styles palette. The New Object Styles dialog box appears.

4. Name the style.

5. Click OK to create the style.

TIP Object styles can be duplicated just like text styles.

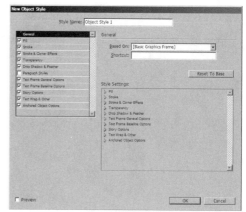

㊾ *Use the* **New Object Styles dialog box** *to define the attributes of an object style.*

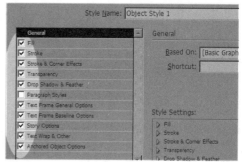

㊿ *Click the* **category controls** *to choose which attributes should be included in the object style.*

Defining Object Styles

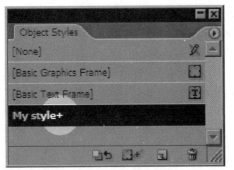

⑤1 *The* **plus sign next to the object style name** *indicates that local formatting was applied to the object.*

Clear Overrides Not
Defined in the Style icon   Clear Overrides icon

⑤2 *There are two ways to clear overrides applied to object styles.*

Working with Object Styles

For the most part, you work with object styles as you would text style, however, with one important difference. There are two types of local formatting changes that can be applied to object styles. There are the local formatting changes that modify attributes that are defined in the style; and there are the local formatting changes that modify attributes that are not defined in the style. Each of these is handled differently.

To clear local formatting defined in the style:

1. Select the object that has the modifications to the object style. A plus (+) sign indicates that local formatting has been applied to the style **⑤1**.

2. Click the Clear Overrides icon to clear the local formatting applied to the object. The plus sign disappears **⑤2**.

TIP You can also use the Redefine Style command from the Object Styles menu to change the style definition to fit the local formatting. This also removes the plus sign.

You may also have made changes to the object in categories that were not selected in the object style. This local formatting is not indicated by a plus sign.

To clear local formatting not defined in the style:

1. Select the object that has the modifications to the object style.

2. Click the Clear Overrides Not Defined in the Style icon to clear the local formatting applied to the object **⑤2**.

TIP The only way to know if that local formatting has been applied to the object is if the icon is visible.

Working with Object Styles

Using the Quick Apply Feature

Once you have defined your text and object styles, there is a very easy way to quickly apply them to text and objects. The Quick Apply feature works entirely from the keyboard — no mouse required!

To use Quick Apply to apply styles:

1. Select the text or object that you want to apply the style to.

2. Press Cmd/Ctrl and then click Return/Enter. The Quick Apply area appears at the top right of the screen **53**.

3. Type a few of the letters that appear in the name of the style. As you type the Quick Apply area shows just those styles that contain the letters.

TIP The letters you type do not have to appear in sequence in the name of the style.

4. Keep typing until you have the style you want **54**.

   or

   Use the up and down arrow keys to move to the style you want.

5. Press the Return/Enter key to select the style **55**.

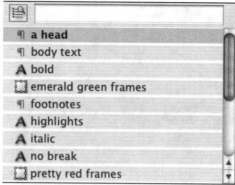

53 The **Quick Apply area** *contains a list of all the text and object styles in a document.*

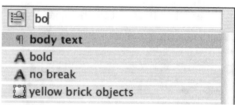

54 *As you type in the* **Quick Apply field,** *the list shows just the styles that contain those letters.*

55 *Click the Return/Enter key to apply the highlighted style in the Quick Apply area.*

TYPOGRAPHY CONTROLS 16

The one thing that truly separates the amateurs from the experts in page layout is the control they take over their text. Amateurs are pleased if they can apply simple formatting such as fonts, sizes, alignment, tracking, and so on.

Experts, though, want more from a page-layout program. They want sophisticated control over kerning. This includes the ability to move one character in so that it tucks under the stroke of another.

They want to control how lines are justified within a text frame. This means that if one line looks too crowded and the next has big gaps between the words, the experts tell the program to reapportion the spaces.

The experts also want to work with the newest typefaces that give more choices for how letters look and act together.

These are advanced text effects. Once you apply these features, you move from being an ordinary designer to a typographer.

Optical Margin Alignment

One of the most sophisticated text effects in InDesign is the ability to apply hanging punctuation to justified text in which a slight adjustment of the margin creates a more uniform appearance for the edge of the text. Hanging punctuation is applied by setting the *optical margin alignment*. This moves punctuation characters slightly outside the text margin ❶. In addition, optical margin alignment moves the serifs of letters outside the margin ❷.

Optical margin alignment is set using the Story palette.

To set optical margin adjustment:

1. Select the text.

2. Choose **Type > Story**. This opens the Story palette ❸.

3. Check Optical Margin Alignment. The text reflows so that the punctuation and serifs lie outside the margin edges.

4. Enter a size for the amount of overhang.

TIP As a general rule, set the overhang the same size as the text.

Off   On

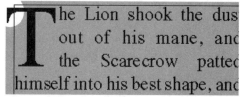

❶ *To create the effect of a straight edge,* **optical margin alignment** *moves punctuation outside the margin edges.*

The Lion shook the dus
out of his mane, and
the Scarecrow patted
himself into his best shape, and

❷ *The* **Optical Margin Alignment** *setting also moves the serifs of letters slightly outside the margin.*

❸ *The* **Story palette** *lets you set the Optical Margin Alignment to hang punctuation in the margin.*

The road was still paved with yellow brick, but these were much covered by dried branches and dead leaves from the trees, and the walking was not at all good.

Off

The road was still paved with yellow brick, but these were much covered by dried branches and dead leaves from the trees, and the walking was not at all good.

On

④ *Turn on* **Adobe Paragraph Composer** *to improve the spacing between words.*

When to Use Paragraph Composition?

Why would anyone want to turn off the miracle of paragraph composition? Well there are times when the paragraph composer insists on breaking a paragraph where you don't want it to break. If that happens, you can turn off the Paragraph Composer.

You may also want to turn off the Paragraph Composer if you have converted a QuarkXPress document into InDesign and you want to keep the text from reflowing.

Also, some statistical data may be easier to work with if you turn off the Paragraph Composer.

Using Adobe Paragraph Composer

InDesign has two ways of composing (laying out) text. Single-line composition looks at the current line and evaluates the best place to break the line or apply hyphenation. Paragraph composition looks at all the text in a paragraph — forward and backward — when it evaluates the best place to break lines. When paragraph composition is turned on, the result is more even spacing for the text and fewer hyphens **④**.

To apply paragraph composition:

1. Select the text.
2. Choose **Type** > **Paragraph** to open the Paragraph palette.
3. Choose Adobe Paragraph Composer from the Paragraph palette menu. The text reflows.

TIP Adobe Paragraph Composer is a paragraph attribute and is applied to all the text in a paragraph.

TIP Adobe Paragraph Composer is turned on by default when you first open InDesign.

TIP Choose Adobe Single-line Composer to apply standard line-by-line composition.

Using Adobe Paragraph Composer

Applying Justification Controls

Justification determines how lines fit between margins. *(See the sidebar below for information on how justification affects text.)* InDesign provides three different ways to control justification: word spacing, letter spacing, and glyph spacing. *Word spacing* changes the space between words.

⑤ *The* **Justification dialog box** *controls word and letter spacing.*

To set word spacing:

1. Select the text.
2. Choose **Type** > **Paragraph** to open the Paragraph palette.
3. Choose Justification from the Paragraph palette menu. This opens the Justification dialog box **⑤**.
4. Set the Word Spacing options as follows **⑥**:
   - **Minimum** controls the smallest amount of space you want between words. For instance, a value of 80% means that you are willing to allow the space to be 80% of the normal space.
   - **Desired** controls the preferred amount of space between words. A value of 100% indicates that you want the same amount that the designer of the typeface created.
   - **Maximum** controls the largest amount of space you want between words. A value of 120% means that you are willing to allow the space to be 120% of the normal space.
5. Click OK to apply the changes **⑦**.

TIP The Minimum, Desired, and Maximum settings apply only to text that is set to one of the Justified settings. Other alignments, such as left-aligned text, use only the Desired setting.

	Minimum	Desired	Maximum
Word Spacing:	80%	100%	133%
Letter Spacing:	0%	0%	0%
Glyph Scaling:	100%	100%	100%

⑥ *The* **spacing controls** *in the Justification dialog box.*

Welcome, my child, to the Land of Oz

Min: 80,
Desired: 100,
Max: 120

Welcome, my child, to the Land of Oz

Min: 80,
Desired: 100,
Max: 100

⑦ *The effect of changing the* **word** *spacing. Notice the change in the amount of space between the words.*

Understanding Justification

The lines in this paragraph are justified—that is, both ends of the line are aligned with the paragraph margins. Not all the words can fit evenly between the margins, so some lines have a bit more space between the words and others have less. The justification settings control how much space is added to make the lines fit between the margins.

Applying Justification Controls

Welcome, my child, to the Land of Oz

Min: 0,
Desired: 0,
Max: 0

Welcome, my child, to the Land of Oz

Min: -4,
Desired: 0,
Max: 4

⑧ *The effect of changing the **letter spacing**. Notice how there is less space between the characters within the words.*

What Are the Best Justification Settings?

Perhaps the most debated issue in desktop publishing is, what are the best settings for the Justification controls. The answer depends on a variety of factors. The typeface, width of the columns, even the type of text all need to be considered in setting the Justification controls.

For body text, such as the text here, I use word spacing of 70%, 100%, and 110%. (Here in New York City, most designers like to set copy tightly.) However, for headlines, I fit letters tighter, with word spacing of 60%, 90%, and 100%.

I keep all the letter spacing values at 0%. I set the glyph spacing values at 100%. I don't like to scrunch up the space between letters, and I definitely don't like to change the shape of the text, which happens with glyph scaling *(see the next page)*.

But that's just me. And that's why they call them preferences!

The space between letters is *letter spacing*, sometimes called character spacing. InDesign lets you change the letter spacing for text whether justified or not.

To set letter spacing:

1. Select the text.

2. Choose **Type** > **Paragraph** to open the Paragraph palette.

3. Choose Justification from the Paragraph palette menu.

4. Set the Letter Spacing options as follows:

   - **Desired** controls the preferred amount of space between letters. A value of 0% indicates that you do not want to add or subtract any space.

   - **Minimum** controls the smallest amount of space between letters. A value of –5% allows the space to be reduced by 5% of the normal space.

   - **Maximum** controls the largest amount of space between letters. A value of 5% allows the space to be increased by 5% of the normal space.

5. Click OK to apply the changes **⑧**.

TIP If a paragraph cannot be set according to the justification controls you choose, InDesign violates the settings by adding or subtracting spaces. Set the Composition preferences to have those violations highlighted *(see page 532)*.

Applying Justification Controls

Another way to control justification is to use *glyph scaling*. (*Glyph* is the proper term for all the letters, numbers, punctuation marks, and other parts of text.) Glyph scaling applies horizontal scaling to the letters themselves so that the text takes up more or less space within the line.

To set glyph scaling:

1. Select the text.

2. Choose **Type** > **Paragraph** to open the Paragraph palette.

3. Choose Justification from the Paragraph palette menu.

4. Set the Glyph Scaling options as follows:

   - **Desired** controls the preferred amount of scaling. A value of 100% indicates that you do not want to apply any scaling to the character shape.

   - **Minimum** controls the smallest amount of scaling that you are willing to apply to the text. A value of 98% means that you are willing to allow the characters to be reduced by 2% of their normal width.

   - **Maximum** controls the amount that you are willing to expand the space between words. A value of 105% means that you are willing to allow the characters to be increased by 5% of their normal width.

5. Click OK to apply the changes ❾.

TIP Glyph scaling distorts the shape of letters. Most people say you can't see the slight distortion. However, typographic purists (such as this author) try to avoid distorting the letterforms whenever possible ❿.

The road was still paved with yellow brick, but these were much covered by dried branches and dead leaves from the trees, and the walking was not at all good.

Min: 100
Desired: 100
Max: 100

The road was still paved with yellow brick, but these were much covered by dried branches and dead leaves from the trees, and the walking was not at all good.

Min: 80
Desired: 100
Max: 120

❾ *The effects of changing the **glyph scaling**.*

❿ *The black area shows the original shape of the character. The gray area shows the effects of 80% glyph scaling.*

Applying Justification Controls

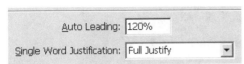

⓫ *The* **Auto Leading field** *controls how InDesign calculates the leading when set to Auto.*

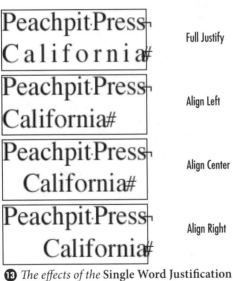

⓬ *The* **Single Word Justification menu** *controls what happens when a single word occupies a line of justified text.*

Peachpit·Press
C a l i f o r n i a#   Full Justify

Peachpit·Press
California#   Align Left

Peachpit·Press
California#   Align Center

Peachpit·Press
California#   Align Right

⓭ *The effects of the* **Single Word Justification** settings.

The Auto Leading field controls how much space is put between the lines whenever automatic leading is chosen *(see page 62).*

To set the Auto Leading percentage:

1. Choose Justification from the Paragraph palette menu.

2. Enter an amount in the Auto Leading field **⓫**.

TIP The Auto Leading percentage is based on the point size of the text. So an Auto Leading of 120% applied to 12-point text creates a leading of 14.4 points $(12 \times 1.20 = 14.4)$.

TIP Most professional designers use an absolute amount for leading by entering a specific number, rather than relying on the automatic leading.

Have you ever seen a paragraph of justified text where a single word stretched out along the entire line? InDesign lets you control what happens to a single word in a justified paragraph.

To set the single word justification:

1. Choose Justification from the Paragraph palette menu.

2. Choose a setting from the Single Word Justification menu **⓬**. Any text that is set to Justify in the Paragraph palette will be set according to the menu command **⓭**.

Applying Justification Controls

Controlling Hyphenation

InDesign lets you turn on hyphenation in the Paragraph palette. Once hyphenation is turned on, you can then control how the hyphenation is applied.

To turn on hyphenation:

1. Select the text.
2. Check Hyphenate in the Paragraph palette 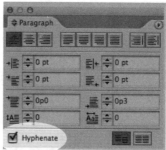.

TIP The Hyphenate checkbox is also controlled from within the Hyphenation dialog box (*see the next exercise*).

⓮ *Click the* **Hyphenate checkbox** *to turn on automatic hyphenation for a paragraph.*

To control the hyphenation:

1. Choose Hyphenate from the Paragraph palette menu. The Hyphenation Settings dialog box appears ⓯. The Hyphenate checkbox displays the controls ⓰.

2. **Words with at Least** controls the minimum number of letters a word must contain before it can be hyphenated.

3. **After First** sets the minimum number of letters that must appear before the hyphen.

4. **Before Last** sets the minimum number of letters that must appear after the hyphen.

5. **Hyphen Limit** sets how many consecutive lines can end with hyphens.

6. **Hyphenation Zone** controls the amount of whitespace at the end of a nonjustified line. This option only affects Single-line Composer text.

7. **Hyphenate Capitalized Words** allows those words to be hyphenated.

8. **Hyphenate Last Word** allows the last word in a paragraph to be hyphenated.

9. Adjust the hyphenation slider to control the total number of hyphens in the paragraph.

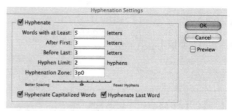

⓯ *The* **Hyphenation Settings dialog box** *lets you control how hyphenation is applied.*

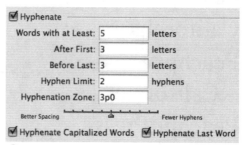

⓰ *The Hyphenation controls let you enter values for how words are hyphenated.*

Hyphenation Units are Nigels

The units in the hyphenation slider are called Nigels in honor of Nigel Tufnel (Christopher Guest), the "Spinal Tap" guitarist, whose amplifier went to 11.

Behold! I am the great and mighty, all-powerful Oz.

Behold! I am the great and mighty, all-powerful Oz.

⑰ *In the bottom example the word* powerful *was selected and the* **No Break command** *was applied to prevent the text from hyphenating.*

A·document· can·not·be·

⑱ *A* **discretionary hyphen** *appears within the word but prints only when it appears at the end of a line.*

Setting Hyphenation Controls

My own preference is to set "Words with at Least" to six or more. This allows a word such as *person* to be hyphenated. I also prefer a minimum of three letters before the hyphen and three after. This avoids breaking words as *un-excited* or *reluctant-ly*.

Hyphenate Capitalized Words?

Some people automatically turn this off so that capitalized words do not hyphenate. I don't. The command doesn't distinguish between proper nouns and words that begin a sentence. So I would rather selectively control how proper nouns break by using the No Break command or by inserting a discretionary hyphen before the word.

Sometimes you may want to prevent words or phrases from being hyphenated or breaking across lines. For instance, you might not want the words *Mr. Cohen* to be separated at the end of a line. You might not want a compound word such as *self-effacing* to be broken with another hyphen **⑰**.

To apply the No Break command:

1. Select the text.
2. Choose **Type** > **Character** to open the Character palette.
3. Choose No Break from the Character palette menu.

You can also control hyphenation by inserting a *discretionary hyphen,* which forces the word to hyphenate at that point if it breaks at the end of a line.

To use a discretionary hyphen:

1. Place the insertion point where you want the hyphen to occur.
2. Press Command/Ctrl-Shift-(hyphen).

   or

   Control-click (Mac) or Right-click (Win) and choose **Insert Special Character** > **Discretionary Hyphen** from the contextual menu.

TIP The discretionary hyphen prints only when it appears at the end of the line **⑱**.

TIP Insert a discretionary hyphen before a word to prevent that instance of the word from being hyphenated.

Controlling Hyphenation

You can control where a word is hyphenated.

To edit the hyphenation in the dictionary:

1. Choose **Edit** > **Spelling** > **Dictionary**.

2. Type the word you want to modify in the Word field as follows 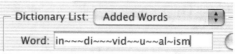:

   - **One tilde** (~) indicates the best possible hyphenation position.
   - **Two tildes** (~~) indicates the next best possible position.
   - **Three tildes** (~~~) indicates the least acceptable position.
   - A tilde before the word prevents the word from being hyphenated.

3. Click Add to add the new hyphenation preferences to the dictionary.

Baseline Grid

InDesign has an electronic grid that you can force text to align to. This ensures that text lines up correctly in two separate frames .

To set the baseline grid:

1. Choose **Edit** > **Preferences** > **Grids** (Win) or **InDesign** > **Preferences** > **Grids** (Mac). This opens the Grids dialog box .

2. Use the Color menu to set the grid color.

3. Use the Start field to control where the grid should start vertically in the document.

4. Use the Relative To menu to choose between the top of the page or the top margin .

5. Use the Increment Every field to control the space between the gridlines.

6. Set View Threshold for the magnification amount above which the grid is visible.

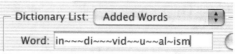

⑲ *The tilde characters control the preference for where hyphenation should occur.*

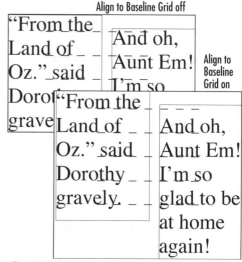

⑳ *When* **Align to Baseline Grid** *is turned on, the text in two different frames lines up.*

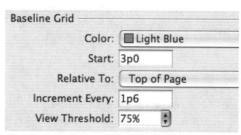

㉑ *The* **Baseline Grid settings** *in the Grids preferences.*

㉒ *The* **Relative To field** *lets you choose where the baseline grid should start.*

Controlling Hyphenation; Baseline Grid

Do not align to baseline grid

Align to baseline grid

②③ *The* **Align to Baseline Grid buttons** *in the Paragraph palette.*

Align to Baseline Grid Off

Chapter·Two:·The·
Council·with·the·
Munchkins¶

Align to Baseline Grid On

She·was·awakened·by·a·shock,·so·sudden·and
severe·that·i
soft·bed·she

As·it·was,

Chapter·Two:·The·
Council·with·the·
Munchkins¶

She·was·awakened·by·a·shock,·so·sudden·and
severe·that·if·Dorothy·had·not·been·lying·on·the
soft·bed·she·might·have·been·hurt.¶

As·it·was,·the·jar·made·her·catch·her·breath

②④ *When text is* **aligned to the baseline grid***, the leading may increase. Also the space between paragraphs may adjust.*

Align all lines to grid

As it was, the jar made her catch her breath
and wonder what had happened; and Toto put
his cold little nose into her face and whined
dismally. Dorothy sat up and noticed that the
house was not moving; nor was it dark, for the
bright sunshine came in at the window, flood-
ing the little room.

This sou
very mu
like the
opening
the movi

Only align first line to grid

As it was, the jar made her catch her breath
and wonder what had happened; and Toto put
his cold little nose into her face and whined
dismally. Dorothy sat up and noticed that the
house was not moving; nor was it dark, for the
bright sunshine came in at the window, flood-
ing the little room.

This sounds
very much
like the
opening for
the movie

②⑤ *Use the* **Only Align First Line to Grid** *command to align just the first line of a paragraph without affecting the leading.*

To align text to a baseline grid:

1. Select the text.

2. Click the Align to Baseline Grid icon in the Paragraph palette **②③**. The text aligns to the grid.

TIP When you align to the baseline grid, the grid setting overrides the leading. Most designers set the baseline grid to the same amount as the leading for the text **②④**.

TIP Aligning to the baseline grid may also change the space between paragraphs **②④**.

In addition to setting the baseline grid, you can choose to set just the first line of a paragraph to the baseline grid.

To align just the first line to the baseline grid:

1. Select the text.

2. Click the Align to Baseline Grid icon in the Paragraph palette. All the lines in the paragraph will be aligned to the baseline grid.

3. Choose Only Align First Line to Grid in the Paragraph palette menu.

    or

    Choose First Line Only from the Align to Grid in the Indents and Spacing area of the Paragraph Styles dialog box.

TIP This forces the first line of a paragraph to align to the grid but allows the other lines in the paragraph to be controlled by the leading **②⑤**.

Baseline Grid

You can also set a custom baseline grid for a text frame. This is especially helpful for formatting margin notes alongside text 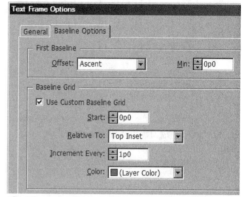.

To create a custom grid for a text frame:

1. Select the text frame.

2. Choose **Object > Text Frame Options** and then click Baseline Options. This opens the text frame baseline controls ㉗.

3. Check Use Custom Baseline Grid to set the options.

4. Use the Start field to control where the grid should start vertically in the document.

5. Use the Relative To menu to choose between the top of the page or the top margin.

6. Use the Increment Every field to control the space between the gridlines.

7. Use the Color controls to set the color of the grid.

8. Don't forget to set the text to align to the baseline grid.

Document grid | Custom frame grid

"All the same," said the Scarecrow, "I shall ask for brains instead of a heart; for a fool would not know what to do with a heart if he had one."

"I shall take the heart," returned the Tin Woodman; "for brains do not make one happy, and happiness is the best thing in the world."

Is the Scarecrow actualy smart here? Does the Tin Woodman show feeling? What does this tell you?

㉖ *A* **custom frame grid** *allows you to have multiple grids in a document.*

㉗ *The* **Baseline Grid settings** *in the Text Frame Options.*

Baseline Grid

Chapter Two: The Council with the
Munchkins

She was awakened by a shock, so sudden and severe that if Dorothy
hurt

Chapter Two: The Council
with the Munchkins

She was awakened by a shock, so sudden and severe that if Dorothy had not been lying on the soft bed she might have been
hurt.

28 *The* **Balance Ragged Lines command**
rearranges text so there is a more equal number
of words in the lines.

Kin

King

Kingd

Kingdom

29 *As you add more letters to an OpenType*
font, the previous letters change.

What is OpenType?

OpenType is a type format that was
developed by Adobe and Microsoft.
OpenType fonts have many advantages over previous type formats. In
addition to containing thousands of
glyphs, OpenType fonts are also cross-
platform. This means you can use the
same font on Mac or Windows without any document reflow.

Adobe sells different types of
OpenType fonts. "Pro" versions of a
font, such as Minion Pro, contain the
extended character sets that give you
access to fractions, ligatures, and other
special effects. "Standard" versions,
such as Futura Std, contain only the
basic characters.

Balancing Ragged Lines

Another nuance for good typography is
to make sure that there are no uneven line
breaks, especially in headlines or centered
type. InDesign's Balance Ragged Lines command makes this easier **28**.

To balance uneven line breaks:

1. Select the text.
2. Choose Balance Ragged Lines from the
   Paragraph palette menu.

   or

   Choose Balance Ragged Lines in the
   Indents and Spacing area of the Paragraph
   Styles dialog box.

Using OpenType

Instead of the paltry 256 glyphs (characters)
in ordinary fonts, OpenType fonts can have
thousands of glyphs. InDesign has special
commands that help you get the most out of
OpenType fonts. For instance, you can set the
commands to automatically swap ordinary
characters with special OpenType glyphs.

To set automatic OpenType alternate characters:

1. Select the text.
   TIP OpenType features can be applied to all
   the text in a document or just part of
   the text.
2. Choose **Type > Character** to open the
   Character palette.
3. Choose the options from the OpenType
   submenu in the Character palette
   menu. InDesign automatically swaps
   characters with the alternate glyphs in
   each category **29**. *(See the chart on pages*
   413 – 414 for a description of the various
   OpenType categories and how they should
   be used.)

You can also manually choose alternate glyphs for each character in the font.

To choose the alternate glyphs:

1. Select the character in the text.

2. Choose **Type > Insert Glyphs** to open the Glyphs palette.

3. Press the triangle next to the selected character in the palette **30**. The alternate glyphs for the selection appear.

4. Choose one of the alternate characters. This replaces the selected text with the alternate character in the Glyphs palette.

You can also set the Glyphs palette to display just certain categories of glyphs.

To view certain categories in the Glyphs palette:

1. Press the Show list in the Glyphs palette.

2. Choose the category of OpenType characters that you want to display **31**.

TIP Not all OpenType fonts contain all the possible glyph features. So the Show list will display different categories depending on the OpenType font chosen. *(See the chart starting on the next page for examples of how to use the OpenType categories.)*

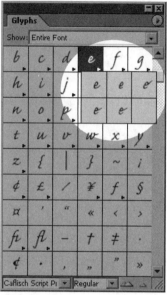

30 *Press a character or letter with a triangle to see the alternate glyphs.*

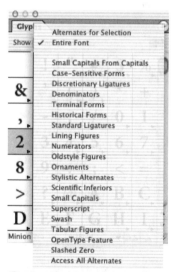

31 *The **Show list** in the Glyphs palette lets you choose to see the categories of specialized glyphs.*

Using OpenType

Open Type Categories

Feature name	Comments	Examples	
All Caps	Changes text to uppercase letters. Also changes punctuation and spacing. Notice how the question mark and hyphens are raised in the OpenType all caps formatting.	*Manually typed all caps*	¡MAMMA-MEXICO?
		OpenType all caps	¡MAMMA-MEXICO?
Small Caps	Changes lowercase text to small capital letters. More appropriate weight for the letters compared to the fake small caps created electronically.	*Electronic small caps*	Smsolutions
		OpenType small caps	Smsolutions
All Small Caps	Changes all text, including uppercase characters, to small capital letters. Use for acronyms such as FBI, CIA, and PDF. The advantage to this setting is that you do not have to retype uppercase characters to make the conversion.	*Without small caps*	The FBI and CIA opened the IRS PDF.
		With small caps	The FBI and CIA opened the IRS PDF.
Ligatures	Applies the special letter combinations such as fi and fl. Other ligatures, such as ffi, ffl, and ff may be present in most Adobe Pro OpenType fonts.	*No ligatures*	difficult flush fish
		With ligatures	difficult flush fish
Discretionary Ligatures	Applies both discretionary ligatures and historical ligatures. These ligatures should be used sparingly as they are not common in contemporary text.	*No discretionary ligatures*	reaction burst
		With discretionary ligatures	reaction burst
Fractions	Converts numbers around a slash into numerator and denominator characters and changes the slash to a virgule. Settings for Numerator and Denominator also use the fraction glyphs.	*Manually styled*	$3\frac{1}{2}\ 4\frac{3}{4}$
		OpenType formatted	$3\frac{1}{2}\ 4\frac{3}{4}$
Ordinals	Converts the characters to the superscript position. Like fractions, the OpenType version is faster to apply and has a better weight than electronic styling.	*Manually styled*	1st 2nd 3rd 4th
		OpenType formatted	1st 2nd 3rd 4th
Swash	Substitutes a stylized alternative for the ordinary glyphs. Swashes are usually found in the italic version of a font. They are contextual and are inserted at the beginning or end of a word.	*Without swash*	Quick Awesome
		With swash	Quick Awesome

Feature name	Comments	Examples	
Stylistic Sets	Substitutes sets of characters that are applied depending on their context in relationship to other letters. Visible in the Glyphs palette.	*Without stylistic set*	*Huddled*
		With stylistic set	*Huddled*
Contextual Alternatives	Substitutes specially designed characters that are applied depending on their context in relationship to other letters.	*Without contextual alternatives*	*bogged who fish stall look lodge*
		With contextual alternatives	*bogged who fish stall look lodge*
Stylistic Alternatives	Created by the type designer, these alternatives are inserted as alternate choices to the selected glyphs.	*Original character*	*&*
		Stylistic alternative	*&*
Superscript/ Superior	Substitutes proper superscript or superior characters for ordinary glyphs. Limited to numbers, punctuation, and a selected set of letters.	*Manually styled*	x^2 $\$4.00$ 2^e
		OpenType formatted	x^2 $\$4.00$ 2^e
Subscript/ Inferior	Like superscript, this substitutes proper subscript characters for ordinary glyphs. Limited to just numbers and punctuation, not letters.	*Manually styled*	H_2O
		OpenType formatted	H_2O
Slashed Zero	Substitute a slashed zero for the normal character. Used in scientific and mathematical writing.	*No slashed zero*	$x-0=y$
		Slashed zero	$x-\emptyset=y$
Figure (number) types	There are four categories of figure types. *Tabular figures* have fixed widths and are used particularly where the numbers need to line up under each other. *Proportional figures* have variable widths. Use these unless it is necessary to line figures up into columns of tabular data. *Lining figures* have a uniform height. Use them with all cap text or for a contemporary look. *Oldstyle figures* have unequal heights. Use them with mixed-case text or when a more traditional look is desired. *Default figure* is the category that the type designer has designated as the default. This is usually tabular lining.	These are the four types of figures:	
		Tabular lining	12: 09/11/2001 34: 07/22/2008
		Tabular oldstyle	12: 09/11/2001 34: 07/22/2008
		Proportional lining	12: 09/11/2001 34: 07/22/2008
		Proportional oldstyle	12: 09/11/2001 34: 07/22/2008

OpenType Categories

COLOR MANAGEMENT 17

I remember when my family got our first color television set. Back then, there weren't many programs broadcast in color, so a color television was a strange and mysterious thing.

No one in the family knew how to make the pictures look realistic. We jumped up to adjust the image whenever we changed channels. My sister and I spent more time fiddling with the TV controls than watching the shows.

Well, not many people understand how color is managed in desktop publishing. They don't know how to make colors look better or how to control images from different applications. They spend most of their time fiddling with the knobs.

Color is a very complex subject — far too deep for the scope of this book. This chapter covers most basic steps for managing color in InDesign. Fortunately, the controls are similar to those in other Adobe products. So if you've set your color management in Photoshop, you will find the same settings in InDesign.

If you are interested in learning more about color, I suggest *Real World Color Management,* by Bruce Fraser, Fred Buntin, and Chris Murphy, published by Peachpit Press.

Choosing Color Settings

The first step for color management is to set up the color system. Fortunately, Adobe provides predefined color settings that are suitable for many users.

To turn on color management:

1. Choose **Edit > Color Settings**. This opens the Color Settings dialog box ❶.

2. Check Enable Color Management. This opens the color settings controls.

3. Choose one of the predefined settings from the Settings menu ❷:

   • **Custom** uses the settings you choose in the Color Settings dialog box *(see the exercises that follow)*.
   • **Color Management Off** uses minimal color management. Use this for video or on-screen presentations.
   • **ColorSync Workflow (Mac)** manages color using the ColorSync 3.0 CMSl.
   • **Emulate Photoshop 4** simulates the color workflow used by Adobe Photoshop 4.0 and earlier.
   • **Europe Prepress Defaults** manages for typical European press conditions.
   • **Japan Prepress Defaults** manages for typical Japanese press conditions.
   • **Photoshop 5 Default Spaces** manages using the default working spaces for Photoshop 5.0 and later.
   • **U.S. Prepress Defaults** manages for typical U.S. press conditions.
   • **Web Graphics Defaults** manages for display on the World Wide Web.

4. Check Advanced Mode only if you want to set the added color controls *(see page 419)*.

5. Click OK to apply the color settings. In many cases, this is all you need to do to set color management in InDesign.

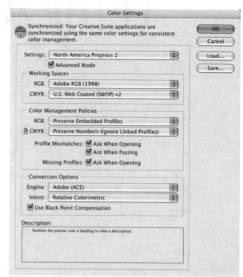

❶ *The* **Color Settings dialog box** *contains the controls for managing how colors are displayed and printed.*

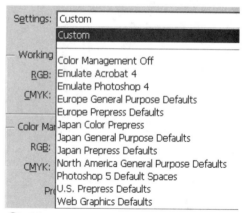

❷ *The* **Settings menu** *lets you choose one of the predefined color management settings.*

RGB:	Adobe RGB (1998)
CMYK:	Other

	Adobe RGB (1998)
Color Mar	Apple RGB
RGB:	ColorMatch RGB
	sRGB IEC61966-2.1
CMYK:	
	Monitor RGB - sRGB IEC61966-2.1

❸ *The* **Working Space RGB menu** *lets you choose the display options for RGB colors.*

CMYK:	U.S. Web Coated (SWOP) v2
	Other
Color Mar	
RGB:	Euroscale Coated v2
	Euroscale Uncoated v2
CMYK:	Japan Color 2001 Coated
	Japan Color 2001 Uncoated
Pr	Japan Standard v2
	Japan Web Coated (Ad)
	U.S. Sheetfed Coated v2
	U.S. Sheetfed Uncoated v2
	U.S. Web Coated (SWOP) v2
escription:	U.S. Web Uncoated v2

❹ *The* **Working Space CMYK menu** *lets you choose the output destination for printing CMYK colors.*

Talk to Your Print Shop

Most designers I know are embarrassed to admit they don't understand color management. It's nothing to be ashamed of. What you need to do is talk to your print shop. Ask them what settings they recommend for color management. And remember, color management also needs to be set in image-creation applications — such as Adobe Illustrator and Adobe Photoshop — that you use to create images placed in InDesign.

The working space applies the default color profiles for RGB and CMYK colors *(see Chapter 5, "Working in Color")*.

To set the RGB working space:

◆ Use the RGB menu to choose one of the following RGB display settings **❸**:

- **Adobe RGB (1998)** has a large color gamut. Use it if you do print work with a broad range of colors.
- **Apple RGB** reflects the characteristics of the Apple Standard 13-inch monitor. Use for files displayed on Mac OS monitors or for working with older desktop publishing files.
- **ColorMatch RGB** matches the color space of Radius PressView monitors.
- **sRGB IEC61966-2.1** reflects the characteristics of the average PC monitor. It is recommended for Web work, but is too limited for prepress.
- **Monitor RGB** sets the working space to the color profile of your monitor. Use this if your other applications do not support color management.
- **ColorSync RGB (Mac)** matches the RGB space specified in the control panel for Apple ColorSync 3.0 or later.

TIP When the Advanced Mode is chosen, the RGB Working Space menu displays additional options.

To set the CMYK working space:

◆ Use the CMYK menu to choose the CMYK output settings **❹**.

TIP Each setting describes the type of ink and paper used in the printing.

Choosing Color Settings

You can also set what happens when placed images contain different color profiles than the current working spaces.

To set the Color Management Policies:

1. Choose a setting in the RGB and CMYK Color Management Policy menus ⑤ and ⑥ as follows:

   - **Off** turns off color management for imported images or documents.
   - **Preserve Embedded Profiles** maintains the profile in the imported image or document.
   - **Convert to Working Space** converts placed images and documents to the working spaces you set for the InDesign document.

2. Check Ask When Opening (under Profile Mismatches) to give a choice when opening documents with different profiles ⑦.

3. Check Ask When Pasting (under Profile Mismatches) to give a choice when pasting information from documents with different profiles.

4. Check Ask When Opening (under Missing Profiles) to give a choice when pasting information from documents that have no color profiles.

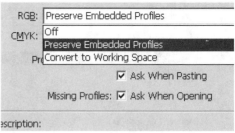

⑤ *The* **RGB Color Management Policy menu** *let you choose what to do with different RGB color profiles.*

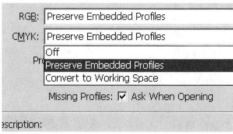

⑥ *The* **CMYK Color Management Policy menu** *lets you choose what to do with different CMYK color profiles.*

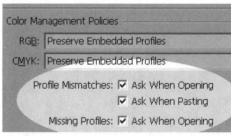

⑦ *The* **Profile Mismatches and Missing Profiles options** *control what happens when different profiles are in the same document.*

Choosing Color Settings

Engine: Adobe (ACE)

Intent: Relative Colorimetric

☑ Use Black Point Compensation

❽ *The* **Conversion Options** *are displayed in the Color Settings when the Advanced Mode is checked.*

Engine: Adobe (ACE)

Intent: Adobe (ACE)
Microsoft ICM

☑ Use Black Point Compensation

❾ *The* **Engine menu (Win)** *lets you choose the Adobe Color Engine or the Microsoft Image Color Management for color management.*

Engine: ✓ Adobe (ACE)
Apple ColorSync
Apple CMM

Intent:

☑ Use Black Point Compensation

❿ *The* **Engine menu (Mac)** *lets you choose the Adobe Color Engine or the Apple ColorSync or Apple Color Management Module for color management.*

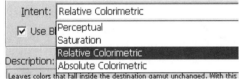

Intent: Relative Colorimetric

☑ Use B Perceptual
Saturation
Relative Colorimetric
Description: Absolute Colorimetric
Leaves colors that fall inside the destination gamut unchanged. With this

⓫ *The* **Intent menu** *lets you choose how the final color display should look.*

Black and White Points?

A *white point* is the most extreme highlight in an image. This is the part of the image that should be totally white without any ink.

A *black point* is the most extreme black part of an image.

The Conversion Options, in the Advanced Mode, control how objects and color data are converted **❽**.

To set the conversion options:

1. Choose one of the settings in the Engine menu **❾** and **❿**:

   - **Adobe (ACE)** uses the Adobe color management system and color engine. This is the default setting for most preset color configurations.
   - **Apple ColorSync (Mac)** or **Apple CMM (Mac)** uses the color management system provided for Mac OS computers. Unless you have an optional color module installed, there is no difference between the two settings.
   - **Microsoft ICM (Win)** uses the color management system provided for Windows computers.

   TIP Choose Adobe (ACE) if you are working with other Adobe products.

2. Choose one of the settings in the Intent menu **⓫**:

   - **Perceptual** preserves the relationships between colors in a way that is perceived as natural by the human eye.
   - **Saturation** is suitable for business graphics, where the exact relationship between colors is not as important as having vivid colors.
   - **Relative Colorimetric** is more accurate than absolute colorimetric if the image's profile contains correct white point information. This is the default rendering intent used by all predefined color management configurations.
   - **Absolute Colorimetric** maintains color accuracy at the expense of preserving relationships between colors.

3. Check Use Black Point Compensation to adjust for differences in black points.

   TIP Adobe strongly recommends you keep the Use Black Point Compensation option selected.

Saving and Loading Color Settings

One of the things that drives my students crazy is when a color in Adobe InDesign looks different when displayed in Adobe Illustrator or Adobe Photoshop. How can the exact same color look totally different? That has to do with different color settings applied in each program. Fortunately, it is rather easy to synchronize all your Adobe application color settings so the color looks the same.

To save the color settings:

1. Set your color settings as described in the previous section.

2. Click the Save button in the Color Settings dialog box.

3. Name the color settings file (.csf) and save it in the following location :

   Disk: Documents and Settings: [User]: Application Data: Adobe: Color: Settings (Win).

   Disk: Users: [User]: Application Support: Adobe: Color: Settings (Mac).

TIP This saves the setting in a location where the other Adobe applications can use the settings file.

Once you have saved the color settings, you can open or load them into InDesign or another Adobe application.

To open the color settings:

1. Click Load in the Color Settings dialog box.

2. Navigate to the Color: Settings folder as described in the previous exercise.

3. Choose the color settings file.

TIP If you have chosen the same color settings for all your Adobe applications, a message appears at the top of the Color Settings dialog box stating that your settings are synchronized 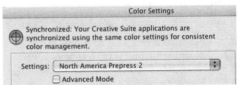.

⑫ *Use the* **Save Color Settings dialog box** *to save your own color settings file.*

⑬ *A message in the* **Color Settings dialog box** *lets you know if all your Adobe applications are using the same color settings.*

Color Management button

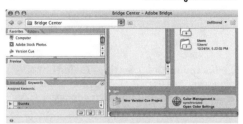

⑭ *The* **Adobe Bridge Center** *allows you to synchronize color management settings across all the Adobe Creative Suite applications.*

⑮ *Use the* **Suite Color Settings dialog box** *to choose the color settings file you want to apply to all the applications.*

If your copy of InDesign is part of the Adobe Creative Suite, you have an additional feature that allows you to easily synchronize all the applications in the suite.

To synchronize color settings using Adobe Bridge:

1. Open Adobe Bridge.

2. Choose **Edit > Create Suite Color Settings**. This opens the Suite Color Settings dialog box.

   or

   Click the Color Management button in the Adobe Bridge Center **⑭**. This opens the Suite Color Settings dialog box.

3. Choose the color setting from the list and then click Apply. This synchronizes the color management across the Adobe Creative Suite applications **⑮**.

TIP If you have chosen the same color settings for all your Adobe applications, a message appears at the top of both the Suite Color Settings and the Color Settings dialog boxes stating that your settings are synchronized.

Saving and Loading Color Settings

Working with Profiles

You can also set profiles and color management for individual imported images.

To control a placed image's color management:

1. If the graphic has already been placed into the layout, select it, and then choose **Object > Image Color Settings** to open the Image Color Settings dialog box .

   or

   If you're about to import the graphic, click the Color tab of the Image Import Options dialog box. This displays the Profile and Rendering Intent menus .

2. Use the Profile menu to choose the source profile to apply to the graphic.

3. Use the Rendering Intent menu to choose a rendering intent.

16 *The* **Image Color Settings dialog box** *allows you to assign a specific profile and rendering intent to an imported image.*

17 *The* **Color tab in the Image Import Options dialog box** *allows you to assign a specific profile and rendering intent to an image that is about to be imported.*

Working with Profiles

INTERACTIVE PDF ELEMENTS 18

At the risk of sounding like an old codger, I can remember when a page-layout program only laid out print files. The idea of creating "push buttons" that sent you flying to other pages — or even other documents — was totally unfathomable. After all, how was someone supposed to press on a weather summary on the front page of a newspaper to jump to the full weather map on the last page?

So it is with some amazement that I write this chapter. Page layout no longer refers to just printed pages. InDesign has a wealth of features that let you create interactive elements for electronic documents.

These interactive features may be simple links that let readers move from one page to another. They may be hyperlinks to Web pages. They may also be special bookmarks that can be used as navigational tools. They may even be rollover buttons that can play movies and sounds in a PDF document.

Of course, if you have no interest whatsoever in creating these types of interactive elements, feel free to skip this chapter entirely. Who cares if this is the future of publishing!

Types of Interactive Elements

There are three different types of interactive elements you can add to InDesign documents: Hyperlinks, Bookmarks, and Buttons. Each has its own particular uses, but some of the features may overlap. Before you start work, decide which type of interactive element is right for you.

Feature	Description	Advantages	Limitations
Hyperlink	Adds a hotspot area to text or objects that is linked to other parts of the document, other documents, or Web pages.	Can be applied directly to the text inside a story. Can be created automatically using the Table of Contents or Indexing feature.	Provides only very primitive visual indications of the linked area.
Bookmark	Adds a navigational element that is visible in the Adobe Reader Bookmark pane.	The Bookmark pane is visible at all times in the document. Can be created automatically using the Table of Contents feature.	Requires some education to teach the reader how to use the Bookmark pane in the Reader. Is not directly on the document page. No special visual indication in the document.
Button	Adds a hotspot area that can contain text or graphics. This hotspot can be set to invoke a wide variety of behaviors including navigation as well as movie or audio playback.	Offers the most navigational and design choices.	Buttons can't be created automatically from text.

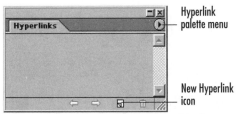

Hyperlink palette menu

New Hyperlink icon

1 The **Hyperlinks palette** *is used to define both the destinations and the hyperlinks.*

2 *The* **New Hyperlink Destination dialog box** *lets you set a page destination.*

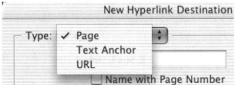

3 *The* **Type menu** *lets you choose the type of hyperlink destination.*

Which Comes First, Source or Destination?

Maybe it's years of working in HTML or JavaScript, but the first time I tried to create hyperlinks in InDesign, I got all fouled up. I started by trying to define a source for the hyperlink—the item that you click—and then setting its destination—the place where the link sends you.

InDesign doesn't work this way. You must set the destination first, and then set the source. I know it seems backward, but that's the way it must be done.

Defining Hyperlinks

A hyperlink is an area of a page that can be clicked to send the reader to a new page, open a new document, move to a Web page, or send an e-mail message. There are two parts to creating a hyperlink. The *source* is the object or text that you click to trigger the hyperlink. The *destination* is the page or Web link you go to.

TIP You must define a destination first, before you define the source.

TIP Hyperlinks are applied when the file is exported as an Adobe PDF *(see page 493)* or when you use the Package for GoLive feature *(see page 517).*

To choose the type of hyperlink:

1. Choose **Window > Interactive > Hyperlinks**. This opens the Hyperlinks palette **1**.

2. Choose New Hyperlink Destination from the Hyperlinks palette menu. This opens the New Hyperlink Destination dialog box **2**.

3. Choose the type of hyperlink from the Type menu as follows **3**:

   • **Page** creates a page destination that links to a specific page in the document. This is the only type of hyperlink that lets you set a magnification for the link. *(See the next exercise for how to create a page destination.)*

   • **Text Anchor** creates a link to a selected area of text. This option is only available if you have selected text. *(See the exercise on page 427 for how to create a text anchor destination.)*

   • **URL** lets you link to an Internet page. *(See the exercise on page 427 for how to create a URL destination.)*

A *page destination* specifies the page and the magnification to use when you move to the link.

To create a page destination:

1. Choose New Hyperlink Destination in the Hyperlinks palette menu to open the New Hyperlink Destination dialog box.

2. Choose Page from the Type menu. This opens the settings for the page destination ❹.

3. Use the Page controls to enter the page number that you want to jump to.

4. If desired, use the Name field to enter a descriptive name for the page.

   or

   Check the Name with Page Number option to automatically name the destination with its page number and whatever Zoom setting has been chosen.

5. Choose the Zoom settings as follows ❺:

   - **Fixed** displays the page as it was when the link was created.
   - **Fit View** displays the visible portion of the page.
   - **Fit in Window** displays the entire page in the document window.
   - **Fit Width** or **Fit Height** displays the width or height of the page.
   - **Fit Visible** displays the areas that contain text or graphics.
   - **Inherit Zoom** displays the same magnification that was active when the link was clicked.

6. Click OK to create the destination.

🆃🅸🅿 Don't worry that you don't see your destination listed in the Hyperlinks palette. Destinations aren't shown there. Destinations are shown when you define the hyperlink source.

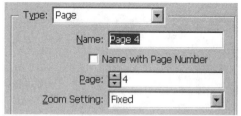

❹ *The New Hyperlink Destination dialog box set for a* **Page destination**.

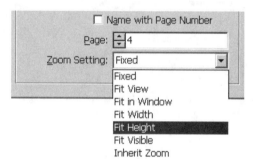

❺ *The* **Zoom Setting menu** *controls the magnification of the destination page.*

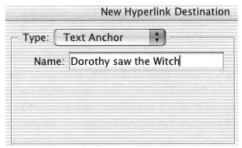

6 *The New Hyperlink Destination dialog box set for a* **Text Anchor destination**.

7 *The New Hyperlink Destination dialog box set for a* **URL destination**.

The second type of hyperlink is a text anchor. A text anchor destination allows you to link to a specific area of text on a page.

To create a text anchor destination:

1. Highlight the text that you want as the destination.

2. Choose New Hyperlink Destination in the Hyperlinks palette menu. This opens the New Hyperlink Destination dialog box.

3. Choose Text Anchor from the Type menu **6**.

4. Use the default name, which comes from the selected text.

   or

   Enter a name for the destination.

The third type of hyperlink is a URL (uniform resource locator). These are the links that can be used to open Web pages, send e-mail, or transfer files.

To create a URL destination:

1. Choose New Hyperlink Destination in the Hyperlinks palette menu to open the New Hyperlink Destination dialog box.

2. Choose URL from the Type menu **7**.

3. Enter a name for the destination.

4. Enter the URL information.

Defining Hyperlinks

You can use the Hyperlink Destination Options dialog box to edit the destinations that you create for the document. This is also the place where you can see which destinations have been defined for your document.

To edit a destination:

1. Choose Hyperlink Destination Options in the Hyperlinks palette menu to open the dialog box.

2. Choose a previously defined destination from the Destination menu.

3. Click the Edit button ❽. The controls for the destination become active.

TIP These controls change depending on the type of destination chosen.

4. Make whatever changes you want to the destination.

   or

   Click the Delete button to delete the destination from the document.

   or

   Click the Delete All button to delete all the destinations from the document.

TIP If you are editing a Text Anchor destination, you can change the text destination by selecting **Set to Current Text Insertion Point**.

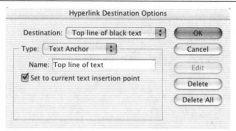

❽ *Use the* **Hyperlink Destination Options dialog box** *to edit the destinations in a document.*

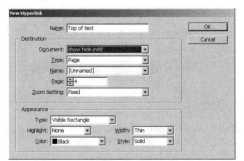

9 *The* **New Hyperlink dialog box** *lets you link to destinations as well as set the appearance of the hotspot area.*

Once you have set the hyperlink destinations, you can then create the hyperlink sources that link to those destinations.

To create a hyperlink from an existing destination:

1. Select the text or graphic that you want to be the hotspot or trigger area for the link.

2. Click the New Hyperlink button in the Hyperlinks palette.

   or

   Choose New Hyperlink from the Hyperlinks palette menu. The New Hyperlink dialog box appears **9**.

3. Use the Name field to name the hyperlink. This is the name that appears in the Hyperlinks palette.

4. Set the hyperlink destination as described on pages 426 – 428.

5. Set the Appearance as described in the exercise on page 432.

6. Click OK to create the hyperlink. The link appears in the Hyperlinks palette.

Defining Hyperlinks

To choose a page destination:

1. In the New Hyperlink dialog box, choose Page from the Type menu. This opens the Page Destination area 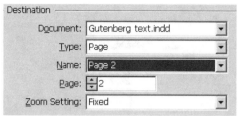.

2. Use the Document menu to choose the destination document. This adds any destinations that were defined in that document to the Name menu.

3. Choose a previously defined Page destination from the Name menu 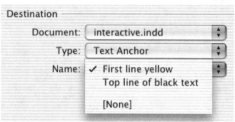.

Of course, it's possible to create a hyperlink without having previously defined a page destination.

To create an unnamed page destination:

1. In the New Hyperlink dialog box, choose Page from the Type menu. This opens the Page Destination area.

2. Choose [Unnamed] from the Name menu. This allows you to define an unnamed destination.

3. Use the Page controls to set the page number.

4. Set the Zoom Setting as described on page 426.

TIP The term [Unnamed] only applies to the destination. The hyperlink still appears in the Hyperlinks palette 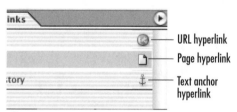.

To choose a text anchor destination:

1. In the New Hyperlink dialog box, choose Text Anchor from the Type menu.

2. Use the Document menu to choose the destination document. This adds any destinations that were defined in that document to the Name menu.

3. Choose a previously defined Text Anchor destination from the Name menu 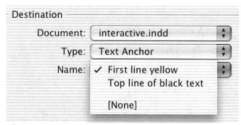.

10 *The* **Page Destination area** *of the New Hyperlink dialog box lets you set the destinations for hyperlinks.*

11 *The* **Name menu** *lets you choose previously defined page destinations for a hyperlink.*

— URL hyperlink
— Page hyperlink
— Text anchor hyperlink

12 *Hyperlinks appear in the Hyperlinks palette. Icons show the type of hyperlink.*

13 *The* **Name menu** *lets you choose a previously defined text anchor as a destination for a hyperlink.*

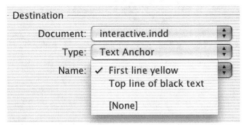

⓮ *The* **URL Destination area** *of the New Hyperlink dialog box lets you set the destinations for URL hyperlinks.*

⓯ *The* **Name menu** *lets you choose previously defined URL destinations for a hyperlink.*

⓰ *The* **URL Destination area** *lets you create an unnamed destination.*

To choose a previously defined URL destination:

1. In the New Hyperlink dialog box, choose URL from the Type menu. This opens the URL Destination area **⓮**.

2. Use the Document list to choose the destination document. This adds any destinations that were defined in that document to the Name menu.

3. Choose a previously defined URL destination from the Name menu **⓯**.

You can easily create a URL destination without having previously defined a URL destination.

To create an unnamed URL destination:

1. In the New Hyperlink dialog box, choose URL from the Type menu. This opens the URL Destination area **⓰**.

2. Choose [Unnamed] from the Name menu. This allows you to define an unnamed destination.

3. Enter the URL in the URL field.

TIP The term [Unnamed] only applies to the destination. The hyperlink itself still has the name you enter at the top of the New Hyperlink dialog box.

TIP You can also create a URL hyperlink by highlighting a URL contained in the text and choosing New Hyperlink from URL in the Hyperlinks palette menu. This adds the hyperlink to the palette and automatically sets the destination as the highlighted URL text.

Defining Hyperlinks

To choose the appearance of a hyperlink:

1. Use the Type menu in the Appearance area to choose a setting for the visibility of the rectangle around the hotspot ⑰.

   - **Visible Rectangle** creates a rectangular area that can be seen.
   - **Invisible Rectangle** creates a hotspot area that is not shown.

2. Use the Highlight menu to choose the appearance of the hotspot area when clicked ⑱:

   - **None** creates no highlight on the area.
   - **Invert** creates the effect of inverting the colors of the hotspot area.
   - **Outline** creates an outline rectangle around the hotspot area.
   - **Inset** creates the effect of a 3D cutout in the hotspot area.

3. Use the Width menu to choose thickness of the visible rectangle ⑲:

   - **Thin** is the most tasteful setting.
   - **Medium** is a more obvious setting.
   - **Thick** is really too ugly to use.

4. Use the Style menu to choose the type of line for the visible rectangle ⑳:

   - **Solid** is the most tasteful setting.
   - **Dashed** doesn't look as nice.

5. Choose a color from the Color menu.

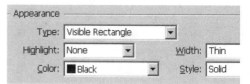

⑰ *The **Appearance area** of the New Hyperlink dialog box lets you set how hyperlinks are displayed in the document.*

⑱ *Examples of the three **Highlight** effects for the rectangle applied to links.*

⑲ *Examples of the three **Width settings** for the rectangle applied to links.*

⑳ *Examples of the **Style settings** for the rectangle applied to links.*

Defining Hyperlinks

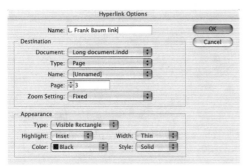

a *The* **Hyperlink Options dialog box** *lets you edit the settings for hyperlinks.*

Tips for Hyperlinks

Hyperlinks don't have to be ordinary text or plain frames. You can use placed images, text inside tables, or even inline graphics as the source object for hyperlinks.

If you use text as the source object for a hyperlink, you may not want to display the clunky rectangle as the link indicator. Instead, consider using an underline with colored text (applied as a character style), to indicate where the hyperlink is located. This changes the link so it is more similar to links in Web pages.

Finally, you can automate some of the process of creating hyperlinks by applying the source object to a master page. The hyperlink can then be visible on all the pages based on that master page.

As you work, you can edit the settings for the hyperlink source.

To edit hyperlinks:

1. Double-click the hyperlink entry in the Hyperlinks palette.

   or

   Choose Hyperlink Options in the Hyperlinks palette menu. This opens the Hyperlink Options dialog box **a**.

2. Make changes in the Hyperlink Options dialog box.

Once you have created a hyperlink, you can change or reset the text selection or frame that was used as the source object.

To reset the hyperlink source:

1. Highlight the text or select the frame that you want to be the new hyperlink source.

2. In the Hyperlinks palette, select the hyperlink that you want to change.

3. Choose Reset Hyperlink from the Hyperlinks palette menu. The original source object is changed to the new selection.

If you have named an external document as a destination, you may need to update the hyperlink to that external document. For instance, if the page name or location has changed, the hyperlink needs to be updated.

To update the hyperlink to an external document:

1. Select the Hyperlink in the Hyperlinks palette.

2. Choose Update Hyperlink from the Hyperlinks menu palette.

3. Choose Reset Hyperlink from the Hyperlinks palette menu.

   TIP If the external document is closed, hold the Opt/Alt key to open the document.

Defining Hyperlinks

Working with Hyperlinks

Once you have set up your destinations and hyperlinks, you can use the Hyperlinks palette to navigate through the document. This lets you easily move to specific locations in your InDesign document.

To move to a hyperlink:

1. Select the hyperlink in the Hyperlinks palette 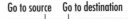.

2. Choose Go to Source from the Hyperlinks palette menu.

   or

   Click the Go to Source icon in the Hyperlinks palette.

To move to a hyperlink destination:

1. Select the hyperlink in the Hyperlinks palette.

2. Choose Go to Destination from the Hyperlinks palette menu.

   or

   Click the Go to Destination icon in the Hyperlinks palette.

TIP If the destination is a URL, the default Web browser will be launched.

To delete a hyperlink destination:

1. Select the hyperlink in the Hyperlinks palette.

2. Choose Delete Hyperlink from the Hyperlinks palette menu.

   or

   Click the Delete Hyperlink icon in the Hyperlinks palette.

Go to source Go to destination

Delete hyperlink

22 *You can use the* **Hyperlinks palette** *to navigate through the document.*

Automatic Hyperlinks

If it seems too much work to create manual hyperlinks, remember that you automatically create hyperlinks when you use the Table of Contents or Index feature.

The manual hyperlinks are best used for those instances when you need to add just a few links to a document. For example, you might want to add a URL address to a sales brochure or a page link to a small document.

Exporting and Testing Hyperlinks

You must export the InDesign file as a PDF in order to test your hyperlinks *(see Chapter 19 "Output," for how to export as a PDF)*. Also, you must remember to check the option to include hyperlinks in order to make them active in the PDF.

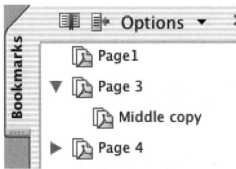

㉓ *The* **Bookmarks pane** *in Acrobat displays the bookmarks created in InDesign.*

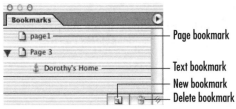

Page bookmark
Text bookmark
New bookmark
Delete bookmark

㉔ *The* **Bookmarks palette** *holds the bookmarks created for the document.*

Working with Bookmarks

Bookmarks provide a different way to navigate within a document. Instead of elements on the page, bookmarks are displayed in the Adobe Acrobat or Adobe Reader Bookmark pane **㉓**. The reader clicks each bookmark to move to that position in the document. One of the advantages to using bookmarks is that the bookmark pane can be always visible next to the area being read. Also, bookmarks can be expanded or collapsed to shorten the length of the bookmark list.

To create a bookmark:

1. Choose **Window > Interactive > Bookmark** to open the Bookmarks palette **㉔**.
2. Do one of the following to create the destination for the bookmark:
   - Place the insertion point at a point within the text. This creates a text bookmark.
   - Select the text. This creates a text bookmark named with the selected text.
   - Select a frame or graphic. This creates a page bookmark.
   - Double-click a page in the Pages palette. This creates a page bookmark.
3. Click the New Bookmark icon in the Bookmarks palette.

   or

   Choose New Bookmark from the Bookmarks palette menu. The bookmark is added to the Bookmarks palette.

TIP Icons show the difference between text and page bookmarks although there are no such differences in Acrobat.

TIP If you already have bookmarks in the Bookmarks palette, the new bookmark is created directly under whichever bookmark is selected in the palette. *(See page 437 for how to move bookmarks to new positions.)*

Working with Bookmarks

New bookmarks are created with the name Bookmark 1, Bookmark 2, and so on. You can rename the bookmark with a more descriptive name to help readers know what is located there.

To rename a bookmark:

1. Select the bookmark in the Bookmarks palette.

2. Choose Rename Bookmark from the Bookmarks palette menu. This opens the Rename Bookmark dialog box 25.

3. Enter a new name in the field and click OK.

You can also rename a bookmark directly in the list area of the Bookmarks palette.

To rename a bookmark in the list area:

1. Click once to select the bookmark in the Bookmarks palette.

2. Click again to open the field that contains the bookmark name 26.

3. Type the new name.

4. Press Return/Enter or click a different bookmark to apply the new name.

You can also delete bookmarks you no longer want in the document.

To delete a bookmark:

1. Select the bookmark in the Bookmarks palette.

2. Choose Delete Bookmark from the Bookmarks palette menu.

   or

   Click the Delete Bookmark icon in the Bookmarks palette.

25 *Use the* **Rename Bookmark dialog box** *to change the bookmark names.*

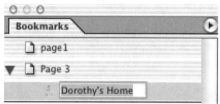

26 **Click the bookmark name** *to type a new name directly in the Bookmarks palette.*

Working with Bookmarks

Black line indicator

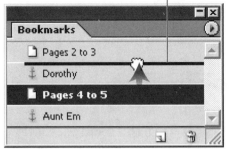

② *Drag the bookmark up to* **move it to a new position** *in the Bookmarks palette.*

Name highlighted

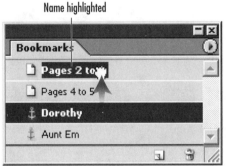

② *Drag the bookmark onto the name* **to nest it under another bookmark**.

Name highlighted

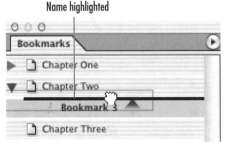

② *Drag the bookmark up until you see the black line* **to unnest it from a bookmark**.

Bookmarks don't have to appear in the order that you create them. You can move important bookmarks up to the top of the list, even if they refer to pages that are at the end of your document.

To move bookmarks to new positions:

1. Drag the bookmark up or down the list to the new position.

2. When you see a black line appear, release the mouse button. The bookmark moves to the new position **②**.

TIP Use the Sort Bookmarks command to rearrange the bookmarks into the order they occur in the document.

You can also *nest*, or move bookmarks so they are contained within others. The top bookmark is called the *parent*; the nested bookmark is called the *child*. This allows you to have a very long bookmark list that can be expanded as necessary.

To nest bookmarks:

1. Drag the bookmark you want to nest onto the name of the parent bookmark.

2. When the name is highlighted, release the mouse **②**. The child bookmark is indented under the parent. A triangle controller appears that lets you open or close the parent bookmark.

TIP When you delete a bookmark, you also delete any bookmarks that are nested within that bookmark.

TIP You can continue to nest bookmarks through as many levels as you want.

To unnest bookmarks:

1. Drag the child bookmark out from the parent so that the black line is no longer indented below the parent bookmark **②**.

2. Release the mouse button. The child bookmark is no longer nested.

Working with Bookmarks

Adding Sounds

Despite the mind-bending concept of adding sound to a page layout, it's actually very simple to add sounds to an InDesign document. Just remember, you won't actually play the sound in InDesign. The sound is played as part of a PDF, when repurposed as part of an XML document, or when packaged for a GoLive Web site.

To add a sound to a document:

1. Choose **File > Place** and then choose the sound file you want to import. The cursor changes into the Sound Clip cursor ⓿.

2. Click the Sound Clip cursor on the document. This adds a sound clip object to the document ⓿.

TIP The sound clip is displayed with an image that Adobe provides as the sound poster. This file is called *StandardSoundPoster.jpg* and can be swapped for any other image you want to use.

You can also add an empty sound clip that can be filled with a sound at some other time.

To add an empty sound clip:

1. Draw a frame.

2. Choose **Object > Interactive > Sound Options**. This opens the Sound Options dialog box ⓿.

3. Enter a name in the Name field and click OK. The frame has been converted to an empty sound clip.

⓿ *The* **Sound Clip cursor** *indicates you are importing a sound file.*

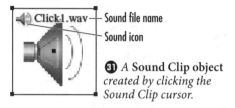

Sound file name
Sound icon

⓿ *A* **Sound Clip object** *created by clicking the Sound Clip cursor.*

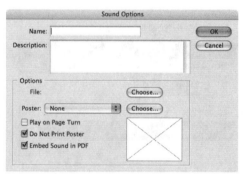

⓿ *A* **Sound Options** dialog box *for an empty sound clip. Notice there is no file specified under Options.*

Sound and Video Requirements

InDesign supports the same media file types as Adobe Acrobat. This means that you can import any sound or video file that can be played by Apple QuickTime, Flash Player, Windows Built-in Player, and Windows Media Player.

On the Mac, QuickTime plays all the media files. So all you need is QuickTime 6 or later. On Windows, you need QuickTime as well as the other players.

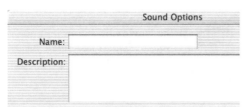

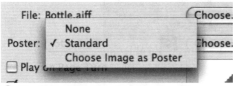

㉝ *You can set a* **name and description for a sound** *in the Sound Options dialog box.*

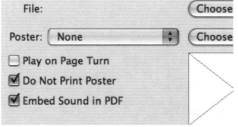

㉞ *The* **Sound Options Poster menu** *lets you choose the image that is displayed in a sound clip.*

File:	Choose
Poster: None	Choose
☐ Play on Page Turn	
☑ Do Not Print Poster	
☑ Embed Sound in PDF	

㉟ *The* **Options controls** *for a sound in the Sound Options dialog box.*

If you have an empty sound clip, you use the Sound Options dialog box to fill it with a sound and set the other sound properties.

TIP You can also edit a filled sound clip by modifying the settings in the Sound Options dialog box.

To set the sound options:

1. Open the Sound Options dialog box by double-clicking the sound clip.

   or

   Select the sound clip and choose **Object > Interactive > Sound Options**.

2. Enter a name for the sound clip in the Name field **㉝**. This name is just to help you identify which sounds have been added to the document.

3. If desired, enter a description that can be read by hearing-impaired users.

4. Use the Choose button to add a sound to the sound clip or to change the sound in the clip.

5. Use the Poster menu to choose an image that will be used to show where the sound is in the document **㉞**:
   - **None** leaves the sound clip frame empty.
   - **Standard** uses the standard icon **㉞**.
   - **Choose Image as Poster** lets you import a custom image to use as the sound poster.

6. Use the Choose button to choose the custom image **㉟**.

7. Check Play on Page Turn to have the sound automatically play when the page is opened **㉟**.

8. Check Do Not Print Poster to prevent the poster image from printing **㉟**.

9. Check Embed Sound in PDF to add the sound file to the PDF. If this is unchecked, you will have to make sure the sound file is kept with the PDF document **㉟**. *(See the sidebar on the next page.)*

Adding Sounds

Adding Movies

Movies can be easily added to an InDesign document. Just remember, you won't actually play the movie in InDesign. The movie is played as part of a PDF, when repurposed as part of an XML document, or when packaged for a GoLive Web page. Consider what it would be like if this book came as a PDF. Instead of the static images, you would see little movies that showed how things work.

To add a movie to a document:

1. Choose **File > Place** and then choose the movie file you want to import. The cursor changes into the Movie Clip cursor **36**.

2. Click the movie cursor on the document **37**. This adds a Movie Clip object to the document.

TIP The movie clip displays the name of the movie and the Movie Clip icon.

TIP The movie clip is displayed with the default poster image that was set for the movie when it was created. *(See page 443 for how to change the movie poster.)*

36 *The* **Movie Clip cursor** *indicates that you are importing a sound file.*

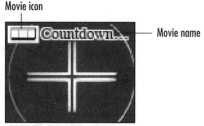

Movie icon

Movie name

37 *A* **Movie Clip object** *appears when you click to import a movie.*

Linking versus Embedding Media Clips

Media clips such as movies and sound files can be linked to the PDF or embedded in the document. You can choose either one, but be aware of the limitations of each method.

Embedding a media clip adds to the size of the PDF. In the case of movies, this can add greatly to the final size of the file. If you embed a movie clip, only those viewers with Acrobat 6 or 7, or Adobe Reader will be able to view the movie. Users with earlier versions of the software will have to upgrade in order to view your documents correctly.

Linking to a media clip keeps the file size down, but then you must remember to keep the media clip with the PDF or it will not play properly.

Also, if you link to a media clip, it resides outside the PDF document. This can cause problems if you distribute your files on CD-ROM. Someone can copy the movie to use for their own purposes. If you don't want people to be able to use your media for their own projects, you can embed the media clip to prevent them from easily snatching the sound or movie to use in their own work.

You can control whether media clips are linked or embedded in the Sound or Movie Options dialog boxes, or when you export the PDF *(see page 493)*.

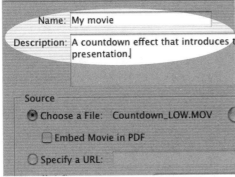

39 The **Movie Options dialog box** *for an empty movie clip frame.*

39 *Use the Movie Options dialog box to set the* **Name** *and* **Description** *for a movie.*

You can also add an empty movie clip that can be filled with a movie at some other time or used as the placeholder for a movie connected via a URL *(see page 442).*

To add an empty movie clip:

1. Draw a frame.

2. Choose **Object > Interactive > Movie Options**. This opens the Movie Options dialog box.

3. Enter a name in the Movie Options dialog box and click OK. The frame holds an empty movie clip **38**.

If you have an empty movie clip, you use the Movie Options dialog box to fill it with a movie and set the other movie properties.

TIP You can also edit a filled movie clip by modifying the settings in the Movie Options dialog box.

To set the name and movie description:

1. Open the Movie Options dialog box by double-clicking the movie clip.

   or

   Select the movie clip and choose **Object > Interactive > Movie Options**.

2. Enter a name for the movie clip in the Name field **39**.

TIP When you fill a movie clip, it uses the name of the actual movie file by default. You can rename it in the Movie Options dialog box.

3. If desired, enter a description to help identify the movie **39**. This description is used if the movie cannot be played or for visually impaired users who use screen readers to hear the description of the file.

Adding Movies

The movie source is the movie clip that will be played. You have several options for how to choose the movie source .

To add a movie to the document movie clip:

1. In the Movie Options dialog box, click Choose a File.

2. Click the Browse button to navigate to find movie you want to add to the document.

3. Click Embed Movie in the PDF to add the movie to the exported PDF. *(See the sidebar on page 440 for more information on embedding and linking movies.)*

40 *The* **Source controls** *set to play a local file within the document.*

You can also play streaming media in your PDF document. This avoids all problems with file sizes. However, it does mean that an Internet connection must be available when the movie is played.

To choose a URL connection for a movie:

1. Create an empty movie frame and then open the Movie Options dialog box *(see page 441)*.

2. In the Movie Options dialog box, click Specify a URL .

3. Type the URL where the movie can be accessed.

4. If you have an active Internet connection, click Verify URL and Movie Size to make sure the settings are correct.

41 *The* **Source controls** *set to play a URL-based movie within the document.*

Adding Movies

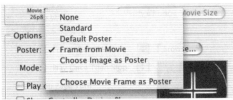

42 Use the **Poster menu** to choose the image that is displayed on the static page.

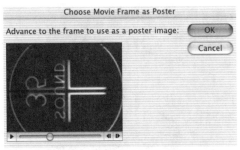

43 Use the **Choose Movie Frame as Poster** dialog box to choose the frame you want to add as the movie poster.

44 Use the **Mode menu** to choose how often the movie plays.

Movie Display Options

You can also set the poster options for the movie. This allows you to set an image that fills the space in the frame for the movie clip.

To set the movie poster options:

◆ In the Movie Options dialog box, choose one of the following from the Poster menu **42**:

- **None** sets no poster for the movie.
- **Standard** uses the image from the StandardMoviePoster.jpg file that Adobe provides with InDesign.
- **Default Poster** uses the poster image that was created when the movie was edited.
- **Choose Image as Poster** lets you click the Browse button to choose an image to use as the poster.
- **Choose Movie Frame as Poster** opens a dialog box that lets you advance through the movie to choose the poster **43**. When this option is chosen, the listing **Frame from Movie** is checked in the menu.

You can also set the options for how often the movie plays.

To set the play options for the movie:

◆ In the Movie Options dialog box, choose one of the following from the Mode menu **44**:

- **Play Once Then Stop** plays the movie a single time.
- **Play Once Stay Open** plays the movie, then leaves the movie player open. This allows the viewer to set the movie to play again.
- **Repeat Play** sets the movie to play over and over in a loop.

Movie Display Options

Movie Display Options

You can also set the rest of the options for how the movie plays **45**.

To set the movie display options:

1. Check Play on Page Turn to have the movie automatically play when the page is opened.

   TIP A movie or sound clip may take a moment to load before it starts playing.

   TIP The automatic page turn isn't the only way to play movies. A movie can be played by clicking the movie object in the PDF page. Also, you can create button behaviors that play movies.

2. Check Show Controller During Play to display the user controls that let you start, stop, rewind, forward, and change the sound of the movie **46**.

3. Check Floating Window to display the movie in a separate window that appears above the Acrobat document.

4. If you check Floating Window, use the Size menu to set the dimensions of the movie window **47**.

   TIP The size options for a floating window movie are listed in multiples of the original movie size. 1/2x means one-half times the size of the original. 3x means three times the size of the original. Max means the maximum size to fit the monitor.

   TIP A movie that is nonfloating is displayed at the size that it was originally created.

5. If you check Floating Window, use the Position menu to set where the movie plays in relation to the Acrobat document **48**.

45 *The settings at the bottom of the Movie Options dialog box that* **control how the movie plays**.

46 *The* **Controller** *is displayed at the bottom of the movie.*

47 *Use the* **Size menu** *to set the size of a movie that plays in a floating window.*

48 *Use the* **Position menu** *to choose where a movie that plays in a floating window is displayed.*

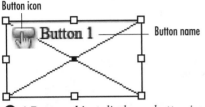

⑨ *The* **Button tool** *in the Toolbox.*

Button icon

Button 1 — Button name

㊿ *A* **Button object** *displays a button icon and a button name.*

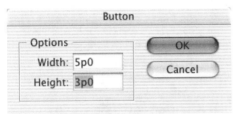

㉛ *You can use the numerical controls in the* **Button dialog box** *to set the size of a button.*

㉜ *An example of how a button can contain text or an image.*

Creating Buttons

Buttons go much further than links. Links let you move to destinations or open Web pages. Buttons contain the code that can send you to destinations, flip pages, open Web pages, play movies, show and hide other buttons, and other tricks. The first thing you want to do is create a button and assign a simple action.

To create a button manually:

1. Select the Button tool in the Toolbox **⑨**.
2. Drag across the page to create the button object. The button appears on the page with a button icon and name **㊿**.

TIP The entire frame is considered the button, not just the little button icon in the frame.

TIP Buttons are drawn like any other object. Use all the same modifier keys and techniques that you use when drawing objects. *(See Chapter 4, "Working with Objects," for more information on drawing objects.)*

To create a button numerically:

1. Select the Button tool in the Toolbox.
2. Click with the Button tool on the page. This opens the Button dialog box **㉛**.
3. Enter the width and height for the button.

You can also convert any existing object into a button. This makes it easy to turn images or text into buttons **㉜**.

To convert an object into a button:

1. Select the object that you want to make into a button.
2. Choose **Object > Interactive > Convert to Button**. The button icon and name appear inside the converted object.

You can also add content, such as text or images, to existing buttons.

To type text in a button:

1. Move the Text tool over the button. The cursor changes to curved edges 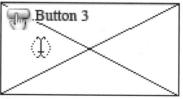. This indicates that text can be added to the button.

2. Click the Text tool. A blinking insertion point indicates that you can type text in the button.

To import text into a button:

1. Select the button.

2. Choose **File** > **Place** and select the text file you want to import. The text flows into the button 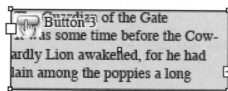.

TIP The text inside a button is in a separate text frame that has been pasted into the button frame. Use the Direct Selection tool to access the text frame.

To add an image to a button:

1. Select the button.

2. Choose **File** > **Place** and select the image file you want to import. The image appears inside the button .

TIP You can also click with a loaded cursor to add an image to a button.

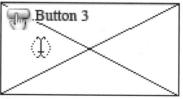

53 *The* **curved text cursor** *indicates that you can click to add text to a button.*

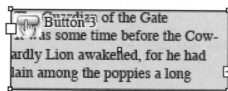

54 *Text can be imported into a button. The overflow symbol lets you flow the text out to another text frame.*

55 *An image can be imported into a button.*

Creating Buttons

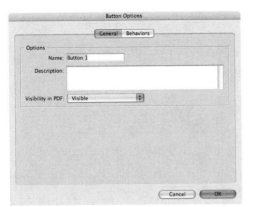

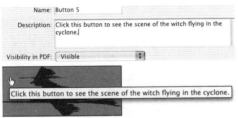

56 The **Button Options dialog box** *set to the General control.*

57 *Enter a description in the General Button Options that the viewer can see while holding the cursor over the button in the PDF viewer.*

58 *The* **Visibility in PDF menu** *in the Button Options dialog box.*

General Button Properties

Once you have created a button, you can set its properties. These are divided into two sections. General properties let you name the button and control how it is viewed in the PDF. The other section is the Behavior properties *(covered on page 453),* which let you apply actions to the button.

To set the General controls of the Button Options:

1. Double-click the button to open the Button Options dialog box **56**.

   or

   Select the button and choose **Object > Interactive > Button Options**.

TIP If you have text in the button, you'll need to use the Object menu command to open it. Otherwise, you'll place an insertion point in the button's text.

2. Click the General control.

3. Choose a name for the button or leave the default name in place.

4. Enter a description for the button. This description is visible when the mouse passes over the button in Acrobat. It is also used as the alternate text heard by visually impaired users **57**.

5. Choose one of the following from the Visibility in PDF menu **58**:

   - **Visible** displays the button. This is the most common setting.
   - **Hidden** hides the button. This setting can be overridden by the Show/Hide Fields behavior *(see page 455).*
   - **Visible but Doesn't Print** allows the button to be seen but keeps it from cluttering up any printouts of the page.
   - **Hidden but Printable** allows you to add information to a printout without cluttering up your onscreen page.

Setting the Button States

Part of the fun of using interactive buttons in PDF documents is that you can make the buttons change their appearance when the viewer passes the mouse over them or clicks the button. Each different appearance for the button is called a button *state*. InDesign lets you add states and control their appearance.

To add button states:

1. If it's not already open, choose **Window > Interactive > States** to open the States palette (59).
2. Select the button. Unless you have already modified it, only the Up state is listed in the States palette.
3. Click the New State icon to add the Rollover state.

   or

   Choose New State from the States palette menu.
4. Click the New State icon again to add the Down state.

TIP After you add the Down state, the New State icon is unavailable, as there are no other states you can add.

To delete button states:

1. Select the state you want to delete.
2. Click the Delete State icon.

   or

   Choose Delete State from the States palette menu.

TIP You cannot delete the Up state.

TIP Instead of deleting states, you may want to use the Enable State setting *(see the next exercise)*.

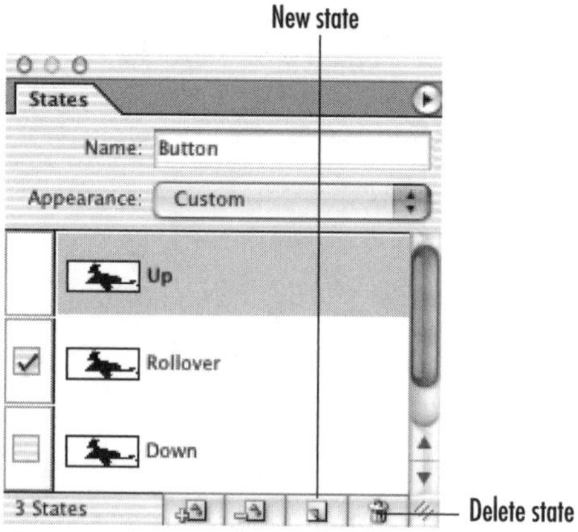

(59) *Use the* **States palette** *to add new states to the button display.*

Understanding the States

The three button states refer to the appearance of the button in relation to the mouse:

- *Up* refers to the state when the mouse cursor is not near the button. This is also the appearance when the user releases the mouse after clicking the button. Some programs may call this the *Normal* state.
- *Rollover* refers to the state when the mouse cursor passes over the boundaries of the button. Some programs call this the *Over* state.
- *Down* refers to the state when the cursor has been positioned over the button and the mouse button has been pressed.

Other programs may have additional states for their buttons, but Acrobat stops at three.

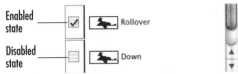

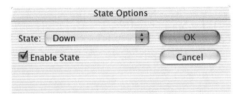

60 *The check marks next to the state names indicate if the state is* **enabled or disabled**.

61 *The* **State Options dialog box** *lets you convert states or change their enable setting.*

Instead of deleting states, which tosses out their content, it may be easier to change whether or not the state is exported with the PDF. This is called *disabling* the state.

To enable a state:

◆ Click the checkbox next to the name of the state **60**. If the check mark is visible, it means the state is enabled and will export with the PDF.

or

Choose State Options and check Enable State in the State Options dialog box.

To disable a state:

◆ Click the checkbox next to the name of the state. If the check mark is not visible, it means the state is disabled and will not export with the PDF.

or

Choose State Options and uncheck Enable State in the State Options dialog box **61**.

If you have only a Down state or a Rollover state, you can turn one type of state into another.

To convert a state:

1. Select the state you want to convert.
2. Choose State Options from the States palette menu.
3. Use the State menu to change the Down state to Rollover or vice versa.

Setting the Button States

One of the reasons you want to create button states is so that the button changes appearance as the mouse cursor passes over or clicks the button. There are two ways to accomplish this. The first way is to use imported artwork to change the appearance of each state. The second way is to modify the art inside the button using InDesign's effects.

To create new states using imported artwork:

1. Create a button. The Up state is automatically selected.

2. Click the Place Content into Selected State icon 62. This opens the dialog box that lets you add imported artwork into the Up state.

3. Click the New State icon. This creates a Rollover state that contains the same artwork as the Up state.

4. With the Rollover state selected, click the Place Content into Selected State icon. This changes the artwork in the Rollover state 63.

   or

   Choose Place Content into State from the States palette menu.

5. Click the New State icon to create the Down state.

6. With the Down state selected, click the Place Content into Selected State icon. This changes the artwork in the Down state 63.

You can use the commands to place content at any time to modify the appearance of a button state.

To edit button states using imported artwork:

1. Select the button state you want to modify.

2. Click the Place Content into Selected State icon to import new artwork into the button state.

Place content into selected state

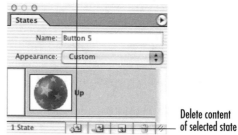

Delete content of selected state

62 Use the **States palette** *to change the artwork in button states.*

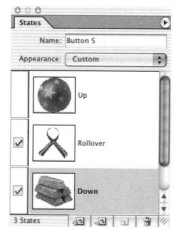

63 *You can change the artwork from one state to another.*

Setting the Button States

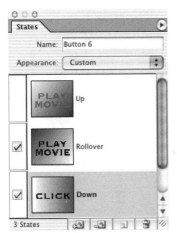

64 *Each one of the states in this button was modified by selecting the text inside the button and making changes.*

The second way to change the appearance of a button is to directly select the object inside the button frame.

To change a button state by selecting the object:

1. Select the button you want to modify.

2. Select the state, in the States palette, that you want to modify.

3. Use the Direct Selection tool to select the object inside the button frame.

TIP You will know you're working on the object inside the button when the states disappear from the States palette.

4. Use any of InDesign's styling features to add a fill, stroke, or effect to the object **64**.

TIP You can also use the **File > Place** command to add text or an image to the object inside the button.

You can also delete the artwork from any state.

To delete the content from a button state:

1. Select the state.

2. Click the Delete Content of Selected State icon. This deletes all the original artwork as well as any effects that you have applied to the state.

   or

   Choose Delete Content from State from the States palette menu.

Setting the Button States

You don't have to work too hard to create different appearances for the button states. Adobe has created three appearance themes that you can instantly apply to buttons. The themes apply different looks to each of the button states.

To apply the appearances to buttons:

1. Select the button.

2. Choose one of the themes from the Appearance menu in the States palette 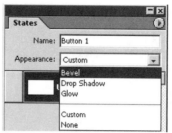:

   - **Bevel** colors the inside of the button and applies a gradient stroke around the edge of the object, creating the look of a beveled rectangle ⑥⑥.

   - **Drop Shadow** colors the inside of the button and applies a drop shadow to the area inside the button frame ⑥⑥.

   - **Glow** applies a multi-colored gradient to the object inside the button ⑥⑥.

   TIP The themes delete any imported images or custom content that was applied to the button states, and they apply their own styled content.

   TIP The appearance themes will delete any nonrectangular shapes from the button.

You can modify the appearance themes that you apply to buttons.

To modify the button themes:

1. Select the button state.

2. Use the Direct Selection tool to select the object inside the button.

3. Use any of the style techniques to change the appearance of the theme ⑥⑦.

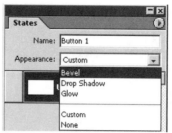

⑥⑤ *Use the* **Appearance menu** *in the States palette to apply preset themes to button states.*

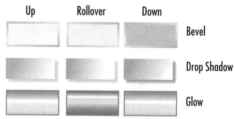

⑥⑥ *The* **appearance themes** *for the button states.*

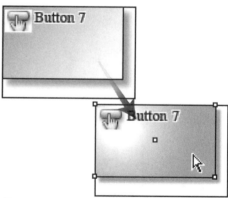

⑥⑦ *Use the Direct Selection tool to* **customize the appearance of a button state.** *Here the Down state of the Drop Shadow theme has been modified by changing the gradient and drop shadow effect.*

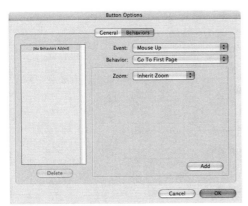

68 The **Behaviors section** *of the Button Options dialog box.*

69 The **Events menu** *lets you set which mouse trigger applies the behavior.*

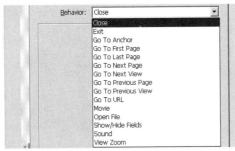

70 The **Behavior menu** *lets you set which behavior is applied to the button.*

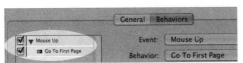

71 The **behavior list** *shows the events and behaviors that have been applied to the button.*

Applying Behaviors

A button without a behavior is like a light switch that is not connected to a lamp. You can flip the button all you want, but nothing changes on the page. Behaviors let your buttons move pages, play movies, or change the appearance of the PDF page.

To apply a behavior to a button:

1. Select the button.

2. Open the Button Options dialog box.

3. Select the Behaviors control in the Button Options **68**.

4. Choose the mouse event that will apply the behavior **69**:

   - **Mouse Up** applies the behavior when the mouse button is released after a click.
   - **Mouse Down** applies the behavior as the mouse button is pressed down.
   - **Mouse Enter** applies the behavior when the mouse cursor is moved over the button.
   - **Mouse Exit** applies the behavior when the mouse cursor is moved away from the button.
   - **On Focus** applies the behavior when the button is prompted by tabbing through the fields.
   - **On Blur** applies the behavior when tabbing takes the focus off the button.

5. Choose the behavior from the Behavior menu **70**. *(See the chart on the next two pages for a description of each of the behaviors and their settings.)*

6. Depending on the behavior, set any additional controls for the behavior.

7. Click the Add button in the Behaviors panel. The event and behavior appear in the list on the left of the dialog box **71**.

8. If desired, you can apply additional behaviors to the button.

Button Behaviors

Behavior name	What it does	Settings
Close	Closes the document.	None
Exit	Exits (quits) the application that displays the PDF document, such as Adobe Reader.	None
Go To Anchor	Moves to a predefined destination that can be a text anchor, page, or bookmark. Lets you choose the document, the destination, and the zoom command.	Document: Chapter one... ⬍ Choose... Anchor: Page 1 ⬍ Page Zoom: Inherit Zoom ⬍
Go To First Page	Moves to the first page of the document. Lets you choose the zoom command.	Zoom: Inherit Zoom ▾
Go To Last Page	Moves to the last page of the document. Lets you choose the zoom command.	Zoom: Inherit Zoom ▾
Go To Next Page	Moves to the next page of the document. Lets you choose the zoom command.	Zoom: Inherit Zoom ▾
Go To Next View	Only available when the Go To Previous View command was active. Then the command moves forward through the views.	None
Go To Previous Page	Moves to the previous page of the document. Lets you choose the zoom command.	Zoom: Inherit Zoom ▾
Go To Previous View	Moves to whatever document, page, or zoom view was previously chosen.	None
Go To URL	Opens a Web page or Web command. Lets you type in the URL.	URL: http://

Behavior name	What it does	Settings
Movie	Controls the play of a movie. Lets you specify the movie and set the play controls.	Movie: [ ] Play Options: [Play] — Play / Stop / Pause / Resume
Open File	Opens an external file which does not have to be a PDF document. Viewer must have the application that created the file. You must specify the full path to open the file.	Select File: [ ] Browse...
Show/Hide Fields	Displays the fields in the document and lets you set them to be hidden or visible by the action of the button.	Trigger 4 / Sunset 4 / Trigger 5 / Button 1 — Show All / Hide All / Clear All
Sound	Controls the play of a sound clip. Lets you specify the sound and set the play controls.	Sound: [ ] Play Options: [Play] — Play / Stop / Pause / Resume
View Zoom	Lets you change the level of zoom as well as change the layout options such as Continuous and Continuous-Facing.	Zoom: [Full Screen] — Full Screen / Zoom In / Zoom Out / Fit In Window / Actual Size / Fit Width / Fit Visible / Reflow / Single Page / Continuous / Continuous-Facing / Rotate Clockwise / Rotate Counterclockwise / Add

Button Behaviors

Applying Behaviors (continued)

The most sophisticated buttons are those that apply multiple behaviors. You can apply multiple behaviors to the same mouse event or to separate mouse events.

To apply multiple behaviors to a button:

1. Select the button and open the Button Options dialog box.
2. Select the Behaviors tab.
3. Choose the event and behavior settings and then click the Add button. The behavior appears in the list on the left side of the dialog box.
4. Choose an additional event and behavior settings, and click the Add button.

TIP If the behavior uses the same event as the first, it appears nested under the event name. If the behavior uses a different event, it appears under that event name (72).

To edit existing behaviors:

1. Choose the behavior in the behavior list that you want to edit.
2. Make whatever changes you want to the behavior settings.
3. Click the Update button.

TIP The Update button replaces the Add button when you edit existing behaviors.

To change the position of a behavior:

- Drag the behavior up or down in the behaviors list (73). The behaviors are applied in the order that they appear in the list.

To change the event associated with a behavior:

- Drag the behavior from one event to another in the behaviors list.

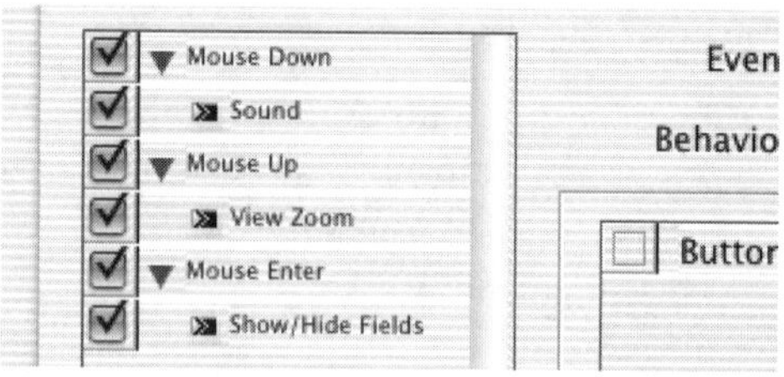

(72) **Multiple behaviors** *appear in the behaviors list.*

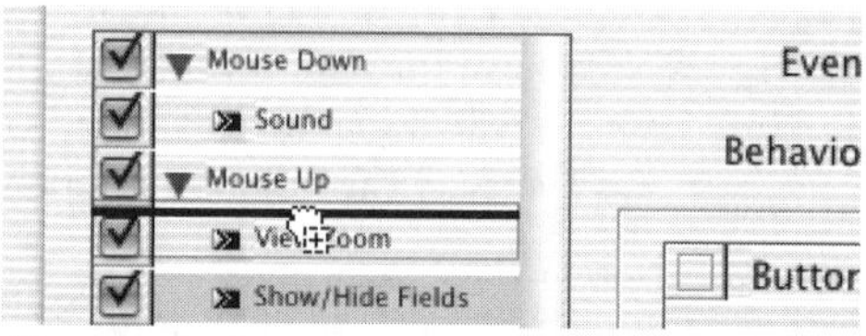

(73) *You can* **drag a behavior** *to a new position or to a different event.*

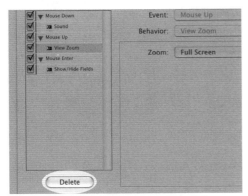

74 *The* **Delete Button** *lets you delete behaviors or events from the behaviors list.*

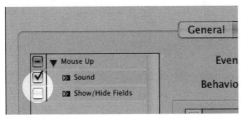

75 *Click the checkbox next to a behavior or an event to* **deactivate the behavior or event**.

Deleting or Deactivating Behaviors

You may have applied a behavior that you no longer want applied to the button. Fortunately, you can delete behaviors from the button.

To delete a behavior:

1. Select the behavior in the behaviors list that you want to delete.

2. Click the Delete button. The behavior will be deleted from the behaviors list **74**.

TIP If that behavior was the only one listed for the event, the event will also be deleted from the list.

Instead of deleting behaviors that you have so carefully defined, you can deactivate them so they are still in the behaviors list but don't get applied to the final PDF. You can also deactivate all the behaviors under a mouse event.

To deactivate a behavior or mouse event:

1. Select the behavior or the mouse event in the behaviors list.

2. Click the checkbox next to the behavior of the event **75**. This deactivates the behavior from the exported PDF.

Deleting or Deactivating Behaviors

Exporting Interactive PDFs

There are a few settings you must be aware of when exporting interactive and multi-media PDFs from InDesign. *(See Chapter 20, "Exporting," for the complete instructions on exporting PDF files from InDesign.)*

To set the interactive/multimedia export controls:

1. Choose **File > Export** and then choose Adobe PDF for the format.

2. Check Bookmarks, Hyperlinks, and Interactive Elements to make sure they are part of the final PDF document ⓴.

3. If you want to embed a movie clip within the file, you must save the document as an Acrobat 6 (PDF 1.5) or Acrobat 7 (PDF 1.6) file ⓴.

4. If you have chosen Acrobat 6 or 7, the Multimedia menu is available ⓴. This lets you override the object embed settings.

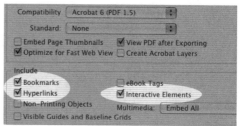

⓴ *Remember to include* **Bookmarks, Hyperlinks,** *and* **Interactive Elements** *when you export the PDF document.*

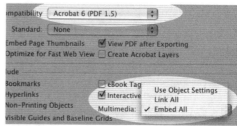

⓴ *You must save as an Acrobat 6 (PDF 1.5) or Acrobat 7 (PDF 1.6) file in order to be able to embed all media clips in the exported PDF.*

OUTPUT 19

everal years ago the title of this chapter would have been "Printing." That was what you did with page-layout documents: You printed them using a desktop printer. Today, however, there are many more choices for publishing your InDesign documents.

Most InDesign files are created as part of the professional prepress process. *(For more information on professional printing, see* The Non-Designer's Scan and Print Book, *by Sandee Cohen and Robin Williams, published by Peachpit Press.)* You need to know more than just how to print to a desktop printer. You need to know how to make sure your document has been set up correctly, and what files are necessary to send to a print shop.

So this chapter is now called "Output." Output refers to preparing documents and printing them — either with an ordinary desktop printer or with a high-end printing device such as an imagesetter.

Printing a Document

When a document is printed, many different instructions are sent to the printing machine. You need to set all those instructions correctly.

TIP Adobe recommends using only the controls inside the InDesign Print dialog box — not the Page Setup (Mac) dialog box or the Printer Properties (Win) dialog box.

To print a document:

1. Choose **File > Print**. This opens the Print dialog box **❶**.

2. Click each of the categories **❷** on the left side of the dialog box to set the options as described in the chart on the following page.

TIP You do not need to set all the controls every time you print unless you need to change a specific setting.

3. Click the Print button to print the document according to the settings.

Before you print a document, you may want to set some objects (such as private notes or alternate designs) to not print.

To set elements to not print:

◆ Select the object and turn on Nonprinting in the Attributes palette *(see page 145)*.

or

Turn off the visibility of the layer in the document *(see page 293)*. This supresses the printing for all objects on the layer.

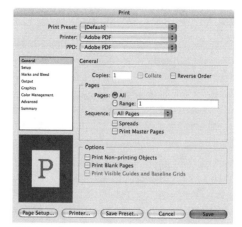

❶ *The* **Print dialog box** *contains all the settings for printing documents.*

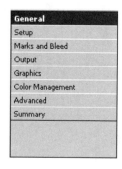

❷ *Click each of the categories to display those settings in the Print dialog box.*

Print Dialog Box Categories

Print category	Settings	Comment
General		Sets the basic printing options *(see page 463)*.
Setup		Controls the dimensions of the printable area *(see page 464)*.
Marks and Bleed		Sets the print control marks and print area *(see page 467)*.
Output		Controls colors and separations *(see page 469)*.

Print category	Settings	Comment
Graphics		Sets how images are printed *(see page 476)*.
Color Management		Controls how colors are handled. (Talk to your service bureau before setting color management controls.)
Advanced		Controls image replacement options and how transparency effects are printed *(see page 477)*.
Summary		Lets you see a summary of all the print settings *(see page 484)*.

Print Dialog Box Categories

③ *The* **Printer list** *lets you choose the printer to print a document.*

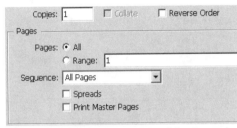

④ *The* **Copies and Pages area** *of the General controls for printing.*

Options
- ☐ Print Non-printing Objects
- ☐ Print Blank Pages
- ☐ Print Visible Guides and Baseline Grids

⑤ *The* **Options area** *of the General controls for printing.*

Setting the General Print Options

If you are printing to a desktop printer, the options in the General category may be all you need to set to print a document.

To choose the printer:

- ◆ Choose the printer from the Printer menu at the top of the dialog box **③**.

To control the copies:

1. Set the number of copies in the Copies field **④**.
2. Choose Collate to print multiple copies as complete sets.
3. Choose Reverse Order to print the copies back to front.

TIP Use Reverse Order for printers that print documents face up.

To control the pages:

1. Choose All to print all the pages **④**.

   or

   Select Range to enter a range of pages.

   TIP Use a hyphen to specify a range of pages, such as 4-6. Use a comma to specify individual pages, such as 8, 9.

2. Choose Collate to print copies as sets.
3. Use the Sequence menu to choose All Pages, Even Pages, or Odd Pages.
4. Check Spreads to print the pages in spreads together.
5. Choose Print Master Pages to print any master pages in the document.

To set the general options:

1. Check Print Non-printing Objects to print objects set to not print **⑤**.
2. Check Print Blank Pages to print pages that have no visible items.
3. Check Print Visible Guides and Baseline Grids to print the guides and grids.

Choosing the Setup Controls

The Setup options contain the controls to set the paper size and orientation.

To set the paper size and orientation:

1. Use the Paper Size menu to choose the size of the paper to print the document on **6**.

TIP This menu changes depending on the type of printer chosen.

2. Click one of the Orientation buttons. This changes the rotation of the document on the printed page.

To choose the setup options:

1. Set the Scale amount for either Height or Width to change the size of the printed document on the paper **7**.

2. Click the Scale to Fit button to have the document automatically resized to fit the chosen paper size.

3. Use the Page Position menu to choose where to position the document on the printed page **8**.

4. Check Thumbnails to print small versions of the pages on a single page.

5. If you have chosen Thumbnails, use the Thumbnails menu to choose how many pages are printed on each page **9**.

TIP See the next exercises for information on how to use the Tile controls.

6 *The* **Paper Size and Orientation controls** *in the Setup category of the Print dialog box.*

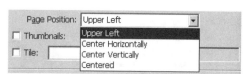

7 *The* **Options controls** *in the Setup category of the Print dialog box.*

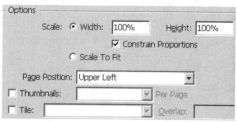

8 *The* **Page Position menu** *in the Setup category of the Print dialog box.*

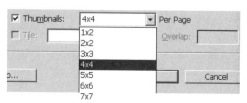

9 *The* **Thumbnails menu** *in the Setup category of the Print dialog box.*

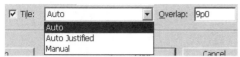

⑩ *The* **Tile menu** *in the Setup category of the Print dialog box.*

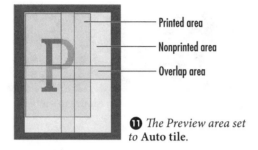

Printed area

Nonprinted area

Overlap area

⑪ *The Preview area set to* **Auto** *tile.*

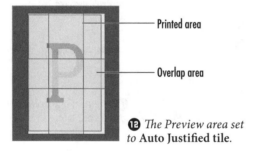

Printed area

Overlap area

⑫ *The Preview area set to* **Auto Justified** *tile.*

Tiling Pages

If your document is larger than the paper in the printer, you can print portions of the document on different pages. You can then assemble the pages together. This is called *tiling*. Auto tiling automatically divides the page into smaller segments.

To set automatic tiling:

1. Check Tile in the Setup category of the Print dialog box.

2. Choose Auto from the Tiling menu ⑩.

3. Set the amount in the Overlap field. This controls how much of one page is repeated on the tile for a second section of the page.

TIP The Preview area in the lower left portion of the Print dialog box shows how the page will be tiled ⑪.

Auto justified tiling divides the pages so that the right edge of the document lies on the right side of a printed page and the bottom edge of the document lies on the bottom edge of a printed page ⑫.

TIP The Auto setting ensures that there is no white space on the right side and bottom of the tiled pages.

To set auto justified tiling:

1. Check Tile in the Setup category of the Print dialog box.

2. Choose Auto Justified from the Tiling menu.

Tiling Pages

You can also tile pages manually. This lets you make sure that the edge of the paper does not cut across an important portion of the document.

To set manual tiling:

1. Use the zero-point crosshairs on the ruler to set the upper-left corner of the area you want to print ⓭. *(See Chapter 2, "Document Setup," for more information on setting the zero point of the ruler.)*

2. Choose **File > Print.**

3. Click the Setup category of the Print dialog box.

4. Choose Manual from the Tiling menu.

TIP The Preview area of the Print dialog box shows the area that will be printed ⓮.

5. Click Print to print that one page.

6. Reposition the zero-point crosshairs to set a new area to be printed.

7. Follow steps 2 through 5 to define and print the second tile.

8. Repeat the process until the entire page has been printed.

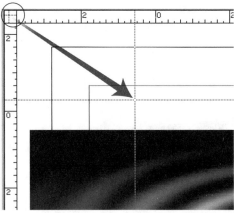

⓭ **Move the zero-point crosshairs** *to set the area to print as a tile on one page.*

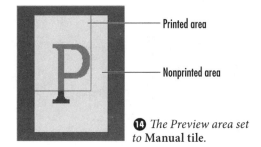

Printed area

Nonprinted area

⓮ *The Preview area set* to **Manual tile.**

Tiling Pages

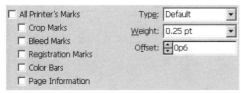

☐ All Printer's Marks   Type: Default ▾
  ☐ Crop Marks   Weight: 0.25 pt ▾
  ☐ Bleed Marks   Offset: ⬍ 0p6
  ☐ Registration Marks
  ☐ Color Bars
  ☐ Page Information

⓯ *The* **Marks settings** *in the Marks and Bleed category of the Print dialog box.*

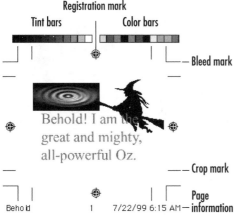

⓰ *The* **page marks and information** *as they appear on the printed page.*

Setting Marks and Bleed

You can also add information that shows where the page is to be trimmed, the document name, and so on. This information is sometimes called *printer's marks* or *page marks.*

To set the page marks:

1. Check All Printer's Marks to turn on all the marks, or use the checkboxes to set each one individually **⓯** and **⓰**.

   - **Crop Marks** indicates where the page should be trimmed.
   - **Bleed Marks** shows how far outside the crop marks you must put graphics so that they are trimmed correctly.
   - **Registration Marks** adds crosshair targets that are used to line up pieces of film.
   - **Color Bars** provides boxes that display the colors used in the document as well as the tint bars that can be used to calibrate the printing press for correct tints of colors.
   - **Page Information** prints the name of the file, the page number, and the time the document was printed.

2. Use the Type menu to choose a custom set of marks such as those used in Japanese printing.

3. Enter an amount in the Weight field for the thickness of the crop marks.

4. Enter an amount in the Offset field to determine how far away from the trim the page marks should be positioned.

Setting Marks and Bleed

You can also control the bleed, or the area that allows objects that extend off the page to print ⑰.

To set the bleed area:

◆ To use the bleed set in the Document Setup dialog box *(see page 19)*, check Use Document Bleed Settings ⑱.

or

Deselect Use Document Bleed settings and then set the custom amounts for the bleed around each side of the page ⑲.

TIP These custom bleed controls make it easy for print shops to set a uniform bleed as part of a print preset *(see page 482).*

If you have set a slug for the document *(see page 19)*, you can choose if that slug area prints.

To set the slug area:

◆ To print items in the slug area, check Include Slug Area.

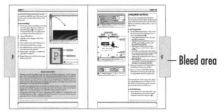

⑰ *An example of an object that bleeds off a page.*

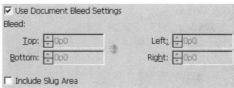

⑱ *Check the option for* **Use Document Bleed Setup** *to have the bleed use the same settings as in the Document Setup dialog box.*

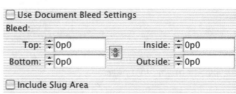

⑲ *The* **Bleed controls** *allow you to define a custom bleed in the Print dialog box.*

Why Do We Need To Bleed?

Why do you need to position objects so they bleed off the page layout? The reason is that the machines that trim books and pages don't always cut perfectly. Take a look at the thumbtabs on the sides of this book. If you flip from page to page, you will see that the gray area isn't always the same size. That's because when the paper for the book is trimmed, some of the pages are cut slightly different from the others. (Yes, I know this will happen, even before the book is printed.)

So instead of trusting that the trim position is always perfect, I set a bleed by extending the gray area outside the edge of the page. That way I don't have to worry if the trim is slightly off. I know that the gray area will still be visible outside the trim.

Unless your print shop is trying to trim pages in the middle of an earthquake, you shouldn't need more than a quarter-inch bleed. However, if you are in doubt, ask your print shop for the size they would like for a bleed.

Setting Marks and Bleed (side margin)

⑳ *The* **Color menu** *in the Output category of the Print dialog box.*

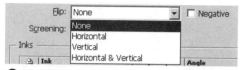

㉑ *The* **Flip menu** *in the Output category of the Print dialog box.*

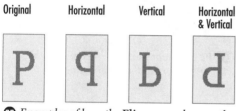

㉒ *Examples of how the* **Flip menu** *changes the readability of a document.*

What Does RIP Stand For?

You may hear people use the term RIP when they talk about printing. *RIP* stands for *raster image processing*.

RIP is simply a fancy term for what happens when a file is processed for output by a high-resolution image-setter. In addition, RIP also refers to the device that does the processing.

Setting the Output Controls

You may need to set the color controls to choose how color documents are printed.

To control how colors are printed:

1. Choose one of the following from the Color menu **⑳**:

   - **Composite Leave Unchanged** prints without converting colors to either RGB or CMYK.
   - **Composite Gray** prints all the colors as a gray image. Use this when printing on one-color laser printers.
   - **Composite RGB** prints all the colors as an RGB image. Use this when printing on RGB ink-jet printers.
   - **Composite CMYK** prints all the colors as a CMYK image. Use this when printing on PostScript CMYK printers.
   - **Separations** prints all the colors onto separate plates or pages.
   - **In-RIP Separations** prints all the colors onto separate plates using the separation controls in the RIP.

   TIP Separations printed on a laser printer are commonly called paper separations and are used to make sure the proper number of plates will be printed by the service bureau.

2. If you choose one of the composite settings, you can check Text as Black.

   TIP The Text as Black command is helpful if you have color text that you want to be more readable when printed on a one-color printer.

3. Use the Flip menu if you need to flip the orientation of the page **㉑** and **㉒**.

4. Check the Negative box in the Output category of the Print dialog box.

   TIP These last two options are not commonly used for desktop printers, but are used by print shops when they create film separations.

You can also change the screen frequency and angle of halftones in the image.

To change the screen settings:

1. Use the Screening menu to set the frequency and angle for the screen applied to images 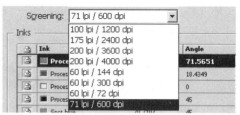.

2. Select a color in the Inks area and then use the Frequency and Angle fields 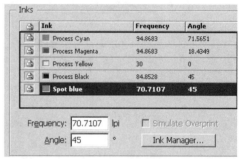.

TIP Always talk to your Print Service Provider for the correct settings.

㉓ *The* **Screening menu** *in the Output category of the Print dialog box.*

Trapping refers to the various techniques that are used to compensate for the misregistration of printing plates. However, if you don't understand trapping, you should consult with the service bureau that will print your file before you set the trapping.

To turn on basic trapping:

◆ Choose Application Built-In or Adobe In-RIP from the Trapping menu 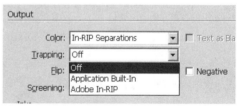.

㉔ *The* **Frequency and Angle fields** *in the Output category of the Print dialog box.*

㉕ *The* **Trapping menu** *in the Output category of the Print dialog box.*

Setting the Output Controls

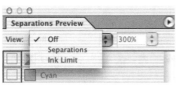

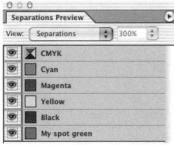

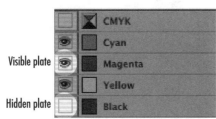

Working with Separations Preview

When a document is printed with more than one color, each color is called a plate. Printing the different colors onto separate plates is called making separations. You use the Separations Preview palette to view the different color plates onscreen. This makes it possible to gauge how a document will look on press.

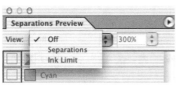

26 *Use the* **View menu** *in the Separations Preview palette to turn on the separations preview.*

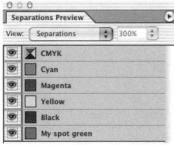

27 *The* **colors in the document** *are displayed in the Separations Preview palette.*

Visible plate

Hidden plate

28 *Click the* **Show/Hide icons** *in the Separations Preview palette to change the display of the colors on the page.*

To turn on separations preview:

1. Choose **Window > Output > Separations**. The Separations Preview palette appears.

2. Choose Separations from the View menu **26**. This displays the controls for the colors in the document **27**.

3. Click each Show/Hide icon next to the color name to change the display of the colors on the page **28**. *(See the chart on the following page for examples of the previews* **29***.)*

TIP Click the Show/Hide icon next to the CMYK listing to show or hide all those plates together.

My Favorite Childhood Book

One of my favorite books I had as a kid was a *World Book Encyclopedia* that had acetate pages that you could flip to see how colors built up to a full-color image. (It's true! At the age of 13 I was into page production and color separations.)

When I worked in advertising we called these color breakdowns *prog proofs* (for progressive proofs). But during many years of working with computer graphics, we had no way to see how colors combine on the page. The best we could do was print color on individual laser prints and then hold them up to the window to see how the colors would separate.

Finally, I am thrilled to see the Separations Preview — an electronic version of my *World Book* acetate pages. Instead of flipping pages, I click ink colors on and off. I can spend hours doing it. It makes me feel like a kid again!

Working with Separations Preview

Separations Preview Plate Settings

Plate	Palette setting	Onscreen preview
All	☑ CMYK / Cyan / Magenta / Yellow / Black / My spot green	**Taste the Grapes**
Cyan	☑ CMYK / Cyan / Magenta / Yellow / Black / My spot green	
Magenta	☑ CMYK / Cyan / Magenta / Yellow / Black / My spot green	
Yellow	☑ CMYK / Cyan / Magenta / Yellow / Black / My spot green	
Black	☑ CMYK / Cyan / Magenta / Yellow / Black / My spot green	
My spot green	☑ CMYK / Cyan / Magenta / Yellow / Black / My spot green	**Taste the Grapes**

㉙ *As you change the colors shown in the Separations Preview palette, the display of the colors on the page changes.*

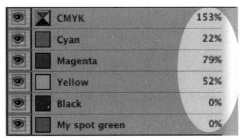

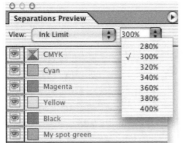

⑳ *Click the* **panel menu icon** *to open the menu for the active panel.*

㉛ *Click the* **panel menu icon** *to open the menu for the active panel.*

Working with Separations Preview (continued)

The Separations Preview palette also lets you view the total amount of ink for each plate.

To view the inks for each plate:

1. Choose Separations Preview from the View menu.

2. Move the cursor around the page. The ink percentages appear next to the name of each color **⑳**.

Separations Preview also shows you the areas of the page that exceed a certain ink limit. For instance, many print shops will request that you not define colors totaling more than 300% of all the inks combined. The Ink Limit setting lets you see if there are any areas that exceed this limit.

To check the ink limit:

1. Select Ink Limit from the View menu in the Separations Preview palette.

2. Use the amount menu to set the ink limit amount **㉛**.

TIP When you switch to the Ink Limit view, the document preview changes to a grayscale image. Any areas that exceed the ink limit are shown in red. The deeper the red, the more the color is over the ink limit.

TIP You can also enter your own custom amount in the Ink Limit field.

Color Separations and Ink Manager

The Inks area of the Output category also lets you control how the inks are separated and printed.

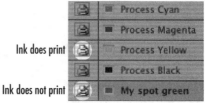

Ink does print

Ink does not print

32 *The* **printer icon next to an ink color** *indicates whether that ink will print or not.*

To set the inks to be printed:

◆ Click the printer icon next to the name of each color. Each click changes how the ink will print as follows **32**:

• If the icon is visible, the color will print.
• If there is a slash through the icon, the color will not print.

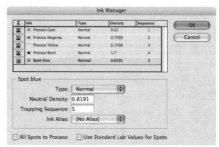

33 *The* Ink Manager dialog box *gives you control over how inks are separated or printed.*

Sometimes you find yourself with a document that contains spot colors that should be process colors. The Ink Manager lets you convert the spot colors to process inks.

To convert spot colors to process:

1. Open the Ink Manager by clicking the Ink Manager button in the Output area of the Print dialog box **33**.

TIP You can also open the Ink Manager from the Swatches palette menu or the Separations Preview palette menu.

2. Click the color icon next to the name of each color. Each click changes how the ink will print as follows **34**:

• A CMYK symbol indicates that the color will separate as a process color.
• A spot color symbol indicates that the color will separate on its own plate.

Spot color

Process color

34 *Click the* color icons *in the Ink Manager to convert spot colors to process.*

3. Click the All Spots to Process option to convert all spot colors to process.

4. If desired, check Use Standard Lab Values for Spots. This converts the spot colors to process using their built-in Lab color values.

35 *An example of how names typed in different cases can create* **too many spot colors** *in a document.*

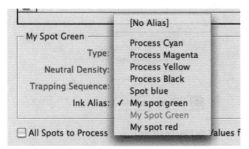

36 *Use the* **Ink Alias menu** *to have one color map to a different one.*

☒		Process Yellow	Normal
☒	■	Process Black	Normal
◎	■	My spot green	Normal
◎	■	My spot red	Normal
⚐		My Spot Green	<My spot green>

37 *An example of how* **one color is used as the alias** *for another.*

When you import artwork that contains spot colors, those spot colors are added to the document and the Swatches palette. There are no problems if the imported colors are named exactly the same as existing colors. But if the name of the imported color differs from the color you have defined, you can wind up with two separate color plates instead of one **35**. Thankfully, InDesign lets you map one color to be an alias of another.

To map one color to be the alias of another:

1. Select the color you want to change in the Ink Manager.

2. Use the Ink Alias menu to choose a different color to map to the selected one **36**. The color is listed in the Ink Manager as mapped to the other color **37**.

TIP You can map the selected color to a spot or process color.

TIP Colors that are mapped to another color are not listed in the Inks area of the Output category. They are also not listed in the Separations Preview palette.

Color Separations and Ink Manager

Setting the Graphics Options

The Graphics options control how much information is sent to the printer. You can control the data that is sent for placed images.

To control the data sent for images:

◆ Choose one of the following from the Images Send Data menu 38:

- **All** sends all the information for the image. This is the slowest setting.
- **Optimized Subsampling** sends only the amount of information necessary for the chosen output device. Use this option if you're proofing high-resolution images on a desktop printer.
- **Proxy** sends only a 72-ppi version of the image.
- **None** replaces the image with crosshairs within the frame. Use this option when you want to proof only the text in the file.

You can also control how much of the font information is sent to the printer.

To control the font information sent for printing:

1. Choose one of the following from the Download menu 39:

- **None** sends no font information, only a reference to the font. Do not use this option unless you understand how to replace the reference in the PostScript data stream.
- **Complete** sends the entire set of glyphs for the font. This is the longest option.
- **Subset** sends only those glyphs used in the document.

2. Choose Download PPD Fonts to send all fonts, even if they have been installed on the printer 40. This option is helpful if you use a variation of the fonts installed on the printer.

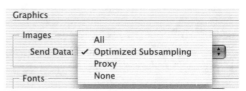

38 *Use the* **Send Data menu** *in the Graphics category to control how images are printed.*

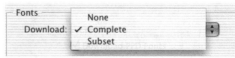

39 *Use the* **Download menu** *in the Graphics category to control how much of a font is sent to the printer.*

40 *Choose* **Download PPD Fonts** *to send printer fonts as part of the print information.*

⬤ *Set the* **OPI Image Replacement options** *to control how images are handled during prepress.*

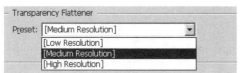

⬤ *Use the* **Preset menu** *in the Transparency Flattener area to set the resolution for converting transparency effects into rasterized images.*

Setting the Advanced Options

The Advanced category lets you set the options for OPI and choose a transparency preset. *OPI* stands for *Open Prepress Interface*. The OPI controls are used when files are sent to Scitex and Kodak prepress systems.

To set the OPI controls:

1. In the OPI area, click the OPI Image Replacement checkbox **⬤**.

2. Choose which types of images should be replaced during an OPI workflow. (An OPI workflow uses low-resolution images for the layout and swaps them with high-resolution images just before printing.)

When you use any of the transparency features, InDesign needs to flatten or convert those effects into vector and raster images as they are sent for output. The Transparency Flattener section of the Advanced category controls how InDesign flattens the image.

To set the flattener preset:

1. Use the Preset menu to choose one of the flattener settings **⬤**.

2. If you have used the Pages palette to flatten individual spreads, you can check Ignore Spread Overrides to override that setting. This means that the setting you choose in this dialog box will be used no matter what flattener settings you have applied to the individual pages.

Setting the Advanced Options

Flattener Presets and Preview

The transparency flattener presets control how the transparency effects, drop shadows, and feathers are handled during output.

To create a transparency flattener preset:

1. Choose **Edit > Transparency Flattener Presets**. This opens the Transparency Flattener Presets dialog box 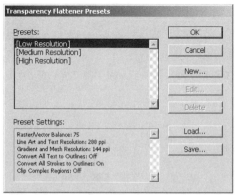.

2. Click the New button. The Transparency Flattener Preset Options dialog box appears 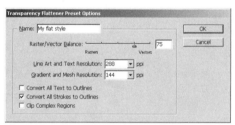.

3. Use the Name field to name the preset.

4. In the Options area, move the Raster/Vector Balance slider to create more vector or more rasterized artwork .

5. Set an output resolution for rasterized artwork in the Flattener Resolution field.

TIP A setting of 300 dpi is sufficient for most output.

6. Set an output resolution for gradient objects in the Gradient and Mesh Resolution field.

TIP A setting of 150 dpi is sufficient for most gradients.

7. Check Convert All Text to Outlines to convert the text to paths.

TIP If this box is not checked, only transparent portions of the text may be converted to outlines, which may make that text thicker than other text. This option makes the text width consistent.

8. If you have strokes that pass through different transparencies, you may want to choose Convert All Strokes to Outlines to convert the strokes to filled paths.

9. Check Clip Complex Regions to ensure that any differences in raster and vector objects always fall along existing paths.

TIP This can result in complex clipping paths, which may not print on some devices.

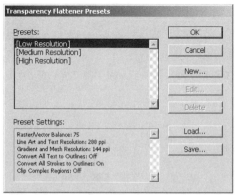

43 *The* **Transparency Flattener Presets dialog box** *lets you define new presets for handling transparency effects.*

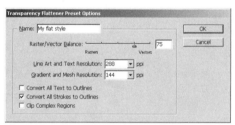

44 *The* **Transparency Flattener Preset Options dialog box** *contains the settings for a custom transparency flattener preset.*

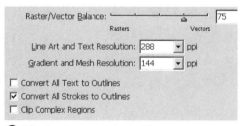

45 *The* **Options area** *in the Transparency Flattener Preset Options dialog box.*

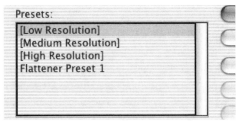

46 *The* **three default transparency flattener presets** *in brackets cannot be edited or deleted.*

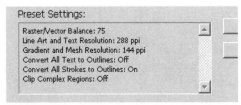

47 *The* **Preset Settings area** *displays a readout of the settings for a particular transparency flattener preset.*

To edit a transparency flattener preset:

1. Choose the preset you want to edit.

TIP The three default presets, surrounded by brackets, cannot be edited **46**.

2. Click the Edit button.

3. Edit the preset in the Transparency Flattener Presets dialog box.

TIP The Preset Settings area displays a readout of the settings for each preset **47**.

To delete transparency flattener presets:

1. Choose the presets you want to delete.

TIP The three default presets, surrounded by brackets, cannot be deleted **46**.

TIP Use the Shift key to select multiple adjacent presets. Use the Cmd/Ctrl key to select multiple nonadjacent presets.

2. Click the Delete button.

You can also save transparency flattener presets to share among others. Once saved, the presets can then be loaded onto other machines.

To save a transparency flattener preset:

1. Choose the presets you want to save.

TIP Use the Shift key to select multiple adjacent presets. Use the Cmd/Ctrl key to select multiple nonadjacent presets.

2. Click the Save button.

3. Name the file.

To load a transparency flattener preset:

1. Click the Load button.

2. Navigate to find the file that contains the presets.

3. Click Open. The presets appear in the Transparency Flattener Presets dialog box.

You can apply a flattener preset to the document in the Advanced category of the Print dialog box *(see page 477)*. However, you may have one page that requires special flattener controls. InDesign lets you apply flattener presets to each specific spread.

TIP Flattening must be handled on a per spread, not per page, basis.

To apply a flattener preset to an individual spread:

1. Move to the spread.
2. In the Pages palette menu, choose one of the following from the Spread Flattening menu:

   • **Default** leaves the spread flattening at whatever setting is applied to the document.

   • **None (Ignore Transparency)** prints the spread without any transparency effect. This setting is useful for print shops that need to troubleshoot during output.

   • **Custom** opens the Custom Spread Flattener Settings dialog box. These settings are identical to ones in the Transparency Flattener Preset Options dialog box *(see page 478)* **48**.

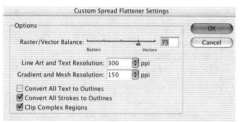

48 *The* **Custom Spread Flattener Settings** dialog box *lets you apply different flattener controls to a specific spread.*

A Short Course in Flattening

You may feel a little overwhelmed by all the controls for flattening transparency. Don't panic, most of the flattening options are best set by the print house that will output your files.

However, there are some simple rules that can make it easier to get successful results when flattening artwork.

Unless you absolutely want text to be part of a transparency effect, keep your text above any transparency effects. For instance, instead of putting text underneath a drop shadow, move it above **51**. If the text is black, you won't see any difference in the final output. If it's a color, set it to overprint.

Try to avoid overlapping two gradients with transparency effects. That combination creates objects that are much too complex.

Run tests. The first time I used transparency and blend modes, I sent ten sample pages to my publisher, who had them output at the print shop. We looked to make sure none of the text had changed and there were no problems with the images. It saved us a lot of worry when the book went to press.

Flattener Presets and Preview

49 *The* **Flattener Preview palette** *lets you see the effects of the flattener presets on your document.*

50 *Use the* **Highlight menu** *to choose which objects will be displayed in the flattener preview.*

Text below shadow   Text above shadow

51 *The* **Flattener preview highlights** *the objects affected by transparency. Here the text below the shadow is highlighted. The text above the shadow is not.*

Instead of waiting for your file to be printed, you can preview how the flattening will occur with the Flattener Preview palette.

To preview the flattener settings:

1. Choose **Window > Output Preview > Flattener**. This opens the Flattener Preview palette **49**.

2. Choose one of the options from the Highlight menu **50**. This controls which objects will be displayed in the flattener preview. *(See the chart on the next page for a description of each of these options.)*

3. Use the Preset menu to choose which flattener preset is used to control the flattener preview.

4. Click the Refresh button to update the screen preview. The page displays the highlighted objects in red against other grayscale objects **51**.

   or

   Check Auto Refresh Highlight to have the screen update automatically.

5. Check Ignore Spread Overrides to use only the setting in the Preset menu.

6. If you want, click the Apply Settings to Print button to apply the settings to the Advanced category of the Print dialog box.

TIP You can open the Transparency Flattener Presets dialog box using the Flattener Preview palette menu.

Flattener Presets and Preview

Transparency Resources

This book can hardly cover all the aspects of setting transparency and flattening. For more information see the InDesign online Help pages.

Also, download the document *Achieving Reliable Print Output with Transparency* on the Adobe Web site.

Finally, if you are a service provider, you should look at the Print Service Provider Resources page of the Adobe Solutions Network (ASN).

Highlight menu setting	Flattener Preview applied
None	Turns off the flattener preview.
Rasterized Complex Regions	Highlights areas that will be rasterized according to the settings in the Raster/Vector Balance slider.
Transparent Objects	Highlights objects that are the sources of transparency effects. This includes objects with opacity settings, blend modes, feathers, drop shadows, alpha channels, and placed images with transparency.
All Affected Objects	Highlights the transparent objects as well as the objects that are affected by transparency.
Affected Graphics	Highlights all placed images affected by transparency or transparency effects.
Outlined Strokes	Highlights the strokes that will be outlined due to transparency or because the Convert All Strokes to Outlines option is selected.
Outlined Text	Highlights the text that will be outlined due to transparency or because the Convert All Text to Outlines option is selected.
Raster-fill Text and Strokes	Highlights text and strokes that have rasterized fills due to flattening.
All Rasterized Regions	Highlights the objects that will be rasterized.

Working with Print Presets

With all the areas in the Print dialog box, you wouldn't want to have to set all the controls each time you have a new document. InDesign lets you save the print settings so you can easily apply them later.

To save a print preset:

1. Set all the categories in the Print dialog box to the settings you want to save.

2. Click the Save Preset button at the bottom of the Print dialog box ⑫. This opens the Save Preset dialog box ⑬.

3. Enter a name for the preset.

4. Click OK. This saves the preset.

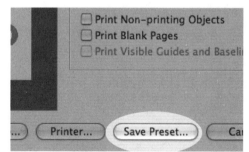

⑫ *Click the* **Save Preset button** *to save the current Print settings as a print preset.*

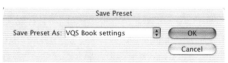

⑬ *Use the* **Save Preset dialog box** *to name your own printer preset.*

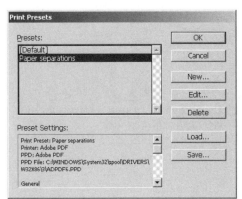

55 *A saved preset can be applied using the* **Printer Preset menu** *at the top of the Print dialog box.*

55 *Saved presets are listed in the* **Print Preset** *dialog box.*

To apply a print preset:

◆ Choose a saved preset from the Print Preset menu at the top of the Print dialog box **54**.

You don't need to go through the Print dialog box to create and save a print preset.

To define a printer preset:

1. Choose **File > Print Presets > Define**. The Print Presets dialog box appears **55**.

2. Click the New button to define a new preset. This opens a version of the Print dialog box that lets you set the various print categories.

   or

   Click the Edit button to make changes to the selected print preset.

To delete a printer preset:

1. Select the presets you want to delete in the Define Print Presets dialog box.

2. Click the Delete button.

One of the benefits of working with printer presets is that you can export them so others can print documents with the same settings.

To export printer presets:

1. In the Print Presets dialog box, select the presets you want to export.

   TIP Use the Shift key to select adjacent multiple presets. Use the Cmd/Ctrl key to select nonadjacent multiple presets.

2. Click Save. A dialog box appears where you can name the document that contains the exported presets.

Working with Print Presets

Your service bureau can provide you with printer presets that you can import to use for printing or packaging documents.

To import printer presets:

1. In the Define Print Presets dialog box, click Load.

2. Use the dialog box to select the document that contains the presets exported from another machine.

3. Click OK. The presets appear in the Define Print Presets dialog box.

Creating a Print Summary

With all the settings in the Print dialog box, you may want to keep track of how a document has been printed. The Summary area gives you a report of all the print settings.

To use the Summary area:

◆ Scroll through the summary area to see all the settings applied to a print job **56**.

or

Click the Save Summary button to save a text file listing all the print settings.

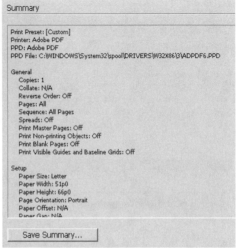

56 *Use the **Summary area** to see all the print settings applied to a document.*

Creating a Print Summary

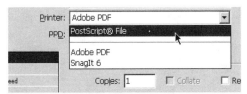

57 *Choose* **PostScript® File** *from the Printer menu to create a file that contains all the information necessary to print the document.*

58 *Choose* **Device Independent** *from the PPD menu to create a PostScript file that can be printed to any printer.*

Creating PostScript Files

Instead of sending the InDesign document to a service bureau, you can create a PostScript file that contains all the information necessary to print the file. (This is sometimes called *printing to disk*.) A standard PostScript file contains all the information necessary to print the file as well as the specific information about the printer.

To create a standard PostScript file:

1. Choose **File > Print**.
2. Choose PostScript® File from the Printer menu **57**.
3. Choose the type of printer that will print the file.
4. Set all the options in the print categories in the Print dialog box.

TIP Check with the service bureau that will print your file for the correct options.

5. Choose a name and location for the file.
6. Click Save.

A device-independent PostScript file does not contain any information about the type of printer or output device.

TIP This lets you create a PostScript file even if you don't know the type of printer that your document will be printed on.

To create a device-independent PostScript file:

1. Choose **File > Print**.
2. Choose Device Independent from the PPD menu **58**.
3. Follow steps 3 through 6 in the previous exercise.

Creating a Preflight Report

When you create an InDesign document, you have two jobs: designer and production manager. As the production manager, you need to know if there could be any problems printing your job. Fortunately, InDesign has a built-in preflight utility that checks all the elements in your document to make sure they print correctly. (The name comes from the list that airline pilots complete before they take off.)

To run the preflight utility:

1. Choose **File > Preflight.** InDesign takes a moment to check all the elements of the document and then opens the Preflight dialog box 59.

2. Review the information in the Preflight Summary 60.

 TIP Any potential printing problems are flagged with an alert symbol in the Preflight Summary.

3. Click each of the categories in the Preflight dialog box 61. *(See the following exercises for details on these categories.)*

4. Click the Report button to create a report of the preflight status.

 or

 Click the Package button to copy all the necessary files into a folder that you choose before you print the document.

 TIP The Package button is the same as the Package command located on the File menu. *(See page 489 for more information on packaging a document.)*

 TIP You can open the preflight report in a text editor.

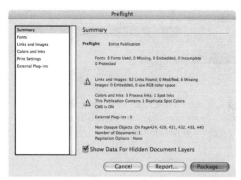

59 *The* **Preflight dialog box** *lets you choose each of the categories for the various aspects of printing a document.*

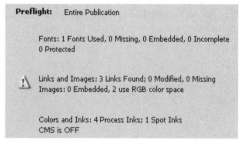

60 *The* **Summary area** *of the Preflight dialog box gives you an overview of the categories checked during a preflight.*

61 *The* **preflight categories** *let you see the details of the preflight report.*

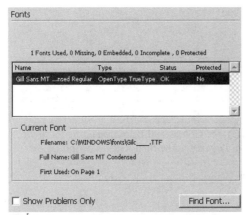

62 *The* **Fonts area of the Preflight dialog box** *shows you the status of the fonts used in a document.*

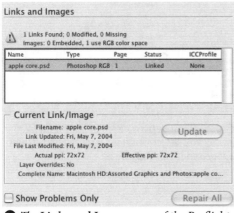

63 *The* **Links and Images area** *of the Preflight dialog box shows you the status of the placed images in the document.*

Your service bureau may ask you to use only Type 1 fonts. The Fonts area lets you make sure that you have used the correct fonts and that they are correctly installed.

To review the fonts information:

1. Choose Fonts from the categories on the left of the Preflight dialog box. This opens the Fonts area, which shows the type of font and whether it is installed in the system **62**.

2. If you want to replace a nonstandard or missing font, click the Find Font button. This opens the Find Font dialog box that lets you replace fonts *(see page 361)*.

You also want to make sure that placed graphics are in the correct format and that they aren't missing or modified.

To review the Links information:

1. Choose Links and Images from the categories on the left of the Preflight dialog box. This opens the Links area, which shows the placed images **63**.

2. Choose the modified or missing image.

3. If the image is modified, click the Update button.

   or

   If the image is missing, click the Relink button. This opens the Find dialog box.

4. Navigate to choose the missing image.

5. Click the Repair All button to have InDesign update all modified images or open the dialog box for all missing images.

Creating a Preflight Report

You should also check the colors and inks to make sure that the right number of colors print.

To review the Colors and Inks information:

◆ Choose Colors and Inks from the categories on the left of the Preflight dialog box. This shows the colors used within the document 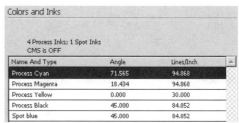.

64 *The* **Colors and Inks area** *of the Preflight dialog box shows the process and spot color plates in the document.*

You can also look at the Print Settings for a complete list of all the print settings currently applied to the document.

To review the Print Settings information:

◆ Choose Print Settings from the categories on the left of the Preflight dialog box. This shows the print settings applied to the document 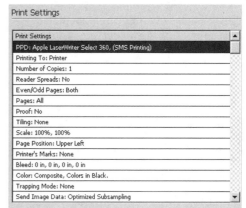.

65 *The* **Print Settings area** *of the Preflight dialog box shows you the current print settings applied to the document.*

You can also look to see if any external plug-ins were used in creating the document. You may need to alert your print shop that these plug-ins are necessary for outputting the document.

TIP You don't need to worry about the plug-ins unless you have installed any special third-party plug-ins.

To review the external plug-ins information:

◆ Choose External Plug-ins from the categories on the left of the Preflight dialog box. This shows any third-party plug-ins that have been installed .

TIP Even though it was installed with the program, the InBooklet SE plug-in is considered a third-party plug-in.

66 *The* **External Plug-ins area** *of the Preflight dialog box shows any third-party plug-ins that have been installed.*

Creating a Preflight Report

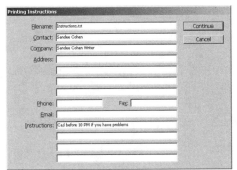

67 *The* **Printing Instructions dialog box** *lets you create a text file with contact information and instructions about the document package.*

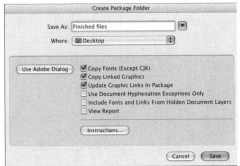

68 *The* **Create Package Folder dialog box** *lets you choose which items should be included in the package folder.*

Packaging a Document

A package is a folder that contains everything necessary to print a document. Instead of manually collecting all the files, the Package command assembles the files for you.

To package files for printing:

1. Choose **File > Package**. InDesign looks through the document and then opens the Printing Instructions dialog box **67**.

2. Fill out the contact and file information.

TIP The information in the Printing Instructions dialog box is kept if you repackage the document later.

3. Click Continue. This opens the Create Package Folder dialog box **68**.

4. Enter a name for the folder that will hold the files.

5. Check the following options for the package:

   - **Copy Fonts (except CJK)** copies the fonts used in the document except double-byte fonts such as those for Chinese, Japanese, and Korean languages. (*See the sidebar on the next page for a discussion of copying fonts.*)

   - **Copy Linked Graphics** copies placed images that are not embedded in the file.

   - **Update Graphic Links in Package** automatically updates any modified graphics.

   - **Use Document Hyphenation Exceptions Only** limits the hyphenation exceptions to only those added to the document.

   - **Include Fonts and Links from Hidden Layers** adds the fonts and graphics from layers that are not visible.

   - **View Report** launches a text editor to open the report created with the document.

6. Click Package to assemble all the necessary files in the folder.

Packaging a Document

Copying Fonts: Legal or Not?

If you choose to send fonts, a warning notice appears about the legalities of copying fonts 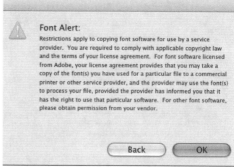. You may have heard stories of people carted off to prison for illegally copying software. While there have been people arrested for software piracy, the rules about fonts are more intricate.

Some font companies, such as Adobe, allow you to send a copy of the font along with your document provided that the service bureau that is going to print your file also has its own copy of the font. Other companies let you send the font along with your file, but the font can only be used to print *your* documents. You must check the license that came with the font.

So why would a service bureau want a copy of your font if it already has a copy? They want to make sure they use exactly the same font as the one you used to create the document.

This is why most service bureaus spend thousands of dollars to buy complete font libraries. If the bureau doesn't have a copy of the font, you should not send the font along with the file. Either the service bureau buys the font or you should create a prepress package.

Of course, if you use a program such as FontLab to make your own fonts, you have total permission to copy the fonts and give them to anyone you want. For instance, the tip bullet in this book is a font I created — I have no problem getting permission to copy that font.

However, the figure numbers are a specialized font I bought. I will have to buy another license to send that font to my service bureau.

Font Alert:

Restrictions apply to copying font software for use by a service provider. You are required to comply with applicable copyright law and the terms of your license agreement. For font software licensed from Adobe, your license agreement provides that you may take a copy of the font(s) you have used for a particular file to a commercial printer or other service provider, and the provider may use the font(s) to process your file, provided the provider has informed you that it has the right to use that particular software. For other font software, please obtain permission from your vendor.

Back   OK

69 *The* **Font Alert** *is a gentle reminder that both you and the service bureau need to own a copy of a font before you can copy and send it with a file.*

EXPORTING 20

Printing your document on paper is not the only way in which your InDesign files can be published. Today there are many more options for publishing documents.

For instance, you might want clients to read your document electronically — even if they don't have the InDesign application. Or you might want to take a design that you created with InDesign and use it as the graphic in another page-layout program. Or you may want to turn your InDesign document into Web pages. You may even want to display your InDesign pages on mobile phones!

When you convert InDesign documents into other formats, you use the export features of the program. Using the export command lets you change InDesign documents into other types of publications such as portable document format (PDF) files or Web hypertext markup language (HTML) pages.

Setting the Export File Options

InDesign gives you many export options. In each case you choose a file format, name the file, and save it to a location.

To choose a file format:

1. Choose **File** > **Export**. The Export dialog box appears **❶**.

TIP You will not see the options for exporting text unless your insertion point is inside a text frame.

2. Give the file a name and set the location.

3. Choose one of the following formats from the Save as File Type (Win) or Format (Mac) menu:

❶ *The* **options for exporting** *InDesign documents.*

Adobe InDesign Tagged Text	Creates a text file formatted with codes *(see page 359)*.
Adobe PDF	Creates an Acrobat file *(see page 493)*.
EPS	Creates a file that can be placed as a graphic *(see page 508)*.
InDesign Interchange	Creates a special format that can be used for converting InDesign CS2 documents so they can be opened by the InDesign CS application *(see page 511)*.
JPEG	Converts the page or selected elements into a raster image that can be used in a Web page *(see page 511)*.
Rich Text Format	Exports selected text with formatting that can be read by most word processing applications *(see page 516)*.
SVG and SVG Compressed	Creates scalable vector graphics that can be viewed on the World Wide Web *(see page 513)*.
Text Only	Exports selected text without any formatting *(see page 516)*.
XML	Creates text formatted with the Extensible Markup Language that offers customizable definitions and tags. *(Working with XML is beyond the scope of this book. I recommend "Real World Adobe InDesign CS2," by David Blatner and Olav Martin Kvern, for their expertise on this topic.)*

4. Click Save. This opens the options dialog box for each format.

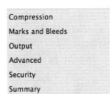

Compression
Marks and Bleeds
Output
Advanced
Security
Summary

② *The Export PDF categories list.*

Creating PDF Files

You can convert your InDesign files into PDF documents so that others can read them — even if they do not have the InDesign application.

To set the PDF export options:

1. Click each of the categories on the left side of the dialog box **②** to display the options as described in the chart below:

   TIP You do not need to set all the controls every time you print unless you need to change a specific setting.

2. Click the Export button to create the PDF file.

PDF Export Options

Print category	Settings	Comment
General	Pages — All, Range: 449–476, Spreads. Options — Embed Page Thumbnails, Optimize for Fast Web View, Create Tagged PDF, View PDF after Exporting, Create Acrobat Layers. Include — Bookmarks, Hyperlinks, Visible Guides and Grids, Non-Printing Objects, Interactive Elements, Multimedia: Use Object Settings	Sets the general PDF export options *(see page 495).*
Compression	Color Images — Bicubic Downsampling to 300 pixels per inch, for images above: 450 pixels per inch, Compression: Automatic (JPEG), Tile Size: 128, Image Quality: Maximum. Grayscale Images — Bicubic Downsampling to 300 pixels per inch, for images above: 450 pixels per inch, Compression: Automatic (JPEG), Tile Size: 128, Image Quality: Maximum. Monochrome Images — Bicubic Downsampling to 1200 pixels per inch, for images above: 1800 pixels per inch, Compression: CCITT Group 4. Compress Text and Line Art, Crop Image Data to Frames	Controls how images and other elements are compressed in the PDF *(see page 498).*
Marks and Bleed	Marks — All Printer's Marks, Crop Marks, Bleed Marks, Registration Marks, Color Bars, Page Information, Type: Default, Weight: 0.25 pt, Offset: 0p6. Bleed and Slug — Use Document Bleed Settings. Bleed: Top: 0p0, Bottom: 0p0, Inside: 0p0, Outside: 0p0. Include Slug Area	Adds printer's marks and a bleed area to the PDF. These are the same controls as in the Print dialog box *(see page 467).*

Creating PDF Files

Print category	Settings	Comment
Output		Sets the controls for color and PDF/X output *(see page 501)*.
Advanced		Sets the controls for fonts, OPI, transparency, and the job definition formats (JDF) of the exported PDF *(see page 503)*.
Security		Sets the controls for passwords, and set permissions that determine whether the document can be printed or edited *(see page 504)*.
Summary		Displays a summary of all the settings for the PDF, organized into categories. The Warnings area provides a quick way to see any problems in the final PDF.

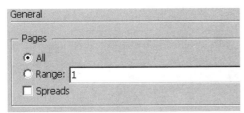

❸ The **Pages area** *in the General category of the Export PDF dialog box.*

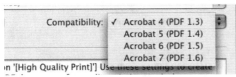

❹ The **Compatibility menu** *lets you choose which PDF version you export.*

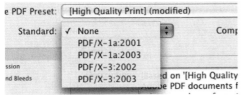

❺ The **Standard menu** *lets you apply an ISO printing standard for PDF documents.*

ISO Standards?

The ISO (International Organization for Standardization) has created standards for PDF documents. When you use these standards you are choosing settings that are relied on as working properly for many publishers. This eliminates many of the color, font, and trapping variables that may create printing problems.

You may be asked to use a PDF/X standard if you are creating PDF documents that will be placed in magazines or newspapers.

General PDF Options

These are the various areas in the General category for exporting as a PDF.

To specify which pages to export:

1. In the Pages area, select All to export all the pages in the document **❸**.

   or

   Select Range to enter specific pages.

   TIP Use the hyphen to select a range of pages such as *4–9*, or use commas to enter individual pages such as *3, 8*.

2. Check Spreads to keep pages that are within spreads together in the Acrobat file.

To set the PDF version and standard:

1. Use the Compatibility menu to choose one of the following **❹**:

   - **Acrobat 4 (PDF 1.3)** creates files that can be opened by a majority of readers.
   - **Acrobat 5 (PDF 1.4)** preserves transparency, text, and spot colors if the PDF is placed into another page-layout program.
   - **Acrobat 6 (PDF 1.5)** and **Acrobat 7 (PDF 1.6)** support the newer PDF features including layers and embedded multimedia.

2. Use the Standard menu to choose one of these four recognized ISO (International Organization for Standardization) standards for PDF files **❺**:

   - **PDF/X-1a:2001** and **PDF/X-1a:2003** are used for CMYK workflows that do not contain color profiles for images.
   - **PDF/X-3:2002** and **PDF/X-3:2003** are used for color-managed workflows that do use color profiles for images.

To set the general options:

◆ Choose one of the following from the Options area in the General category ⑥:

- **Embed Page Thumbnails** adds a thumbnail image for each page in the PDF. This option is not necessary for PDFs that will be viewed in Acrobat 5 and higher.
- **Optimize for Fast Web View** restructures the file to prepare for downloading from Web servers.
- **Create Tagged PDF** adds tags to the final PDF. These tags allow the PDF to be read by screen readers or reflowed onto handheld devices.
- **View PDF after Exporting** opens the finished Adobe PDF file in Acrobat.
- **Create Acrobat Layers** is available for PDF 1.5 and PDF 1.6. It converts the layers in InDesign into layers that can be viewed in Acrobat.

To control what to include in the PDF:

◆ Choose one of the following from the Include area in the General category ⑦:

- **Bookmarks** creates bookmarks for table of contents entries, preserving the TOC levels.
- **Hyperlinks** creates Acrobat hyperlinks from InDesign hyperlinks, table of contents entries, and index entries.
- **Visible Guides and Grids** exports the guides and grids currently visible in the document.
- **Non-Printing Objects** exports objects that have the nonprinting option applied.
- **Interactive Elements** exports InDesign's buttons as interactive PDF elements.

⑥ *The* **Options** controls *in the General category of the Export PDF dialog box.*

⑦ *The* **Include** settings *in the General category of the Export PDF dialog box.*

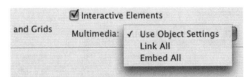

8 *The* **Multimedia menu** *in the General category of the Export PDF dialog box.*

Talk to Your Service Bureau

If you create PDF files for onscreen viewing or to be downloaded from the Web, you can use the compression settings to reduce the file size.

However, if you create PDF files to be output by a service bureau for print work, you should not apply too much downsampling or compression.

Ask your service bureau for the correct settings. Better yet, ask them to create a PDF preset that you can load onto your machine *(see page 506)*.

If you have movie or sound clips in the document, you can choose whether those files should be linked or embedded in the PDF document.

To set the multimedia embedding options:

1. Check the option for Interactive Elements. This activates the Multimedia menu.

2. Choose one of the following from the Multimedia menu in the General category **8**:

   - **Use Object Settings** embeds or links the movie or sound clip according to the settings applied to each media clip.
   - **Link All** overrides any object setting and links all media clips to the PDF. Both the PDF and the media files must be kept together for the media to play properly.
   - **Embed All** overrides any object setting and embeds all media clips in the PDF. This option creates the largest file size.

Compression PDF Options

One of the benefits of creating PDF files is that they can be compressed to take up less space. You use the same types of controls for compressing both color and grayscale bitmap images ❾.

To set the color or grayscale downsampling:

1. Choose one of the following from the Sampling menu ❿:

   - **Do Not Downsample** does not throw away any pixel information. Use this to maintain all information in the image.
   - **Average Downsampling to** averages the pixels in a sample area.
   - **Subsampling to** reduces processing time compared to downsampling, but creates images that are less smooth.
   - **Bicubic downsampling to** is the slowest but most precise method, resulting in the smoothest tonal gradations.

2. When you have set a downsampling method, enter an amount in the resolution field ⓫.

   TIP For print work this setting is usually 1.5 times the line screen of the printing press.

   TIP For onscreen viewing this setting is usually 72 pixels per inch.

3. Enter an amount in the field for images above a certain resolution ⓫.

   TIP This helps you downsample only high-resolution images without losing information in lower-resolution images.

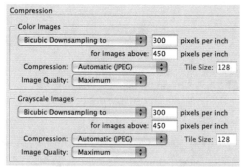

❾ *The* **compression controls** *in the Export PDF dialog box for color and grayscale bitmap images.*

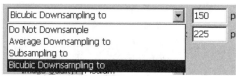

❿ *The* **Sampling menu** *for color and grayscale bitmap images.*

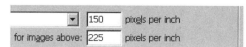

⓫ *The* **Resolution fields** *for color and grayscale bitmap images.*

Compression PDF Options

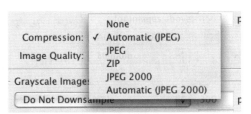

⓬ *The* **Compression menu** *for color and grayscale bitmap images.*

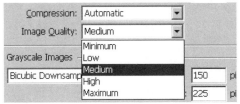

⓭ *The* **Image Quality menu** *for color and grayscale bitmap images.*

⓮ *The* **compression controls** *for monochrome images.*

⓯ *The* **Sampling menu** *for monochrome images.*

To set the color and grayscale compression:

1. Choose one of the following from the Compression menu **⓬**:
   - **None** applies no compression to the image.
   - **Automatic (JPEG)** lets InDesign automatically determine the best quality for color and grayscale images.
   - **JPEG** applies a compression that is best for images with tonal changes.
   - **ZIP** applies a compression that is best for images with large areas of flat color.
   - **JPEG 2000** is the international standard for the compression and packaging of image data. This option is only available for Acrobat 6 (PDF 1.5) or higher.
   - **Automatic (JPEG 2000)** automatically determines the best quality for color and grayscale images. This option is only available for Acrobat 6 (PDF 1.5) or higher.

2. Choose a setting from the Image Quality menu **⓭**:
   - Maximum sets the least amount of compression.
   - Minimum sets the most.

   TIP Use Maximum for high-end output.

There are different resolution and compression options for monochrome bitmap images (such as 1-bit scanned art) **⓮**.

To set the monochrome bitmap downsampling:

- Choose one of the following from the Sampling menu **⓯**:
   - **Do Not Downsample** does not throw away any pixel information. Use this setting if you want to maintain all the information in the image.
   - **Average Downsampling to** averages the pixels in a sample area.
   - **Subsampling to** is faster than downsampling, but creates images that are less smooth.
   - **Bicubic downsampling to** is the slowest but most precise method, resulting in the smoothest tonal gradations.

Compression PDF Options

To set the monochrome bitmap resolution:

1. When you have set a downsampling method, enter an amount in the resolution field **16**.

TIP For print work, this setting is usually the resolution of the output device with a limit of 1500 dots per inch.

2. Enter an amount in the field for images above a certain resolution **16**.

TIP This helps you downsample only high-resolution images without losing information in lower-resolution images.

To set the compression for monochrome images:

1. Choose one of the following from the Compression menu **17**:

   • **None** applies no compression to the image.
   • **CCITT Group 3** is similar to the compression used for faxes.
   • **CCITT Group 4** is a general-purpose method that produces good results for most monochromatic images.
   • **ZIP** works well for black-and-white images that contain repeating patterns.
   • **Run Length** produces the best results for images that contain large areas of solid black or white.

2. Check Compress Text and Line Art to further reduce the size of the file.

3. Check Crop Image Data to Frames to delete the image outside the frame.

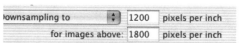

16 *The* **resolution fields** *for monochrome images.*

17 *The* **Compression menu** *for monochrome images.*

⑱ *The* **Color Conversion menu** *allows you to control how colors in a PDF are handled.*

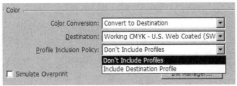

⑲ *The* **Profile Inclusion Policy menu** *controls how color management profiles are handled.*

More Info on Color Profiles

If you are interested in learning more about color profiles, you should visit www.color.org. This is the home of the International Color Consortium. From their Web site:

The International Color Consortium was established in 1993 by eight industry vendors for the purpose of creating, promoting and encouraging the standardization and evolution of an open, vendor-neutral, cross-platform color management system architecture and components. The outcome of this cooperation was the development of the ICC profile specification.

The intent of the International Color Consortium (R) profile format is to provide a cross-platform device profile format. Device profiles can be used to translate color data created on one device into another device's native color space.

Output PDF Options

The Output category contains the controls for how color is handled as well as the PDF/X settings.

To set the color controls:

1. Choose one of the following from the Color Conversion menu **⑱**:
   - **No Color Conversion** does not convert the colors in the document.
   - **Convert to Destination** converts all colors to the profile selected for Destination.
   - **Convert to Destination (Preserve Numbers)** converts colors to the destination profile only if the embedded profiles differ from the destination profile.

2. Choose a profile for the type of output device from the Destination menu. This is typically the type of printing machine that will handle the file.

3. Choose one of the following from the Profile Inclusion Policy menu to control how the color profiles are handled in the document **⑲**.
   - **Don't Include Profiles** removes all color management from the document.
   - **Include Destination Profile** creates a color-managed document. If the application or output device that uses the Adobe PDF file needs to translate colors into another color space, it uses the embedded color space in the profile. Before you select this option, turn on color management and set up profile information.

4. Check Simulate Overprint to show onscreen a representation of how overprinting will look when printed.

5. Click the Ink Manager button to control how process and spot colors are handled. *(See page 474 for more information on using the Ink Manager.)*

If you have chosen a PDF/X standard, you can control the output profiles for the document.

To set the PDF/X profile controls:

1. Use the Output Intent Profile Name menu to select the profile that matches how the document will be printed ⑳.

2. If desired, enter an optional description of how the file will be output in the Output Condition Name field. This information is then stored in the PDF/X file.

3. If desired, enter the registration name for the output condition in the Output Condition Identifier field. This field is automatically filled in when you choose one of the standard output profiles.

4. If desired, enter the URL in the Registry Name field where the output information is stored. This field is automatically filled in when you choose one of the standard output profiles.

⑳ *The **PDF/X area** controls the profiles for PDF/X files.*

Subsetting Fonts?

One reason why PDFs became popular is you don't have to worry about someone having particular fonts in order to view the file. You can *embed* the entire font or you can *subset* only a portion.

If you embed the entire font, you add to the file size, but you allow anyone who has the font to make changes to the text. If you subset the font, it makes a smaller file, but it also means that the person on the other end won't be able to make changes to the text.

The default setting of 100% means that only a subset of the font will be embedded unless you have used every single character in the font. If you lower the threshold to, let's say 35%, InDesign embeds only the characters used in the document up to a maximum of 35% of the characters. If you use more than 35% of the characters, InDesign embeds all the characters in the font.

There is no option to embed, but if you set the amount to 1% then you will most likely embed all the characters in the font.

(sidebar, left margin) **Output PDF Options**

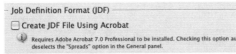

㉑ *The* **Subset fonts when percent of characters used is less than field** *in the Advanced area of the Export PDF dialog box.*

Job Definition Format (JDF)

☐ Create JDF File Using Acrobat

ⓘ Requires Adobe Acrobat 7.0 Professional to be installed. Checking this option auï deselects the "Spreads" option in the General panel.

㉒ *The* **Job Definition Format (JDF) option** *in the Advanced area of the Export PDF dialog box.*

What's a Job Definition Format File?

A Job Definition Format (JDF) file describes the intent of the final ouput of a file. These specifications are used to produce the final printed piece. This file can specify the paper and ink, production quantities, and customer information.

The JDF file and associated PDF files travel together as part of the JDF workflow, from JDF device to JDF device. When the JDF file is submitted to production, the information it contains is used to define the processes for print production.

Advanced PDF Options

The Advanced category contains the controls for handling colors and fonts, and for setting the transparency flattener options.

TIP The OPI controls are the same as the ones in the Print dialog box *(see page 477).*

TIP The Transparency Flattener controls are the same as the ones in the Print dialog box *(see page 477).*

To control how much of a font is embedded:

◆ Enter an amount in the Subset Fonts field for the threshold amount **㉑**. That threshold determines at what point all the characters of the font will be embedded. *(See the sidebar on the opposite page for an explanation of embedding and subsetting fonts.)*

To add a Job Definition Format to the file:

◆ Select the option to Create JDF File Using Acrobat **㉒**. This adds Job Definition Format (JDF) information to the PDF document.

TIP You must have Acrobat 7 Professional installed on your machine in order to add the JDF information to the file.

Security PDF Options

You can also set security options for PDF files to restrict who can open the file or to limit what they can do to it.

The Document Open Password area allows you to set the password that readers must enter in order to open the file.

To set the document password:

1. Check Require a Password to Open This Document 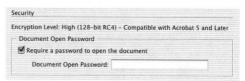.
2. Type a password in the Document Open Password field.

The Permissions area sets up what edits and modifications people can make to the PDF once they have opened it. The Permissions password is needed in order to change the settings in the Permissions area.

To set the permissions password:

1. Check Use a Password to Restrict Printing, Editing, and Other Tasks .
2. Type a password in the Permissions Password field.

TIP This can't be the same as the Document Open Password.

To set the printing permission:

◆ Choose one of the following from the Printing Allowed menu :

- **None** turns off all printing from the document.
- **Low Resolution (150 dpi)** prints only low resolution versions of the images.
- **High Resolution** prints the full resolution of the images.

The **Document Open Password area** *of the Security category of the Export PDF dialog box.*

The **Permissions area** *of the Security category of the Export PDF dialog box.*

The **Printing Allowed menu** *of the Security category of the Export PDF dialog box.*

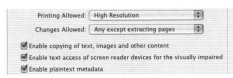

② The **Changes Allowed menu** *of the Security category of the Export PDF dialog box.*

② *The other permissions you can set in the Security category of the Export PDF dialog box.*

Limits of Security

Even when you set security options, there are some additional things to remember.

First, if you e-mail a PDF document, send the password in separate e-mail. That makes it less likely that the password will be found if your e-mail is hijacked.

Next, passwords are case-sensitive. Use a combination of uppercase and lowercase letters as well as numbers to make the password more secure. Don't use ordinary words as passwords.

Finally, if you feel that you would lose your entire livelihood if the PDF were to fall into the wrong hands, then don't distribute it as a PDF. There are plenty of people who take it as a challenge to break into password-protected PDF documents.

To set the changes that are allowed:

1. Choose one of the following from the Changes Allowed menu **②**:
   - **None** allows no changes whatsoever.
   - **Inserting, deleting and rotating pages** allows the user only to add, remove, or change the position of pages in the document. It does not allow changing the content of the pages.
   - **Filling in form fields and signing** allows changes to form fields or applying a security signature to the document.
   - **Commenting, filling in forms fields, and signing** allows adding comments, changing form fields, or applying a security signature to the document.
   - **Any except extracting pages** allows all changes except removing pages from the document.

2. Check any of the following as desired **②**:
   - **Enable copying of text, images and other content.**
   - **Enable text access of screen reader devices for the visually impaired.**
   - **Enable plaintext metadata.**

Working with PDF Presets

Just as you can create printer presets for printing documents *(see page 482)*, you can also create PDF presets that contain settings for generating different types of PDF documents. For example, you may want to post a PDF file on the Web or send the file to a print shop for output.

To save the current PDF settings as a PDF preset:

1. Set the options in the Export PDF dialog box.

2. Click the Save Preset button 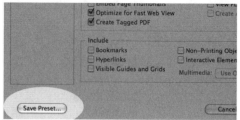. This opens the Save Preset dialog box **29**.

3. Enter a name for the preset and click OK. The new preset appears at the top of the Export PDF dialog box.

Once you have saved a preset, you can easily apply it.

To apply a PDF preset:

◆ Choose a saved preset from the Preset menu at the top of the Export Adobe PDF dialog box **30**.

or

Choose **File** > **Adobe PDF Presets** and then pick the preset listed in the menu.

You can also define PDF presets without going through the Export PDF dialog box.

To create a PDF preset:

1. Choose **File** > **Adobe PDF Presets** to open the Adobe PDF Presets dialog box **31**.

2. Click New. This opens the New PDF Export Preset dialog box.

3. Name the preset.

4. Choose each of the categories and set them as described earlier in this chapter.

28 *Click the* **Save Preset** *button to create a preset based on the current settings in the Export Adobe PDF dialog box.*

29 *Enter a name for a PDF preset in the* **Save Preset dialog box**.

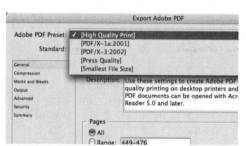

30 *Choose a preset to apply to a PDF from the* **Preset menu** *in the Export PDF dialog box.*

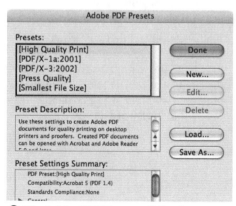

31 *The* **Adobe PDF Presets** *dialog box displays the PDF presets.*

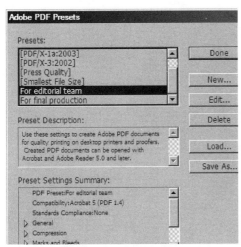

32 A **custom PDF preset**, *listed without brackets, can be edited, deleted, exported, or imported.*

To edit a PDF preset:

1. Select the custom preset you want to edit in the Adobe PDF Presets dialog box **32**.

2. Click the Edit button. This opens the Edit PDF Export Preset dialog box.

TIP There is no difference between the New PDF dialog box and the Edit PDF dialog box except the name in the title bar.

3. Choose each of the categories and make changes as described earlier in this section.

To delete a PDF preset:

1. Select the preset you want to delete in the Adobe PDF Presets dialog box **32**.

TIP Use the Shift key to select multiple adjacent presets.

TIP Use the Cmd/Ctrl key to select multiple nonadjacent presets.

2. Click the Delete button.

3. Click OK to confirm your choice.

To export PDF presets:

1. In the Adobe PDF Presets dialog box, select the presets you want to export **32**.

TIP Use the Shift key to select multiple adjacent presets.

TIP Use the Cmd/Ctrl key to select multiple nonadjacent presets.

2. Click the Save As button. This creates a file that contains the exported presets.

To import PDF presets:

1. Click the Load button in the Adobe PDF Presets dialog box **32**.

2. Use the dialog box to select the document that contains the presets exported from another machine.

3. Click OK. The presets appear in the Adobe PDF Presets dialog box.

Creating EPS Files

You might create a special shape or design in InDesign that you would like to use in another layout program. Export the file as an EPS, or Encapsulated PostScript, file so that you can use it in other applications.

TIP Most of today's layout programs import PDF files. Use the EPS format for older programs than can't import PDF files.

To create an EPS file:

◆ Click the General tab in the Export EPS dialog box to display the pages, bleed, and general controls ③③.

or

Click the Advanced tab to display the production controls ③④. These are the same as the graphic options for printing *(See page 476 for information on setting the graphic options.)*

To set the EPS pages options:

1. In the General area, choose All Pages to export all the pages in the document as EPS files ③⑤.

TIP Each page is exported as its own EPS file.

or

Choose Ranges and enter the numbers of the pages you want to export.

TIP Use hyphens to export a range of pages, such as *4-9*.

TIP Use commas to export individual pages, such as *3, 8*.

2. Check Spreads to export spreads as a single EPS file.

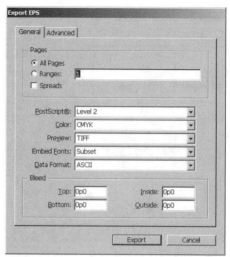

③③ *The* **Export EPS dialog box** *lets you create an EPS file that can be placed in other programs.*

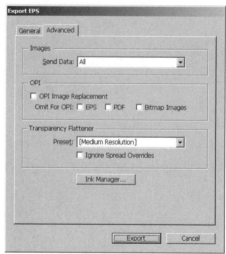

③④ *The* **Advanced section** *in the Export EPS dialog box contains production controls for creating an EPS file.*

③⑤ *Choose the pages to convert with the* **Pages controls** *in the Export EPS dialog box.*

36 *Use the* **PostScript menu** *in the Export EPS dialog box to set the type of printing instructions.*

37 *Use the* **Color menu** *in the Export EPS dialog box to control the colors in the file.*

38 *Use the* **Preview menu** *in the Export EPS dialog box to give a preview to the image.*

The PostScript level sets the complexity the instructions that are sent to the printer.

To set the EPS PostScript level:

♦ In the General area, use the PostScript menu to choose the following **36**:

- **Level 2** is used with older printers.
- **Level 3** is used with newer printers. Use Level 3 only if you know the printer can handle Level 3 PostScript.

You can control the color space in the file.

To set the EPS colors:

♦ In the General area, use the Color menu to choose one of the following options **37**:

- **CMYK** forces the colors to CMYK. Use this setting for process separations.
- **Gray** converts the colors to their grayscale values. Use this to limit the colors to a black plate.
- **RGB** converts the colors to the RGB color space. Use this for onscreen presentation programs.
- **PostScript® Color Management** lets a PostScript printer use its own in-RIP separations to control the color.

Not all programs can create a preview directly from a placed EPS file. For those that can't, you need to set a preview.

To set the EPS preview:

♦ In the General area, use the Preview menu to choose one of the following **38**:

- **None** adds no preview to the file.
- **TIFF** creates a preview that is visible on both the Mac and Windows platforms.
- **PICT** (Mac only) creates a preview that is visible on the Mac only.

Creating EPS Files

Just as you can embed fonts in a PDF file, you can also embed fonts in an EPS file.

To embed fonts in the EPS file:

◆ In the General area, use the Embed Fonts menu to choose one of the following options  ③:

- **None** does not embed any fonts in the file.
- **Complete** includes all the characters in the fonts.
- **Subset** includes only the characters you have used in the file.

EPS files need to be formatted with a specific type of data.

③ *Use the* **Embed Fonts menu** *in the Export EPS dialog box to control how many characters in a font are added to the EPS file.*

To set the data format of the EPS file:

◆ In the General area, use the Data Format menu to choose one of the following options  ④:

- **Binary** is acceptable for most instances.
- **ASCII** is used for a PC network that requires ASCII data.

TIP Choose Binary. If you have trouble printing, then switch to ASCII.

④ *Use the* **Data Format menu** *in the Export EPS dialog box to specify the formatting language of the EPS file.*

Just as you can add a bleed area when printing a document, you can add a bleed to an EPS file. *(See page 468 for additional discussion on creating a bleed.)*

To set the size of a bleed:

◆ In the General area, use the Bleed fields to create a bleed area  ④.

④ *Set the size of the bleed in the* **Bleed fields** *in the Export EPS dialog box.*

Creating EPS Files

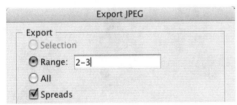

42 *Use the* **Export JPEG dialog box** *to convert an InDesign document into a JPEG file.*

43 *The* **Export options** *in the Export JPEG dialog box.*

InDesign Interchange Format

The InDesign Interchange Format creates a InDesign Interchange Format file (INX). This INX file can then be opened using InDesign CS.

To open CS2 files using InDesign CS:

1. Choose File > Export to open the Export dialog box.

2. Choose InDesign Interchange from the Format (Mac) or Save as Type (Windows) menu.

3. Name the INX file and click Save.

4. In InDesign CS, choose File > Open and navigate to open the INX file. The INX file is converted into an InDesign CS file.

TIP There are no further controls for the Interchange format.

JPEG Options

You might want to convert an InDesign document into a JPEG file that can be posted on the Web. This can be done using the Export JPEG dialog box 42.

To set the area or page to be converted:

1. Use the Export area in the Export JPEG dialog box to choose one of the following:

   - **Selection** exports just the selected items as the JPEG. (The selection must be made before you choose **File > Export**.
   - **Range** exports a range of pages as individual JPEG files.
   - **All** exports all the pages as individual JPEG files.

2. If you are exporting pages, you can select Spreads to export both pages in the spread to a single JPEG file 43.

You can also control the quality of the JPEG image and how it is displayed in the browser.

To set the JPEG quality and display:

1. Use the Export JPEG dialog box's Image Quality menu to choose the quality of the JPEG image as follows .

   - **Maximum** creates an image that is closest to the original but is the largest in file size.
   - **High** creates an image that has a small amount of compression artifacts but is smaller in file size than the Maximum setting.
   - **Medium** creates an image that contains a noticeable amount of compression artifacts but is smaller in size than the Maximum setting.
   - **Low** creates an image that contains the most amount of compression artifacts but is the smallest file size possible.

2. Choose a Format Method as follows :

   - **Progressive** creates an image that appears gradually on the page. This is similar to the Interlaced GIF .
   - **Baseline** creates an image that appears all at once, after the entire image has been downloaded.

44 The **Image Quality menu** *controls the size and the quality of JPEG images.*

45 The **Format menu** *controls how JPEG images are revealed.*

46 *An example of how a **progressive** JPEG image appears.*

SVG or SVG Compressed?

If you choose to export as SVG, you may wonder about the choice for SVG or SVG Compressed. There is no difference between the settings for SVG and SVG Compressed files. However, SVG Compressed files are smaller.

Depending on how you want to use the SVG format, you may not want to compress your SVG files. For instance, the compression may make it harder to edit the SVG file.

Check with your Web designer about which format you should choose.

JPEG Options

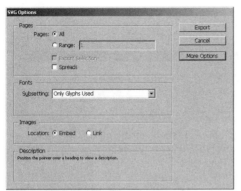

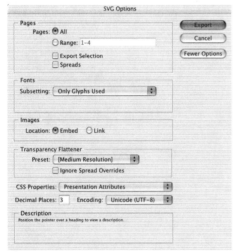

47 *The* **SVG Options dialog box** *contains the controls for creating SVG and SVG Compressed files.*

48 *The* **More Options for the SVG Options dialog box** *contains additional controls for creating SVG and SVG Compressed files.*

49 *The* **Pages options** *in the SVG Options dialog box let you control which pages are exported into SVG files.*

Exporting SVG Files

InDesign also lets you export documents in SVG (scalable vector graphics) format, which can be viewed on the Web. This format is also being used as the file format for graphics on mobile phones.

To set the basic SVG options:

1. Choose SVG or SVG Compressed from the Save as File Type (Win) or Format (Mac) menu. The SVG Options dialog box appears **47**. *(See the sidebar on the opposite page for the difference between the two SVG options.)*

2. Click the More Options button to see the complete set of controls for exporting SVG files **48**.

You can choose which pages or even which selected objects are exported as an SVG file.

To set the area or pages to be converted:

1. In the Pages area, select All to export all the pages in the document **49**.

   or

   Select Range to enter specific pages.

TIP Use the hyphen to select a range of pages such as *4-9*, or use commas to enter individual pages such as *3, 8*.

2. If you have any objects selected, you can check Export Selection to convert just those objects into an SVG file.

3. Check Spreads to keep pages that are within spreads together in the SVG file.

Exporting SVG Files

SVG files often contain dynamic content, which can be changed by databases that supply new information. You may want to embed fonts so that there are characters available for the new text.

To set the fonts for an SVG file:

1. In the Fonts area, use the Subsetting menu to choose one of the following ⑩:

   - **None (Use System Fonts)** does not embed any characters in the file.
   - **Only Glyphs Used** embeds only the characters in the file. This may limit the ability to edit the text later.
   - **Common English** embeds all the characters in English documents.
   - **Common English & Glyphs Used** adds any non-English characters used in the document as well as the Common English characters.
   - **Common Roman** embeds characters used in Roman language documents.
   - **Common Roman & Glyphs Used** adds characters used to Common Roman.
   - **All Glyphs** uses all characters in a font such as characters in Japanese fonts.

You can also control how placed images are embedded within an SVG file.

To set the images for an SVG file:

1. In the Images area, choose Embed to add the image into the SVG file ⑪.

   or

   Choose Link to have the image exist outside the SVG file.

   TIP Use the Link setting if you have many SVG files that use the same image.

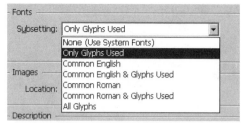

⑩ *The* **Fonts Subsetting menu** *lets you choose how much of a font is embedded in a SVG file.*

⑪ *The* **Images Location controls** *let you choose to embed or link images in the SVG file.*

52 *The* **CSS Properties** *let you choose how much of a font is embedded in a SVG file.*

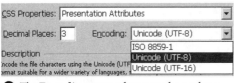

53 *The* **Encoding menu** *lets you choose how much of a font is embedded in a SVG file.*

If you select the More Options button, you have additional controls for SVG files **48**. The Transparency Flattener section is identical to the controls in the Print dialog box *(see page 477)*. You can also control the CSS (Cascading Style Sheets) properties in the exported SVG document.

To set the CSS properties:

◆ Choose one of the following from the CSS Properties menu **52**:

- **Presentation Attributes** has the highest level of properties and allows the most flexibility during editing.
- **Style Attributes** creates a slightly larger file but is necessary if the file is used in XSLT (Extensive Stylesheet Language Transformation).
- **Style Attributes** (**Entity References**) creates a smaller file.
- **Style Elements** is used when sharing files with GoLive documents.

You can also set how precisely the curves are drawn for vector shapes in the SVG file.

To set the decimal precision:

◆ Enter a value of 1 to 7 in the Decimal Places field to set how precisely the curves should be drawn.

TIP The highest value results in a larger file size but creates the best image quality.

You can choose the encoding for the character set in the SVG file. Ask your Web designer which encoding is preferred.

To set the encoding:

◆ Choose one of the following from the Encoding menu **53**:

- **ISO 8859-1** uses ASCII character encoding.
- **Unicode (UTF-8)** uses an 8-bit level of Unicode encoding.
- **Unicode (UTF-16)** uses an 16-bit level of Unicode encoding.

Exporting Text

You may find it necessary to export text from InDesign. For instance, you may want to send the text to someone who works with Microsoft Word. You can send them a text file by exporting the text.

To export text:

1. Place an insertion point inside the frame that contains the text. All the text within that story will be exported.

TIP Select an area of text to export only that portion of the text.

2. Choose **File > Export.** This opens the Export dialog box.

3. Choose a text export format:

   • **Rich Text Format** keeps all the styles and text formatting. This format can be opened by most word processors, especially Microsoft Word.

   • **Text Only** exports only the characters of the text and discards any styles and text formatting. Use this option only if you want to strip out the text formatting or if the application you are working with does not support the Rich Text Format.

   • **Adobe InDesign Tagged Text** format exports the text with special codes for local character formatting and styles. *(See page 359 for more information on working with tagged text.)*

4. Name the file and choose a destination.

5. Click Save to export the file.

Working with InCopy

In addition to exporting stories as text files, you can also export them for use with Adobe InCopy. InCopy is the word processing and editing program that works in tandem with InDesign.

A designer lays out InDesign pages and then exports them to InCopy. A writer or editor can work on the text for those pages. The designer doesn't have to worry that the writer will inadvertently move something or change the layout. And the writer has many more word processing tools than are available in InDesign.

For instance, InCopy lets you edit text using automation text macros, dynamic spell checking, a built-in thesaurus, and powerful Find/Change controls. You can even track changes using electronic notes.

If you are using InCopy, you will find many of its commands and tools very similar to the ones described in this book. There are other commands, however, that are unique to InCopy.

There are two ways to purchase InCopy. If you are a small company with just a few designers and editors, you can purchase InCopy directly from Adobe. If you are a large organization, you should consider using a systems integration specialist to configure InDesign and InCopy specifically for your needs. See the Adobe Web site (www.adobe.com) for more information.

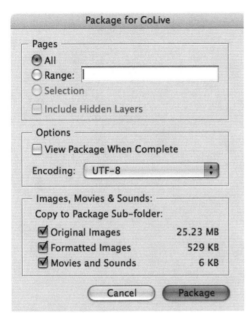

54 The **Package for GoLive dialog box** *lets you control how InDesign documents are converted to Web pages.*

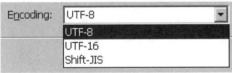

55 The **Encoding menu** *in the Package for GoLive dialog box.*

Packaging for GoLive

One of the great struggles in desktop publishing is how to convert print publications into a format that can be viewed on the Web. Perhaps the best way to convert InDesign documents for the Web is to use the Package for GoLive command.

The General area sets the most basic options for the GoLive package.

To package a file to be opened by GoLive:

1. Choose File > Package for GoLive. The Package for GoLive dialog box appears **54**.

2. Use the Pages area to choose which pages in the document should be packaged.

3. In the Options area, choose View Package When Complete to automatically open GoLive with the finished package open.

4. Choose one of the options from the Encoding menu **55**. Ask the Web master for your site what this setting should be so that it matches the encoding of the GoLive Web Page.

5. Choose whether or not to include the following:

    - **Original Images** if you plan to optimize the images later in GoLive.
    - **Formatted Images** to copy images as they appear in the InDesign document after being modified.
    - **Movies and Sounds** to copy any placed movie and sound files.

Designing Documents for Use in Adobe GoLive

The Package for GoLive feature can't maintain every attribute of your InDesign layout. Package for GoLive uses CSS (Cascading Style Sheets) to preserve typeface (if available on the viewer's computer), size, leading, underline and strikethrough, alignment, indents, space before and after paragraphs, and text color.

Attributes not preserved in CSS include baseline shift, ligatures, tracking, kerning, paragraph rules, justification, hyphenation, no-break settings, keep options, and tab positions.

CUSTOMIZING INDESIGN 21

Working with computer software is a personal thing. I'm always impressed with how emotional my students are (maybe *too* emotional) about how their software should work. One student tells me she hates the way a certain feature works; yet another insists it's his favorite thing in the entire program.

The InDesign team recognizes that some people want the program to work one way, and others want it exactly the opposite. That's why there are many ways to customize the program.

You can change the keyboard shortcuts so that they are similar to other software you use. You can modify the settings for the display of images and onscreen elements. You can control how text wraps around other objects. You can even throw away all your own customized settings and start back at the out-of-the-box settings.

It's all your choice.

Modifying Keyboard Shortcuts

Keyboard shortcuts are the fastest way to invoke program commands. However, if you are used to working with other programs, your fingers may be trained to use those other shortcuts. You may also want to assign a shortcut to a command that doesn't have a shortcut. InDesign lets you change the keyboard shortcuts to keystrokes that match your preferences.

InDesign ships with three sets of shortcuts. The default set is the one that the Adobe engineers created. This set uses most of the shortcuts found in Adobe products such as Adobe Illustrator or Adobe Photoshop. The second set contains the shortcuts used in PageMaker 7.0. The third set contains the shortcuts used in QuarkXPress 4.0.

To change the shortcut set:

1. Choose **Edit** > **Keyboard Shortcuts**. The Keyboard Shortcuts dialog box appears ❶.
2. Choose one of the shortcuts from the Set menu ❷.
3. Click OK. The new shortcuts appear in the menus ❸.

TIP Some keyboard shortcuts are "hard-wired" to the program and do not change to match the keystrokes in PageMaker or QuarkXPress. For instance, the Zoom tool does not change to the XPress Control key (Mac) or Ctrl-Spacebar (Win) shortcuts.

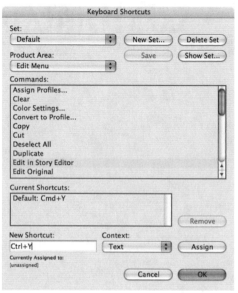

❶ *The* **Keyboard Shortcuts dialog box** *lets you change the shortcuts used for commands, tools, and palettes.*

❷ *The* **Set menu** *lets you choose a set of keyboard preferences.*

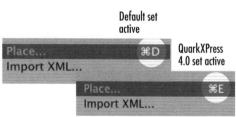

❸ *You can switch the InDesign default shortcuts to the set for other applications.*

❹ *The* **New Set dialog box** *lets you name a new shortcut set and choose which set it should be based on.*

Creating Your Own Keyboard Shortcuts

I use quite a few different programs from many different software companies. I've taught QuarkXPress for more than 15 years. I work with both Adobe Illustrator and Macromedia FreeHand. I also know Adobe Photoshop and Macromedia Fireworks. And I use InDesign to lay out all my books.

I don't change InDesign's keyboard shortcuts to follow all those other programs. I find it easier to concentrate on learning InDesign's shortcuts. It's the primary program I use when working on a book—so I'd rather remember its shortcuts.

If you work with other programs such as Macromedia FreeHand, you may want to create your own shortcut set to match it.

To create a new shortcut set:

1. Choose **Edit > Keyboard Shortcuts**.
2. Choose New Set. This opens the New Set dialog box ❹.
3. Enter a name for the set.
4. Choose a set that the new set will be based on.

TIP A set must be based on another set so that it starts with some shortcuts. However, if you later change something in the original set, the one that was based on it does not change.

5. Click OK. You can now edit the set as described on the next page.

If you want a list of keyboard shortcuts to print out and post next to your computer, you can create a file with all the shortcuts.

To create a list of the keyboard shortcuts:

1. Choose **Edit > Keyboard Shortcuts**.
2. Use the menu to choose the set.
3. Click the Show Set button. This opens the list of shortcuts in Notepad (Win) or TextEdit (Mac).
4. Print the text file.

TIP I can't always remember where a specific shortcut is located. So I create the text file of shortcuts and then use the Find command in the text editor to search for the location of the shortcut.

Modifying Keyboard Shortcuts

You can change the shortcut applied to a command. However, not all commands have shortcuts assigned to them. So you can also assign a shortcut to commands.

To change or assign a shortcut:

1. Choose a shortcut set in the Keyboard Shortcuts dialog box.

   or

   Create a new set.

2. Use the Product Area menu to choose the part of the program that contains the command to which you want to assign a shortcut ❺.

3. Choose a command from the list under the Product Area menu ❻.

4. Use the Context menu to choose in what portion of the program the keystroke will work ❼.

5. Click inside the New Shortcut field to make that field active.

6. Press the keys on the keyboard that you want to assign to invoke the command.

TIP If the keystroke is already assigned to another command, the command that uses the shortcut is listed in the Currently Assigned To area ❽.

7. Change the keys if necessary by selecting them and typing a new combination.

   or

   Click Assign to apply the new shortcut.

8. Click Save to save the set as modified.

To delete a set:

1. Use the Set menu to choose the set you want to delete.

2. Click the Delete Set button.

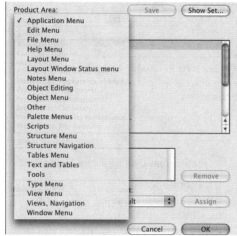

❺ The **Product Area menu** *lets you choose which parts of the program you want to*

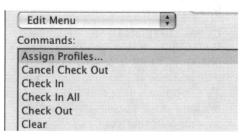

❻ The **Commands field** *contains a list of the commands available for a specific product area.*

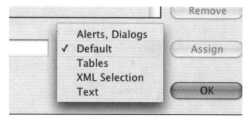

❼ The **Context menu** *lets you choose in which context a keyboard shortcut is applied.*

❽ The **Currently Assigned to area** *shows what command a keystroke is assigned to.*

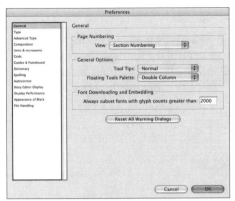

⑨ *The* **Preferences dialog box** *set to the General category.*

General
Type
Advanced Type
Composition
Units & Increments
Grids
Guides & Pasteboard
Dictionary
Spelling
Autocorrect
Story Editor Display
Display Performance
Appearance of Black
File Handling

⑩ *The* **preferences categories** *in the Preferences dialog box.*

Setting the Preferences Categories

InDesign has nine different categories that let you customize how the program works.

To choose a preference category:

1. Choose **Edit > Preferences (Win)** and then choose one of the preferences categories. This opens the Preferences dialog box **⑨**.

   or

   Choose **InDesign > Preferences (Mac)** and then choose one of the preferences categories.

2. Click the categories on the left side of the dialog box to open a new category **⑩**. *(See the chart below for the settings for each category and its description.)*

The Preference Categories

Print category	Settings	Comment
General	Page Numbering — View: Section Numbering; General Options — Tool Tips: Normal, Floating Tools Palette: Double Column; Font Downloading and Embedding — Always subset fonts with glyph counts greater than: 2000; Reset All Warning Dialogs	The General preferences *(see page 527)* contain the settings for page numbering, tool tips and tool palette, font embedding, and warning dialog boxes.

Setting the Preference Categories

Setting the Preference Categories

Print category	Settings	Comment
Type	Type Options ☑ Use Typographer's Quotes ☑ Automatically Use Correct Optical Size ☑ Triple Click to Select a Line ☑ Adjust Text Attributes when Scaling ☐ Apply Leading to Entire Paragraphs ☑ Adjust Spacing Automatically When Cutting and Pasting Words ☑ Font Preview Size: Medium Drag and Drop Text Editing ☐ Enable in Layout View ☑ Enable in Story Editor Links ☐ Create Links When Placing Text and Spreadsheet Files When Pasting Text and Tables from Other Applications Paste: ○ All Information (Index Markers, Swatches, Styles, etc.) ● Text Only	The Type preferences *(see page 529)* control the settings for selecting and formatting text, dragging and dropping text, linking imported text, and pasting text.
Advanced Type	Character Settings Size Position Superscript: 58.3% 33.3% Subscript: 58.3% 33.3% Small Cap: 70% Input Method Options ☐ Use Inline Input for Non-Latin Text	The Advanced Type preferences *(see page 531)* control the character settings and how non-Latin text can be input.
Composition	Highlight ☐ Keep Violations ☑ Substituted Fonts ☐ H&J Violations ☑ Substituted Glyphs ☐ Custom Tracking/Kerning Text Wrap ☐ Justify Text Next to an Object ☑ Skip By Leading ☐ Text Wrap Only Affects Text Beneath	The Composition preferences *(see page 532)* control which text problems are highlighted and the rules for text wraps.
Units & Increments	Ruler Units Origin: Spread Horizontal: Picas points Vertical: Picas points Point/Pica Size Points/Inch: PostScript (72 pts/inch) Keyboard Increments Cursor Key: 0p1 Size/Leading: 2 pt Baseline Shift: 2 pt Kerning: 20 /1000 em	The Units & Increments preferences *(see page 534)* let you set the units for rulers, palettes, and dialog boxes, the number of points per inch, and how much keyboard shortcuts move and modify items.
Grids	Baseline Grid Color: Light Blue Start: 3p0 Relative To: Top of Page Increment Every: 1p0 View Threshold: 75% Document Grid Color: Light Gray Horizontal Vertical Gridline Every: 6p0 Gridline Every: 6p0 Subdivisions: 8 Subdivisions: 8 ☑ Grids in Back	The Grids options *(see page 535)* let you set the colors and increments for the baseline grid and the document grid.

Print category	Settings	Comment
Guides & Pasteboard	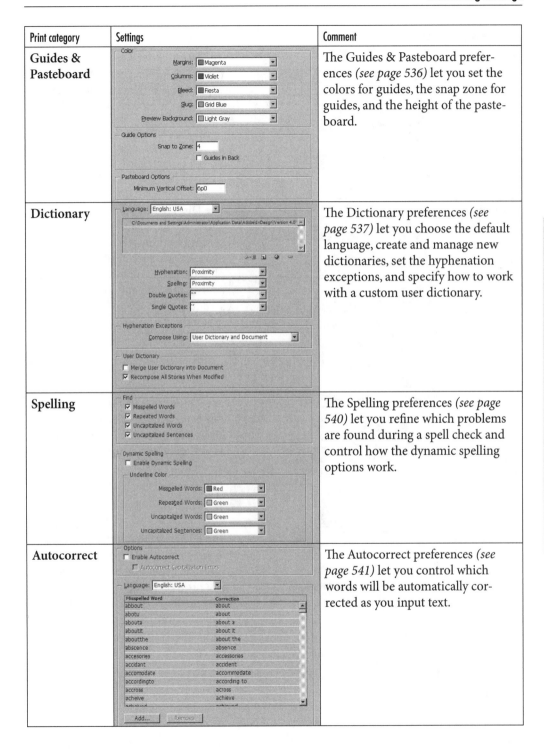	The Guides & Pasteboard preferences *(see page 536)* let you set the colors for guides, the snap zone for guides, and the height of the pasteboard.
Dictionary		The Dictionary preferences *(see page 537)* let you choose the default language, create and manage new dictionaries, set the hyphenation exceptions, and specify how to work with a custom user dictionary.
Spelling		The Spelling preferences *(see page 540)* let you refine which problems are found during a spell check and control how the dynamic spelling options work.
Autocorrect		The Autocorrect preferences *(see page 541)* let you control which words will be automatically corrected as you input text.

Setting the Preference Categories

Print category	Settings	Comment
Story Editor Display	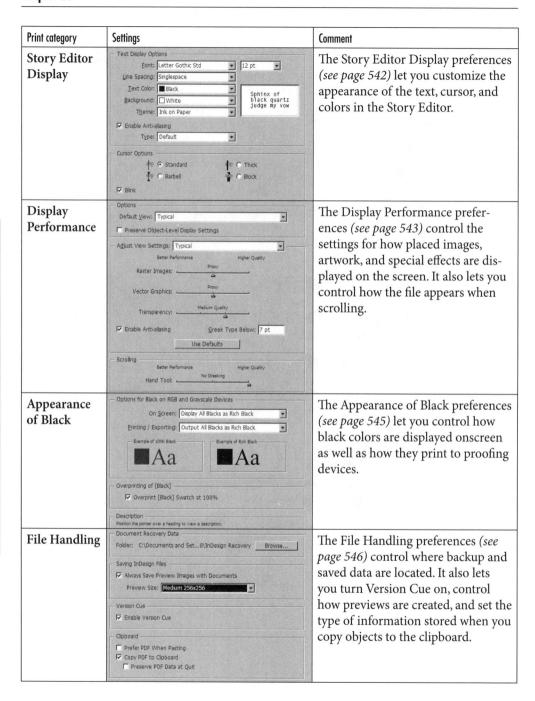	The Story Editor Display preferences *(see page 542)* let you customize the appearance of the text, cursor, and colors in the Story Editor.
Display Performance		The Display Performance preferences *(see page 543)* control the settings for how placed images, artwork, and special effects are displayed on the screen. It also lets you control how the file appears when scrolling.
Appearance of Black		The Appearance of Black preferences *(see page 545)* let you control how black colors are displayed onscreen as well as how they print to proofing devices.
File Handling		The File Handling preferences *(see page 546)* control where backup and saved data are located. It also lets you turn Version Cue on, control how previews are created, and set the type of information stored when you copy objects to the clipboard.

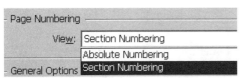

Section Numbering

⓫ *The **Page Numbering View menu** lets you choose the section numbers or absolute numbers.*

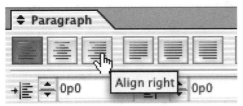

⓬ *The difference in the Pages palette between using absolute numbers and section numbers. The black triangles indicate the start of a new section.*

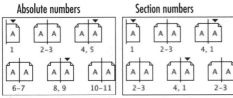

⓭ *An example of a **tool tip** that appears when you pause over an interface element.*

General Preferences Controls

Ordinarily, you want page numbers to be displayed in the Pages palette according to their section numbers. This usually starts at number 1 and ends with the last page of the document. However, if you have several sections in the same document, they could all have a page number 1. The page numbering preferences change how the page numbers are displayed.

To set the page number preferences:

◆ Choose one of the following from the Page Numbering View menu ⓫:

- **Absolute Numbering** ignores any section numbers and uses the physical placement number of the page in the document ⓬. Use this if you want to print a page that has the same number as another page in a separate section.
- **Section Numbering** uses the numbers set from the section options ⓬.

Tool Tips are explanations and notes that appear when you pause your cursor over a tool or onscreen element. You can control how fast Tool Tips appear.

To control the tool tips:

◆ Use the Tool Tips menu to choose one of the following ⓭:

- **Normal** waits a moment before displaying the tip.
- **None** turns off the display of the tips.
- **Fast** displays the tips almost immediately after the cursor pauses over the tool or feature.

General Preferences Controls

You can also change the orientation and arrangement of the Toolbox.

To change the display of the Toolbox:

◆ Use the Floating Tools Palette menu to choose how the Toolbox is displayed :

- **Single Column** displays the palette in a single vertical column 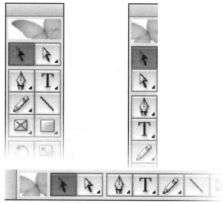.
- **Double Column** displays the palette in two vertical columns .
- **Single Row** displays the palette in a single horizontal row .

TIP You can also change the shape of the Toolbox by double-clicking the Toolbox title bar.

The Font Downloading and Embedding section controls the threshold below which a font is subset.

To choose the threshold for font subsetting:

◆ Enter an amount in the Always Subset Fonts With Glyph Counts Greater Than field **16**.

TIP A number such as 2000 ensures that fonts with large character sets are always subset, creating smaller files. But custom fonts with only one or two characters are set in their entirety. (The word TIP in this book is just such a custom, single-character font.)

Every once in a while you may see a dialog box that warns you about doing something. These alerts have boxes you can check so you never see the warning again. If you've turned them off, you can reset them all to turn back on.

To turn the warning dialog boxes back on:

◆ Click the Reset All Warning Dialogs button at the bottom of the General preferences **17**. An alert box informs you that you will now see the warnings.

14 *The* **Floating Tools Palette menu** *lets you choose the configuration of the Toolbox.*

15 *The* **three arrangements** *for the Toolbox.*

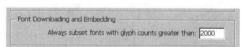

16 *The* **Font Downloading and Embedding** *lets you control if fonts are embedded or subset.*

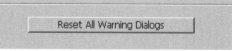

17 *Click the* **Reset All Warning Dialogs** *to bring back those annoying alert messages when you perform certain actions.*

General Preferences Controls

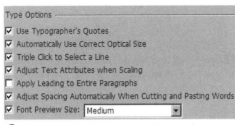

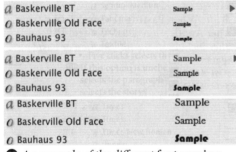

18 *The* **Type Options** *let you change the preferences for how text is set.*

"The Wizard of Oz" Off

"The Wizard of Oz" On

19 *An example of using* **typographer's quotes**.

20 *An example of the different* **font preview sizes.**

Type Preferences

Use the Type Options controls for working with text **18**.

To set the type options preferences:

1. **Use Typographer's Quotes** automatically changes typewriter quotes into the proper curly quote characters **19**.

2. **Automatically Use Correct Optical Size** sets the correct value for the optical size of Multiple Master fonts.

3. **Triple Click to Select a Line** does the following:
   - Three clicks selects a line.
   - Four clicks selects a paragraph.
   - Five clicks selects the story.
   TIP If this option is unchecked, three clicks selects the paragraph and four clicks selects the story.

4. **Adjust Text Attributes when Scaling** lets the text point size increase or decrease when scaled.

5. **Apply Leading to Entire Paragraphs** lets InDesign work more like QuarkXPress.

6. **Adjust Spacing Automatically When Cutting and Pasting Words** avoids adding two spaces when pasting text from one position to another.

7. **Font Preview Size** lets you choose the size of the preview of fonts in the Type menu. Larger previews take longer to display **20**.

   TIP Deselect this option to turn the font preview off. This helps the Font menu display faster.

Type Preferences

You can also control whether or not drag-and-drop text is activated.

To turn on drag-and-drop text:

1. Select Enable in Layout View to have drag-and-drop text active when working within frames on the pages **21**.

2. Select Enable in Story Editor to have drag and drop text active when working within the Story Editor **21**.

TIP I love drag-and-drop text, so I have mine turned on for both views. But most designers keep it off in the layout view so they don't inadvertently drag text to new positions.

Very early versions of InDesign automatically linked text and spreadsheet documents back to their original file. Now, a preference controls whether placed text files are automatically linked to their source.

To choose if text files are linked or embedded:

◆ Click the option **Create Links When Placing Text and Spreadsheet Files** to link those styles back to the original files **22**. If you make changes to the word processor or spreadsheet file, those changes will automatically update in InDesign.

TIP All local formatting you have applied will be discarded when the text is updated.

If you paste text from a word processor or Web page, you may not want all the formatting that comes with the text. Fortunately, there is a preference that strips out the gunk.

To control how text is pasted:

◆ Choose one of the following from the When Pasting Text and Tables from Other Applications Paste options **23**:

• **All information** includes markers, swatches, and styles.

• **Text** includes only the text characters.

21 The **Drag and Drop Text Editing controls** *let you turn on the drag-and-drop feature in either the layout or the Story Editor.*

22 The **Create Links When Placing Text and Spreadsheet Files option** *allows you to link your text files to their original documents.*

23 The **When Pasting Text and Tables from Other Applications Paste controls** *let you either include all the information or paste just the text.*

Type Preferences

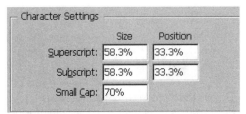

㉔ *The **Character Settings** control the size and position of superscript, subscript, and small cap characters.*

㉕ *The **Input Method Options** let you choose to enter non-Latin characters without a keyboard.*

Advanced Type Preferences

The Character Settings control the size and position of superscript, subscript, and small cap characters **㉔**.

To set the character settings preferences:

1. Enter amounts in the Size field to control the size of the characters **㉔**.

2. Enter amounts in the Position field to control how far above or below the baseline the characters are positioned **㉔**.

TIP The percentage amount is based on the total space between the two lines.

A non-Latin typeface is one that uses 2-byte and 4-byte characters. Japanese, Korean, and Chinese are examples of non-Latin typefaces. If you work with non-Latin typefaces, you may need to use features in the operating system to enter characters instead of the keyboard.

To use the operating system to enter non-Latin text:

◆ Click the option **Use Inline Input For Non-Latin Text** to allow you to input text using the operating system features **㉕**.

Advanced Type Preferences

Composition Preferences

The Highlight settings let you control which parts of the text are highlighted to indicate composition or typographic violations or substitutions **26**.

To set the highlight options:

◆ Set the Highlight options as follows **27**:

- **Keep Violations** displays lines that have been broken in violation of the Keep With settings that you chose for the paragraph options.
- **H&J Violations** highlights those areas that violate the hyphenation or justification controls.

TIP H&J Violations occur when InDesign has no other way to set the text except to break the H&J controls.

- **Custom Tracking/Kerning** highlights the text with tracking or kerning applied to it.
- **Substituted Fonts** highlights characters that are substituted for a font that is not installed in the computer system.

TIP This is the famous pink highlight for a missing font that many people see when they import text or change typefaces.

TIP If the shape of the uninstalled font exists in the Adobe Type Manager database, the shape of the font is approximated. If not, a default font is used.

- **Substituted Glyphs** highlights Open Type characters that have been substituted with alternate glyphs.

26 *The* **Highlight Settings** *let you choose which typographic problems are displayed with a highlight.*

27 *An example of text with a* **highlight** *applied.*

Composition Preferences

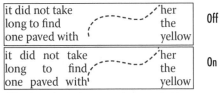

🔵 *The* **Text Wrap controls** *in the Composition category.*

You can also control the effect of the Text Wrap settings and how text wraps around objects 🔵.

To set the text wrap options:

◆ Choose one of the following from the Text Wrap options:

- **Justify Text Next to an Object** forces text next to an object to be justified if it wraps around an object inside the frame 🔵.

- **Skip by Leading** forces text that has wrapped around an object to move to the next available leading increment. This avoids problems where text may not line up across columns or frames 🔵.

- **Text Wrap Only Affects Text Beneath** causes InDesign text wrap to work only on text below the object, rather than text above and below the object.

🔲 Some designers turn this on because they want InDesign work more similarly to QuarkXPress. Don't do it! You're only limiting yourself from some of the more interesting effects that InDesign offers.

🔵 *The effect of setting the* **Justify Text Next to an Object**.

🔵 *Notice how, when* **Skip By Leading** *is turned off, the text does not line up across columns. When it is turned on, the text does line up.*

Composition Preferences

Units & Increments Preferences

InDesign ships with measurements in picas and points. You may be more comfortable working in something else.

To set the ruler units:

1. Use the Origin menu to select one of the following 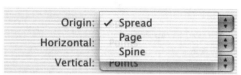:

   - **Spread** sets the horizontal ruler to stretch across the pages in a spread.
   - **Page** sets the horizontal ruler to reset for each individual page in a spread.
   - **Spine** sets the horizontal ruler to stretch across the spine of the document.

2. Use the Horizontal and Vertical menus to select the unit of measurement for each of the rulers 32.

   or

   Set an amount, in points, for a custom unit of measurement 33.

3. Use the Points/Inch field to choose between the PostScript or the Traditional numbers of points per inch.

TIP Although the purists insist there are 72.27 points per inch, today's electronic work is done with the measurement of 72 34.

TIP Change these settings with no document open to create the defaults for all new documents.

The keyboard increments control how much the objects move or the text changes 35.

To set the keyboard increments:

◆ Enter an amount in the fields as follows:

   - **Cursor Key** lets you choose the amount that the arrow keys move objects.
   - **Size/Leading** controls the amount that the type size and leading change.
   - **Baseline Shift** lets you set the amount that the baseline shift changes.
   - **Kerning** controls the amount that the kerning changes.

31 *The* **Origin menu** *lets you choose how the rulers stretch across the page.*

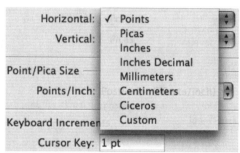

32 *The* **Ruler Units menu** *lets you choose a unit of measurement for the horizontal and vertical menus.*

33 *The* **Custom menu** *lets you choose how many points per tick appear on the ruler.*

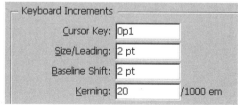

34 *Use the* **Points/Inch field** *to choose between the PostScript measurement for points per inch or the Traditional measurement.*

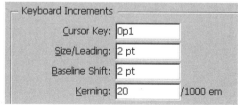

35 *The* **Keyboard Increments fields** *in the Units & Increments category.*

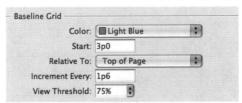

36 *The* **Baseline Grid controls** *in the Grids category.*

37 *The* **Document Grid controls** *in the Grids category.*

38 *The* **Grids in Back option** *in the Grids category.*

Grids Preferences

The Baseline Grid options let you control the color and position of the baseline grid, which is used to align text across frames and columns. Change these preferences when the default color is difficult to see on the screen **36**.

To set the baseline grid options:

1. Use the Color menu to choose a color for the baseline grid.

2. Use the Start field to position where the grid should start on the page.

3. Use the Relative To menu to position the start of the grid relative to the top of the page or the top margin.

4. Use the Increment Every field to set the distance between the lines of the grid.

5. Use the View Threshold field to set the lowest magnification at which the grid is visible.

TIP Set this for something like 75% to make it easier to see the entire page when you zoom out.

To set the document grid preferences:

1. Use the Color menu to choose a color for the document grid **37**.

2. Enter a value for the Horizontal and Vertical fields as follows:

   • **Gridline Every** sets the distance between the major lines of the grid.

   • **Subdivisions** sets the number of secondary lines of the grid.

To set the positioning of the grids:

◆ Check Grids in Back to position the grids behind graphics and text **38**.

Grids Preferences

Guides & Pasteboard Preferences

The Colors area is a rainbow of choices for how to color onscreen guides and areas .

To set the onscreen elements colors:

♦ Use the menus to set the colors for each of the following:

- **Margins** sets the color of the guides created by the margins settings.
- **Columns** sets the color of the guides created by the column setting.
- **Bleed** sets the color of the guide around the bleed area.
- **Slug** sets the color of the guide around the slug area.
- **Preview Background** sets the color of the area that surrounds the page in the preview mode.

To set the Guide Options:

1. Use the Snap to Zone field to set how close the objects should be when they snap to guides ❹. This amount is set in pixels.

2. Check Guides in Back to hide the guides when they appear behind objects.

To set the Pasteboard Options:

♦ Enter an amount in the Minimum Vertical Offset ❹ to increase or decrease the amount of pasteboard space above and below the page ❹.

❸❾ *The* **Margins Color menu** *in the Guides category.*

❹⓿ *The* **Guide Options** *in the Guides category.*

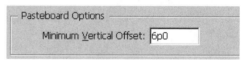

❹❶ *Use the* **Minimum Vertical Offset** *to control how tall the pasteboard area is.*

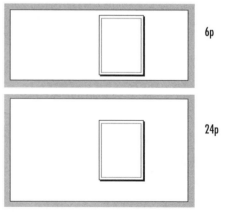

❹❷ *The effect of increasing the minimum vertical offset.*

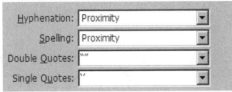

🔢 *The* **Language menu** *in the Dictionary category.*

🔢 *The* **Language options** *in the Dictionary category.*

Double quote choices

Single quote choices

🔢 *The* **Quote menus** *in the Dictionary preferences.*

Dictionary Preferences

The language setting is used to choose which language dictionary should be used to check whether words are correctly spelled. Consider that the word *cinema* is correctly spelled if English is the chosen language. However, the word is incorrectly spelled if French is chosen as the language. In that case the word should be *cinéma*.

To set the language options:

1. Use the Language menu to set the default language **🔢**.

2. If you have installed special hyphenation preferences, choose a preference from the Hyphenation menu **🔢**.

3. If you have installed special spelling preferences, choose a preference from the Spelling menu **🔢**.

4. Use the Double Quotes menu to choose the characters for double quotation marks **🔢**.

5. Use the Single Quotes menu to choose the characters for single quotation marks **🔢**.

TIP The Quotes menus list the marks used for different languages, such as Spanish and French. Or you can enter your own characters in the field **🔢**.

Sharing Dictionaries

You may want to create a single dictionary that everyone in your workgroup can share. *(See the next page for how to choose a specific dictionary.)* Make sure that each station in your workgroup has the same customized user dictionaries installed and added, so that a document uses the same spelling and hyphenation rules regardless of who is working on it. You can either make sure that everyone adds the same dictionaries to their computer, or you can share a user dictionary over the network server.

When a user dictionary is stored on a server, the first user to load the dictionary locks the file; all subsequent users see that the dictionary is locked. Files can also be locked through the operating system, which makes the file read-only. If you share a user dictionary over the network server, you may want to lock the file so that it's read-only for all users, allowing only the administrator to add words.

Dictionary Preferences

You use the dictionary management tools to create, link to, add, and delete new user dictionaries. This allows you to create several dictionaries for InDesign.

To create a new user dictionary:

1. Click the New Dictionary button in the Dictionary preferences ➏.

2. Name and save the dictionary file (.udc) to a location. The new dictionary appears in the Dictionary list ➐.

You don't have to create your own new dictionary. You can use the dictionary management tools to add someone else's dictionary to your version of InDesign.

To add a dictionary:

1. Click the Add Dictionary button in the Dictionary preferences.

2. Navigate to select the new dictionary. The dictionary appears in the Dictionary list.

To delete a dictionary:

1. Select the dictionary that you want to delete in the Dictionary list.

2. Click the Delete Dictionary button in the Dictionary preferences.

To relink a dictionary:

1. Select the dictionary that has a missing or modified icon next to its name in the Dictionary list ➑.

2. Click the Relink Dictionary button in the Dictionary preferences.

3. Navigate to find the missing dictionary.

New Dictionary Delete Dictionary
Relink Dictionary Add Dictionary

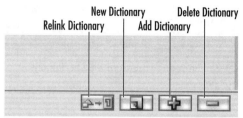

➏ *The* **Dictionary buttons** *in the Dictionary preferences.*

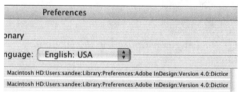

➐ *The* **Dictionary list** *displays the list of dictionaries installed in the Dictionary preferences.*

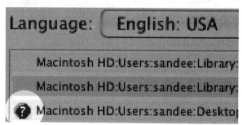

➑ *The* **Missing icon in the Dictionary list** *indicates that you need to relink to the dictionary.*

The hyphenation exceptions let you choose to apply the hyphenations created by editing the Dictionary or those built into the application.

To set the hyphenation exceptions:

- Choose one of the following from the Compose Using menu ⑲:
  - **User Dictionary** uses only the hyphenation exceptions set by editing the Dictionary.
  - **Document** uses the hyphenation exceptions list stored inside the document. *(See the next exercise for how to add the user dictionary hyphenation exceptions to a document.)*
  - **User Dictionary and Document** merges the exceptions in both the document and the user dictionary. This is the default setting.

The User Dictionary options let you merge hyphenation exceptions into a document and create new hyphenation exceptions that affect the document ⑤⓪.

To set the user dictionary preferences:

1. **Merge User Dictionary into Document** adds the hyphenation exceptions in the user dictionary to the document. This is on by default.

   TIP This is especially useful if you send the native InDesign document to a service bureau for output.

2. **Recompose All Stories When Modified** applies the new exceptions in the user dictionary to all the stories in the document.

⑲ *The* **Compose Using menu** *in the Dictionary category.*

⑤⓪ *The* **Language controls** *in the Dictionary category.*

Dictionary Preferences

Spelling Preferences

The Find section of the Spelling preferences controls what types of problems the spelling checker flags during a spelling check 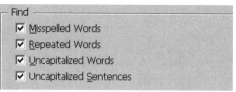.

To set the Find options for Spelling:

1. Select **Misspelled Words** to find words that are not known in the spelling dictionary.

2. Select **Repeated Words** to find instances of words that are repeated, such as "the the spelling checker."

3. Select **Uncapitalized Words** to find words that are listed in the dictionary as capitalized. For instance, proper names of countries are capitalized in the dictionary.

4. Select **Uncapitalized Sentences** to flag uncapitalized words that begin sentences. For instance, the figure numbers I use in this book are interpreted by the spelling checker as uncapitalized sentences. So I can turn off this option to avoid having those numbers flagged.

Dynamic spelling highlights errors right on your page. If you want to work with dynamic spelling, you have a choice as to which colors the errors are underlined with.

To set the Dynamic Spelling options:

1. Select Enable Dynamic Spelling in the Spelling preferences 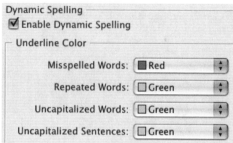.

2. Use the Underline Color menus to specify the color used to highlight misspelled words, repeated words, uncapitalized words, and uncapitalized sentences.

51 *Use the* **Find controls** *in the Spelling category to choose which words are flagged during a spelling check.*

52 *Use the* **Dynamic Spelling controls** *to turn on dynamic spelling and specify colors for each of the error categories.*

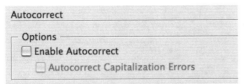

⓼ *Use the* **Autocorrect Options controls** *to turn on autocorrection for word errors and for capitalization errors.*

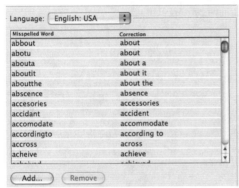

⓾ *Use the* **Autocorrect Options controls** *to turn on autocorrection for word errors and for capitalization errors.*

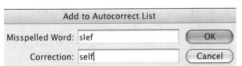

⓭ *Use the* **Add to Autocorrect List dialog box** *lets you enter the mispelling for a word and its correction.*

Autocorrect Preferences

The Autocorrect preferences not only turn on the Autocorrect feature, they allow you to add or remove those words that you want to have automatically corrected.

To turn on Autocorrection:

1. Choose Enable Autocorrect to turn on the basic correction for words ⓼.

2. Choose Autocorrect Capitalization Errors to also automatically correct errors in uppercase and lowercase words.

The Autocorrect list contains the words that are commonly mistyped. In addition to the words the Adobe engineers felt you would mistype, you can easily add your own.

To add words to the Autocorrect list:

1. Use the Language menu to choose the language for the autocorrection.

2. Click the Add button at the bottom of the Autocorrect Preferences ⓾. This opens the Add to Autocorrect List dialog box ⓭.

3. Type the typical misspelling in the Misspelled Word field.

4. Type the correct spelling in the Correction field.

5. Click OK to add the word to the list.

To delete words from the Autocorrect list:

1. Select the word in the list that you want to delete.

2. Click the Remove button.

Autocorrect Preferences

Story Editor Display Preferences

If you work in the Story Editor, you can choose the preferences for its display .

TIP None of these settings affect the appearance of the text in the layout.

To set the preferences for text display:

1. Use the Font menu to set the typeface.
2. Use the point size menu to set the size.
3. Use the Line Spacing menu to choose the leading between the lines 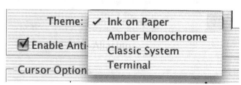.
4. Use the Text Color menu to set the color of the text.
5. Use the Background menu to set the color of the Story Editor window background.

    or

    Use the Theme menu to select a preset text and background color scheme .
6. Choose Enable Anti-Aliasing to soften the edges of the text.
7. If you choose Enable Anti-Aliasing, choose an anti-aliasing Type option .

    - **Default** is the typical anti-aliasing.
    - **LCD Optimized** works best on light-colored backgrounds with black text.
    - **Soft** produces a lighter, fuzzier appearance than Default.

You can also change how the cursor, or insertion point, is displayed within the Story Editor. This is helpful for those who are used to editing text on mainframe terminals.

To set the preferences for cursor display:

1. Choose **Edit > Preferences > Story Editor Display** (Win) or **InDesign > Preferences > Story Editor Display** (Mac).
2. Choose one of the Cursor Options .
3. Select Blink to make the cursor turn on and off within the text.

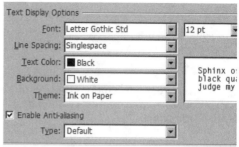

56 *The* **Text Display Options** *section of the Story Editor preferences.*

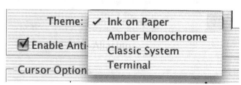

57 *The* **Line Spacing menu** *of the Story Editor preferences controls the space between the lines of text.*

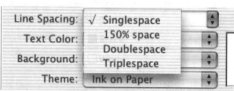

58 *The* **Theme menu** *lets you quickly change the text and background colors.*

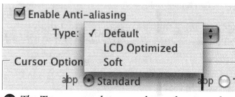

59 *The* **Type menu** *lets you choose how much anti-aliasing is applied to the text.*

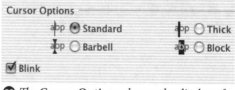

60 *The* **Cursor Options** *change the display of the cursor within the text.*

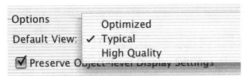

61 *The* **Default View Settings controls** *in the Display Performance category.*

Adjust View Settings: Typical

Better Performance — Higher Quality

Raster Images: Proxy

Vector Graphics: Proxy

Transparency: Medium Quality

62 *The* **Adjust View Settings** *in the Display Performance category.*

☑ Enable Anti-Aliasing   Greek Type Below: 7 pt

Use Defaults

63 *The controls for anti-aliasing, greeking type, and resetting the defaults in the Display Performance category.*

Dorothy On

Dorothy Off

64 *The effect of applying* **anti-aliasing** *to type.*

Display Performance Preferences

The default view is the view that is used when documents are first opened.

To set the default view:

1. Use the Default View Settings menu to choose which of the display performance settings is automatically applied to new documents **61**.

2. Check Preserve Object-level Display Settings to maintain any individual settings applied to graphics.

The Adjust View Settings control how images appear onscreen for each of the three view choices **62**.

To choose the options for Adjust View Settings:

1. Choose one of the options from the Adjust View Settings menu:

2. Drag the slider controls to set the quality for raster images, vector graphics, and the transparency effects.

3. Repeat for the other two view settings.

TIP It takes longer for the screen to redraw if you choose the highest quality previews.

Anti-aliasing is the term used to described the soft edge applied to either text or graphics **63**.

To control the anti-aliasing of text and graphics:

◆ Check Enable Anti-Aliasing to add a soft edge to the type and graphics displayed on the monitor **64**.

Display Performance Preferences

Greeking is the term used to describe the gray band that is substituted for text characters **65**.

To set text to be greeked:

◆ Enter an amount in the Greek Type Below field. This sets the size below which the text characters will be replaced with gray bands onscreen.

When you use the Hand tool to scroll around a document, InDesign needs to determine how text and images that were not originally in the window appear when you move them into view. You use the Hand Tool preferences to control how the images appear or how fast you can move while scrolling.

To set the scrolling preferences:

◆ Drag the Hand Tool slider to one of the following **66**:

• The left position greeks both text and images. This is the fastest setting but it loses the appearance of the page as text and images come into view **67**.
• The middle position greeks images but maintains text visibility **67**.
• The right position turns off all greeking of text and images. This is the slowest setting but it maintains the appearance of the page as text and images come into view **67**.

On

Off

65 *The effect of applying* **greeking** *to type.*

66 *The* **Scrolling** *controls for the Hand tool for how text and images are displayed when new areas of the page come into view.*

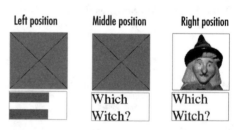

67 *The appearance of text and images for each of the Hand Tool slider settings.*

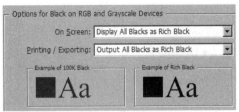

68 *Use the Options for Black on RGB and Grayscale Devices to control how 100%K ink appears.*

69 *The On Screen menu controls how black appears on the computer monitor.*

70 *The Printing/Exporting menu controls how black appears when printed on RGB or grayscale devices.*

Appearance of Black Preferences

What could be so difficult about the color black? As the old rock and roll song goes, "Black is Black. I want my baby back." However, as many designers have discovered, when a color-corrected black is displayed on a computer screen, 100% black ink winds up looking very washed out. The Appearance of Black preferences allow you to choose how 100% black ink is displayed and printed **68**.

To control the appearance of black on screen:

◆ Choose one of the following from the On Screen menu **69**:

- **Display All Blacks Accurately** displays 100%K as dark gray. This setting allows you to see the difference between pure black and rich black.
- **Display All Blacks As Rich Black** displays 100%K as jet black (RGB=000). This setting makes pure black and rich black appear the same on-screen.

You can also control how 100%K appears when printing to a non-PostScript desktop printer or exporting to an RGB format. This helps control the appearance of blacks in PDF and JPEG files.

To control the appearance of black when printing or exporting to an RGB format:

◆ Choose one of the following from the Printing/Exporting menu **70**:

- **Output All Blacks Accurately** outputs 100%K using the color numbers in the document. This setting allows you to see the difference between pure black and rich black in the finished document.
- **Output All Blacks As Rich Black** outputs 100%K as jet black. This setting makes pure black and rich black appear the same.

File Handling Preferences

If InDesign crashes or the computer is shut down before you can save the InDesign documents, a file is created that contains the recovered document. The Document Recovery Data area lets you choose where that recovered document is located.

TIP Although most people will use the same drive that contains the application, this option lets you specify a folder on a drive that has more space than the one that contains the InDesign application folder.

To set the temporary folder:

1. Click the Choose button in the Temporary Folder area **71**.
2. Use the dialog box to choose the location of the recovered documents.

The Saving InDesign Files area lets you add a thumbnail preview to the file. You can also control the size of the preview.

To create a preview with saved documents:

1. In the Saving InDesign Files area, choose Always Save Preview Images with Documents **72**.

TIP You can change the preview option in the Save As dialog box.

2. Choose one of the sizes from the Preview Size menu **73**.

TIP Larger previews increase the file size and the time it takes to save the document.

If you work in a collaborative setting, you may want to use the Adobe Version Cue software to help coordinate the workflow.

To turn Version Cue on or off:

1. Select or deselect Enable Version Cue in the Version Cue area **74**.
2. Restart InDesign.

71 The **Document Recovery Data setting** *lets you choose where to save temporary files that contain recovery data for your current work.*

72 The **Save Document Preview Image option** *lets you add a preview to show what the file looks like before you open it.*

73 The **Preview Size menu** *lets you choose the size for the preview image that is saved with the file.*

74 The **Version Cue control** *lets you set your copy of InDesign to be part of a collaborative environment.*

Working with Previews

You may not see a document preview if you open the file using the Macintosh Finder or Windows Explorer. That's why I recommend using Adobe Bridge to open InDesign documents.

If you save a document with a preview, you will only see a preview of the first spread. However, you will be able to see a preview of all the pages of a template.

File Handling Preferences

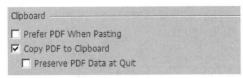

75 The **Clipboard options** *control the type of information that is copied to the clipboard.*

76 The **Delete InDesign Preference Files** dialog box *lets you start from scratch with factory-fresh default settings.*

The clipboard contains the information stored during a copy or cut command. You may need to change the options for what type of information is included in the clipboard. This is especially helpful when pasting objects to and from Adobe Illustrator and InDesign.

To set the clipboard format:

◆ Check the Clipboard options as follows **75**:

- **Prefer PDF When Pasting** lets you add Illustrator graphics as self-contained PDF files that retain all the effects, such as transparency and drop shadows, applied to the PDF.
- **Copy PDF to Clipboard** lets you copy data as complete PDF files. Select this option in order to copy and paste paths from InDesign into Illustrator or Photoshop.
- **Preserve PDF Data at Quit** maintains any copied PDF information on the clipboard for use in other applications.

TIP If you want to copy and paste plain paths from Illustrator, you must change Illustrator's Clipboard preferences to AICB (no transparency): Preserve Paths before you copy the item.

Trashing Preferences

Sometimes InDesign may start to act strangely. This may mean that the files that hold all your preferences and settings have become corrupt. In that case you need to trash those files and let InDesign start over with the factory settings.

To restore all preferences and default settings

1. As you launch InDesign, immediately press Ctrl-Alt-Shift (Win) or Cmd-Opt-Shift-Control (Mac).

2. Click Yes when asked if you want to delete your preference files **76**.

File Handling Preferences; Trashing Preferences

Configuring Plug-Ins

InDesign uses a large set of plug-ins as its core set of commands and features. You may want to control which plug-ins are loaded each time you launch the program.

To select the plug-ins set:

1. Choose **InDesign > Configure Plug-ins** (Mac) or **Help > Configure Plug-ins** (Win) to open the Configure Plug-ins dialog box ⑰:

2. Choose a set from the Set menu ⑱.

To modify a plug-in set:

1. Select the plug-in set.

2. If the set is one of the default sets, choose Duplicate to make a copy of the set.

3. Click the checkbox column to the left of the name to enable or disable the plug-in from the set.

4. Use the Display checkboxes to see the types of plug-ins.

To see the information about a plug-in:

♦ Click the Show Info button in the Configure Plug-ins dialog box to open the Plug-in Information dialog box.

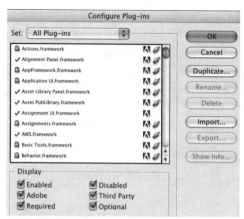

⑰ *The* **Configure Plug-ins dialog box** *is where you can control which plug-ins get loaded when you launch InDesign.*

⑱ *The three* **default plug-ins sets** *cannot be modified. Custom plug-ins sets are shown at the bottom of the Sets menu.*

INDEX

A

absolute offset, 209
Acrobat. *See* Adobe Acrobat
Add Anchor Point tool, 15, 186, 192
Adjust View Settings menu, 228, 229
Adobe Acrobat
  bookmarks, 435
  exporting interactive file format, 458
  media file format supported, 438
  PDF export file format, 492
Adobe Bridge
  additional options, 48
  Bridge Center (Web browser), 48
  display options, 46–47
  graphics, placing from Bridge, 196
  installing, 45
  launching, 45
  libraries, 300
  navigation options, 46
  opening InDesign files via Bridge, 46
  synchronizing color settings, 421
  using, 45
Adobe Creative Suite 2, 45
Adobe dialog box, 42
Adobe Illustrator
  AI file format, 195
  AICB (Adobe Illustrator Clipboard), 199
  importing swatches from, 133
  and InDesign
    converting paths, 199
    Erase tool, 191
    importing native Illustrator files, 200
    Pen tool, 180
    Pencil tool, 188
    Smooth tool, 190
    Spiral tool and Pen tool, 180
  Preferences dialog box, Clipboard/
  AICB option/Preserve Paths, 199
Adobe InCopy, 516
Adobe InDesign
  Interchange file format, 492, 511
  Version Cue, 42
    preferences, 546

Adobe InDesign Tagged Text format
  Adobe InDesign Tags Import
  Options dialog box, 360
  Export dialog box, 359, 492, 516
Adobe Paragraph Composer, 401
Adobe PDF. *See* Adobe Acrobat
Adobe PDF Presets dialog box, 506–507
Adobe Photoshop and InDesign
  clipping paths, 220–221
  layers
    controls, 293
    layer comps, 201
    visibility, 219
  PSD file format, 195, 200, 201
  transparencies, 224, 225
Adobe Reader Bookmark pane, 435
Adobe Single-line Composer, 401
Adobe Stock Photos controls, 48
Adobe Swatch Exchange (.ase) files
  importing, 131
  saving, 130
Advanced category
  Export PDF dialog box, 494, 503
  Print dialog box, 462, 477–482
AI (Adobe Illustrator) file format, 195
AICB (Adobe Illustrator Clipboard), 199
Align palette, 2
  Control palette options, 110
American Standard Code for Information
Interchange (ASCII) text, 261, 263
ANPA Color swatch library, 133
Appearance of Black preferences, 526, 545
Apple QuickTime media file format, 438
Arrange menu commands
  Bring All To Front, 41
  Bring Forward, 102
  Bring to Front, 102
  Cascade, 41
  New Window, 41
  Send Backward, 102
  Send to Back, 102
  Tile, 41
arrow key keyboard shortcuts, 55
arrowhead styles, paths, 166

artwork placement. *See also* graphic frames; graphics; images
  from Bridge, 196, 203
  into existing frames, 195
  file formats for display/printing, 195
  moving/copying between frames, 195
  replacing in existing frames, 195
  without drawing frames, 194
ASCII (American Standard Code for Information Interchange) text, 261, 263
Attributes palette
  fills or strokes, overprinting, 145
  opening, 2, 145
Automation menu
  Script Label palette, 7
  Scripts palette, 7

B

background color, 36
baseline grids
  aligning text, 409
  custom grids for text frames, 410
  preferences, 408, 535
Baseline Shift controls, 63
  wrapping on paths, 239
batch commands, Bridge, 48
bevel effect, 452
beveled stroke joins, 155
Bezier curves, 180
Black color palette, 120
black eyedropper, 176–177
Blatner, David, 9, 286
Bleed Mode, 35
Bleed tool, 15
bleeds, 19, 23
  EPS output, 510
  guides, 28
  print options, 461, 468
blend modes
  adding, 168
  drop shadows, 171
  knockout groups, 168
  list, 169
BMP (Windows Bitmap) file format, 195
Book palette
  Add/Remove Document, 277
  Book Page Numbering Options, 280

Document Page Numbering Options, 280
documents
  opening, 278
  order, 278
  updating, 279
Export Book to PDF, 281
opening, 277
Package, 281
Preflight Book, 281
Print Book, 281
Repaginate, 280
Replace Document, 279
Synchronize Book, 278
Synchronize Options, 279
bookmarks
  creating, 435
  deleting, 436
  nesting/unnesting, 437
  opening Bookmarks palette, 2, 435
  renaming, 436
  repositioning, 437
  sorting, 437
Bookmarks palette
  Delete Bookmark, 436
  New Bookmark, 435
    destinations, 435
  opening, 2, 435
  Rename Bookmark, 436
  Sort Bookmarks, 437
books (electronic book file)
  changes, controlling, 281
  creating, 277
  documents
    adding/removing, 277
    changing order, 278
    numbering, 280
    opening, 278
    replacing, 279
    synchronizing files to source, 278, 279
    updating, 279
  exporting files as PDF, 281
  indexes
    generating, 288
    index reference markers, 287
  packaging, 281
  pagination
    adjustment settings, 280
    forcing, 280
  preflighting, 281

printing, 281
table of contents (TOC)
  alphabetizing, 286
  defining styles, 282
  document preparations, 282
  formatting styles, 284, 285
  generating, 282
  indenting entries, 286
  option settings, 286
  selecting listings, 283
  separator characters, 285
  titling, 283
bounding box handles, 86
Bridge. *See* Adobe Bridge
  Bridge Center (Web browser), 48
  display options, 46–47
  graphics, placing from Bridge, 196
  installing, 45
  launching, 45
  libraries, 300
  navigation options, 46
  opening InDesign files via Bridge, 46
  synchronizing color settings, 421
  using, 45
Bullets and Numbering dialog box, 354, 372
  bullets and numbers
    converting to text, 355
    hanging bullet or numbered list, 68
    positioning, 355
  finding/replacing, 350–351
  inline objects, 244
  numbered lists, 355
  positioning, 355
Butin, Fred, 415
Button dialog box, 445
Button Options dialog box
  Behaviors controls, 453–455
    Add, 453, 456
    Delete, 457
    repositioning, 456
    Update, 456
  Behaviors controls and mouse events, 453
    changing, 456
    deactivating, 457
  General controls, 447
  Visibility in PDF, 447
Button tool, 15, 445
buttons
  appearance themes

applying, 452
  modifying, 452
behaviors
  applying, 453
  applying multiple, 456
  changing associated events, 456
  deactivating behaviors or events, 457
  definitions, 454–455
  deleting, 457
  editing, 456
  repositioning, 456
button states
  adding, 448
  changing, 451
  converting, 449
  creating, 450
  definition, 448
  deleting, 448
  deleting content, 451
  editing, 450
  enabling/disabling, 449
converting objects into buttons, 445
creating, 445
General controls, 447
images, placing, 446
text, importing or typing in, 446

C

Cascading Style Sheets (CSS)
  Package for GoLive, 517
  properties, 515
CellStyles. *See* Teacup Software
changing text. *See* text, finding/changing
Character palette
  baseline shift, 63
  distortions
    finding/replacing, 350
    skewing, 64
    vertical/horizontal scaling, 64
  font menu, 59
  kerning list, 62
  language, 65
    finding/replacing, 350
  leading, 62
    finding/replacing, 350
  local formatting, 382
  opening, 2, 58

Character palette *(continued)*
  OpenType, 411
  point size menu, 59
  Show options, 58
  strikethrough options, 61, 372
    finding/replacing, 350
  styles, 59
    electronic styles, 60, 65, 350
    keyboard commands, 59
  tracking, 63
  underline options, 61, 372
    finding/replacing, 350
character styles
  applying, 382
  breaking links, 384
  case sensitive, 378
  defining, 375
    basing one style on another, 376
    by example, 375
  deleting, 385, 386
  drop caps, 387–388
  duplicating, 376
  importing Word styles, 380–381
  keyboard shortcuts, 377
  local formatting, 382
    clearing, 383–384
  nested styles, 389–391
  redefining, 385
  resetting base style, 376
  resolving conflicts, 379–380
  transferring to another document, 378
Character Styles palette, 3
  Advanced formats, 370
  Basic formats, 370
  Break Link to Style, 384
  Character Style Conflicts menu, 380
  Character Style Options
    Drop Caps, 387–388
    keyboard shortcuts, 377
    redefining styles, 385
  Delete Character Style alert box, 386
  Delete Styles, 385–386
  Load Styles commands, 378–379
  New Character Style, 375
    Based On menu, 376
    keyboard shortcuts, 377
  Preserve Formatting, 386
  Reset to Base, 376
  Select All Unused Styles, 385

characters
  alternative characters, 72
  hidden characters, 268
  inserting, 72
  styles (*See* Character Styles palette)
checkerboard grid over pages, 253
checking spelling. *See* spell check
clipboard
  Adobe Illustrator Clipboard (AICB), 199
  Copy/Paste commands *versus*
  Duplicate command, 57
  preferences, 547
clipping paths
  choosing
    alpha channels as paths, 222
    as InDesign path, 221
  Clipping Path dialog box, 221–223
  converting to frames, 221
  creating
    from images, 222
    in Photoshop, 220
  deleting, 223
  modifying
    effects of paths, 223
    shapes, 221
Cohen, Sandee, 118, 459
color
  CMYK color
    blend modes, 169
    color management, 418
    converting out-of-gamut
    colors to CMYK, 122
    creating, 118
    defining, 120
    EPS output, 509
    mixed inks, 134
    printing, 118, 121
    uses, 118
    working space, 417
  compression output settings, 498–500
  conversion output settings, 501–502
  finding/replacing, 350
  ICC (International Color Consortium), 501
  LAB color
    creating, 119
    luminance, 122
    mixing, 122
    out-of-gamut symbol, 122
    uses, 119

Mixed Ink Groups, 118
  creating, 135
mixed inks
  controls, 134, 135
  creating, 119
  creating swatches, 134
  uses, 119
printing
  unnamed colors, 125, 131
  unused colors, 130
profiles, 501–502
RGB color
  color management, 418
  creating, 118
  EPS output, 509
  mixing, 121
  onscreen display color, 118, 121
  out-of-gamut symbol, 122
  uses, 118
  working space, 417
sampling/downsampling
output settings, 498–499
spot color
  blend modes, 169
  creating, 119
  versus four process color, 127
  mixed inks, 134
  uses, 119
tints
  creating, 119
  creating swatches, 138
  modifying swatches, 139
  storing swatches, 139
  tinting swatches, 138
  uses, 119
Color blend mode, 169
Color Burn blend mode, 169
Color Dodge blend mode, 169
color management
  Bridge, 48
    synchronizing color settings, 421
  conversion options, 419
  enabling, 416
  Engine menu, 419
  Intent menu, 419
  policies, 418
  PostScript Color Management, 509
  profiles, 418, 422
  settings

opening saved settings, 420
predefined, 416
saving, 420
white and black points, 419
working space, 417
Color Management category,
Print dialog box, 462
Color palette
  CMYK color, 120
  colors
    adding to Swatches, 125
    applying, 123, 128
    transferring to Swatches palette, 123
  Fill icon, 128, 148
  LAB color, 120
  opening, 3, 120
  RGB color, 120
  Stroke icon, 128
  unnamed colors, 125
Color Picker
  adding colors to Swatches palette, 125
  defining colors and swatches, 140
  opening, 140
Color Settings dialog box
  Advanced Mode, Conversion Options, 419
  Color Management Policy,
  RGB and CMYK, 418
  Enable Color Management, 416
  Engine menu, 419
  Intent menu, 419
  Missing Profiles, 418
  Open (saved color settings), 420
  Profile Mismatches, 418
  Save (color settings), 420
  Settings menu, 416
  working space, RGB and CMYK, 417
Color tool, 15
column guides (ruler), 28
  moving, 29
  unlocking, 29
columns, 22
  Keep Options, 362, 371
  text break characters, 268
  text frames, 76
    Fixed Column Width, 77
    inline objects, 244
  text rules, 242
Compact Mode, Bridge, 46, 196

compound shapes
adding images, 197
creating, 197
splitting, 197
Compression category, Export
PDF dialog box, 493, 498–500
Configure Plug-ins dialog box, 548
container objects, 107–109
fill effects, 148
gradient fills, 149
selecting, 108
stroke effects, 152
content objects, 107–109
moving, 108
selecting, 108
content offset, 209
context sensitive, Control palette, 110
contextual menus, 16
opening, 16
Control palette, 3
Align palette, 110
Bridge, 45
character settings, 79
context sensitive, 110
Fit icons, 208
with grouped or pasted-in objects, 110
local formatting, 382
objects
flipping, 100
rotation settings, 100
paragraph settings, 79
Select commands, 110
with single/multiple objects, 110
Stroke palette options, 110
table controls, 339
Transform Content, 205
Transform palette options, 110
Convert Direction Point tool, 15, 187
Corners list, dashes and gaps, 158
Create Guides dialog box, 30
CSS (Cascading Style Sheets)
Package for GoLive, 517
properties, 515

D

Darken blend mode, 169
dash strokes, 158, 159, 161

DCS (Desktop Color Separation)
file format, 195
Default fill and stroke tool, 15
Default workspace, 14
Define Print Presets dialog box, 483–484
Delete Anchor Point tool, 15, 186, 192
Delete Workspace dialog box, 14
Desktop Color Separation
(DCS) file format, 195
Details view, Bridge, 47
DIC Color Guide swatch library, 133
Dicolor spot color libraries, 119
Difference blend mode, 169
Direct Selection tool, 15
keyboard shortcuts, 204, 211
objects, resizing, 91
path segments, 187
paths, moving anchor points
and control handles, 184
distortion
text, 64
Transform palette, Shear field, 99
Document Presets dialog box, 24, 25
document rulers
contextual menus, 26, 27
guides
appearance, changing, 31
column guides, 29–30
creating, 29
deleting, 31
hiding/showing, 28
locking, 31
moving, 31
preferences, 28
repositioning, 30
row guides, 29
snap to guides, 29
types, 28
unlocking, 29
origin settings, 27
preferences, 534
showing/hiding, 26
units of measurement, changing, 26
zero points, repositioning, 27
Document Setup dialog box
default settings, 22
document presets, 24
Make Same Size icon
margins, 21

slugs, 19
pages
Bleed area, 23
Columns, 22
Facing Pages, 20, 23
Gutter, 22
Margins, 21
Number of Pages, 23
Orientation, 21, 23
Page Size, 20, 23
Slug area, 23
documents, 18
bleeds
Bleed Mode, 35
changing, 23
setting, 19
columns
changing, 23
setting, 22
converting for Web sites, 517
copying, 43
default settings, 22
facing pages
changing, 23
setting, 20
grids
appearance, changing, 32
preferences, 535
showing/hiding, 32
snap to document grid, 33
gutters
changing, 23
setting, 22
island spreads
creating, 259
dismantling, 259
joining pages, 260
keeping pages together, 259
separating pages, 260
magnification
commands, 33
keyboard shortcuts, 34
magnification list, 34
Make Same Size icon
bleeds, 19
margins, 21
slugs, 19
managing with Bridge, 48

margins
changing, 23
setting, 21
media files
linking *versus* embedding, 440
movies, 440–444
sound, 438–439
minimum vertical offset, 36
More Options button, 19
movie clips
adding empty movie clips, 441
adding movie clips, 440
adding movie to empty clips, 442
selecting images, 443
navigating
Hand tool, 38
keyboard shortcuts, 40
Navigation palette, 39–40
Zoom tool, 37
number of pages, 23
opening
within InDesign, 44
QuarkXPress or PageMaker files, 44
recently saved documents, 44
orientation
changing, 23
setting, 21
page size
changing, 23
setting, 20
pasteboard area, 18
background color, 36
presets
applying/editing, 24
creating, 25
deleting, 25
importing/exporting, 25
preview settings, 226–228
preferenes, 546
printing
bleed areas, 468
choosing printers, 463
CMYK color, 118, 121
color options, 469
color output, 469
controlling pages, 463
font information, 476
general options, 463
images send data, 476

documents *(continued)*
  Ink Manager, 474–475
  Object Attributes, Nonprinting, 460
  OPI (Open Prepress
    Interface) controls, 477
  page marks, 467
  paper size and orientation, 464
  PostScript files, 485
  Print dialog box categories, 460–462
  print presets, 482–483
  print summary, 484
  screen settings, 470
  separations preview, 471–474
  setup options, 464
  slug areas, 468
  suppressing printing, layer visibility, 460
  tiling pages, 465–466
  Transparency Flattener, 477–479, 481–482
  Trapping menu, 470
  recovering, 44
    preferences, 546
  reverting to saved versions, 43
  saving/naming, 42
    keyboard shortcuts, 43
  sections
    creating, 275
    marker characters, 276
    page numbering options, 275
    section numbering *versus*
      absolute numbering, 276
  slugs
    changing, 23
    setting, 19
    Slug Mode, 35
  sound clips
    adding empty sound clips, 438
    adding sound clips, 438
    selecting images, 439
  starting, 18
  undo/redo steps, 43
  View modes, 35
dotted strokes, 159
drop caps, 70, 371
  finding/replacing, 350
drop shadows
  adding, 171
  applying, 230
  blend mode, 171

buttons, 452
checkerboard grid, 253
flattener presets, 478–480
flattener previews, 481–482
flattening transparency effects, 480, 481
removing, 172
Transparency slider, 229

E

Edit Glyph Set dialog box, 74
Edit menu (Mac and Win)
  Check Spelling dialog box, 342–343
  Clear
    segment, 187
    table cell content, 321
  Color Settings, 416
  Copy, 56, 88
    cell content, 322
    graphics, 195
  Create Suite Color Settings, 421
  Cut, 56, 88
    cell content, 322
    graphics, 195
    objects, 107
    pasted-in content, 109
  Duplicate, 57, 88
  Edit in Story Editor, 353
  Find/Change dialog box, 346
    Change All, 347
    Find Format Settings, 349–351
    Find Next, 347
    Find What, 347
    Find What, wildcard characters, 348
    More Options, 348
  Keyboard Shortcuts
    Context menu, 522
    Delete Set, 522
    New Set, 521
    New Shortcut, 522
    opening list in Notepad (Win)
      or TextEdit (Mac), 521
    Product Area menu, 522
    Set menu, 520
  Paste, 56, 88
    cell content, 322
    inline objects, 244
  Paste in Place, 88

Paste Into
  graphics, 195
  nesting frames, 210
  objects, 107
  pasted-in content, 109
Select All, 85
  cell text, 317
Spelling
  Autocorrect, 345
  Dynamic Spelling, 345
  Edit Dictionary, 344
  hyphenation, 408
Step and Repeat, 89
Edit menu (Win), Preferences
  Advanced Type category, 524
    Character Settings, 531
    Input Method Options, 531
  Appearance of Black category, 526
    Printing/Exporting menu, 545
    On Screen menu, 545
  Autocorrect category, 525
    Add to Autocorrect List dialog box, 541
    Autocorrect Options controls, 541
  Autocorrect preferences, 525, 541
  choosing categories, 523
  Composition category, 524
    Highlight settings, 532
    Text Wrap controls, 533
  defaults, 547
  Dictionary category, 525
    Compose Using (hyphenation) menu, 539
    Language menu, 537
    manipulating dictionaries, 538
    Quote menu, 537
    User Dictionary controls, 539
  Display Performance category, 226, 228, 526
    Adjust View Settings menu, 543
    Default View Settings controls, 543
    Hand tool slider settings, 544
    type and graphics, anti-aliasing, 543, 544
    type and graphics, greeking, 544
  File Handling category, 526
    Clipboard options, 547
    Document Recovery Data area, 546
    Preview Size menu, 546
    Save Document Preview Image option, 546
    Temporary Folder area, 546
    Version Cue control, 546
  General category, 523

Floating Tools Palette menu, 528
Font Downloading and
  Embedding section, 528
  Page Numbering View menu, 527
  Reset All Warning Dialogs section, 528
  Tool Tips menu, 527
Grids category, 32, 524
  Baseline Grid controls, 408, 535
  Color menu, 535
  Document Grid controls, 535
  Grids in Back option, 535
Guides & Pasteboard category, 28, 36, 525
  color for onscreen elements, 536
  Guide Options, 536
  Pasteboard Options, 536
Spelling category, 525
  Dynamic Spelling controls, 540
  Find options, 540
Story Editor Display category, 526
  Cursor Options menu, 542
  Line Spacing menu, 542
  Text Display Options, 542
  Theme menu, 542
  Type menu, 542
Type category, 524
  Create Links When Placing Text
  and Spreadsheet Files, 530
  Drag and Drop Text Editing controls, 530
  Type Options, 529
  When Placing Text and Tables from
  Other Applications Paste controls, 530
Units & Increments category, 26, 524
  Custom menu, 534
  Keyboard Increments fields, 534
  Points/Inch field, 534
  Ruler Units menu, 534
Effect menu options, text wrap on paths, 238
electronic rulers. See document rulers
Ellipse dialog box, 83
Ellipse Frame tool, 15
  graphic frames, 82, 83
Ellipse tool
  text frames, 50
  unassigned frames, 82
elliptical graphic frames, 83
elliptical text frames, 50
em spaces, 80
EMF (Enhanced Metafile) file format, 195
en spaces, 80

Encapsulated PostScript file format. *See* EPS

Enhanced Metafile (EMF) file format, 195

EPS (Encapsulated PostScript) file format
  Export EPS dialog box, 492, 508–510
  import file formats, 195
  Import Options dialog box, 200, 201

Erase tool, 15, 190, 192

Excel files. *See* Microsoft Excel files

Exclusion blend mode, 169

exporting InDesign files
  to Adobe InCopy, 516
  EPS dialog box, 492, 508–510
  Export dialog box
    Adobe InDesign Tagged Text
      format, 359, 492, 516
    text export formats, 516
  Export PDF dialog box, 492
    Adobe PDF Presets dialog box, 506–507
    Advanced category options, 494, 503
    Compression category
      options, 493, 498–500
    General category options, 493, 495–497
    Marks and Bleed category options, 493
    Output category options, 494, 501–502
    Security category options, 494, 504–505
    Summary category options, 494
  Interchange file format, 492, 511
  JPEG file format, 492, 511–512
  RTF file format, 492, 516
  SVG/SVG Compressed format,
    492, 513–514, 515
  Text Only file format, 492, 516
  XML file format, 492

Eyedropper tool, 15
  black eyedropper, 176
  Eyedropper Options dialog box, 176
  keyboard shortcuts, 144
  sampling/applying object attributes, 176
  sampling/storing placed graphics colors, 144
  white eyedropper, 176

F

facing pages, 20, 23
  Fit Spread In Window, 33, 34
  keeping together in Acrobat file, 495

Favorites tab, Bridge, 46

feathering

checkerboard grid, 253
  flattener presets, 478–480
  flattener previews, 481–482
  Transparency slider, 229

fifth color. *See* color, spot color

figure spaces, 80

File menu commands
  Close, 43
  Document Presets, 24
    Define, 24, 25
  Export
    Adobe InDesign Tagged Text, 359, 492
    Adobe PDF, 458
    Format (Mac), 492
    InDesign Snippet, 304
    Save as File Type (Win), 492
  New
    Book, 277
    Document, 18–19
    Library, 5, 298
  Open, 44
  Open Recent, 44
  Package, 489
  Place
    files with clipping paths, 220–223
    graphics, 194–196
    graphics into tables, 328
    image file into button, 446
    image file to object inside buttons, 451
    Import Options dialog box, 200–203, 380
    inline objects, 244
    Movie Clip cursor, 440
    Sound Clip cursor, 438
    tables from Word or Excel, 313
    tagged text, 360
    text, 261
    text file into button, 446
    text file to object inside buttons, 451
    text into tables, 316
    transparencies, 224, 225
  Preflight, 486
  Print, 460
    categories, 460–462
    Device Independent from PPD menu, 485
    PostScript File, 485
    Tiling, 465–466
  Print Presets, Define, 483
  Revert, 43
  Save a Copy, 43

Save/Save As, 42
  recovering files, 44
  Undo/Redo, 43
files
  creating copies, 43
  managing with Bridge, 48
  opening
    within InDesign, 44
    QuarkXPress or PageMaker, 44
    recently saved documents, 44
  recovering, 44
  reverting to saved versions, 43
  saving/naming, 42
    keyboard shortcuts, 43
  undo/redo steps, 43
Fill tool, 15
  object fills
    applying, 148
    applying to text, 149
    default, 178
  opening
    Color Picker, 140
    Swatches palette, 128
Filmstrip view, Bridge, 47
finding/changing text. *See*
text, finding/changing
Flash Player media files, 438
flat color. *See* color, spot color
Flattener Preview palette, 3
flush spaces, 80
fly-out panels, 15
  opening related tools, 16
Focoltone swatch library, 133
Folders tab, Bridge, 46
FontLab, 490
fonts (typefaces), 59
  Character palette menu, 59
  embedding in files
    EPS, 510
    PDF, 502–503
    preferences, 528
  Find Font
    making changes, 361
    replacing missing fonts, 361
  FontLab, 490
  legalities of copying, 490
  OpenType fonts, 372
    finding/replacing, 350
  service bureaus, 490

subsetting, 502–503
  SVG output, 514
footnotes
  baseline, 358
  formatting, 357
    references, 357
    styles, 356
  importing from Word, 358
  inserting, 356
  placement options, 358
  separator rules, 358
  spacing options, 357
Format container tool, 15
Format text tool, 15
four process color. *See* color, CMYK color
frames. *See also* graphic frames; text
frames; unassigned frames
  compound shapes, 197
  converting text to frames (paths), 197
  importing paths as frames, 199
  nesting, 210
    selecting/moving nested elements, 211
  text break characters, 268
Fraser, Bruce, 415
Free Transform tool, 15, 95
Freehand. *See* Macromedia Freehand

G

General category
  Export PDF dialog box, 493, 495–497
  Print dialog box, 461, 463
GIF (Graphics Interchange
Format) file format, 195
glow effects, buttons, 452
Glyphs palette, 3
  alternate glyphs, 412
  characters
    accessing alternative characters, 72
    inserting, 72
  glyth set characters, 73
  Show list (categories), 412
GoLive Web site
  movie files, 440
  sound files, 438
Grabber tool. *See* Hand tool
Gradient palette, 4
  gradients

Gradient palette *(continued)*
   Linear or Radial, 143
   process *versus* spot color, 143
   unnamed, 143, 144
  opening, 4, 143
  options, 143
Gradient tool, 15
  fills
   adjusting, 150
   applying, 149
  strokes, applying, 153
gradients, flattening transparency
effects, 480, 481
graphic frames. *See also* artwork
    placement; graphics; images
  diagonal lines convention, 82
  drawing, 82
  elliptical, 83
  modifying, 205
  moving, 204, 206
  nesting, 210
  placed graphics, 205–206
  polygonal, 84
  rectangular, 83
  resizing frames to graphic size, 208
  selecting, 204, 206
   Selection tool *versus* Direct
    Selection tool, 115
  text, 82
graphics. *See also* artwork placement;
graphic frames; images
  embedding/unembedding, 218
  in graphic frames
   centering within frames, 208
   moving both, 204
   numerically positioning on pages, 209
   numerically positioning within frames, 209
   offset, content and absolute, 209
   resizing both, 206
   resizing just graphics, 207
   resizing to fill frames, 208
   selecting within frames, 204
   transforming within frames, 209
  linking
   editing linked graphics, 216
   editing links, 216
   examining, 214
   finding linked files, 217

   jumping to linked graphics, 216
   link information, 217
   relinking, 215
   updating modified links, 216
   opening QuarkXPress or PageMaker files, 44
Graphics category, Print dialog box, 462, 476
Graphics Interchange Format
(GIF) file format, 195
grayscale images
  coloring, 213
  downsampling, 498
  EPS output, 509
Group Selection tool
  keyboard shortcuts, 211
  resizing objects, 91
Guides & Pasteboard Preferences dialog box,
    document's minimum vertical offset, 36
  guides, 28
guides (ruler)
  appearance, changing, 31
  column guides
   creating, 30
   moving, 29
   unlocking, 29
  creating, 29
  deleting, 31
  hiding/showing, 28
  locking, 31
  moving, 31
  preferences, 28
  repositioning, 30
  row guides, creating, 30
  snap to guides, 29
gutters, 22
  text frame columns, 76

H

hair spaces, 80
Hand tool, 15
  display preferences, 544
  keyboard shortcuts, 38
  navigation guidelines, 40
handles, bounding boxes, 86
hanging bullets, 68
Hard Light blend mode, 169
Help menu (Win), Configure Plug-ins, 548
hidden characters, 71

highlighting
  Highlight preferences, 532
  with underlining, 61
HKS swatch library, 133
horizontal alignment, 103
horizontal distribute icon, 104
horizontal gridlines, 32
horizontal ruler settings, 26
horizontal scale controls, 64
horizontal space controls, 104
Hue blend mode, 169
hyperlinks
  appearance, 432
  destinations
    choosing, 430
    creating, 424
    creating from existing, 429
    deleting, 434
    editing, 428
    moving to, 434
    setting before sources, 435
  editing, 433
  exporting, 434
  hotspots, 429
  indexes, 434
  link indicator suggestions, 433
  moving, 434
  resetting sources, 433
  Table of Contents, 434
  testing, 434
  updating, 433
Hyperlinks palette
  Delete Hyperlink, 434
  Go to Destination, 434
  Go to Source, 434
  Hyperlink Destination Options
    Delete, 428
    Edit, 428
  Hyperlink Options, 433
  New Hyperlink
    Appearance area, 429, 432
    Color menu, 432
    Document menu, 430, 431
    Highlight menu, 432
    Name menu, 429, 430, 431
    Style menu, 432
    Width menu, 432
  New Hyperlink Destination, 429
    Type menu, 425

  Type menu, Page, 426, 430
  Type menu, Text Anchor, 427, 430
  Type menu, URL, 427, 431
  Zoom settings, 426, 430
  opening, 4, 425
  Reset Hyperlink, 433
  Update Hyperlink, 433
hyphenation, 71, 371

I

ICC (International Color Consortium), 501
Illustrator. See Adobe Illustrator
Image Import Options dialog box. See
    also Import Options dialog box
  Alpha Channel, Transparency, 224, 225
  clipping paths, 220–223
  Color tab (profile and rendering intent), 422
  Crop to list, 202
  EPS, 200, 201
  JPEG, 200
  PDF, 200, 202–203
  Photoshop layers, 293
  PSD, 200, 201
  TIFF, 200
images
  clipping paths
    choosing alpha channels as paths, 222
    choosing as InDesign path, 221
    converting to frames, 221
    creating from images, 222
    creating in Photoshop, 220
    deleting around images, 223
    modifying effects of paths, 223
    modifying shapes, 221
  embedding/unembedding, 218
  file formats for printing, 200–203
  placed images
    applying effects, 230
    coloring frame fills or strokes, 213
    coloring grayscale images, 213
    embedding/unembedding, 218
  previewing
    default settings, 226
    default settings, switching, 227
    individual images, 227
    raster and vector settings, 228
    transparency effects settings, 229

images *(continued)*
transparencies
applying alpha channels, 225
in Photoshop and Illustrator files, 224
Images Send Data menu, 476
Import Options dialog box. *See also*
Image Import Options dialog box
Microsoft Word
Style Mapping, 381
styles, 380
text, 261, 263
importing
color swatches, 131, 133
document presets, 25
images, 200–203
inline objects, 244
master frames, 264
paths as frames, 199
text
ASCII text, 261, 263
into existing or master frames, 264
Import Options dialog box, 261
Microsoft Excel files, 263
Microsoft Word files, 262
into new frames, 264
RTF (Rich Text Format)
file format, 261, 262
In-RIP (raster image processing)
Separations, 469
InCopy (Adobe), 516
Indent to Here character, 69
InDesign. *See* Adobe InDesign
InDesign menu (Mac), Preferences
Advanced Type category, 524
Character Settings, 531
Input Method Options, 531
Appearance of Black category, 526
Printing/Exporting menu, 545
On Screen menu, 545
Autocorrect category, 525
Add to Autocorrect List dialog box, 541
Autocorrect Options controls, 541
choosing categories, 523
Composition category, 524
Highlight settings, 532
Text Wrap controls, 533
Configure Plug-ins, 548
defaults, 547
Dictionary category, 525

Compose Using (hyphenation) menu, 539
Language menu, 537
manipulating dictionaries, 538
Quote menu, 537
User Dictionary controls, 539
Display Performance, 226, 228
Display Performance category, 226, 228, 526
Adjust View Settings menu, 543
Default View Settings controls, 543
Hand tool slider settings, 544
type and graphics, anti-aliasing, 543, 544
type and graphics, greeking, 544
File Handling category, 526
Clipboard options, 547
Document Recovery Data area, 546
Preview Size menu, 546
Save Document Preview Image option, 546
Temporary Folder area, 546
Version Cue control, 546
General category, 523
Floating Tools Palette menu, 528
Font Downloading and
Embedding section, 528
Page Numbering View menu, 527
Reset All Warning Dialogs section, 528
Tool Tips menu, 527
Grids, 32
baseline grids, 408
Grids category, 32, 524
Baseline Grid controls, 408, 535
Color menu, 535
Document Grid controls, 535
Grids in Back option, 535
Guides & Pasteboard, 28, 36
Guides & Pasteboard category, 28, 36, 525
color for onscreen elements, 536
Guide Options, 536
Pasteboard Options, 536
Spelling category, 525
Dynamic Spelling controls, 540
Find options, 540
Story Editor Display category, 526
Cursor Options menu, 542
Line Spacing menu, 542
Text Display Options, 542
Theme menu, 542
Type menu, 542
Type category, 524
Create Links When Placing Text

and Spreadsheet Files, 530
Drag and Drop Text Editing controls, 530
Type Options, 529
When Placing Text and Tables from
Other Applications Paste controls, 530
Units & Increments, 26
Units & Increments category, 26, 524
Custom menu, 534
Keyboard Increments fields, 534
Points/Inch field, 534
Ruler Units menu, 534
Index palette, 4
Generate Index, 288
New Page Reference, 287
opening, 4, 287
indexes
generating, 288
index reference markers, 287
Info palette, 4, 111
Ink Manager, 474–475475
inset spacing (text frames), 77
.inst files (strokes), 163
interactive elements
bookmarks, 424
creating, 435
deleting, 436
nesting/unnesting, 437
opening Bookmarks palette, 2, 435
renaming, 436
repositioning, 437
sorting, 437
buttons, 424
appearance themes, 452
behaviors, 453–457
button states, 448–451
converting objects into buttons, 445
creating, 445
General controls, 447
images, adding, 446
text, adding, 446
export controls, 458
exporting PDF files, 497
hyperlinks
appearance, 432
destinations, 424, 428–430, 434–435
editing, 433
exporting, 434
hotspots, 429
indexes, 434

link indicator suggestions, 433
moving, 434
resetting sources, 433
Table of Contents, 434
testing, 434
updating, 433
media clips
movies, 440–444
sounds, 438–439, 440
page hyperlink destinations, 425–426, 430
text anchor hyperlink
destinations, 425, 427, 430
URL hyperlink destinations, 425, 427, 431
Interactive menu
Bookmarks, 2, 435
Button Options, 447
Convert to Button, 445
Hyperlinks, 4, 425
Movie Options, 441
Sound Options, 438, 439
Interchange file format, 492, 511
International Color Consortium (ICC), 501
International Paper, 118
ISO (International Organization
for Standardization), 495
Unicode encoding, 515

J

JDF (Job Definition Format), 503
JPEG (Joint Photographic
Experts Group) file format
exporting InDesign files, 492, 511–512
importing files, 195, 200

K

Keep Options dialog box, 362, 371
kerning, 62
keyboard shortcuts
assigning, 522
changing, 522
character styles, 59, 377
contextual menus, 16
creating
list of shortcuts, 521
new set, 521
personal shortcuts, 521

keyboard shortcuts *(continued)*
  Direct Selection tool, 204, 211
  drawing text frames, 52
  Eyedropper tool, 144
  Group Selection tool, 211
  Hand tool, 38
  hiding all palettes, 10
  Insert Break Character, 268
  magnification, 34
  objects
    moving and copying, 87
    resizing, 90
    transform tools, 91
  paragraph styles, 377
  saving/naming documents, 43
  Selection tool
    graphic frames and images, 204
    selecting multiple objects, 85
  shortcut sets
    changing, 520
    deleting, 522
  text
    formatting, 59
    insertion point, 53
    selecting, 55
    Type tool, 55
  Toolbox tools, 16
  Zoom tool, 37
Keyboard Shortcuts dialog box
  Context menu, 522
  Delete Set, 522
  New Set, 521
  New Shortcut, 522
  opening list in Notepad (Win)
    or TextEdit (Mac), 521
  Product Area menu, 522
  Set menu, 520
knockout groups, 165, 168
Kvern, Olav Martin, 9, 286

L

landscape orientation, 21
language settings, 65
  preferences, 537
Layer Options dialog box
  Color list, 292
  Lock Guides, 294

  Lock Layer, 292
  Name field, 292
  Show Guides, 294
  Show Layer, 293
  text wrap options, 235, 294
layers
  creating, 290
    while pasting, 291
  deleting, 291
  duplicating, 290
  guide controls, 294
  highlight color settings, 292
  layer comps, 201
  locking, 292
  merging, 295
  naming, 292
  objects
    applying, 295
    moving from layer to layer, 295
  reordering, 295
  text wrap, 235
    for hidden layers, 294
Layers palette
  applying/moving objects, 295
  Delete Layer/Delete Unused (layers), 291
  Hide Others, 293
  Merge Layers, 295
  New Layer, 290
  opening, 5, 290
  Paste Remembers Layers, 291
  Photoshop layers, 293
  Toggle Lock space, 292
  Toggle Visibility, 293
Layout menu commands
  Create Guides, 30
  Layout Adjustment, 274
  navigating pages, 256
  Numbering & Section Options, 275
  Ruler Guides, 31
  Table of Contents dialog box, 282
    additional options, 286
    Between Entry and Number menu, 285
    Include Paragraph Styles list, 283–286
    Page Number menu, 285
    Style menu, 283
    Title field, 283
leading, 62
libraries
  Bridge, 300

creating, 298
display, changing, 301
items
    adding, 298
    adding all items separately, 299
    adding to documents, 300
    deleting, 299
    modifying information, 301
    updating, 300
pages, 299
saving, 298
searching, 302
sorting, 303
uses, 299
Library palette, 5
Add Item, 298
Add Items on Page, 299
Delete Item(s), 299
Item Information Object Type, 301
List View, 301
Place Item(s), 300
Save (new library), 298
Search Entire Library, 302
Show All, 303
Show Subset, 302
Sort Items, 303
Thumbnail View, 301
Update Library Item, 300
Lighten blend mode, 169
Line tool, 15
straight lines, 84
    constraining to 45-degree angle, 84
    drawing from center point, 84
    inline objects, 244
linear gradients, 141, 143
Links palette commands, 5
Embed icon, 218
Link Information dialog box, 217
links
    editing, 216
    finding, 217
    information, 217
    jumping to linked graphics, 216
    relinking, 215
    status icons, 214
    updating, 216
opening, 5, 214
locking
  guides (ruler), 29, 31

objects for alignment, 105
luminance, 122
Luminosity blend mode, 169

M

Macintosh
AppleScripts, 365
Macintosh Picture (PICT) file format, 195
    EPS preview, 509
System swatch library, 133
Macromedia Freehand
AICB (Adobe Illustrator Clipboard), 199
compared to InDesign
    converting paths, 199
    Pen tool, 180
magnification
changing, 34
commands, 33
keyboard shortcuts, 34
Margin and Columns dialog box, 23
margins
changing, 23
guides, 28
indents, 370
    finding/replacing, 350
    hanging bullets, 68
    numbered lists, 68
Make Same Size icon, 21
optical margin adjustment, 400
Optical Margin Alignment setting, 400
setting, 21
Marks and Bleed category
Export PDF dialog box, 493
Print dialog box, 461, 467–468
marquee zoom, 37
masks, 107
master frames, 264
master pages. See pages, master pages
Measure tool, 15
Microsoft Excel files
importing, 263
tables
    formatting, 314
    importing, 313
Microsoft Word files
exporting footnotes, 358
formatting tables, 315

Microsoft Word files *(continued)*
  importing, 262
    styles, 380–381
    tables, 313
mitered stroke joins, 155
mouse events and button behaviors, 453
  changing events, 456
  deactivating events, 457
Move dialog box, 86
movie clips
  display options, 444
  documents
    adding empty movie clips, 441
    adding movie clips, 440
    adding movie to empty clips, 442
    selecting images for clips, 443
  linking *versus* embedding, 440
  naming, 441
  play options, 443
  URL connections for movie, 442
Movie Options dialog box
  Embed Movie in the PDF, 442
  Floating Window, 444
  Mode menu, 443
  Name field, 441
  opening, 441
  Play on Page turn, 444
  Poster menu, 443
  Show Controller During Play, 444
  Size and Position menus, 444
  Specify a URL, 442
  Verify URL and Movie Size, 442
Multiply blend mode, 169
Murphy, Chris, 415

N

Navigator palette, 5
  navigation guidelines, 40
  Palette Options, 40
  Preview area, 40
  View All Spreads option, 39
  View Box color, 40
  Zoom In/Zoom Out buttons, 39
  Zoom slider, 39
New Document dialog box, 18–19
New Glyph Set dialog box, 73
The Non-Designer's Scan and Print Book, 118, 459

The Non-Designer's Type Book, 65
None tool, 15, 151
Normal blend mode, 169
Normal view, 15
Normal View Mode, 35
numbered lists, 68, 355
  finding/replacing numbers, 350–351

O

Object menu commands
  Anchored Object
    Insert, 245
    Options, 248–249
  Arrange
    Bring All To Front, 41
    Bring Forward, 102
    Bring to Front, 102
    Cascade, 41
    New Window, 41
    Send Backward, 102
    Send to Back, 102
    Tile, 41
  Clipping Path, 221, 223
  Compound Paths, Make/
  Release, 151, 173, 197
  Content, 245
  Convert Shape, 249
  Corner Effects, 166
  Display Performance, 227
  Drop Shadow, 171–172
  Feather, 172
  Fitting
    Center Content, 208
    Fit Content Proportionally, 207, 210
    Fit Content to Frame, 207, 210
    Fit Frame Proportionally, 208
    Fit Frame to Content, 207, 208
  Group, 106, 168, 170
  Image Color Settings, 422
  Interactive
    Button Options, 447
    Convert to Button, 445
    Movie Options, 441
    Sound Options, 438, 439
  Path
    Open Path/Close Path, 185
    Reverse Path, 185

Pathfinder, 173–174
Select
  available in Control palette, 212
  Container, 108, 212
  Content, 107, 108, 212
  Next Object in Group, 107
  Previous Object in Group, 107
Text Frame Options, 76, 236
Transform
  Move, 87
  Rotate, 93
  Scale, 92
  Shear, 94
  Transform Again/Again Individually, 101
Ungroup, 107
object styles
  anchored objects, 395
  corner effects, 394
  creating, 393
  drop shadow, 394
  feather, 394
  fill, 394
  paragraph styles, 395
  Quick Apply feature, 398
  Story options, 395
  text frame options
    baseline, 395
    general, 395
    text wrap, 395
  transparency, 394
Object Styles palette
  anchored objects, 395
  Clear Overrides Not Defined, 397
  corner effects, 394
  drop shadow, 394
  feather, 394
  fill, 394
  New Object Styles, 396
  Object Style Options, 393
  opening, 6, 393
  paragraph styles, 395
  Quick Apply feature, 397
  Redefine, 397
  Story options, 395
  text frame options
    baseline, 395
    custom baseline grids, 410
    general, 395
    text wrap, 395

  transparency, 394
objects
  aligning, 103
    Control palette options, 110
    Lock command, 105
  anchored objects
    alignment, above line, 247
    creating, 245
    editing settings, 249
    options, 248
    options, content, 245–246
    releasing, 249
  changing shapes, 84
  compound paths, 151
  constraining width and height
      to same amount, 84
  contextual menus, 16
  Control palette options, 110
  copying, 88
  cutting, 88
  defaults, 178
  distributing, 104–105
  drawing from center, 84
  drop shadows
    adding, 171
    applying, 230
    blend mode, 171
    buttons, 452
    checkerboard grid, 253
    flattener presets, 478–480
    flattener previews, 481–482
    flattening transparency effects, 480, 481
    removing, 172
    Transparency slider, 229
  duplicating, 88
    creating grids, 89
    many objects, 89
  Eyedropper
    precision eyedropper, 177
    sampling/applying attributes, 176
    sampling new attributes, 177
    setting options, 176
  feathered edges, 172
    Transparency slider, 229
  fill effects
    adjusting, 150
    applying, 148–149, 151
    applying defaults, 178
  flipping, 100

objects *(continued)*
  grouping, 106
    Control palette options, 110
    nesting groups, 106
    ungrouping, 107
  Info palette display, 111
    documents, 113
    placed objects, 113
    text, 113
  inline objects
    creating, 244
    importing images, 244
    options, 246
    uses, 244
  locking/unlocking, 114
  measuring angles, 112
  moving
    and copying, 87
    dragging with Selection tool, 86
    measuring lines, 112
    with Move command, 87
    with Transform palette, 97
  pasted-in content
    Control palette options, 110
    deleting, 109
    moving along with containers, 109
    swapping one for another, 109
  pasting into another, 107
  pasting/pasting in place, 88
  Pathfinder commands, 173
    changing shapes icons, 174
    paths, 175
    separating results, 173
  preview settings, 226–228
  repositioning points, 112
  resizing, 90
    versus scaling, 90
    with Transform palette, 97
    with transform tools, 91
  rotating
    with Rotate command, 93
    with Rotate tool, 93
    with Rotate tool, numerically, 94
    with Transform palette, 96
    with Transform palette,
      Rotation Angle field, 99
  scaling, 92–93
    with Scale command, 92
    with Scale tool, numerically, 93

  with Transform palette, 98
  selecting
    all page objects, 85
    Control palette options, 110
    dragging a marquee, 85
    objects within groups, 106–107
    Selection tool, 85
    Selection tool *versus* Direct
      Selection tool, 115
  shearing
    with Shear command, 94
    with Shear tool, 94–95
    with Shear tool, numerically, 95
    with Transform palette, 99
  spacing settings (between objects), 105
  stacking order, 102
  stroke effects
    alignment, 156
    applying, 152–153
    arrowheads, 166
    caps, 155
    corner effects, 166
    end shapes, 166
    weight, 154
  stroke styles, 157
    applying defaults, 178
    dashed stroke, 158
  stroke styles (custom), 159
    dashed stroke, 161
    deleting from documents, 163
    dotted stroke, 162
    gap color, 157
    joins, miter limits, 155
    saving, 163
    stripe stroke, 160
    transferring from another document, 163
    uses, 163–164
    weight, 154
  styles (*See* object styles)
  transparencies
    blend modes, 168, 169
    isolating blending, 170
    knockout groups, 168
    reducing opacity, 167
objects styles
  anchored objects, 395
  corner effects, 394
  drop shadow, 394
  feather, 394

fill, 394

general options, 394

Object Styles dialog box, 393

opening, 6, 393

paragraph styles, 395

Story options, 395

text frame options

baseline, 395

baseline, custom grids, 410

general, 395

text wrap, 395

transparency, 394

onscreen display color. *See* RGB color

Opacity slider, 167

Open dialog box

Adobe dialog box, 42

OS (operating system) dialog box, 42

OpenType fonts, 372

finding/replacing, 350

OPI (Open Prepress Interface) controls

Export dialog box, 503

Print dialog box, 477

orientation, 21, 23

print options, 463

origin settings on rulers, 27

OS (operating system) dialog box, 42

swatches

importing from other documents, 131

saving as Adobe Swatch Exchange files, 130

out-of-gamut symbol, 122

Output category

Export PDF dialog box, 494, 501–502

Print dialog box, 461, 469–475

Overlay blend mode, 169

overprinting colors, 145

rules, 145

P

Package for GoLive feature

CSS (Cascading Style Sheets), 517

packaging files for opening in GoLive, 517

packaging documents

Create Package Folder dialog
box options, 489

Font Alert, 490

Printing Instructions dialog box, 489

page hyperlinks, 425. *See also* hyperlinks

destinations

choosing, 430

creating, 426

creating unnamed, 430

Page origin of rulers, 27

PageMaker

files, opening, 44

Powerpaste command, 88

pages

adding

Insert command, 254

manually, 253

checkerboard grid, 253

deleting, 257

document pages, 253

duplicating, 257

Keep Options, 362, 371

local override, 253

magnification/magnification list, 33–34

master items on document pages

changing display, 273

detaching single items, 272

modifying all, 272

overriding all, 272

removing overrides, 273

separating all, 273

stacking order of items, 273

master pages, 253

adding objects, 269

applying to pages, 271

basing on existing master pages, 270, 271

calculating number needed, 273

creating, 270

creating from document pages, 270

definition, 253

opening, 269

uses, 269

moving, 255

within documents, 258

navigating

Layout menu commands, 256

Pages palette, 255

Page list/maximum pages, 257

page numbering

automatic, 275

continued to/from characters, 276

preferences, 527

section numbering *versus* absolute
numbering, 276

pages *(continued)*
  print options, 463
    page marks, 467
  rearranging, 258
  sizes, 20, 23
  text break characters, 268
Pages palette
  Allow Pages to Shuffle
    deselecting, 258–260
    selecting, 258–259
  Delete Pages, 257
  Duplicate Spread, 257
  Insert command, 254
  Keep Spread Together, 259
  master pages, 253
    Apply Master to Pages, 271
    Detach All Objects From Master, 273
    Detach Selection From Master, 272
    New Master, 270
    Override All Master Page Items, 272, 273
    Save as Master, 270
    Show/Hide Master Items, 273
  Move Pages, 258
  navigation techniques, 40, 255
  New Page, 253
  opening, 6, 252, 269
  Pages Options dialog box, 252
  Remove All Local Overrides, 273
Palette Options dialog box, 40
palettes
  Align, 2
  Attributes, 2, 145
  Automation menu
    Script Label, 7
  Book, 277
  Bookmarks, 2, 435
  Character, 2, 58
  Character Styles, 3, 373
  closing, 10
  Color, 3, 120
  Control, 3
  displaying
    palette menu, 10
    small palette rows, 11
  docking/undocking, 13
  Flattener Preview, 3
  Glyphs, 3
  Gradient, 4

  hiding, 10
  Hyperlinks, 4, 425
  Index, 4, 287
  Info, 4, 111
  Layers, 5, 290
  Library, 5
  Links, 5
  Navigator, 5
  nesting/unnesting, 12
  Object Styles, 6, 393
  opening palettes, 10
  options, revealing, 10
  Pages, 6, 252, 269
  Paragraph, 6
  Paragraph Styles, 6
  Pathfinder, 7
  screen display, collapsing/expanding, 11
  Script Label, 7
  Scripts, 7
  Separations Preview, 7
  side tabs
    collapsing/expanding, 13
    creating, 12
    nesting, 13
  States, 448
  Story, 7
  Stroke, 8, 154
  Swatches, 8, 124
  Table, 8
  Tabs, 8, 371
  Tags, 9
  Text Wrap, 9
  Transform, 9, 99
  Transparency, 9, 167
  Trap Presets, 9
Pantone color library, 119, 133
Paper color, 125
Paragraph palette, 6
  Adobe Paragraph Composer, 401
  Adobe Single-line Composer, 401
  alignment, 67, 370
    finding/replacing, 350
  attributes, 66
  Balance Ragged Lines, 411
  Bullets and Numbering, 354
    Add Bullets, 354
    Convert Bullets and
    Numbering to Text, 355

Numbering, 355
Position list, 355
drop caps, 70, 371
Drop Caps and Nested Styles, 387, 392
New Nested Style, 390
Repeating Element menu, 390–391
hyphenation, 71, 371
Hyphenation Settings dialog box, 406
Indent to Here character, 69
Justification
Auto Leading, 405
Glyph Scaling options, 404
guidelines, 403
Letter Spacing options, 403
Single Word, 405
Word Spacing options, 402
Keep Options, 362, 371
margin indents, 68, 370
finding/replacing, 350
hanging bullets, 68
numbered lists, 68
space between, 70
text formatting, 66
paragraph rules, 371
appearance, 241
applying, 240
offset, 242
reversed text, 243
width, 242
Paragraph Rules dialog box, 371
Gap Color/Tint, 241
Offset, 242
Overprint Stroke, 241
reversed text, 243
Rule Above/Below, 240
Text Color/Tint, 241
Weight, 241
Width, 242
paragraph styles
applying, 382
breaking links, 384
case sensitive, 378
defining
Basic Paragraph attributes, 368
manually, 369
deleting, 385, 386
drop caps, 387–388
by example, 373

general options, 370
importing Word styles, 380
mapping one style on another, 381
keyboard shortcuts, 377
local formatting, 382
overriding, 383–384
naming guidelines, 377
nested styles, 389–390
changing order, 392
inserting End Nested Style
Here character, 391
repeating elements, 391
next paragraph style
applying to multiple paragraphs, 374
setting, 373
redefining, 385
resolving conflicts, 379
automatically, 380
transferring to another document, 378
Paragraph Styles palette, 6
anchored objects, 245
Basic Paragraph style, 368
Break Link to Style, 384
Clear Overrides, 383–384
Delete Paragraph Style alert box, 386
Delete Styles, 385–386
General options, 370, 373
Load Styles, 378–379
Conflict with Existing Style, 379
New Paragraph Style, 369
keyboard shortcuts, 377
Next Style, 374
Paragraph Style Conflicts, 380
Paragraph Style Options, 368
Drop Caps, 388
keyboard shortcuts, 377
redefining styles, 385
Preserve Formatting, 386
Redefine Style, 368
Same Style from Next Style list, 373
Select All Unused Styles, 385
paragraphs
alignment, 67, 370
finding/replacing, 350
attributes, 66
drop caps, 70, 371
finding/replacing, 350
hanging bullets, 68

paragraphs *(continued)*
  hyphenation, 71, 371
  Indent to Here character, 69
  margin indents, 68, 370
  numbered lists, 68
  space between, 70
  styles *(See* Paragraph Styles palette)
  transforming to tables, 312
passwords and permissions, output, 504–505
pasteboard
  Entire Pasteboard, 33
  preferences, 525, 536
  View modes, 35–36
Path Type tool, 237
Pathfinder palette, 7, 173
  Convert Shape commands, 84, 174
    special shapes, 175
  paths, 175
  separating results, 173
paths
  anchor points, 180
    adding/deleting, 186, 192
    modifying, 187
    moving, 184
  clipping paths
    choosing alpha channels as paths, 222
    choosing as InDesign path, 221
    converting to frames, 221
    creating from images, 222
    creating in Photoshop, 220
    deleting around images, 223
    modifying effects of paths, 223
    modifying shapes, 221
  closing
    with smooth curves, 182
    with straight lines, 181
  control handles, 180
    extending handles from points, 183
    moving, 184
    pivoting, 182
    retracting handles, 183
  converting text to paths, 198
  corner points, 181
  deleting, 191
  drawing, 188
  editing, 188
  elements, 180
  importing as frames, 199
  opening/closing, 185

  reversing, 185
  segments, 180
    curved, 182
    deleting, 187
  smoothing, 190
  splitting, 185
PC Paintbrush (PCX) file format, 195
PDF (Portable Document Format) file format
  Export PDF dialog box, 492
    Adobe PDF Presets dialog box, 506–507
    Advanced category options, 494, 503
    Compression category
      options, 493, 498–500
    General category options, 493, 495–497
    Marks and Bleed category options, 493
    Output category options, 494, 501–502
    Security category options, 494, 504–505
    Summary category options, 494
  importing graphic file formats, 195
  layer visibility, 219
  PDF Import Options dialog
    box, 200, 202–203
Pen tool, 15
  curves
    Bezier curves, 180
    corner curves, 182
    smooth curves, 182
  One-Third Rule, 183
  straight lines, 181
    closing paths, 180
  text wrap, 235
  tutorial at www.zenofthepen.org, 179
  uses, 180
Pencil tool, 15
  editing and drawing paths, 188
  preference settings, 189
Photoshop. *See* Adobe Photoshop
PICT (Macintosh Picture) file format, 195
  EPS preview, 509
plug-ins
  Configure Plug-ins dialog box, 548
  duplicating, 548
  Plug-in Information dialog box, 548
  preflighting documents, 488
  TableStyles and CellStyles, 311
PNG (Portable Network
Graphic) file format, 195
*Pocket Pal Graphic Arts
  Production Handbook,* 118

point sizes, 59
  preferences, 534
Polygon Frame tool, 15
  graphic frames, 82, 84
Polygon Settings dialog box, 51
Polygon tool, 15
  converting frames to text frames, 51
  unassigned frames, 82
polygonal graphic frames, 83
Portable Document Format
file format. *See* PDF
Portable Network Graphics
(PNG) file format, 195
portrait orientation, 21
Position tool, 15
  graphic frames, 206
PostScript Color Management, 509
PostScript language, 180
PostScript (PS) file format, 195
  Print dialog box, 485
Preflight dialog box
  Colors and Inks, 488
  External Plug-ins, 488
  Fonts, 487
  Links and Images, 487
  Package, 486
  Preflight Summary, 486
  Print Settings, 488
  Report, 486
Premedia Systems, 365
Preview area, Navigator palette, 40
Preview mode, 15
Preview panel and slider, Bridge, 47
Preview tool, 15
Print dialog box
  Advanced category, 462, 477–482
  Color Management category, 462
  General category, 461, 463
  Graphics category, 462, 476
  Marks and Bleed category, 461, 467–468
  Output category, 461, 469–475
  PostScript files, 485
  Save Preset dialog box, 482–484
  Setup category, 461, 464–466
  Summary category, 462, 484
Print Presets dialog box, 483
printing by professionals. *See* service bureaus

printing documents
  choosing printers, 463
  CMYK color, 118, 121
  color output, 469
  controlling pages, 463
  font information, 476
  general options, 463
  images send data, 476
  Ink Manager
    converting spot colors to
    process colors, 474
    mapping one color to alias of another, 475
  Object Attributes, Nonprinting, 460
  OPI (Open Prepress Interface) controls, 477
  paper size and orientation, 464
  PostScript files, 485
  Print dialog box categories, 460–462
  print presets, 482–483
  print summary, 484
  screen settings, 470
  separations preview
    inks, 473
    inks, setting for printing, 474
    plate settings, 472
    turning on, 471
  settings
    bleed areas, 468
    color options, 469
    page marks, 467
    slug areas, 468
  setup options, 464
  suppressing printing, layer visibility, 460
  tiling pages, 465–466
  Transparency Flattener
    flattener presets, 477, 479, 481–482
    flattener settings, 481
    transparency flattener presets, 478–479
  Trapping menu, 470
Printing Instructions dialog box, 489
process color. *See* color, CMYK color
PS (PostScript) file format, 195
PSD (Photoshop) file format, 195, 200, 201
  layer visibility, 219
punctuation spaces, 80

Q

QuarkXPress
  compared to InDesign
    character style sheets, 382
    Content tool and Direct Selection tool, 85
    frames or line effects and
    stroke effects, 152
    multi-ink color and mixed inks, 134
    Object tool and Selection tool, 85
    text frames, flowing in text, 75
  files, opening, 44
  graphic frames, diagonal
  lines convention, 82

R

Radial gradients, 143
radial gradients, 141
raster images, 228
Reader. *See* Adobe Reader
Real World Color Management, 415
Real World InDesign CS2, 9, 286
Rectangle dialog box, 83
Rectangle Frame tool, 15
  graphic frames, 82–83
Rectangle tool, 15
  rectangular frames, 52
  unassigned frames, 82
rectangular frames
  graphic, 83
  text, 52
Registration color, 125
RGB color
  color management, 418
  creating, 118
  EPS output, 509
  mixing, 121
  onscreen display color, 118, 121
  out-of-gamut symbol, 122
  uses, 118
  working space, 417
Rich Text Format (RTF) file format
  exporting InDesign files, 492, 516
  importing, 261, 262
Rotate dialog box, 93, 94
Rotate tool, 15, 93–94
rotation settings, 100
round stroke joins, 155

RTF (Rich Text Format) file format
  exporting InDesign files, 492, 516
  importing, 261, 262
Ruler Guides dialog box, 31
rulers. *See* document rulers

S

sampling/downsampling files, 498–499
Saturation blend mode, 169
Save Preset dialog box, 482–483
  Print dialog box, 482–484
Save/Save As dialog box
  Adobe dialog box, 42
  OS (operating system) dialog box, 42
  saving/naming files, 42
Save Workspace dialog box, 14
scalable vector graphics. *See* SVG/
SVG Compressed file formats
Scale dialog box, 92, 93
Scale tool, 15, 92–93
Scissors tool, 15
  splitting paths, 185, 192
Scitex Continuous Tone (SCT) file format, 195
Screen blend mode, 169
Script Label palette, 7
scripts
  Bridge, 48
  running in InDesign, 365
  writing, 365
Scripts palette, 7
second color. *See* color, spot color
Security category, Export PDF
dialog box, 494, 504–505
Selection tool, 15
  keyboard shortcuts, graphic
    frames and images, 204
  objects
    moving by dragging, 86
    resizing, 91
    selecting, 85
  ruler guides, 31
Separations Preview palette, 7
  opening, 7, 471
  plate settings, 472, 473
  View menu
    Ink Limit, 473
    Show/Hide (previews), 471

service bureaus
  color management, 417
  exporting PDFs, 497
  graphic formats recommended, 195
  grayscale images, 213
  JDF (Job Definition Format), 503
  legalities of copying, 490
  unnamed colors, 125
  unused colors, 130
Setup category, Print dialog box, 461, 464–466
shapes, 84
Shear dialog box, 94, 95
Shear tool, 94–95
shortcut keys. *See* keyboard shortcuts
sixth color. *See* color, spot color
skewing text, 64
slug guides, 28
Slug Mode, 35
Slug tool, 15
slugs, 19, 23
  print options, 468
Smooth tool, 15
  paths, 190
  preference settings, 190
snippets, 304
Soft Light blend mode, 169
Sound Clip cursors, 438
sound clips
  documents
    adding empty sound clips, 438
    adding sound clips, 438
    selecting images, 439
  linking *versus* embedding, 440
  naming, 439
  opening Sound Options dialog box, 438, 439
Sound Options dialog box
  opening, 438, 439
  sound clips
    adding to documents, 438
    Name field, 439
    Poster menu, 439
special characters, 80
specialty color. *See* color, spot color
spell check, 342
  correcting errors, 343
    while typing, 345
  dictionary
    adding words, 344
    editing, 344

hyphenation, 408, 539
  importing/exporting words, 345
  preferences, 525, 537–539
dynamic spelling, 345
  preferences, 540
  ignoring specialized words, 343
  InCopy, 516
  limitations, 343
  preferences, 525, 540
Spine origin of rulers, 27
Spread origin of rulers, 27
spreads. *See* facing pages
stacking order, objects, 102
StandardSoundPoster.jpg, 438
star frames
  Star Inset field, 84
  text, 51
State Options dialog box, Enable State, 449
States palette
  Appearance menu, 452
  Delete Content from State/Selected State, 451
  Delete State, 448
  Down state to Rollover, 449
  New State, 448, 450
  opening, 448
  Place Content into State/Selected State, 450
Step and Repeat dialog box, 89
Story Editor, 353
  display preferences, 526, 542
Story palette, Optical Margin Alignment, 400
Strikethrough options, 60–61, 372
striped strokes, 159, 160
Stroke palette, 8
  Align Stroke controls, 154
    options, 156
    uses, 156
  Cap and Join icons, 155
  Control palette options, 110
  Corners list options, 158
  Edit Stroke Style dialog box, 162
  Gap Color menu, 157
  Gap Tint controls, 157
  New Stroke Styles dialog box, 159–162
  opening, 8, 154
  Stroke Styles options, 159, 162
    custom strokes, 163
    custom strokes, uses, 164–165
  Stroke Type menu, 157
    Dash, 158, 161

Stroke palette *(continued)*
  Dotted, 159, 162
  Stripe, 159, 160
Stroke tool, 15
  coloring frame strokes, 213
  default, 178
  opening
    Color Picker, 140
    Swatches palette, 128
styles. *See* character styles; paragraph styles
Summary category
  Export PDF dialog box, 494
  Print dialog box, 462, 484
SVG (scalable vector graphics)/
SVG Compressed file formats
  exporting InDesign files, 492, 513–514, 515
    CSS (Cascading Style Sheets)
    properties, 515
  SVG *versus* SVG Compressed, 512
Swap fill and stroke tool, 15
Swatches palette
  Add Unnamed Colors, 129
  color swatches, 372
    adding new color, 125, 132
    applying colors, 128
    default colors, 131
    defining in Swatches palette, 126
    defining with Color Picker, 140
    deleting, 128, 129
    duplicating, 130
    finding/replacing, 350
    importing, 131, 133
    merging, 129
    modifying, 127
    moving, 130
    naming unnamed colors, 131
    saving, 130
  Convert Mixed Ink Swatches to Process, 136
  default swatches
    None, 128
    Paper, 128
    Registration, 128
  Delete Swatch, 128–129
  display options, 124
  Duplicate Swatch, 130
  Fill icon, 148
  Gradient Options, 142
  gradient swatches, 372
    adding/deleting color stops, 142

  defining, 141
  finding/replacing, 350
  linear and radial gradients, 141
  modifying, 142
  Inks list, 136
  Load Swatches, 131
  Merge Swatches, 129
  Mixed Ink Group Options
    Ink controls, 135
    Inks list, 136
  mixed ink swatches
    combining spot colors, 134
    creating, 134
    modifying, 136–137
  modifying, 127, 136–137
  moving, 130
  naming unnamed colors, 131
  New Color Swatch, 126
    Color Mode list, 126, 132, 133, 137
    Color Type list, 126, 137
  New Gradient Swatch
    color stops, 141, 142
    midpoint controls, 141
  New Mixed Ink Swatch, 135
    Ink controls, 134
  New Tint Swatch, 138–139
  opening, 8, 124
  Preview Swatches button, 135
  Save Swatches For Exchange, 130
  saving, 130
  Select All Unused, 129
  swatch libraries, 126, 132
    third-party, 133
  Swatch Options, 127
    mixed ink swatches, 136, 137
    tints, 139
  tint swatches
    creating, 138
    modifying, 139
    storing, 139
  types, 124
System (Macintosh) swatch library, 133
System (Windows) swatch library, 133

T

table of contents (TOC)
  alphabetizing, 286

document preparations, 282
entries
  defining styles, 282
  formatting styles, 284, 285
  indenting, 286
  separator characters, 285
generating, 282
option settings, 286
selecting listings, 283
titling, 283
Table palette, 8
  Cell Alignment menu, 314
  Cell Options
    Diagonal Lines, 338
    Rows and Columns, 323, 324
    Strokes and Fills, 333, 334
    Text, 329
    Text, baseline, 331
    Text, graphics display, 328
    Text, vertical justification, 330, 331
  Control palette table controls, 339
  Convert Rows To Header/
    To Footer/To Body, 327
  Convert Table to Text, 315
  Convert Text to Table, 312
  Delete, Column/Row/Table, 321
  Distribute Columns/Rows Evenly, 324
  formatting options, 314
  Go to Row, 316
  Insert, Column/Row, 320
  Insert Table, 311
  Merge/Unmerge Cells, 329
  Select options, 318
  Split Cell Horizontally/Vertically, 329
  Table Options
    Alternating Column Strokes, 336
    Alternating Fills, 337
    Alternating Row Strokes, 335
    Headers and Footers, 326
    Preserve Local Formatting, 332
    Table Setup, 319, 325
    Table Setup, stacking order, 334
tables
  borders
    adding around tables, 332
    stacking order, 334
  cells
    content, copying/pasting, 322
    content, deleting, 321

diagonal lines, 338
graphics, inserting/controlling display, 328
merging/unmerging, 329
moving from one to another, 316
placing tables in cells, 315
preserving formatting, 332
proxy lines, 333
splitting, 329
strokes around cells, 333
tab characters, inserting, 316
TableStyles and CellStyles plug-in, 311
columns
  adding/deleting, 321
  alternating strokes, 336
  changing number, 319
  changing width, 323
  distributing, 324
  inserting, 320
  selecting, 317
converting
  cells to headers/footers, 327
  header or footer cells into body cells, 327
  tables to text, 315
  text into tables, 312
creating, 311
deleting
  cell content, 321
  columns, 321
  entire tables, 321
  rows, 321
fills
  alternating in rows/columns, 337
  customizing inside cells, 334
formatting with third-party plug-in, 311
graphics, 328
headers/footers
  adding, 326
  converting cells to, 327
  converting header or footer
  cells into body cells, 327
  setting repeat options, 326
importing Excel tables, 313
  specific cells, 313
  specific cells, formatting, 314
importing Word tables, 313
  formatting, 315
rows
  adding/deleting, 321
  alternating strokes, 335

tables *(continued)*
  distributing, 324
  height, 322, 323
  inserting, 320
  jumping to specific row, 316
  number, 319
  options, 324
  red dot warning, 322
  selecting, 318
  width, 323
  selecting, 318
  strokes
    alternating for columns, 336
    alternating for rows, 335
    around cells, 333
    stacking order, 334
  Table palette or Control palette options, 339
  TableStyles and CellStyles plug-in, 311
  versus tabs, 310
  text frames
    flowing tables between frames, 325
    spacing around tables, 325
  text in cells
    first baseline, 331
    inserting into, 316
    options, 330
    selecting, 317
    vertical alignment, 330
    vertical justification, 331
  updating all in documents, 311
TableStyles and CellStyles plug-
  in (Teacup Software), 311
tabs
  tab characters
    custom characters, 309
    indenting paragraphs, 306, 370
    inserting, 306
    inserting, one per column, 306
  tab leaders, 310
  tab stops
    aligning, 307
    changing, 308
    clearing all, 309
    removing, 309
    repeating, 308
  versus tables, 310
  transforming to tables, 312
Tabs palette, 371
  Clear All, 309

Decimal Tab, 309
Leader field, 310
opening, 8, 307
positioning, 307
Repeat Tab, 308
tab alignment, 307, 308
Tagged Image File Format
  (TIFF) file format, 195
  EPS preview, 509
tagged text. *See* Adobe InDesign
Tagged Text format
Tags palette, 9
Teacup Software's TableStyles
  and CellStyles plug-in, 311
templates, opening QuarkXPress
  or PageMaker files, 44
text
  balancing ragged lines, 411
  break characters, 268
    keyboard shortcuts, 268
  Contour Options Type menu options, 234
  converting to frames (paths), 197
  copy/pasting, 56
  defaults, 58
  distorting, 64
  dragging to another location, 57
  duplicating, 57
  exporting
    to Adobe InCopy, 516
    formats, 516
  fill effects, 149
    gradient fills, 149
  finding
    formatting options, 349–351
    wildcard characters, 348
  finding/changing
    applying, 347
    expanding options, 348
    ignoring instances, 347
    InCopy, 516
    metacharacters, 347
    text string settings, 346
  formatting, 58
    changing, 352
    fonts (typefaces), 59
    keyboard shortcuts, 59
    with Paragraph palette, 66
    point size, 59
  graphic frames, 82

importing
ASCII text, 261, 263
into existing or master frames, 264
import options, 261
loaded text cursor, 261, 264
Microsoft Excel files, 263
Microsoft Word files, 262
into new frames, 264
RTF (Rich Text Format)
file format, 261, 262
Keep Options, 362, 371
placeholder text, 268
styles, 59
electronic, 60
electronic, *versus* actual typefaces, 65
electronic finding/replacing, 350
finding/changing, 350
text anchor hyperlinks, 425. *See also* hyperlinks
destinations
choosing, 430
creating, 427
Text Frame Options dialog box
columns, 76
fixed width, 77
frame insets, 77
justification, 78
spacing limits, 78
text wrap, ignoring, 236
vertical justification, 78
text frames
columns, 76
Fixed Column Width, 77
converting unassigned frames, 52
creating, 82
elliptical frames, 50
polygon frames, 51
rectangular frames, 52
star frames, 51
drawing, 50
keyboard shortcuts, 52
flowing text into frames
autoflow cursor, 267
existing frames, 264
into fixed number of pages, 267
fixed-page autoflow cursor, 267
manually, 265
master frames, 264
overflow symbol, 265
semi-autoflow cursor, 266

frame insets, 77
inline objects, 244
insertion point, keyboard shortcuts, 53
inset spacing, 77
justification, 78
master frames, 264
nesting, 210
none *versus* white fills, 151
numerically sizing, 52
object styles options
baseline, 395
baseline, custom grids, 410
general, 395
text wrap, 395
overflow symbol, 53, 75
paragraph spacing limitations, 78
selecting, 54
keyboard shortcuts, 55
Selection tool *versus* Direct
Selection tool, 115
skewing, 64
special characters, 80
strokes, 153
text
changing links, 75
embedding files, 218
importing into new frames, 264
linking, 75
linking files, 216
scaling, 98
showing, 75
text break characters, 268
text threads, 75
vertical justification, 78
Text Import Options dialog box, 263
Text Only file format, 492, 516
Text tool
fills, 149
strokes, 153
text frames, creating, 82
text wrap, 232
around inline objects, 244
around invisible objects, 235
contour options, 234
custom wraps, 235
flowing inside objects, 232
ignoring wraps, 236
offset controls, 232
preferences, 533

text wrap *(continued)*
  text on paths
    applying effects, 238
    positioning on paths, 237
    running on outside of, 237
    vertical alignment, 237
Text Wrap palette, 9
  Bounding Box, 232–233
  Jump Object, 232–233
  Jump to Next column, 232–233
  No Wrap, 232–233
  Object Shape, 232–235
thin spaces, 80
thumbnails, 463
Thumbnails view, Bridge, 47
TIFF (Tagged Image File Format)
    file format, 195, 200
  EPS preview, 509
Tiling menu
  Auto/Auto Justified, 465
  Manual, 466
TOC. *See* table of contents
tool tips
  preferences, 527
  tool names and keyboard shortcuts, 16
Toolbox
  fly-out panels, 15
    opening related tools, 16
  tools
    keyboard shortcuts, 16
    selecting, 15
Toyo color library, 119, 133
tracking controls, 63
Transform palette
  Control palette options, 110
  Link icons, 98
  objects
    flipping, 100
    moving, 97
    repeating transformation, 101
    resizing, 97
    rotating, 99
    scaling, 98
    shearing, 99
  opening, 99
  reference points, 99
  Reset Scaling to 100%, 154
  Show Content Offset, 209
  Transform Content, 205

  X and Y coordinates, 209
transparency effects
  checkerboard grid, 253
  flattener presets, 478–480
  flattener previews, 481–482
  Transparency slider, 229
Transparency Flattener, Print
options, Advanced category, 503
  flattener presets, 477, 479, 481–482
  flattener settings, 481
  transparency flattener presets, 478–479
Transparency palette
  blend modes
    adding, 168
    knockout groups, 168
    list, 169
  Opacity slider, 167
  opening, 9, 167
Trap Presets palette, 9
Trumatch swatch library, 133
Truskier, Peter, 365
Type menu commands
  Character palette
    No Break, 407
    OpenType, 411
  Character Styles, New Character Style, 375
  Create Outline, 198
  Document Footnote Options, 356–358
  Fill with Placeholder Text, 268
  Find Font
    making changes, 361
    replacing missing fonts, 361
  Font, 59
  Glyphs, 72
  Hidden Characters, Show/Hide, 71
  Insert Footnote, 356
  Insert Glyphs, 412
  Insert Special Character, 80
    Auto Page Number, 275
    Discretionary Hyphen, 407
    End Nested Style Here, 391
    Indent to Here, 69
    Next/Previous Page Number, 276
    right tabs, 306
    Section Marker, 276
  Insert White Space, 80
  Paragraph
    Adobe Paragraph Composer, 401
    Justification, 402–405

Paragraph Styles, New Style, 373
Show Hidden Characters, 268, 306
  End Nested Style Here, 391
Size, 59
Story, 6, 400
Tabs, 307
Type on a Path options
  Align menu, 239
  Effect menu, 238
  Path menu, 239
Type on a Path tool, 15
type preferences, 524, 529–531
Type tool
  keyboard shortcuts, 55
  text frames, 50
typography controls
  Adobe Paragraph Composer, 401
  Adobe Single-line Composer, 401
  baseline grid
    aligning text, 409
    custom grids, 410
    setting, 408
  hyphenation, 406
    capitalized words, 407
    discretionary hyphens, 407
    editing in dictionary, 408
    Nigel measurement, 406
    No Break command, 407
  justification
    auto leading, 405
    glyph scaling, 404
    guidelines, 403
    letter spacing, 403
    single words, 405
    word spacing, 402
  OpenType
    categories, 413–414
    definition, 411
    selecting alternate glyphs, 412
    setting alternate characters
    automatically, 411
    viewing glyphs, 412
  optical margin adjustment, 400
  uneven line breaks, balancing, 411

U

Ultra-Compact Mode, Bridge, 46
unassigned frames
  converting to text frames, 52
  with Rectangle, Ellipse, or Polygon tools, 82
  Selection tool *versus* Direct
    Selection tool, 115
Underline option, 60–61, 372
Unembed alert box, 218
Unicode and ISO encoding, 515
Units & Increments dialog box, 26–27
URL hyperlinks, 425. *See also* hyperlinks
  destinations
    choosing, 431
    creating, 427
    creating unnamed, 431

V

vector images, previewing, 228
Versions and Alternates view, Bridge, 47
vertical gridlines, 32
vertical justification, text frames, 78
vertical scale controls, 64
vertical settings, rulers, 26
View All Spreads option, Navigator palette, 39
View Box color, Navigator palette, 40
View menu commands
  Entire Pasteboard, 33
  Fit Page In Window, 33
  Fit Spread In Window, 33
  Grids & Guides
    Lock Column Guides, 29
    Lock Guides, 31
    Show/Hide Baseline Grid, 32
    Show/Hide Document Grid, 32
    Show/Hide Guides, 28
    Snap to Grids, 33
    Snap to Guides, 29
  Overprint Preview, 145
  Show/Hide Rulers, 26
  Show Text Threads, 75
  Zoom In/Zoom Out, 33
view threshold
  grids, 32
  ruler guides, 31

W

Web (Web-safe colors) swatch library, 133
white eyedropper, 176–177
white space, Insert White Space command, 80
Williams, Robin, 65, 459
Window menu
  Arrange
    Bring All To Front, 41
    Cascade, 41
    New Window, 41
    Tile, 41
  Attributes, 2, 145
  Automation
    Script Label, 7
    Scripts, 7, 365
  Color, 3, 120
  Control, 3
  Gradient, 4, 143
  Info, 4, 111
  Interactive
    Bookmarks, 2, 435
    Hyperlinks, 4, 425
    States, 448
  Layers, 5, 290
  Links, 5, 214
  Object & Layout
    Align, 2, 103
    Navigator, 5, 39
    Pathfinder, 7
    Transform, 9, 96
  Object Styles, 6, 393
  Output
    Flattener, 3
    Separations, 7, 471
    Trap Presets, 9
  Pages, 6, 252
  Stroke, 8, 154
  Swatches, 8, 124
  Tags, 9
  Text Wrap, 9
  Transparency, 9, 167
  Type & Tables
    Character or Type>Character, 2, 58
    Character Styles or
    Type>Character Styles, 3
    Glyphs or Type>Glyphs, 3
    Index, 4, 287

    Paragraph, 6, 66
    Paragraph Styles, 6
    Story, 7
    Table, 8
    Tabs or Type>Tabs, 8, 307
    Text Wrap, 8, 232
  Workspace>Save/Delete Workspace, 14
Windows
  System swatch library, 133
  VisualBasic scripts, 365
  Windows Bitmap (BMP) file format, 195
  Windows Metafile (WMF) file format, 195
Windows Built-in Player media files, 438
Windows Media Player media files, 438
WMF (Windows Metafile) file format, 195
Word files. *See* Microsoft Word files
workflow automation, Bridge, 48
workspaces
  applying, 14
  Default, 14
  deleting, 14
  managing cluttered space, 5
  multiple, managing with
    multiple monitors, 5
  saving custom workspaces, 14

X – Y

X and Y coordinates, 97
  positioning graphics numerically, 209
XML file format
  exporting InDesign files, 492
  PDF files
    movie files, 440
    sound files, 438

Z

zero points on rulers, repositioning, 27
zoom button (Mac)
  palette display, 11
Zoom In/Zoom Out buttons/
commands, 33, 34, 39
Zoom slider, Navigator palette, 39
Zoom tool, 15
  keyboard shortcuts, 37
  marquee zoom, 37